VICTORIA FORNER

PROSCRIBED HISTORY

The Role of Jewish Agents in Contemporary History

II

THE SILENCED HISTORY
OF THE INTERWAR PERIOD

ꙮMNIA VERITAS.

VICTORIA FORNER

PROSCRIBED HISTORY
The Role of Jewish Agents
in Contemporary History
II
THE SILENCED HISTORY OF THE INTERWAR PERIOD

Cover illustration:
"Unser täglich Brot (Our Daily Bread) 1946
Painted by Ulrich Leman (1885-1988)
Düsseldorf, Stadtmuseum

HISTORIA PROSCRITA II
La actuación de agentes judíos en la Hª Contemporánea
La historia silenciada de entreguerras
First published by Omnia Veritas in 2017

Translated from Spanish and published by
OMNIA VERITAS LTD

ⓞMNIA VERITAS®
www.omnia-veritas.com

© Omnia Veritas Limited - Victoria Forner - 2025

CHAPTER VIII 9

THE SILENCED HISTORY OF THE INTERWAR PERIOD 9

Part 1 The Peace Conference 9

    RIIA, CFR, IPR 12

    The Treaty of Versailles 14

    The creation of the League of Nations and its failure 18

    San Remo Conference, *Balfour Declaration* and British Mandate 20

Part 2 Despoilment, civil war and terror in Russia. Lenin's death and
Trotsky's defeat 29

    The biggest heist in history 32

    The civil war against the whites 46

    Civil war against the peasants 64

    Civil war against the Kronstadt workers and seafarers 68

    Civil war against the Cossacks 73

    Red terror and Jewish terror 75

    Lenin's death. Trotsky and Stalin vie for power 79

Part 3 Failure of International Communism in Germany and the Triumph of
Nationalism 88

    Germany, a key player in the international revolution 89

    The Treaty of Rapallo and the assassination of Rathenau 97

    Hitler and the "Munich Putsch" 101

    Numerous "anti-Semitic" Jews in Hitler's entourage 103

    Jewish bankers finance Hitler 111

    As Judea declares war, Zionism collaborates: the Haavara Agreement 130

Part 4 Roosevelt in the White House. Congressman McFadden denounces
the conspiracy 139

    McFadden's speech delivered on 10 June 1932 145

    McFadden's speeches in 1933 149

    The 1934 speeches 153

Part 5 Terror in the USSR and genocide in Ukraine 159

    The elimination of the kulaks 161

    Forced collectivisation 166

    New attacks on priests and churches 170

    Holodomor: the ignored genocide of the Ukrainian peasants 173

Part 6 The Moscow Trials and the purge of Trotskyism 186

    The Kirov assassination 189

    The Trial of the Sixteen 198

    The Pyatakov trial 216

    The purge in the NKVD and the Red Army 231

    The Trial of the Twenty-One 247

    Yezhovschina 276

CHAPTER IX 278

REPUBLIC, REVOLUTION AND CIVIL WAR IN SPAIN 278

Part 1 Religion and the Church in Spain 278

    Apostles of atheism bring the Internationale to Spain 287

Part 2 Harassment of the Monarchy and overthrowing it 290

    Fourteen months without respite 292

The bloodless coup d'état 302

Part 3 The Second Republic *309*

The tide of Freemasons is flooding in...310
Anti-clericalism 313
The Constitution of the Second Republic...316
The social-Azharist or Masonic biennium 321
The centre-right governs without CEDA...328
Companys' coup d'état in Catalonia 335
Bloody coup d'état and civil war in Asturias...340
From crisis to crisis towards the Popular Front...346

Part 4 Popular Front, revolution and civil war *351*

The assassination of Calvo Sotelo..360
Failed coup 367
The revolution..370
Catalonia, spearhead of the revolution 371
The situation in Madrid 378
Largo Caballero and Negrín present gold to Stalin 385
Government flight and mass killing of prisoners 391
Towards Stalinist rule of the Republic 402
Civil war on the Republican side and the overthrow of Largo Caballero............411
Trotskyist Jews and Stalinist Jews 424
Repression against poumists and anarchists. The assassination of Andreu Nin.430
The situation in Franco's Spain..434
On the myth of Guernica and the Northern Campaign.................................438
Two decisive battles to win the war 440
Casado's coup d'état and new civil war on the Republican side............446
On repression in national Spain 449

OTHER BOOKS **455**

CHAPTER VIII

THE SILENCED HISTORY
OF THE INTERWAR PERIOD

PART 1
THE PEACE CONFERENCE

From 28 to 30 June 1917, almost three months after the United States declared war on Germany, a very important international Masonic conference was held at the headquarters of the Grand Orient in Paris, 2 rue Cadet. Viscount Léon de Poncins, one of the most widely written scholars on Freemasonry, says it was "a top-secret meeting of absolutely vital historical significance". Nearly all the lodges of the Allied and neutral countries were present. The purpose of the meeting was to lay the foundations of a peace treaty and to prepare for the creation of a future League of Nations. A commission presented the result of its work through Brother Lebey, who read aloud a resolution consisting of thirteen articles. Six months later, Brother Woodrow Wilson, supported by Brother Mandell House and his Jewish advisors Baruch and Brandeis, presented to the United States Congress his famous fourteen points, thirteen of which repeated verbatim the text read at the Masonic Congress in Paris. This fact, unknown or ignored by historians, is demonstrated by Léon de Poncins as an undeniable truth in his book *Société des Nations, super-état maçonnique*, published in 1936. This book quotes the motion presented by Brother Peigné, which became the resolution that Congress addressed to President Wilson, who in 1919 was to receive the Nobel Peace Prize for promoting the League of Nations:

> "This Congress sends to Mr. Wilson, President of the United States, the tribute of its admiration and the tribute of its appreciation for the great services he has rendered to humanity; declares that it is happy to collaborate with President Wilson in this work of international justice and democratic brotherhood, which is the very ideal of Freemasonry; and affirms that the eternal principles of Freemasonry are entirely in harmony with those proclaimed by President Wilson in defence of civilisation and the liberty of peoples."

In the absence of the representatives of the defeated countries, to whom the agreements were presented for signature, the Peace Conference began in Paris on 18 January 1919, attended by thirty-two countries. It lasted until 20 January 1920. The creation of the League of Nations was high on the victors' agenda. The sessions were led by Wilson, Lloyd George and Clemenceau. Vittorio Emanuele Orlando, who headed the Italian delegation, played a very minor role and eventually resigned in June 1919.

In reality, as has been explained, these men were only the instruments of the Occult Power which completely dominated the Conference. These politicians were surrounded by Jewish advisers whose influence was preponderant in the debates. George Lloyd's privy councillor was the Jew Sir Philip Sassoon. The Sassoons, enriched by the illicit opium trade, are related to the Rothschilds and control the banks in India and China. Naturally Lord Milner, the British Rothschild super-agent, was part of the British delegation and, along with Bonar Law and George Lloyd, signed the Treaty of Versailles. The British Jew Edwin Samuel Montague, a British Jew, attended the Conference as Secretary of State for India. As for the French, Georges Clemenceau himself was a Freemason close to the Rothschilds. His inseparable adviser was George Mandel, a Jew who was his private secretary and whose real name was Louis Georges Rothschild, the natural son of a Rothschild. Even Clemanceau's interpreter, Paul Mantoux, was Jewish. Another French Jewish signatory to the Treaties was Louis-Lucien Klotz. The Italian Foreign Minister, Baron Sidney Sonnino, who signed the Treaty of Versailles, was also the son of a Jew. Sonnino was also a man of the Olivetti trust, founded in 1908 by Camillo Olivetti, a Jewish socialist who foresaw that typewriters would be a cutting-edge market.

The contingent of Jews in the American delegation was scandalous. Paul Warburg, the architect of the Federal Reserve System, headed it. Four men surrounded Woodrow Wilson: Edward Mandell House, an illuminati agent of the Rothschild-Warburg-Rockefeller cartel, whom the president considered his "alter ego", Bernard Mannes Baruch, "Judah's proconsul in America", Supreme Court Justice Louis Dembitz Brandeis, a champion of Zionism in America, and Henry Morgenthau. The delegation also included nine members of the American Jewish Committee, whose president, Louis Marshall, was also vice-president of the American Jewish Congress. Following in Marshall's footsteps were Rabbi Stephen Wise, Rabbi B. L. Levinthal, Judge Julian Mack, Harry Cutler, Jacob de Haas, Jacob Syrkin, Joseph Barondess and Leopold Benedict.

The German delegation included Paul Warburg's brother, Max Warburg, who as head of the German Secret Service had financed Trotsky and Lenin. Almost all the members of the German representation who reviewed the Treaty of Versailles and accepted the peace terms were also Jewish. The most prominent were Walter Rathenau, foreign minister of the Weimar Republic; Edgar Jaffé, a Bavarian communist who had been finance minister of the Soviet Republic of Bavaria and was a friend of Kurt Eisner; Professor Albrecht Mendelssohn-Bartholdy, grandson of the composer Felix Mendelssohn; Professor Jacob Wassermann, author of several novels with Jewish themes; Oscar Oppenheimer and others.

As if all this were not enough, the Jews in the various diplomatic representations formed the "Comité des Delegacions Juives". Their claims concerned the rights of minorities, which they succeeded in putting into practice in a Treaty on National Minorities signed on 28 June 1919, which was basically applied in countries where Jewish minorities existed. The architect was Lucien Wolf, who attended the Peace Conference as part of the British delegation. Wolf, who was said to have all the secrets of the Foreign Office and whose secretary was also a Jew, David Mowshowitch, brought his diplomatic contacts into play to achieve the Treaty, which allowed Jews to appeal to the League of Nations whenever they felt their privileges had been violated by a sovereign state[1]. The Zionist Organisation, in addition to having its agents placed on the backs of the Allied leaders, also had its own representation at the Conference. Its head, the ubiquitous Chaim Weizmann, had just signed an agreement with Amir Feisal Ibn Hussein on Palestine on 3 January 1919 that was never implemented. Another must-mention Zionist present in Paris was Felix Frankfurter, a judge confidant of his colleague Louis Brandeis, who headed the American Zionist delegation. Frankfurter would later become an advisor to Franklin D. Roosevelt.

On May 13, 1919, while the Jewish element predominated in all the delegations to the Peace Conference, Senator Adrien Gaudin de Villaine denounced in unequivocal words in the French Senate the subversion which the Jews were engaged in. Among other prescient accusations he said: "the Russian Revolution and the Great War are only phases of the supreme mobilisation of the cosmopolitan powers of money, and this culminating crusade of Money against the Cross is nothing other than the furious aspiration of the Jew for the domination of our world. It is the Jewish High Bank that has provoked in Russia the revolution prepared by the Kerenskys and finally perpetrated by the Lenins, Trotskys and Zinovievs, as was yesterday's Communist coup d'état in Hungary, for Bolshevism is a Talmudic uprising."

---

[1] Article VI of the Treaty allowed Jews to have representation in national parliaments and town councils, as well as institutions of self-government. Any measure they considered a violation of their privileges gave them the right to complain to the League of Nations, which was to interfere with the supposedly sovereign state. In Poland, in particular, the Jewish minority succeeded in prohibiting elections from being held on the Sabbath, their public holiday. Nor could they be summoned to court on the Sabbath, nor could they be required to pay their debts or the wages of their employees.

RIIA, CFR, IPR

It can be said that they were all in Paris. It was a matter of taking advantage of the results of the war to advance the internationalist pretensions of the illuminati bankers, the ultimate victors of the world conflict that they had sponsored and financed. In addition to the negotiation and drafting of the Treaties, the Peace Conference provided the attendees with the opportunity to hold multiple meetings and contacts of the highest level in parallel. On 19 May 1919, Edward Mandell House convened a number of British and American delegates for a working meeting at the Hotel Majestic in Paris. On 30 May 1919, a second meeting was held at the same hotel to discuss the creation of the Royal Institute of International Affairs (RIIA), also known as the Chattan House Study Group, as its headquarters were initially located in this headquarters owned by the Astors, one of the great Illuminati families. Lionel Curtis had previously been commissioned by the Round Table Group, the secret society founded by Lord Milner, to assemble a staff of experts to prepare for the founding of the RIIA.

In Paris, Alfred Milner's men established excellent relations with the technicians sent by Morgan and Rockefeller, including Georges Louis Beer and Thomas Lamont, one of the two Treasury representatives at the Conference, who is already known for his activities in favour of communism. Both were among the organisers of the "Council on Foreign Relations" (CFR), the equivalent of the RIIA in the United States, which was also planned in Paris. It was at a meeting on 5 June 1919 that the formula of separate organisations that were to collaborate with each other was decided upon. Despite the initial agreement reached in Paris, the CFR, headquartered in New York, was not officially formed until 29 July 1921. Another subsidiary body of the RIIA conceived by the financial elite at the Paris meetings was the Institute of Pacific Relations (IPR), founded to deal exclusively with Far Eastern affairs.

These globalist organisations have since their inception acted as "think tanks" whose purpose in theory would be to advise their respective governments on international issues. In practice they are instruments of control of the Hidden Power that moves permanently in the shadows, which through these organisations dictates or imposes on nations the policies to be adopted in the international arena. In short, the internationalists, mundialists or globalists, and today it is becoming crystal clear, intended to take sovereignty away from the national states and hand it over to a clique of technicians at the service of the international bankers. The financial backing for the RIIA initially came from the Astors. In an act of recognition, Waldorf Astor, son of John Jacob Astor, was made an honorary fellow of the Royal Institute of International Affairs. Another prominent financier involved in the creation of the RIIA was Baron Edmond de Rothschild of France, who played a major role in the Paris Peace Conference. Edmond de Rothschild gave his personal approval to each of the founding members. From the RIIA, new supervisory bodies such as the Tavistock Institute and the Club of Rome were subsequently born.

The money for the founding of the Council on Foreign Relations was provided by J. P. Morgan, Paul Warburg, Bernard Baruch, Jacob Schiff, Otto Kahn and John D. Rockefeller, among others. In other words, the same Jewish bankers who were behind the creation of the Federal Reserve. The first Board of Directors of the CFR included Paul Warburg, Otto Kahn, Isaiah Bowman, William Shepard, Whitney Shepardson, Stephen Duggan, John W. Davis, Norman H. Davis and Archibald Coolidge. This institution was eventually to become America's shadow government. Here are the names of some of the famous politicians who were directors of the CFR: Zbigniew Brzezinski, Paul Volker, George H. W. Bush, David Rockefeller, Henry Kissinger, Alan Greenspan, George Shultz, Jeane Kirkpatrick, Richard B. Cheney, etc... For a long time the most powerful man in the CFR was David Rockefeller, grandson of John D. Rockefeller, who served as Chairman of the Board of Directors of the Council from 1970-85. David Rockefeller served for thirty-six years as one of the Council's directors, a position he complemented with the chairmanship of the Chase Manhattan Bank.

International bankers and their agents now dominate these bodies, which work towards a global monopoly of banking, regardless of what kind of power eventually takes control of a world government. Since Adam Weishaupt and enlightened Freemasonry, the expression New World Order signifies the coming of a single government for the whole world, one of whose symbols, the pyramid with the eye of Osiris (The All-Seeing Eye) and the inscription "Novus Ordo Seclorum", was placed on the US dollar note by Franklin Delano Roosevelt. The existence of these bodies is generally unknown even to university-educated people. Secrecy, as in Weishaupt's time, is considered essential. This is why it is never known when and where the meetings are held at which the most important decisions for the whole of humanity are taken.

The Institut of Pacific Relations, also an offshoot of the Milner Group, i.e. the Round Table, though conceived in Paris, was finally born in 1925. Later, in the pages of Chapter Eleven, there will be an opportunity to delve into the struggle that the maligned Senator McCarthy waged almost single-handedly to dismantle the Communist conspiracy in the United States, of which the IPR was one of the main bastions. Professor Carroll Quigley admits that the IPR was dedicated to the spread of communist ideology, which became public knowledge thanks to US Senate investigations. What is often not known, however, is the Wall Street sponsorship. The IPR, a tax-exempt private association, was governed by a body of ten National Councils. The constituent nations were the United States, Britain, USSR, China, Australia, New Zealand, Canada, the Netherlands, the Philippines and

THE SILENCED HISTORY OF THE INTERWAR PERIOD

France. The American Council of the IPR had its headquarters in New York. Its main financiers were the Carnegie Foundation and the Rockefeller Foundation. Both foundations were linked to Wall Street through the alliance of Morgan and Rockefeller. The rest of the contributions came from firms associated with these Jewish bankers, such as Standard Oil, International Telephone and Telegraph (ITT), International General Electric, National City Bank and Chase National Bank. The Institute of Pacific Relations arguably came to control US policies in the Far East. Among IPR's little-known moves is the role it played in the fall of China to communism. But we will now move on chronologically to other aspects of the Peace Conference, for all of this will be covered in due course.

The Treaty of Versailles

At the beginning of this section, it is pertinent to recall the words of Adolphe Isaac Crémieux in 1861: "In place of the Popes and the Caesars, a new kingdom will arise, a new Jerusalem. And our good Masons, blindfolded, assist the Jews in the 'Great Work' of building that new Temple of Solomon, that new Caesarean-Papist Kingdom of the Kabbalists!". Five years later, in 1866, Rabbi Isaac M. Wise had also confirmed the absolute control they exercised over Freemasonry: "Freemasonry is a Jewish institution, whose history, degrees, costs and enlightenments are Jewish from beginning to end". Versailles was thus the embodiment of a long-sought triumph: Europe's most powerful monarchies had been overthrown, Russia was in the grip of communism, and the Zionists could at last lay the foundations of the Jewish state in Palestine. Leon Motzkine, in an article published in September 1933 in the magazine *Les Juifs. Témoignages de notre temps*, acknowledges this in these words: "At Versailles everything had been meticulously prepared and nothing had been left to chance. It was a moment of triumph savoured in silence". The words of these Jewish ideologues thus confirm that the Treaty of Versailles was the embodiment of a victory achieved with the collaboration of the "good Masons", who since they were enlightened by Adam Weishaupt's sect had been the best instrument of the conspiracy.

If Lord Curzon acknowledged that the Treaty of Versailles "was not a peace treaty but a rupture of hostilities", Ezra Pound referred to it on Radio Rome with this blunt statement: "The real crime is to end one war in order to make the next one inevitable". The spectral pretensions of a peace without winners and losers, i.e. on the basis of President Wilson's programme, not only fizzled out dramatically in Paris, but were transformed into humiliating conditions that cruelly punished the German people. What is astonishing, however, is that hopes for a negotiated peace could have been conceived after witnessing the anti-German campaign manufactured in the international press and after seeing who and how the United States had been pushed into war against Germany. Even Stalin declared that the Treaty of Versailles was "a dictate of hatred and larceny." In Paris, a three-tiered system of operation was adopted. The first of these was the public conference, held in full view of all, which was shown to the swarm of journalists from all over the world who had come to cover the proceedings extensively and all the paraphernalia openly staged. The second level were the secret conferences of the allied presidents, the co-opted politicians, who met privately and compared notes and instructions passed to them by their hidden masters. The third level was the nightly conferences of the Jewish leaders and their good masons, known only to a select group of chosen ones, where the real agenda was discussed and decided.

After the signing of the Armistice of Compiègne on 11 November 1918, the Allies gave Germany thirty-six days to sign the Peace Treaty. Plunged into chaos by the demobilisation of the army and the communist revolution, Germany was only able to buy the extension of the armistice with deliveries of raw materials, patents, machinery and even foodstuffs. In these circumstances, Britain and France imposed a starvation blockade to support their demands. On 3 March 1919 Winston Churchill declared before the House of Commons: "We shall continue to practise the starvation blockade with all rigour. Germany is on the point of starvation. In a very few days she will be in full collapse. Then it will be time to deal with her." Count Brockdorff-Rantzau, the ambassador in Copenhagen who in 1917 had fallen into Alexander Parvus' trap and had recommended him to his country's secret services, arrived in Paris on 29 April at the head of the German delegation aspiring to negotiate peace. On 7 May, the first session began and Clemenceau, who had been appointed President of the Conference, without remembering Poincaré's warmongering and incendiary speeches in favour of war in St. Petersburg, accused Germany of being solely responsible. Brockdorff-Rantazu claimed, of course, that this was not true. A text containing 440 articles was then submitted to the German delegation and they were asked to respond within a week. No one wanted to know anything about Wilson's fourteen points which the German representative had put forward for peace negotiations and about the demand for a union of Austria and Germany.

On 9 May Walter Rathenau, who as a Jew loved Germany and felt German, wrote in *Die Zukunft* that if no improvement in the conditions of the Treaty could be achieved, Count Brockdorf-Rantzau would have to present to the enemy governments the decree for the dissolution of Parliament, the collective resignation of the Reich President and his ministers, and the invitation to the Allies to take over power in Germany. In this way," said Rathenau, "the enemy will bear the responsibility for peace and for all Germany's actions, and they will have, before the world, before history and before their own people, the duty to take charge of the fate of sixty million individuals. This would be an unprecedented event, the unprecedented downfall of a state, but, at the same time, a decision compatible with honour and conscience." On 12 May, Chancellor Scheidemann obtained an overwhelming majority in the Assembly against the signing of the Treaty. Counter-proposals were then tabled. The text of the diplomatic letter sent reminded the Assembly of the following:

> "By the exchange of notes between President Wilson and the German Government in the course of October 1918, a compromise was reached which was valid from the point of view of international law. Under this compromise, Germany laid down her arms on 11 November on the basis of the fourteen points defined by President Wilson in his message to the American Congress on 8 January 1918 and in his subsequent statements, especially in his speech of 27 September 1918.... According to the principles enunciated in these various speeches, peace was to be established on the basis of the free right of peoples to dispose of themselves, and treaties were to be discussed by all, without discrimination between victors and vanquished. To impose on Germany a treaty different from the principles accepted by both sides would thus be tantamount to a violation of the pact entered into prior to the armistice. However, there is, so to speak, not a single clause which is in accordance with the principles previously agreed upon".

Much more important than this diplomatic letter, which was practically underestimated, was the famous telegram that Jacob Schiff sent from New York to Woodrow Wilson on 28 May, a text that has gone down in history as "the two-thousand-word cablegram". Both Cyrus Adler, the banker's biographer, and Count de Saint-Aulaire in *Geneva versus Peace* comment on its contents. The latter refers to Schiff's instructions to the US President on the Palestine Mandate, on German reparations in relation to Upper Silesia, the Saar, and the Danzig Corridor, and on Fiume. Wilson immediately changed the direction of the negotiations and yielded in everything to the demands of the banker who was financing Trotsky. It is bitterly sarcastic to note that the one who was most interested in the victory of the Communist dictatorship in Russia and in the immediate recognition of the Government of the Soviets sent the cable in the name of the "Association of the League of Free Nations", headed by the same Jacob Schiff and financed by five American bankers.

It has already been noted in the previous chapter that Article 231 of the Treaty of Versailles obliged Germany to assume full responsibility for the war, and it has also been seen that on 16 June 1919 there was even a note of extension to this article, in which Germany was directly accused of having planned and initiated the war. Moreover, it was added that the German people were responsible for the deeds of their Government. This was a moral condemnation of an entire people, which was historically unprecedented. It was on 16 June itself that the Allied reply to the diplomatic letter was handed to the German delegation. When Chancellor Scheidemann saw that the arguments put forward by the German government had been ignored, he refused to sign the letter and resigned. On 21 July a new government was formed under the leadership of Gustav Bauer, which succeeded in getting the Reichstag to approve the signing of the Treaty. The conditions stated: "The German Reich Government is prepared to sign the peace treaty, without, however, acknowledging that the German people are responsible for the war".

Count Brockdorff-Rantzau, claiming that his concept of honour prevented him from signing the document, resigned and left Paris. France and Britain threatened to resume the blockade if the Treaty was not signed. In these circumstances an unknown person named von Haniel, whose name appears in no other historical event, replaced Brockdorff-Rantzau and announced on 23 June that the German Government would bow to all the demands of its enemies. Some of the clauses of the treaty," the acceptance text said, "have only been included in it in order to humiliate the German people. We bow before the violence to which we are subjected because, after all that we have suffered, we no longer have any means of replying. But this abuse of force cannot tarnish the honour of the German people." Two days earlier, at the base at Scapa Flow, where the German war fleet was held, German Admiral von Reuter, taking advantage of the fact that the British surveillance squadron had put to sea for firing exercises, had ordered the hatches, hatches and torpedo tubes of all the ships to be opened and then ordered the German flag to be lowered from the masts. As the boats were lowered, sirens wailed and alarm bells sounded. Seventy ships slowly sank to the bottom of the sea.

On 28 June 1919, Germany signed the Treaty in the Hall of Mirrors of the Palace of Versailles, the "Diktat", which contained three types of clauses: territorial, military and financial. Under the first, Germany lost 88,000 km2 and eight million inhabitants: France annexed Alsace-Lorraine and the territory of the Saar was placed under its administration, allowing it to exploit the mining region for fourteen years. Belgium took over the counties of Eupen and Malmedy. The territory of Memel, the northern part of East Prussia on the Baltic, came under French administration, and in 1924 the League of Nations awarded it to Lithuania without a plebiscite. Denmark annexed North Schleswig. Poland, which had not existed as a state since 1795, received Posen and part of West Prussia in order to give it an outlet to the sea. This created the Danzig Corridor, which separated East Prussia from the rest of Germany. Danzig, a city inhabited almost exclusively by Germans, became a so-called "free city" under the theoretical protection of the League of Nations. The southern part of Upper Silesia, a very important mining region, also became part of the new Polish state. To these losses must be added the Sudetenland, which by the Treaty of Saint-Germain was handed over to Czechoslovakia, a newly created country whose moral, social and political cohesion was non-existent. As for the German colonies, they were transformed into mandates and assigned, under League of Nations tutelage, to France, Great Britain and Commonwealth countries such as Australia, New Zealand and the South African Union.

The military clauses imposed: the seizure of the merchant and war fleets, the reduction of the German army to 100,000 soldiers, the abolition of military schools, of the General Staff, of heavy artillery, of tanks and of aviation. The manufacture of war material was prohibited. As for the financial clauses, Germany had to pay for the reconstruction of the regions it had occupied militarily in France, Belgium and Romania. It was also required to repair the damage caused by French troops in Alsace-Lorraine and to pay for the war damage suffered by the civilian population in the unoccupied regions. It also had to bear the costs of the occupying troops on its own territory. Germany was forced to accept control of inland navigation on its major rivers, which meant the internationalisation of its waterways. It was required to pay 20 billion gold marks by 1 May 1921, and a reparations commission was set up to calculate the final amount to be claimed from Germany. Finally, on 27 April 1921, this commission, which was chaired by the ineffable Raymond Poincaré, established that Germany should pay 132 billion gold marks. Germany refused to accept this impossible sum, which was equivalent to the total assets of the country in 1914. On 5 May 1921, an ultimatum was issued: if this debt was not recognised, the Anglo-French fleet would resume its blockade of Germany and would occupy the Ruhr, Germany's mining and industrial heartland, which Franco-Belgian troops did on 11 January 1923.

The creation of the League of Nations and its failure

President Wilson, a great promoter of the League of Nations, succeeded in getting the League of Nations Covenant adopted by the Peace Conference on 25 April 1919 and annexed to the various peace treaties. It actually came into force on 28 June, the date on which the Treaty of Versailles was signed, although it was founded in Geneva on 10 March 1920. This project of "universal justice and democratic fraternity" was a prime example of the hypocrisy of its promoters, who pursued only their own ends and the aims of those who aspired to world government. After dismembering four empires, the internationalists intended the League of Nations to be a supranational body that would neutralise all the problems arising from the multiple shifting of borders and the location of populations within the new states.

On the other hand, while according to the Treaty on National Minorities the Jewish minority was to be fully respected in all countries, France and England, which had expanded their colonial dominions, ignored the aspirations of the colonised peoples of Africa and Asia. While the

Zionists imposed their claims on Palestine, the rights of the Palestinian people, who had inhabited that land for thousands of years before Christ, were disregarded. While in Poland the Jews could force the entire population to respect their Sabbath, in the United States the rights of the black minority were continually violated. Despite all these contradictions, the rabbis of France affirmed: "This League of Nations is the first application in the political order of the principles of peace and fraternity that Judaism has proclaimed since the prophets in the civilised world". For his part Rabbi Simon Tor Yacal demanded the liberation of Jerusalem and asserted that "the League of Nations, a chaste creature born of the spirit of Israel, must live and breathe the air of its father. The League must have its headquarters in Jerusalem". With all this, then, it is not surprising that some detractors of the new body referred to it as the League of Aluci-Nations. The first President of the Council of the League of Nations was a famous Freemason, Léon Bourgeois, who in 1895 had presided over a government in France in which eight of the ten ministers were also Freemasons. If in 1919 Brother Wilson had received the Nobel Peace Prize, in 1920 it was Brother Bourgeois' turn. The second president of the League of Nations was Paul Hymans, a Jew who had represented Belgium at the Peace Conference and who was a member of the lodge *Les Amis Philantropes* of the Grand Orient of Belgium.

When Woodrow Wilson returned to the United States, he had with him precious gems and gifts worth a million dollars in gold, offered by his Masonic brethren and other "friends" in order to secure his efforts on behalf of the League of Nations, the body that was to guarantee world peace and establish a new order. Clemenceau had asked Wilson to create an international force that would be under the executive control of the League of Nations, but the American president had refused on the grounds that his country's constitution did not permit such a surrender of sovereignty. In any case, everything seemed to be on track until the surprise: the Senate reminded Wilson that the signing of treaties required the approval of the House by a two-thirds majority. With his Democratic administration living side by side with a Republican majority in the Senate, a deal had to be struck. It might have been wiser to go to the Peace Conference with strong Republican representation to avoid such a setback. In any case, there was a belief in Europe that President Wilson would overcome the obstacle.

However, the president's request for US membership in the League of Nations was not approved. The Senate's rejection of the Treaty of Versailles and the Covenant of the League of Nations jeopardised the whole scheme laid out in Paris. Republicans did not accept, among other things, that the United States should cede its national sovereignty to an international body, nor were they willing to commit military or naval force to intervene in conflicts between nations without congressional authorisation. They did not consider it admissible that the United States could be subject to arbitration or investigation by the Assembly of the League of Nations, nor that they should be obliged to contribute to any of the expenses of that body. Despite the impasse, Wilson was determined to play one last trick and set out on a tour of the country to try to sell the idea of the League of Nations directly to the American people. In 22 days he travelled 8,000 miles and his health began to fail. At the end of September, after suffering constant headaches, he collapsed in exhaustion in Pueblo, Colorado, and had to return to Washington, where on 2 October he suffered a stroke that nearly killed him and left him paralysed. When he recovered, he tried to resume his campaign, which ended in an election defeat in 1920. Warren Harding was sworn into office in March 1921 and began a Republican term that was to last until 1933, when the Democrats put Franklin D. Roosevelt in the White House. Thomas Woodrow Wilson died on 3 February 1924. His alter ego, Edward Mandell House, ended up alone and forgotten in his New York flat. Both had been nothing but puppets in the service of the powerful bankers who had used them until they were useful to them.

In 1922, two years after its noisy founding in Geneva, the first General Assembly of the League of Nations met. Despite the disappointment of the withdrawal of the United States, it was proclaimed that it was an international of the peoples which should bring about the constitution of a Super-State with all powers, i.e. executive, legislative and judicial. It was also openly declared that the more it relied on Masonic groupings throughout the world, the more moral and real strength it would have. It is clear that the idea of World Government, opposed to the principle of the existence of nation states, was pursued in two formally different ways. While the League of Nations, "a Jewish idea", according to the Zionist leader Nahum Sokolov, aspired to an international of the peoples, to a Super-State; the Communists, for whom the bourgeoisie was not part of the people, proclaimed the international dictatorship of the proletariat. The conspiracy had set two systems in motion in order to achieve the same goal, and the international Jewish bankers were ready to use either of them to reshape the world to suit their interests. The communist experiment was to cost over a hundred million lives across the globe. After the United States' non-participation, the League of Nations was bound to fail: it failed to exercise any authority and struggled to survive until it was replaced in 1946 by the UN.

San Remo Conference, *Balfour Declaration* and British Mandate

In addition to the Treaty of Versailles, the Peace Conference gave rise to other treaties. The boundaries of Austria, which became a country of 84,000 square kilometres with a population of six and a half million, were defined in the Treaty of Saint-Germain, signed on 10 September 1919, which reordered Central and Eastern Europe. The Treaty of Trianon, signed on 4 June 1920, established the Hungarian borders. The new state was reduced to

92,000 km2 for a population of eight million. The Treaty of Sèvres, signed on 10 August 1920, was never ratified by Turkey, which lost Eastern Thrace and Smyrna to Greece, as well as Armenia and Kurdistan, which gained independence. The Bosphorus Straits and the Dardanelles were transferred to an international commission. The Sultan's acceptance of these peace terms prompted a reaction from the Young Turks, who declared war on Greece. Mustafa Kemal Ataturk and many of his followers were Jewish apostates, "doenmes", who took advantage of the situation to overthrow Mehmet VI and establish the Republic on 29 October 1923. Earlier, on 23 July 1923, the Treaty of Lausanne annulled the clauses of the Treaty of Sèvres concerning the above-mentioned territories, which were returned to Turkey. In 1936, by the Montreaux international agreement, Turkey regained control of the straits.

The imperative need to reasonably limit the length of this work prevents us from expanding on the relevant events that took place in the Ottoman Empire, as well as to dwell on the silenced genocide of one and a half million Armenian Christians, which took place between 1915 and 1923 under the rule of the Young Turks, who, through the Committee for Union and Progress, had organised a coup d'état against Sultan Abdul Hamid II in 1908 and seized power. Here are just a few facts. The founder of the Young Turks movement was a Jewish Freemason named Emmanuel Carasso, the leader in Salonika of the Italian lodge *Macedonia Risorta*, to which all the members of the movement belonged. Carasso shared with his co-religionist Alexander Parvus the lucrative business of supplying supplies to the Ottomans during the World War. In addition to various publications and numerous pamphlets, Carasso financed the newspaper *The Young Turk*, edited by the Zionist Vladimir Jabotinsky. One of his partners in the journalistic enterprise was again Alexander Parvus, who was the financial director of another Young Turk newspaper, *The Turkish Homeland*. Emmanuel Carasso was a protégé of the Venetian banker Volpi de Misurata, of whom he was also a partner. This banker was closely allied with the City of London. As a result, in 1909 Sir Ernest Cassel, an Ashkenazi Jew who was the banker to the British Royal Family, established and headed the National Bank of Turkey and command of the Ottoman fleet was handed over to a British admiral. The Young Turks were quick to halt the construction of the Orient Express, which was to link Berlin and Baghdad. Control of the Ottoman Empire had been planned in the Masonic lodges of Thessaloniki, Paris and Vienna. The Salonika Committee, in addition to Carasso, included the Jews Salem, Sassun, Fardji, Meslah, and Doenmes or crypto-Jews such as David Bey and the Baldji family. It can be said that the so-called Young Turk Revolution was equivalent in the Ottoman Empire to the Judeo-Bolshevik Revolution in the Russian Empire. David Bey, who was Minister of Finance surrounded by numerous British advisors, and other Doenmes of Thessaloniki who carried out the revolution were descendants of the followers of an 18th century Jewish cult, whose leader was the false messiah Baruchyah Russo, in whom the soul of Shabbetay Zeví was believed to have been reincarnated through the process of metempsychosis. It seems clear that the responsibility for the Armenian genocide must be attributed, with all the relevant connotations, to those in power, i.e., the Young Turks.

With regard to the dismemberment of the Ottoman empire, which was designed in 1916 in the secret Sykes-Picot agreements, and the division of its territories in the Middle East between France and Britain, we are interested in the San Remo Resolution for Palestine, signed on 25 April 1920 and based on the *Balfour Declaration* of 1917. This Resolution is the fundamental document that made it possible to establish the British Mandate for Palestine. On 24 July 1922 the Council of the League of Nations confirmed the Resolution, which was signed by fifty-one states. As a consequence of the San Remo Resolution, all previous agreements affecting the region, including the Sykes-Picot agreement, were abolished. Zionism has always considered the legal implications of this Resolution to be decisive, since, according to Zionists, it granted the Jewish people de jure sovereignty over Palestine and obliged Britain to honour its *Balfour Declaration* promises to the Mandate nation. However, Lord Curzon, the Secretary of State in the Foreign Office who with Lloyd George led the British delegation to San Remo, interpreted the *Balfour Declaration* with more caution and less euphoria. Initially, the Conference established a national home for the Jewish people in Palestine, whose territory comprised both sides of the Jordan River, i.e. Transjordan (present-day Jordan) and the Gaza Strip included. However, in 1922 the British partitioned Transjordan and created an emirate that was handed over to Abdullah I, a member of the Hashemite family that had been expelled by Ibn Saud from Saudi Arabia.

The minutes of the meeting on Palestine of the Supreme Council of the Allied Forces on 24 April 1920 show that the *Balfour Declaration* was not as emphatic and definitive a document as the Zionists claimed, and that at San Remo they sought to expand and improve it. Lord Curzon resisted the pressure and absolutely refused to move one iota beyond the original text. "The fairest thing to do is to abide strictly by the original terms," he said, "beyond which the British Government was not prepared to go." It should be made clear that Lord Curzon was one of the members of the British Cabinet who had opposed the Zionist project when the terms of the Declaration were being discussed. He argued that Palestine's resources were too limited to sustain a Jewish state and that any move in this direction would provoke antagonistic reaction from the Arabs in the region. According to the minutes, Lord Curzon was convinced that the French delegation would not refuse to accede to the text as originally drafted.

However, Philippe Berthelot, France's top foreign ministry representative, disagreed and suggested that the proposal might have to be submitted to the League of Nations. Berthelot asked whether the *Balfour*

Declaration in favour of the Zionists had been generally accepted by the Allies. After pointing out that he had no wish to offend the British Government, he reported that as far as he could remember, "there had never been any official acceptance of the Declaration by the Allies of the British Government". Against these words, Lord Curzon argued that Berthelot was not entirely familiar with the history of the matter and reminded him that in February 1918 Nahum Sokolov had communicated the terms of the Declaration to the then French Foreign Minister, Stéphen Pichon. Lord Curzon pointed out that the Declaration envisaged, firstly, the creation of a national home for the Jews, whose privileges and rights were to be safeguarded by a military power; secondly, it was of the utmost importance to guarantee the rights of minorities, first the Arabs and then the Christian communities, as stated in the second part of the text. He therefore argued that, in the interests of these communities, to which Berthelot had referred, it was unwise to delete the second part of the Declaration. Berthelot then asked for the text to be read out and added that, as far as he knew, Pichon had agreed to establish the traditional home for Jews, but it was not clear that he had accepted the Declaration in full. Lord Curzon rejected Berthelot's arguments and told him that he could hardly maintain that Pichon was unaware of the full text of the document and its meaning. Curzon reminded him that Pichon had not only endorsed the *Balfour Declaration* on behalf of his government, but had written in his letter of reply to Sokolov that "the agreement between the French and British governments on the question was complete".

When there were virtually no Jews in Palestine and those who were there did not share Zionist views, it is puzzling that the British and French should refer to "minorities" to refer to the native inhabitants, the Palestinian people, who owned one hundred percent of the land and had inhabited it since time immemorial. In probing or exploring the possibilities of deleting the second part of the *Balfour Declaration,* the part referring to the Arab population, it seems clear that Berthelot represented the interests of the Zionists, for whom the Palestinians did not exist. Pressure at San Remo to amend the text of the Declaration in favour of Zionism was therefore unsuccessful. This little diplomatic spat between Lord Curzon and Philippe Berthelot serves as a preamble to go back and explain in some detail how this famous document came into being and how the British Mandate for Palestine was prepared.

From the very beginning the Zionists understood that in order to take the land from the people who inhabited it, they needed the protection of a great power and its army. Already in 1915 Dr. Weizmann had foreseen it in these words: "The taking possession of the country by the Jews, on whom the whole weight of the organisation rests, will have to be carried out during the next ten or fifteen years under a temporary British protectorate". When the British government realised what Zionism intended, it became alarmed at the prospect of acting as the sole protector of Zionist Jews in Palestine and looked to the United States to share in the occupation of the country. In order to raise the issue, Lord Balfour crossed the Atlantic. Before setting out, Balfour had a long conversation with Weizmann, who learned first-hand that the British were anxious to agree to an Anglo-American protectorate. Since the Zionists feared the reaction of American public opinion, they decided to reject this approach. On 8 April 1917, Weizmann wrote to Justice Brandeis asking him to oppose the plan and to work to get the US government to support the proposal for a single British protectorate. It was eighteen days after Britain had entered the war when Lord Balfour arrived in Washington. President Wilson decided to leave the matter in the hands of the Zionists around him, namely Brandeis, Mandell House and Rabbi Wise. To the latter he said specifically, "When the time comes that you and Justice Brandeis think the matter is ripe for me to step in and act, I shall be ready." It appears that the Foreign Office Secretary did not even meet Woodrow Wilson, as he accepted without complaint the Zionists' wishes for British administration of Palestine. His biographer writes that he "pledged his personal support for Zionism".

Of the highest order was the role of the Rothschilds both in the Mandate affair and in the drafting and reception of the *Balfour Declaration*. The Damascus Affair marked the beginning of the progressive involvement of the French and British Rothschilds in the task of making Palestine the future Jewish state. It was the French house which, through Baron Edmond de Rothschild, youngest son of James de Rothschild, became directly involved in colonisation projects in Palestine. In 1882 Edmond sponsored the establishment of the first colony at Rishon LeZion and bought land from Ottoman landowners. Today, Edmond de Rothschild's face appears on the 500 shekel note, several towns in Israel are named after him and there is a Rothschild Boulevard in Tel Aviv. His son James Armand, Jimmy to his friends, financed the Knesset (Parliament) building. Jimmy's wife, Dorothy de Rothschild, Dolly, donated the most significant building of the Zionist state, the Supreme Court of Justice in Jerusalem, where one can admire an architectural display of all the symbols of Masonic Illuminism, dominated by a huge green pyramid with The All Seeing Eye, symbol of the New World Order.

On 9 November 2004, a Jew named Jerry Golden published on the internet (goldenisraelreport.com/EvilRoots.htm) a report entitled *The Roots of Evil in Jerusalem in* which, after accepting that he will be branded an anti-Semite, he exposes the existence of a diabolical force based in Jerusalem, which has spread from there throughout Israel. In this report, illustrated with startling photographs, he denounces the architectural design of the Supreme Court of Justice, a building designed and financed by the Rothschilds, as visible proof of the diabolical plot of illuminati Freemasonry and those who seek to establish the New World Order. The report explains in detail the meaning of all the Masonic elements architecturally displayed inside the Supreme Court. Two photographs show from different positions a huge green pyramid, the same as the one on the US dollar note, with The All Seeing Eye at the top. In the first picture the pyramid is seen from inside the building. One of the faces with the Eye of Osiris is cut out perfectly centred behind the glass of a large rectangular-shaped window that opens up to the light in a darkened room. The second is an aerial photograph of the palace as a whole. The top of the four-sided pyramid with the famous Eye, which protrudes above the building through a large circle, is clearly visible. The entire journey inside the courthouse is intended to be a journey from darkness to enlightenment. There is a dimly lit area with a staircase leading up to an all-encompassing luminosity. The steps total 30 and form three groups of ten separated by two landings. At the top of the staircase is a glassed-in bay window overlooking Jerusalem. From there you enter the great library, which has three floors or levels, the number required to reach 33, the high degree reserved for the enlightened in Scottish Rite Freemasonry. The first level of the library is for lawyers only; the second, for serving judges only; the third, for retired judges only. The display of symbols is constant throughout this Masonic temple. Perfectly assembled, forming part of the ingenious architectural design of the building, are all the usual elements of Freemasonry: inverted crosses on which one walks, an Egyptian obelisk, combinations of figures that add up to six, the square and compass forming part of the floor of a large inner courtyard, the letter "G", and so on.

In addition to the Rothschilds mentioned above, Niall Ferguson comments that after Nathaniel (Natty)'s death in 1915, his two sons, Walter and Charles, shared with their French relatives the Zionist fervour. The latter's wife, Rozsika von Wertheimstein, was introduced by Jimmy to Zionist leader Chaim Weizmann in July 1915. Through her Weizmann made contact with influential people such as Lord Robert Cecil, under-secretary of the Foreign Office, and General Allenby, the future 'liberator' of Jerusalem. However, Weizmann himself declared that the best way to "associate the name of the most important house of Jewry with the granting of the Magna Charta of Jewish liberation" was to secure the support of Walter, Nathaniel's heir and the new head of the New Court, who was considered a king by world Jewry. Shortly before his death, Nathaniel had in January 1915 endorsed the memorandum of the Zionist Herbert Samuel, who in 1920 was to be appointed High Commissioner for Palestine. The title of the document was *The Future of Palestine* and it called for a British protectorate "in which the scattered Jews would gradually concentrate en masse from the four corners of the globe and in due course achieve autonomy". The idea of Britain sharing power in Palestine with France was rejected by Walter himself, who wrote a letter to Weizmann opposing the idea: "England must have sole control," were his words. The English Rothschilds were unwilling to see the experiment of shared control of the Suez Canal in Egypt repeated in Palestine.

In 1917 the moment of decision came. The final outcome logically depended on the balance of power within the government. Walter Rothschild had the most influential members on his side: Prime Minister David Lloyd George, Alfred Milner and Arthur Balfour, the Foreign Office Secretary, who asked Lord Rothschild to send him a text that could serve as a proposal for a declaration. On 18 July 1917 Lord Rothschild wrote a letter to Lord Balfour, quoted by B. Jensen in his *The Palestine Plot*, which reads as follows:

"Dear Mr. Balfour,
At last I can send you the formula you asked for. If Her Majesty's Government would send me a message along the lines of this formula and they and you would approve it, I would present it to the Zionist Federation at a conference convened for this purpose.
The draft tax return is as follows:
(1) His Majesty's Government accepts the principle that Palestine should be reconstituted as a national home for the Jewish people.
(2) His Majesty's Government will use its best endeavours to ensure the achievement of the said objective and will discuss the necessary methods and means with the Zionist Organisation".

The crucial meeting of the British government took place on 17 October 1917. According to Niall Ferguson, Lord Rothschild himself was responsible for pressuring and urging Lloyd George through Lord Milner, his agent in the War Cabinet, to put the Palestine issue on the agenda, for if the decision was delayed, the Germans could pre-empt it and issue their own pro-Zionist declaration in order to win Jewish support in the United States and Russia. Finally, on 2 November 1917, the British government sent the famous *Balfour Declaration* to Sir Walter Lionel Rothschild, President of the Jewish communities in Britain, which was drafted by the Jew Leopold Amery, Assistant Secretary to the War Cabinet, who in 1925 went to Palestine as Colonial Secretary to the British government. The reader can compare similarities and differences with the above text:

"His Majesty's Government view with sympathy the establishment in Palestine of a national home for the Jewish people and will use their best endeavours to facilitate the attainment of that objective, it being clearly understood that nothing shall be done which would prejudice the civil and religious rights of existing non-Jewish communities in Palestine, or the rights and political status enjoyed by Jews in another country."

This text is regarded as one of the most important documents of the 20th century. To emphasise the Rothschilds' contribution to this historic achievement, on 2 December there was a great celebration at the Covent Garden Opera House, during which Walter and Jimmy addressed the audience. Lord Rothschild told the enthusiastic audience that this was "the greatest event in Jewish history for the last eighteen hundred years". For his part, Jimmy declared that the British government had "ratified the Zionist plan".

The *Balfour Declaration* received almost total support from the international community; however, a comparison of the texts cited above now provides a better understanding of the dialogue held in San Remo on 24 April 1920 between Lord Curzon and the French diplomat Philippe Berthelot. In the text initially proposed by Lord Rothschild, the Arabs or "non-Jewish communities" did not deserve any consideration; but the *Balfour* Declaration spoke of "the civil and religious rights of the non-Jewish communities in Palestine". It seems clear that the theses of Lord Curzon and the non-Zionist members of the Cabinet had managed to find expression in the text of the *Balfour Declaration*. Also striking is the reference to "the rights and political status enjoyed by Jews in another country", which raises the suspicion that the intention was to safeguard non-Zionist Jews from any migratory pressure. It is therefore understandable that at the San Remo Conference the Zionists sought to improve or modify the document in their favour.

The facts on the ground were to demonstrate the aims of international Zionism. Before the Peace Conference began, under the pretext of liaising between the British Military Administration and the Jews, a Zionist Commission was sent to Palestine, which arrived in early March 1918. Its real intentions were to "advise" General Clayton that his Administration should collaborate with them in everything. Predictably, Chaim Weizmann travelled with the Commission. James de Rothschild, Jimmy, Edmond de Rothschild's son, was another prominent member. He was joined by Israel Sieff and Major Ormsby-Gore, the future Lord Harlich, who was a director of the Midland Bank and who, as a director of the Standard Bank of South Africa, had contributed to the Boer War for control of South Africa's gold and diamonds. Israel Sieff was a director of Marks & Spencers and a partner of several international bankers. Sieff was appointed chairman of the Economic and Political Planning Committee and was a permanent member of the brain trust that advised successive British governments. As a reward for his services to international Jewish banking, he was appointed head of the Order of the Maccabees. Leon Simon, later knighted, was in charge of the British General Post Office and controlled all telegraphic and telephone communications. Propaganda was in the hands of Edwin Samuel, who during World War II acted as chief censor for the British government. When the State of Israel was proclaimed in 1948, Samuel was appointed Chief Director of Broadcasting.

In *Palestine, The Reality* (1939) J. M. N. Jeffries recounts an episode which gives an insight into the extent of Zionist arrogance in Palestine before the Mandate was established. In 1919 the parade of leaders was continuous. One of those who travelled from the United States was Louis Dembitz Brandeis, the judge imposed on President Wilson in the Supreme Court. Once in Jerusalem, Brandeis went to the British military barracks on the Mount of Olives and told General Money that the ordinances of the military authorities should be subordinate to the Zionist Commission. The general was stunned by such an arrogant demand, but his aide argued hotly: "For a government to do this would be to abdicate its position. As a lawyer you realise that." Brandeis retorted, "It has to be understood that the British government is committed to supporting the Zionist cause. Unless this is accepted as a guiding principle, I shall have to inform the Foreign Office." A few hours later the Foreign Office, through the War Office, overruled the military. As it was, several officers requested a transfer and Colonel Meinertzhagen, a leading Zionist, was sent to Palestine.

During the decade that followed, despite attempts to encourage illegal immigration to Palestine by all means and to buy land from the Arabs through the Jewish National Fund, it became clear that Weizmann's vision of occupying the country in ten to fifteen years was not feasible. It then began to be thought that a new war would be necessary in order to take the country from the Palestinians and to convince or force hundreds of thousands of Jews from all over the world to migrate to the Promised Land. At the end of August 1929 serious riots between Jews and Palestinians led to the appointment of a commission of enquiry, the Hope-Simpson Commission, whose findings denounced the activities of the Jewish Agency and the Histadrut (General Federation of Labour) as detrimental to the economic development of the Arab population.

In 1930 Lord Passfield, the British colonial secretary, issued the 'Passfield White Paper', an official report on British policy in Palestine, in which he proposed suspending Jewish immigration and curtailing the authority of the Jewish Agency. Chaim Weizmann immediately sought an audience with the British Prime Minister, then Ramsay Macdonald, who, intimidated by the Zionist leader's reproaches, behaved as if threatened with a gun: he not only rescinded the Passfield White Paper, but humbly asked Weizmann whom he wanted him to appoint as the new High Commissioner for Palestine. Despite the increasingly obvious fiasco of the Jewish National Home project and despite the realisation that, as many had predicted, Jews would not themselves go en masse to Palestine, neither American nor British politicians dared to disobey Dr. Weizmann, the emissary of international Zionism.

PART 2
DESPOILMENT, CIVIL WAR AND TERROR IN RUSSIA.
LENIN'S DEATH AND TROTSKY'S DEFEAT

"What is the most difficult thing of all?" Goethe asked himself. He himself gave the answer: "what seems the simplest: to see with our eyes what lies before them". Perhaps this is the reason why so many short-sighted historians fail to explain or ignore that international Jewish bankers conspired with Marxists to overthrow traditional capitalism and replace it with communism. Despite all the evidence, it must be admitted that it is not easy to accept that the Rothschilds, the Morgans, the Warburgs, the Rockefellers, the Schiffs, the Guggenheims..., the most powerful men in the world, supported professional revolutionaries who were supposed to fight them. It may seem contradictory, but that is exactly what happened with the establishment of communism halfway around the world.

Both Dr. Quigley, the "insider" who in his amazing *Tragedy in Hope* offered the keys to the conspiracy, and W. Cleon Skousen in *The Naked Capitalist* make it clear that the contradiction is only apparent. Quigley openly confesses: "the international bankers who have set out to remake the world were absolutely certain that they could use their money to gain the co-operation and control of the Communist and Socialist conspiratorial groups". The aim of these internationalists, the same ones who are globalists today, was to appropriate all the wealth and resources of the planet. To achieve this they used Marxism as their ideology and thousands of agents as political conspirators to overthrow existing governments and replace them with a socialist world dictatorship. John Ruskin, Cecil Rhodes and Alfred Milner were persuaded that through socialist patterns the whole world could be federated. These select agents of the big financiers founded the Round Table, the secret society that was in coalition with the communist conspiracy. Both groups worked for a world run by chosen political leaders, who, advised and financially supported, were to take control of all property, industry, agriculture, education and politics in general. The apostle of the world revolution par excellence, Adam Weishaupt, had already announced this long before: "It is necessary to establish a universal regime of domination, a form of government that will embrace the whole world."

As has been seen, the groups of financiers running the conspiracy from Wall Street and the City of London devoted large sums of money to finance the Marxist revolutionaries. It will be seen below that it did not matter in the least to them that, once in power, the communists would impose a ferocious dictatorship and commit crimes against humanity on a scale unprecedented in history. Studies have shown that the Judeo-Bolsheviks, sick criminals if ever there was one, would never have been able to seize and maintain power in Russia without the financial support they received from the bankers. Let us recall once again that in 1917 the greatest financial aid was organised by Sir George Buchanan and Lord Alfred Milner, the founder of the Round Table who worked as an agent of the Morgan-Rothschild-Rhodes confederation. Trotsky was reportedly married to the daughter of the wealthy banker Givotovsky and was financed by Jacob Schiff of Kuhn Loeb & Company. Other key Jewish bankers in the conspiracy were the Warburgs. Felix Warburg was married to Frieda Schiff, the daughter of Jacob Schiff; Paul Warburg married Nina Loeb, daughter of Salomon Loeb. Max Warburg financed the Russian revolution from Germany, which did not prevent him from later collaborating with the Nazis in the Reichsbank until 1938.

In our opinion, the impunity that the Judeo-Bolsheviks have always enjoyed in the eyes of history is proof that they were agents of the occult power, of the Illuminati, i.e. of the international bankers. While the crimes of Nazism are continually magnified through Hollywood and the media, the world is still waiting for the first film of the film industry, in the hands of Jewish tycoons, to denounce the red terror and the countless crimes of communism in Russia, China and so many other countries. While Himmler or Eichmann are identified as great criminals, Dzerzhinsky, Yagoda, Yezhov or Beria are unknown to the general public. While Hitler, Goebbels or Goering symbolise the worst of humanity, Lenin and Trotsky are still revered by large sections of the public as prestigious leaders of the working class. While Nazi concentration camps are visited by millions and students in Germany and England are scheduled to make annual pilgrimage visits to Auschwitz, the Soviet Gulag remains lost in oblivion as if it had never existed. While nonagenarians are still being prosecuted for alleged crimes committed against Jews during the war, communist criminals have lived free from any prosecution by the courts of justice.

Seventy years after the end of World War II, Germany still imprisons people for their National Socialist past[2]. By contrast, hardly anyone knows,

---

[2] In 2009, the US extradited John Demjanjuk, an 89-year-old man who had been tried in Israel and acquitted in 1993, to Germany. A Munich court had claimed jurisdiction to try him because he had lived near the Bavarian capital in 1952. On 2 May 2011, Demjanjuk, now aged 91, was convicted of complicity in the murder of Jews in Sobibor and sentenced to five years in prison. Finally placed in a nursing home because of his failing health, he died on 17 March 2012. On 22 December 2010, a German prosecutor in the city of Dortmund brought charges against a ninety-year-old man, Samuel Kunz, a former Belzec concentration camp guard, accusing him of helping to kill hundreds of thousands of Jews. On 1 August 2012 the press in Hungary reported that Laszlo Csatary, a ninety-seven-year-old man accused by the Simon Wiesenthal Centre of having overseen the deportation of thousands of Jews, had been arrested at the request of the French Foreign Minister. On 7 August 2012, Reuters reported that Nadja Drygalla, a German athlete planning to participate in the London Olympics, had a boyfriend who was a neo-Nazi, prompting Germany to consider forcing all athletes to pledge their commitment to democracy. On 27 January 2013, Chancellor Angela Merkel declared, "Germany bears eternal

since it has never been publicised, that the Soviet concentration camps, called colonies or labour camps, were run by Jews who were never accused of anything, despite the fact that, according to Robert Conquest's figures in *The Great Terror,* twelve million people no one remembers perished in the Gulag. Prominent among these Jews was Naftaly Frenkel, who proposed to Stalin the construction of a canal linking the Baltic Sea to the White Sea. The chief engineer was the Jew Gregory Davidsohn Afanasjew and the supervisors of the work were the Jews Aron Solts and Jacob Rappoport. This pharaonic project cost the lives of 250,000 prisoners. In volume II of *Gulag Archipelago,* Alexander Solzhenitsyn provides valuable information, illustrated with photos and drawings, on the construction of the canal, on Naftaly Frenkel and on his "hired killers". Among the most prominent Jewish criminals in the general administration of the concentration camps denounced by Solzhenitsyn are Matvei Davidovich Berman, director of the concentration camps; Semion Firin and Abraham Appeter, directors of prisons; Lazarus Josephsohn Kagan, head of the Baltic Sea camps; Abraham Isaaksohn Rottenberg, chief in charge of prisoners in isolation and at the same time head of the Atheist Action League; Samuel Kwazenskij, political instructor. There are several others not mentioned by the author of the *Gulag Archipelago,* whose names we have spared.

The economic plundering of Russia also reigns in silence. The opposite is true when it comes to denouncing the intrinsic evil of National Socialism in this respect. In the mid-1990s, a series of sensationalist reports appeared on the laundering of Nazi-stolen money in Switzerland. A worldwide campaign was triggered by a lawsuit filed by the World Jewish Congress. Alleged Holocaust survivors represented by US Senator Alphonse D'Amato filed suit against Swiss banks. Nazi gold made front-page headlines around the world. The BBC proclaimed to be "the greatest robbery in history". The campaign was supported by the publication of books such as Adam Lebor's, which was immediately translated into several languages. It was published in Spain in 1998 under the title *Hitler's Secret Bankers: How Swiss Bankers Profited from Nazi Geonocide.* According to Lebor, the Nazis looted $289 million from the central banks of the occupied countries.

The looting of Russia by the Bolsheviks is the subject of Professor Sean McMeekin's 2008 book, *History's Greatest Heist. The Looting of Russia by the Bolsheviks.* According to McMeekin, who suggests multiplying the 1918 figures by a hundred to calculate the equivalence of the 1918 figures with those of today, the sales of stolen gold by the Bolsheviks in just eighteen months far exceed the figure given by Lebor. The reason, of

---

responsibility for the crimes of National Socialism, for the victims of World War II and above all for the Holocaust." Six months later, on 13 June 2013, the German parliament passed a resolution to combat anti-Semitism, protect Jewish life in Germany and deepen the relationship with the racist state of Israel, whose crimes have enjoyed impunity since its founding.

course, that there are no campaigns to denounce the plunder and slaughter of gentiles in Russia is because the criminals and thieves were Jews in the service of the secret power that had financed them. "The day is not far off when all the riches and treasures of the world will be the property of the children of Israel", Adolphe Crémieux had announced in the founding manifesto of the Universal Israelite Alliance.

The biggest heist in history

Unlike the Swiss bankers who concealed their collaboration with the Nazis, the main financiers of the genocide in Russia did not bother at all to hide their contribution to the cause of the revolution, but even, as in the case of Jacob Schiff and J. P. Morgan, proudly proclaimed it to the whole world. These same bankers more than recouped their investment, for, once in power, their agents took it upon themselves to launder the gold, silver, platinum and precious stones compulsively stolen by the Judeo-Bolsheviks. For them were the future contracts and the exploitation of Russia's enormous wealth and resources, which they had always coveted. Without this self-interested collaboration it would have been impossible for the communists to stay in power, since the economic ruin of an unproductive country was compounded by civil war. The State Bank of Russia held the largest gold reserves in the world, but there were also the private banks, competitors of the international Jewish banks, as well as the wealth of private individuals and the Church. Therefore, to the imperial gold reserves, one had to add cash, bonds, watches, platinum, jewellery, diamonds and other gems, cutlery, paintings, icons, engravings, books. In other words, all the wealth of a continent accumulated over centuries.

Sean McMeekin recounts in the above-mentioned work the problems that Lenin, Trotsky and their henchmen had in running the banks without the collaboration of employees skilled in financial techniques and the methods of accounting. Anthony C. Sutton writes in *Wall Street and the Bolshevik Revolution* that in this context Trotsky remembered his good friend Bernard Baruch and said: "What we need here is an organiser like Bernard Baruch". A week after the coup, the private banks, which knew of Lenin's nationalising intentions, closed their doors. The State Bank and the Treasury remained open, but throughout November refused to accede to the request for funds made on behalf of the Council of People's Commissars (Sovnarkom). The Council then issued a decree threatening to arrest bank managers who refused to facilitate the withdrawal of funds. I. P. Shipov, the director of the State Bank, persuaded his colleagues not to give in and informed the Sovnarkom that the State Bank had earmarked 600 million roubles for army pay and public charity, which maintained kitchens for the poor.

On 23 November the employees of the State Bank went on strike. On 24 November, after unsuccessful attempts to obtain money, Lenin sent the new Commissar of Finance, Vyacheslav Menzhinsky, with an ultimatum: If Shipov did not give in, all the bank's employees would be dismissed, lose their pensions and the younger ones would be drafted. In the face of the new refusal, Shipov was dismissed and replaced by a financial team of Bolsheviks, who, although they had knowledge of the books and manuals of the banking system, did not know the technical procedures of the State Bank of Russia, whose endless corridors and complicated machinery were inaccessible to them. They needed to know how many cash boxes there were, how many safe deposit boxes and where the keys were hidden. They opted for hostage-taking: the manager of the Petrograd branch, the chief cashier, the chief accountant and the vault keeper were forced to cooperate at gunpoint.

In December 1917 almost all state officials refused to collaborate with the Bolshevik government, which was considered illegal: teachers, telegraph and telephone employees, water transport workers, municipal officials in Petrograd and Moscow went on strike against the so-called workers' government. Lenin then chose Felix Dzerzhinsky to head the Cheka (Extraordinary Commission for Combating Counterrevolution and Sabotage), set up on 20 December with the task of liquidating practically without any legal limits any counter-revolutionary acts. It should not be forgotten that in November, eighteen days after the coup d'état, elections for a Constituent Assembly had been held and the Bolsheviks had been left in a minority. Parliament was scheduled to be constituted on 18 January 1918. It was only natural, therefore, that the bank managers and the whole country expected the formation of a legal government to emanate from these elections. As if that were not enough, on 27 December 1917, the Jew Grigori Sokolnikov (Girsh Yankelovich Brilliant), appointed as the new director of the State Bank, abolished private banks by decree, and the Bolsheviks demanded all bank deposits of more than 5,000 roubles. The decree stipulated that, upon receipt of the notification, owners of safes had three days to present themselves at the bank with the keys to their safes. Not surprisingly, everyone ignored the decree of a government that wanted to blatantly steal people's property, since there was the conviction that the days of the Bolsheviks were numbered. Nobody expected that on 18 January there would be a second coup d'état and that the parliamentarians would be dissolved by the Red Guards and the Latvian regiments acting as shock troops of the Soviet government. On the same day, thousands of people demonstrating outside the Tauride Palace, where the Constituent Assembly was meeting, were dispersed by gunfire and around 20 were killed.

The system put in place by Sokolnikov to proceed with the looting consisted of calling out in alphabetical order all the owners of safes. The names of those who did not show up or refused to cooperate were marked as "enemies of the people". As early as February 1918, the letter "L" had already been reached in Petrograd. Max Laserson, commercial director of the Shuvalov Mining Company, turned up with the keys to his safe and became a collaborator of the communists. Laserson later described how the operation was carried out to steal valuables: gold bars and coins, platinum, silver, precious stones and foreign currency. According to Laserson, "the confiscated silver, gold, precious stones and pearls... were accumulated in such enormous quantities that they can hardly be conceived of.... I passed through large rooms filled to the ceiling with all sorts of boots, suitcases, boxes, baskets, bags, etc.". Actually that was the easiest part of the general looting that was intended to be carried out. The banks, in addition to gold reserves, jewellery and cash, had depositary obligations, shares and government bonds. But it was not all assets: taking control of the banks also meant taking over the liabilities. In any case, many owners of safes had fled abroad or were in hiding, so on 10 November 1918 the Trotskyite Nikolai Krestinsky, another Jew who had recently been appointed Commissar of Finance, issued a decree granting certain advantages to those who turned up and collaborated with the government.

In the same month of November 1918, an agency was formed to register all kinds of art objects. Leonid Krasin and Maxim Gorky were the two men commissioned to carry out this task. The writer and Maria Andreeva, his common-law wife, naively believed that it was a matter of saving the Russian cultural heritage and that the confiscated objects were destined for display in "proletarian museums". They soon had occasion to understand the real purpose of the operation. In February 1919, Gorky's agency was subordinated to the Commissariat of Trade, specifically to its Foreign Trade Commission (Narkomvneshtorg), in order to prepare the most valuable antiquities and works of art for possible export. Krasin (Goldgelb), the former Comrade Nikitich, the Judeo-Bolshevik linked to Olof Aschberg (Obadiah Asch) who as director of Siemens-Schuckert in St. Petersburg had established important contacts in Stockholm and Berlin, was empowered by Lenin to supervise the project and to explore the possibility of business with Swedish and German firms. The search that was made of the confiscated antiquities and valuables has enabled researchers such as Sean McMeekin to provide a comprehensive study of the operation, which is the subject of chapter three of his book. The following data is therefore taken from *History's Greatest Heist. The Looting of Russia by the Bolsheviks.*

Most of the treasure stolen by the Bolsheviks left Russia via the Estonian port of Tallinn. Leonid Krasin himself personally drafted the terms of the Tartu Peace Treaty, which Estonia ratified on 2 February 1920. The Treaty granted the communists almost unlimited use of Estonian railway lines and ports. The next day, 3 February, a decree of the Council of Commissars signed by Lenin appointed the Jewish Trotskyite Nikolai Krestinsky as director of the "Gokhran" (State Treasury for the Storage of

Valuables), whose responsibility was to centralise and record in ledgers all valuables on Soviet territory. Professor McMeekin writes: "From Siberia to the Polish border, from the Black Sea to the Baltic, Russia's tremendous wealth was to be accumulated and prepared for export". Two weeks after the signing of the Treaty of Tartu, Krasin ordered the Gorky-Andreeva commission to begin collecting in the vicinity of Petrograd the most valuable objects for possible export. In his brief he emphasised "articles made of gold, silver and platinum, as well as precious stones and pearls".

On 16 March 1920, Krestinsky ordered the Gokhran workers to start preparing the precious metals in piles of platinum, iridium, gold and silver. The jewellery was to be stacked into pearls and precious stones, which, at the same time, were to be separated by size. Separately, diamonds were to be disassembled from the objects containing them and sorted by carat. By mid-July, the 'harvest' accumulated at Gokhran amounted to 21,563 carats of diamonds, 20,305 carats of pearls, three thousand gold, silver and platinum watches, two hundred kilos of artistic jewellery, about one hundred kilos of gold bars and nuggets, thirty tonnes of silver, about eight thousand gold-plated artistic objects, half a tonne of gold fragments and 41,845 pieces of silver, the weight of which is not specified. On the world markets the value of all this amounted to 225 million roubles, about 112.5 million dollars. By the end of November 1920 the value of the art objects accumulated in Gokhram had exceeded 490 million roubles or $245 million, or about $25 billion in today's dollars. It has been said that in order to calculate the approximate present value of the figures, it is necessary to multiply by a hundred.

Krestinsky had a mandate to amass the loot of the entire Eurasian continent, but for the first six months the Gokhran focused on the bank vaults in Moscow and Petrograd that remained unopened. Thirty-five thousand were opened during the summer of 1918, but the pace of looting stagnated. Approximately fifty-one thousand boxes confiscated by the communists remained, the owners of which had not turned up. Two years later, in September 1920, only about twelve thousand seven hundred had been emptied, another fourteen thousand nine hundred were opened by force, but there remained about twenty-three thousand three hundred which had resisted all efforts. In view of the slow pace of the process, Krestinsky decided to set up another body, the Seifovaia Komissiia (Seifovaia Komissiia), subordinate to the Commissariat of Finance, which began its operations in August 1920, supervised by the Cheka. In the effort to structure the logistics of looting, yet another bureaucratic apparatus was created, the Financial Inspectorate (Finninspektsiia).

The massive dumping of Russian diamonds on the Tallinn, Stockholm and Copenhagen markets became a problem, as it threatened to destroy the artificial price ceiling set by the Oppenheimer family, who dominated the world market after taking control of South African diamonds. In 1920,

Krasin himself sold £40,000 worth of diamonds in London. All this led the communists to court the De Beers consortium, with the intention of selling them the diamonds stored by the Gokhran in bulk. In general, the flooding of the markets with the precious metals and stones that the communists were trying to sell distorted prices, which plummeted.

The mass confiscation of the wealth of the Church, whose assets and movable property had been nationalised in January 1918, did not begin until early 1922. It was in the context of the civil war against the peasantry and the great famine of 1921, which caused five million deaths, that the communists organised a campaign to justify the theft in the eyes of the population, mostly united with the Orthodox Church. In the summer of 1921, famine in the Volga region began to alarm the Soviet government, which publicly admitted that 25 million Russians were on the verge of starvation. With the onset of winter, Trotsky took centre stage, as Lenin was forced to withdraw from the limelight due to health problems that two years later would lead to his ultimate demise. In January 1922 Trotsky wrote an article that was widely circulated in the Soviet press. In it, accused the Orthodox Church of failing to provide assistance to the needy. It was asked to sell its gold and silver valuables to help the hungry. The campaign was supplemented by thousands of letters from supposed readers of *Izvestia and Pravda,* supporting the confiscation of church property. Many of these letters were written by clerics collaborating with the regime, the so-called "renovationists", who even let slip that Patriarch Tikhon was threatening generous Christian donors who sought to help with excommunication. "Turn gold into bread" was the slogan coined by Trotsky for his "agitprop" campaign, inviting the masses to steal from the churches on the grounds that the reactionary clerics were sabotaging the authorities' relief efforts.

Sean McMeekin describes these arguments as "a lie from beginning to end" and claims that in 1921 the communists had sold gold and other precious metals worth 200 million dollars at the time, money that had not been used to alleviate the hunger of the population, but for strategic imports, especially in the field of armaments. McMeekin adds that in the context of the famine, instead of buying grain and seeds for the affected regions, imports of items considered luxury goods for party members were made, for example, chocolate bought in London worth 30 million Tsarist roubles; fruit, tobacco and opium from Persia worth 63 million roubles; and thousands of tons of Swedish herring, Finnish seasoned fish, German bacon and French pork fat. Georg Solomon writes in *Unter den Roten Machthabern* (*Among the Red Rulers*) that, "while the people starved", Soviet elites consumed such delicacies as "truffles, pineapples, mandarin oranges, mandarins, bananas, nuts, sardines and God knows what else".

In January 1922 Leonid Krasin paid 16,400 gold roubles in London for spare parts for the fleet of Rolls-Royces in which the Communist Party bigwigs were travelling. The impudence and arrogance of the Judeo-

Bolshevik leaders was such that they did not even bother to keep up appearances. Trotsky, Lenin, Dzerzhinsky and company drove through the streets of Petrograd and Moscow in luxurious Rolls-Royces. Lenin claimed for himself the enjoyment of three luxury cars from the garage of Alexander's palace at Tsarkoye Seló, two Rolls-Royces and Nicholas II's old Delauney-Belville Limousine. At first Lenin went from place to place in this vehicle. Professor McMeekin amusingly explains that in March 1918 the limousine was stolen from him at gunpoint, an ironic twist on the phrase "loot the looters", coined by Lenin to justify widespread robbery. From then on Lenin made use of a 1915 Rolls-Royce model that had belonged to Mikhail Romanov. Earlier Kerensky had already set an example of how to behave when in power. In July 1917, installed in the Winter Palace, he decided to make use of Tsar Alexander III's bedroom. Kerensky also requisitioned a Rolls-Royce from a rich foreigner and used it for his travels.

In June 1921 Patriarch Tikhon had organised a committee to help the starving. On 7 July, Tikhon launched an anguished appeal to his parishioners through a pastoral read in all the churches, asking them to quickly take the suffering into their arms "with hearts full of love and desire to save your starving brethren". Here is a significant excerpt: "Carrion has become a choice dish for the starving population, and even that dish is hard to find. The cries and groans are heard everywhere. It has already reached the point of cannibalism? Lend a helping hand to your brothers and sisters! With the agreement of the faithful you can use the treasures of the churches which have no sacramental value to help the hungry, such as rings, chains and bracelets, as well as the ornaments which adorn the holy icons...". Over two hundred thousand copies of this appeal were distributed throughout the nation. On 22 August 1921 the patriarch wrote to the Soviet authorities. He asked for permission for the Orthodox Church to buy supplies directly and to organise relief kitchens in famine areas. Not only was the request denied, but in September 1921 the communists also dissolved the relief committee and arrested its leaders. On 23 February 1922, the expropriation of the Orthodox Church's valuables was ordered by decree. The Archbishop of Petrograd, Veniamin, and Patriarch Tikhon were arrested and declared "enemies of the people."

It was the Americans who were allowed to help. On 13 July 1921 the Soviet government appealed for international relief through Maxim Gorky. The future President Hoover's American Relief Administration (ARA) sent substantial aid to Russia from 20 August onwards. A total of $45 million was allocated and food distribution began. The ARA and its partner organisations fed some 12.5 million mouths. The American Commission on Russian Relief, whose relief efforts Stalin oversaw, estimated that in 1922 there were some three million homeless children and that another two million were on the verge of starvation at home. In *The Harvest of Sorrow* Robert Conquest charges that the Moscow government deliberately failed to inform American aid organisations about the famine areas in Ukraine and furthermore obstructed contact with the areas in need. Most shamefully, as it demonstrates once again the criminal nature of the communist leaders and their disregard for human life, between 1 August 1921 and 1 August 1922 some 500,000 tons of grain were exported from the Ukraine for distribution abroad.

To properly understand the systematic assault on Church property, one must consider that after four years of continuous payments in gold, the communists had exhausted Imperial Russia's reserves. The last consignment of gold, forty tons, left the port of Tallinn on 6 February 1922 aboard the steamship *Gladiator*. The urgent need for more gold was decisive in the campaign of Church robberies, which was directed by Trotsky and entrusted to the Cheka, which at the beginning of the year had been renamed the GPU (Political State Administration). Under Trotsky's full command, the offensive was planned in a series of sessions of the Sovnarkom, the Politburo and the Central Committee of the Communist Party, held in December and January 1921-22. A resolution of the Central Executive Committee of 2 January 1922, which did not contain a single word for the victims of the famine, explicitly stated that church valuables that could be sold would go to the Gokhran. Two further successive decrees, issued on 14 and 23 January, ordered that consignments from all regions should be delivered to the Gokhran without delay. All trains in which the Church's booty was transported were escorted by Red Army officers.

In Trotsky's strategy the propaganda justifying the confiscation was essential, as it was to be presented as a wave of popular anger against the Church. The expected defence of many churches and monasteries by parishioners was to serve at the same time as a justification for the Red Army to crush resistance. In a letter of 19 March 1922 to the members of the Politburo, from which the following extract from Sean McMeekin's book is taken, Lenin expressed himself in these terms:

> "...With so many starving people feeding on human flesh, with the roads congested with hundreds and thousands of corpses, now and only now can we (and consequently must we) confiscate the property of the Church with ferocious and merciless energy. Precisely now and only now can the overwhelming majority of the peasant masses support us, or, more precisely, can they not be in a position to support that handful of clerical Black Hundreds and reactionary petty-bourgeois.... We can thus provide ourselves with a treasury of several hundred million gold roubles. Without this treasury, no state activity in general, no economic realisation in particular, and no defence of our positions is conceivable. We must, at all costs, seize this treasure of several hundred million roubles (perhaps several billion roubles!). All this can only be carried out successfully now."

In mid-April 1922 *Izvestia* reported over fourteen hundred "bloody excesses" as a result of clashes between church supporters and the GPU. In reality, each new clash was perfectly in line with Trotsky's plans and his accusations that the Church was preventing aid to the starving. On 28 March 1922 *Izvestia* had issued instructions on what workers and peasants should do if they wanted to avoid the deaths of millions of dying people: "Despise this band of 'solemn' rabid priests. Burn the holiest counter-revolution with hot iron. Take the gold from the churches. Exchange the gold for bread." Estimates of the number of victims of this particular campaign of terror vary. Official figures acknowledge that twenty-eight bishops and 1,215 priests were killed. Church sources put the murder figures at 2,691 priests, 1,962 monks and 3,447 nuns. "Another twenty thousand parishioners," writes McMeekin, "also lost their lives, most of them old believers who defended their beloved churches with pitchforks and were shot with machine guns."

In Moscow alone there were seven hundred and sixty-four Orthodox churches and another seventy-four chapels. Pieces of art and treasures from a thousand years of Russian history were preserved in them. Each of the city's seven districts was assigned to a looting commission. More than twenty heavily armed men, half of whom were Red Guards or members of the GPU, made up these commissions. By 5 April 1922, they had raided forty-three Orthodox churches and monasteries, from which they had stolen about six and a half tons of treasures. In his research, Professor McMeekin claims that in just three days the raids multiplied and notes that between 5 and 8 April "no less than one hundred and six Moscow churches were plundered and a haul of thirteen tons of valuables was obtained." Between April 24 and 26 "one hundred and thirty churches and three chapels were attacked and thirteen tons of silver and about twenty-five kilos of gold were carried off, besides unspecified quantities of vases and vessels." In Petrograd the looting committees had accumulated by the end of April thirty tons of silver, about seventy kilos of gold, three thousand six hundred and ninety diamonds and three hundred and sixty-seven other precious stones. Valuable Orthodox icons, the oldest of which were from the 15th and 16th centuries, were also confiscated in large quantities. Many ended up in bazaars and antique shops where they were sold at bargain prices. The banker Olof Aschberg personally bought some 280 of them. The Moscow Gokhran received almost all the gold and silver. At the beginning of 1923 there was so much silver accumulated in the Gokhran, some five hundred and fifty tons, that a nearby building had to be emptied for storage.

In addition to systematic looting, tens of thousands of Christian churches were destroyed throughout Russia. Many were turned into public urinals, warehouses and storerooms. An anti-God museum was set up in St. Basil's Cathedral. However, not a single synagogue suffered the slightest damage. While orthodox priests were imprisoned, tortured and even crucified, the rabbis had nothing to fear. In contrast to the numerous anti-

Christian measures, the communists passed a law against anti-Semitism that could lead to the death of the accused. Possession of a copy of the *Protocols of the Elders of Zion* could also lead to imprisonment and even death. Robert Wilton denounces the Talmudic vengeance character underlying many actions perpetrated by the Judeo-Bolsheviks. Perhaps the most significant act was the erection of a monument to Judas Iscariot, a symbolically charged act carried out in 1918 on Trotsky's initiative. In *The Orthodox Encyclopaedia*, Father Alexey Uminskiy reports that Trotsky wanted to be present at the unveiling of the statue. Before his arrival, Bishop Ambrose was hastily assassinated. The reason given for the commemoration of the figure of Judas was that he was considered the "first revolutionary". The image, described by eyewitnesses, depicted a man with a face distorted by anger, looking up to heaven with a clenched fist.

The Judeo-Bolsheviks more than compensated their bosses, the international Jewish bankers. It has already been noted that during 1918, after the signing of the Treaty of Brest Litovsk, Germany and the Entente powers competed for business concessions in Russia: mining, railways, electrification were the most desired contracts. In May 1918 an internal German Foreign Office report described the Bolshevik leaders as "Jewish businessmen". Agents of the Deutsche Bank and the Jewish Mendelssohn bank were courting Krasin and Joffe, who had been granted diplomatic pouches by the German Foreign Ministry. The Swedish government, from where Olof Aschberg, the man behind J.P. Morgan's Guaranty Trust, operated, had facilitated the use of a diplomatic code for Soviet agents in their communications with Moscow. Sweden, while not formally recognising the Bolsheviks, acted as a de facto ally. Again Olof Aschberg became the financial genius who channelled the illegal Russian gold traffic abroad. The Communists themselves leaked a report in the summer of 1919 in which they acknowledged that Aschberg's banking expertise enabled them to send Russian gold, so long coveted by the Morgans, Schiffs, Warburgs, Rothschilds and company, wherever they wished. Another Jewish financial expert who worked as an adviser to the Soviet government was Aaron Sheinman, who worked in close association with Aschberg, Krasin, Litvinov and Sokolnikov, all of whom were Jewish co-religionists. Sheinman was an expert in the gold and platinum markets. In 1918 he was dispatched to Stockholm with 17 million gold roubles, and in 1920 he travelled to Tiflis with several million French francs to buy fifty planes with Fiat engines.

Traffic in Russian Imperial gold bullion was channelled through the Estonian port of Tallinn, where bankers' agents came to buy it at bargain prices before it was remelted by the Swedish mints. Supervising the sales of this gold were the Jews Isidor Emmanuilovich Gukovsky and Georg Solomon, who headed the Soviet Trade Mission in Tallinn. The former had been Finance Commissioner after the revolution. The latter was a former colleague of Krasin's at Siemens-Schukert. Professor McMeekin reveals that Leonid Krasin, the Trade Commissioner, gave Solomon the droll title of "minister of state smuggling". In *Unter den Roten Machthabern* Georg Salomon cynically describes his own work in one sentence: "I worked therefore as a plunderer and thief" ("Ich arbeitete also für Plünderer und Diebe"). Gukovsky had set up his headquarters in the Petersburg Hotel, whose rooms had all been rented out cheaply by courtesy of the Estonian government. Solomon was based at the Hotel Goldener Löewe (Golden Lion), where he received suppliers. Georg Solomon himself reports on his shady business dealings. Solomon acknowledges the receipt of lavish 'tips' and also admits to the corrupt habits of his colleague Gukovsky, who sometimes sold Russian gold 30 percent below market price to G. Scheel and Company, Tallinn's largest private bank, then run by Paul Heinrich Scheel.

The man credited as "financial representative" of the Soviet Mission was Olof Aschberg, an old friend of Georg Solomon and Leonid Krasin since the Siemens-Schukert days in Stockholm. Aschberg himself explains how gold smuggling worked in collaboration with the Swedes: "They hoarded Russian gold, put another stamp on the ingots and melted the coins. The royal mint worked under full pressure. Then the gold with the Swedish stamp could be sold at a fantastic profit". It is worth noting that the Swedish government was presided over three times (1920, 1921-1923 and 1924-1925) by the social democratic Freemason Hjalmar Branting, who had already been Minister of Finance in 1917-1918. Transactions were conducted through Aschberg's bank, which in 1918 had changed its name from Nya Banken to Svensk Economiebolaget. This was where the orders from the buyers were received. Gukovsky delivered Soviet gold or other precious metals to Aschberg or other intermediaries, who for a fee transported the goods across the Baltic.

Aschberg usually set sail on the *Kalewipoeg* and on one voyage passed a cargo of gold worth many millions of kroner. In Stockholm the gold was melted down and the old Tsarist insignia was exchanged for a Swedish one. It was then sold mainly to the United States, specifically to J.P. Morgan's Guaranty Trust. In the same year, 1918, Aschberg opened a branch of Svensk Economiebolaget opposite the Soviet Embassy in Berlin, at 69 Unter den Linden, the city's most famous boulevard. Isaak Steinberg, known as "the engineer", another Bolshevik Jew, one more, who had been the Commissar of Justice until March 1918, was one of the bank's directors. In London, it has already been said in the previous chapter, the agent of the new bank of Aschberg was Earl Grey, a former associate of Cecil Rhodes who presided over the British Bank of North Commerce. Professor McMeekin reports that in the autumn of 1920, Olof Ascheberg's boldness reached such a point that he even promised Maksim Litvinov that he could send the gold directly to the US mint and avoid the high premiums paid in Stockholm. This offer was made before the US government cracked down in November on the movement of Russian gold, which was being sold to the Federal Reserve without proper certificates of ownership.

In *Wall Street and the Boshevik Revolution,* Professor Sutton reports on the departure from Tallinn for the United States of three ships carrying Soviet gold: the *S.S. Gauthod,* with a cargo of two hundred and sixteen boxes of gold, supervised by the Freemason Yuri Lomonosov[3]; *the S. S. Carl Line,* also loaded with another two hundred and sixteen boxes of gold; and the *S. S. Ruheleva,* with one hundred and eight boxes. The contents of each box were valued at sixty thousand gold roubles. Sutton still cites the name of a fourth ship, the *S. S. Wheeling Mold,* but gives no figures. Deposited by the Guaranty Trust of New York, the gold arrived at the Valuation Office. The Guaranty Trust then inquired of the Federal Reserve regarding acceptance. The Federal Reserve in turn asked the Treasury. The superintendent of the New York Valuation Office informed the Treasury that approximately seven million dollars worth of gold had no identifying marks and that the deposited bullion had already been melted down in the United States.

The Superintendent of the Treasury explained on 17 November 1920 to James Hecksher of the Irving National Bank in New York that there were reports of gold shipments from certain Baltic countries and that all shipments were suspected to be of Russian gold, and that he should therefore forward to the Treasury all enquiries about gold of Russian or Bolshevik origin in order to receive instructions before it was introduced into the market by those who offered it or wished to make payments with it. Kunh, Loeb & Company, apparently on behalf of the Guaranty Trust, made inquiries at the State Department as to the official position on the receipt of Soviet gold. On 26 November, S. P. Gilbert, Assistant Secretary of the Treasury, warned in no uncertain terms to the bankers who sought to recast Russian gold in Swedish style: "All gold of Soviet origin will be rejected by the United States Mint, regardless of who offers it".

In early 1919 the Soviet government had opened the "Soviet Bureau" in New York, headed by Ludwig Martens, a German-born Bolshevik who acted de facto as ambassador and whose secretary was Santeri Nuorteva (Alexander Nyberg). As early as 1919 a Scotland Yard report quoted by Anthony Sutton associated Martens with the Guaranty Trust Company:

---

[3] Yuri Lomonosov, a railway engineer, had been the right-hand man of the Minister of Communications in the Masonic Provisional Government. Between 1918 and 1919 Lomonosov lived in the United States, but after the triumph of the revolution he returned to Russia and collaborated with the Bolsheviks. With the help of Kuhn, Loeb & Company, he worked in Sweden with Olof Aschberg on the export of Russian gold to the United States. In November 1920 the Council of People's Commissars appointed him responsible for the purchase of railway equipment. In Berlin he organised the purchase of German and Swedish locomotives for the Bolsheviks, who had ruined Russia's once stupendous railway infrastructure, vital in the midst of the civil war. Before the revolution, Russia imported neither locomotives nor wagons, as its industry supplied its own needs. Russia produced 56% of the world's manganese, the ore needed to make steel.

'Martens is in the limelight. There is no doubt of his connection with the Guaranty Trust Company, though it is surprising that such an influential firm should have business with the Bolsheviks." In mid-June 1919 a committee chaired by Senator Clayton R. Lusk, the "Lusk Committee", investigating seditious activities, obtained a search warrant for the Manhattan offices of the Soviet Bureau and seized important documents. Martens was summoned to testify before the Committee, but refused to appear, claiming diplomatic immunity. He finally admitted that he had received $90,000 to finance communist activities in the United States, and it also became clear that the Guaranty Trust was financially supporting the communists.

With Woodrow Wilson's failure with regard to the League of Nations and after his paralysis due to stroke, the plotters' plans suffered a slight setback, which was accentuated by the arrival of the Republican Warren Harding in office. Mandell House gradually disappeared from the scene and the Communists lost important supporters in the government. However, although it was not until the arrival of Democrat Franklin D. Roosevelt in 1933 that the US officially recognised the USSR, nothing prevented Jewish Wall Street bankers from continuing to work closely with the communists, as evidenced by the fact that in November 1922 Olof Aschberg opened a bank in Moscow to handle wire transfers.

As part of the NEP (New Economic Policy), the communists authorised the opening of certain private banks, and Aschberg founded the Ruskombank (Bank of Foreign Trade), in which the Bank of England had a major shareholding. Its chief operating officer was Max May, vice-president of the Guaranty Trust Company, a J. P. Morgan man who had already worked with Aschberg in importing Russian gold for the Guaranty Trust. Thanks to Aschberg's contacts in Berlin and Stockholm and May's contacts on Wall Street, the Ruskombank attracted many billions of dollars in foreign capital to Moscow. The communists obtained credit from Ruskombak by depositing gold, platinum, diamonds, pearls and other precious stones from the Gokhran, which were then sold abroad or directly to buyers in Moscow. In short, concludes Anthony Sutton, 'a syndicate of Wall Street bankers expanded its horizons on a global scale. The giant Russian market was to become a captive market, technically a colony to be exploited by a group of powerful financiers and the corporations they controlled".

Once the gold laundering system was at its height, the communists were able to pay for all the imports they needed. Bank notes had been greatly devalued, so much so that they had lost 96% of their value in relation to the gold rouble. Logically, if they could be paid in gold or platinum, of which Russia produced 95% of the world's currency, no one was willing to accept paper. Paying suppliers in gold opened almost every door to the communists, who in four years squandered Tsarist Russia's enormous reserves. Gold was disappearing at such a rate that in February 1921 the Politburo commissioned Krasin to explore the possibility of selling diamonds and jewellery to finance arms purchases abroad. However, the Bolsheviks' failure to recognise the debts and commitments made by previous governments led to a wave of protests and was initially a stumbling block in trade relations with European countries. Dutch bankers, for example, asked in April 1918 why the capital that "neutral Holland" had invested in Russia had been confiscated. Krestinsky, the new Finance Commissioner, replied that the bank holdings "were being nationalised, not liquidated".

The man in charge of managing the Lloyd George government's collaboration with the communists in London was again the ubiquitous Leonid Krasin. The British share of the debt contracted by Tsarist Russia, mainly between 1914 and 1917, was larger than the French, amounting to more than £600 million. Alexandre Millerand, Prime Minister of France, told Lloyd George in June 1920 that the British government's negotiations with Krasin gave the Bolsheviks a prestige and authority they did not deserve. Lloyd George hypocritically replied that he was negotiating with representatives of the Soviet regime "not as a Government, but as de facto controllers". Lloyd George cared little for the moral objections, also raised on 7 June by several MPs in the Commons, who warned of the aberrant nature of the Soviet regime, whose commercial pretensions were based on stolen gold.

At the same time, Louis Delavaud, the French ambassador in Stockholm, protested indignantly to the Swedish foreign minister, Baron Erik de Palmstierna, to whom he made it known that France regarded the Russian gold reserves as collateral for his country's creditors and that the gold "would be legally confiscated" in Western countries if it was re-exported from Sweden. The Swedes turned a deaf ear and the prime minister, the socialist Hjalmar Branting, even reproached the French for refusing to participate in the London negotiations. The truth is that in Europe, everyone was waiting for the outcome of the crucial Anglo-Soviet negotiations, which were to decide the legal status of Russian gold in the continent's capitals. In London, the main opponents of the negotiations were Lord Curzon and Winston Churchill, who had not yet been won over by the international conspirators. Churchill, then Minister of War, went so far as to threaten to resign if any agreement was signed with Krasin. The Anglo-Soviet trade agreement was finally signed on 16 March 1921 and was as favourable to the interests of the Communists as the Treaty of Tartu with Estonia had been. On the crucial issue of debt, Krasin accepted that the Soviet Government would make a declaration that "it was responsible for paying compensation to private persons who had supplied goods or services to Russia which had not been settled". However, this probability referred to a general peace treaty that would have to be negotiated later, after the end of the civil war in which Britain, France and the United States had a more than ambiguous position, as will be seen in the next section.

Once the communists could sell gold in England, they could sell it anywhere. It should not be forgotten that a Rothschild fixed the price of gold in the City of London on a daily basis then and now. Sean McMeekin writes: "By ceding the right to seize gold, funds, securities or commodities from Soviet Russia, the British Government undermined its own case for the responsibility of the Bolsheviks to compensate private persons whom they had expropriated, since it recognised as legal Soviet property the spoils obtained through expropriation. Surprisingly, imported Soviet gold received better conditions for re-export than gold entering Britain from South Africa, which was a member of the Commonwealth. The former was granted an export licence valid for six months, as opposed to forty-two days for the latter."

Lloyd George insisted in the House of Commons that the Anglo-Soviet agreement did not grant Moscow diplomatic recognition, but was "merely a commercial agreement". In reality, the agreement included the use of codes and ciphers, as well as diplomatic pouches and the recognition of valid passports. In May 1921 the British Court of Appeal, urged by Lloyd George himself, overturned an earlier High Court decision that had allowed creditors of Tsarist Russia to seize Bolshevik assets. The High Court itself ruled in July that Soviet gold imported into the UK was legally inviolable. From this point on, the only major countries reluctant to give in as Britain had done were France, the United States and Japan. In the words of Professor McMeekin, "the Anglo-Soviet agreement signified the transformation of the Bolshevik regime from a conspiracy beset by political activists into a billionaire criminal oligarchy that could tap into Western capital markets to finance the war against its own people".

After the agreement, the Soviet government gorged itself on imports and gold reserves were disappearing at a faster rate. In six months one hundred and fifty tons of gold were shipped abroad. During the summer of 1921, many shipments of Soviet gold were no longer in bullion, but in coins. Of course, there was always the Gokhran. Olof Aschberg estimates that between 1921 and 1924 he alone processed platinum, gold, diamonds and pearls from the Gokhran worth 200 million Swedish kronor, about 50 million dollars. In their quest to further accumulate wealth, in 1922 the Judeo-Bolsheviks even dared to desecrate the tomb of Catherine the Great in order to steal a famous necklace. Also in March 1922, after a frantic search, they discovered the imperial crowns of the Romanovs hidden in the Kremlin armoury and were ready to sell them to the highest bidder. The Communists' intention to smuggle Catherine's necklace and the imperial crowns was so widely publicised that a Russian passenger ship, the *White Star,* on its arrival in New York harbour was thoroughly searched by Treasury agents. A tip-off that turned out to be false placed the imperial jewels on board the ship.

As the gold reserves were depleted, Soviet leaders decided they needed to share on credit and thought of offering mining rights and oil exploration. Guggenheim Exploration, General Electric, Standard Oil won lucrative contracts. The General Electric Company, a multinational controlled by Morgan, electrified the USSR for two decades, thus fulfilling Lenin's dictum that socialism equalled electrification. Standard Oil, a Rockefeller clan company, took over 50% of the Caucasus oil fields, which were supposedly nationalised. The Rockefellers' Chase Manhattan Bank, after securing a deal in 1927 to distribute Soviet oil to European markets, gave the communists a $75 million loan. No wonder, then, that Frank Vanderlip, president of the National City Bank of New York and Rockefeller's representative at the Jekill Island meeting that led to the creation of the Federal Reserve, compared Lenin to George Washington. It is also understandable that publicist Ivy Lee, John D. Rockefeller's right-hand man in communications, launched a publicity campaign explaining that the communists were in fact "misunderstood idealists" who had to be helped "for the good of mankind".

Following the Anglo-Soviet agreement, attempts were made to delay payment of the debts as long as possible. In preparation for the Genoa Conference, which was to be held in April 1922, Georgi Chicherin, a foreign commissar who was considered Russian, but who was considered Jewish by Jüri Lina because his mother, named Meierdorf, was Jewish, sent a proposal to London and Paris on 28 October 1921,, suggesting payment of pre-1914 debts, but not of the large loans contracted during the war. The final terms the Politburo presented to the Conference called for the debt to be repaid after fifteen years in exchange for a large loan of one trillion dollars. Sean McMeekin writes that "the diplomatic problem facing Chicherin and Krasin was how to politely frustrate the Entente's expectations without delivering a strident slap in the face to Lloyd George". To cushion the blow to the British premier, Trotsky made before his Politburo colleagues a brazen proposal: "We should announce that in the event of the Entente powers confiscating all the money of Russian capitalists abroad, we would regard it as an act of reciprocity and undertake not to protest." As the saying goes, the thief believes that all are of his own kind. In other words, Trotsky was inviting the bondholders and bondholders, having been robbed by the Bolsheviks, to rob themselves in return. The contempt with which the Soviet government treated the Genoa Conference was so evident that even Lloyd George could not prevent its failure. The first international meeting after the world war, attended by thirty-four countries, ended without any agreement.

The civil war against the whites

There are few books translated into English that deal monographically with the Russian Civil War, a little-known historical disaster. Some two million Russians lost their lives in the First World War, but the civil war caused nearly thirteen million deaths. Although figures vary according to sources, B. T. Urlanis, quoted by Robert Conquest in *The Harvest of Sorrow* as an authority on the subject, gives the figure of 300,000 combatants killed on both sides. If this is true, the rest would be victims of repression in the civil war against the bourgeoisie, peasants, workers and Cossacks who opposed the communist dictatorship. This figure includes five million people who died as a result of the famine of 1921-22. The civil war, rather than a war of major military operations, was a rearguard war in which Whites and Reds pursued opponents in the areas they controlled.

That said, the crimes of the one and the other do not bear comparison, since the communist policy of terror openly preached the extermination of class enemies. Nicolas Werth in *The Black Book of Communism* states that "the communist policy of terror was systematic, organised and put into operation long before the war against whole groups of society". When they seized power, the Bolsheviks had between 100,000 and 200,000 members in a country of 175 million people. This party, whose leaders were not even Russians, but professional revolutionaries of Jewish origin financed from abroad, persecuted all its political opponents, from anarchists to monarchists. There is a tendency to believe that the bourgeoisie was the only class enemy they wanted to eradicate; however, as will be seen, the victims included workers and soldiers who demanded bread and work; peasants who opposed requisitions and collectivisation; the Cossacks, an ethnic and social group considered hostile; and, in short, anyone who opposed their policies. Those who did not accept his dictatorship were branded as "enemies of the people", whom the Jewish communist leaders claimed to represent.

Civil war had been an aspiration of both Trotsky and Lenin. In 1914, in a letter to Schliapnikov already mentioned above, Lenin wrote that the war had to be transformed into a civil war. Let us now complete the quotation from the text: "When this will happen is another question, and it is not yet clear. We must let the moment ripen and force it to ripen systematically..... We can neither promise civil war nor decree it, but we have a duty to act - for as long as it takes - in that direction". In September 1916, in the midst of the world war, Lenin again wrote along the same lines: "Anyone who accepts the class struggle must accept civil war, which in every class society represents the continuation, development and accentuation of the class war." In 1918 Trotsky insisted before the Central Executive Committee that the party was in favour of civil war. In other words, the recipe of these two "friends" of the proletariat was more war and more suffering for the Russian people. With utter contempt for the lives of the workers and the people, after the terrible world conflagration which had cost millions of dead, they openly intended that the Russians should tear each other to pieces so that they could more easily eliminate all those who opposed them.

Because of the internal doubts and struggles between supporters and opponents of recognition of the Communists, Allied intervention in Russia, especially the British and the Americans, was characterised by ambiguity.

The agents of the conspiracy tried hard to get their governments to recognise Lenin's government. If Lord Milner, as he wished, had managed to get into the Foreign Office, it is certain that he would have pushed for recognition. The disagreements between the Foreign Office and the War Cabinet are confirmed by Bruce Lockhart, who writes in *Memoirs of a Britsh Agent* that Lord Milner, disappointed by the lack of initiative of Lord Balfour, "a harmless old gentleman", wished to be at the head of the Foreign Office for six months. Mandell House, the agent of the bankers who had created the Federal Reserve and financed the revolution in Russia, pressed Wilson to the end to get the President to recognise the Communists. Recall that Rabbi Judas Magnes, convinced of the imminent triumph of the theses of Trotsky's friends, declared in April 1918 that President Wilson intended to convene a Peace Conference to bring about a general peace based on the Bolsheviks' views.

To achieve a general peace rather than a separate peace was the plan of those who wanted the Bolsheviks at Versailles. As we know, one of the aims of Lockhart's mission to Moscow was, in his own words, "to put a stick in the wheels of a possible separate peace negotiation". Trotsky, the war commissar, wanted the US and Britain to intervene in Russia as allies against Germany and offered the British to assist him in reorganising the fleets. However, uncertainty over the outcome of the Bolshevik infighting, apparently culminating in 1918 with the attempted assassination of Lenin, led to ambiguity and impeded decision-making. Lockhart, a victim on the ground of the lack of a clear line of action, lamented that there was no British policy, "unless seven different policies at once could be considered one policy". Indeed, in the House of Commons, angry parliamentarians in the name of decency demanded explanations from the government for the continued presence in Moscow of a British agent "before a government of criminals who boasted of their intention to destroy Christian civilisation".

By the end of April 1918, Allied contradictions and indecision were apparent. While France was clearly advocating support for the anti-Bolshevik forces, the US and Britain seemed to be leaning in favour of the Soviets: President Wilson opposed intervention without the consent of the Communists, and the British were pressing their agents to get the Soviets to accept military aid with a supposed commitment not to interfere in their internal affairs. Initially, at Trotsky's request, British, French and American soldiers landed small contingents at Murmansk, Archangel and Vladivostock to prevent the Germans from capturing the supplies stored in these ports. By the end of May, the Japanese were determined to intervene, but President Wilson was absolutely opposed to such intervention. In June the British were still undecided, although the White generals were trying to organise themselves and hoped for the support, financial and/or military, of their former allies, which they considered decisive. They expected two British divisions to land in Archangel and several Japanese divisions in Siberia.

Bruce Lockhart, Lord Milner's man, writes that on 4 August rumours spread that the Allies had landed a powerful force at Archangel, which some put at 100,000 troops and others at two divisions. The Japanese were to send seven divisions to help the Czech[4]. Despite the great confusion, the landing at Archangel was understood to be anti-Bolshevik in character. On 10 August 1918, the Soviet Press appeared with shocking front-page headlines reporting a great naval victory over the Allies at Archangel. Lockhart recounts that he went to Lev Karachan (Karakhanyan), another Jew who was deputy foreign minister. Karakhanyan, who along with his co-religionists Joffe and Trotsky had been secretary of the delegation that negotiated at Brest-Litovsk, immediately told Lockhart the whole truth. The situation is not serious," he told him, "the Allies have landed only a few hundred men. The great naval victory was therefore nothing more than pure propaganda by the Communists to encourage their followers. In reality, General F. C. Poole, who commanded the landed troops, was once again under orders to resist German influence and penetration. Lockhart admits that the travesty of the landing in the north resulted in the loss of the Volga line and the temporary collapse of the anti-Bolshevik movement in European Russia. Moreover, the perception that the Allies were unwilling to engage seriously provoked dissension and bitter quarrels among opposition groups.

Boris Brasol asks in *The World at the Crossroads* what the real intentions of the small Allied contingents were, since no one in Russia could understand what they intended. One of the British expeditions for which detailed information is available is that of Colonel John Ward, whose 25th Battalion of the Middlesex Regiment was sent in July 1918 from Honk-Kong to Vladivostok (Siberia), originally for garrison duty. Ward published *With the "Die-Hards" in Siberia* in 1920, a book in which he recounts his experiences during the Russian Civil War in 24 chapters. Particularly significant is the 22nd chapter, entitled *American Policy and its Results*. In it, John Ward provides some clues to understanding certain actions. Ward writes that Admiral Kolchak, appointed head of the Provisional Government in Omsk, expressed to him his conviction that American troops were being used for purposes other than what was expected and that the American

---

[4] The actions of the Czechs require a brief explanation, although if there were room it could be lengthy, for the facts are complex. We will only say that at the outbreak of the war the Tsar accepted the request of a group of Czech immigrants who wanted to fight with the Imperial Army. Thus was born the Czechoslovak Company, which soon grew in size thanks to the incorporation during the war of deserters and prisoners from the Austro-Hungarian army. By the end of 1917 it had grown to a corps of some 60,000 soldiers. The Bolsheviks agreed to evacuate the Czech Legion to France, but this had to be done via Vladivostock. Therefore, the Czechs had to travel by the Trans-Siberian Railway. As soon as the transfer began, the Soviets went back on their word and tried to arrest the Austrian army deserters in order to repatriate them to Austria. Finally, Trotsky ordered the disarmament of the Czech Legion, which led the Czechs to take up arms against the Bolsheviks in May 1918 after seizing the city of Chelyabinsk.

expeditionary force commanded by General William Graves was collaborating with the Communists. Here are some excerpts from the chapter:

> "His (Kolchak's) agents had informed him that out of sixty liaison officers and translators, fifty were Russian Jews or relatives of Russian Jews, some of whom had been exiled from Russia for political or other crimes and had returned as American citizens, capable of influencing policy in a direction contrary to that desired by the American people. I assured him that this could not be..., but he replied that the reports were so voluminous and so categorical that he felt that I, as a representative of the English people and an officer in His Majesty's Army, must have knowledge of the situation."

Colonel Ward writes that some time after he received Kolchak's complaint, a key railway point at Kraevesk station was seized by a detachment of Red Guards, who quietly entered the station and arrested the American soldiers guarding it. Suspecting collaboration, Ward decided to investigate Kolchak's accusations for himself and held several interviews with American officers and soldiers. He discovered that many felt that they were merely helping the Bolsheviks, who had even been given territory in which they could carry out propaganda in order to win over the population:

> "I learned from these American troops that their officers and their officers, from General Graves downwards, were in constant touch with officers of the Red Guards, with whom they had come to more than one understanding; that even ordinary soldiers thought that the understanding between the two forces was of so general and friendly a character that future hostilities between them were not contemplated.... The Kraevesk affair seemed to be only the symptom of a wider policy and not the foolish act of a negligent officer."

Through his investigations, Colonel Ward managed to get hold of a letter from an American captain addressed to a Red Army officer operating in the Svagena district, which clearly spoke of fraternisation between the two troops. Ward regards the letter as clear evidence of the understanding that had existed for months between the American authorities and the communists in the Maritime Provinces. Colonel Ward denounces in his book that "the presence of American forces in Siberia was being used by someone for other than purely American purposes". He considers it quite obvious that "this sinister subterranean influence had diverted American policy from its straight and honest course". Ward states bluntly that American policy produced "a state of indecision among the Allies, and of unrest and anarchy among the population of the Transbaikal and Ussurie provinces". Here is another excerpt:

"Contrary to general opinion, the American command declared a zone in the Suchan district to be neutral. Armed operations by Admiral Kolchak's Russians or the Red Army were forbidden within this zone. Lenin's and Trotsky's officers did not respect the order and immediately began to assemble their scattered forces. Within three weeks they raised the red flag in their own barracks, under the protection of the American flag. From this American neutral zone the Bolsheviks organised their forces to attack the Japanese in the Amur province, to destroy the British supply trains on the Ussurie line, and finally exchanged fire with the Russian sentries near Vladivostock, always escaping to the American zone when attacked by the governor's forces."

The reaction of the US command to the Allied complaints was the opposite of what was desired. Instead of eradicating the evil and extirpating the communists from the area, it was concluded that, in order to prevent a recurrence of regrettable acts in the future, a broader and more binding agreement between the American forces and the communists was needed. It was then learned that General Graves had arranged a conference with Red Army commanders. Faced with an indignant reaction from the Governor of Vladivostock, who told Graves that the Russian government would consider such a meeting a hostile act, the American general gave up his efforts. The breakdown of negotiations provoked the wrath of the Soviet Government in Moscow, which ordered its commissars in Ussurie to use forces organised under American protection to attack their protectors.

In short, it can be said that at no time during 1918 did the Entente governments have any intention of overthrowing the Bolsheviks. Apart from this American contingent infiltrated by Jewish agents friendly to the Bolsheviks, the Allied intervention was a disappointment. Fourteen countries sent troops to Russia; but, except for the sixty thousand Czechs, who, as explained in the previous note, were already on the ground, they only deployed between them one hundred and thirty thousand soldiers on Soviet territory, half of whom were Japanese. The Japanese intervention, moreover, was in their own interests, since, after the Treaty of Brest-Litovsk, they were convinced of Germany's victory in the world war. In any case, 130,000 troops is a ridiculous figure considering the enormous size of a country spanning two continents.

By contrast, Trotsky recruited an army of five million men in two years. On the nature of command in the Red Army, several authors refer to a quotation from the newspaper *The Communist*, edited in Kharkov, which in its edition of 12 April 1919 published an article by M. Cohen boasting that the revolution was the work of the Jews. About the army, Cohen writes: "It is true that in the ranks of the Red Army there are soldiers who are not Jews, as far as the rank and file soldiers are concerned, but in the committees and in the social organisations, as with the commissars, the Jews bravely lead the masses of Russian proletarians to victory.... The symbol of Judaism has also become the symbol of the Russian proletariat, as can be seen by its adoption of the red five-pointed star, which in earlier times was the symbol of Zionism and Judaism." According to the *Jewish Virtual Library,* in Kharkov, which between 1919 and 1934 was the capital of Ukraine and became an important Jewish centre, numerous publications were published at that time in Yiddish and Hebrew, so it can be assumed that if *The Communist* was not written in Russian, it must have been in one of these two languages.

The composition of the Red Army is studied by Jüri Lina, who cites the monthly magazine *Molodaya Gvardiya,* founded in 1922 in Moscow. In issue 11 of 1990, this historic publication reported that almost all the army commanders were Jewish, as were 80% of the commissars of the Commissariat for Military Affairs. As many as a hundred names are cited. Here are a few of them, some of whom will reappear later when we examine Stalin's purges against the Trotskyists. The Deputy People's Commissar for Military Affairs was Yefraim Shchlyansky, who had travelled with Lenin from Switzerland on the famous train. Among his collaborators were Semyon Nakhimson and Yemelyan Yarovslaski (Minei Izrailevich Gubelman), who was editor of the satirical newspaper *Bezbozhnik* (*The Atheist*) and chairman of the Anti-Religious Committee of the Central Committee. Later Yaroslavsky was also an official party historian. Among the members of the Military Council *Molodaya Gvardiya* mentions twelve other Jews. Three names stand out: Arkady Rosengoltz, a close collaborator of Trotsky, who after the civil war worked in the Commissariats of Transport, Finance and the Air Force Directorate of the Red Army. Between 1925 and 1927 he was ambassador to the United Kingdom, a post from which he supervised Soviet espionage. Rosengoltz, like so many other Trotskyists, was executed in 1938. Mikhail Lashevich, according to the *Jewish Encyclopaedia of Russia* also known as Gaskovich, another Trotskyite persecuted by Stalin who disappeared (suicide or car accident) in 1928. Joseph Unschlicht, together with Rosa Luxemburg and Leo Jogiches a member of the Polish and Lithuanian Social Democratic Party. A Jew of Polish extraction, Unschlicht was one of the most active mass criminals in the elimination of political opponents. He too was liquidated by Stalin in 1938. Among the most important military commanders were Naum Zorkin; Iona Yakir; Boris Feldman, who in July 1934 became head of the Army Personnel Administration and, together with Yakir, was also shot in June 1937; Vladimir Lazarevich, commander-in-chief of the Fourth Army between December 1918 and March 1919, and later commander of the Third Army between June and October 1920. Lazarevich headed the Air Force Academy from 1925 to 1927. Based on the information in the above-mentioned magazine, Jüri Lina gives an account of more than fifty Jews who were important leaders of the Red Army, half of whom commanded a division. In the interwar period the power of Jews in the Red Army did not diminish. According to Andrei Sverdlov, son of the man responsible for the assassination of the Imperial family, there were three hundred and five Jewish generals in the Red Army during the Second World War.

Although all political forces had taken a stand against the Bolshevik dictatorship, by the beginning of 1920 the die was already cast and the defeat of the Whites was inevitable, although the war lasted until 1922. Once again, the partisan struggle is one of the keys to understanding the events that led to the communists' victory. On the one side were the left-wing revolutionary socialists, whose leader, Maria Spiridonova, imprisoned after the coup attempt of July 1918, had remained in detention until she was amnestied in November. In December 1918 she chaired a party congress tolerated by the Bolsheviks, where she condemned the systematic terror of the Cheka. Arrested again on 10 February 1919 along with 210 other party members, she was deemed hysterical by a revolutionary court, which ordered her internment in a sanatorium for the mentally ill. During 1919 some two thousand SRs were arrested and about sixty organisations of the Left Socialists were suppressed. On the other hand, the revolutionary right-wing socialists met in September 1918 with all the anti-Soviet forces and agreed to form a new provisional government in Omsk, which was headed by a five-member directory: Avksentiev, Boldyrev and Zenzinov of the Social-Revolutionary Party, and Vinogradov and Volgogodski of the Constitutional Democratic Party (Kadets).

Colonel John Ward's book is again a valuable source for first-hand accounts of events in Omsk. Ward recounts that when he arrived with his battalion of 800 men on 18 October 1918, the city was decorated with flags of all nations. The aim in that October was to unite the forces of the Directory of Five and those of Admiral Kolchak's Siberian Government. The Directory, composed of moderate revolutionary socialists and "intellectuals" of the Kadet party, had received its authority from the Constituent Assembly meeting in Ufa and was recognised as the Government of all the Russias. Kolchak's government was the result of the Siberian districts of the Duma and was considered reactionary, since it was royalist and was supported and guarded by the tsarist Cossacks. Both the military and the Cossacks blamed the former for the destruction of the army, and the also accused them of having handed the country over to the forces of anarchy and Bolshevism through Kerensky. Colonel Ward confirms that Russians of all classes generally agreed in regarding Kerensky as the cause of all evils, and acknowledges that "combining these hostile and divergent elements into a united force for the resurrection of Russia seemed to him impossible". It succeeded, however, despite scepticism, in forming a unitary government of which Kolchak was appointed Minister of War. Soon events were to prove that this was a mirage.

During the negotiations for the formation of the government a serious complication arose. General Boldyrev, through whom the revolutionary

Socialists were to control the new army, and his colleague Avksentiev asked for a member of their party to head a newly created militia which was to act as a kind of police under the new regime: they aspired to have revolutionary and social control of all the forces of the new government. Only pressure from Allied representatives succeeded in getting the request accepted and overcoming the stumbling block. On 6 November a banquet was held in honour of the new All-Russian Government. The representatives of the Allied forces present in Omsk were all invited, including Colonel Ward, who does not fail to mention in his chronicle that the temperature outside was sixty degrees below zero. The ceremony was presided over by Avksentiev, the new Chairman of the Council of Ministers. At the time of the speeches, General Knox, head of the British military mission, spoke, calling for the Russians to work together to form an army and a government capable of establishing law and order. Next to speak were General Boldyrev, a member of the Ufa Directorate who had been appointed commander-in-chief of the new Russian army, and Admiral Kolchak, who spoke only a few short sentences, which were received with little enthusiasm.

According to Ward, while shortages of arms and equipment were a sad reality at the front, the militia controlled by the revolutionary socialists was perfectly equipped. The generals' protests to Boldyrev forced War Minister Kolchak to back up their demands and present their grievances to the commander-in-chief. Boldyrev's reply was that the complaints from the front were fictitious, and he further intimated that the matter was none of his business. In the course of the discussion, Boldyrev told him frankly that he had been accepted into the government under pressure from the Allies and that if he continued to interfere he would be excluded from it. Kolchak immediately resigned; but the Western Allies persuaded him to remain in the government. Apparently in order to draw him away from Omsk, he was authorised to make an inspection visit to the front line. Admiral Kolchak learned that Colonel Ward had been ordered to travel to the front as well, so he asked him if he could hitch his carriage to the train. Thus, in early November 1918, the two soldiers travelled together on the same train. On the presence of Kolchak at the front, Colonel Ward writes: "The presence of Admiral Kolchak seemed to galvanise the whole army with life and energy. The Russian soldiers, whose boots had long since disappeared, and whose feet were bandaged with sacks to protect them from the snow, felt the assurance that after the minister's visit they would receive proper boots and clothing".

While at the front, news came that made it advisable to return urgently to Omsk. At one of the stations it was learned that General Boldyrev, who had left the city and was on his way to the Ufa front, asked Admiral Kolchak to wait for him to meet him. Ward writes that he was invited by Kolchak to his carriage and explained that the situation in Omsk was critical, as the two government groups were at loggerheads and were ready to destroy each other. On 6 November, the train of Commander-in-Chief Boldyrev entered the Ekaterinburg station. At twelve o'clock noon Kolchak boarded Boldyrev's train and began an interview that lasted until five o'clock in the afternoon. What happened between the two soldiers only they know. A lot can be said during five hours of conversation. On 17 November, the train carrying Admiral Kolchak and Colonel Ward arrived in Omsk. Colonel Ward describes the state of the city as "indescribable": "Every night, as soon as darkness came, shouts and rifle and revolver shots could be heard everywhere. In the morning, sanitary carts collected between five and twenty bodies of dead soldiers".

A coup d'état was imminent and took place on 18 November. The Directory was arrested and absolute authority was offered to Admiral Kolchak, who, although initially refusing the post, was appointed Supreme Governor of all the Russias, with a fourteen-member Council of Ministers to account to him for his responsibilities. Kolchack summoned the French representative in Omsk, Eugene Renault, and Colonel John Ward, who was then the highest British representative in the city. It was the admiral himself who went to British headquarters where, in addition to Colonel Ward, he was received by Lieutenant Colonel J. F. Neilson, Captain Stephani, Colonel R. Frank, a Russian army officer who was Ward's liaison, and Mr. Frazer, the correspondent of *The Times*. Before them all the admiral, who spoke perfect English, explained the reasons and circumstances which had led him to assume supreme authority over all Russia. The Admiral was questioned as to the fate of the Socialist Revolutionaries and other members of the Directory who had been arrested, and he replied that he had no information as to their whereabouts.

The next day, 19 November, Colonel Ward wrote the following text to Admiral Kolchak: "After our interview last evening I sent you a note asking for information and some assurance for the arrested members of the Council. So far I have not received any news of this. I have already told you that I have the assurance that my country will view with great concern any harm done without a proper trial to these state prisoners. I would appreciate it as a favour if you could provide me with information on this matter." The same day Cossack Ataman Krasilnikov, Colonel Volkov and Lieutenant Colonel Katanaev presented themselves at British headquarters and reported that the responsibility for the arrest of the government members was entirely theirs, that they had not suffered the slightest harm, and that they were ready to hand over the prisoners to the authorities, together with the intercepted papers and several million roubles which were supposed to have been stolen. The three officers assured that Admiral Kolchak was responsible for their safety, and added that he intended to take them out of the country at the earliest opportunity.

To get the full picture of what happened during the civil war, it must be considered that, in addition to the disputes, clashes and betrayals among the Russians, the divergent interests of the Allies and mistrust among them prevented coordination with the White generals. The appointment of General Maurice Janin as head of the Allied and Russian forces in Siberia was the cause of serious disputes with Admiral Kolchak, who did not accept that Russian troops should be under the command of a foreign military officer. On 16 December 1918, Janin arrived in Omsk. This French general believed that the British had installed Kolchak in power to serve their interests. As early as the 19th, he wrote a report on the Omsk government in which he said that an admiral of great prestige had replaced the coalition government "thanks to the complacency of an Englishman who wanted to keep a firm grip on his stirrup". In addition to General Graves' Americans, infiltrated by the Judeo-Bolsheviks, the Japanese, whose erratic attitude was due to their initial miscalculations, were also waging war on their own. The Japanese government, which had some 60,000 troops on the ground, thought that a German victory in the war would allow it to make territorial gains in Asiatic Russia.

When Bóldyrev returned to Omsk from Ufa, Admiral Kolchak, who had declared that as soon as order had been restored in the country he intended to convene a national assembly elected by universal suffrage, offered him a post in his government, but he refused. Boldyrev pleaded that he wished to leave the country, as he did not believe that a dictatorial government could extricate Russia from its difficulties. His request was granted. The Japanese representative in Omsk soon afterwards asked to be informed whether General Bóldyrev had been forced to leave the country or had done so voluntarily. He also wanted to know whether the British had supplied the train and the guard who had led the members of the Directorate, who had left the country via Chang-Chun, a Chinese border post, into exile. Curiously enough, the only general who refused to obey the orders of the Kolchak government was the Ataman G. M. Semyonov, whose headquarters were next to those of the Japanese at Chita, from where he insolently refused to recognise Kolchak's authority. When the latter prepared to act against the mutinous general's adventurism, the Japanese prevented him and informed him that Semyonov was under their protection and that they would not tolerate interference from the Omsk government. General Semyonov became notorious for his cruelty: he carried out indiscriminate executions of workers and imprisoned and flogged numerous people in his district. The scandal and alarm among the population reached such an extent that the Allies were forced to ask Japan to explain its unacceptable behaviour.

Soon, however, the Japanese were able to redirect their relations with the Omsk government. The ambiguous and hypocritical attitude of the Allies culminated in a declaration issued in Paris by the Allied Council in mid-January 1919. It said that they could neither help nor recognise either side, and that the various existing governments should reach an armistice and send representatives to the "Isle of Dogs" near Constantinople in order to reach a mutual compromise. The news hit Russia like a bombshell. It was tantamount to overlooking more than a year of communist crimes and plunder and accepting their legitimacy. Taking advantage of the bewilderment and anger, the Japanese were quick to declare that the only country capable of helping Russia was Japan, since the other countries were war-weary, incapable of fighting the Bolsheviks and clamouring for demobilisation. In their propaganda they offered to liquidate the Bolshevik army in two months and to establish a monarchy in Russia in return for a reasonable agreement with the Omsk Government. These were the circumstances that had to be faced at the beginning of the decisive year 1919.

We have left aside an issue of great importance for a proper understanding of the figure of Admiral Aleksander Kolchak. This is the famous "Admiral Kolchak's gold", the story of which we will now briefly summarise. In 1915, faced with the possibility that the Germans might take Petrograd, half of the Russian Imperial gold reserves, some five hundred tons of gold, were placed in the armoured cellars of the Kazan bank. More gold stored in branches of the State Bank in Moscow, Samara and Tambov was also moved to Kazan. In the summer of 1918 the Bolsheviks, who had charged the Cheka with guarding the treasury, tried to move the city's reserves, but only managed to remove about 100 boxes of gold. In early August 1918 Kazan fell into the hands of the Czech Legion and the Army of KOMUCH (People's Army of the Committee of Members of the Constituent Assembly), commanded by General Vladimir Kappel. On 2 August the city of Kazan was besieged and ships sailed up the Volga. The Red Guards were attacked even by revolutionary socialists, who, like the Czechs, wanted to continue the war against Germany. On 6 August the White Army seized 8,400 boxes of gold bullion and platinum bullion, as well as some 2,500 sacks of silver and with gold pieces. On 13 October, following Kolchak's instructions, most of the treasure was transported by train to Omsk. It is not surprising, then, that tensions arose over the control of these impressive resources. A shipment of gold sent by train from Omnsk to Vladivostock was captured by General Semyonov. The Ataman used the bullion to support his troops, deposited 13 million gold roubles in Japanese banks, and even tried to persuade the Mongols to fight against the Third International. To this end he sent Baron R. F. Ungern to Mongolia with several million gold roubles.

The news that part of the imperial treasury had fallen into white hands whetted the insatiable appetite of the bankers, who, as usual, had no problem financing both sides, especially when the loans were guaranteed by gold. Anthony Sutton reveals that the same bankers who had financed the revolution contacted Secretary of State Robert Lansing in August 1919, who received a letter from the National City Bank of New York (Rockefeller) asking for an opinion on a $5 million loan to Admiral Kolchak. Also J. P. Morgan & Co advised the Secretary of State of their willingness to offer Kolchak an additional credit of ten million pounds sterling through a consortium of British and American bankers. The loan was secured by Kolchak's gold, which, according to Sutton, was sent by ship to San Francisco. The lack of equipment among the white soldiers, only two out of ten of whom had rifles, forced the admiral to spend whatever was necessary to equip his army adequately. Two American firms, Remington Arms and Union Metallic Cartridge, sold armaments worth 125 million rubles gold.

In addition to Aleksander Kolchak, whose army operated in Siberia, the leading White generals included Anton Denikin, who advanced from the south with a volunteer army, supported by the Don Cossacks and reinforced by the Caucasian army of Pyotr Wrangel, Baron of Wrangel. In August 1919 this southern army unleashed an offensive that began with major victories and even managed to break through the Bolshevik security perimeter. Between September and October 1919 the cities of Kiev, Kursk and Orel, the latter located 250 miles from Moscow, were conquered. The Tula munitions factory almost fell into their hands. Captain George Pitt-Rivers[5], an English anthropologist who returned to England after being seriously wounded during the First World War, wrote several texts on the civil war. We reproduce one of them particularly significant on Denikin's advance, quoted by Boris Brasol in *The World at the Cross Roads*:

"The White Armies were defeated because they were inefficient, they were inefficient because political traitors were allowed to conspire to ensure their inefficiency..... The Whites could not unite in one policy because they had no common policy, because all their efforts were nullified by intrigue, conspiracy and sabotage, and finally because no movement made up of a hodge-podge of incompatible and contradictory elements can defeat another movement which at all times knows what it wants and accepts no compromise. Even the Russian peasants understand

---

[5] Captain George Pitt-Rivers was a cousin of Clementine Churchill, wife of Winston Churchill, who ordered his arrest and imprisonment on 27 June 1940 for his declared sympathies with National Socialism. The "Pitt-Rivers Papers" in the archives of Churchill College, Cambridge University, have recently become available. These are a collection of letters and writings that offer new insights into this anthropologist, who during the 1920s-1930s was considered an eminent and respected scientist, praised for his work and publications. After his death in 1966, Pitt-Rivers was completely forgotten by historians. Considered an anti-Semite, the fact that he had been on the "wrong side" of the war led to his disappearance. Already in his writings on the First World War, Pitt-Rivers publicly denounced his country's duplicity and hypocrisy vis-à-vis Tsarist Russia. "It was in England," Pitt-Rivers wrote, "the home of the Jews, that the Czar's Government was systematically denigrated, made for years the centre of the blackest and most oppressive tyranny in the world." Bradley W. Hart, a young scholar who in the course of his PhD research contacted the family in 2009, gained access to thousands of personal papers found in the attic of the family home in Dorset. With the family's permission, Hart reported on the importance of the papers to the staff of the Churchill Archives Centre, and today the Pitt-Rivers papers, which shed new light on Anglo-German relations, can be consulted in this archive, which he finds fascinating.

this better than the Allied statesmen and politicians. When Denikin made his rapid advance towards Moscow, the enthusiasm of the peasants of the liberated territories was unbridled. They came out en masse to welcome their liberators, carrying on their heads the sacred icons and the image of the Tsar. Imagine their bewilderment and sadness when the officers of Denikin's entourage told them to bury their trinkets and that their struggle with the Bolsheviks had nothing to do with the Tsar."

Denikin certainly did not represent the tsarists but the democratic constitutionalists, but the absence of unity in the ranks of the Whites, as Pitt-Rivers rightly points out, allowed any assumption about their ultimate intentions. Nor could one speak of uniformity among the Ukrainians, who years later would culminate their misfortunes with the famine of 1932-33 (Holodomor) and became the greatest victims of the catastrophe unleashed after the Revolution. On Ukrainian soil, the tragedy of the civil war took on the worst levels of repression, for within two years this republic was repeatedly seized by both sides. On 11 October 1919, almost simultaneously with Denikin's offensive, the North-Western Army, commanded by Nikolai Yudenich, tried to conquer Petrograd.[6] Yudenich reached the Tsarkoye Seló summer palace and some suburbs of the city. His forced retreat from the gates of the former tsarist capital dealt another blow to the hopes of the Whites, who had thought that if they could gain control of the big cities they

---

[6] In the November 1917 Constituent Assembly elections, the Bolsheviks won only 10% of the vote in Ukraine. At the Congress of Soviets convened in Kiev on 16-18 December 1917, their delegates won 11% of the vote and rushed to Kharkov, a city in the east of the country that had been occupied by the Red Army. There on 25 December 1917 they proclaimed a Soviet government (Ukrainian People's Republic); but on 22 January 1918 the Rada (Supreme Council or Parliament) declared Ukrainian independence and sent a delegation to Brest-Litovsk to appeal to Germany for support against the Bolsheviks. On 12 February the puppet government in Kharkov entered Kiev escorted by the Red Army. Following Lenin's instructions, the Bolsheviks seized grain in the villages and shipped it to Russia. According to Robert Conquest, between 18 February and 9 March 1918 some eleven hundred railway wagons loaded with grain were sent to Russia from Kherson province alone. This first Soviet government, which suppressed all Ukrainian schools and cultural institutions, lasted only a few weeks. The Jew Latsis, the head of the Cheka, shot people for merely speaking Ukrainian in the streets. With the advance of the Germans and Austrians, the Soviet government was dissolved. On 29 April 1918, the Germans put General Pavel Skoropadsky in power, and he remained in power as "Hetman" until December. After the armistice of Compiègne, Skoropadsky lost German support and the Whites could not prevent his downfall. On 5 February 1919, the Soviets launched an attack and the Ukrainian government was forced to abandon Kiev. The second communist regime was installed and lasted for about eight months, before being dissolved on 2 October 1919 on Lenin's orders in the face of the imminent arrival of Denikin's Whites. Finally, in March 1920, the Soviets occupied Ukraine for the third time. The occupation was temporarily interrupted in May by the conquest of the western part of the country, including Kiev, by the Poles. It is not hard to imagine what all this back and forth meant in terms of repression for the long-suffering Ukrainian population.

would cause panic among the Bolsheviks' supporters. In their eagerness to achieve this goal both Denikin and Yudenich overstretched their lines and neglected the flanks. The Red attack forced them to retreat in haste in November, a retreat in complete disarray that presaged disaster.

Also fighting against the Communists near Petrograd in late 1919 were General Johan Laidoner's Estonians, who were waging their own war of liberation and had refused to supply Yudenich with supplies for his autumn offensive. On 31 December 1919, two Estonian newspapers published a text found in the possession of a Jewish commander named Shunderev, who had fallen in battle while commanding a Bolshevik battalion. Estonian writer Jüri Lina reproduces in *Under the sign of the Scorpion* excerpts from the document that appeared in full in the Tartu newspaper *Postimees*. It is a circular letter containing an appeal to all Jewish leaders for the formation of a Zionist secret society. The letter, written in Russian by the central committee of the department of the Israeli World Union in Petrograd, was dated 18 March 1918. The text is in line with the same ideas as always:

> "Children of Israel! The time of our final victory is at hand. We are at the beginning of our world domination and prestige. That which we had dreamed of has become almost a reality.... Despite the fact that Russia has been subdued and lies under the chastisement of our foot, we must still be careful. We have transformed Russia into an economic slave, we have taken practically all her wealth and gold and forced her to kneel before us. But we must be careful to keep our secret. We must have no mercy for our enemies. We must eliminate their best and most talented individuals, so that subjugated Russia will be left without its leaders. In this way we shall destroy any possible rebellion against us. We must provoke class struggle and discord among blind peasants and workers. Civil war and class struggle will annihilate the cultural values which the Christian peoples have acquired.... Trotsky-Bronstein, Zinoviev-Radomyslsky, Uritsky, Kamenev-Rosenfeld, Steinberg, these and many other loyal sons of Israel occupy the highest offices of the nation and rule over the enslaved Slavs. We will utterly defeat Russia. Our people hold leading positions in the citizens' committees, in the commissariats, in the victualling committees and in other institutions, but do not let victory go to your heads!"

The possibility that the letter is a forgery must be ruled out. Juri Lina adds that in February 1994 information was published in Russia about the result of an investigation of the materials of the Trotskyite Uritsky. Among his papers had been found a secret document copied on 17 May 1918 which reproduced the very text of the circular Shunderev was carrying.

The decisive battles of Denikin and Yudenich coincided with a statement by the British Premier, Lloyd George, the puppet used time and again by Zionism and the sponsors of the Communist conspiracy. On 8 November 1919 Lloyd George made a speech at the London Guildhall in which he announced a change of policy towards Russia. Britain was leaving the game because, in his words, Russia was "a swamp" that had swallowed up foreign armies in the past. The time had come to admit that "Britain could not afford the luxury of such a costly intervention in an endless civil war". The prime minister said he hoped the winter months would give all sides a chance to reflect and reconsider the situation. In *History's Greatest Heist*, Professor McMeekin quotes an English journalist accompanying Denikin's army as saying that the effect of this speech on white morale "was electric". The white volunteers had believed they were fighting the last battles of the world war with Britain as a powerful ally. "Suddenly - writes Meekin - they realised in horror that Britain considered the war over and that the fighting in Russia was simply a civil conflict.... The atmosphere in southern Russia changed completely. George Lloyd's view that the volunteer cause was doomed to failure helped to certify the debacle. In December 1919 the Black Sea port of Novorossiysk was the scene of desperate scenes as crowds of civilians and white soldiers, fearing capture by the Reds, tried to board the last French and British ships leaving the port.

Nevertheless, on 4 April 1920 General Wrangel, who earlier in the year had been accused of plotting against Denikin, accepted the post of commander-in-chief of a new army in the Crimea, offered by a new General Staff. Wrangel, it seems, naively tried to curry favour with certain influential Jews in the United States, England and France. He soon had some installed in his rearguard. In the Crimea, for example, the French representative, Count Damien de Martel, was married to a Jewess from Odessa. One of Count de Martel's liaison officers with Wrangel was a certain Peshkov, whose real name was Sverdlov, an adopted son of Gorky who was the brother of the Jew who had ordered the assassination of the imperial family. Fully equipped with the woollen clothing, boots, helmets, coats and all the armaments they had received during the year, the Reds in November 1920 intensified their campaign to drive Wrangel out of the Crimea. During the evacuation of the last White units and fleeing civilians, a large-scale massacre took place, culminating in the summary execution of no less than fifty thousand civilians, according to official figures, who were shot or hanged between mid-November and the end of December. It has already been mentioned in the previous chapter that some sources put the number of victims as high as 120,000, and that the Red Army political commissar who led the massacre was Bela Kun, supported by two other Jews, Roza Zemlyachka and Boris Feldman.

In Siberia, after the winter fighting, Admiral Kolchak began a three-pronged offensive in March 1919. Aided by desertions and anti-Bolshevik uprisings in several cities, he advanced more than 300 kilometres in three months; but in early summer the Soviet counteroffensive began, and by July the admiral's troops had retreated back to the starting point. On 29 October, General Mikhail Dieterichs, who from January to July 1919 had personally supervised Judge Sokolov's investigation into the assassination of the royal family, ordered the evacuation of Omsk, but Kolchak rescinded the order and opted for an impossible defence of the city. Allied diplomatic missions left Omsk on 7 November, and Kolchak himself left on the night of 13 November. Five trains leaving the city with him on their way to Irkutsk, where he planned to meet his ministers, were carrying the Tsars' gold reserves. During the journey he learned that the commanders of the Czech Legion had decided to abandon their activities in favour of the Omsk government and leave Russia. Shortly afterwards he also learned of the social-revolutionary uprising in Vladivostock, which was crushed.

The behaviour of French General Maurice Janin and that of the Czech Legion, which was under his command and supported the Socialist Revolutionary Party uprisings in Siberia, was key to Kolchak's tragic end. The Czechs demanded that Janin give priority to their evacuation and General Janin agreed to their terms. Within days the Czechs seized control of the Trans-Siberian and imposed their evacuation order on the Russian stationmasters, which meant priority over the admiral's troops, who were travelling slowly towards Irkutsk with the intention of reaching the port of Vladivostock. More than 120 refugee trains got stuck on the tracks in the middle of the Siberian winter and were captured by the Soviets. Kolchak's convoy, faced with Janin's refusal to give priority to his trains, was held up in Krasnoiarsk from 17 to 21 December. After lengthy negotiations and with Janin's undertaking to guarantee his freedom and safety, Admiral Kolchak was able to leave the city and proceed to Nizhneudinsk, where he arrived with his cargo of gold on 27 December. It seems that there he was both detained and protected by the Czechs, who are accused by investigators on both sides of having stolen part of the Russian treasure.

When Kolchak arrived in Irkutsk on 15 January 1920, the city was in the hands of the revolutionary socialists. On the 16th, two Czech officers boarded the train, parked on the outskirts of the city, and arrested Kolchak. Although the Admiral's safe conduct was guaranteed by the Allies, i.e. Britain, France, Italy and Japan, the Czech military, who were under the command of the French general, handed the Admiral over to the local authorities of Mensheviks and revolutionary socialists, who handed him over to the Bolsheviks on 21 January. In the early morning of 7 February 1920 Aleksander Kolchak was executed on the banks of the Angara River by decision of the Bolshevik Provincial Committee. The executioners threw his body into the frozen waters of the river through a hole cut in the ice. Today there is a monument at the execution site, which was erected a few years ago.

When the French government obtained information about what had happened, it relieved General Janin of his command and ordered his immediate return to France. Janin left Russia via the port of Kharbin, near

Vladivostock, in April 1920. When he arrived in Paris, he was received at the Ministry of Foreign Affairs, where he must have heard serious reproaches for his performance that tarnished his career, as he was eventually posted to a minor assignment. As noted in note 55 of the previous chapter, before leaving Russia, General Janin met Judge Sokolov and Pierre Gilliard, the French teacher of the Tsar's daughters, in his train parked on the platforms of the port of Kharbin, near Vladivostock, They managed to hand him the investigation dossiers and three valuable chests containing some 300 imperial relics, documents and photographs of the family of Nicholas II that Gilliard and General Dieterichs had rescued from the house of Ipatiev.

A legend about the so-called "Admiral Kochak's gold" has grown over the years. Books, films, documentaries and research articles offer various versions of the final fate of the treasure. The following is the most reliable information. Professor Meekin, whose study of what happened to Russia's immense wealth deserves the greatest credibility, believes that most of the treasure fell into Soviet hands and writes that the Bolsheviks' gold reserves increased by $210 million ($21 billion today) after Kolchak's capture at Irkutsk in February 1920. According to other sources, between Nizhneundinsk and Irkutsk, the Soviets seized 333 tons of gold and platinum, although the Czechs, as has been said, also took some of the loot. Everything suggests, as several researchers have suggested, that the Czechs shipped a large number of crates of gold to Vladivostock, which was used to found a bank that laid the foundations for the economic development of Czechoslovakia, a country born after the Treaty of Versailles. There are, of course, no documents to prove this, but this is the only way to explain why the value of the Czech koruna soared immediately after the establishment of the bank and why the Czechoslovak currency became one of the strongest in Europe until 1939.

Pavel Nokilov, an expert on the history of the White Movement, refers to a curious document of the head of Kolchak's counter-intelligence service in the State Archives of the Russian Federation. It is a report dated 14 August 1919 on the shipment of gold to France to pay for the purchase of aircraft. According to the document, the French government kept the gold as payment for the debt incurred by the Russian Provisional Government. Oleg Budnitskii, a researcher at the Russian Academy of Sciences in Moscow, in addition to downplaying the amount of the treasure, tries to prove that all the gold ended up in banks abroad, because it was used to pay for loans and the purchase of tanks, planes, locomotives and all the necessities of the White armies. Finally, it is believed that some of the gold is at the bottom of Lake Baikal, the deepest lake in the world with depths of more than 1,600 metres. It would have ended up there after a derailment caused by the blasting of a tunnel in the mountains surrounding the lake near Irkutsk. In 2010, Russia's Interfax news agency reported that part of Kolchak's imperial treasure had been found in the depths of the lake. The Mir-1 and Mir-2 bathyscaphs, in the context of a scientific expedition by the Foundation for the Protection of Baikal, reportedly discovered gold bars at a depth of 400 metres below the surface of the lake.

Civil war against the peasants

Theoretically, the civil war so longed for by Lenin and Trotsky had as its fundamental enemy the bourgeoisie, the social class which in 1789 had been used by the world conspiracy with two aims: to put an end to all thrones and all religions and to introduce liberalism to replace mercantilism. As is well known, state intervention in the economy, protectionism of one's own production and the strengthening of nations were the characteristics of mercantilism, which had to be replaced by a new economic and political system advocating the "laissez faire, laissez passer" that prevails today in the form of savage neo-liberalism. In 1917, the proletariat was the new social class that was to be used to do away with the bourgeoisie and private property, with the ultimate aim of taking over all the resources of the planet and establishing the dictatorship of the proletariat. It was a second way to take control of all wealth. It was a quicker system than liberalism, as it advocated large-scale robbery. The foundations of communism, as has been explained, were already established when Adam Weishaupt died in 1830. The *Communist Manifesto* basically reproduces the doctrine of enlightenment. In Russia, in order to replace the bourgeoisie by the proletariat Lenin blithely appealed for extermination. On 31 August 1918 an appeal to this effect was made in *Pravda:* "Workers, the time has come to annihilate the bourgeoisie, otherwise you will be annihilated by it. The cities must be ruthlessly cleansed of all bourgeois rot. All these lords will be brought to book and those who represent a danger to the revolutionary cause will be exterminated". Soon, however, the communist dictators realised that they were opposed not only by the bourgeoisie, but by eighty per cent of the population, comprising all strata of Russian society.

More terrible than the war against the White armies was the war against the civilian population, most especially the war against the Russian peasantry, whose revolts and uprisings in the rear of the Red armies had been a constant since the spring of 1918. Already then Lenin referred to the kulaks as "leeches and parasites" because they refused to hand over their foodstuffs and proclaimed "merciless war against the kulaks". For tactical reasons, on 8 November 1917 the Bolsheviks, under pressure from the revolutionary socialists, had issued a decree intended to win the support of the peasantry. It stated that all land, including state-owned land, should be "for the tiller" and that the "forms of occupation of the land should be free". However, it stated that any final decision would be taken by the Constituent Assembly, which was famously shot to pieces. Lenin admits that the Bolsheviks at the time signed a law they did not want "because they did not want to oppose the will of the majority of the peasants". On 19 February 1918 there was a new decree on land distribution which was related to the previous one; but it already spoke of the "socialisation" of the land and the virtues of "collectivisation". The situation before Stolypin's reforms was then reversed and the communes reappeared. In *The Harvest of Sorrow* Robert Conquest states that in May 1918 "the Bolsheviks decided that the initial phase of alliance with the peasantry as a whole was finished and that the socialist revolution could now begin in earnest."

The new Soviet constitution of 1918 meant a demotion of the peasantry in favour of the workers. The confrontation of the village proletariat against the kulaks was the formula for the new phase of socialism. That is, an alliance with the poorest peasants was intended in order to neutralise the middle-class peasants. However, the party was extremely weak in the villages. Conquest writes that "before the revolution only four hundred and ninety-four peasants belonged to the Bolshevik Party and there were only four rural cells". He adds that the Bolshevik leaders frankly admitted the necessity of originating class warfare in the villages and reproduces Sverdlov's speech to the Central Executive Committee in May 1918: "We must seriously set ourselves the problem of dividing the villages into classes, of creating in them two opposing hostile camps, setting the poorer elements of the population against the kulak elements. Only if we are able to break the villages into two camps, to excite the same class struggle there as in the towns, will we achieve in the villages what we have achieved in the towns."

Although the bulk of the poor peasants remained aloof, the regime managed to create some sort of base in the rural areas. As antagonism grew in the villages, small gangs who accepted communist patronage, with the help of armed intruders from the cities, began to rob and murder with more or less impunity. The result was widespread revolt. In the course of 1918 there were two hundred and forty-five anti-Soviet rebellions in twenty regions of Central Russia. According to official figures, between July and November 1918 there were one hundred and eight "kulak rebellions", as the regime called them, in which entire villages participated without distinction of social class. On 10 August 1918, in directives to the Penza Soviet, Lenin ordered: "Comrades! The kulak uprising in your five districts must be ruthlessly crushed." The specific instructions for action called for the public hanging of at least a hundred kulaks, the publication of their names, the seizure of all grain and the selection of hostages. The Cheka archives, open to researchers since 1991, confirm that between 15 October and 30 November 1918 there were 44 explosions that turned into peasant revolts. Nearly a thousand people were shot and six hundred and twenty others lost their lives as a result of the repression.

Nicolas Werth in the first chapter of *The Black Book of Communism,* entitled *A State against its People,* argues that at the beginning of 1919 the requisitioning system was already centralised and well planned. Each province, district, canton or village community had to hand over to the state a quota fixed in advance on the basis of estimated harvests. These quotas included a score of products: potatoes, honey, eggs, butter, meat, milk, etc. Another reason for the peasant revolts was the forced conscription ordered by Trotsky. At least three million peasants deserted between 1919 and 1920. Government repression was not limited to shooting thousands of them, but also to taking their families hostage. A decree signed by Lenin on 15 February 1919 ordered local chekas to take hostages to force the peasants to clear snow from the railways. If they refused, the hostages were to be "taken by force of arms".

In 1919 there were in the Ukraine real peasant armies of tens of thousands of men, whose demands were: "land for the peasants, freedom of trade and freely elected soviets without Muscovites and Jews". Werth comments on the great April revolts in the Ukraine against the Bolshevik requisitioning detachments and provides Cheka data on the first twenty days of July, which refer to more than two hundred revolutions, "implying about a hundred thousand armed fighters and several hundred thousand farmers." Grigoriev's peasant armies, consisting of mutinous units of the Red Army with fifty guns and seven hundred machine guns, seized cities in southern Ukraine in April-May 1919, shouting the following slogans: "All power to the Soviets of the Ukrainian people!" "Ukraine for the Ukrainians without Bolsheviks and Jews!" "Land distribution!" "Freedom of enterprise and trade! Among the occupied cities were Cherkassy, Kherson, Nikolayev and Odessa. Some historians claim that this uprising made the planned invasion of Romania by the Red Army,, which wanted to come to the aid of Bela Kun's Hungarian Soviet Republic, impossible. Another army commanded by a certain Zeleny, under the slogan "Long live Soviet power, down with the Bolsheviks and the Jews!" came to control the province of Kiev except for the big cities. The rebellion in the Ukraine and in parts of the Volga can be said to have become widespread.

During the months of February and March 1920, in Kazan, Simbirsk and Ufa, provinces subjected to unbearable requisitions, the so-called "gallows insurrection" took place, led by some 30,000 peasants. The rebellion grew in strength, and a peasant army of 50,000 men was formed, which fought with farm implements against regular Red Army units armed with cannons and machine guns,. Within days, thousands of peasants were fighting against the Red Army. Within days thousands of peasants were killed and hundreds of villages burned down. In the autumn and winter of 1920, after the last contingents of foreign troops had left Russia, the fiercest peasant rebellions against the dictatorship of Lenin and Trotsky broke out. In the eastern Ukraine, Nestor Makhnov's army gathered fifteen thousand men and two and a half thousand horsemen, armed with a hundred machine guns, about twenty cannon and two tanks. In western Siberia an army of over

60,000 men was formed. In the North Caucasus another thirty thousand peasants rose up against the communist government.

The chairman of the North Caucasus Revolutionary Committee, Serge Ordzhonikidze, a Trotskyite of Georgian origin who during Stalin's purges ended up "committing suicide" in 1937, ordered on 23 October 1920 that all the inhabitants of Ermolovskaia, Romanovskaia, Samachinskaia and Mikhailovskaia be expelled from their homes and that the houses and land be redistributed to poor peasants. All men between the ages of eighteen and fifty were deported to the North, sentenced to forced labour. The Cheka henchmen seized the property of the aforementioned towns and all the livestock. In mid-November two of the towns were completely emptied of their inhabitants, and one of them was razed to the ground. In addition, the Caucasus was cleansed of ten thousand "class enemies" and more than five thousand awaited deportation. Lenin justified the measures by arguing that the peasants were "far more dangerous than all the Denikins, Yudenichs and Kolchaks put together, since we are dealing with a country where the proletariat (he meant the industrial proletariat) represents a minority." This statement is not without aberration, for it implies the admission that the dictatorship of a minority was intended to be imposed

The longest revolt was in Tambov province, which had broken out as early as 1918 and lasted until the end of 1920. Tambov, a densely populated province some 500 kilometres southeast of Moscow and controlled by the revolutionary socialists, was the breadbasket of the regime's new capital. Since the autumn of 1918, the requisitions had led to numerous riots, which had been ruthlessly suppressed. If the quotas were surrendered, the people were condemned to starvation. In August 1920, in the village of Jitovo, where the requisitioning detachments committed all kinds of abuses, one of which was the beating of old men whose children had deserted and were hiding in the woods, serious incidents occurred and spread throughout the province. In early September, all the government representatives of three Tambov districts who could not flee were killed by an army of more than 14,000 men, mostly deserters, armed with rifles, pitchforks and sickles.

This revolt developed into an insurrectionary movement organised by a social revolutionary military leader named Aleksandr Stepanovich Antonov. Peasant militias were formed and an information service was set up which managed to infiltrate the Tambov Cheka. Antonov launched a propaganda campaign denouncing the "Bolshevik commissariat". In addition to railway and other workers, thousands upon thousands of deserters joined his army. According to Richard Pipes in *A Concise History of the Russian Revolution*, Antonov made use of no less than one hundred and ten thousand deserters, of whom he managed to arm fifty thousand, whom he divided into eighteen or twenty regiments. On 19 October 1920 Lenin ordered Dzerzhinsky to "quickly and exemplarily crush this movement". By October the government controlled only the provincial capital and a few urban centres; but by the end of the year, with special troops from the Crimea and other Red Army detachments, was able to muster a force of 100,000 soldiers. General Mikhail Tukhachevsky was responsible for "operations to liquidate the Antonov gangs in Tambov province". Tukhachevsky used special Cheka detachments equipped with heavy artillery and aircraft. He carried out Lenin's orders by ruthless repression, even using asphyxiating gas to exterminate the rebels who continued to gather in the forests.

These peasant wars reached their peak in the first months of 1921. The Cheka reported in February that one hundred and eighteen uprisings were under way. The communists only controlled the cities and the countryside was left to the mercy of gangs or armies of starving peasants. Vladimir Antonov Ovseenko, commander of the Red Army, admitted in January 1921 that half the farmers were starving. On 12 February the Volga military commander reported that in Samara province the army had fired on several thousand starving peasants besieging the hangars where grain had been stored. In Saratov heavily armed peasants seized the stocks in the state warehouses. Between January and March 1921 control of the provinces of Tyumen, Omsk, Chelyabinsk and Ekaterinburg was lost. The city of Tobolsk was seized by a people's army of peasants and could only be recaptured by army units on 30 March. In the two big cities, Petrograd and Moscow, a government decree had imposed bread rationing in January.

The situation was so explosive that the Tenth Party Congress, in the context of the NEP (New Economic Policy) which began to be implemented from March 1921, proposed to end requisitions and replace them with a tax in kind. This measure did not put an end to the riots, which only subsided as a result of the famine of 1921-1922. As for the NEP, it was a recognition that the socialisation and collectivisation plans for the countryside were leading the country to ruin and endangering the regime itself. Lenin referred to this new policy,, which was intended to prevent the collapse of industrial production and made certain concessions to capitalism, as "breathing space". In his own words, it was "a strategic retreat which will enable us to advance on a wider front in the near future." Robert Conquest transcribes these lines from a letter from Lenin to Kamenev dated 3 March 1922, but which only became known in 1959: "It is a great mistake to think that the NEP puts an end to terror; we shall resort again to terror and economic terror."

Civil war against the Kronstadt workers and seafarers

The Soviet regime adopted the label "bandits" for all those who opposed its dictatorship. The term was adopted after the operation against anarchists carried out on the night of 11-12 April 1918. Bruce Lockhart, an eyewitness to the events, recounts that Trotsky decided to cleanse Moscow of anarchists, who, following the example of the Bolsheviks, had occupied the houses of the rich and applied Lenin's advice to "plunder the plunderers".

The raid began at 3 a.m. and consisted of a simultaneous attack on twenty-six houses seized by the anarchists. Lockhart describes the raid as a complete success, despite the fact that, in order to clear the buildings, Dzerzhinsky's and Peters' chekists killed a hundred anarchists and another five hundred were arrested, of whom twenty-eight were executed on charges of being "bandits". Later in the morning, Bruce Lockhart and Raymond Robins, the American colleague who considered Trotsky the most important Jew after Christ, were invited on a macabre sightseeing tour, guided by Yacov Peters. Lockhart describes one of the scenarios:

> "In the luxurious main hall of the Gracheva house, the anarchists had been caught in the middle of an orgy, the long table that had served for the feast was lying flat, and broken plates, glasses and champagne bottles were unpleasant islands in a pool of blood and spilt wine. A young woman lay with her face to the floor. Peters turned her over. Her hair was dishevelled. She had been shot in the neck and the blood had coagulated into a sinister purple lump. She couldn't have been more than twenty years old. Peters shrugged. 'Prostitute,' he said, 'Maybe it was for the best.' It was an unforgettable scene."

From then on the workers could become bandits if they opposed the government. The soviets controlled by Menshevik opponents and revolutionary socialists were dissolved on 14 July 1918. Protests and strikes took place in many cities. In Kolpino, near Petrograd, a Cheka detachment opened fire on a demonstration of workers protesting against starvation, and ten workers were killed. On the same day in Ekaterinburg, at the Berezovsky factory, fifteen people were killed by the Red Guards during a protest rally against the Bolshevik commissars. The next day martial law was decreed and the local Cheka shot fourteen people. Nicolas Werth notes that Moscow was not even informed of these executions and adds that in the summer of 1918 numerous demonstrations in various industrial cities were suppressed at the cost of workers' blood. According to this author, "one of the episodes of repression most carefully concealed by the new regime was the violence exercised on the workers' world, in the name of which the Bolsheviks had seized power".

During 1919, the wave of workers' protests in the factories was increasing. According to the Russian Centre for the Preservation and Study of Contemporary Historical Documentation (CRCEDHC), a source cited again and again by the half-dozen authors of *The Black Book of Communism*, on 10 March 1919, ten thousand Putilov factory workers gathered in general assembly issued a proclamation denouncing the government as nothing but "the dictatorship of the Central Committee of the Communist Party, which rules with the Cheka and the revolutionary courts." It demanded the release of political prisoners of the "genuine revolutionary parties". Lenin went to Petrograd and on 12 and 13 March tried to speak in the factories, but he and

Zinoviev were booed by the workers, who shouted "Down with the Jews and the commissars!". On 16 March, Cheka detachments raided the Putilov factory and arrested about a thousand workers. In the following days, two hundred strikers were executed without trial in the fortress of Schüsselbourg. Strikes in various Russian cities followed one after another in the spring of 1919, and all were severely repressed. The workers demanded the same bread rations as the soldiers, the abolition of privileges for communists, an end to forced conscription, free elections to the factory committee, freedom of association, of speech and of the press.

In early March 1919, workers in the town of Astrakhan, near the mouth of the Volga, went on strike. On 10 March the 45th regiment refused to fire on the workers marching through the town, and the soldiers joined the strikers. After the sacking of the Communist Party headquarters and the murder of its leaders, Astrakhan fell into the hands of the workers and deserters. The town, considered a key to preventing the connection between Kolchak's and Denikin's armies, was soon recaptured. Sergei Kirov, chairman of the Revolutionary Military Committee of the region "ordered the merciless extermination of the dirty White Guards by all means". The troops who remained loyal and detachments of the Cheka blockaded Astrakhan and recaptured it. The prisons were filled with mutinous soldiers and strikers.

The method of Carrier, the famous inventor of the Loire drownings, was then put into practice. The crimes of this fanatical criminal have already been described in the second chapter of this work, and it has been remarked that the Judeo-Bolshevik Chekists imitated his method in Astrakhan. We remember, then, that strikers and soldiers were thrown from barges into the Volga with a stone around their necks. Between 12 and 14 March between two and four thousand prisoners were drowned or shot. From the 15th the persecution of the city's bourgeoisie began, who were accused of having instigated a conspiracy that had made use of the workers and deserters. The houses of Astrakhan merchants were ransacked and their owners shot. Figures on the number of victims considered to be bourgeoisie are close to a thousand. On 18 March, the anniversary of the Paris Commune, as the authorities pointed out, the forty-seven dead of the communists were buried with great pomp and ceremony.

In March 1920 Trotsky launched a campaign for the militarisation of labour. Here is a quotation from the historian E. H. Carr in *The Bolshevik Revolution 1917-1923*, one of the volumes of his *History of Soviet Russia*: "Militarisation is unthinkable without militarising the trade unions as such, without the establishment of a regime in which every worker feels that he is a soldier of labour, that he cannot freely dispose for himself; if he is given the order to move, he must carry it out; if he does not carry it out, he is a deserter who is punished. Who takes care of that? The union; it creates the new regime. This is the militarisation of the working class." These ideas were intended to convince the workers that communism was the ideology that would liberate them from their supposed slavery.

In early 1921 the Kronstadt rebellion took place, one of the best-known episodes of the civil war against workers and soldiers. On 21 January a government decree ordered a one-third reduction in bread rations in a number of towns, including the Kronstadt naval base. At the end of February, hunger marches, strikes and factory occupations followed one after another, reaching their peak in the big urban centres, especially in Petrograd and Moscow. In the former capital, workers tried to enter the barracks to fraternise with the soldiers, and there were heavy clashes with Cheka units in which several workers lost their lives and hundreds were wounded. In Petrograd the workers of the big factories, meeting in assemblies, demanded the abolition of the communist dictatorship. Several Petrograd regiments met and adopted declarations of support for the workers. On February 23-25, thousands of workers marched through the streets of Petrograd to protest against the dictatorship. On the 24th Cheka detachments opened fire on a demonstration, killing twelve people. On the same day about a thousand socialist militants were arrested, which did not prevent thousands of soldiers from deserting to join the workers.

On 28 February, the *Sevastopol* and *Petropavlosk, the* two battleships at the Kronstadt base on Kotlin Island, finally mutinied. The sailors issued an ultimatum to be answered within 24 hours. The demands were set out in a fifteen-point programme. Among other things, they demanded: secret elections to the soviets, since the present ones "did not represent the will of the workers and peasants"; freedom of speech, press and organisation; an end to the supremacy of the Communist Party; equal rationing for all; and the release of political prisoners, including members of the SRs, workers, peasants, soldiers and sailors. It also called for the abolition of the requisitions, the abolition of the Cheka detachments and the expulsion of Jews from all the high positions they held. According to Alexander Berkman, an anarchist writer of Jewish origin, this last demand was considered among the most important.[7]

On 1 March a mass meeting was held in Kronstadt, which was attended by fifteen thousand people. Half of the two thousand Bolsheviks in Kronstadt joined the insurgents. Mikhail Kalinin, chairman of the Central Executive Committee of the Soviets, went to the naval base to try to calm things down, but was booed away. During the first week of March the Cheka issued daily reports on the situation, fearing a general uprising in Petrograd,

---

[7] Alexander Berkman, a Lithuanian of Jewish origin, spearheaded the anarchist movement in the United States together with Emma Goldman, who like him was Lithuanian and Jewish. After the repression of Kronstadt, Berkman left Russia in horror and published several books denouncing the myth of Bolshevism. In his own words, "terror and despotism had crushed the hope born in October 1917". He finally committed suicide on 28 June 1936.

since the mutineers had contacted the workers' assemblies in a large number of factories. One of the visible leaders of the rebellion was the first officer of the *Petropavlosk*, named Perichenko, who imprisoned the local committee of the Communist Party. On 6 January Trotsky had declared that all those who demanded freedom of speech and of the press should be shot "like ducks in a pond" or "like dogs". On 7 March the Cheka was ordered to act against the workers, and more than two thousand sympathisers with socialist or anarchist sympathies were arrested in order to crush the rearguard of the rebellion.

Operations against the mutineers, organised by Trotsky himself and directed by General Tukhachevsky, began on 8 March 1921. Trotsky ordered the women and children of the rebels to be taken hostage and promised the mutineers that they would be "shot like partridges". The island was bombarded with aircraft and shore artillery before the 561st Infantry Regiment launched the attack. Some units refused to attack and almost all members of the 2nd Battalion went over to the mutinous Marines. The fighting was fierce and resulted in thousands of deaths on both sides. The frozen waters of the Gulf of Finland were littered with corpses, and the Finnish government called for the bodies to be removed, fearing that they would wash up on Finnish shores and pose a health hazard. Ten thousand Red soldiers lost their lives in the assault. Mikhail Tukhachevsky later declared that he had never seen fighting like in Kronstadt: "The sailors fought like beasts. I cannot understand where they got the strength for their fury. Every house had to be dynamited".

In the days following the fall of Kronstadt, ruthless repression was unleashed and large-scale executions were carried out. Over the course of two months, summary trials were held which, according to official figures, sentenced more than 2,100 people to death. According to the Kronstadt documents cited by Nicolas Werth, some 6,500 people were interned in prisons and concentration camps. Before the fall of the naval base, about 8,000 people managed to flee across the Gulf of Finland and ended up in concentration camps. Five thousand of these prisoners ended up in Jolmogory, a camp near Archangel, and within a year three and a half thousand of them had died. In Jolmogory, as in Astrakhan, the Carrier method was used: the prisoners were loaded onto barges, tied by the arms and with a stone around their necks, and thrown into the waters of the Dvina River. A Jewish chekist, a psychopath named Mikhail Kedrov (Zederbaum) had inaugurated this cruel system of mass murder there in June 1920. Kedrov's barbarity and cruelty are described by Donald Rayfield in the book *Stalin and the Executioners*, published in English in 2003. He explains that in northern Russia Kedrov "massacred schoolchildren and army officers so viciously that he had to be committed to a mental hospital". The mentally ill man was soon released and was again given command of a Cheka unit in the Caspian Sea. Several testimonies confirm that many mutineers from

Kronstadt, as well as large numbers of Cossacks and peasants from Tambov province deported to Khomolgory were drowned in the river in 1922. About 2,500 civilians from Kronstadt were deported to Siberia just for having remained at the base at the time of the events.

Civil war against the Cossacks

The elimination of the Don and Kuban Cossacks was the goal of the civil war against this ethnic group, a people of freedom-loving warriors. The Bolshevik leaders themselves called their actions aimed at the extermination and deportation of the entire population of these territories the "Soviet Vendée". The historical precedent of the French Vendée, one of the most brutal massacres in contemporary history, was thus the model for the communists. In chapter two it has been studied that the Jacobin revolutionaries achieved a proclamation of the Convention which in unequivocal terms declared that it was a matter of "exterminating the bandits of the Vendée in order to completely purge the soil of liberty of that accursed race". The same genocidal will animated the Soviet leaders, who as early as the spring of 1918 planned war against the Cossacks, considered class enemies.

On 24 January 1919, a secret resolution of the Central Committee of the Communist Party envisaged a series of measures against the Cossacks, including the confiscation of their lands, which were redistributed; the obligation for them to surrender their weapons on pain of death; and the dissolution of their administrative districts. Isak Reingold, a Jewish Trotskyite who chaired the Don Revolutionary Committee and who years later would be eliminated by Stalin, took over the repression in these Cossack lands. In a few weeks, between February and March 1919, detachments of Bolsheviks executed more than 8,000 people. In the Cossack villages, revolutionary courts needed only a few minutes to sentence to death for "counter-revolutionary behaviour". In June 1919 Reingold acknowledged: "We have had a tendency to carry out a policy of mass extermination of the Cossacks without the slightest distinction". Faced with the evidence of mass shootings, the Cossacks decreed the general mobilisation of all men between the ages of sixteen and fifty-five and called for a region-wide uprising against the communists. The text of the call for rebellion explained that they were "for free elections and against communists, communes and Jews. We are against the requisitions, robberies, and executions carried out by the chekas". By early June, the Don and Kuban Cossacks had joined the bulk of Denikin's White armies.

The defeat of the Whites led to a second military occupation of the Cossack lands, which were again subjected to Red terror. Another Jew, Karl Lander, one of the main leaders of the Cheka, was appointed plenipotentiary in the North Caucasus and the Don. Lander set up special three-member tribunals (troikas) to carry out decosatisation. In October 1920 alone, these troikas sentenced more than 6,000 people to death. Those members of Cossack families who had not been captured were taken hostage and many ended their days in concentration camps, veritable death camps, as Martin Latsis, another Latvian-born Jew like his colleague Karl Lander, acknowledged. Latsis, whose real surname was Sudrabs, was chairman of the Ukrainian Cheka in 1919 and a member of the Cheka's Presidium from 1918-1921. In a CRCEDHC (Russian Centre for the Conservation and Study of Documents in Contemporary History) report quoted by Nicolas Werth, Martin Latsis wrote on that women, children and old people, in terrible conditions, in the mud and cold, "died like flies", adding: "women are ready to do anything to escape death. The soldiers guarding the camp take advantage of the situation to have relations with them". Latsis, who was singled out as a Trotskyite by Stalin, was also executed in 1938. In *A State against its People,* Werth estimates that between 300,000 and half a million people from the Cossack regions of the Don and Kuban were killed or deported during 1919 and 1920. He explains that one of the most effective means of de-Cossackisation was the destruction of villages and the deportation of all their inhabitants.

However, the most harrowing episode for the Cossacks came 25 years later when, having surrendered to the British in southern Austria, the British, knowing that they were being sent to death or internment in the Soviet Gulag, repatriated 50,000 Cossacks to the USSR. The officers were executed and the rest were sentenced to concentration or labour camps. It is estimated that half of them died during internment. The book that recounts the events in detail is Nicholas Bethell's *The Last Secret,* published in 1974. From official archives opened to researchers in 1972, Lord Bethell reveals that the 50,000 Cossacks were among two million people, men, women and children who were in Allied hands and repatriated to the Soviet Union against their will. Many had left Russia in 1917 and were exiles, dissidents who therefore did not have Soviet passports.

Our champions of freedom and democracy, despite knowing full well the bloodthirsty nature of the communist dictatorship, which by then had killed more than 20 million people, had no moral problem in collaborating once again with communism. Alexander Solzhenitsyn, who regards Churchill and Roosevelt as criminals who sent political refugees back to Russia to be persecuted and executed, calls this little-known fact "the last secret of the Second World War". Certainly, the Cossacks had fought with the Germans, but their wives and children had not. Moreover, it should be noted that after the communists' victory in the civil war and the subsequent wave of terror unleashed against them, tens of thousands of Cossacks fled to western Europe and were not Soviet citizens, as they were already a generation of émigrés who had never recognised the legitimacy of the Soviet state. Under the terms of the Yalta Treaty, most of them were not to be repatriated. Hugh Trevor-Roper, author of the introduction to Bethell's book, is more moderate than Solzhenitsyn in his criticism and charges that there was "an excess of pro-Soviet zeal on the part of the British authorities responsible for repatriation".

Red terror and Jewish terror

The Cheka (Extraordinary Commission for Combating Counterrevolution and Sabotage), later known under various acronyms (GPU, OGPU, NKVD, MVD and KGB) was created on 20 December 1917 by Lenin's decree. Lenin placed Felix Dzerzhinsky, a Polish Jew whose real name was Rufin, at the head of this political police. "We don't need justice", Dzerzhinsky, a sadistic drug addict whom Zinoviev considered "the saint of the revolution", once declared. In October 1918 Dzerzhinsky's mental disturbances reached such an extreme that he had to be sent incognito to a sanatorium in Switzerland, where he stayed for a month for psychiatric treatment. Precisely in October 1918, after the attempted assassination of Lenin, the Cheka ordered between 10,000 and 15,000 summary executions without trial. Thus, in just a few weeks, the Cheka doubled the number of death sentences carried out in the tsarist empire during ninety-two years.

Another Jew named Gleb Boky, the main organiser of the Gulag, seemed destined to succeed Dzerzhinsky after his death at the end of 1926. Boky was his protégé and most trusted confidant. However, it was a Stalinist named Vyacheslav Menzhinsky who took over. Except for the aforementioned Menzhinsky, the communist chiefs who presided over the Cheka were either Jewish or had a Jewish wife. Among them, as will be seen below, were Yagoda, Yezhov (married to a Jewish woman) and Beria, three of the greatest criminals in contemporary history. The Jewish historian Leonard Shapiro writes that "anyone unlucky enough to fall into the hands of the Cheka stood a good chance of being confronted with, and possibly shot by, a Jewish investigator". W. Bruce Lincoln, an American professor of Russian history, confirms that in Ukraine "Jews constituted 80% of the regular Cheka agents". Half of the members of the secret police operating under the orders of the Jewish directors of the Cheka were also Jewish, although many of them, as was customary, concealed this fact by adopting Russian names. The rest were recruited from the dregs of society. This last fact was even denounced by two veteran Bolsheviks, Olminsky and Petrovsky, who, finding that the Cheka acted "with full powers over the Soviets and the party itself", called for measures to "limit the excesses of zeal of an organisation full of criminals and sadists, of degenerate elements of the lumpen-proletariat".

Werth relies on Central Committee files to confirm that the local chekas were in the hands of degenerate elements, bloody, uncontrolled and uncontrollable tyrants. He quotes a report by the regional organising secretary of the party in Yaroslavl, dated 26 September 1919, which states: "The Chekists plunder and arrest anyone. Knowing that they will go unpunished, they have transformed the Cheka headquarters into a huge brothel where they take the 'bourgeois women'. The drunkenness is general. Cocaine is widely used by the bosses". Another report arrived on 16 October 1919 from Astrakhan confirms the above: "Drunkenness and orgies are daily occurrences. Almost all the Chekists consume a lot of cocaine. This enables them, they say, to better withstand the daily sight of blood. Drunk on violence and blood, the Chekists do their duty, but they are uncontrolled elements who need to be closely watched".

The intention to use terror as a fundamental instrument to get rid of opponents and to hold on to power was first announced by Trotsky on 1/13 December 1917 before the delegates of the Central Executive Committee of the soviets: "In less than a month, terror will take on very violent forms, after the example of what happened during the great French Revolution. It will no longer be prison alone, but the guillotine, that remarkable invention whose recognised advantage is to cut off a man's head, which will be available to our enemies." Days later Lenin, at a rally before an assembly of workers, alluded to the use of terror as "revolutionary class justice". The first victims of terror were the intellectuals, independent thinkers who were active in denouncing the communist dictatorship. The "intelligentsia", the intellectual elite guardian of Russian culture, was singled out as a target in the circular letter of the Zionist secret society mentioned above: "We must eliminate its best and most talented individuals, so that subjugated Russia will be left without its leaders. In this way we shall destroy any possible rebellion against us".

After the fall of communism, numerous works began to appear in Russia which, not being initially translated into English or any other Western language, could only be read in Russian. Estonian researcher Jüri Lina drew on many of these sources and cites them in *Under the Sign of the Skorpion*. One such work, published in Moscow in 1992, is *In the Light of the Day*. Its author, Vladimir Soloukhin, who died in 1997, was a prominent poet and writer of the "Village Prose" group, a literary movement interested in the traditional life of rural communities. In his last work, Soloukhin denounces that, in addition to persecuting intellectuals, the Chekists also arrested young people wearing a student cap and some of them were liquidated because Lenin thought that future intellectuals could also be a threat to the Soviet regime. This author reveals that the Chekists were interested in good-looking girls and boys: guided by the strange belief that among attractive people there would be more intellectuals, they considered them a potential danger to society.

In 1924, one of the first books to appear in the West on communist terror, *Red Terror in Russia (1918 to 1923),* by the revolutionary socialist S. P. Melgunov, was published in Berlin,. This work has become a classic consulted by almost all researchers and can now be read in English on the internet in a 2014 translation by Terri Fabre (Kuznetsoff). This pioneering book gives an account of the major mass killings and executions perpetrated by the communists. Melgunov's quotations from the report of the Rohrberg Commission, which entered Kiev at the end of August 1919 after the capture of the city by the Whites, are well known. In the execution room of the Kiev Provincial Czech, a large garage, "the whole floor was flooded with blood, and it did not run, but formed a layer of a few inches. It was a horrible mixture of blood, brains, pieces of skulls, locks of hair and other human remains. All the walls pierced with thousands of bullets were splattered with blood, and pieces of brains and scalps were stuck on them." Another extract from the report describes a mass grave found in a corner of the garden containing some eighty bodies showing the cruelty of the murderers: "There lay disembowelled corpses; others had several limbs amputated; some were quartered; others had their eyes gouged out and their heads, faces, necks and trunks covered with deep wounds... others had no tongues."

The Kiev Cheka had published the first issue of its newspaper *Krasnyi Mech* (*The Red Sword*) in August 1919. Nicholas Werth gives an excerpt from its editorial article, in which the criminal excesses described in the preceding paragraph are ideologically justified:

> "We reject the old systems of morality and 'humanity' invented by the bourgeoisie in order to oppress and exploit the 'lower classes'. Our morality is unprecedented, our humanity is absolute because it rests on a new ideal: to destroy all forms of oppression and violence. For us everything is permitted because we are the first in the world to raise the sword not to oppress and reduce to slavery, but to free humanity from its chains.... Blood? Let blood flow in rivers! For only blood can forever colour the black flag of the pirate bourgeoisie into a red banner, the banner of the Revolution, for only the final death of the old world can free us forever and ever from the return of the jackals!"

Let us recall that the chairman of the Cheka for the whole Ukraine between 2 April and 16 August 1919 was the aforementioned Martin Latsis, a close collaborator of Dzerzhinsky who had replaced another Jew named Isaak Izrailevitch Schvarts. Latsis published a book in 1920 in which he advocated unlimited violence against class enemies. According to his thesis, sentences should not be passed on the basis of guilt or innocence, but on the basis of social class. This is how Latsis explains the Red Terror: "We are committed to the extermination of the bourgeoisie as a class. It is not necessary to prove that a man acted against Soviet power. The first thing to ask when a person is arrested is what class he belongs to, what is his origin, his education, his profession." Melgunov picks up a text of the Central Committee of the Communist Party in which it is openly recognised that the Extraordinary Commissions "are not organs of justice, but of merciless extermination". The Central Committee defines the Cheka as "a combat organ working on the internal front of the civil war. It does not judge the enemy, but exterminates him, nor does it spare the one on the other side of the barricade, but crushes him".

With these guidelines as a backdrop, atrocities were the order of the day. Rape and all sorts of other abuses, as one can easily imagine, were commonplace; although, rape aside, one of the cruelest tortures for women was the stuffing of burning coals into their vaginas. As for the religious, priests, monks and nuns, the methods were varied. One of them consisted of pouring molten lead down their throats before being burned alive. Crucifixions were common. In a recent film documentary entitled *The Russia We Lost*, director Stanislav Govorukhin tells how the priests of Kherson were crucified. In Pern, Archbishop Andronnikov was horribly tortured: his eyes were gouged out and his ears, nose and tongue were cut off. The bishop of Voronezh was boiled alive in a large cauldron and then the monks were forced at gunpoint to drink the broth.

One of the cruelest methods involved rats: victims were put in coffins full of hungry rats, or voracious rats were locked in a bottomless cage on the detainee's bleeding stomach to watch the rodents devouring his intestines. Various sources describe a torture called "skin-pulling", practised by the Kharkov Chekists. Detainees were lined up and their hands were nailed to a board, then their wrists were cut with a knife, boiling water was poured over their hands and the skin was pulled off. Another cruelty of the Chekists consisted in crushing the skulls of the victims with screws or drilling them with dentists' tools. Once the top was cut off or sawed off, the next in line was forced to eat the brains. Whole families were often arrested and children were tortured in front of their parents and wives in front of their husbands. Jüri Lina refers to the book *Nomenklatura*, published in Stockholm in 1982 by Mikhail Voslensky, a former Soviet official. Victims dipped in boiling oil or tar, victims impaled, roasted alive in ovens, soaked in water in the middle of winter and left in the snow to become human ice cubes, and other methods that we can spare you are described in the book.

Lina, who is assiduous with newspaper archives in her research, cites a Russian-Jewish newspaper, *Yevreyskaya Tribuna*, which reports in its 24 August 1922 edition that Lenin had asked the rabbis whether they were satisfied with the cruel executions. The Estonian author denounces an ideological background that goes beyond the class struggle and quotes a biblical passage, modified in some European Bibles after the Second World War. It is found in the second book of Solomon and refers to the "victory over the Ammonites". The original version narrates the massacre of King David in all the cities inhabited by the sons of Ammon. The original text reads: "he cut them with saws and with iron picks and threw them into the furnace". In the modified passage it reads, "he brought out the inhabitants of the city and set them to work with saws, traces and iron picks". Certainly, it is very easy to find in the books of the Pentateuch and in the historical books texts in which Yahweh, the God of Israel, in addition to the destruction of other religions, orders extermination and ethnic cleansing, sometimes with the sole exception of virgin girls. On the other hand, it has already been seen that in the *Talmud*, in addition to fostering a pathological hatred of Christianity, only Jews are considered to be human beings.

Despite the display before the eyes of the whole world of this visceral hatred of Christian civilisation and of an unprecedented terror based on utter contempt for human life, some leaders of the nations which should necessarily have defended these values, subjected to the interests of those who had financed communism, shamelessly collaborated with the Judeo-Bolshevik criminals. Although the war against the Whites was won in early 1920 and a cease-fire with Poland was signed in October of the same year, the new British predisposition after Lloyd George's declaration definitely allowed the communists to make all sorts of purchases from their still abundant gold reserves. 1920 was the year of massive purchases of war material, which was used by the Soviets to massacre their own people in the face of the indifference and customary hypocrisy of the famous democracies.

Lenin's death. Trotsky and Stalin vie for power

On 6 February 1922 the Cheka was abolished by decree and replaced by the GPU (State Political Directorate). The name was changed, but the perpetrators and methods remained the same. On 20 May Lenin proposed by letter to Dzerzhinsky a plan to expel writers and teachers considered counter-revolutionary. On 22 May a commission was set up to identify a number of intellectuals to be arrested. On 1 June a new Penal Code came into force, legalising violence against political enemies. These were arguably the last actions under Lenin's leadership, as he had his first stroke on 25 May 1922. Although he was not removed from all responsibility until 10 March 1923, the struggle for power began from that moment onwards.

Lenin's health improved in June and, although he did not return to the Kremlin, he tried to write letters and take part in some public events, until on 13 December 1922 he suffered two more strokes which made it advisable to curtail his activities. Stalin had been appointed General Secretary of the Central Committee of the All-Russian Communist Party on 3 April, which is perhaps why on 18 December the Central Committee appointed him to be responsible for Lenin's medical supervision. The post of general secretary was then seen as a lesser post. Some even referred to Stalin as the "comrade archivist". But it so happened that Stalin also controlled the "Orgburo" (Organisational Office of the Central Committee of the Party). The two positions combined enabled him to place his allies in key positions in the party. All this coincided with Lenin's serious health problems and caught

Trotsky and his associates by surprise, who tried to react before the leader's death.

On 22 December, the day Lenin had a new attack, Stalin, who must have already been pondering his strategy for asserting himself as leader, learned that Lenin had written to Trotsky to congratulate him on his victory over the trade monopoly. The next day Stalin called Nadezhda Krupskaya, Lenin's Jewish wife who was working in the shadows to make Trotsky her husband's successor, and verbally abused her for having let Lenin write in his delicate state of health. Instead of complaining to her husband, Krupskaya wrote to Kamenev and explained that she had been subjected to a storm of rude expletives for having written a letter to Trotsky, dictated by Lenin with medical permission. She asked for protection against interference in her private life. Stalin had threatened to bring her before the Party Control Commission. Although she was confident of the Commission's unanimous support, she told Kamenev that she had no time for such a "farce" and that her nerves were "on the point of breaking". Robert Conquest confirms that among other coarse words Stalin called Krupskaya a "syphilitic whore". Another source on the incident is Maria, Lenin's sister who was with him until the end. According to her, "Krúpskaya was completely broken after the conversation with Stalin; she was not herself, she cried and rolled on the floor."

On 29 December 1922 the creation of the USSR was approved, and on 30 December the Treaty making Russia the Union of Soviet Socialist Republics was signed. On 4 January 1923 Lenin added a postscript to his will, proposing Stalin's resignation:

"Stalin is too coarse, and this defect, though quite acceptable in our milieu and in dealings among us communists, is intolerable in a general secretary. I therefore suggest that the comrades think of a way of removing Stalin from this post and of appointing another man who in every respect differs from Comrade Stalin in his superiority, that is to say, more loyal, more polite and more considerate of comrades, less capricious, etc. This circumstance may seem a trifle; but I believe that, from the point of view of preventing the split and from the point of view of what I have written before about the relations between Trotsky and Stalin, it is not a trifle, or it is a trifle which may acquire decisive importance."

The will with its postscript, which was given to Krúpskaya in a sealed envelope to be opened and handed over to the party when she died, was not known until Lenin's disappearance. In these circumstances, Lenin dictated several articles for *Pravda* in the following weeks, one of which, written on 10 February and finally published on 4 March, attacked Stalin. A majority of the Politburo opposed its publication, and it was even considered to print the article in a single copy of the paper in order to deceive Lenin. Finally

Trotsky persuaded Zinoviev and Kamenev to have *Pravda* publish the text. In February 1923 Stalin had told the Politburo that Lenin had asked for poison. Trotsky replied that Lenin's doctor, who was also his own, thought that he could recover with slight disabilities. Stalin insisted that the poison was only to be kept on hand in case the pains became intolerable; but his request was not supported.

At the beginning of March 1923, Lenin wrote a letter to Stalin, copies of which he sent to Zinoviev and Kamenev. The whole letter referred to the telephone conversation in which he had severely insulted his wife. Robert Conquest, a Sovietologist and author of numerous works on the USSR, reproduces the text in his biography *Stalin, Breaker of Nations*, published in 1991:

> "Most respectable Comrade Stalin,
> You allowed yourself to be so rude as to call my wife on the phone and insult her. She has agreed to forget what you said. However, she has informed Zinoviev and Kamenev about the incident. I have no intention of forgetting what has been done against me, and of course I consider that whatever has been done against my wife has been done against myself. I therefore ask you to consider whether you would be prepared to take back what you said and apologise, or whether you would prefer to break off relations with us.
> Respectfully yours,
>
> Lenin".

One of Lenin's secretaries, Maria Volodicheva, personally handed the letter to Stalin, who opened it in front of her. She reacted calmly and said slowly that "it was not Lenin speaking, but his illness", although agreed to apologise to Krúpskaya if Lenin insisted. Volodicheva returned with the oral apology.

Conquest relates that one of Lenin's secretaries told Trotsky that Lenin was preparing "a bomb" against Stalin. Moreover, Kamenev learned from a second secretary that Lenin had decided to "crush Stalin politically". It seems clear that the Krupskaya and Trotsky were playing their cards in order to get rid of Stalin. It is almost certain that they would have succeeded if on 7 March 1923 Lenin had not suffered the last stroke, which permanently deprived him of his ability to speak. On 17 April 1923, a few weeks after Lenin was finally incapacitated, the Twelfth Party Congress was held. Trotsky seemed well placed and many assumed he would be the new leader. On 23 April, doctors decided to operate on Lenin in order to remove the bullet that had been lodged three millimetres from his carotid artery since Dora Kaplan's assassination attempt in 1918. The agony lasted until 21 January 1924. Although there were rumours that Lenin had been poisoned, there is little chance that this was the case.

The evidence and facts recounted throughout this work leave no room for doubt: Trotsky, besides bringing Russia money and powerful international aid, had rallied the entire revolutionary left wing around the insignificant Bolshevik party by his authority over the Bund. He was the man the Jewish financiers behind the revolution had wanted from the beginning at the head of Russia. With Lenin's demise the time had finally come. His prestige in the United States and Europe was well established and in the USSR he was the leading figure in the Politburo. War Commissar and Generalissimo of the Armed Forces, he had at his command the Red Army that had won the civil war and which he himself had created. A Jewish woman who knew very well what Trotsky stood for, Nadezhda Krupskaya, had stood by Lenin to the end and had managed to get a postscript written in his will rejecting Stalin as his successor. Trotsky's failure to seize power was surprising and of decisive historical importance, since years later his international backers, faced with the evidence that Stalin was ruthlessly liquidating all Trotskyist Jews, devised a way to regain control of the Soviet state.

In *My Life* Trotsky himself explains why at the moment of the decisive struggle he was disabled by fever, unable to take part in the debates that were to decide the future. In the late autumn of 1923, only a few months before Lenin's death, Trotsky was hunting ducks in the marshes in unsuitable footwear:

> "As soon as I stepped onto the ground, wearing felt slippers as I was, my feet were soaked with water. Before I could jump into the car, my feet were completely frozen. I sat down next to the driver, took off my shoes and warmed my legs in the engine. But the chill got the better of me and I had to crawl into bed. The flu was followed by a cryptogenic fever. The doctors forbade me to leave my bed, which I had to keep for the rest of the autumn and through the winter. That is to say, while the discussion about Trotskyism was going on, I had to be tied to my bed. One can foresee revolutions and wars. On the other hand, it is not so easy to foresee the consequences of a duck hunting trip in the autumn."

The end of the quotation is significant: wars or revolutions can be foreseen, especially if you provoke them or know how to provoke them; but chance or chance can condition events. An unforeseen event, an accident or, if you like, fate forced Trotsky to disappear from the political scene just as the struggle for power was unfolding. The sum of resources he had in his hands was sufficient to achieve this. Once set up as dictator, Lenin's letter drafted by the Krupskaya would have enabled him to eliminate Stalin at once with ease. The discussion on Trotskyism referred to in the text had been prompted by Stalin, who reproached Trotsky for a series of "errors". For their part, the Trotskyists defended themselves by accusing Stalin of wanting to intimidate the party, to which he replied that he was only trying to intimidate the factions.

After Lenin's death, Petrograd was renamed Leningrad at the suggestion of Stalin, who telegraphed Trotsky, who after months of illness was convalescing in the Caucasus, and announced that the funeral would take place before he could reach Moscow, and advised him to continue his recuperation. However, the funeral was held six days later, on 27 January 1924; in other words, Trotsky would have been able to arrive in time to be present at such an important moment, at which Stalin took centre stage. Besides being the organiser of the grandiloquent ceremonies, he made a speech in which he pledged eternal loyalty to Lenin. Trotsky later declared that Stalin had deliberately deceived him.

In May 1924 the Thirteenth Congress of the Communist Party was held. A few days earlier, Krupskaya sent Kamenev, who was married to Olga, a sister of Trotsky's who had been shot on Stalin's orders on 11 September 1941 along with Maria Spiridonova, Lenin's secret will with a letter stating that her husband had expressed the wish that after his death it should be presented to the party congress for information. Again Robert Conquest reveals the actual words spoken by Stalin when he read the document. He again referred to Krupskaya as an "old whore" and even cursed Lenin, of whom he said: "He shits on me and shits on himself". Before the Congress began, the Central Committee met to examine the documents. Kamenev read out the text. The situation was embarrassing, but Stalin, seated on one of the benches in the rostrum of the Presidium, knew how to control himself and keep calm. Trotsky, with a sneer on his face, kept silent. When Stalin took the floor, he said that Lenin was not himself when he wrote the text, but "a sick man surrounded by women".

Oleg Agranyants, a Soviet agent who defected in 1986, shares Stalin's idea and attributes to Nadezhda Krupskaya the authorship of the documents to be submitted to the Thirteenth Congress. According to Agranyants, during the period in which they were written Lenin's health was so bad that at times he could not even remember his own name, which was known to the Politburo members. Moreover, Agranyants claims that a comparison of the text with Lenin's other writings shows that the language is markedly different. Finally, the Central Committee decided that the testament should not be read before the Congress or published. It was allowed, with comments by the Committee to the effect that Stalin had proved his ability and Lenin had been ill, to be read only at restricted meetings in the provincial delegations. Stalin tendered his resignation as General Secretary, which was unanimously rejected.

Realising that they could not prevail for the time being, the Trotskyists decided on the tactic of forming groups. Thus Zinoviev and Kamenev initially pretended to support Stalin in order to maintain a permanent underground struggle until they found some possibility of undermining his leadership from within. The triumvirate that was formed was generally accepted as the core of the Politburo. The order in which they were named placed Zinoviev, who controlled the party machine in Leningrad, first; Kamenev, who supposedly dominated in Moscow, second; Stalin was assumed to be third, though nothing could be further from the truth. Soon Zinoviev and Kamenev realised that the tactic of splitting up only favoured Stalin, who took advantage of the situation to play one against the other and thus prove his loyalty.

Once again circumstances worked against Trotsky. At a time when the ideological struggle and arguments were fierce and Stalin had unleashed a campaign to weaken him, the fever returned and he was once again out of action in the autumn of 1924. In October Stalin began to denigrate him publicly. Among other things, his disagreements with Lenin were alluded to, his political opportunism was criticised, and it was recalled that it was only at the end that he had joined the Bolsheviks. On 17 December 1924 came one of the decisive moments. Stalin rejected Trotsky's idea of "permanent revolution" and advocated building "socialism in one country" in principle. This perplexed the Trotskyists, as it clashed head-on with their internationalist plans. They believed that the revolution in a backward and non-proletarian Russia could only be consolidated with the support of revolutions in Western Europe, where the conditions for a proletarian upsurge were in place and would allow world government and the dictatorship of the proletariat. Reality, however, showed that the repeated attempts of the communist parties in Austria, Hungary and, above all, in Germany had failed and that the only aim achieved by the Bolsheviks had been to hold on to power at the cost of the complete ruin of Russia.

Stalin actually intended to place the International at the service of the USSR and subject to its orders. When the choice between Stalin's national communism and international communism was posed at the end of 1924, Zinoviev and Kamenev decided to fight against socialism in one country. It thus became clear that they were Trotskyists. In January 1925 Trotsky lost his key position in the People's Commissariat for War to Mikhail Frunze, a trusted confidant of Zinoviev. Frunze was short-lived as Commissar. In October Stalin asked him on behalf of the Politburo to undergo surgery for stomach ulcers. He died during the operation, allegedly from an overdose of chloroform. Since the operation seemed unnecessary, rumours spread that he had been murdered, although nothing was ever proved. In his place Stalin placed a man he trusted most, Kliment Voroshilov. The appearance in the West of the American writer Max Eastman's *Since Lenin Died*, which published Lenin's will, prompted another show of force by Stalin. The Politburo asked Trotsky to do the party a service. It was that he should repudiate Eastman and also deny the existence of the will. The text was imposed on Trotsky, who, humiliated, had only to sign it.

The 14th Congress was held in December 1925. Before it began, Kamenev's trusted confidant, Nikolai Uglanov, who was the party's organising secretary in Moscow, defected with his entire staff and sided with Stalin. The trick infuriated Kamenev, who during the congress sessions made a very critical speech which ended with these words: "I have come to the conviction that Comrade Stalin cannot perform the function of uniting the whole party." During the speech the uproar had been increasing. At the end there were cries of disapproval such as: "Lies!" "Bullshit!" "Bullshit!" From the place occupied by the Zinovievievite delegation from Leningrad a faint clamour of support was raised. But immediately the delegates rose to their feet and cheered Comrade Stalin with thunderous applause and shouts of "Long live Comrade Stalin!". The strategy of Zinoviev and Kamenev had failed and their defeat was publicly staged.

In the spring of 1926 Trotsky travelled to Berlin with his wife, Natalia Sedova. The doctors in Moscow could not explain the severe fevers he was suffering from, and he decided to consult German doctors. As soon as he returned to the USSR, he openly resumed his relations with Zinoviev and Kamenev. At their meetings they frequently criticised Stalin, who they parodied: they made fun of him by imitating his behaviour and manner of speaking,. But at the same time, convinced of the Georgian's harshness and implacable temperament, they feared that he might be tempted to take them out of their way, as he finally did during the purges. The three Jews denounced the Stalinists' anti-Semitic campaigns against them in Moscow. In the summer of 1926, the trio formed a united opposition group.

A fourth Jew, Nikolai Bukharin, who was playing the same role before Stalin that Zinoviev and Kamenev had played, tried to make Trotsky understand that his fellow oppositionists were no longer an option for the party. Trotsky replied that Stalin was less so. The three of them formally intervened before the Central Committee plenum in July 1926, and Zinoviev was immediately removed from the Politburo. In October, under threat of expulsion from the party, they were forced to cease their dissident activities. A few weeks later, however, during stormy Politburo sessions in which many members of the Central Committee were present, Trotsky could not restrain himself and launched a terrible attack on Stalin. Specifically, he said: "The First Secretary offers his candidature for the post of gravedigger of the Revolution." Stalin, pale, rose to his feet. He looked at first as if he was going to lose his temper and retort intemperately, but he did not. After remaining silent for a few seconds, he left the room, slamming the door. The next day the Central Committee voted Trotsky out of the Politburo. It was the beginning of the Mexican end written with an ice axe by Ramon Mercader in 1940.

From this point onwards the situation for Trotsky became untenable. The episode that precipitated his expulsion from the party and his confinement in Alma Ata was the failure of the Chinese Communists to start the war in that country. On 12 April 1927, Chian Kai-Shek, after accusing them of acting socially and economically against China's interests, had thousands of members of the still fledgling CCP (Communist Party of China), founded in 1921, executed. Exporting and implanting communism in China was for the internationalists a matter of the highest order. The Trotskyist opposition could not remain silent and took advantage of the situation to blame the Stalinist leadership for the debacle in China, which had led to the dispersal of the Communist Party. Stalin forced Trotsky and Zinoviev to appear before the Control Commission of the Central Committee with the intention of preparing their expulsion. The opponents then prepared a platform for the next party congress, which was to be held in December 1927. Stalin banned it. They resorted to the old propaganda tactics of illegal printing of pamphlets and various printed matter, which in Stalin's eyes constituted a real underground conspiracy.

On 7 November, the tenth anniversary of the Revolution, Trotskyites and Zinovievites joined the official demonstration, but unfurled their own banners and shouted their own slogans. Stalin, informed in advance of his enemies' intentions, had prepared the response. The police, aided by groups of Stalinists and other sympathisers mobilised for the occasion, cracked down hard on the dissidents. In the end, Trotsky and Zinoviev were expelled from the party and Kamenev and other opponents were expelled from the Central Committee. Zinoviev and his supporters surrendered and, without being readmitted, were allowed to sing the Palinody at the 15th Congress, held between 2 and 19 December 1927, where they publicly acknowledged that they were anti-Leninist and wrong. Trotsky, for his part, rejected any compromise and was confined in 1928 in Kazakhstan's capital, Alma Ata. His staunchest supporters were deported to Siberia and Central Asia.

With Trotsky and Zinoviev out of action and Kamenev seriously wounded, Stalin then set his sights on Bukharin and his allies, Mikhail Tomsky (Honigberg), who committed suicide in 1935 before being arrested by the NKVD, and Aleksei Rykov, executed in 1938 on charges of having conspired with Trotsky against Stalin. All three headed a moderate section, called by some the right wing of the party. In August 1928 Bukharin began to show signs of nervousness and discomfort and met Kamenev and Sokolnikov (Brilliant), who, like him, were later to be among the Jewish Trotskyists purged by Stalin. Bukharin regretted that neither Zinoviev nor Kamenev were any longer on the Central Committee and admitted that only he, Tomsky and Rykov held out in a Politburo totally dominated by Stalin, whom he compared to Genghis Khan. Bukharin agreed with his interlocutors that Stalin's line was bad for the revolution. Robert Conquest claims that Bukharin feared for his life, since he told his interlocutors verbatim that Stalin, whose tactic was to make verbal commitments, would kill them ("he will slay us"). This rapprochement with Kamenev and Sokolnikov, who until he was recalled to London as ambassador in 1929 was negotiating contracts with Western oil companies, served no purpose except to mark Bukharin, who had sought to establish alliances with his co-religionists in view of a possible future struggle. Despite Bukharin's insistence that the meeting should be kept secret, it became known almost immediately to Stalin's secret police, who were to establish themselves as one of history's great police geniuses, perhaps comparable only to Joseph Fouché.

PART 3
FAILURE OF INTERNATIONAL COMMUNISM IN GERMANY AND THE TRIUMPH OF NATIONALISM

When Lord Curzon warned that the Treaty of Versailles was a declaration of war, he did not point out that the war could be civil. We have already seen that both Trotsky and Lenin conceived of civil war in Russia as the best way to settle the class struggle. Their intentions in Germany were the same, as will be seen below. The absurd economic limitations imposed on Germany and the impossible war reparations demanded of the new Weimar Republic, which forced the surrender of the production of all the nation's labour, could only plunge the country into misery and permanent social unrest, i.e., create the conditions for spreading the revolution to Germany. Famine, misery, unemployment and continuous coups d'état were foreseeable consequences of the ill-fated Treaty of Versallles.

On 18 November 1919 Hindenburg appeared before a Parliamentary Committee of Inquiry into the causes of the war and the collapse. The old marshal read a statement he had prepared with Karl Helfferich and Ludendorff in which he reaffirmed his belief in treason. Paul von Hindemburg claimed that the Army could have ended the war favourably if it had not been disintegrated in the rear, and quoted a British general who acknowledged that the German Army had been "stabbed in the back". The general, whose name he did not give, was Sir Frederick Maurier, whose articles in the London *Daily News* had been translated in the *Neue Zürcher Zeitung.* In his texts appeared the word "Dolchstoss", meaning "stabbed in the back".

Perhaps this statement, which provoked commotion and shouting within the parliamentary committee, helped trigger the so-called "Kapp Putsch", which took place between 13 and 17 March 1920. It was a desperate attempt to reject the Treaty of Versailles by means of a coup d'état whose planning was almost non-existent and therefore doomed to failure. Wolfgang Kapp, a conservative nationalist, and General Walther von Lüttwitz, who had little support in the army, were the visible heads of the attempt. Kapp was born in New York and his mother was Jewish, according to the memoirs of Heinrich Brüning, chancellor from 1930 to 1932. Initially, the coup plotters easily seized power in Berlin, but Social Democratic President Friedrich Ebert called the trade unions out on general strike and they were forced to give in within two days.

Immediately the communists, who were still biding their time, seized the opportunity and called for armed struggle. Through revolutionary committees they seized political power in Essen, Duisburg, Düsseldorf and Mülheim. Thus began an insurrection that lasted two weeks, especially in the metallurgical and coal-mining areas of the Ruhr region, where there was bloody fighting between the revolutionary militias and the army, which finally had to intervene to restore constitutional order. The pro-communist media proudly claimed that a "Red Army" of fifty thousand men had been formed in the Ruhr. According to these media, the workers were armed because they had buried their weapons after the uprisings of 1919. Hundreds of people lost their lives in the fighting. All this provoked a feeling of antagonism which throughout 1920 took the form of continuous strikes and fierce street battles in the industrial cities.

Germany, a key player in the international revolution

Twice the communists tried to seize power in Germany: the first time in March 1921, the second time in October 1923. Trotsky and other theorists of communism agree that the failure of the German revolution of 1923 was decisive for the aspirations of the internationalists, who aspired to permanent revolution in order to achieve the world dictatorship of the proletariat. In August 1920 Trotsky sought to lead the Red Army to the borders of Germany, which, with its large industrial proletariat, was the ideal country in which to expand the revolution. Having defeated the army of Jósef Pilsudski, commander-in-chief of the Polish forces, the Soviets pursued the retreating Poles in order to gain the longed-for common border with the new Weimar Republic. However, a crucial defeat near Warsaw dashed Trotsky's hopes. In 1921 communism was still stuck in one country and the fall of Germany was considered vital.

After the failure of the November 1918 revolution and the Spartacist uprising of January 1919, a Jewish son of bankers, Paul Levi, succeeded Rosa Luxemburg. His first aim was to turn the KPD into a mass party. To this end, as we said in the previous chapter, he began to receive abundant funding from Russia through Jacob Reich, comrade Thomas. With the money, "proletarian centuries" were organised, which were to be the embryo of a future Red Army after the seizure of power through guerrilla warfare. The administrator of the dollars flowing from Moscow to the Russian Embassy in Berlin was the Jew Leo Flieg, a bank clerk who passed for the party's grey eminence. Flieg, who had been the right-hand man of Leo Jogiches (Tischa), served as secretary of the organisational office of the KPD Central Committee until 1932. In addition, he acted as a clandestine liaison with the OMS (Comintern's Secret Service). His conspiratorial work must have played an important role in the preparation of the coup attempt of 1921.

Twenty-four Russian experts went to Germany in January 1921 to organise a military uprising. They were supposedly experts in civil war. At their head was an old acquaintance, Bela Kun. As usual, his main companions were Jews. Prominent among them were: Joseph Pogány and Samuel Guralsky. The former, known as the "Red Napoleon", had been part of the group that assassinated Count Tisza. Under Bela Kun's regime in Hungary Pogány had been successively in the course of three months Commissar for Foreign Affairs, Commander-in-Chief of the Red Army and Commissar for Education of the Hungarian Soviet Republic. The second was a Polish Jew named Abraham Heifetz, who had belonged to the Zionists of Poale Zion. In *Anti-Semitism, Bolshevism and Judaism* Rogalla von Bieberstein notes that Guralski, who was very small and therefore nicknamed "le petit" by the Comintern agents, was to head the General Staff of the Revolutionary Committee. On 18 March 1921 Bela Kun pointed out the necessity of civil war in *Rote Fahne* (*Red Flag*), the party newspaper permanently controlled by Jewish intellectuals and propagandists. "The proletarian revolution," he said, "implies the arming of the proletariat and the disarming of the bourgeoisie. Kun openly declared that the law should not be an impediment to the proletariat.

A few days before the uprising began, Zinoviev authorised the assassination of the army chief, General Seeckt, whom he called "the German Kolchak and the greatest danger to the workers". Comintern hitmen tried to kill him while he was riding a horse in the Berlin Zoo, but failed. The man who took responsibility for preparing General Seeckt's assassination was Skoblewsky, a Trotskyite who had been sent to Germany to prepare the insurrection and who in Berlin was known as General Wolf and Helmuth; in Hamburg, he was Hermann; in Dresden, Goresoski. When he was arrested he said his name was Alexander Skoblewsky. During the Spanish Civil War, as will be seen, he was the famous General Gorev, who together with Miaja led the defence of Madrid in November 1936. In *The Night Was Left Behind*, Jan Valtin, pseudonym of Richard Krebs, recounts this time when he worked for him and claims that Skoblewsky had also planned the assassination of Hugo Stinnes, one of Germany's great industrialists.

Bela Kun was convinced that the triumph of the revolution in Germany would have consequences in Hungary and the countries of Eastern Europe. Supported by Zinoviev and Ernst Meyer, who in February had replaced a dissenting Paul Levi in the leadership of the KPD, Kun put forward his "Theory of the Offensive", according to which a communist party should always be on the offensive against the bourgeoisie. When it became clear that the insurrectionary movement intended to overthrow the parliamentary system, President Ebert declared a state of siege on 24 March. The insufficiently prepared uprising was isolated in some industrial areas of the country. Nevertheless, on 27 March the Communist Party decided to launch the revolutionary offensive in support of the miners in central Germany. In the large factories of Leuna in Saxony-Anhalt, south of Leipzig, some 4,000 workers armed with machine guns staged the uprising. Not far from Weimar, other towns in this industrial area of central Germany joined the rebellion. Merseburg, Halle and Mansfeld, where coal miners had been at loggerheads with the authorities since mid-March, were the main centres of the insurrection. On 29 March the Prussian riot police and an army battery crushed the 4,000 workers in Leuna. Thirty-five policemen and about 150 workers lost their lives during the fighting. Impatience, lack of coordination and improvisation led the "March Action" (Märzaktion) to disaster.

Paul Levi, a supporter of the united front policy, disagreed with Bela Kun's strategy, which led to his expulsion for indiscipline. Levi, who called the theory of the permanent offensive "nonsense", referred to the "March Action" as an attempted coup d'état, thus agreeing with the social democratic newspaper *Hamburger Echo*, which denounced what had happened as an "attempted communist coup d'état". In June 1921 the Third Congress of the International was held in Moscow. Victor Serge writes in his memoirs that Lenin was furious with the performance of Bela Kun, whom he repeatedly called "stupid" during his speech. It should not be forgotten, however, that both Zinoviev, who was head of the Comintern, and Bukharin and Radek, the latter a representative of the International in Germany, had supported the "Märzaktion", despite the fact that, as the analysis of the Congress concluded, there was no revolutionary situation.

Reinhard Kühnl, author of *The Weimar Republic*, a work which we have checked against our sources, presents what happened in March 1921 and October 1923 without writing a single word about the role of Moscow. He insists, as Marxist historians generally do, that the workers "were fighting to bring about social transformations on the model of the revolution in Russia". Kühnl overlooks the fact that simultaneously, in the same month of March, while Bela Kun, Zinoviev and company were using the German workers as cannon fodder to achieve their aims, the Russian workers in the big factories of Petrograd were parading through the streets of the city demanding an end to the Communist dictatorship. The Cheka, fearing a general uprising, had arrested more than two thousand socialist workers who supported the Kronstadt sailors. At the same time, Trotsky said that all those who demanded freedom of speech should be shot and threatened the mutineers with the murder of their wives and children, whom he had taken hostage. Naturally, Kühnl prefers to ignore the fact that the social transformations proposed as a model had led to a famine in Russia in 1921, which caused five million deaths.

German October" was decided on 28 August 1923 at a secret meeting of the Politburo in the Kremlin. Already the name indicates what its aims were. The October revolution in Germany was to be the trigger for the revolution in Central and Western Europe, which was to make the continuation of the world revolution possible. It was therefore a large-scale operation, a re-enactment of the Russian October Revolution. In *Das Scheitern des Kommunismus in deutschen Oktober* (*The Failure of Communism in German October*), Karsten Rudolph writes that posters were printed in Russia for young people with the slogan: "Russian youth, learn German, the German October is coming! On 10 October 1923, a letter from

Stalin to August Thalheimer, the Jewish leader of the KPD, who had been the newspaper's chief ideologue since the death of Rosa Luxemburg, was reproduced *in Rote Fahne*. In it he wrote: "The coming revolution in Germany is the most important world event of our time. The triumph of the revolution will have a greater significance for the proletariat of Europe and America than the triumph of the Russian revolution six years ago. The victory of the German proletariat will undoubtedly shift the centre of the world revolution from Moscow to Berlin."

The political background to the German October in the USSR cannot be overlooked. In April 1923 Lenin had been incapacitated. Trotsky and Stalin were preparing to fight the battle to succeed him. A triumph of the revolution in Germany would have endorsed the Trotskyist theory of permanent revolution and Stalin would never have been able, as he did in December 1924, to advocate national communism and advocate the initial establishment of socialism in a single country. In general, the decisions taken on Germany in the summer of 1923 were conditioned by internal struggles within the Soviet party. Shortly before the mechanisms for unleashing the revolution were set in motion, for example, it was put to Stalin that the most senior members of the Politburo, perhaps Zinoviev, Stalin and Trotsky, should jointly exercise responsibility for the Secretariat, the importance of which was beginning to be correctly appreciated by the Trotskyists. Robert Conquest points out that Stalin responded by proposing that Trotsky, Zinoviev and Bukharin join the Orgburo. Conquest adds that at a meeting of the Central Committee held shortly before the German October, "a ridiculous scene" took place: Trotsky in a huff offered to resign from all his posts and go to Germany to fight in the revolution. Zinoviev, for his part, said that he would do the same. Naturally, neither of them met with the approval of the Central Committee. Many of the discussions and positions of the Soviet leaders were later made known in the *Lessons of October*, a text in which Trotsky made his "critical analysis" of what had happened. Despite the cult of communists all over the world, it is a rather unobjective text of relative value, for, as usual, Trotsky gives the version of events that interests him.

The year 1923 had begun with the French occupation of the Ruhr, which led to chaos and an economic and political crisis that was an ideal breeding ground for revolution. On 11 January 1923, five French and one Belgian division equipped with heavy artillery and tanks stormed into the Ruhr, a territory of 3,300 square kilometres and three million inhabitants that was the largest industrial region in Germany and Europe. Essen and Gelsenkirchen were the first urban centres to be occupied. Machine guns were placed at strategic points in the cities, such as the stations and on the roofs of houses overlooking the squares. Mines, coal and fuel reserves were confiscated. Customs, railways, ships and means of transport in general were taken over by the occupiers, and hundreds of German officers were imprisoned. The revanchist Poincaré government justified the military occupation on the grounds that Germany had fallen behind in paying war reparations. The government headed by the liberal Wilhelm Cuno, who had been in office since 23 November 1922, opted for a policy of passive resistance and civil disobedience to the occupation authorities, which meant closing down all production facilities. Even prominent industrialists such as Thyssen, Krupp, Stinnes, Kirdorf and Kloeckner helped to organise passive resistance in the factories. Fritz Thyssen and other coal entrepreneurs were arrested by the French authorities and imprisoned in Mainz. Accused at his trial of inducing workers to disobey the occupation authorities under martial law, Thyssen fearlessly pleaded: "I am a German and I refuse to obey French orders on German soil. Instead of sentencing him to five years' imprisonment, the court martial preferred to fine him 300,000 gold marks.

Walter Krivitsky (Samuel G. Ginsberg), a Jewish Trotskyite murdered in New York in 1941, reveals in *I, Chief of the Soviet Military Secret Service* that in 1923 he and other agents were immediately sent to Germany in order to "mobilise agitators in the Ruhr region and to gather arms for an uprising when the time was ripe". Krivitsky explains that they created three organisations in the German Communist Party: "the Party Secret Service, under the direction of the fourth department of the Red Army; military formations, nuclei of the future German Red Army; and the 'Zersetzungsdienst' (Corruption Service), whose mission was to demoralise the Army and the Police." Krivitsky adds that the German Communists formed small terrorist groups, called "T" units, whose mission was the assassination of military and police. These criminal units, according to Krivitsky, "were made up of fiercely courageous fanatics".

On 13 May 1923 a strike began in the industrial centre of Dortmund which spread to all the mining and metallurgical centres of the Ruhr and involved about 300,000 workers. There were intense battles between the police and the "proletarian centurie", which took control of the markets and shops. The Cuno government fell in August as a result of the strike wave. The Social Democrat Gustav Stresemann, who declared that his would be "the last bourgeois parliamentary government", then formed a unity executive without the KPD, which had experienced a sharp rise in membership and advocated a united front policy, adopted after the failure of the "Märzaktion". In autumn unemployment was around 30%, industrial production was only 20% of what it had been in 1913, and inflation was absolutely out of control. There is even a medal commemorating the inflation of that year which reads: "On 1 November 1923 a pound of bread cost three million marks, a pound of meat thirty-six million marks and a glass of beer four million marks". To buy one dollar required an astronomical amount of marks. In other words, paper money had lost all its value. It was in this way that the middle classes were robbed of their life savings.

The leader of the KPD at the time was Heinrich Brandler, the first major Communist Party leader who was not Jewish. Brandler had returned to Germany from Moscow in August 1922. At the Eighth Congress of the KDP, held in Leipzig on 28 January 1923, the faction represented by Brandler and August Thalheimer was supported by Karl Rádek and thus prevailed over the more radical faction led by Ruth Fischer, Arkadi Maslow and Ernst Thälmann. In August 1923 Trotsky decided that a revolutionary situation existed in Germany. Radek and Zinoviev, who despite the failure of the "Märzaktion" still headed the Comintern, were hesitant. Stalin was in favour of waiting and containing the KPD; but he knew that he could not oppose the German revolution and did not do so. It was Trotsky, therefore, who demanded that the Communist International and the German Communist Party organise the seizure of power. In September, in view of the supposed suitability of the situation for relaunching the revolution, Brandler and two Jewish leaders of the radical faction, Ruth Fischer and Arkadi Maslow, were summoned to Moscow for consultations. On Trotsky's proposal, the Politburo had agreed that the German uprising would take place on 7 November 1923, the sixth anniversary of the Bolshevik Revolution. Brandler, however, proposed that the German Communists should set the date at the most appropriate time. Brandler apparently said that he was not Lenin and asked Trotsky to go to Germany to personally lead the revolution. It was agreed that technical and military aid would be sent, and numerous agents and specialists travelled clandestinely to Germany to prepare the uprising.

Brandler returned to Germany and Zinoviev, with Trotsky's approval, supported the KPD in forming coalition governments with the left Social Democrats of the SPD in Saxony and Thuringia, which took place in early October. On 1 October Zinoviev sent a telegram to the National Committee of the German Communist Party stating that according to the estimates of the Communist International (Comintern) "the decisive moment will come in four, five or six weeks". The communists were urged to "proceed at once to arm some sixty thousand men". The proletarian army of Saxony was to move towards Berlin and that of Thuringia towards Munich. Trotsky publicly defended in several speeches the entry into the governments of Saxony and Thuringia, since, according to him, it would allow a "training camp" until the main battalions of the proletariat were ready to break decisively with the bourgeois order and begin the insurrection under Communist leadership. In two reports, on 19 October to the Union of Metalworkers of Russia, and on 21 October to the Conference of Political Workers in the Red Army and Red Navy, Trotsky insisted on this approach.

Unexpectedly, in mid-October, the government of the Weimar Republic had declared a state of siege throughout the country, and the conflict with the Saxon cabinet was already under way, which, on Zinoviev's instructions, was hastily arming the proletarian centuries. In response to the demand for the dissolution of the centuries, the Minister of the Interior of the Saxon Government declared at a meeting of the Lepizig Workers' Councils that a choice had to be made between the red dictatorship or the white dictatorship, and added that the proletarian centuries were workers' organisations preparing for struggle. At the session of the Saxon Parliament on 17 October, a letter from the military governor of Saxony was read out. General von Müller asked whether the government agreed with the Minister of the Interior or accepted the dissolution of the centuries. The chairman of the Saxon Council of Ministers declared that the government was not accountable to the military governor and demanded that the government of the Republic overrule the general. Müller, however, received the support of the Stresemann government, so that street demonstrations were banned, the publication of communist newspapers was suspended, and the Reichswehr (Army) entered Saxony.

In these circumstances, the united front strategy pursued by Heinrich Brandler, outlined by his predecessor Paul Levi and supported by the Kremlin leadership, did not work, since the left wing of social democracy did not back the communists at the crucial moment. On 21 October a conference of factory committees was held in Chemnitz at which it was taken for granted that the Congress of Workers' Councils throughout the country would proclaim a general strike and the dictatorship of the proletariat. When Brandler moved a motion for a general strike, the SPD delegates objected, and this caused the communist leader to hesitate, opting to postpone the call, since in his opinion it was impossible to attempt the insurrection without the unconditional backing of the left wing of the SPD. The stand-by order was therefore given; but in Hamburg, allegedly because of a communication problem, the counter-order was ignored, and during the early hours of 23 October the proletarian centuries began the armed uprising. Their military commander was a Soviet brigadier of Jewish origin, Manfred (Moses) Stern, who years later would be sent to Spain, where he made a name for himself during the civil war as commander of the XL Brigade.

The Trotskyite Victor Serge narrates in heroic tones the capture of Hamburg in *Memoirs of Vanished Worlds (1901-1941)*, where he spares no praise for the Jewish leaders of the KPD: Ruth Fischer, Arkadi Maslow, Heinz Neumann and Arthur Rosenberg, "the only possible leaders - according to him - of a German revolution". His account begins: "The counter-order does not reach Hamburg, where three hundred communists start the revolution. The city is glacial with silence and concentrated waiting; they rush in with terrible enthusiasm, methodically organised. Police stations fall one after another, sharpshooters are installed in the garrets overlooking the crossroads, Hamburg is taken, those three hundred have taken it." Less romantic is the information provided by Rogalla von Bieberstein, who explains that the communists erected barricades and armoured car traps and that the assault on the police stations was aimed at getting hold of more weapons. Seventeen policemen and twenty-four revolutionaries lost their lives during the clashes. Twenty-six policemen were wounded and numerous insurgents were also wounded or arrested before their retreat. This author reveals that secret archives opened in Russia confirm that most of the strategists of the German October were international Jewish revolutionaries. Among them he mentions Radek, who travelled expressly to Germany to assume the top leadership of the revolution; Joseph Unslichlicht, "who held senior positions in both the Red Army and the Cheka and was to supervise the formation of a Red Army in Germany"; Lazar Stern, "who was to command military operations"; and again Samuel Guralski, "le petit", who, as in 1921, was to lead the Revolutionary Committee (REVCOM). Among the Soviet military experts of Jewish origin Victor Serge adds Solomon Abramovich Losovsky.

Chancellor Stresemann issued an ultimatum to Saxony's prime minister, the left-wing Social Democrat Erich Zeigner, demanding that he dismiss all communist ministers from his cabinet. Zeigner refused to capitulate, so on 27 October, pursuant to Article 48 of the Weimar Constitution, the President of the Republic, Friedrich Ebert, ordered his replacement. On 30 October 1923 a Social Democratic government was formed without communists. The German October had failed and there had been almost no struggle. With the defeat of the German communists, the world revolution had been knocked to death. The impossibility of putting the internationalists' proposals into practice would allow Stalin to formulate his plan to establish socialism in one country and to establish national communism in the USSR.

Zinoviev and Trotsky, although they had agreed with the united front strategy and had authorised the entry of the KPD into the governments of Saxony and Thuringia, blamed Brandler and his colleague Thalheimer for the debacle. In January 1924 Brandler was recalled to Moscow and it was decided to send him to Kazakhstan in Central Asia. At the German Communist Party congress in Frankfurt in April 1924, the same culprits were also singled out and, with Moscow's help, replaced. The new KDP leadership was headed by Ruth Fischer, Arkadi Maslow, Werner Scholem, Ivan Katz, Paul Schlecht and Ernst Thälmann. Only the last two were not Jewish. The real leaders were in fact the first two. The head of Agitprop (agitation and propaganda) was Alexander Emel, another Jew whose real name was Moses Lurje. A Fischer supporter, Arthur Rosenberg, a baptised Jewish Christian, became the most prestigious intellectual in German radical communism. Rosenberg, who in July 1924 became a member of the Comintern Presidium, insisted in a speech in the German Parliament that the Communists should put an end to the bourgeois republic. In 1925, as the Trotskyists lost power in the USSR, these leaders were progressively removed from the leadership. Most of them ended up in Stalin's hands and were executed during the purges.

The Treaty of Rapallo and the assassination of Rathenau

In the interval between the revolutionary episodes of 1921 and 1923, two events of great importance and complexity took place which require this brief section, as both are significant. We refer to the baffling Treaty of Rapallo and the assassination of Walter Rathenau, one of its architects. On 16 April 1922, two Jews, Georgi Chicherin (Ornatsky) and Walter Rathenau, both foreign ministers of their respective countries, were the protagonists of a historic agreement signed in the Italian town of Rapallo. His Jewishness did not prevent Rathenau from being a convinced German nationalist. Oswald Hesnard, a French Germanist who knew him personally, notes with admiration that "his person revealed nothing but wisdom, moderation and modesty". Rathenau openly declared that Jews should oppose both Zionism and communism and integrate normally into German society. Charles Sarolea, professor at Edinburgh University, in *Impressions of Soviet Russia*, a masterly work, writes that one evening, while conversing with Rathenau about the dominant role of the Jews in the Bolshevik Revolution, he asked him what he thought would be the end of the Russian tragedy. His reply was: "There can be no doubt that the end of the Russian tragedy will be the most terrible pogrom that the Jewish race has ever suffered". Convinced of the aberration of the Treaty of Versailles, Rathenau argued in vain to France and Britain that only if his country was allowed to develop economically would it be possible to pay the reparations demanded. Germany's raw materials were plundered, and Great Britain levied a 26% tax on its goods in order to prevent their recovery. Along with the fleet and other resources, as mentioned above, Germany had been forced to surrender five thousand locomotives, one hundred and fifty thousand wagons and its transport vehicles. The industrial machinery had been dismantled and transported to France and England. In short, it was an enslaved country.

Therefore, despite being profoundly anti-Communist, Rathenau realised that the only alternative was to reach trade agreements with the other country that had not signed the Versailles Treaty. Preliminary secret negotiations had taken place before the signing of Rapallo. Already in 1920 and 1921 Soviet Russia had shown interest in acquiring German-made military equipment and had placed long-term orders worth hundreds of millions of gold roubles. However, the involvement of Moscow agents in the "March Action" of 1921 caused the Germans to hesitate, who then proposed that any commercial dealings should be done on a strictly private basis. "The Soviets," writes McMeekin, "agreed as long as it was done through Olof Aschberg's S.E.A. (Svenska Ekonomie Aktiebolaget). The Reichbank, when it learned that Aschberg's bank was willing to sell Soviet gold - to the tune of 38 metric tons - as an import credit, jumped at the chance to obtain gold, which was becoming increasingly scarce in inflation-ridden Germany." Professor McMeekin points out that the German government was more desperate and in greater need than the Russians for a broad agreement. "That is why," he goes on to write, "the Wilhelmstrasse (Foreign Office headquarters) was willing to overlook repeated attempts by the Communists in 1919 and 1921 to overthrow the Weimar Republic government by coup d'état, apparently on the paradoxical principle that only a long-term agreement with the Bolsheviks could save Germany from Bolshevism."

So great was Germany's need to find a way out of its isolation that the Treaty of Rapallo was extraordinarily advantageous to Russia. The draft, revised in Moscow by German experts in the winter of 1922, received Rathenau's approval almost without amendment. It is a cruel irony that he who had been the German Foreign Ministry's greatest sceptic about relations with the Soviets should be forced to make a pact with them and establish diplomatic relations. So generous were the Germans that, in addition to cancelling the entire debt owed by Russia, they provided the communists with an almost unlimited line of credit to buy arms in Germany. "The commercial provisions in Article 5 of the Treaty of Rapallo," explains Sean McMeekin, "in which Berlin promised its best efforts to honour contracts, revealed the harsh reality: the Germans were so desperate for business with the Bolsheviks that they did not even bother to ask how they would get paid." There was, however, a secret clause in the Treaty which satisfied the demands of the military, since it provided for the training of German troops and the manufacture of weapons on Soviet territory. The opportunity to agree to the winter draft and sign the final text of the Treaty came at the Genoa Conference, held between 10 April and 22 May 1922. Some thirty countries participated, as discussed above. Soviet and German negotiators travelled from Genoa to the nearby seaside resort of Rapallo and signed the Treaty.

English, French and Americans were shocked by the news of the German-Soviet agreement and were outraged at Walter Rathenau. John Coleman, author of *The Conspirator's Hierarchy: The Committee of 300*, believes that there is no doubt that Rathenau was murdered by SIS (British Secret Intelligence Service) agents. According to him, Rathenau thwarted the plans of the ruling elite and put his nationalism before the interests of the so-called Committee of 300. Coleman points out that Rathenau had for a time been an adviser to the Rothschilds and this may have made him think that he was safe from reprisals against them. He also belonged to the German hierarchy. His father, Emil Rathenau, had founded the giant AEG (Allgemeine Elektricitäts-Gesellschaft) and he had succeeded him as chairman of the company in 1915. Rathenau, who had been a financial adviser to Kaiser Wilhelm II, was so well informed about the nature of power that on 24 December 1921 he had published an article in the *Wiener Freie Presse* from which various researchers extract these words: "Only three hundred men, each of whom knows all the others, govern the destiny of Europe. They choose their successors from among their own entourage. These men have in their hands the means to end the form of a state which they deem unacceptable". According to Coleman, Rathenau made the mistake of placing limits on the wickedness of men who can shake the world.

Two months after the signing of the Treaty, on the morning of Saturday, 24 June 1922, Walter Rathenau, who had rejected as ostentatious the protection offered to him by three policemen, was assassinated while travelling in an open car from his home in Grunewald to the Foreign Office. A vehicle occupied by three men overtook him. The driver was Ernst Werner Techow and sitting in the back seat were Erwin Kern and Hermann Fischer. Kern shot him from close range with an automatic pistol and then Fischer threw a hand grenade which exploded in the back seat where Rathenau was sitting. A job of true professionals, who, according to official history, belonged to the Consul Organisation, an ultra-nationalist underground organisation. Techow was arrested on 29 June, but the two assassins tried to escape to Sweden. Three weeks after the attack, Kern was liquidated by the police when he was surrounded in his hiding place. Fischer allegedly committed suicide. Thus they could neither be interrogated nor brought before a court of law, which is very significant.

Walter's mother Rathenau demonstrated in a letter to Techow's mother that her and her son's values were more Christian than Jewish. These were her words, transcribed in *Walter Rathenau* by Hans Lamm: "It is with indescribable sorrow that I extend my hand to you. Tell your son that in the name of the spirit of the victim, I forgive him, as God will surely forgive him, if he fully confesses before an earthly court and repents before God. Had I known my son, the noblest person on earth, I would have directed the murder weapon at himself rather than at him. May these words bring peace to his soul. Mathilde Rathenau.

The misinformation that often surrounds the comments on Walter Rathenau, who is condemned in some media with absolute levity, without knowing anything about him, for the fact that he is Jewish, prompts us to write a few lines of biographical content that do him some justice. Walter was the eldest of the three children of Emil Rathenau and Mathilde Nachmann. Emil Rathenau founded the Allgemeine Electricitäts-Gesellschaft in 1883 with a relatively modest capital of five million marks, which by 1914 had become one of the most important companies in the world. Although he shared his mother's passion for music and the arts, he studied mathematics, physics, chemistry and philosophy with the most eminent scholars of his time. His abilities encompassed literature, painting, science, philosophy, politics and metaphysics. Emil Ludwig wrote that Walter Rathenau could paint a portrait, design a house, build turbines and factories, write poetry, write treatises or play a sonata. Little known is the fact that Robert Musil, author of *Der Man ohne Eigenschaften* (*The Man without Attributes*), a monumental novel left unfinished by Musil's death, was inspired by Walter Rathenau to create Arnheim, his main character.

Thomas Edison was another of the personalities who were amazed by his many abilities.

Eugene Davidson, author of *The Making of Adolf Hitler*, refers to him as a man of extraordinary perceptions and contradictions. Rathenau wrote of the blue-eyed northern races, which he called "Mut-Menschen", people of courage, of prowess, of deep soul, as opposed to the "Furcht Menschen", the fearful, more intelligent, dark-haired races of the south, who were the artists and classical thinkers. Davidson sees both types as projections of his two souls, and adds that it was the Germans he admired, for their courage, for their virtues, for their integrity; even though it was the people of the south who had bequeathed the world's culture, religions, as well as its decadence.

Rathenau felt deeply German and loved his country without restraint. Hans Lamm, author of the book *Walther Rathenau*, highlights these words of his: "I have nothing but German blood, no other tribe and no other people". Although he identified himself as a Jew and did not want to convert to Christianity, he believed in the revelation of Christ, to the extent that at his father's funeral he quoted a text with words of Jesus. In a letter to a friend he expressed his desire to travel to Seville, "our home", he wrote, alluding to his Sephardic roots. In May 1921, Chancellor Joseph Wirth offered him the post of Minister of Reconstruction. His mother, for whom he was particularly fond, begged him to decline the offer. Acceptance meant giving up his positions in industry, giving up his many facets as a writer, his personal interests and business, and the possibility of retiring to his country estates. He initially promised his mother that he would decline the offer; but his personal commitment to Germany led him to reflect that he should accept the appointment. Rathenau resigned as chairman of the power company and as a member of several boards of directors, but he only served as Minister of Reconstruction for three or four months: although two-thirds of the population of Upper Silesia had expressed their wish to remain German in a referendum, the League of Nations Council decided on 20 October 1921 that Upper Silesia should pass to Poland, which led to the collapse of the government due to the withdrawal of the Centre Party ministers, Rathenau among them.

Later, as we know, he was to be appointed foreign minister. A few weeks before he was assassinated, even though he was only fifty-four years old, he wrote: "In reality I don't have much left, the flame is dying out". The fact that one day after his death a million people rallied at the Lustgarten in Berlin and hundreds of thousands in Hamburg, Leipzig and other German cities gives an idea of the people's emotion and shock. About death, Walther Rathenau made the following reflection, which we take from the work *Walter Rathenau, sein Leben und sein Werk* (*Walther Rathenau, his life and work*), written a few years after his death by Count Harry Graf Kessler: "Death is an appearance, we suffer it because we look at only a part, and not at the whole structure of life. The leaves die, but the tree lives, the tree dies, but the forest lives, the forest dies, but the earth that feeds and consumes its creatures is green. If the planet dies, then thousands more like it are born under the rays of new suns. In all the visible world we do not know death. Nothing essential on earth dies. Only appearances change.

Hitler and the "Munich Putsch"

No sooner had the communist conspiracy to overthrow the Weimar Republic been defeated than another attempted coup d'état took place, this time of a diametrically opposed nature, led by Adolf Hitler, assisted by Hermann Göring, Rudolf Hess and Alfred Rosenberg, members of the National Socialist Workers' Party of Germany (NSDAP). The coup plotters were further supported by General Erich Ludendorff. Among the turbulences and dangers facing the young Republic were separatist tendencies. From this consideration, the "Munich Putsch" can be understood somewhat better, since it took place when the conservative government of Bavaria, headed by Gustav von Kahr, intended to declare Bavarian independence. In this context, Hitler planned to pre-empt the separatists and stage a coup of his own; not to separate Bavaria from the rest of the country, but to use it as a platform for overthrowing the government of the Republic.

At eight o'clock in the evening of 8 November 1923, von Kahr was giving a speech to three thousand people in the great hall of the Bürgerbräu, a large beer hall on the outskirts of Munich. Hitler entered the hall accompanied by party members, ordered a few beers and endured the speaker's boring speech for half an hour. Meanwhile, six hundred members of the party's Storm Troopers (Sturmabteilung), the SA, surrounded the building. When at 8.30 p.m. Göring burst into the beer hall and placed a machine gun at the entrance, Hitler took advantage of the tumult, climbed on a chair, and after firing at the ceiling shouted, "The national revolution has begun!" Hitler immediately invited von Kahr, General Otto von Lossow, who was in charge of the Army in Bavaria, and Colonel Seisser, Chief of Police, to enter with him into an adjoining room in order to discuss plans for overthrowing the Berlin Government. All three demanded the presence of General Ludendorff, whose prestige in the army was undisputed. Once it was clear that Ludendorff supported the coup, they all returned to the beer hall and made short speeches, which were greeted with cheers from an excited audience.

News then came from abroad that the SA was having difficulties with army troops. Hitler decided to leave and commissioned Ludendorff to control the brewery. The general asked von Kahr, Lossow and Seisser to give him their word of honour that they were loyal to Hitler. Once the promise was received, he naively told them that they were free and free to go. None of them had the slightest intention of supporting the coup and they rushed for reinforcements. During the night the troops began to manoeuvre and the coup plotters were unable to occupy the strategic centres of the city. At dawn Hitler realised that they had been betrayed by von Kahr and company. Then Ludendorff, convinced that his presence would be enough to keep soldiers and policemen from shooting at them, proposed to Hitler a public march into the city centre to take it. About 2,000 men, with Hitler and Ludendorff in the lead, began the march from the Bürgerbräu along the Isar River to the Marienplatz, where the Town Hall is located, at eleven o'clock in the morning.

People came out en masse to watch the column pass and some joined the march as a sign of support. They intended to head towards the Ministry of Defence, where SA vans were parked with 150 men under the command of Gregor Strasser. A police cordon was blocked by a street leading to the Odeon Square. After a time of silent contemplation of each other, a shot was heard. The police immediately fired a hail of bullets. Sixteen Nazis fell to the ground dead, among them the engineering doctor Max Erwin von Scheuber-Richter, a personal friend of General Ludendorff who had financed the party with large sums of money. Ludendorff continued to walk in a straight line through the hail of fire until he reached the police ranks intact. Göring was seriously wounded in the groin and Hitler fractured the head of the humerus in his left shoulder. Four policemen were also killed in the firefight.

General Ludendorff was acquitted, but Hitler, accused of high treason, was sentenced to five years in prison, of which he was to serve only nine months. The party offices were closed and its newspaper, the *Völkischer Beobachter* (*The People's Observer*), was seized and banned. Göring managed to escape, but the heavy treatment he received for his wound temporarily turned him into a morphinomaniac. The leaders who were not arrested took refuge in Austria. Everything suggested that after the failure of the coup the political chances of Adolf Hitler and the NSDAP had vanished. This was not the case, for after writing *Mein Kampf* in prison, Hitler emerged convinced that in order to seize power it was necessary to turn the NSDAP into a mass party and win elections.

Hitler had begun his political career in 1919, a year after he had been admitted to Passewalk hospital near Berlin for gas inhalation at the front. There he was stunned by the news that his country had lost the war without being defeated on the battlefield. Like many Germans, he took up the theory that Germany had been "stabbed in the back" by a gang of communists led by Jews. When he was discharged, he remained attached to the army, for which he did information work. On 12 September 1919, he was commissioned to attend a political meeting in Munich of the DAP "Deutsche Arbeitpartei" (German Workers' Party), founded nine months earlier by a railway worker named Anton Drexler under the patronage of the Thule-Gesellschaft (Thule Society). The programme of this small party was nationalist and anti-Semitic. A mere fifty people attended the event, including Gottfried Feder, who spoke about the vileness of interest. Hitler was about to leave when another speaker rose, a professor named Baumann,, who made a speech advocating the separation of Bavaria from Germany and its union with Austria in order to found a new Germanic state in the south. Excited and in complete disagreement with these separatist ideas, Hitler decided to intervene and made a fiery, impromptu speech in which he refuted the professor's arguments and declared himself in favour of the union of all Germans. When he had finished speaking, he went out into the street without a word. Drexler ran after him and declared that he agreed with what he had said. A few days later he asked him to join the party, and Hitler accepted the invitation.

After joining the DAP, Hitler worked hard for four years in search of membership and funding. Since 24 February 1920, that small grouping of railway workers had become the NSDAP, a party whose benefactors or financial donors included the Bechsteins, Helene and Carl Bechstein, the famous Jewish piano manufacturer, and Fritz Thyssen, the steel magnate. Hitler also had the sympathies of Henry Ford, who, according to a report in *The New York Times* on 20 December 1922, financed Hitler's nationalist and anti-Semitic movement in Munich.

Numerous "anti-Semitic" Jews in Hitler's entourage

Much has been written about Hitler, but the aspects that will be discussed in the following pages are largely ignored. In this section it will be seen that Jews, sometimes Zionists, supposedly anti-Semitic, repeatedly appear around him, whether in his family background, in his ideological formation as a young man, or in his political career. In a second section we will see that, before coming to power, Hitler was financed by the same international Jewish bankers who had financed the Bolshevik Revolution and who put Franklin Delano Roosevelt in the White House. Thirdly, we will discuss the *Haavara Agreement*, a "Nazi" agreement, signed on 25 August 1933 between Nazis and Zionists, which promoted the emigration of German Jews to Palestine. If one considers that the racism of both sides contributed to the pursuit of overlapping goals, the facts have an undeniable logic. In reality, Hitler's nationalism and anti-Semitism were the tools used by international Zionism to finally achieve the founding of the State of Israel, impossible without "pushing" the great masses of Ashkenazi Jews, therefore non-Semitic, to Palestine.

A key book to address the first point is *Bevor Hitler kam* (*Before Hitler came*), published in 1964 by Dietrich Bronder, a German professor of Jewish origin who in 1952, after studying law, economics, medicine, theology and philosophy between 1940 and 1950, presented his doctoral thesis in history at the University of Göttigen on the subject of *Leadership and Organisation of the Socialist Workers' Movement in the German Empire from 1890 to 1944.* As far as we know, there is no English edition of this work, but a few copies can still be found in old bookshops in Germany. This writer spent August 2011 in Berlin and was able to find out from a colleague, a professor of Latin, that only one copy of Bronder's work was kept in the library of her university, which could not be borrowed and therefore had to be consulted in the library. extremely scholarly *Bevor Hitler kam* examines the intellectual and ideological baggage that laid the foundations of Prussian racial nationalism, which even before the First World War influenced an intellectual and military elite and was later to be a key factor in National Socialist thought. Professor Bronder begins his work with a significant quotation from Engelbert Pernstorfer, co-founder of the Austrian Social Democratic Party who died in 1918, which deserves to be reproduced as it is relevant in the context under consideration:

> "Every culture is national... Socialism and national thought are not only not contradictory, but necessarily go together. Every attempt to weaken national thought must, if successful, reduce the wealth of mankind..... Nationalism must therefore be something more than an atavistic phenomenon, like a reprehensible chauvinism; its roots must penetrate deep into the soil of human beings. History is nothing other than the history of peoples and states, in which they live their lives. The people are the motive and the trigger of all human events. Whoever tries to overlook this fact or to overcome it theoretically, will always be shipwrecked".

Published in 1974 in Switzerland, another interesting work that can be read online in PDF format is *Adolf Hitler - Founder of Israel. Israel in War with Jews,* whose author Hennecke Kardel, also of Jewish origin, was acquitted in 1982 of a lawsuit brought against him in 1979 by the German state, which also confiscated his property. In 1998, together with Anneliese Kappler, Kardel published *Marcel Reich -Ranicki: der Eichmann von Kattowitz (Marcel Reic-Ranicki: the Eichmann of Katowice),* for which he was sued for libel, presumably by Reich-Ranicki himself, a Polish Jew known as the 'Pope of German Literature' for his literary criticism. On 9 March 1999, Hennecke Kardel was informed by the Public Prosecutor's Office of the Hamburg District Court that the investigations against him on suspicion of possible insult or libel had been unsuccessful and that the case had therefore been dropped. Kardel, who seems to have been persecuted all his life, draws heavily from Dietrich Bronder's book, the source mentioned in the previous paragraph. Much of the following information is taken from both works.

Based on his own research, Bronder lists a number of National Socialist hierarchs of Jewish origin, among whom he places the Führer and Reich Chancellor Adolf Hitler in first place. Many false certificates of racial purity were fabricated at the time in order to conceal unwanted parentage.

Kardel claims that in Hitler's case, although the documents are not available because they were made to disappear, there is a very high probability that the Führer's paternal grandfather was a wealthy Jew named Frankenberger. Some authors, most notably Greg Hallett, author of *Hitler Was a British Agent*, point out that this Frankenberger was merely a middleman hiding the identity of Hitler's real grandfather. Hitler's father, Alois, an only child born in 1837, was thus a bastard conceived at the age of forty-two by Maria Anna Schicklgruber. On 10 May 1842, five years after the birth of her illegitimate son, Maria Anna Schicklgruber married Johan Georg Hiedler. Little Alois, who carried his mother's name for forty years, went to live with his uncle Johan Nepomuk Hüttler. The author of *The Making of Adolf Hitler,* Eugene Davidson, considers it unlikely that Adolf Hitler's grandfather was the Jewish Frankenberger and believes that the most plausible thesis is that Hitler's father Alois was actually the son of Johan Nepomuk, a well-to-do farmer with whom Alois Hitler lived until he was sixteen.

In 1847 Schicklgruber died, and ten years later her husband followed her. In January 1877, three unlettered persons who signed their declaration with the letter "X" swore before Pastor Zahnschirm that Johan Georg Hiedler had said before his death that he wanted to adopt Alois as his son. After hearing this testimony, the pastor of the parish of Döllersheim amended the entry of 7 June 1837. From that day on, Alois Schicklgruber was officially called Alois Hitler. Alois thus changed his patronymic from Hiedler to Hitler, a Jewish surname that also appears in three other forms: Hütler, Hüttler and Hittler. Adolf Hitler's mother, Klara Pölzl, was the third wife of Alois Hitler, whom she called "Onkel Alois" (Uncle Alois), as she was his niece. Konrad Heiden, a Jewish journalist and historian who sometimes wrote under the pseudonym Klaus Bredow, is the author of a two-volume biography of Adolf Hitler published in Zurich in 1936-37. In it he reveals that an ancestor of Klara Hitler was Johann Salomon and confirms that Hitler is a common surname on Jewish graves in parts of Austria.

Another testimony to the Führer's Jewish origin comes from Hans Frank, governor-general of occupied Poland and Hitler's lawyer during the war. Frank, who according to Bronder and Kardel was also half-Jewish, was sentenced to be hanged at Nuremberg. Before his death he admitted that he knew Hitler's origins. He confirms this in his memoirs, *In the Face of the Gallows,* written shortly before he went to the gallows. Kardel writes that Hans Frank was commissioned by Hitler to trace documents that could link him to his Jewish grandfather. Frank is said to have discovered years of correspondence between the Frankenbergers and Hitler's grandmother, Maria Anna Schicklgruber.

In *I Paid Hitler,* a book by Fritz Thyssen published in 1941 and supposedly written by himself, although he later denied his authorship, grandmother Schicklgruber is said to have been a maid in the Rothschild family home in Vienna, where she became pregnant. Eugene Davidson, however, mentions the Frankenberger family and not the Rothschild family. If Fritz Thyssen is correct in placing Grandmother Schicklgruber as a servant in the Viennese house of Salomon Rothschild, the Frankenberger Jew could be the intermediary appointed by the Rothschilds themselves, thus confirming Greg Hallett's thesis. In this connection, Niall Ferguson, authoritative biographer of the Rothschild family, confirms Salomon Rothschild's sexual excesses and perversions in Vienna: "He had a lascivious passion for 'very young girls' and his 'affairs' with them had to be covered up by the police". The inverted commas within the quotation obviously indicate the euphemisms used by Ferguson to avoid two words: girls and scandals.

According to Kardel, Hitler learned of his Jewish grandfather's existence through his mother, who, fearing for her life after an operation for breast cancer, spoke to her son a few months before she died. Klara Hitler gave him an address in Vienna in case he might need it, and explained that his paternal grandmother had become pregnant while working for Mr Frankenberger in Graz. Klara told her son that his father, Alois, had received financial support from the Frankenberger family until he was 14 years old. On 21 December 1907, Klara Hitler died, and at the beginning of 1908, young Adolf, who had failed the entrance examination for the Academy of Fine Arts in Vienna, decided to visit the Frankenbergers in the hope that they might be able to help him get into that institution. He met a man in his sixties, who admitted to him that his family had helped his father financially, although it was not proven that his father had been one of them. In addition to being disappointed, Hitler, who was eighteen at the time, came away from the interview humiliated. From that moment on, his interest in Jewish culture and his contacts with Jews in Vienna, where some 200,000 Jews lived, took on a new dimension.

By the autumn of 1908 Hitler was already a regular reader of the journal *Ostara*, founded in 1905 by Adolf Josef Lanz, a former Cistercian monk who had been expelled from the order in 1899 because of his racist interpretation of sacred history and for being part of a movement that preached separation from Rome. Lanz, who since 1908 had been editor and sole writer of the magazine, justified his racial theories from Gnostic and Kabbalistic viewpoints modified to suit his racial aims. In 1909 Hitler visited the Cistercian abbey of the Holy Cross in Wienerwald in order to find out the address of the creator of the magazine *Ostara*, a name that evoked an ancient Germanic divinity of spring. Hitler reportedly wanted to buy back issues from him, and Lanz gave them to him. From then on, the friendship between the two was born.

Brother Jörg, as he was known in the monastery, despite his preaching of Aryan racial purity and anti-Semitism, had taken up with a Jewish woman named Liebenfels and from then on called himself Dr. Georg Lanz von Liebenfels. He later decided to become a nobleman and claimed to be the son of Baron Johann Lancz and Katharina Skala. His father, Johann Lanz, was not actually a nobleman, but a professor in Vienna, but his real mother's surname was Hoffenreich, the daughter of a Slovakian merchant of Jewish origin named Abraham Hoffenreich. It is clear that this Nazi ideologue, who was neither a doctor nor a baron, sought to conceal his origins.

In 1907 the supposed Baron von Liebenfels formed the ONT (Order of the New Templars). Dietrich Bronder states that the idea came to him after attending a performance of Heinrich Marschner's romantic opera *Der Templer und die Jüdin (The Templar and the Jewess)*. The Order of the New Templars was based at Werfenstein Castle, where the swastika flag was flown for the first time in Germany. It was a flag with a red swastika on a gold background. Bronder adds that what is most surprising is that, 'after von Lanz had lent them Werfenstein Castle, the Jewish community in Vienna also celebrated its Feast of Tabernacles there, in memory of the wandering of the children of Israel through the desert. The alliance was forged with Rabbi Moritz Altschüler, one of the Jewish friends of the masters of the Order, known as co-editor of *the Monumenta Judaica*, in which the anti-Semite Lanz also collaborated!" Evidently, the fact that the quotation ends with an exclamation indicates Bronder's astonishment at the lack of logic in the behaviour of the sinister von Liebenfels, who was in reality a Zionist who granted the Jews full rights over Palestine.

Hennecke Kardel quotes the text of a letter from Lanz von Liebensfels to a brother of the ONT, Brother Aemilius, written on 22 February 1932, a year before Hitler came to power: "Do you know that Hitler is our greatest student? You will see that he and through him we too will triumph and stir up a movement that will shake the world. Heil you!" Lanz's influence on Hitler is the subject of a dozen-page article entitled "The Man Who Gave Hitler the Ideas" ("Der Mann, der Hitler die Ideen gab. Jörg Lanz von Liebenfels"), published in 1958 by Wilfried Daim. The German text can be read in PDF format on the Internet. Lanz von Liebenfels also belonged to the Thule-Gesellsachft, of which he was Master.

Of particular importance for the launch of the NSDAP was the acquisition of the newspaper *Völkischer Beobachter (People's Observer)*, whose main shareholders were members of the Thule Society (Thule-Gesellschaft), a secret order initially claiming Germanic antiquity, to which prominent Nazi leaders belonged. On Christmas Day 1920, a small advertisement appeared in the newspaper informing that the Nazi party had acquired the newspaper at great sacrifice "in order to turn it into a ruthless weapon of Germanism". Dietrich Bronder and Hennecke Kardel confirm that it was two Jewish friends of Hitler's who made the purchase possible: Moses

Pinkeles, alias Trebitsch-Lincoln, one of the most mysterious men of the 20th century[8], and Ernst Hanfstängl.

Kardel explains that Hitler met Ignaz Trebitsch-Lincoln through Dietrich Eckart, a party ideologue and member of the Order of Thule who died prematurely in 1923. According to his account, the meeting had been arranged to explore the possibilities of Trebitsch contributing money for the purchase of the newspaper and took place in a beer hall. Hitler asked Trebitsch-Lincoln what he thought about Palestine as a solution to the whole anti-Semitism racket. His interlocutor expressed his opinion on the merits of the union of the National Socialists and the Zionists. He added that the British should hand over Palestine to them and they would then take the people there. Kardel recounts that at one point in the conversation about the Jews, Trebitsch-Lincoln put his hand on Hitler's forearm and said, "I know who you are, Frankenberger". Hitler forcefully withdrew his arm and looking defiantly at him replied, "Never say Frankenberger or I will speak loudly about you, Moses Pinkeles! Moses Pinkeles of Hungary!" Asked how much money he needed, Hitler replied 100,000 Marks. Pinkeles then took out of his pocket three bundles of banknotes totalling 30,000 marks and placed them on the table. Dietrich Bronder claims that the remaining 70,000 marks were contributed by Ernst Hanfstängl, "Putzi" to his close friends, including Hitler, for whom he sometimes played the piano.

The fact that Hanfstängl, the son of a wealthy German art publisher and a Jewish American woman named Katharine Heine, had American

---

[8] The mystery of Ignaz Trebitsch-Lincoln has aroused the interest of many researchers. René Guenon, a specialist in esotericism, believes that Trebitsch-Lincoln, born in Hungary in 1879 into an orthodox Jewish family, was an agent of occult forces. Jean Robin, another writer on occult subjects, places Trebtisch-Lincoln in the service of an elite he calls the Unknown Superiors, linked to the Green Dragon Society. The historian Guido Preparata, by contrast, believes that, like Parvus (Alexander Helphand), he was a specialist in the art of subversion working for Britain. Bernard Wasserstein in *The Secret Lives of Trebitsch-Lincoln* argues that he was already engaged in espionage before the First World War. The thesis that he was a double or even triple spy is supported by other researchers. Donald McCormick in *Peddler of Death: The Life and times of Sir Basil Zaharoff* links him with the "Merchant of Death", the Jew Basil Zaharoff, of whom he was a close friend, and adds that he worked as a secret advisor to David Lloyd George. McCormick believes that there was a triangular partnership between Zaharoff, Lloyd George and Trebitch-Lincoln based on the fact that "each knew a secret about the other". Preparata writes that by the time he arrived in Berlin in the summer of 1919, he had lost his English nationality and had been expelled from England. This historian considers that there is a possibility that he was a communist agent in the service of the Bolsheviks. Ultimately, neither the known facts nor the speculation about this character allow us to unravel the enigma of his true personality. Two further facts, on which several sources agree: in 1930 Moses Pinkeles, alias Ignaz Trebitsch-Lincoln, was initiated, supposedly in Tibet, and became the venerable Chao Kung. He was officially reported missing in Shanghai in 1943, although this is not certain either. He is believed to have died on 6 October, but some sources speak of suicide and murder. The *Times of Ceylon* reported after the war that he had been seen in India, in the vicinity of Tibet, living quietly.

nationality and was Jewish did not prevent him from remaining for twenty years in Hitler's elite circle. Until 1937, Hanfstängl was head of the NSDAP's Foreign Press Department, but something must have happened in 1941, for he lost the Führer's confidence and was asked to leave the country. After the US intervention in the World War, this friend of Hitler's became an advisor to the US president, the also Jewish Franklin Delano Roosevelt, whom he had already met when they were both studying at Harvard. Was Putzi an agent placed alongside Hitler from the beginning?

That the top leaders of the NSDAP were related to families of Jewish origin is certainly a surprising revelation, since they all claimed to be anti-Semites. As Dietrich Bronder points out, the contradiction of this circumstance with "völkisch" (racial) theories seems insurmountable. Bronder insists that the data he offers in his book are the result of his own research on the National Socialist leaders. Of the 4,000 leaders he researched, Bronder found that 120 were foreigners by birth, and in many cases both parents were foreigners. A percentage," he adds, "were even of Jewish origin, therefore 'intolerable' for the purposes of the racial laws of National Socialism".

The names on the list in *Bevor Hitler kam* include, in addition to Hitler himself, the following: Karl Haushofer, considered one of the architects of the spiritual theories of National Socialism and the originator of geopolitics, a subject in which he was a professor at the University of Munich. A prominent leader of the Society of Vril or Luminous Lodge and of the Order of Thule, Haushofer, although a pious Catholic and an enthusiastic advocate of Aryan racial theories, was of Jewish origin and married to a Jewess. Rudolf Hess was his assistant at the University and was also initiated into the Vril Society. Hess, secretary to the Führer, Reich Minister and also a conspicuous member of the Thule-Gesellschaft, whose Grand Master was Baron Rudolf von Sebottendorf, also had, according to Bronder, ancestors of Jewish origin. Among the most important names cited in *Bevor Hitler kam* are: Hermann Göring, Reich Marshal; the Reich and NSDAP leader Gregor Strasser; Dr. Josef Goebbels; Alfred Rosenberg; Hans Frank and Heinrich Himler; Reich Minister von Ribbentrop (who pledged close friendship with Zionist leader Chaim Weizmann, first head of the State of Israel who died in 1952); SS high commander Reinhard Heydrich; Erich von Bach-Zelkewski; bankers Ritter von Stauss and von Stein, powerful backers of Hitler before 1933; Field Marshal and Secretary of State Erhard Milch; Under-Secretary of State Friedrich Gauss; physicists and former party members Philipp von Lenard and Abraham Robert Esau...

A separate comment deserves the aforementioned R. Heydrich, one of the worst figures of the regime, as he was the head of the Einsatzgruppen (Action Groups or operatives), who shot thousands of Jews in Poland and the USSR. Both Kardel and Bronder allude to the predominantly Jewish origin of Reinhard Tristan Eugen Heydrich, but in this case we have additional information from the Jewish writer Henry Makow (Henrymakow.com, 4 October 2009), who confirms that Heydrich's father was the Jew Bruno Suess, son of the Jew Robert Suess and Ernestine Linder. Bruno changed his surname to Reinhard, which in German means of impeccable purity. Graf Kessler in *Die Familennamen der Juden in Deutschland (The Surnames of Jews in Germany)*, explains that many German Jews with the surname Goldman changed their name to Reinhard, which was a favourite. Thus Bruno Suess became Bruno Reinhard, a Wagnerian opera singer and composer who wanted to be accepted as a non-Jew. Makow claims that Bruno Reinhard, who married his teacher's daughter and opened a music school in Halle, was a Freemason and a Frankist. He adds that Reinhard Heydrich did his military service in the navy and was called the blond Moses by his comrades. Felix Kersten, Himmler's doctor, writes in *The Kersten Memoirs* (1957) that Hitler knew that Heydrich was half-Jewish. The fact that Heydrich was one of the most ferocious Nazis against the Jews could perhaps be explained by his need to make a point of ensuring that, despite his origins, he would not be doubted. In Spain, the Dominican Tomás de Torquemada is a similar case. This converted Jew, confessor to Queen Isabella and the first Inquisitor General of Castile and Aragon, was noted for his implacable zeal in persecuting his brothers of his race. Torquemada was one of the main supporters of the expulsion of the Jews from Spain.

Julius Streicher, district chief, head of the SA, prominent member of the Order of Thule and famous editor of the famous newspaper *Der Stürmer*, is also singled out by Kardel for his Jewish origins. Founded in 1923, the paper was uncompromising for twenty years in denouncing the worst aberrations attributed to Jews, including ritual crime and certain sexual perversions. The paper's cartoonist, whose drawings were extremely aggressive and vicious, was the Jew Jonas Wolk, alias Fritz Brandt. Although he could not be charged with blood crimes, Streicher was sentenced to death in Nuremberg. Every day, more and more jurists denounce what happened in Nuremberg as the antithesis of law. Streicher's case is illustrative in this respect. It is known, thanks to a note that his lawyer Hans Marx managed to pass on, that blacks and Jews tortured him horribly in his cell: a photo was even taken of him naked with black and blue marks and a sign around his neck reading "Julius Streicher, King of the Jews". When the lawyer reported the incident to the court, the judges indignantly rejected the protest and ordered that it should not appear in the trial notes and recordings as "grossly inappropriate".

The executioner who hanged the Nazi hierarchs was the Jew John Clarence Woods, a US Army sergeant who delighted in prolonging the suffering of the condemned on the gallows. Rosenberg's agony was the shortest and lasted ten minutes. Ribbentrop took eighteen minutes to die and General Keitel twenty-four. When it was Streicher's turn, he was asked what his name was, and he replied: "You know it already". As he climbed the steps to the gallows, he shouted "Heil Hitler! Streicher's strangulation lasted fourteen minutes. Kardel notes that the box in which his body was placed bore the inscription Abraham Goldberg, according to him, his real name. On the other hand, Giles MacDonogh, author of *After the Reich* (2010), a work recently translated into Spanish and published in Barcelona, confirms that the name Abraham Goldberg was also written in the log book of the crematorium where Streicher's remains were cremated. According to MacDonogh, this was a false name. If so, why was the sign "King of the Jews" put up? Why was he asked his name when he was on the scaffold? What was the point of changing his name? The executions "coincidentally" took place on 16 October, the Jewish holiday of Hoshanah Rabbah, the seventh day of Sukkot, considered by the Zohar to be a day of judgement for the nations of the world. Thus, they were presented to the Jewish community as an act of Talmudic revenge.

Jewish bankers finance Hitler

A book that has gone down in history as the *Sidney Warburg* is the irrefutable proof that Hitler was used as a tool by the international Jewish bankers: the Rockefellers, the Warburgs, the Morgans, i.e. the same conspirators who had financed the Bolshevik Revolution. Antony Sutton, author of *Wall Street and the Rise of Hitler*, devotes a chapter of this work to studying the matter. Sutton, who believes that the book is authentic and that Sidney Warburg is in fact James Paul Warburg, son of Paul Warburg, quotes from Franz von Papen's *Memoirs*, published in 1953, in which the statesman considers the book in question to be genuine. Von Papen writes: "The best documented explanation of the National Socialists' sudden acquisition of funds was in a book published in Holland in 1933 by the prestigious publishing house Van Holkema & Warendorf, entitled *De Geldbronnen van Het Nationaal-Socialisme (Drie Gesprekken Met Hitler),* under the name of Sidney Warburg".

The book was only in Dutch bookshops for a few days, as it was soon suppressed. Sutton claims that three copies survived the purge, one of which was translated into English under the title *The Financial Sources of National Socialism (Three conversations with Hitler)* and subsequently deposited in the Britsh Museum, although it is currently unavailable to the public and therefore cannot be used by researchers. A second copy belonged to Chancellor Schuschnigg of Austria and is no longer known. The third copy was translated into German in Switzerland. Sutton makes it clear that the text in his possession was translated into English from an authenticated copy of the German translation purchased by him in 1971. He makes no reference, however, to an edition that appeared in Spain in 1955, published by Mauricio Carlavilla's NOS publishing house under the title *El dinero de Hitler*. This edition is the one we handle. Surprisingly, Carlavilla reproduces the cover of the Dutch edition and claims that this original copy had been in his possession for eight years. Comparing the texts of the Spanish edition with those published in English by Professor Sutton, we can confirm that, except for a few irrelevant nuances due to the Spanish translation, the contents are essentially the same.

On 24 November 1933 *The New York Times* reported the publication of the book with the headline "Hoax on Nazis Feared". A brief article noted that a pamphlet had appeared in Holland and that the author was not Paul Warburg's son. The translator was reported to be J.G. Shoup, a Belgian journalist living in Holland, and the editors and Shoup himself were said to be "wondering whether they had been the victims of a swindle". In our opinion, the immediate attempt to discredit the book through the publication of an article in that newspaper is only further proof of its authenticity. It has already been noted in the previous chapter that a Jew named Adolph Ochs bought *The New York Times* in 1896. We will now add that Adolph Ochs married the daughter of an important member of Reform Judaism. This marriage produced a daughter who married Arthur Hays Sulzberger, who ran the paper. The paper is therefore owned by the Ochs-Sulzberger clan and serves the interests of those who financed Hitler and Rossevelt in the 1930s.

Since we have a copy of *Hitler's Money*, we will comment in some detail on the text allegedly written by James Paul Warburg under the pseudonym Sidney Warburg. The reasons that prompted Paul Warburg's son to hand over a text in English to the renowned Dutch publicist are not known to us. What we do know is that his family disapproved of his vagaries and was able to withdraw the book from circulation. Thanks to the aforementioned *Memoirs* of von Papen, it is also known that an associate of the Warburgs who worked at the firm Warburg & Co. in Amsterdam reported the publication of the book to Holkema & Warendorf. The publishers, having been advised that there was no person by the name of Sidney Warburg, decided to withdraw the work from circulation. In von Papen's book is the text of an affidavit made by James Paul Warburg in 1949, in which he stated that the book was a forgery. In any case, even granting that Sidney Warburg was not Paul Warburg's offspring, the facts are narrated in the first person with complete accuracy and detail. Whoever wrote the text must necessarily have been someone very close to the financiers who brought Hitler to power.

The book, which consists of three chapters entitled with three dates: '1929', '1931' and '1933', begins with a brief account of the conversation between 'Sidney Warburg' and I. G. Shoup, the translator of the conversations with Hitler. In it Warburg justifies why he gives him the English manuscript for translation into Dutch: "There are times," says Warburg, "when I would like to escape from a world so full of intrigues, stock exchange manoeuvres, deceit and lies. I talk to my father about these things from time to time. Do you know what I have never been able to understand? How it is possible for people of good and honest character to engage in scams and deceit knowing that they will affect thousands of people." Shoup knows perfectly well who his interlocutor is, for he refers to him as "the son of one of the most powerful bankers in the United States, a partner in the New York bank Kuhn, Loeb & Co." The translator asks, "Why did he want to tell the world how National Socialism had been financed?"

In the first chapter, "1929", Warburg says some things that are impossible to believe, such as, for example, that the Treaty of Versailles, although inspired by Wilson, had never had the sympathy of Wall Street because France had benefited and had the economic reconstruction of Germany in its hands. It should be remembered that Wilson was accompanied to Paris by Wall Street bankers, including Bernard Baruch, Thomas Lamont of J. P. Morgan and Paul Warburg himself. Bernard Baruch, economic adviser to the Peace Conference, approved and pushed through the very harsh reparations imposed on Germany. We do not know who "Sidney Warburg" is trying to deceive, who self-righteously argues, as if it were not good business, that "the more France pressed for its war reparations, the more loans had to be granted by the United States and Great Britain so that Germany could pay and ensure the economic reconstruction of the country". After some political and economic reflections intended to "expose the errors of a system that rules the world", Warburg goes on to recount how he was commissioned to travel to Germany and meet Hitler.

Warburg, who spoke perfect German, having worked for four consecutive years in a Hamburg bank, tells how on a certain day in June 1929 he had an interview in New York at the offices of the Guaranty Trust with J. H. Carter, the bank's president commissioner. At a second meeting the next day at the Guaranty Trust, attended by the young Rockefeller; a Royal Dutch representative named Glean; presidents of the Federal Reserve Banks and five other private bankers, Carter proposed the young Warburg's name for the mission to Hitler: "all agreed that I was the man they needed:" Warburg writes that there was a further conference "at which Carter and Rockefeller called the shots and the others merely listened and nodded". There, all agreed that "there was only one way to save Germany from the French financial pincer, and that way was a revolution. This could be effected by two different political groups: either the German Communist Party - which meant, in the event of the success of its Soviet revolution, the domination of the USSR over Europe and the increase of the Communist danger throughout the world - or the unleashing of the revolution by the group of nationalists". The justificatory arguments of "Sidney Warburg" seem neither credible nor honest, not least because the communist revolution had already failed three times. Moreover, it is unreasonable that "to save Germany from the French financial pincer" a revolution should be thought of. The real motives, of course, were different and far more far-reaching, as we shall have occasion to discuss later, for the actual events that took place are of interest here. It was agreed that Hitler was not to know the purpose of Wall Street's economic assistance, and that he must be left to his own wits and reasoning to discover the latent motives behind the proposal.

Warburg left New York for Cherbourg aboard the *Ile de France.* "I was travelling with a diplomatic passport and letters of introduction from Carter, Tommy Walker, Rockefeller, Glean and Herbert Hoover". Once in Munich, the American consul failed in his attempt to put him in touch with the Nationalist group: "This cost me eight days". He finally managed to reach Hitler thanks to the efforts of the Munich municipal authorities. Deutzberg, the mayor, informed him that Hitler would receive him in the Bräukeller. The story of the first meeting follows. In an old, rustic room behind the great hall of the brewery Hitler was seated between two men behind a long table. "The three men stood up when they saw me coming and introduced themselves one by one. The waiter brought me a large tankard of beer and I began to talk." Warburg implied that he wanted a conversation alone and that preferred that no third parties were present. "It is not my custom," said Hitler, "but if you show me your papers, I will think about it." A couple of letters of introduction shown, the escorts withdrew after an indication with a glance. "Then I took out all my letters of recommendation and spread them out on the table, inviting Hitler to enquire about their contents. After reading them, he asked me if I intended to publish my conversation with him in an American newspaper. I replied in the negative. More calmly, he immediately said: 'It's just that I don't trust journalists very much. Especially American journalists'. I didn't ask why, as I didn't want to know either".

There can be no doubt that from this moment on Hitler knew with whom he was dealing, for the names on the letters of recommendation were quite significant. Then began a monologue by Hitler, who wanted to know what they thought about his Movement, since his programme had been translated into English. This was followed by denunciations of the consequences of the Treaty of Versailles on the population, denunciations of Marxists and Jews, of political parties and their servitude, of treason and corruption. Against all this stood his party, which aimed to win the hearts of the people, which promised work and bread with an all-German programme, and which was beginning to win the support of many unemployed, the middle classes and the people of the countryside. He then spoke of the need for strength and money to achieve the objectives and denounced the attitude of the Jewish banks. Hitler then handed him the party's programme: "Here you will find what we intend to achieve and what we consider our goal". Warburg thought the time had come to state the reason for his mission, but "he almost did not let me begin." Again he picked up the packet and began to refer to the difficulties and the necessity of carrying out a great propaganda, for which he needed money. Warburg declares that he was tired of listening to speeches and writes: "It became more and more difficult for me to carry out my task and to state the object of my interview. Hitler seemed to listen to himself with pleasure, and when I tried to interject a few words as an introduction to explain what I wanted, he would move on to another subject". When the moment finally came, Warburg reflects it in the text with these words.

- "'President Hindenburg does not look with sympathy on our movement, but when the time comes he will not try to turn the people against us. The aristocracy around him is afraid to see the people in power. For we could call them to account for their cowardly attitude towards the foreigner and their indecision towards Jewish capitalism'.
Suddenly he fell silent. He looked at me long and hard and questioned me rudely.
- Are you perhaps Jewish?
- No; I am of German descent'.
- 'Yes, of course; your name makes that clear'.
Then I had an opportunity to talk again about the difficulties that stood in the way of Hitler's programme, and I managed at last to start talking about the financial aid plan I wanted to propose to him.
- 'If this were true,' Hitler interrupted, 'how many things we could achieve!'"

When the Wall Street envoy asked him how much money he needed for his plans, Hitler was momentarily surprised and pressed a bell. He spoke to the waiter and shortly afterwards a tall, thin man in his forties came in, dressed in a brown uniform. Hitler, without introducing him to his interlocutor, asked him bluntly "what amount of money would be needed for intensive propaganda for the Movement". Warburg indicates that he later learned that the man who had come in was the banker von Heydt, who wrote down some numbers and passed them on to his boss, who thanked him in a tone that meant he could leave. "You see," said Hitler, "it is not easy to make a calculation in our circumstances. I must first know the maximum that the gentleman who sent you is prepared to give, and also whether he would be prepared to make a further donation if we should need his help again." Warburg then explained that he could not reply. His mission was to make contact with him, and he needed to inform those who had sent him of the maximum amount they would make available to him. "He didn't seem to like my answer very much. Perhaps he thought it was all a bit complicated, and in a rather dry tone he asked if I could give him even a rough idea of how much he might be able to count on eventually. I repeated that it was not possible." For its interest, the full quote from the dialogue follows:

- "When can I have the money?
I replied that I hoped it would be as soon as my telegraphic report was received in New York, provided there was agreement on the exact sum.

Hitler took me at my word again. He did not wish the money to be sent to Germany; it was too dangerous.
- I have no confidence in any German bank. The money must be deposited in a foreign bank, from which it would be made available to me.
Again he looked at the amount they had added up and, as if giving a sharp command, said:
- One hundred million marks'.
I made an effort not to let my astonishment at the magnitude of the sum show. I promised to telegraph to New York and promptly let him know what answer I got. He interrupted me:
- As soon as you hear from him, write to von Heydt. His address is Lützow-Ufer, 18, Berlin. He will get in touch with you immediately if necessary'.
Hitler stood up. He shook my hand - which I took as a good sign - and I left. On the way to my hotel I was mentally crunching the numbers. 100 million marks was about $24 million. I began to doubt that Carter would want to give such a large sum to a European political movement in 'fond perdu'. Finally I thought that New York would like to know the result of my efforts and I secretly sent an extract of the conversation I had with Hitler.
The next day, in the evening, I went to a meeting which was held in the circle of the National Socialist Party; in the morning I had received at my hotel an invitation to attend. Hitler spoke in person; afterwards a certain Falkenhayn took the floor."

The reply from New York came three days later. "A brief reply, and also in cipher writing. In it Hitler was offered ten million dollars. I was expected to inform to which European bank this amount was to be sent on account in my name". In relation to the amounts given, it must be considered that the hyperinflation which between 1921-23 destroyed the German currency had been able to be curbed by the temporary replacement of the Reichsmark by the Rentenmark, supported by mortgages on German property and by industrial production. Warburg goes on to say that he wrote to von Heydt, who telephoned him the next day and they arranged to meet at his hotel. Von Heydt arrived accompanied by another man who was introduced as Frey, and "I informed them that New York was prepared to make available to them ten million dollars to be sent to a European bank in my name. I would gladly place it at Hitler's disposal. The payment and transfer of this money would have to be regulated." Two days later both men presented themselves again at the hotel with the instructions the Führer had given them. The proposition was as follows:

"I should telegraph to New York and tell them to place the ten million dollars at my disposal at the Mendelssohn & Co. bank in Amsterdam: I would have to fetch the money myself in that city and get this banker to give me ten cheques for one million dollars to be exchanged for marks and to place them in ten different towns in Germany. I would make the cheques out to ten different people, who would make them available to Heydt. He would come with me to Amsterdam. Once in Amsterdam, I could return to America".

The fact that Hitler's bank of choice was the Mendelssohn Bank of Amsterdam is significant, since it was a Jewish bank in the Warburg orbit. The Mendelssohns, moreover, had been the bankers most favoured by the Rothschilds in the 19th century, even though Samuel Bleichröder tried to supplant them in Berlin. It is therefore not surprising that "Sidney Warburg" was received with extraordinary kindness by the director when he asked to meet him. It surprised the young Warburg that von Heydt "was treated by all employees, both junior and senior, as if they considered him to be one of the bank's best customers". This indicates, of course, that the Nazis, despite speeches against Jewish banking, routinely dealt with Jewish banks without any problems.

"Sidney Warburg embarked on the *Olympia* at Southhampton and returned to New York, where he reported everything to J. H. Carter, Morgan's man and the Guaranty Trust, who proposed to call a plenary meeting so that he could report in detail. At the new meeting," writes Warburg, "the same gentlemen were present as in July; but this time beside Glean, who represented the Royal Dutch, sat an English representative, Angell, one of the most important men in the Asiatic Petroleum Company.... They all found the sum of 24 million excessive, but I got the impression that it was precisely the size of the sum which indicated to them that one could have confidence in the firmness and truthfulness of the Führer's actions." Among other details, Warburg notes Rockefeller's "enormous interest in Hitler's statements about the Communists." He also notes that within weeks of his return, certain newspapers "began to take a special interest in the new German party" and adds that "newspapers such as *The New York Times, Chicago Tribune, Sunday Times,* etc. began to publish news reports on Hitler's speeches.

At the beginning of 1924, the NSDAP had 24 deputies. After the failure of the "Munich Putsch", the party fell into disrepute, and in the elections at the end of that year it won 14 representatives. Things were even worse in 1928, when the Nazis won only 12 seats. Surprisingly, everything began to change in the elections of 14 September 1930, when the NSDAP increased its results tenfold and, with almost six and a half million votes, won 107 seats. Overnight Hitler's party had become the second largest political force in Germany, behind only the Social Democratic Party, which was the party with the most votes and 143 seats. The Communists, the sworn enemies of the Nazis, with almost two million fewer votes, won 77 seats. It seems clear that the injection of money from Wall Street had had an effect.

The second chapter of *Hitler's Money*, entitled "1931", begins with a reflection on monetary policy. The fact that in September 1931 the Bank of England abolished the gold standard[9] prompted the French government to withdraw part of its gold reserves stored at the Federal Reserve: "Enormous quantities of gold were shipped," writes Warburg, "from New York to Europe, a good part of which went to France, though I cannot say for certain.... By the end of September 1931 and the beginning of October we saw that between 650 and 700 million dollars had already been sent to Europe. The gold deposits still held by the French Government with the Federal Reserve Bank at the end of October were valued at about $800 million." Warburg attributes the weakening of sterling to the French tactic, which was supposedly intended to wear London down financially so that it could not come to Germany's aid. The visit to Washington by Pierre Laval, President of the French Council of Ministers, and two financial experts, Parnier and Lacour-Gayet, is reported. "Sidney Warburg" comments that the Federal Reserve and Treasury experts "were of the opinion that the French Government had lost a few millions to sink the pound and bring down the gold standard in London".

The topic then returns to the financing of the NSDAP, as "Sidney Warburg" reports receiving a letter from Hitler at the end of October 1931, from which he transcribes the following text in his book:

> "Our Movement is growing so rapidly throughout Germany that it needs a great deal of financing. The sum which you have already given me for the development of the Party has already been used up, and I foresee that I shall not be able to go ahead unless I receive further help soon. I do not, like our enemies the Communists and Social-Democrats, have at my disposal the great financial sources of governments, but I have to stick strictly to the sums provided by the members of the Party. Of the sum you sent me there is nothing left. Next month I have to undertake a great action which can bring us to power. But for this I need a lot of money. I

---

[9] The gold standard, as is well known, allowed paper money to be exchanged for gold. Thus, for example, in 1930 anyone could obtain an ounce of gold in exchange for a $20 note. As a result of the Great Depression caused by the stock market crash of 1929, people panicked to the point that in 1931 many people exchanged their paper money for gold, and the Bank of England's reserves began to fall. Montagu Norman, Governor of the Bank of England from 1920-1944, agreed to abandon the gold standard, although he had always been its staunchest advocate. The move stimulated a worldwide exchange of paper for gold, for if the City of London, the world centre of finance, could make such a move, others could follow suit. In 1933 F. D. Roosevelt ended gold convertibility for citizens. From then on only governments and world banks could exchange banknotes for gold. It went so far as to prohibit Americans from owning gold. In 1934 the United States readopted the gold standard, but not at 20 dollars an ounce, but at 35. T. McFadden's criticism of Roosevelt's policy in relation to his gold measures.

would be grateful if you would let me know what amount I can count on from you."

"Sidney Warburg" comments on the tone of the letter and considers it to be rather that of "a person who thinks he has more right to ask than to beg for a favour." Another detail that catches his attention is that, although the letter was dated Berlin, the envelope had reached him with a postmark from an American post office, indicating that Hitler had a confidant in the United States and probably in New York itself. It then goes on to report a further meeting at the offices of the Guaranty Trust Co, to which a Rothschild man, Montagu Norman, the Governor of the Bank of England, who was in New York, was also invited. "Sidney Warburg" puts the following words in J. H. Carter's mouth: "If he wants to come, we can claim victory ". Montagu Norman was informed of the 1929 administration and felt that the ten million dollars was a very large sum for the financing of a political movement; but it was finally decided that "Sidney Warburg" should go back to Europe.

Once in Germany, the young Warburg visited various cities to assess the situation on the ground. In Hamburg he met a Jewish banker who was a supporter of Hitler, and asked him how, as a Jew, he was a supporter of the Nazis. In Berlin he met an industrialist who was an enthusiastic supporter of National Socialism. After seeing that the party had taken root among the population, he felt it was time to contact Hitler, to whom he wrote to his Berlin address. Staying at the Hotel Adlon, he received in his rooms the banker von Heydt and a stranger who was introduced to him as Lütgebrunn. Both explained to him the party's work with the unemployed, whom they integrated into the militias, which entailed high expenses, for in the NSDAP houses in the various German cities "the men eat there, sleep there, and all at the party's expense." After justifying the expenses for uniforms, arms purchases from smugglers, means of locomotion, etc., von Heydt announced that Hitler would receive him the next day at his house at Fasanenstrasse 28. "Sidney Warburg" comments that, from the appearance of the building, he had the impression that he was going to visit an ordinary citizen: "I found Hitler rather aged, but less nervous; he had more poise, and he was also better dressed. I got the impression that he knew what he wanted and who he was".

The account of the second interview begins with an intervention by Hitler, who assures his interlocutor: "If you give us a year of activity, power will fall into our hands". He proudly states that "the red gang is trembling with fear" and adds that they will make them see what they are capable of. He explains that they have "a mobilisation plan that cannot fail", which is "in charge of Göring, one of our best collaborators. In two hours our formations can be ready all over the country to take to the streets. In the first place would be the storming parties, whose mission is to occupy the buildings, to capture the political leaders and also the members of the Government who are not on our side.... If blood is to flow, let it flow. A revolution can be made in no other way; only by force can traitors be taught what honour is."

After listening to him, Warburg asks what his intentions are in international politics. Hitler then got up and began to walk around the room and began a long monologue, in the middle of which "Sidney Warburg" interjects the following: "I must make it clear before I go any further that as soon as I got back to my hotel I wrote down this conversation verbatim. I have the sheets of paper in front of me, so I am not responsible for anything incomprehensible or incoherent. You must protest to Hitler if you find anything strange or if you are surprised by his ideas on foreign policy". Hitler's speech contains some noteworthy things. For example, he assures that he will imprison Jews, Communists and Social Democrats; that the Reich Army is with them "to the last man"; that the only two world leaders he respects are Mussolini and Stalin, especially the former, and adds, "Too bad Stalin is a Jew." When he considered that his long speech had answered the question, Hitler immediately inquired how much money he could be offered. He then set forth the existence of two plans for seizing power. The first is the "revolutionary plan". The second is the legal seizure of power, i.e., the "change of government". It seems clear that at the beginning of the interview Hitler had tried to sell him the first, which, he said, was a matter of three months, while the second would take three years. "Which do you think is preferable?"

"Sidney Warburg" writes that he merely shrugged his shoulders in ignorance. At this attitude, Hitler said, "You Americans do not know the circumstances; therefore it is very difficult for you to get this dilemma right; but what do you think your friends will say?" Since Warburg could not give him an answer either, Hitler felt it necessary to explain the matter further: "You see, neither I nor my collaborators know for certain which way to go. Göring is in favour of revolution; the others are rather in favour of a change of government. I am in favour of both.... There is one reason why we are in doubt as to the best method, and that is that we do not know how much money we can count on from you. If you had been more generous in 1929, everything would have been in order long ago; but with ten million dollars we could not realise half the plan." At last, according to Warburg's account, Hitler sat down at the table, picked up a little notebook and sentenced, "The revolution costs 500 million marks; the change of government, about 200 million marks. What do you think your friends will decide?" Warburg promised him that he would quickly contact New York and as soon as he had an answer he would let him know immediately. Then Hitler got up again, started pacing again and said: "Your friends in America have an undoubted interest in our party gaining power in Germany; otherwise you would not be with me now, nor in 1929 would they have given me ten million dollars. I do not care what motives impel them to help me; but they must be well aware that without sufficient financial means I can do nothing."

As has been said, the Jewish bankers who financed Hitler intended that he himself should interpret the reasons for their financial assistance. Of course, in two years Hitler had had time to know exactly who wanted him in power. Whether he had understood their true intentions is another matter. In this respect it is very significant that he acknowledges that he does not care about the reasons. "Sidney Warburg ends his account of his interview with the Führer with these words: "From the tone of the last sentences, it seemed that Hitler was addressing a large audience and attacking me as if I were his worst enemy. I had had enough of it. I told him again that I would speak to New York and give him the answer as soon as I received it." It took five days for New York to reply. Apparently, the first reply was not clear and "Sidney Warburg" telegraphed again for a repeat reply. He then received a long cablegram which he transcribes:

> "The sums proposed are out of line. We do not want to and we cannot. Explain to the man that such a turnaround would disrupt the European market. Completely unknown in the international arena. I await a more extensive report before making a determination. Continue there. Keep investigating. Convince the man of the impossibility of his demands. Don't forget to include in the report your own opinion on the future possibilities offered by the man."

Warburg wrote a letter to Hitler and informed him of the news he had received. Two days later he was visited at his hotel by two people he had never met before: Göring and Streicher. "The former, elegant-looking, firm-stepping, brutal; the latter had a rather effeminate appearance." The meeting with Göring was unpleasant in the extreme, for, despite Warburg's insistence that he was a mere intermediary whose opinions or ideas had "nothing to do with the development of things", Göring spoke to him in an infuriated tone, to the point where he went so far as to tell him verbatim: "You are all phonies." These words outraged Warburg: "I stood up and pointed to the door for Göring to leave; he did so, in the company of Streicher, without even saying hello." The text continues:

> "I wrote Hitler a letter in which I asked him to deal with me personally from now on and not to send any more emissaries to me, especially to Göring. I explained to him in a few words what had happened and added that I did not wish for the world to meet Göring again. I do not know what happened between Hitler and Göring; the fact is that the next day I received a letter from the latter in which he apologised to me, attributing his excitement to the great tension they were experiencing, since after Hitler he was the second in command of the party."

Three days later a cablegram finally arrived with the following text: "Report received. We are prepared to give ten, maximum fifteen million dollars. Advises man of the necessity of aggression against foreign danger." The ambiguity of the last sentence allows for all sorts of speculation, for in it may lie the key to the real purposes of the financing. After communicating the news to Hitler in a new letter, Strasser and von Heydt visited Warburg with full powers to act on behalf of the Führer, who, they said, had to rest for two weeks on his doctor's orders. Von Heydt accepted the sum of fifteen million and warned that the revolutionary option was out of the question. Strasser asked when the money could be in Germany: "I told him that I thought it would be a matter of a couple of days at the most, as soon as I knew whether Hitler was satisfied with the figures, but that I would take steps to ensure that the money would not be sent until I had spoken to Hitler. Von Heydt replied that the Führer needed absolute rest, but Warbug insisted that "nothing would be arranged until I had spoken to Hitler."

The next day, while dining in his hotel rooms, "Sidney Warburg" was told that a chauffeur was waiting for him at the entrance. After reading a letter in which Hitler begged him to come and see him in the car at his disposal, he got into the car and was driven to the house in Fasanenstrasse, where the meeting with Hitler finally took place. The latter confirmed that he accepted the fifteen million dollars, but thus chose the longer way, that of a change of government. Von Heydt," Hitler announced, "will get in touch with you about how to send the money transfer. The narrative goes on: "I tried to make him understand that it was not possible for those I represented to send the fifteen million dollars in one draft. They would first send ten and then five million, and that they needed to receive my instructions. I repeated to Hitler the importance of the conditions which Carter laid down in the telegram with regard to the foreign country. This time he did not throw out the usual phrases about the programme, but replied sharply: 'Leave that to me. What I have already achieved is a guarantee for what I can still achieve'. That was the end of the conversation.

Three days later a counter-order arrived, according to which the fifteen million was to be handed over "to a certain European bank" as soon as it was collected. After having communicated this news to Hitler, Warburg was again visited by von Heydt, who asked him to have the amount drawn as follows: Five million to Warburg, to be paid to Mendelssohn & Co. in Antwerp; five million to the Rotterdam Banking Union in Rotterdam; and another five million to the Banca Italiana in Rome. The details of the operation are set out below:

> "In the company of Von Heydt, Gregor Strasser and Göring I went to these three points to collect the money orders. Then we had to send a large number of cheques to cities and towns in Germany to an endless series of names on very long lists kept by the National Socialist chiefs. In Rome, Strasser, von Heydt and Göring were received in the main bank building by the President Commissar. We had not yet been in the office five minutes when two men in Fascist uniforms, who apparently must

also have been chiefs, were introduced to us: Rossi and Balbo. Göring took the floor and spoke to them in Italian. I heard nothing. We were invited to lunch at Balbo's house. I was the only one not in uniform. The National Socialist leaders wore brown uniforms; the Fascists wore black."

Regarding the fact that the money was split into numerous cheques, Anthony Sutton considers that this was a common practice, the purpose of which was to launder the money in order to disguise its Wall Street origin. Days after his European tour with the Nazis, "Sydney Warburg" embarked in the port of Genoa and sailed on board the *Savoy* for New York. On arrival, he reported extensively on the talks with Hitler and the circumstances in Germany. Again, Rockefeller was one of those most interested in specific details. They also wanted to know all about the Führer's collaborators, and the young Warburg told them about the incident with Göring.

At the beginning of 1932, the Great Depression that began in 1929 with the crash of the New York Stock Exchange was raging in Germany. Some six million workers were registered at the employment offices; but if one includes those doing small part-time jobs and unregistered people who were also looking for work, the figure was close to ten million. On 3 July 1932, the NSDAP achieved spectacular results and became the leading political force. The nearly six and a half million votes won in 1930 became fourteen million. From 107 seats in the Bundestag it went to 230. This meant that 37.4% of the votes cast had gone to the Nazi party. Although the success was undisputed, Hitler did not succeed in bringing about the desired political change, as Hindenburg, President of the Republic, and General Kurt von Schleicher, a close associate of the old marshal, did not endorse him as chancellor. After a long tug-of-war between the various political players, an impasse was reached and a new election was called, which was held on 6 November 1932. The results were not what Hitler had hoped for, and the NSDAP lost two million votes and thirty-four deputies, but remained by far the party with the most votes.

The intrigues for the Chancellorship began again. Schleicher convinced Hindenburg that he could divide the Nazis by appointing him Chancellor. The old marshal acceded to his request on 2 December 1932. The man who could challenge Hitler for the leadership of the party was Gregor Strasser. Schleicher, convinced that some sixty National Socialist deputies would follow him, offered him the Vice-Chancellorship. Göbbels' diary gives us an insight into the mood within the NSDAP. In an entry on 8 December, he notes: "There are rumours that Strasser is planning some kind of palace revolution.... At noon the bomb exploded. Strasser has written a letter to the Führer in which he informs him that he is resigning from all posts". At a meeting between Göbbels, Himmler, Röhm and Hitler, the Führer threatened to commit suicide if the party broke up. Specifically, as

Göbbels writes, he said, "If ever the party breaks into pieces, then I will put an end to it all with a pistol in three minutes."

The struggle within the party between Strasser and Hitler ended in the latter's favour, and Chancellor Schleicher was unable to remain in office. On 4 January 1933, under the auspices of the banker Kurt von Schröder, Hitler met with von Papen, who had belonged to the Catholic Centre Party and had the support of the conservative DNVP (German National People's Party). The two reached an agreement to form a coalition government in which Hitler would be chancellor and von Papen vice-chancellor. On 28 January 1933 Schleicher resigned and von Papen proposed a government with the Nazis to Hindenburg. On 30 January Hitler took the oath of office before Hindenburg at mid-morning and was appointed Chancellor of Germany. On 1 February 1933, Ludendorff, the general who had participated with Hitler in the "Beer Hall Putsch", wrote a letter to Hindenburg which Eugene Davidson quotes in *The Making of Adolf Hitler*. From the text we extract this extract: "By appointing Hitler Reich Chancellor, you have handed over our fatherland to one of the greatest demagogues of all time. I solemnly predict to you that this accursed man will plunge our Reich into the abyss and lead our nation into inconceivable misery. Because of what he has done, generations to come will curse him in his grave." This was the situation when "Sidney Warburg" arrived in Berlin to meet Hitler again.

In the third chapter, entitled "1933", Warburg recounts that on the very night the Reichstag building burned down, i.e. 27 February 1933, he sent a letter to Hitler's former home in Berlin announcing his arrival. Warburg confesses that on this occasion it was Carter, the man from the Guaranty Trust Co. who had received a letter from Hitler with the request to "send his old confidant immediately for an interview", which proves beyond doubt, as "Sidney Warburg" himself proclaims, that Hitler knew that "he was dealing with the most powerful financial group in the world".

The now Reich Chancellor received him in the same house on Fasanenstrasse. Hitler, very excited, spoke to him for half an hour about the Reichstag fire, for which he blamed the Communists: "The Communists have gambled everything for everything and lost by setting fire to the Reichstag". Warburg writes the following about the burning of the Reichstag building: "Only later have I been able to read in America and elsewhere of different theories; now, if it is true that Hitler's party took part in the fire, it must be admitted that Hitler is the best comedian I have ever met in the five parts of the world. Göring and Göbbels are no slouches either; their despair was so spontaneous, or they expressed themselves so stupendously well, that when I recall those conversations I still doubt whether it was all fictitious." In other words, Warburg had the impression that the Nazi leaders were honest when they talked to him about the fire.

Eighty years later, Communists and National Socialists are still accusing each other of an event from which both tried to make political capital. Now, official history has concluded beyond doubt that it was all the work of the Nazis, and this is what is being taught in academic institutions all over the world. However, since the official story is false, it must be assumed that it is lying in this matter as in so many others. Only two days after the fire, for example, the *Daily Worker, the* official organ of the British Communist Party, claimed without any evidence that the Nazis had set fire to their own parliament. Willi Münzenberg, the genius of Communist propaganda in Europe, and the OGPU fabricated false evidence implicating the Nazis in the fire. The only thing clearly established is that a young Dutch socialist, Marinus Van der Lubbe, was arrested at the scene and admitted that he had set the fire. Van der Lubbe declared that he intended the burning of the building as a signal for the revolution and that he had done it alone. Again and again he stuck to this story; but the communists accused him of being a degenerate, an imbecile who had been put on the spot as a scapegoat, and began to spread the rumour that it was all the work of the Nazis. Van der Lubbe explained that he had bought ignition material and oil to start the fire. The police were able to prove all these things. Non-political interrogators thought he was telling the truth. The fire brigade also declared that Van der Lubbe's account was consistent with the results of their investigations at the scene.

We could write at length about the communist propaganda campaign, as it was mainly the work of Otto Katz, the Jew from Jistebnice, a triple or quadruple agent who, as we shall see in due course, was hanged in 1952. A work on Katz, whom we will find again in Spain directing the propaganda of the Second Republic in tune with Álvarez del Vayo, appeared in 2010, *The Nine Lives of Otto Katz*, which offers a wealth of information on this wandering Jew, whom Molotov once called "Globetrotter". Jonathan Miles, the author of the book, devotes two chapters to discussing the details of the international campaign on the Reichstag fire organised by Katz, who, as Miles notes, never had the slightest scruple about lying with absolute naturalness. In April 1933 Münzenberg travelled to Moscow, where the campaign to blame the Nazis for the fire was decided. Katz, Münzenberg's protégé, travelled to England, France, Holland, the United States and wherever else was necessary to obtain information and support to write and edit the *Braunbuch uber Reichstagsbrand und Hitlerterror* (*The Brown Book about the Reichstag Fire and Hitler's Terror*), the centrepiece of the propaganda, which in a show of means and funding was translated into some twenty languages, including Hebrew and Yiddish. An edition of 135,000 copies was smuggled into Germany in August 1933. Its front cover is not to be missed: against a backdrop of the burning Reichstag, the image of Göring appears. His deformed head resembles that of a rabid dog. In his right hand he holds a huge bloody axe. From the waist down he wears a butcher's apron splattered with bloodstains. Amongst other fables, the book attributes to the young Marinus van der Lubbe an entanglement with a mysterious Dr. Bell,

THE SILENCED HISTORY OF THE INTERWAR PERIOD

a supposed pimp of Ernst Röhm. Otto Katz also organised a parallel trial in London, for which support committees were formed in numerous countries. Katz attributed the highest authority to his court: he declared that "its mandate emanated from the conscience of the world".

With this background, we can return to the meeting between Hitler and Warburg, which took place a few days before the new elections, called for 5 March 1933. At the first government meeting on 30 January, Hitler had proposed the dissolution of Parliament and the calling of new elections, as he was convinced that he could obtain an absolute majority. Von Papen, his ally and vice-chancellor, had agreed on the condition that he would not change the government regardless of the results[10]. In addition to explaining his immediate plans to the young Warburg, Hitler told him that von Heydt was no longer with them, nor was von Pleffer. He called the brothers Gregor and Otto Strasser ridiculous: "Instead of attacking, the Strassers and their henchmen prepared everything in the greatest silence, but I was aware of their every move". He then told him that he had waited for him earlier in Berlin, that it was necessary to act quickly, and asked him if his friends wanted to help him further."

Warburg's assessment of Hitler on this occasion is very negative: "There are times when Hitler gives the impression of being ill. It was never possible for me to hold an orderly, ordinary conversation with him. From time to time he made such sudden and absurd changes that one had no choice but to doubt his mental equilibrium. I am convinced that he is of a hypernervous nature." At one point in the interview Hitler began to speak of the Jewish problem. "Good God! -Warburg exclaims, "he compared this German problem to the Negro problem in America. This was enough to give me an idea of Hitler's intelligence and his way of thinking. The two problems could not be compared. I will spare you the useless comparisons that Hitler made." It was already three o'clock in the morning when the question of the amount of the new aid was finally raised. Hitler said he needed "at least a hundred million marks to get everything and to have a chance of a complete and final victory." Warburg told him that such a large sum was out of the question, and recalled that $25 million had already been sent. He promised to telegraph to New York at once, which he did at 4.30 a.m., the time he arrived at his hotel.

Carter telegraphed that he could send him seven million dollars. "Five would be wired from New York to Europe, to the banks I had indicated, and the other two million would be delivered to me personally by the Rhineland Joint Stock Company in Düsseldorf, the German subsidiary of the Royal

---

[10] In the elections of 5 March 1933 the NSDAP won 17,200,000 votes, which translated into 288 seats. 43.9% of Germans voted for the National Socialists. The second party was the SPD, which with 7,100,000 votes won 120 seats. The Communists were supported by 4,800,000 voters and won 81 seats. On 21 March 1933 Hitler succeeded in passing the Enabling Act, which made him a constitutional dictator.

Dutch." After transmitting the reply to Hitler, "Sidney Warburg" was visited by Göbbels, who took him to the Fasanenstrasse. He was received by Hitler and Göring. "The conversation was very short. I had the impression that the three men were displeased by the amount announced and that they were making efforts not to be rude to me; but it ended well. Hitler asked me to have the five million dollars wired to the Italian Bank in Rome; Göring would accompany me. The other two millions were to be handed over to Göbbels in German money, in fifteen cheques of equal value. Thus ended the interview.

Perhaps we have gone on longer than necessary in this synopsis, but we have chosen to do so because this purged book is not available in the Netherlands. In any case, interested readers may still be able to find a copy of the 1955 NOS edition in Spain. Antony Sutton admits that some of the information is known today, but adds that it should be borne in mind that the Dutch edition appeared in 1933 and that in it the author reveals facts and names that only became known much later, such as, for example, that the von der Heydt bank was a financial conduit for Hitler. The author, whether or not he is James Paul Warburg, demonstrates that he has access to very specific data and knows things that few people could know without being in a privileged position.

The evidence of Wall Street's financing of the Nazis has been demonstrated by various researchers. The first name that appears intimately connected with international bankers is Hjalmar Horace Greeley Schacht, the so-called "Wizard of Finance". In his *Memoirs* (Barcelona, 1954) Schacht recounts that in 1903 the elder Emil Rathenau offered him a job at the A.E.G., but he preferred a position at the Dresdner Bank, run by the Jews Eugen Gutmann and Henry Nathan. Schacht reveals that in 1905 this bank signed a "very interesting and beneficial agreement for me" with Morgan & Co., in whose negotiations in New York he was involved. Hjalmar Schacht was appointed president of the Reichsbank on 22 December 1923, a position he held until 1930. His first business was in London, where he went on 29 December 1923 to meet Montagu Norman, Governor of the Bank of England. Montagu Norman was the godfather of Schacht's daughter Inge's third child, who was named Norman Schacht in his honour.

In 1932 Schacht, who in his memoirs readily admits his good relations with Zionist Jews, persuaded the industrialists to claim the Chancellorship for Hitler from Hindenburg, who reappointed him president of the Reichsbank on 17 March 1933, a position he held until 1939. Three prominent Jewish Zionist bankers, Warburg (Max), Mendelssohn and Wasserman, were on the bank's General Council and signed the appointment alongside Hindenburg and Hitler. While at the head of the bank, he was instructed that no official who had been a Freemason could be appointed to positions of trust. In his memoirs, he writes that he replied "that I was not in a position to carry out the provision as long as a Freemason was at the head of the Reichsbank. This was myself. On his membership of Freemasonry, he refers specifically to a Berlin lodge, "Urania zur Unsterblichkeit" (Urania towards immortality), and writes: "In 1908 I became a member of a Masonic lodge. Freemasonry runs in my family. My father belonged to an American lodge. My great-grandfather, Christian Ulrich Detlev von Eggers, was one of the great Freemasons of his time". In another passage he reveals that in 1909 he was in Salonika, where "almost all the leaders of the Young Turks movement were Freemasons and their secret meetings were held under the cover of the lodge." He does not reveal, however, that, in addition to Freemasons, they were also Jewish converts, "doenmés". Hjalmar Schacht, who had studied Hebrew because he considered it necessary for advancement in the banking business, was appointed Minister of Economics on 2 August 1934, and Hitler made him an honorary member of the party.

Schacht was," writes Sutton, "a member of the international financial elite that wields power behind the scenes through a nation's political system. He was the key link between the Wall Street elite and Hitler's inner circle ". It was thanks to the creditors' confidence in Hjalmar Schacht that the Dawes (1924) and Young (1928) plans, both designed by Federal Reserve bankers, were conceived. Schacht was the man who implemented both plans, acting as a kind of comptroller who administered the German debt on behalf of the Wall Street bankers. In *Tragedy and Hope* Carroll Quigley claims that the Dawes plan was a creation of J. P. Morgan. Specifically, some $800 million in loans were arranged and the proceeds flowed to Germany in the form of investments that were used to create and consolidate giant chemical (I.G. Farben) and steel (Vereignigte Stahlwerke) companies that first helped Hitler to power and then produced most of the materials used in World War II. In *Wall Street and the Rise of Hitler* Professor Sutton explains:

> "Between 1924 and 1931, under the Dawes and Young plans, Germany paid the Allies about 36 million marks in reparations. At the same time Germany borrowed abroad, mainly in the United States, 33 billion marks, amounting to a net payment of three billion marks for reparations. Consequently, the burden of monetary reparations was in fact borne by foreign underwriters of German bonds issued by Wall Street finance houses, at a significant profit, of course. And, incidentally, these houses were owned by the same financiers who regularly took off their bankers' hats and put on statesmen's hats. As statesmen, they prepared the Dawes and Young plans to 'solve' the reparations 'problem'. As bankers, they issued the loans."

The Young Plan was named after its formulator, Owen D. Young, an agent of Morgan who was president of the General Electric Company. In reality, Sutton believes, the Plan was the result of the exchange of ideas and collaboration between Schacht in Germany and Morgan in New York, i.e., the form of a vast and ambitious system of international cooperation and alliance for world control. It was intended to occupy Germany with American capital and to pledge German assets through a gigantic mortgage held by the United States. Insider Carroll Quigley states that the aim was to "create a global system of financial control in private hands capable of dominating the political system of each country and the world economy as a whole". The idea of the BIS (Bank for International Settlements), key to implementing this scheme, came from Hjalmar Schacht himself, who foresaw a new world war. He himself explains how he proposed it at a meeting with international bankers. The quote, taken from *Wall Street and the Rise of Hitler,* is a most interesting document:

> "...Such a bank will require financial cooperation between victors and vanquished that will lead to a community of interests, which in turn will produce mutual trust, understanding, and promote and secure peace.
> I can still vividly remember the setting in which this conversation took place. Owen Young was sitting in an armchair puffing on his pipe, his legs outstretched, his shrewd eyes never leaving me. As is my wont when I propose arguments of this kind, I was pacing quietly up and down the room. When I had finished there was a brief pause. Then his whole face lit up, and his resolution was expressed in these words: 'Dr. Schacht, you have given me a wonderful idea, and I am going to sell it to the world."

With loans from the Federal Reserve bankers, the big German cartels began to be built up. The syndicate National City Corporation, led by Morgan and Rockefeller, lent $35,000,000 to the General Electricity Company (Allgemeine Elektricitäts Gesellschaft). The same banking syndicate lent another $30,000,000,000 to I. G. Farben, which was to become the world's largest chemical manufacturing company. This cartel, sponsored by Hermann Schmitz with financial assistance from Wall Street, was born in 1925 from the union of six large German chemical companies (Badische Anilin, Bayer, Agfa, Hoechst, Weiler-ter-Meer and Griesheim-Elektron). The Steelworks Union (Vereinigte Stahlwerke) received an astronomical loan of 70,225,000 dollars, issued by Dillon, Read & Co. a banking association whose main shareholder was Clarence Dillon. This banker's real name was Lapowski, son of Samuel Lapowski, a Polish Jew who had emigrated to the United States.

The General Electric Company, controlled by Morgan and Rockefeller, which was doing the big business with the electrification of Soviet Russia, was the US equivalent of the German A.E.G. (Allgemeine Electricitäts Gesellschaft). In 1929 General Electric took over 25% of the shares of A.E.G. in an agreement that meant the provision of American technology and patents to the German company. In this agreement, however, it was stipulated that A.E.G. would have no share in the American company. The German financial press also reported that A.E.G. would not be represented on the board of General Electric in the United States. Instead, Owen D. Young became the director of A.E.G. and Osram in Germany. In 1930 Young, who was already Chairman of the Executive Committee of the Radio Corporation of America, was appointed Chairman of the Board of General Electric in New York. It can be said that through these operations the American electrical industry had conquered the world market.

In 1939 the German electrical industry was controlled by American corporations. Companies not connected with the United States, such as Siemens and Brown Boveri, were targeted for bombing during the war, but companies affiliated with the Americans were hardly attacked. Antony Sutton writes the following about the financing of Hitler by these companies: "there is no evidence that Siemens, without American directors, financed Hitler. On the other hand, we have irrefutable documentary evidence that both A.E.G. and Osram, both with American directors, financed Hitler". Sutton attaches photocopies of two documents that prove such funding. The first is a transfer order dated 2 March 1933. A.E.G. instructs the "Delbrück, Schickler Bank" to pay 60,000 marks into the "Nationale Treuhand" fund. The second document is dated 9 March 1933. Gunther Quandt, the main shareholder in Accumulatoren Fabrik and a member of A.E.G.'s management, orders the payment of DM 25 000 to the same fund via the same bank.

In *Wall Street and the Rise of Hitler* Antony Sutton shows that the Warburgs, in addition to sending one of their own to offer money to Hitler, also financed the NSDAP with a very substantial amount through I. G. Farben, a company to which they were closely linked. In Germany, Max Warburg was a director of this chemical conglomerate, while in the United States Paul Warburg, the father of "Sidney Warburg", was a director of the American I. G. Farben. Sutton again reproduces a photocopy of the transfer from I. G. Farben to the Delbrück Bank, Schickler in Berlin. This document is dated 27 February 1933 and gives payment instructions for 400,000 marks to the "Nationale Treuhand", a fund managed by Hjalmar Schacht and Rudolf Hess which was used to elect Hitler in March 1933. The bank in question had been formed in 1910 as a result of the union of two families of Jewish origin: Gebrüder Schickler & Co. and Delbrück Leo & Co.

As Judea declares war, Zionism collaborates: the Haavara Agreement

In 1917 the plotters who aspired to the subjugation of nations through a communist world government had achieved two goals: the triumph of the Judeo-Bolsheviks in Russia and the promise of Palestine to international Zionism, contained in the *Balfour Declaration*. In the inter-war period, however, things had not gone according to plan either in Russia, where Trotsky had been ousted from power, or in Germany, where the communist revolution had repeatedly failed, or in Palestine, where immigration did not satisfy Zionism's desires. The financial support of the international Jewish bankers for Hitler and the triumph of nationalism in Germany were ultimately to serve to redirect the situation in all three scenarios through a new strategy leading to another war. In 1933, as soon as Hitler had been placed in power, the conspiratorial capacity of international Jewry was set in motion without delay: on the one hand, Talmudic Jewish organisations around the world declared war on Germany; on the other, almost simultaneously, Zionists worked hand in hand with the Nazis for the transfer of German Jews to Palestine. The result of this collaboration took the form of a transfer agreement (Haavara heskem), which has gone down in history as the Haavara Agreement.

After Hitler's election as chancellor, a conference took place in Amsterdam at which Jewish leaders from all over the world called for a boycott of German goods and agreed to put pressure on shipping companies with international connections to refuse to transport German goods. At the same time they called for Germany to be denied access to international capital. In the United States, the Jewish War Veterans Association also called for a boycott. On 23 March, 20,000 American Jews rallied at City Hall in New York in support of these calls. Finally, the next day, 24 March 1933, the London *Daily Express* reported on the front page with the following seven-column headline: "Judea declares war on Germany". According to the London paper, prominent international leaders, some of whom were well-known Zionists, called for the unification of all the world's Jews against Germany and announced a boycott of its goods. The text of the article stated that German trade, industry and finance would be the object of an international boycott and claimed that in London, Paris, New York and Warsaw Jewish businessmen were united in waging an "economic crusade". The Jewish newspaper *Natscha Retsch* also reported on the Amsterdam conference and encouraged that the war against Germany be waged by all communities, conferences and congresses, as well as individually, "in this way," it argued, "the war against Germany will ideologically promote and enliven our interests, which require that Germany be completely destroyed". One of the most prominent agitators was Samuel Untermayer, the powerful New York lawyer who had imposed on President Wilson the appointment of Zionist Louis Dembitz Brandeis as a Supreme Court justice. In his campaign Untermayer called for the "holy war" called for in the *Daily Express*.

The German government reacted by demanding an immediate halt to the campaign. Hitler threatened reprisals if the plan against Germany was not stopped immediately, and warned that he would order a one-day boycott of Jewish shops throughout the country. Naturally, the campaign continued with equal intensity, and the government announced that a boycott of all Jewish-run businesses would take place on 1 April. While 1 April is described by most historians as an act of aggression against the German

Jewish community, the "Judean" declaration of war and the campaign of hatred against the German people as a whole is generally ignored by official historiography. On 7 August 1933 *The New York Times* reproduced a lengthy speech by Samuel Untermayer, radioed to the nation the day before, appealing to humanity in the name of idealism and justice: "Every one of you, Jew and Gentile alike, who has not already enlisted in this sacred war should do so here and now. It is not enough that you do not buy German-made goods. You must refuse to deal with any merchant or shopkeeper who sells goods made in Germany or who sponsors German transports or shipments." The consequences of the campaign were very negative for the German economy, which saw its exports reduced by ten percent. On the other hand, however, it had positive effects, as it helped to kick-start trade through "barter", a system of exchange of goods that made it possible to dispense with Jewish capital.

The boycott stoked anti-Jewish sentiments among the German people and actually promoted the anti-Semitism desired by the Zionists, who needed Hitler's retaliatory actions to be sufficiently severe to convince German Jews that their place was in Palestine. It was in this context that the Nazis began to collaborate decisively with the ZVFD, "Zionistische Vereinigung für Deutschland" (Zionist Union for Germany) in order to send German Jews to Palestine. The Nazis lent themselves absurdly from the outset to this perverse scheme. It must be remembered that it was the Zionists who betrayed Germany during World War I and not the ordinary German Jews, twelve thousand of whom died in the war fighting alongside their German compatriots. It was international Zionism that proposed victory to Britain in exchange for the *Balfour Declaration*. Through Mandell House, Justice Brandeis, Bernard Baruch and other agents influencing the puppet president in the White House, American and British Zionists lobbied for America's entry into the war and the subsequent defeat of Germany. The Nazis could not and should not ignore this.

Research on Nazi-Zionist collaboration is still very incomplete, as most of the documents referring to it, many of which are locked away in Israel, cannot be accessed by researchers. In 2002 an American writer of Jewish origin, Lenni Brenner, published *51 Documents: Zionist Collaboration with the Nazis*, which, the editor presumes, 'contains explosive information that historians ignore'. It contains, for example, the full text of the Haavara Agreement. There is also a very interesting article, "The Secret Contacts: Zionism and Nazi Germany, 1933-1941", published in 1976 by Klaus Polkehn in the *Journal of Palestine Studies*. Let us look at some of the information contained in these works.

Statistics show that between 1871 and 1933 the population of Jewish origin in Germany decreased from 1.05% to 0.76%. In 1933 there were 503,000 Jews living in Germany, one third of whom resided in Berlin. Most of these Jews were not Zionists. In 1925, for example, less than nine thousand people were members of Zionist organisations. The CV, "Centralverein deustscher Staatsbürger jüdische Glaubens" (Central Union of German Citizens of Jewish Faith), founded in 1893, was the most representative organisation and openly declared its rejection of Zionism. A statement of the CV made on 10 April 1921 is quite significant in this respect: "If the work of settlement in Palestine were only a work of aid and assistance, then from the point of view of the CV nothing would be said against the promotion of this work. However, settlement in Palestine is first and foremost a Jewish national policy objective, and from there its promotion and assistance should be rejected". Despite the fact that history shows that Jews are for the most part unassimilable, the VC fought anti-Semitism and, as Rathenau had proposed, advocated the assimilation and integration of Jews into German society. In contrast, the ZVFD rejected these approaches, took up the Talmudic argument that Jews cannot be assimilated and declared itself against the integration and participation of German Jews in public life, i.e. it fully shared the Nazis' views. In fact, the VC went so far as to accuse the ZVFD of having given "a stab in the back" to its fight against anti-Semitic nationalism.

In March 1933 Hitler's government began to act against non-Zionist Jewish organisations. The premises of the VC itself were occupied by the SA and closed down. On 5 March the VC in Thuringia was banned after being accused of "intrigues of high treason". Among the banned groups, two stood out for their nationalist character: the "League of Jewish Empire Veterans" and the "National Union of German Jews"[11]. Newspapers published by communists, trade union organisations and social democrats were banned, and other publications came under the supervision of the Propaganda Ministry. Only the Zionists were free to continue their work and their newspaper, *Jüdische Rundschau*, was allowed to appear without hindrance. Freedom of action for Zionists also included the publication of books: works by Zionist leaders such as Chaim Weizmann, David Ben Gurion and Arthur Ruppin were legally published. On the other hand, it is worth noting that while Masonic lodges were banned, until 1939 B'nai B'rith was allowed to continue its subversive activities. It was only when the war broke out that its documents were confiscated. In any case, the ban must not have mattered too

---

[11] The existence of these organisations may come as a surprise to some readers, but they are only examples of a reality that Dietrich Bronder documents extensively in *Bevor Hitler kam*. Although the loyalty of some of the personalities cited in his work is highly debatable, Bronder discusses a list of names of Jewish origin who stood out for their nationalism in the 19th and 20th centuries. Many were high-ranking military officers, including numerous generals. Recently, Bryan Mark Rigg, a professor of history at the American Military University in Virginia, has published a book in which he claims that more than 100,000 soldiers with Jewish family backgrounds served in the Wehrmacht during World War II.

much to Freemasonry, for traditionally Freemasons and Illuminati have always operated without problems in hiding.

Klaus Polkehn places contacts between Nazis and Zionists even before 1933. He mentions a Zionist officer, Leo Plaut, who had a connection to the political police through Rudolf Diels, a personal friend of Göring's who was to be appointed first chief of the Gestapo in 1933. Plaut had Diels' secret telephone number and could call him at any time. Although documents on these contacts remain secret in the archives of Yad Vashem in Jerusalem, Polkehn assumes that through this connection, on 26 March 1933, Hermann Göring held a meeting with Zionist leaders, including Kurt Blumenfeld, chairman of the ZVFD, who moved to Palestine shortly afterwards. At this meeting, the basis for the collaboration that led to the Haavara Agreement, signed on 25 August 1933, was allegedly laid.

One step prior to the agreement was the founding in Palestine of a Zionist citrus plantation company, 'Hanotea', which was supported by the German Ministry of Economics in the transfer of capital. The first German Jews to migrate to Palestine did so within the scope of this agreement, whose architect was Sam Cohen, a Jewish financier of Polish origin, a friend of Nahum Goldman, who owned a castle in Luxembourg. The Zionist organisation soon replaced him with a member of the Executive Committee of the Jewish Agency in Palestine, Chaim Arlozoroff, who together with David Ben Gurion and Moshe Sharett was part of the Agency's leading troika. He was also a close friend of Weizmann, the leader of world Zionism and the future first president of Israel. Arlozoroff, a Russian Jew trained in Germany, was the lover of the future Magda Göbbels, who was a friend of the Zionist leader's sister. Arlozoroff was assassinated on 16 June 1933, shortly after returning to Tel Aviv from a round of negotiations in Germany. Despite self-serving confusion, even suggesting that Göbbels was behind the assassination attempt, all indications are that the assassins acted on the orders of Zeev (Vladimir) Jabotinsky's Revisionist movement. In fact, this was established by the Labourites.

The work that recounts the disagreements and infighting among Zionists is *The Transfer Agreement: the Untold Story of the Secret Pact Between the Third Reich & Jewish Palestine*, published in 1984 by Jewish historian Edwin Black. His account suggests that there was a short-sighted sector that did not accept or understand the medium- and long-term plan laid out by Chaim Weizmann and the grand strategists of Zionism, a plan that was supported by the B'nai B'rith lodge. This radical or ultra-nationalist sector, headed by Jabotinsky, fervently advocated the economic boycott and wanted to end German nationalism before it had fulfilled the function for which it had been raised to power. The revisionists were manoeuvring to do battle at the 18th Zionist Congress, which was to be held in Prague in August 1933. It was in this context that the assassination of Arlozoroff, the declared enemy of Jabotinsky and revisionism, took place.

His death, probably a miscalculation, was well exploited by the Mapai Labourites to gain an easy victory. It was during the Congress sessions that the press leaked on 25 August that the Transfer Agreement had been signed, the text of which was published by the Nazis on 31 August. According to Edwin Black, in order to silence any protest, Mapai Labour, supported by allies from other parties, imposed a resolution that "banned all forms of anti-Nazi protest, including campaigning against the Transfer Pact. Under the resolution, anyone who broke discipline would be suspended and tried by a special tribunal, with power to expel the person or party from the Zionist Organisation." Jewish author Ralph Schönman confirms in *The Hidden History of Zionism* that at the 18th Congress of the World Zionist Organisation a resolution against Hitler was defeated by 240 votes to 43.

The Haavara Agreement, the centrepiece of the 'Nazi' collaboration, was signed by the Zionist Federation of Germany (ZVFD), the Anglo-Palestinian Bank, which obeyed the orders of the Jewish Agency, and the German Ministry of Economic Affairs. According to the text of the decree, the aim was to "promote Jewish emigration to Palestine by releasing the necessary sums of money, but without putting excessive pressure on the foreign currency funds of the Reichsbank, and at the same time to increase German exports to Palestine". As a consequence of the agreement, two companies were founded: the Haavara company in Tel Aviv and a sister company called Paltreu in Berlin. The mode of operation was as follows: the Jewish emigrant deposited a minimum of one thousand pounds sterling in German accounts of the Haavara company opened at the Wassermann Bank in Berlin or at the Warburg Bank in Hamburg. The money was used for the purchase of German products: agricultural tools, building materials, fertilisers, water pumps, etc., which were then exported to Palestine and sold there by the Jewish-owned Haavara Company in Tel Aviv. With the money from the sales, the emigrant was given the same amount as he had contributed when arrived. German goods entered Palestine en masse, but at the same time the Zionists brought in Jewish settlers and capital for the development of the country. Poorer German Jews were excluded from the agreement: the fact that only members of the Jewish bourgeoisie could contribute the required amount implied selectivity in emigration. It is therefore no coincidence that the most important projects in Israel were founded or led by German emigrants. Future prime ministers of Israel such as Ben Gurion, Moshe Sharret (then Moshe Shertok), Levi Eshkol and Golda Meir were involved in the Haavara enterprise. Eshkol was its representative in Berlin and Golda Meir supported it from New York.

In 1934 *Der Angriff* (*The Attack*), Göbbels' newspaper, published a laudatory report entitled "A Nazi travels to Palestine", signed by LIM, the pseudonym of Leopold Itz von Mindelstein, a member of the SD, the SS Security Service (Sicherheitsdienst). Mindelstein, an enthusiastic Zionist, headed a department within the Secret Service called "Judenreferat" (Office for Jewish Affairs). To commemorate this trip, Göbbels had a coin minted with the Star of David on the obverse and the swastika on the reverse. Next to the star an inscription read: 'A Nazi travels to Palestine'. On the side of the swastika the text read: "And it is published in *Der Angriff*'. So successful was the cooperation that the Zionists bought a German passenger ship, the *Hohenstein*, renamed it *Tel Aviv* and set up their own shipping company. The first voyage from Bremerhaven to Haifa took place in early 1935. While the stern of the ship read its name in Hebrew script, the swastika flag flew on the mast. In these circumstances, in August 1935 the 19th Zionist Congress in Lucerne overwhelmingly approved the pact with Hitler's Germany.

Another episode of the good understanding between Nazis and Zionists is contained in a memorandum by Professor Franz Six, a member of the SS Secret Service. Classified as 'Secret Matter for the Command', the document, cited by Klaus Polkehn, is dated 7 June 1937 and is in the archives of the American Commission for the Study of War Documents. It details the visit to Berlin of Feivel Polkes, a Zionist who was commander of the Haganah, the Jewish underground army. Polkes was in Berlin from 26 February to 2 March 1937 and had several meetings with agents of the German Secret Service. In two of these meetings the contact was Adolf Eichmann, who in December 1961 was to be tried in Israel and sentenced to be hanged. The first meeting between Eichmann and Polkes took place at the Traube restaurant near the zoo. Polkes offered cooperation and told Eichmann that his main interest was "to accelerate Jewish emigration to Palestine, so that the Jews would achieve a majority over the Arabs." Polkes explained that for this purpose he was working together with the British and French secret services and offered information about the Middle East that might be of interest to Germany. The Haganah commander invited Eichmann to Palestine and he accepted the invitation.

On 26 September 1937, disguised as editors of the *Berliner Tageblatt*, Adolf Eichmann and Herbert Hagen, Mindelstein's replacement at the Office for Jewish Affairs (Judenreferat), left Berlin for Haifa, where they arrived on 2 October. The British authorities prevented the two SS chiefs from disembarking, so they went to Egypt, where they contacted Polkes. The report of the trip contains the conversations held at the Café Groppi in Cairo, noted down by Eichmann and Hagen. Polkes expressed himself with absolute frankness: "The Zionist state," he said, "must be founded by whatever means and as soon as possible, in such a way as to attract a stream of Jewish emigrants to Palestine. When the State has been established in accordance with the proposals expressed in the Peel report, and in accordance with the partial promises of England, then the frontiers must be expanded according to our wishes." Polkes expressed words of thanks to his interlocutors for the anti-Semitic policies, which were noted in these terms: "Nationalist circles expressed their joy at the radical policy towards the Jews, since this policy would help to increase the Jewish population in Palestine, so that a Jewish majority could be counted on in Palestine in the immediate future."

As a result of these meetings, further plans for collaboration emerged: "Mossad Le'aliyah Bet", a division of the Haganah set up to boost clandestine immigration, was established at Meineckestrasse, 10, in the Berlin-Charlottenburg district. Two emissaries, Pina Ginsburg and Moshe Auerbach, travelled from Palestine to Germany for the purpose of arranging with the Gestapo everything necessary to promote and expand the illegal entry of Jewish immigrants without permission from the British authority. After the "Anschluss" (union) of Austria and Germany, a Central Office for Jewish Emigration was established in Vienna, and in the early summer of 1938 Eichmann met in the Austrian capital with Bar-Gilead, an emissary of the Mossad, who asked him for permission to establish training camps for emigrants. Eichmann consulted on the request and after receiving a positive response provided everything necessary for the establishment of these camps. By the end of 1938 about a thousand young Jews had been trained for their future work in Palestine. Also in Germany, with the help of the Nazi authorities, Pina Ginsburg set up training camps similar to those in Austria.

The first criticism of the Haavara Agreement came in the wake of the Palestinian revolt that began in April 1936. In protest at the illegal immigration of Jews, the Palestinians went on a general strike that lasted until October. The Foreign Ministry began to question how useful it was for Germany to continue with the transfer agreement. The German consul general in Jerusalem, Hans Döhle, submitted a lengthy memorandum on 22 March 1937, in which expressed his fears about the repercussions of the policy of supporting Jewish immigration. German and Arab businessmen lamented the monopoly of the Haavara company in Tel Aviv on the sale of German goods. Official support for Zionism could lead to the loss of markets in the Arab world. The Ministry of the Interior also issued a memorandum in December 1937 acknowledging that the agreement had made a decisive contribution to the development of Palestine; but it agreed with Consul Döhle's report that the disadvantages outweighed the benefits and should therefore be terminated. In the end, Hitler reviewed the situation and settled the controversy with a decision to proceed with the agreement, since the objective of getting the Jews out of Germany justified the disadvantages. On 12 November 1938 a new Foreign Office memorandum advised the cancellation of the Haavara Agreement; but again Hitler personally ordered the promotion of mass immigration to Palestine "by all possible means".

Between 1933 and 1941 some sixty thousand German Jews emigrated to Palestine under the Haavara Agreement and were able to take with them more than $100 million, then a huge sum. Edwin Black confirms that many managed to transfer their personal wealth from Germany to Palestine. According to this Jewish historian, the influx of goods and capital into Palestine thanks to the Haavara Agreement "led to an economic explosion and was an indispensable factor in the creation of the state of Israel". Perhaps the irony of Hennecke Kardel, who in the title of his book alluded to Hitler as one of the founders of Israel, is now better understood. The persecution of the Jews was in fact pre-designed by Zionism for later use in the creation of the state of Israel. As conceived, the Jews harassed and persecuted by Hitler, displaced to Eastern Europe and interned in labour and concentration camps, were the least well-off. After the war they could be transferred relatively easily to Palestine.

PART 4
ROOSEVELT IN THE WHITE HOUSE.
CONGRESSMAN MCFADDEN DENOUNCES THE
CONSPIRACY

This fourth part of the chapter will be mainly taken up by the texts of Louis Thomas McFadden, a congressman of those who are not left, a patriot who denounced the conspirators in the right place, in the House of Representatives of the American people; but first it is necessary to outline the circumstances of the coming to power of Franklin Delano Roosevelt, an illuminati mason who on 28 February 1929 had acquired the 32nd degree of the Scottish Rite, a circumstance which made him "Sublime Prince of the Royal Secret". Five years later he was appointed first Honorary Grand Master of the International Order of Molay. Roosevelt, the only man in history to have won four elections, was sworn in as President of the United States on 4 March 1933. Hitler won the final election on 5 March with 44% of the vote. Both came to power simultaneously and both were to remain in power for a period of twelve years. In America, Rabbi William F. Rosenblum referred to Roosevelt as "a divine messenger, the favourite of destiny, the Messiah of tomorrow's America". Douglas Reed in *The Controversy of Zion* comments that a Jewish friend told him in 1937 that the rabbi of his synagogue, a pious old man who tried to interpret events in terms of Levitical prophecy, preached that Hitler was "the Jewish Messiah."

After a period of three Republican presidents, the arrival of another Democrat in the White House was to allow a return to the policies of Woodrow Wilson. With *Wall Street and FDR*, Antony Sutton completes his trilogy on the bankers of the Federal Reserve. Sutton traces the career of Roosevelt, a financial speculator since the early 1920s, and presents Roosevelts and Delanos as historical associates of the New York financiers. According to this author, Roosevelt was related to one of the oldest banking families in the United States and his great-grandfather, James Roosevelt, founded the Bank of New York in 1784. Some researchers trace his Jewish origins to Claes Rosenfelt, a Dutch ancestor who came to America in 1649. Another of his predecessors was the Illuminati Freemason Clinton Roosevelt, a disciple of Adam Weishaupt introduced in Chapter V, author in 1841 of a communist manifesto whose economic programme was very similar to FDR's New Deal. Clinton Roosevelt proposed a totalitarian government led by an elite that would enact all laws.

For his part, John Coleman sees the election of Roosevelt as clear evidence of the control of the '300' over US policy, although in view of the legion of Zionist Jews who surrounded the president, he could have been referring to a new puppet of international Jewry and Zionism. Coleman writes that the Delano dynasty had an enormous fortune from the opium trade with China through the East India Company, with which they made an agreement in 1657 on the colonisation of Curaçao. F. D. Rossevelt's father had married Sara Delano, who was already in her seventh generation from a Jewish family of Sephardic origin. As in the case of Woodrow Wilson, Roosevelt had been selected as a future president well in advance. His wife, Eleanor Roosevelt, daughter of a brother of President Theodore Roosevelt, a distant cousin of Franklin Delano Roosevelt and a Zionist to the core, confirms this: "Mr. Baruch was a trusted advisor to my husband both in Albany and in Washington". Bernard Baruch was only the tip of the iceberg, for Roosevelt was surrounded by Jewish socialists in Albany, the capital of New York State, of which he was governor for four years before becoming President. Two other men close to Wilson, Justice Brandeis and Rabbi Stephen Wise, had also rallied around Roosevelt, who, with the backing of socialists and communists, came to the White House on a promise to end Wall Street rule. As soon as he took office, however, he appointed a Wall Street man, James Paul Warburg ("Sidney Warburg"), as Budget Director.

The number of Zionist, Socialist and Communist Jews who installed themselves in power during the F. D. Roosevelt years is scandalous. More than seventy important positions were held by Jewish agents, most of them Zionists, who for twelve years controlled the US government. Perhaps one of the most influential was Felix Frankfurter, who played the role with Roosevelt that Mandell House had played with Wilson. Frankfurter, indoctrinated by Justice Louis Brandeis, had been a Zionist delegate to the Paris Peace Conference in 1919. Later, in 1939, Roosevelt would appoint him to the Supreme Court to replace Benjamin Cardozo, another Jewish justice who moved in the orbit of Bernard Baruch. Among the members of the Administration of Jewish origin allied with Frankfurter were Herbert Feis, adviser for economic and international affairs at the State Department; Benjamin V. Cohen, a lawyer in the service of the Zionist Movement who in 1919 had travelled to Paris with Frankfurter and was part of Roosevelt's brain trust; Jerome Frank, who openly asked Frankfurter to bring him into the Administration and ended up being appointed by Roosevelt as a judge of the Court of Appeals; David E. Lilienthal, a jurist recommended by Frankfurter, about whom there will be occasion to write in Chapter XI, as he chaired the Atomic Energy Commission after the war; Charles E. Wyzanski, another judge, a student of Frankfurter's at Harvard Law School, who was brought into the Department of Labor as legal adviser; Harold Joseph Laski, a Briton whose Jewish name was Frankenstein, a member of the Executive Committee of the Fabian Society, who became a friend and adviser to President Roosevelt through Frankfurter.

Bernard Mannes Baruch spent forty years at the pinnacle of power. While under Wilson his position was always dominant and key due to the importance of the positions he held, under Roosevelt he was considered by some to be the unofficial shadow president. Baruch advised Roosevelt to prepare for a new war and proposed strengthening the War Industries Board (WIB), which he himself had chaired during the First World War. The new agency Baruch devised was the National Recovery Administration (NRI). An associate of Bernard Baruch's, Gerard Swope, became one of the key players within the Roosevelt Administration. Swope, one of the promoters of the New Deal, as president of the General Electric Company between 1922 and 1939, held half a dozen important positions in different departments of the Administration. Two other Jews in Baruch's orbit were Mordechai Ezekiel, economic adviser to the Secretary of Agriculture, who became a captains of the FAO (Food and Agriculture Organization) in 1945, and Adolph J. Sabath, an ardent supporter of the war against Germany.

Another prominent member of the powerful Jewish clan that dominated President Roosevelt was Henry Morgenthau junior, advisor to the president and Secretary of the Treasury from 1934 to 1945, a position from which he was able to finance the war by issuing so-called 'war bonds'. Morgenthau and Baruch worked to get the United States to enter the war against Germany and did not stop pressuring Roosevelt until they achieved their goal. As is well known, Morgenthau wanted to turn Germany into a country of farmers and put forward the so-called Morgenthau Plan, about which there will be occasion to write more later. Other Jews who moved within his sphere of influence were: R. S. Hecht, Finance Counsellor. Hecht, adviser to Finance; Jacob Viner, a rate economist who worked closely with Morgenthau as an assistant to the Secretary of the Treasury and was one of the mentors of the Chicago School; Emmanuel Goldenweiser, director of the Division of Research and Statistics of the Board of Governors of the Federal Reserve; David Stern, also a member of the Federal Reserve Board; Herman Oliphant, another rate expert very influential in Treasury policy who was also Roosevelt's adviser; Harold Glasser, Assistant Director of the Monetary Research Division, where he worked as an agent of Soviet espionage; Solomon Adler, also infiltrated into the Treasury Department, was sent to China as a Treasury representative during World War II and turned out to be a spy working for international communism; Irving Kaplan and David Weintraub, both members of the Communist Party, were other Jewish spies brought into the Treasury Department.

Justice Louis Dembitz Brandeis, who had said that to be a good American you had to be a good Zionist, even though he had in Felix Frankfurter a man he trusted alongside the president, was often on the prowl to exert pressure when necessary. Samuel I. Rosenman, one of the Jewish Supreme Court justices close to Brandeis, was Roosevelt's speechwriter, and later wrote Harry Solomon Truman's most important speeches as well. It was he who proposed and organised the brain trust that formulated the policies that later constituted the New Deal. It was in one of Rosenman's speeches that the phrase that was to make history appeared, the one in which he promised "a new deal for the American people". Rosenman served on the White House Council between 1943 and 1946, and was therefore also an advisor to Truman, the Jewish president and 32nd degree Scottish Freemason who ordered the atomic bombings of Japan. Although Rosenman was a key figure in the investigation of war crimes, he saw no problem with the genocides of Hiroshima and Nagasaki. Another judge, in this case of the New York Supreme Court, who had connections to Brandeis was Samuel Dickstein, who played a key role in the formation of the Un-American Activities Committee, which persecuted dissidents and those suspected of sympathising with Germany. To these names of people close to Brandeis who swarmed in Roosevelt's entourage must be added two other well-known Zionists, Samuel Untermayer and Rabbi Stephen Wise.

Another Jewish adviser with great influence over the President was Edward A. Filene, who had been associated with Franklin D. Roosevelt since 1907. Filene succeeded in getting the Roosevelt Administration to pass the Federal Credit Union Act in 1934, a law to regulate credit that gave rise to CUNA (Credit Union National Association). One of Filene's associates, Louis Kirstein, was often an advisor to the President on Palestinian affairs. Kirstein, one of America's most prominent Zionists, was chairman of the Executive Committee of the American Jewish Committee, honorary chairman of the United Jewish Appeal and national director of the Jewish Welfare Board. The United Jewish Appeal was dedicated to raising funds to promote immigration to Palestine. The Kirstein Committee worked to seek the cooperation of all Jews with Zionism. Another Zionist who served first as an aide to Roosevelt and later to Truman was David Niles, an immigrant of Russian origin. His apologists attribute to him great influence over the president and claim that he was able to get Roosevelt to yield to the demands and arguments of the Zionists, to whom he provided permanent access to the White House.

The appointments of ambassadors to the USSR were also very significant. The first of these was William C. Bullitt, a close friend of Roosevelt's and a member of the brain trust, whose mother, Louise Gross (Horowitz), daughter of Jonathan Horowitz, was of Jewish origin. Bullitt was the first ambassador to Moscow and served from 1933 to 1936. His next posting was to the embassy in Paris, from where he held daily talks with the American president. Bullitt became a kind of roving ambassador working on behalf of the world war. The first US Secretary of Defence, James Forrestal, whose "suicide" will be recounted in Chapter XI, wrote in *The Forrestal Diaries* (1951) a very famous paragraph about Bullitt and the war boosters:

"27 December 1945
Today I played golf with Joe Kennedy (Joseph P. Kennedy, who was Roosevelt's ambassador to Britain in the years before the war). I asked him about his conversations with Roosevelt and Neville Chamberlain

from 1938 onwards. He said that Chamberlain's position in 1938 was that Britain had no reason to fight and could not risk war with Hitler. Kennedy's point: That Hitler would have engaged Russia without a subsequent conflict with Britain had it not been for Bullitt's exhortations to Roosevelt in the summer of 1939 about the need to confront Germany in favour of Poland; neither the French nor the British would have made Poland a cause for war had it not been for Washington's constant demands. Bullitt, he said, insisted to Roosevelt that the Germans would not fight. Kennedy said they would, and that they would invade Europe. Chamberlain, he (Kennedy) says, declared to him that America and world Jewry had forced England into war."

Bullit's successor to Stalin was a Zionist linked to Wall Street and also a personal friend of Roosevelt, Joseph E. Davies, an admirer of the USSR who remained in office until June 1938. His replacement was once again a Zionist Jew, Laurence A. Steinhardt. Steinhardt, who was the nephew of Samuel Untermayer and a member of the Federation of American Zionists and the American Zion Commonwealth.

The string of names of Jewish agents in the various departments of the Roosevelt Administration is particularly numerous in the field of labour relations. First and foremost is Sidney Hillman, who organised labour's support for the president chosen by Wall Street. An advisor to Roosevelt, this Lithuanian-born Jew, the grandson of a Talmudic rabbi, was able at the age of thirteen to memorise several volumes of the Talmud and was on his way to become a rabbi; but Marx's communist doctrines pushed him towards revolution and he became an activist for the Jewish Bund. In the United States he founded the Congress of Industrial Organisations and was one of the communist leaders infiltrating the Administration. Another Jew of Lithuanian origin was the economist Isador Lubin, who was appointed director of the Bureau of Labor Statistics by Frances Perkins, the Secretary of Labor, also of Jewish origin, although this is not fully confirmed, as she was adopted at birth. Isador Lublin was a prominent Zionist who worked for over twenty years as an advisor to the United Israel Appeal and the Jewish Agency for Israel. In addition to being a close associate of Perkins, Lublin became a trusted confidant of Roosevelt. Frances Perkins brought many Jewish immigrants from Eastern European countries into the Department of Labour, another of whom was David Joseph Saposs (David Saposnik). Born in Kiev, Saposs was in 1935 the chief economist of the newly created NLRB (National Labor Relations Board) and was later hired by Nelson Rockefeller as an advisor on labour issues. Other Jewish members or associates of Frances Perkins' Department of Labour were: Max Zaritsky, son of a rabbi in Russia, a very active Zionist who belonged to the Jewish National Workers Alliance and was also treasurer of the National Labor Committee for Palestine; David Dubinsky (David Isaac Dobniesky), a member of the Bund born in Belarus and emigrated to the United States in 1911; William

M. Leiserson, Benedict Wolf, a member of the National Labor Relations Board (NLRB) and a member of the National Labor Relations Board (NLRB). Leiserson, Benedict Wolf, A. H. Meyers, Frances Jerkowitz, Rose Schneiderman, Leo Wolman, Edward Berman, Jacob Perlman...

If in Russia the international bankers wanted to take control of the country's wealth and resources through the actions of the agents they had placed in power, in the United States the corporate or business socialism associated with Roosevelt sought to eliminate competition and, under philanthropic social façades and thanks to state protection, aspired to take control of the nation's main companies. In other words, it was about favouring a few and guaranteeing their profits to the maximum through a legislative policy that allowed the concentration of business in the hands of "corporate socialists" who would provide public services from their private companies. Their top ideological representatives were Wall Street "financial philosophers" such as Bernard Baruch, the Warburgs or Otto Kahn of Kuhn Loeb & Co, the same people who had financed the Bolshevik revolution.

With this brief review of Roosevelt and who was behind him, it is now time to get to know the texts of Louis Thomas McFadden. Much of what has been said so far in this book is confirmed by the brilliant speeches of a Congressman of integrity and honesty, whose speeches are sensational documents that should be translated into several languages and widely disseminated. McFadden's denunciations are astounding for their courage, as they ultimately cost him his life. This Republican congressman from Pennsylvania was for ten years chairman of the Congressional Banking and Currency Committee, so he was an expert on the subject and knew very well what he was talking about when he exposed the crimes of the Federal Reserve bankers.

On 14 October 1936, *Pelley's Weekly* published a report on the death of Louis T. McFadden on 3 October 1936. According to this publication, the congressman's relatives reported that he had suffered two attempts on his life. The first attempt was made when he was getting out of a taxi in front of a hotel in the capital. Someone who was ambushed fired two shots with a revolver, but missed and the bullets became embedded in the body of the vehicle. The second attempt took place during a political banquet in Washington. After eating, McFadden suffered violent convulsions. Fortunately, a doctor friend who happened to be there was able to prevent his death by poisoning and saved him by emergency treatment. Shortly afterwards, a sudden cardiac arrest caused his instant death. Richard C. Cook, an expert on politics and economics in the United States, is convinced that "on the third attempt, the assassins succeeded in killing the most eloquent critic of the Federal Reserve System".

McFadden's congressional speeches are edited in a book entitled *Federal Reserve Exposed. Collective Speeches of Congressman Louis T. McFadden.* On 10 June 1932, McFadden delivered a historic speech to the

United States Congress in which he called for an audit of the Federal Reserve Banks and demanded the repeal of the Federal Reserve Act. The following is a summary of the text of the speech, delivered at the height of the Great Depression.

McFadden's speech delivered on 10 June 1932

"Mr. President, in these sessions of Congress we have considered emergency situations. We have talked about the effects and not the causes of the events. In this speech I will deal with the causes that have led us into this situation. There are underlying principles that are responsible for the conditions we are now experiencing, and I will deal with one of them in particular that is tremendously important in terms of the considerations of this proposition.

Mr. President, we have in this country one of the most corrupt institutions ever known in the world. I am referring to the Federal Reserve Board and the Federal Reserve Banks. The Federal Reserve Board has bilked the United States Government and the American people out of enough money to pay off the national debt. The plunder and iniquities of the Federal Reserve Board and the Federal Reserve Banks acting in concert have cost this country enough money to pay off the national debt several times over. This evil institution has ruined and impoverished the people of the United States, has brought about its own bankruptcy, and has brought about the near bankruptcy of our government.. It has done this through the shortcomings of the Federal Reserve Board and the Federal Reserve Banks. It has done so through the defects in the law under which it operates, through the disastrous administration of the Act by the Federal Reserve Board, and through the corrupt practices of the money vultures who control it.

Some people believe that the Federal Reserve Banks are institutions of the United States government. They are not government institutions. They are private credit monopolies that prey on the people of the United States for their own benefit and that of their foreign proxies; domestic and foreign speculators, swindlers and wealthy predatory lenders. In the shadowy crew of financial pirates are some who would cut a man's throat to get a dollar out of his pocket; there are those who send money to the States for votes to control our legislation; and there are those who sustain international propaganda for the purpose of deceiving us into granting new concessions that will enable them to cover up their felonies and put their gigantic crime train back in motion.

These twelve private credit monopolies (he means the twelve Federal Reserve Banks) were deceitfully and unfairly imposed on this country by bankers who came here from Europe and thanked our hospitality by undermining our American institutions. These bankers took money out of this country to finance Japan in its war against Russia. They created the reign of terror in Russia with our money in order to promote war. They induced a separate peace between Germany and Russia and thus furthered the division between the Allies in the world war. They financed Trotsky's trip from New York to Russia so that he could contribute to the destruction of the Russian empire. They encouraged and instigated the Russian revolution and placed at Trotsky's disposal a large fund of American dollars in one of their bank branches in Sweden, through which Russian homes could be completely broken up and Russian children taken away from their protectors.

It has been said that President Wilson was deceived by these bankers' entertainments and by the philanthropic appearances they adopted. It has been said that when he discovered how he had been deceived by Colonel House, he turned on this busybody, this 'holy monk' of the financial empire, and showed him the door. He had the elegance to do this; and in my opinion he deserves praise for it. President Wilson was a victim of deception. When he became President, he had certain qualities of mind and soul which qualified him for a prominent place in this nation. But there was one thing he was not and never aspired to be. He was not a banker. He said he knew very little about banking. It was therefore on the advice of others that the perverse Federal Reserve Act - the death knell of American liberty - became law during his tenure.

In 1912 the National Monetary Association, under the chairmanship of Senator Nelson W. Aldrich, reported and introduced a perverse law called the National Reserve Association Act. It is generally known as the Aldrich Act. He was the tool, if not the accomplice, of the European bankers who for nearly twenty years have been plotting to found a central bank in this country, and who in 1912 had spent and were going to continue to spend enormous sums of money to accomplish their purpose. We opposed the plan for a central bank. The men who lead the Democratic Party then promised the people that if they returned to power there would be no central bank here as long as they held the reins of power. Thirteen months later this promise was broken and the Wilson Administration, under the tutelage of those sinister Wall Street figures behind Colonel House, established here in our free country the rotten institution to control us from top to bottom and to chain us from cradle to grave.

One of the great battles for the protection of this Republic was fought here in Jackson's time, when the second bank of the United States was created, founded on the same false principles which are exemplified in the FED. After that, in 1837, the country was warned against the dangers that might befall if these same predatory interests, having been banished, were to return in disguise and ally themselves in order to seize control of the Government. This is what they did when they returned in the livery of hypocrisy and under false pretenses obtained the text of the Federal Reserve Act. The danger that this country was warned about has fallen upon us and is demonstrated in the chain of horrors that have to do with the treacherous and dishonest FED. Look around you as you leave this

House and you will see evidence of it everywhere. This is a time of misery and for the conditions that caused this misery the Federal Reserve Board and the Federal Reserve Banks are fully responsible. This is a time of economic crimes and in the financing of the crimes the Fed does not play the role of a disinterested bystander.

... The infamous Colonel House, economic advisor to President Woodrow Wilson, was largely responsible not only for the first Great Depression, but for the artificial indebtedness, eviction and cyclical collapse that resulted from the misleadingly named Federal Reserve Act. House was primarily responsible for the creation of the Federal Reserve. He was reportedly constantly seen alongside the president, always confusing him with inappropriate economic jargon. The President himself joked that House had become his alter ego. In truth, House dominated the President with the hidden intentions of the authors of the Aldrich Plan, without making available to him certain science.... On the eve of December 23, 1913, they passed the Federal Reserve Act during the Christmas absence of many legislators who opposed it. Thus the law was not only passed without public consent, but in explicit violation of the public mandate.

In the meantime, and because of it, we ourselves are now in the midst of the greatest depression we have ever known. From the Atlantic to the Pacific our country has been ravaged by the dismal practices of the Fed and the interests that control it. At no time in our history has the general welfare of the people been at such a low ebb or the minds of the people so full of despair. Recently, in one of our states sixty thousand private homes and farms were put up for auction in a single day. According to the Reverend Charles E. Coughlin, who recently testified before a committee of this House, seventy-one thousand homes and farms in Oakland County, Michigan, were sold and their former owners dispossessed. Similar cases have surely taken place in every county in America. The people who have been evicted are thus the refuse of the Federal Reserve Act. They are victims of the dishonest and ruthless Fed banks. Their children are the new slaves of the auction room in the resurgence here of the slavery of human beings."

McFadden's speech continued with quotations from statements made by various experts in 1913 before the Senate and Congressional Banking and Currency Committees. The predominant tone in all of them was the denunciation of the Federal Reserve System as an attack on the nation's liberties and sovereignty. The Congressman went on to criticise the flight of his banks' reserves abroad and again accused Fed bankers of acting as agents of foreign central banks and of using depositors' money for the benefit of major European banking houses, all of which was at the expense of the US government and to the detriment of the American people. McFadden called for America to be saved for the Americans and demanded that the Fed be destroyed, as national reserves were seized for the benefit of foreigners. Since we have already seen the investments of Wall Street bankers in

Germany in order to take control of German companies, we reproduce the part of the speech which refers to these operations and follows with some figures on the magnitude of the racket set up by the international "banksters" who today are squeezing nations with the same methods.

"Mr. President, trillions and trillions of our money have been pumped into Germany and money is still being pumped into Germany by the Federal Reserve Board and by the Federal Reserve Banks. Their worthless paper is still traded and renewed here with public credit from the United States Government. On April 27, 1932 the Federal Reserve gang sent to Germany $750,000 in gold belonging to depositors in American banks. A week later another $300,000 in gold was sent to Germany in the same way. In mid-May $12,000,000 in gold was remitted to Germany by the FED. Almost every week there is a shipment of gold to Germany. These remittances are not made to make money on the exchange rate, as the German mark is below parity with the dollar.

Mr. Chairman, I believe that American depositors in the National Bank have a right to know what the Federal Reserve Board and the Federal Reserve Banks are doing with their money. There are millions of depositors in this country who do not know that a percentage of every dollar they deposit in a member bank of the Federal Reserve System automatically goes to the American agents of foreign banks, and that all their deposits may be paid out to foreigners without their knowledge or consent by the fraudulent organisation of the Federal Reserve Act and by the dubious practices of the Federal Reserve banks.

Mr. President, the American people should know the truth from the mouths of their public servants. The Federal Reserve Board and the Federal Reserve Banks have been international bankers from the beginning - with the US Government as their compulsory banker, and supplier of currency. But it is not, nevertheless, extraordinary to see these twelve private credit monopolies buying up again and again foreign debts in all parts of the world and asking the US government for new issues of banknotes in exchange for these debts. The magnitude of the racket as it has been developed by the Federal Reserve banks, their foreign correspondents, and the predatory European bankers who set up the Federal Reserve institution here and taught our own pirates how to rob the people... the magnitude of this racket is estimated to approach $9,000,000,000 (nine trillion dollars) a year. In the last ten years it is said to have amounted to $90,000,000,000,000 (ninety billion). Linked with this, you have, to the tune of trillions of dollars, the gambling with U.S. debt securities, which takes place in the same stock market, a gambling on which the Federal Reserve Board is now spending $100,000,000 a week. Federal Reserve notes are taken from the United States Government in unlimited quantities. Is it any wonder that the burden of supplying these immense sums of money to the gambling fraternity has become too heavy a burden on the American people?"

The Congressman's historic speech ended with a call for an audit of the Federal Reserve Banks, which more than eighty years later has still not been carried out. McFadden charged that the Federal Reserve Board had usurped the US government: "It controls everything here. It controls our international relations and sets up or dismantles governments when it wants to".

McFadden's speeches in 1933

With Franklin D. Roosevelt in the White House, Louis T. McFadden denounced that the new president was under the orders of the international bankers, which corroborates Antony Sutton's thesis mentioned at the beginning of this section. On 23 May 1933, Louis T. McFadden formally charged the Board of Governors of the Federal Reserve, the Comptroller of the Currency and the Secretary of the Treasury with numerous criminal acts, including conspiracy, fraud, exchange rate illegality and treason. There follows, then, a further summary of the most significant of his speeches during 1933, beginning with his denunciation of the bankers' plan to enslave the world.

> "Mr. President, when the Fed was passed, the people of the United States did not realise that a world system was being installed here.... That this country was going to supply financial power to an 'international superstate'. A superstate controlled by international bankers and international industrialists acting in concert to enslave the world for their own pleasure. Americans are being enormously harmed. They have lost their jobs, been dispossessed of their homes, been evicted from their rented accommodation, lost their children and been left to suffer and die for lack of shelter, food, clothing and medicine. The wealth of the United States and the capital of labour has been stolen and locked away in the vaults of certain banks and corporations or exported to foreign countries for the benefit of the foreign clients of these banks or corporations. As far as the people of the United States are concerned, the pantry is empty. It is true that the warehouses and coal depots and grain silos are full, but they are padlocked and the big banks and corporations have the keys. The looting of America by the Fed is the greatest crime in history."
> ... Mr. President, what is needed is a return to the Constitution of the United States. The old fight that was fought here in Jackson's time must be repeated. The independent Treasury of the United States should be re-established and the Government should lock up its own money in the people's building designed for this purpose. The Fed should be abolished and state borders should be respected. Bank reserves should be kept within the boundaries of the states to whose people they belong, and this stock of people's money should be protected so that international bankers

cannot steal it. The FED should be abolished and its banks, having violated its charter, should be liquidated immediately. Disloyal government employees who have violated their promise should be dismissed and brought to trial. If this is not done, I predict that the American people, outraged, plundered, insulted and betrayed in their own land, will rise up in anger and sweep the money changers from the temple. Mr. President, America is bankrupt: it has been bankrupted by the corrupt and dishonest Fed. It has repudiated debts to its own citizens. Its main foreign creditor is Britain and a British henchman has been in the White House and British agents are in the US Treasury taking inventory, arranging the timing of settlements. Sir, President, the Fed has offered to meet British demands at the expense of the American people through deceit and corruption, in return for Britain helping them hide their crimes. The British are protecting their agents at the FED because they do not want the system of theft to be destroyed. They want it to continue for their benefit. Through it, Britain has become the financial director of the world. It has regained the position it held before the world war. For several years it has been a silent partner in the business of the Fed. Under threat of blackmail or through its bribery or through the treachery of American citizens to the people of the United States, the agents at the head of the FED have recklessly granted Britain immense gold loans running into hundreds of millions of dollars. It has done this against the law! These gold loans were not mere transactions. They have given Britain the power to borrow billions. Britain takes billions out of the country through its control of the Fed."

The following passage refers to Britain's abandonment of the gold standard in 1931 and the measures subsequently taken by President Roosevelt. These measures have been alluded to in passing in footnote 9, and we can now appreciate McFadden's criticism. To properly understand the following passage, Roosevelt's first proposal before Congress on 9 March 1933, five days after his inauguration, was the Emergency Banking Act (EBA). This law was passed with such urgency that a copy of the text was not even circulated in the House of Representatives so that members of Congress could at least study it, if not read it. The text was passed after a read aloud by Banking Committee Chairman Henry Steagall. Four days before the passage of the Emergency Banking Act, President Roosevelt had decreed a closure of all banks, which did not open until 13 March. The closure did not, of course, affect the Federal Reserve banks, which were the only ones allowed to operate nationwide. It is perhaps of interest to add, in order to better assess McFadden's interventions, that by July 1932 the Dow Jones index had lost 90% of its value since 1929, that American GDP had fallen by 60% and that more than four thousand banks had disappeared.

"...Mr. President, the closure of the banks in the different states was caused by the corrupt and dishonest FED. This institution manipulated money and credit and was the cause of the bank holiday order. This holiday was a set-up! There was no national emergency here when Franklin D. Roosevelt took office, with the exception of the bankruptcy of the FED, a bankruptcy which had been covered up for several years and which had been hidden from the people so that they would continue to allow their bank deposits and their bank reserves and their gold and the funds of the US Treasury to be seized by these bankrupt institutions. Protected, the predatory international bankers have been stealthily shifting the burden of the Fed's debts to the Treasury and to the people themselves, who pay for their swindle. That is the only national emergency here since the depression began. The week before the bank closures were declared in New York State, deposits in the New York savings banks were greater than withdrawals. There was no fear in New York banks. There was no need for a bank closure either in New York or in the country. Roosevelt did what the international bankers ordered him to do! Do not be deceived, Mr. President, or allow yourself to be deceived by others into believing that Roosevelt's despotism is somehow intended to benefit the people: Roosevelt is preparing to sign on the dotted line! He is preparing to cancel the war debts fraudulently! He is preparing to internationalise this country and to destroy the Constitution itself in order to keep the FED intact as a monetary institution for foreigners.

Mr. President, I do not see why citizens should be terrorised into surrendering their property to the international bankers who own the FED. The statement that gold will be confiscated from its rightful owners if they do not surrender it voluntarily, for private interests, shows that there is an anarchist in our government. The statement that it is necessary for people to surrender their gold - the only real money - to the banks in order to protect the currency is a statement of calculated dishonesty! Through this disloyal usurpation of power on the night of March 5, 1933, and by his proclamation, which in my opinion was a violation of the Constitution, Roosevelt separated the currency of the United States from gold, and the currency of the United States is no longer protected by gold. It is therefore pure dishonesty to say that the people's gold is necessary to protect the currency. Roosevelt ordered the people to hand over their gold to private interests, i.e. the banks, and took control of the banks so that all the gold and gold securities they held could be handed over to the international bankers who own and control the FED. Roosevelt ties his fate to the usurers. He chooses to save the corrupt and the dishonest at the expense of the American people. He took advantage of the confusion and exhaustion of the people and spread the ambush throughout the country to grab anything of value. He made a big raid on the international bankers. The Prime Minister of Great Britain (referring to Ramsey McDonald's trip) came here for money. He came here to cash in! He came here with Fed currency and other claims on the Fed that Britain had hoarded all over the world and presented them for cash in gold.

Mr. President, I am in favour of forcing the Fed to pay its own debts. I do not see why the general public should be forced to pay the gambling debts of international bankers. By his action of closing the banks of the United States, Roosevelt seized gold bank deposits worth forty trillion or more. These deposits were deposits of gold securities. By this action he forced himself to pay depositors only in paper, if at all. The paper money which he proposes to pay out to the depositors of the banks and to the people in general in lieu of their hard-earned gold values is of negligible value, for it is not based on anything with which the people can convert it. It is the money of slaves, not of free men.

At noon on March 4, 1933, FDR with his hand on the Bible promised to preserve and protect the Constitution of the United States. At midnight on March 5, 1933, he confiscated the property of American citizens. He rejected the internal debt of the Government to its own citizens. It destroyed the value of the American dollar. It released, or attempted to release, the Fed from its contractual responsibility to settle its currency in gold or in lawful money at parity with gold. It depreciated the value of the national currency. The people of the United States are now using unredeemable pieces of paper as money. The Treasury cannot settle this paper in gold or silver. The Treasury's gold and silver have been illegally turned over to the corrupt and dishonest Fed. And the Administration has had the gall to plunder the country to get more gold for private interests by telling patriotic citizens that their gold is needed to protect the currency. It is not being used to protect the currency! It is being used to protect the corrupt and dishonest FED. The directors of these institutions have perpetrated an affront against the United States Government, and must include the crime of making false entries in their books of account and the even more important crime of withdrawing funds from the United States Treasury. The looting of Roosevelt's gold is intended to help them out of the hole they dug for themselves when they gambled away the savings of the American people. The international bankers have established a dictatorship here because they want a dictator to protect them. They want a dictator who will make a proclamation granting the Fed unconditional and absolute freedom. Has Roosevelt relieved other debtors in this country of the need to pay their debts? Has he made any proclamation telling farmers that they need not pay their mortgages? Has he announced that mothers who have starving children need not pay for milk? Has he freed homeowners from having to pay rent? Certainly not. He has only issued a proclamation to reassure international bankers and foreign debtors of the US government.

Mr. President, the gold in the banks of this country belongs to the American people, who have paper money contracts for it in the form of national currency. If the FED cannot honour its contracts with the citizens of the United States to redeem their paper money for gold, or lawful money, then the FED must be relieved by the United States Government and its managers must be put on trial. There must be a day of reckoning.

If the FED has stolen from the Treasury, so that the Treasury cannot settle in gold the currency for which it is responsible, then the FED must be expelled from the Treasury. Mr. President, a gold certificate is equivalent to a receipt of deposit in the Treasury's gold store, and the person holding a gold certificate is the present owner of a corresponding amount of gold piled up in the Treasury. Now along comes Roosevelt who wants to melt down the value of money by illegally declaring that it can no longer be converted into gold at the will of the holder.

Roosevelt's next robbery for the international bankers was the reduction of the pay of federal employees. Next are the veterans of all the wars, many of whom are old and infirm or disabled..... I see no reason why these veterans of the civil war should be forced to give up their pensions for the financial benefit of the international vultures who have looted the Treasury, bankrupted the country and treacherously handed it over to a foreign enemy. There are many ways to raise public revenue that are better than this barbaric act of injustice. Why not collect from the FED the amount they owe the US Treasury in interest on all the money they have taken from the government? This would bring in trillions of dollars to the Treasury. If FDR were honest as he pretends, he would have done this immediately. And furthermore, why not force the Fed to disclose its profits and pay the government its share? Until this is done, it is nauseatingly dishonest to talk about maintaining the government's reputation."

The congressman's speech went on to denounce the international bankers as "enemies of the people" and continued with further accusations of FDR for being in their service and for covering up their crimes instead of "forcing the vultures and swindlers at the Fed to pay back what they stole." He ended with a string of names of people linked to various crimes, the chief of which was the appropriation of Treasury funds. Among those accused by McFadden were government servants, members of the Federal Reserve Board and a handful of agents in its employ. He asked the House Judiciary Committee to investigate and report to Congress so that those found guilty could be removed from office and brought to justice.

The 1934 speeches

As a result of his speeches in the House of Representatives during 1934, the usual accusations of anti-Semitism against Louis T. McFadden soon arose. As is well known, those who criticise the criminal actions of certain Jews are branded as anti-Semites, which is often a fallacy. Today, those who condemn the crimes of Zionism are even considered anti-Semitic. Just as there are different Semitic languages, there are different Semitic peoples, including, of course, the Palestinians. Paradoxically, the Zionists, who are not Semites, being mostly Ashkenazi descendants of the Khazars, are the world's leading anti-Semites, since they have been trying for almost seventy years to wipe out a Semitic people in Palestine. McFadden was given the label because he denounced the Roosevelt administration as Jewish-controlled and because he opposed the Jewish Henry Morgenthau as Secretary of the Treasury. The written records of the 1934 speeches show that during the first few months McFadden continued his accusations against Roosevelt, the Federal Reserve and Britain. On 15 June 1934, however, McFadden made a speech about Jacob Schiff which we reproduce almost in full below, as it is a document that confirms once again what we have been writing about this Jewish banker and his very prominent role in the destruction of Tsarist Russia.

> "...At that time a man by the name of Jacob Schiff came to this country as an agent for certain moneylenders. His mission was to take control of the American railways. This man was a Jew. He was the son of a rabbi. He was born in one of the Rothschild houses in Frankfurt, Germany. He was a small fellow with a pleasant face and, if I remember correctly, his eyes were blue. At an early age he left Frankfurt to make his fortune and went to Hamburg, Germany. In Hamburg he went into the banking business of the Warburgs. The Hamburg Warburgs were lifelong bankers, with branches in Amsterdam and Sweden.... Some time before Schiff's arrival there was in Lafayette, Indiana, a firm of merchants known as Kuhn & Loeb. I think they were already here around 1850. They probably made money at the expense of new settlers passing through Indiana on their journey northwest. This Jewish firm eventually moved to New York, where they set up shop as private bankers and became wealthy.
> Jacob Schiff married Teresa Loeb and became the head of Kuhn Loeb & Co. Schiff made a lot of money for himself and the London moneylenders here. He started giving orders to presidents almost on a regular basis. He seems to have been a man who would stop at nothing to achieve his goals. I do not reproach him for being a Jew, I reproach him for being a provocateur of conflicts. Russia had in Jacob Schiff a powerful enemy. The American people came to believe that their enmity was caused by wrongs done to Russian Jews. I looked elsewhere for the motives behind it. In 1890 Jacob Schiff was the agent in this country of Ernest Cassell and other London moneylenders. These moneylenders were eager for a war between England and Russia and were making propaganda designed to support England in the United States. The United States was then a debtor country and paid a large amount annually to Schiff and his bosses. Consequently he took it upon himself to bias the United States against Russia. He did this by presenting to the American people alleged iniquities against Russian Jews. Unpleasant stories began to appear in the press. Children in this country were told in schools that Russian soldiers crippled Jewish children for life with the whip. Hostility between Russia and the United States was fomented by infamous means.

One of Schiff's schemes was the large-scale importation of Russian Jews to the United States. He planned various and sundry ways for the temporary transfer of these Jewish emigrants. He said that he would not have them enter this country through the port of New York because they might like New York too much and then not want to go to the outposts for which they had been selected. He said it was preferable to have them come in through New Orleans and leave them there for two weeks, 'so they could get a little English and get a little money' before they left for what he called the 'interior of America'. How they were to get money, he did not say. Aided by Schiff and his associates, many Russian Jews came to this country at that time and were naturalised. Many of these naturalised Jews later returned to Russia. As soon as they returned to that country, they immediately claimed exemption from the domiciliary regulations imposed there on Jews, that is, they claimed the right to live anywhere in Russia because they were American citizens, or 'Yankee' Jews. There were riots which were exploited by the American press. There were riots, bombings and murders that were paid for by someone. The perpetrators of these atrocities appear to have been protected by powerful financial interests. While this was going on in Russia, a shameful campaign of lies was orchestrated here, and vast amounts of money were spent to make the public believe that the Jews in Russia were a simple and innocent people crushed by the Russians who needed the protection of the world's great benefactor, Uncle Sam.

I now come to the moment when war was declared between Russia and Japan. It was brought about by the skilful use of Japan in order that England should not have to fight with Russia in India. It was cheaper and more convenient for Britain to let Japan fight Russia rather than do it herself. As expected, Schiff and his London associates financed Japan. They took large amounts of money out of the United States for this purpose. The environment for the issuance of the loans had been skilfully prepared. The moving stories, at which Schiff was a master, touched the hearts of sympathetic Americans. The loans were a great success. Millions of American dollars were sent to Japan by Schiff and his London associates. England's dominance in India was secured. Russia was prevented from entering through the Khyber Pass and reaching India from the north-west. At the same time Japan was strengthened and became a great world power, which as such now confronts us in the Pacific. All this was achieved by controlling the American media, which communicated that Russian Jews and 'Yankee' Jews were being persecuted in Russia, and by selling Japanese war bonds to American citizens. While the Russo-Japanese war was raging, President Theodore Roosevelt offered to act as mediator, and a conference between the belligerents was arranged in Portsmouth, New Hampshire. When the conference was held, Jacob Schiff attended and used all his influence over Theodore Roosevelt to favour Japan at Russia's expense. His main objective, then and now, was the humiliation of the Russians, whose only crime was to be Russians rather than Jews. He tried to humiliate the Russians, but Count Witte, the Russian plenipotentiary, would not allow it. Schiff's power and that of his organised propaganda were well understood by Witte. He was therefore not surprised when President Roosevelt, who was often deceived, twice asked him to give special consideration to Jews with American citizenship who had returned to Russia. Witte took with him to Russia a letter from Roosevelt containing this plea.

Mr. President, the restrictions on Jews in Russia at that time may have been heavy, but heavy or not, before the Russians had a chance to change them, Schiff had condemned the eighty-year old treaty of friendship and goodwill between the United States and Russia. Speaking on this matter, Count Witte says in his biography: 'the Russians lost the friendship of the American people'. Mr. President, I cannot believe that those people, the real Russians, ever lost the friendship of the American people. They were wiped out to fulfil the ambitions of those who claim to be the financial masters of the world, and some of us were duped into believing that in some mysterious way they themselves were to blame. The gulf that suddenly opened up between us and our old friends and admirers in Russia was a gulf created by Jacob Schiff, the vengeful in his inhuman greed, and he created it in the name of the Jewish religion.

Mr. President, the people of the United States should not allow financial or any other particular interests to dictate the government's foreign policy. But on this issue history repeats itself. You have heard, no doubt, about the so-called persecutions of Jews in Germany. Mr President, there is no real persecution of Jews in Germany. Hitler, the Warburgs, the Mendelssohns and the Rothschilds seem to be on the best of terms. There is no real persecution of Jews in Germany, but there has been a pretended persecution because there are two hundred thousand unwanted communist Jews in Germany, mostly Jews from Galicia who entered Germany after the world war, and Germany is very anxious to get rid of these particular communist Jews. The Germans wish to preserve the purity of their own race. They are willing to keep rich Jews like Max Warburg and Franz Mendelssohn, whose families have lived in Germany for so long that they have acquired some of the national characteristics. But the Germans are not willing to keep the Jews from Galicia, the upstarts."

"Sidney Warburg" writes something very similar when he alludes to a conversation with a Jewish friend, a bank manager in Hamburg, who is a supporter of Hitler. He tells him: "By Jews, Hitler means Jews from Galicia, who infest Germany. Jews of purely German origin are considered by Hitler to be as much German citizens as anyone else; you will see that he will not bother them at all. Do not forget that in the Social-Democratic and Communist parties it is the Jews who have the upper hand. Hitler will attack them not because they are Jews, but because they are Communists or Social-Democrats." It so happens, as has been said, that these Jews in Galicia were not Semites. McFadden's speech continued with further allusions to Roosevelt's policies and concluded with sharp references to the role of international Jewish bankers in the Russian revolution.

"This big show has been put on, mainly by the German Jews themselves, in the hope that Uncle Sam will show that he is still as crazy as before and allow these Communist Jews from Galicia to come here. For this reason Miss Perkins has been put in charge of the Department of Labour. She is there to relax the immigration bans. It is believed that because she is a woman she can appease the critics. She is in tune with the international bankers. Otherwise she would not be in a Jewish-controlled administration. When the so-called "anti-Semitic campaign" designed for American consumption was launched in Germany, France was alarmed because it feared that the Jews of Galicia might end up on French soil. French newspapers published articles alluding to this threat; but now that France has realised that the purpose of the anti-Semitic campaign is to dump two hundred thousand Communist Jews in the United States she is no longer worried. Ah, just think, old Uncle Sam is going to pay the piper, all right!

Mr. President, I consider it a pity that there are Americans who like to be servile to wealthy Jews and to praise them. Some of these wretches are in the hands of moneylending Jews and dare not cross them. You have witnessed Franklin D. Roosevelt's indecent seizure of the gold reserves and other valuables of the American people, the destruction of the banks, the attempted laundering of the Federal Reserve Banks, whose corruption Roosevelt had admitted in his campaign harangues, and you will have seen that what has been confiscated is not in the hands of the present constitutional Government, but in the hands of the international bankers who are the nucleus of the new government which Roosevelt intends to establish here. Roosevelt's actions are not in line with the Constitution of the United States, but with the plans of the Third International. There was a time when Trotsky was a favourite of Jacob Schiff. During the war Trotsky published *Novy Mir* and addressed mass meetings in New York. When he left the United States to return to Russia, it is well known that he did so with Schiff's money and with Schiff's protection. He was captured by the British at Halifax and immediately, on the advice of a personage on high, was released. No sooner had he arrived in Russia than he was informed that he had credit in Sweden, in the Swedish branch of the bank owned by Max Warburg in Hamburg. This credit enabled him to finance the Russian revolution for the benefit of international Jewish bankers. He helped them to disrupt it for their own ends.

Today the Soviet Union is in debt. Since Trotsky's return to Russia, the course of Russian history has certainly been influenced by the operations of the international bankers. They have acted through German and British institutions and have kept Russia in their servitude. Their relatives in Germany have drawn immense sums of money from the United States and have financed one by one their agents in Russia at a handsome profit. Treasury funds have been contributed to the Soviet Government by Federal Reserve banks, acting through the Chase Bank and the Guaranrty Trust Co. and other New York banks. England, no less than Germany, has taken money from us through the Federal Reserve banks and either lent it back at high rates of interest to the Soviet Government or used it to subsidise its sales to Soviet Russia and its engineering work on Russian territory. The dam on the Dnieper River was built with funds illegally taken from the US Treasury by the corrupt and dishonest Federal Reserve Board.

Mr. President, an immense sum of United States money has been used abroad in war preparations and in the procurement and manufacture of war supplies. Germany is said to be co-owner of a large gas production plant at Troitsk on Russian soil (this probably refers to I. G. Farben, whose directors were Max Warburg in Germany and Paul Warburg in the United States). China is almost completely Sovietised and huge stocks of munitions are thought to be stockpiled inside Asia, awaiting the day when the US warlords will send American troops into Asia.

Mr. President, the United States should try to stay out of another war, particularly a war in Asia. It should decide whether it is worth joining Russia and China in a war against Japan. I say and have said to often that America should remember George Washington's advice. It should mind its own business and stay at home. It should not allow the international Jewish bankers to get it involved in another war, so that they and their Gentile front men and sycophants can reap tasty profits from it all. An army needs everything from toilet bags to aeroplanes, submarines, tanks, gas masks, poison gas, ammunition, bayonets, cannon and other paraphernalia and instruments of destruction."

Louis Thomas McFadden fought an unequal battle, as he must have known that no one would dare to support him. For this reason, his attitude can be considered heroic. The magnitude of the accusations he made publicly in Congress were of great magnitude and importance, hence unacceptable to the accused. Some resorted to the usual insinuation that he had lost his mind. His disappearance from the political scene in 1936 deprived Americans of a patriot, an unrepeatable congressman worthy of going down in their country's history.

PART 5
TERROR IN THE USSR AND GENOCIDE IN UKRAINE

A GPU decree dated 18 January 1929 ordered Trotsky's expulsion from the USSR. Thus the possibility of the Jewish bankers' chief agent seizing power was at least temporarily removed. Trotsky arrived in Turkey in February and settled there until July 1933, when he opted to move to France, from where he thought he could relaunch a full-scale political offensive. Stalin later declared that his expulsion had been a mistake, which seems obvious, since Trotsky was able to conspire from abroad, as demonstrated during the purges, which he would never have been able to do while in the USSR. An example of his activities against Stalin was the *Opposition Bulletin*, which he himself founded and edited as early as 1929. Printed in Cyrillic characters in Berlin, Zurich, New York or Paris (depending on the period), sixty-five copies were published over the years. Trotsky's son, Leon Sedov, who in 1929 was twenty-three years old, acted as editor and organised its distribution in the USSR. Trotsky's first political objective was the cohesion of the opposition to Stalin. Isaac Deutscher, one of his followers, writes that he had pinned his hopes on the creation of the Fourth International. In any case, with their leader out of the country, the Trotskyist opposition remained crouched and waiting, so that by 1929 Stalin had apparently consolidated his hold on power. Under him, communism continued the genocidal methods practised by Lenin and Trotsky against the so-called class enemies.

There is a tendency to think that Stalin brought an end to Jewish predominance in the leading cadres of the party, which is false. Stalin's strongman was his brother-in-law, the Ukrainian Jew Lazar Kaganovich, whose sister Rosa was Stalin's wife or concubine. There is controversy over whether Iosif David Vissarionovich Djugaschvili, known as Joseph Stalin, was himself of Jewish origin. Hitler considered him to be Jewish and told "Sidney Warburg" so in one of his interviews. According to some sources, including the Soviet official Ivan Krylov, the Georgian surname Djugaschvili means son of a Jew. It has also been claimed that the name Kochba or Koba, an alias used by Stalin early in his career, alludes to Simon bar Kochba, a Jewish leader before Christ. Russian researcher Gregory Klimov claims that Stalin was half-Jewish. Jewish author David Weismann claimed in 1950 in *B'nai B'rith Messenger*, a Los Angeles publication, that Stalin was fully Jewish. Another Jewish publicist, Solomon Schulman, revealed in Sweden that Stalin spoke Yiddish and that this was one of his best-kept secrets. All this is of relative importance, since what is relevant is that those who held power alongside Stalin were mostly Jews, many of whom hid their loyalty to Trotsky.

Denis Fahey in *The Rulers of Russia* cites the names of the fifty-nine members of the Central Committee of the Communist Party of the USSR in 1935 and only three were not Jewish, but were married to Jewish women. Fahey also cites the ambassadors who in 1935-36 held office in the major countries of the world and almost all of them were Jewish or married to Jewish women. The Soviet delegation to the League of Nations, headed by Litvinov, consisted of eight members, only one of whom was not Jewish. Also Alfred Rosenberg, the Nazi hierarch who himself had Jewish blood, gives a nominal list of Jews who in 1935-36 were still in power in Russia. In the administration of the armaments industry the percentage was over 95% and in the People's Commissariat for Food it reached 96%. As for the leaders of trade, 99% were also Jewish. It has already been mentioned above that both the People's Commissariat for Internal Affairs, the GPU or former Cheka, and the General Administration of the Labour Camps were in the hands of Jewish criminals. At the same time, the Censorship Department in Moscow was staffed by Jewish officials. Douglas Reed accompanied Anthony Eden, Secretary of the Foreign Office, on his visit to Moscow as a journalist for *The Times*. In his book *Insanity Fair* he writes:

"The Censorship Department, that is, the whole machinery for controlling the internal press and muzzling the international press, was entirely staffed by Jews... there seemed to be not a single non-Jewish official in the whole staff. They were the same sort of Jews one finds in New York, Berlin, Vienna and Prague, well-groomed, well-fed and dressed with a touch of the 'dandy'. I had been told that the proportion of Jews in the Government was small, but in this department which I had occasion to know intimately they seemed to have a monopoly, and I asked myself where the Russians were".

Jüri Lina points out that it is generally ignored that Stalin's chief personal aides were Jewish. This was, for example, his personal secretary Leon (Leiba) Mekhlis, who in turn, according to Boris Bazhanov, had two Jewish assistants, Makhover and Yuzhak. Bazhanov, one of the Estonian author's sources, was himself Stalin's secretary between 1923 and 1925 and then secretary of the Politburo until January 1928, when he defected from the USSR. Bazhanov writes in his memoirs that of Stalin's forty-nine secretaries, forty were Jews. According to Lina, in 1937 seventeen of the twenty-two People's Commissars were Jewish. In the Presidium of the Supreme Soviet, seventeen of its twenty-seven members were also Jewish. Lina introduces one by one the Jewish members of the Commissariat for Foreign Trade, whose commissar from 1930 to 1937 was Arkady Rosengoltz, a Trotskyite executed in 1938. We will have the opportunity to get to know the characters as they appear as protagonists. There follows an abbreviated account of the terror practised by the communist state in its struggle against the peasantry, the first episode of which took place in 1918-1922.

The elimination of the kulaks

In January 1928, fearing a grain shortage, the Politburo unanimously decided to adopt emergency measures allowing the expropriation of grain from the kulaks, which was in contradiction with the NEP, the New Economic Policy adopted in 1921, which meant the theoretical end of the requisitions. The NEP, which allowed for a certain functioning of the market, then recognised that the measures of socialisation and collectivisation were inapplicable; although Lenin himself warned that this was a "strategic retreat". A letter of Lenin's written on 3 March 1922 has been quoted above, in which he told Kamenev that it should not be thought that the NEP put an end to terror: "we shall again have recourse to terror and economic terror". Ten years later these words proved to be prophetic. The seizure of grain produced with the supposed guarantee that it could be marketed and made money was an unmistakably bad signal to the peasants, even though Stalin declared that these were "absolutely exceptional" measures. The Communist Party proceeded to mobilise its cadres and thirty thousand activists were sent to the agricultural regions. In the villages, troikas were set up with power over the local authorities, and the peasants were allowed to grind only the amount necessary for their own consumption.

At the end of 1928 the State Planning Commission warned of a downward trend in the grain harvest. Stalin decried the idea of making "exceptional measures" a permanent principle; but the Politburo pointed out that there were large supplies of grain in the hands of the kulaks and insisted on the need to increase the quotas. The party plenipotentiaries sent to the villages not only ordered the requisitioning of produce, but demanded that it should be pointed out in the assemblies which kulaks should be subjected to the greatest pressure. Many peasants saw the kulak as an example and accepted his authority. The elimination of the kulaks was inextricably linked to the end of the market, since in economic terms it meant destroying the farmers' incentive to produce. This was sensed or understood in the towns and villages, where people often voted against the measures proposed by the party. Leaders who made immoderate use of the word were denounced as kulaks, against whom measures such as arrests, house searches, fines, confiscations and sometimes even shooting were taken.

The climate was becoming increasingly tense, and resistance against the officials, described by the regime as "terrorist acts", became more widespread. Moreover, in the cities, where small shops and artisans' workshops regarded as capitalist enterprises were closed down by the authorities, ration cards, which had disappeared since the beginning of the NEP, were once again used. In the spring of 1929 meat also began to be forcibly collected. In Siberia, for example, meat supplies rose from 700 tons in 1928 to 19,000 tons in 1929.

In May 1929 the Council of People's Commissars (Sovnarkom) defined a kulak as a peasant who provided work, or who owned a mill or other facilities, or who rented farm machinery, or who was capable of commercial activity. It was said at the time that there was no intention to eliminate them and mass deportation was not contemplated either; however, in the spring of 1929 the cases of proceedings against kulaks increased and in the autumn arrests and requisitions became more widespread, which caused even the poorest farmers to put up increasingly fierce resistance: grain was buried or sold at low prices; but sometimes it was even burned or thrown into rivers, which was interpreted as an attempt to undermine the Soviet regime by the "rural capitalists".

In April-May 1929 the first Five-Year Plan was adopted and the government announced a new phase of mass collectivisation. The Plan initially provided for the collectivisation of five million households, but in June of the same year the figure was increased to eight million in 1930 alone, and in September the figure of thirteen million small family farms was given. Stalin in an article published in *Pravda* on 7 November 1929 painted an idyllic picture and announced that a radical change had taken place in agriculture: "From small and backward individual farming to large-scale farming, to advanced collective farming, to cultivation of the land in common." According to Stalin, farmers were massively adhering to the system of collective farms: "Not in small groups, as had happened before, but whole villages, whole regions, whole districts, even whole provinces. And what does this mean? - he asked rhetorically, "It means that the average farmer has joined the collective farming movement. And that is the basis of the radical change in the development of agriculture which represents the most important achievement of Soviet power during the past year."

A few days after the publication of this article the Plenum of the party's Central Committee met for a week, from 10 to 17 November 1929. The members were told that voluntary collectivisation was taking place, and Vyacheslav Molotov, First Secretary of the Moscow Communist Party, who was to be appointed Chairman of the Council of Commissars in December 1930, addressed the plenum, calling for the moment to be seized to settle the agrarian question once and for all. Molotov, who was married to a Jewish Zionist named Polina Zhemchúzhina[12], urged immediate collectivisation in

---

[12] Polina Zhemchúzhina (Perl Karpovskaya) came from a family of Ukrainian Jews. A Propaganda Commissar during the civil war, she married Vyacheslav Molotov, already a member of the Central Committee, in 1921. A sister of his, a Zionist like herself, emigrated to Palestine in the 1920s. According to historian Zhores Medvedev, Stalin was always suspicious of Polina and on several occasions advised Molotov to divorce her. When Golda Meir arrived in Moscow in November 1948 as ambassador of the newly created Zionist state, Polina immediately befriended her, but in December of the same

provinces and republics and called for a new impetus to be given in the coming months. He would later be in charge of supervising the entire collectivisation process from the head of the government. As for the kulaks, Molotov warned against their incorporation into the collective farms ("kolkhozes") and called for them to be treated as "the most malicious and not yet defeated enemies". On 27 December 1929 Lazar Moiseyevich Kaganovich (Kogan), a Ukrainian Jew, Stalin's brother-in-law after his marriage to Rosa Kaganovich, announced the aim of "liquidating the kulaks as a class". Deskulakisation and agrarian collectivisation were thus two processes that took place simultaneously.

Although during 1929 there had already been numerous evictions and arrests of kulaks in Ukrainian villages, in Cossack settlements ("stanitsas") and elsewhere, the official party resolution which marked the beginning of the destruction of the kulak as a class was known on 30 January 1930, when the Politburo approved the "Measures for the Elimination of Kulak Houses in Districts Subject to Collectivisation". The reader may think that the kulaks were rich farmers who operated large estates and lived like well-to-do bourgeoisie; but this was not the reality. The kulaks in 1929 were very impoverished and could hardly cope with the increasingly heavy taxes. Only a minority owned half a dozen cows and two or three horses, and only one per cent employed more than one labourer for farm work.

A Political Bureau commission chaired by Molotov defined three categories of kulaks: in the first, those "involved in counter-revolutionary activities" were to be arrested and transferred to GPU labour camps or executed if they resisted. Their families were to be deported and their property confiscated. The second category included those who were to be arrested and deported with their families to remote regions because, although less actively opposed, they were "naturally inclined to help the counter-revolution". The third category kulaks were those considered "loyal to the regime", those who could be tried to be integrated into the collectivised farms on a probationary basis.

In *The Harvest of Sorrow* Robert Conquest gives figures that show how meagre the resources of the expropriated kulaks were in Kryvti Rih province (central Ukraine). In January and February 1930, 4,080 farms were expropriated there, which contributed only 2,367 buildings, 3,750 horses, 2,460 head of cattle, 1,105 pigs, 446 threshing machines, 1,747 ploughs, 1,304 seed drills and 2,021 tons of grain and millet to the "kolkhoz" (collective farm). The excuse given to justify such miserable results is that these farms had already been requisitioned in the 1928-29 offensive, which

---

year she was arrested on charges of treason. Sentenced to five years in a labour camp, she was released in 1953 by Lavrenti Beria, the Jew who was to replace Stalin after his death, as he was the chosen agent of the financiers of the revolution. As will be seen in another chapter, there is an almost general consensus that Beria was responsible for Stalin's assassination.

only goes to show that they were acting against farmers who were already badly ruined. Conquest gives the testimony of an activist with a bad conscience who attends the intervention and requisitioning of a house, which serves as an example to understand the situation of many of the expropriated kulaks: "he has a sick wife, five children and not a crumb of bread in the house. And this is what we call a kulak! The children wear rags and rags. They all look ghostly. I saw the pot on the stove with a few potatoes in the water. That was their dinner." Nicolas Werth gives more examples and denounces that peasants were arrested only for having sold grain at the market during the summer, for having employed a farm labourer for two months, or for having slaughtered a pig in September 1929 "with the aim of consuming it and thus subtracting it from socialist appropriation." Humble peasants who sold products made by themselves were arrested for having "indulged in commerce". Some were deported because a family member had been a Tsarist officer, others because they were regular churchgoers. In general, any peasant who opposed collectivisation was labelled a kulak.

During 1930 some two and a half million peasants took part in about fourteen thousand revolts, uprisings and demonstrations against the regime. There were bloody clashes between detachments of the GPU and peasant groups armed with pitchforks, sickles and axes. Hundreds of soviets were looted and peasant committees temporarily took control of some villages. In the Ukraine twenty-six thousand people were arrested by the GPU between 1 February and 15 March, six hundred and fifty of whom were shot. Also, at the end of March 1930, more than fifteen thousand "counter-revolutionary elements" were arrested in some districts of Western Ukraine alone. According to official GPU data, twenty thousand people were sentenced to death in 1930 by the exceptional jurisdictions of the political police alone. Conquest writes that in February 1931 the decision was taken to proceed with a second wave of deportations of kulaks, which was more thoroughly prepared. According to Conquest, within two years "a relentless and merciless struggle took place in the camps, claiming millions of lives ". Conquest summarises the estimates of various unofficial Russian researchers and concludes that some fifteen million human beings, men, women and children, were uprooted. Two million were transferred to industrial projects and the rest were deported to the Arctic. One million men went directly to internment in labour camps.

But behind the cold, dry numbers lie millions of stories of human beings who suffered injustice and terror. *The Harvest of Sorrow* tells some of these stories, first-hand accounts that give a glimpse of the barbarity in some detail. Take, for example, the case of a former peasant who had served in the Red Army and who in 1929 had thirty-five acres, two horses, a cow, a pig, five sheep, forty chickens and a family of six. In 1928 he had to pay a tax of 2,500 roubles and 7,500 bushels of grain. He was unable to do so and was forced to hand over his house, valued at about 2,000 roubles. An activist bought it for 250 and the goods were also sold. The tools and implements were sent to the new kolkhoz. The peasant was arrested and imprisoned. Although he had previously been labelled a subkulak, he was accused of being a kulak who refused to pay taxes, of inciting against collectivisation, of belonging to a counter-revolutionary organisation, of having owned five hundred acres, five pairs of oxen, fifty head of cattle, of exploiting the workers, and so on. His sentence was ten years' hard labour.

Another story is told by a Ukrainian girl, whose family had a horse, a cow, a heifer, five sheep and some pigs. Her father refused to enter the kolkhoz and was demanded a quantity of grain that he did not have. "For a whole week - the young woman continues to narrate - they did not let my father sleep and beat him with sticks and revolvers until he turned black and blue and ended up swollen." Finally, a GPU officer, chairman of the village Soviet, went to the house in the company of others and confiscated everything after taking an inventory. The father, mother, eldest son, two younger sisters and a small baby were locked up in the church overnight. Then they were taken to the station and put into cattle cars. Near Kharkov the train stopped and a kindly guard allowed the girls to get off to get some milk for the baby. At a nearby hut they got milk and some food, but when they returned the train had left. The two girls wandered through the countryside. The narrator explains that, after being separated from her sister, she was taken in temporarily by a farming family.

Another description paints a line of deportees in Sumy oblast (northern Ukraine), stretching in both directions as far as the eye can see, continually swelling with people from new villages, on their way to a station to board a train that will take them to the Urals. Robert Conquest gives specific details of these deportee trains. He refers to a train with sixty-one wagons that on 26 May 1931 left Yantsenovo, a small station in Zaporizhia province (Ukraine), with three and a half thousand people on board, members of kulak families who arrived in Siberia on 3 June. Generally in each carriage, with little air and little light, there were about sixty people, who were poorly fed. Nicolas Werth in *A State against its People,* the first of five parts of *The Black Book of Communism, a* work already mentioned, written by several authors, writes that correspondence between the GPU and the People's Commissariat for Transport shows that convoys could be immobilised on a secondary road for weeks in temperatures of minus 20 degrees Celsius. There are letters signed by collectives of railway workers and employees, by citizens of Rostov, Omsk, Vologda and other marshalling yards, denouncing the "slaughter of innocents". According to various reports, sometimes up to 20% of the passengers, mostly young children, died during the journey. Alexander Solzhenitsyn refers to numerous stories in his *Gulag Archipelago.* In one of them, he tells how a Cossack mother gave birth to a baby inside a deportation wagon. The baby, as usual, died and two soldiers threw its body out of the moving train.

In reality, the arrival in the taiga or tundra could be worse than the journey. Conquest refers to some cases: at a destination for kulaks near Krasnoyarsk, there was no reception centre, just barbed wire and a few guards. Of the four thousand people deported there, about half had died within two months. In another camp near the Yenisei River in the Arctic Ocean, the kulaks lived in underground shelters. A German communist tells how in Kazakhstan, between Petropavlovsk and Lake Balkash, kulaks from the Ukraine and Central Russia walked in the open until they came to stakes driven into the ground with signs bearing only the number of the settlement. They were told to take care of themselves and began by digging holes in the ground. Camp No. 205 in the Siberian taiga near Kopeisk, south of Ekaterinburg, consisted of shacks built by the prisoners. The men were sent to saw wood or to the mines, where childless women were also sent. In November, the elderly, the sick and children under the age of 14 were forced to build huts for the winter. Their ration consisted of a quart of broth without substance and ten ounces of bread a day. Almost all the children died.

Forced collectivisation

One of the most important Russian intellectuals of the 19th century, Konstantin Leontiev, who died in 1891, warned of catastrophic revolutionary ideas entering Russia from the West. Leontiev, who advocated a cultural and territorial expansion of Russia eastwards, prophesied a bloody revolution in Russia led by an anti-Christ of a totalitarian nature that would be socialist: "Socialism is the feudalism of the future", Leontiev warned. In *The Harvest of Sorrow* Conquest claims that it was common among peasants to refer to communism as a "second serfdom" and alludes to official reports that reproduce verbatim complaints of peasants lamenting that they had been turned "into something worse than slaves". Conquest refers to a *Pravda* newspaper report of a silent meeting in a Ukrainian village where collectivisation has been approved. A crowd of women blocked the road and tractors soon arrived. Among other things it is shouted: "The Soviet government wants to return us to serfdom". Other Soviet reports contain the same denunciation: "You want to put us on collective farms so that we are your serfs and so that we perceive the local leaders as the masters".

The middle peasants, or subkulaks, were the ones who opposed it most fiercely; but also the poor peasants, who had managed to improve their social and economic status through hard work and effort, were mostly opposed to forced entry into the kolkhoz. The individualist peasants were stigmatised by the authorities as if they were criminals. From the early 1930s, threats, slander and coercion intensified. The range of coercive measures was varied: camouflaged people could be stationed in front of the recalcitrant peasants' houses; the postman could be ordered not to deliver mail to the "individualists"; their relatives could be refused medical care in medical centres; their children could be expelled from school; their grain could be refused to be milled in the mills; blacksmiths could even be pressured to refuse to work for them.

Stalin once told Churchill what happened between 1930-1931 in very similar terms to what is recorded in *The History of the Communist Party*. According to this official version, "the peasants drove the kulaks off the land, deskulakised it, confiscated their cattle and machinery, and asked the Soviet power to arrest and deport the kulaks". Obviously, this version, according to which collectivisation was a revolution carried out from above, but supported from below, has nothing to do with what happened. It is true that at first some peasants took advantage of the situation for revenge and settling of scores, or simply to indulge in plunder; but in general the peasant community opposed both deskulakisation and collectivisation. In fact, since Stolypin's time, the medium and small farmers had been asking for a bit of land in order to be able to work it and to progress, i.e., they aspired to become kulaks.

Compesino revolts against the government's forced collectivisation measures multiplied during the first months of 1930. According to official GPU figures, in January there were four hundred and two "mass demonstrations"; in February, one thousand forty-eight; and in March more than six thousand five hundred, of which more than eight hundred had to be "crushed by armed force". The forced collectivisation measures were to put an end for ever to the dream of millions of small and medium-sized farmers who did not want to join the kolkhoz, and were therefore subjected to expropriation and persecution, as had happened to the kulaks.

In the face of this massive peasant resistance, something unexpected happened. On 2 March 1930, *Pravda* and all the Soviet newspapers published a famous article by Stalin entitled "The Vertigo of Success". In it he condemned "the numerous violations of the principle of voluntariness in the membership of the peasants in the kolkhozes". According to Stalin, the local leaders, "drunk with success", had committed "excesses". Surprisingly, a passage in the text offered the possibility that in the future the peasants would be allowed to leave the collective farm if they so wished. Werth claims that the article had an immediate impact, and while mass uprisings continued in Ukraine, the North Caucasus and Kazakhstan, some five million peasants left the kolkhozes in the same month of March. For his part, Conquest attributes Stalin's article to protests from moderate sections of the Politburo and quotes Anastas Mikoyan as saying that the mistakes had "begun to undermine the loyalty of the farmers to the alliance of workers and peasants". Conquest adds that Stalin continued to denounce the coercive measures against the peasants in various articles and speeches, which prompted many local communists, startled by his reproaches, to try to suppress them and considered his attitude of offloading responsibility for the excesses onto local officials as wrong.

Normally, the peasants were convinced of the advantages of collective farms by means of assemblies and propaganda rallies. The next step was the arrival of a party envoy who asked who was against the kolkhoz and the plans of the Soviet government, but the peasants were also exhorted with imperative phrases: "You must enter the kolkhoz immediately. Whoever does not do so is an enemy of the Soviet regime". On the other hand, more than once *Pravda* had reported on the desertion of sceptical local communists who disagreed with the collectivisation campaign. On 28 February 1930, only two days before Stalin's article appeared, *Pravda* quoted the words of a young agricultural expert who had left the party after seven days in a village: "I do not believe in collectivisation. The pace is too fast. The party has taken a wrong turn. Let my words serve as a warning." Dissenting activists were generally arrested and accused of conspiring with the kulaks, for which they could be sentenced to two or three years in prison.

In April it seemed that Stalin's article would have a positive effect. Letters calling for a slower pace of collectivisation were sent to the local authorities. The collectivised peasants were allowed to have a cow, sheep and pigs of their own, as well as work tools for their own plots. In other words, as an incentive for the peasants to remain in the kolkhozes, they were allowed to keep their land, grow fruit and vegetables and keep their animals, provided they complied with the requirement to work certain days on the collective farm. Leaving the kolkhoz meant the loss of this right. They had to agree to work for the state at low wages as a condition for keeping their plots of land.

The formula amounted to a new type of feudalism in the sense prophesied by Leontiev. In place of the feudal lords of the castles, there were party plenipotentiaries, on whose willingness it depended whether or not the peasants were given facilities to leave the kolkhoz: once the land was seized, it was not so easy to set it aside again, and the possibilities of interpretation and enforcement of the decree were in the hands of the local gerifaltes. In general, the best lands were retained for the collective farm and the poor farmers were granted land with bushes, marshes and wastelands. Nevertheless, according to figures provided by various authors, during the months of March and April 1930 the amount of collectivised land fell from 50.3 per cent to 23 per cent and continued to fall until the autumn. Altogether nine million farmhouses left the collective farms. Where the greatest disbandment took place was in the Ukraine, and consequently the authorities accused those responsible of allowing the peasants to leave without having made sufficient efforts to dissuade them.

During 1930, according to GPU figures, some two and a half million peasants took part in about fourteen thousand revolts, riots and mass demonstrations against the regime. From the spring onwards, with the adoption of the above-mentioned measures, the agitation diminished and the uprisings became progressively less frequent. While in April 1930 the GPU recorded about two thousand cases of peasant disturbances, in June there were only about nine hundred riots, about six hundred in July, and only two hundred and fifty-six in August. In September 1930, however, the pressure on the individualist peasants was again increased, and demands were made for large quotas of grain and other products. In *Pravda* it was flatly asserted that the best way to force collectivisation was to make small individual farms unprofitable. The truth was, however, that despite the unfavourable conditions, the individual farms had done better than the kolkhozes in the 1930 harvest. Therefore, in its issue of 16 October 1930, the newspaper asked: "If the peasant can develop his own economy, why should he join the kolkhoz?" Thus in the autumn a new wave of deskulakisation took place, directed mainly against the peasants who had been the standard-bearers in the abandonment of the collective farms, who were again regarded as kulaks opposing collectivisation.

According to official figures provided by Naum Jasny in *The Socialized Agriculture of the USSR. Plans and Performance* (1949), the Government's demands for grain increased steeply during the years under consideration: in 1928-29 it obtained 10.8 million tons; in 1929-30, it increased the quota to 16.1; for the 1930-31 harvest the figure rose to 22.1 million tons; in 1931-32, the grain procurement was 22.8 million tons, i.e., the quantity doubled in three years. Whatever the conditions, these quantities had to be delivered to the state, and this requirement had to be fulfilled regardless of the food needs of the peasantry itself, which were not even taken into consideration.

A law of 16 October 1931 forbade the kolkhozes to set aside grain for their internal needs until the government's demands had been met. In the second half of 1931 meat also began to be collected by the same methods. Not only did these demands far exceed the possibilities of the peasants to replenish their stocks, but, thanks to the system of contracts with the collective farms, the produce was paid for at arbitrarily low prices. A decree of 6 May 1932 allowed private trade in grain once the state quotas had been met. Shortly afterwards, two further decrees, one of 22 August and the other of 2 December 1932, stipulated sentences of up to ten years in concentration camps for those who sold grain before they had complied with the state. To get an idea of the extent to which the peasants were being squeezed, it is useful to know that in 1933 the market prices of the products of forced delivery were 25 times higher than those paid by the government. This fact, of course, undermined the incentives of the collective farms to develop their socialised production. The system of compulsory delivery of meat, milk, butter, cheese, wool and other products was regulated in the same way as that of cereals by decrees of 23 September and 19 December 1932.

From exile, Leon Trotsky, despite his irreversible enmity towards Stalin, declared himself an enthusiastic supporter of collectivisation. In his *Problems of Development in the USSR* (1931) he wrote that collectivisation was "a new era in the history of man and the beginning of the end of idiocy in the countryside". However, faced with the unbearable circumstances of peasant life, many "idiotic", indeed desperate, peasants began to move en masse to the cities, causing the countryside to lose labour power at an accelerated rate. Christian Rakovsky, a Trotskyite Jew of Bulgarian origin deported to Central Asia in 1928, proposed in an article as a solution to the problem of the peasants' flight: "Can our proletarian government enact a law that would subject the poor peasants on collective farms to ". This suggestion met with an immediate response in the form of an "internal passport", introduced in December 1932, which effectively prohibited the kulaks and peasants from moving to the towns without permission. A law of 17 March 1933 stipulated that a peasant could not leave the collective farm and enter a town without a contract of employment from the employer, ratified by the kolkhoz authorities. The adoption of internal passports and the farmers' subjection to the land implied greater servitude than before the emancipation decreed in 1861 by Alexander II, the liberating tsar.

New attacks on priests and churches

In 1918 the property of the Churches, as well as that of the landowners, was nationalised without compensation. Clergymen and priests, considered "servants of the bourgeoisie", were deprived of their civil rights and were deprived of ration cards. Most of the ecclesiastical lands were linked to the parishes, whose parish priests gave work to the peasants or rented them out to them, although there were those who ploughed the land themselves. Almost all monasteries were closed and their property confiscated. With the NEP, however, there was a lull and the attacks on religion softened, even though Lenin had on numerous occasions shown his utter contempt for religiosity and the idea of God, which he considered "an indescribable and abominable vileness". In a letter to Maxim Gorky written in November 1913 Lenin had declared: "Millions of sins, disgusting deeds, acts of violence... are far less dangerous than the subtle, spiritual idea of God".

After the death of Patriarch Tikhon in April 1925, his temporary successors, Metropolitans Peter and Sergey, were sent to Siberia. Ten other temporary substitutes were also imprisoned until a pact was reached in 1927 that led to the release of Metropolitan Sergey. A year later, in the summer of 1928, a new anti-religious campaign began: the few remaining monasteries were closed and the monks were sent into exile. In April 1929 a law prohibited religious organisations from establishing assistance funds, organising meetings with parishioners, conducting excursions, opening libraries or reading rooms, providing medical or health care and other activities. In May 1929 the Commissariat for Education replaced the policy of no religious instruction in schools with that of teaching against religion.

In June 1929 a congress of the Union of Militant Atheists was held, and shortly afterwards the campaign was intensified throughout the country. In the civil war, Trotsky's orchestrated despoilment of the churches and murder of thousands of churchmen had been justified on the grounds that the church wealth would be used to alleviate that first famine which had caused five million deaths. During the years of deskulakisation and collectivisation the excuse for the attacks was solidarity and mutual protection between peasants and priests. From the point of view of the party, the church organised the agitation campaigns of the kulaks. For this reason, the priests were usually deported with the kulaks.

The same patterns of action as in 1921 were repeated between 1929 and 1931: opposition of the priest to the closure or destruction of the church, supportive support of the peasants, arrest and deportation, if not murder on the spot, of peasants and priests. Collectivisation usually involved the closure of the local church. Icons were routinely confiscated and then burned along with other objects of worship. Robert Conquest quotes a confidential letter from a Provincial Committee dated 20 February, which speaks of drunken soldiers and konsomols (young communists) "arbitrarily closing churches in the villages, breaking icons and threatening the peasants". At the end of 1929, under the pretext that they were needed for industry, a campaign was launched to requisition church bells. By January 1930, in the Pervomaysk district (north-west Ukraine) alone, one hundred and forty-eight church bells had been dismantled. A huge collective farm in the Urals proudly reported on 11 January that all the church bells in the area had gone to scrap and that a large number of icons had been burnt at Christmas. Interestingly, these actions were also criticised by Stalin in the famous letter of 2 March 1930, so that weeks later a resolution of the Central Committee spoke of "distortion" in the struggle for the kolkhozes and included a condemnation "for the administrative closing of churches without the consent of the majority of the people." As with collectivisation, there was a moderation in the campaign against the churches, but the pause was used to better organise the actions and from the autumn onwards it continued inexorably. By the end of 1930, 80% of the village churches had been closed.

The Moscow Academy of Sciences was forced to withdraw the protected status of all monuments that had any connection or could be associated with religious themes. Architects protested when even inside the Kremlin, on Moscow's Red Square, the Iversky Gates and the small Iversky Chapel in front of them, now rebuilt, were destroyed. Kaganovich, a Zionist who had belonged to "Poale Zion" and was the head of the party in Moscow, rejected criticism and went ahead with the destruction of monasteries and churches of priceless artistic and architectural value. One of his greatest feats in this respect was the blowing up of the Cathedral of Christ the Saviour in Moscow on 5 December 1931. On the same site Stalin and Kaganóvich had planned to build the Palace of the Soviets, a pharaonic project designed by the Jewish architect Boris Yofan. The palace was to be 415 metres high, topped by a seventy-metre, six-thousand-tonne statue of Lenin. The new Saviour of the Russian people, the alternative God for the international proletariat, had preached civil war, terror and the extermination of a social class; in other words, instead of loving one another, kill one another. Before the revolution there were in Moscow four hundred and sixty orthodox churches, of which only two hundred and twenty-four remained on January 1, 1930, and only about one hundred on January 1, 1933.

Particularly destructive was the action in Ukraine, which must be understood as a prologue to the genocide planned by Kaganóvich and his henchmen, which was to take place between 1932 and 1933. In Kiev, a church built in the 10th century, the Church of the Tithes (Desyatynna), the first church in the city, was destroyed along with other religious buildings erected between the 12th and 18th centuries. St. Sophia Cathedral in Kiev and other churches were converted into museums and barns. Of the hundreds of churches in Kiev, only two very small ones remained active in 1935. In Kharkov, Poltava and other cities, churches were used as warehouses for spare parts, cinemas, radio stations, and were even converted into public urinals. At the parish level, some 2,400 priests were arrested. There are records of 28 Ukrainian priests imprisoned in the prisons of Poltava (central Ukraine), of whom five were shot, one lost his mind and the others ended up in concentration camps. In 1931 the Mariupol Theological Seminary was converted into barracks for labourers, but a barbed-wire enclosure was set up around it, in which about 4,000 priests and some lay prisoners were imprisoned, forced to hard labour with little food, and some of them died every day. By the end of 1932 more than a thousand churches had been closed all over the Ukraine; but by the end of 1936 80% of the remaining ones were destroyed. Successive metropolitans of the Ukrainian Autocephalous Church died at the hands of the political police. Between 1928 and 1938 fourteen Ukrainian archbishops and bishops lost their lives in Soviet prisons. Some 1,500 priests and about 20,000 members of parishes and district churches ended their days in camps in the Gulag Archipelago.

The measures supposedly applied to all religions. The official decrees in the European part of the USSR expressly refer to "churches and synagogues". This was, of course, a phraseology to save face for the Judeo-Bolsheviks, all of whom were supposedly atheists. The crimes and persecutions mainly affected Orthodox Christians and Catholics. The persecution of Catholics in the USSR from the revolution until the Second World War is well documented in Irina Osipova's *If the World Hates You* (1998). Protestant Christians were harassed on another, much less destructive level. As for Judaism, no evidence has been found of either the destruction of synagogues or the persecution or murder of rabbis. Not even Rabbi Marvin S. Antelam, who time and again viciously denounces Shabbetaics, Freemasons, Frankists and Communists as part of the international conspiracy, offers a single example in *To Eliminate the Opiate*, a work whose title clearly alludes to the phrase attributed to Marx that religion is the opium of the people.

Holodomor: the ignored genocide of the Ukrainian peasants

In the previous chapter, in summarising the conditions in Russia before the catastrophic revolution financed by the Jewish bankers, an abbreviated account has already been given of the starvation of six to seven million people in Ukraine, a figure which the *Encyclopaedia Britannica* increases, estimating that between seven and eight million died. A crime against humanity that was finally recognised on 23 October 2008 by the European Parliament. The fact that in March of the same year the Ukrainian Parliament and nineteen other countries denounced to the world that the Soviet government had carried out a planned genocide forced the Strasbourg Chamber, the ineffective European Parliament, to issue a resolution. From then on, it was never heard of again and a wall of silence and oblivion settled over Europe and the world.

In June 2009 the Ukrainian authorities published a list of names of Soviet officials linked to the genocide. When it became clear that most of them were Jews, the leader of the Ukrainian Jewish Committee, a lawyer named Aleksander Feldman, was quick to warn those who sought to investigate that it was a farce to dig into the facts and publicise the case, since all the organisers of the extermination were already dead. In other words, while the UN calls on the Spanish Government to dig into the past and search for those possibly responsible for the crimes of Francoism, while hundreds of books and films annually grind international public opinion about the Jewish holocaust, while in various European countries researchers who question the imposed version and seek to revise the figures are imprisoned for thought crimes, while in Germany nonagenarians are persecuted and imprisoned for the terrible crime of having been guards in concentration or labour camps, Mr Feldman considers it ridiculous that Mr Feldman should be the only one to be held responsible for the crimes of the Franco regime, and that he is not the only one to be held responsible for the crimes of the Holocaust. Mr. Feldman finds it ridiculous that those guilty of an unprecedented mass murder are being singled out.

For his responsibility for the Ukrainian genocide and the atrocities of communism, Stalin, one of the greatest criminals in history, must be singled out; but it must be borne in mind, as will be seen from now on, that there is an enormous number of books which, since Lenin's death, lay all the crimes of communism on Stalin's shoulders, as if he alone were responsible for them. Most of them are written by Trotskyists or paid propagandists who seek to establish moral differences between Stalin and the untouchable Lenin and Trotsky, martyrs of internationalism who have always been venerated on the altars of the left. The genocide of the Ukrainian peasantry is one of these crimes usually attributed entirely to Stalin, although, in reality, the main perpetrator was Lazar Kaganóvich, who, after helping Stalin to stuff the Krupskaya's mouth and recover through her the money Lenin had deposited in Switzerland, became the grey eminence and was instrumental in the fight against Trotsky.

In addition to marrying Rosa Kaganóvich, years later Stalin strengthened his family ties with this Jewish family by marrying his daughter Svetlana to Mikhail Kaganóvich, son of Lazar Kaganóvich. On 15 July 1951 the *London Sunday Express* and other London newspapers reported the news and quoted the international Associated Press as a source. "Nuptials of Dictator's daughter cost a reported $900,000" was one of the headlines. Two other Jews played a key role alongside Kaganóvich in organising the famine. The first was Yakov Yakovlev (Epstein), who in 1922/23 had been head of the Agitation and Propaganda (Agit-Prop) section of the Russian Central Committee. Yakovlev was from 1929 Commissar of Agriculture, a post from which he promoted forced collectivisation. The second, Grigory Kaminsky, a Ukrainian like Kaganovich, became secretary of the Moscow State Committee in 1930.

Before beginning the account of events, it is necessary to recall the underlying background to the anti-Ukrainian animosity. The attacks on Ukraine and its national culture have been briefly discussed in footnote 6 of this chapter. The fact that on 28 January 1918 the Rada (Ukrainian Parliament) declared independence provoked a confrontation between the Bolshevik internationalists and the Ukrainian nationalists. Even then Lenin requisitioned all the grain and sent it to Russia. As the note explains, repression of language and culture led the Bolsheviks to close schools and cultural institutions, and even the head of the Cheka, the Jew Latsis, went so far as to shoot people for speaking Ukrainian. The constant changes of political colour during the civil war unleashed an ongoing repression in Ukraine that plunged the suffering Ukrainian population into permanent terror.

Lenin and Trotsky's phobia of Ukraine was fully inherited by Stalin and Kaganóvich, who as early as April 1929 launched a campaign through the OGPU against nationalist academics and intellectuals. In July some 5,000 members of the clandestine Ukrainian Liberation Union were arrested, and between 9 March and 20 April 1930 a public trial was staged in the Kharkov Opera House against 40 alleged members of the organisation. A linguist and lexicographer, Serhiy Yefremov, a federalist socialist who in the last days of tsarism had claimed Ukrainian identity, was the leading figure among the defendants. In February 1931 there was a new wave of arrests of intellectuals, mostly former revolutionary socialists, accused of having created the Ukrainian National Centre. This time there was no trial and almost all were sent to prison camps. Some authors consider these moves to crush the Ukrainian intelligentsia as the first assault preceding the all-out attack on the peasantry.

It was officially recognised that one of the aims of collectivisation in Ukraine was the "destruction of the social basis of Ukrainian nationalism". The Union for the Liberation of Ukraine was widespread in the villages, and many teachers and professors were shot for their links with it. Doctors and even some peasants were also executed, accused of belonging to the organisation. Stanislas Kossior, the alleged Trotskyite who was shot in 1939 and who in July 1928 had replaced Lazar Kaganóvich as head of the Ukrainian Communist Party, declared after the genocide that "the nationalist deviation in the party had played an exceptional role in the origin and deepening of the crisis in agriculture". Similarly, the head of the Kossior political police, Vsevolod Balitsky, another Trotskyite also executed in the context of the Great Purge on 27 November 1937, declared in 1933 that "the fist of the OGPU struck in two directions. First, at the kulak elements in the villages, and second, at the main centres of nationalism". The fact that resistance to collectivisation was greater in the Ukraine than in Russia was attributed to the fact that nationalist ideas had been instilled in the kulaks.

To understand how the starvation of so many millions of people could be organised, it must be borne in mind that forced collectivisation established new relations between the peasantry and the communist state. Under the NEP, the peasants only marketed a maximum of 20% of their harvest. They could set aside up to 15% for seed and up to 30% for livestock. The rest was for their own consumption. The collective farms were intended to ensure the delivery of agricultural products to the state, which were requisitioned every autumn. Each season became a struggle between the state and the peasants, who tried by all means to ensure their survival by keeping a reasonable share of the harvest for themselves. In 1930 the state demanded 30% of Ukraine's production, 38% of the harvest from the Kuban plains in the North Caucasus and 33% from Kazakhstan. In 1931 the season was much worse and production decreased, but the required percentages increased to 41.5%, 47% and 39.5% respectively. If one takes into account how the farmers distributed the harvest when the NEP was in force, it is easy to understand that the exorbitant demands of the state in 1931 would disrupt the entire production cycle. In 1932, faced with the prospect of famine, the kolkhoz farmers began to hide part of the harvest at. In *A state against its people* Nicolas Werth writes: "A real 'passive resistance front' was formed, strengthened by the tacit and reciprocal agreement that often went from the kolkhoz to the brigade commander, from the brigade commander to the accountant, from the accountant to the head of the kolkhoz, from the head of the kolkhoz to the local party secretary. The central authorities had to send 'shock brigades' recruited in the city to seize the grain."

On 7 August 1932, despite the fact that even then reports had reached the Kremlin about the existence of "a real threat of famine even in districts where the harvest had been excellent", a law of unhappy memory was promulgated for the people, who christened it the "law of the ears of corn". It provided for the death penalty or sentences of up to ten years in labour camps "for any theft or squandering of socialist property". Incredible as it may seem, those who had promised to free the Russian people from slavery were prepared to sentence a person to death for stealing a few ears of wheat or barley from a field in the kolkhoz. This law stipulated that all collective farm property, such as livestock and grain, was considered "sacred and inviolable" property of the state. In application of the law, from August 1932 to December 1933, more than 125,000 people were convicted, 5,400 of whom received death sentences.

In *The Harvest of Sorrow*, a seminal work for an in-depth study of the Holodomor, R. Conquest refers to stories in the Ukrainian press reporting on executions of kulaks who "systematically rationed grain". In the province of Kharkov five courts of justice heard fifty such cases, and in the province of Odessa the same happened. Here are a few cases in brief: In the village of Kopani, in the Dniepropetrovsk province, a gang of kulaks and subkulaks cut a hole in the floor of a granary and stole wheat: two of them were executed and the rest imprisoned. In Verbka, another village in the same province, the chairman of the local Soviet and a deputy, as well as three chairmen of kolkhozes and eight kulaks were tried: three kulaks were sentenced to death. A farmer from Novoseltytsya (Zhytomyr province) was shot for being in possession of twelve kilos of wheat, collected in the field by his ten-year-old daughter. A woman whose husband had starved to death two weeks earlier was sentenced to ten years for cutting 100 ears of corn from her own field. A father of four received the same sentence for the same offence. Another woman was also sentenced to ten years for picking ten onions from collective land. Another ten-year sentence was justified for "stealing" potatoes.

Despite the terror, the state did not receive the quantities of grain demanded, so on 22 October 1932 Vyacheslav Molotov was sent to the Ukraine and Lazar Kaganóvich to the Caucasus. Both headed two extraordinary commissions whose aim was to speed up the harvests. Kaganóvich arrived in Rostov-on-Don on 2 November. Gendrij Yagoda (Hirsh Yehuda), who exercised de facto control of the secret police (OGPU), was part of his commission. Yagoda, People's Commissar for Internal Affairs from 10 July 1934 to 26 September 1936, established himself at the head of the OGPU/NKVD as one of the greatest criminals of the 20th century. Kaganóvich summoned all the district party secretaries in the North Caucasus region. It was decided to force the local party organisations to act against the "counter-revolutionary kulaks" and to "annihilate the resistance of the local communists and kolkhoz chairmen who had placed themselves at the head of the sabotage".

For the districts placed on the "black list", N. Werth cites these measures: "withdrawal of all products from the warehouses, total suppression of trade, immediate reimbursement of all current credits, exceptional imposition and arrest of all 'saboteurs', 'alien elements', and 'counter-revolutionaries' following an accelerated procedure, under the direction of the GPU. In case of further 'sabotage' the population would be liable to mass deportation." In November 1932 alone, five thousand rural communists, accused of "collaborating with sabotage", and fifteen thousand kolkhozsians were already arrested. In December the mass deportations of kulaks and whole populations of Cossacks, whose villages, "stanitsas", had already suffered the same measures in 1920-21, began. In the Ukraine, too, the Molotov commission drew up a "black list" of districts which did not deliver the required grain quotas, and the same measures were taken.

With the ban on trade and following the requisitioning of goods from the warehouses ordered by Kaganóvich, including grain that was kept as a reserve for seed, supplies in the Ukraine were running low. In November 1932 there were peasant revolts and cases of dissolution of the kolkhozes. Not all the grain had been exported abroad or sent to the cities or to the army. The local granaries had stocks, state reserves for emergencies, such as war. However, it was clear that famine was not considered an emergency. The peasants were furious to learn that, while they were starving, there was grain that could be used for their sustenance. In Poltava province, for example, the warehouses were known to be full to bursting. Milk was processed into butter in plants near villages where people were dying of starvation. The butter was packaged and the paper was marked in English: "USSR butter for export".

There were still peasants who remembered the famines of the time of Nicholas II. The authorities had helped them then. The peasants went to the cities to beg for help "in the name of God". Kitchens where hot soup was served and students contributed donations received through collections had been set up. It was incomprehensible that the self-styled government of the workers and peasants had the possibility to help the starving and did not do so. There were, of course, peasants who twenty-five years earlier had known about the land reform decree of November 1906, by which Stolypin had given the peasants title to the plots of land they had worked in the communes. This historic decree had become law in June 1910.

The fact that the Ukrainian-Russian border was blocked in order to prevent food from entering Ukraine is irrefutable proof that Holodomor was a planned criminal decision. Troops were deployed along the border to prevent Ukrainians from crossing into Russia. At stations and on trains, OGPU men checked passengers and their travel permits. Mikhaylivka, the last station between Kiev and the border, was taken over by armed OGPU detachments. Those without special passes were detained and sent back to Kiev in freight trains. Everyone in Ukraine knew that things were different in Russia, so some people risked their lives to cross the border. Those who managed to circumvent the blockade and get through tried to sell or trade carpets, linen or their fur coats in order to get food for their starving families. Especially cruel was the return after so much sacrifice, as grain and food was confiscated from those who tried to bring it into Ukraine.

Robert Conquest cites the example of a Ukrainian peasant who had been hired to work on the Moscow railways. On learning of the plight of his relatives, he left the Russian capital with some thirty-five kilos of bread. In Bakhmach, at the border, thirty-two kilos were confiscated and, thanks to the fact that he was registered as a Russian worker, he was allowed to keep the rest. However, two Ukrainian peasant women who were also trying to smuggle bread into their country were arrested and everything was seized. Sometimes people with bread hid in empty wagons returning to Ukraine after having unloaded Ukrainian grain in Russia; but these trains were also checked, either by officials who confiscated and arrested, or by employed personnel who often blackmailed the unfortunates who had been discovered. Conquest draws the following conclusion from this: "The bottom line is that there were in fact clear orders to stop peasants entering Russia where food was available, and to confiscate food from those who had managed to circumvent the controls and return with it. This can only have been an order from above: and it can only have had one motive." There were hungry peasants who tried to enter the areas near the border with Poland and Romania, but the police did not allow them to do so either. Some of the most desperate who tried to cross the Dniester River into Romania were shot by members of the OGPU.

As winter approached, things got worse and worse. On 20 November 1932, a decree of the Ukrainian Government stopped, until the required quota of grain had been delivered, any shipment of grain to the kolkhoz peasants in payment for their work. On 6 December the Central Committee of the Communist Party of Ukraine and the Soviet Government of Ukraine by decree singled out six villages in three provinces (two in Odessa, two in Kharkov and two in Dnipropetrovsk) for sabotage of grain deliveries. They were immediately punished by suspension of supplies, cancellation of any trade with the state, and requisitioning of all supplies from the cooperative and state warehouses. In addition, the purge of those elements considered hostile and counter-revolutionary from all collective farms in the above-mentioned villages was carried out. The next step was the blockade of the villages which had not been able to deliver the quotas in order to prevent products from the towns from entering them. On 15 December 1932, a list was even published of all the districts which had been penalised by the interruption of the delivery of commercial products until they had achieved a substantial improvement in the fulfilment of the grain collection plans. Out of three hundred and fifty-eight districts across Ukraine, eighty-eight were penalised and many of their inhabitants were deported en masse to the north.

Despite all the measures, by the end of 1932 the tons of grain delivered were only seventy percent of what had been planned.

Various sources refer to large movements of up to three million people, who as early as the beginning of the summer of 1932 were trying to move to more prosperous areas. The stations were crowded with people from the countryside seeking to enter the cities. Victor Serge gives this description:

> "Grimy crowds fill the stations, men, women and children huddled together, waiting for God knows what trains. They are shooed away, and they try again without money or tickets. They get on the first train they can and stay inside until they are pulled out. They are silent and passive. Where do they go? Only in search of bread, potatoes or work in the factories where the workers are better fed? Bread is the great mobiliser of these masses. What can I say about the robberies? People steal everywhere, everywhere...".

The entry of starving peasants into the towns became almost impossible after 27 December 1932, when the government introduced the internal passport and the compulsory registration of town dwellers in order to "liquidate social parasitism" and "combat the infiltration of kulak elements into the towns". The real intention of the internal passport was to prevent the exodus of starving peasants trying to save their lives by entering the big cities.

At the beginning of 1933 new exactions were announced and a new inhuman assault was made on the already non-existent Ukrainian reserves. On January 7, 1933, an editorial in the daily *Pravda* declared that the Ukraine had failed in grain deliveries because the Ukrainian Communist Party allowed the organisation of the class enemy in the Ukraine. At a plenum of the Central Executive Committee in the same month of January Stalin said that the causes of the difficulties in the grain collection were to be sought within the party itself. Kaganóvich presented a report in which he insisted that in the villages there were still representatives of the kulak class who had not been deported and kulaks who had escaped from exile and were being protected by their relatives and, occasionally, by "sympathetic party members, who in fact behaved as traitors to the interests of the workers". He also denounced that there were still "representatives of the white bourgeoisie, the Cossacks and the rural intelligentsia". Related to the latter, he singled out teachers, agricultural engineers and experts, doctors, etc., as targets of an anti-Soviet purge. Once again Kaganóvich called for a struggle against the class enemy. He laid particular stress on the kulaks, whom he accused of "sabotaging sowing and grain deliveries". According to his report, the kulaks had taken advantage of the "petty-bourgeois tendencies of the peasants" and he accused them of "terrorising the honest workers of the kolkhozes".

On 22 January 1933, a circular signed by Stalin and Molotov was issued which put the final nail in the coffin of millions of starving people. It called on the local authorities and the OGPU to prohibit "by all means the mass marches of peasants from the Ukraine and the North Caucasus to the cities". It also ordered that counter-revolutionary elements be arrested and that the other fugitives be taken to their places of residence. Nicolas Werth, who partially transcribed the text, quotes the terms used in the circular: "The Central Committee and the government have proof that this mass exodus of peasants is organised by the enemies of Soviet power, counter-revolutionaries and Polish agents for the purpose of propaganda against the kolkhoz system in particular and Soviet power in general. In application of the circular, the sale of railway tickets was immediately suspended and police cordons controlled by the OGPU were set up to prevent the peasants from leaving their districts.

Mortality was very high throughout the winter, but it was from March 1933 onwards that mortality was on a large scale in the camps. Typhus was added to famine, so that there were villages with thousands of inhabitants in which only a few dozen survived. Numerous testimonies are available. An Italian historian, Andrea Graziosi, published in 1989 in *Cahiers du Monde Russe et Sovietique* a series of letters written in Kharkov by Italian diplomats. These are reports written between 1932-1934. The following report by the Italian consul appears in *The Black Book of Communism*:

> "Since a week ago, a reception service for abandoned children has been set up. Indeed, there are more and more peasants who flow into the city because they have no hope of survival in the countryside, there are children who have been brought here and who are immediately abandoned by their parents, who return to their village to die there. The latter hope that in the city someone will take care of their children. [...] For a week now, the 'dvorniki' (doormen) in white coats have been mobilised to patrol the town and take the children to the nearest police station. [Around midnight they begin to be transported by lorry to the Severo Donetz goods station. Here, the children found at the stations or on the trains, the families of the peasants, the isolated older people, are also gathered. [...] There are medical personnel who do the 'selection'. Those who have not swollen and offer a chance of survival are directed to the Golodnaya Gora barracks, where in hangars, on straw, a population of about 8,000 souls, composed mainly of children, is dying in agony. [...] The bloated people are transported by goods train to the countryside and abandoned fifty to sixty kilometres from the city, so that they die unseen. [...] On arrival at the unloading sites, large pits are dug and the dead are removed from the wagons."

While local party and OGPU elites survived the famine well fed, reports from the OGPU itself point to cases of cannibalism, some of which are recounted in Conquest's work, such as families feeding on their own dead, or starving people trapping children or ambushing strangers. A party activist who had worked in the collectivisation campaign in Siberia returned to Ukraine in 1933 to find that the population of his village had almost died out. Her younger brother told her that they survived on bark and grass, but that their mother had told them they must eat it if she died. These cases of cannibalism are also reported by Italian diplomats serving in Kharkov:

> "Every night about 250 corpses of people who have died of starvation or typhus are brought to Kharkov. It is noticeable that many of them no longer have a liver: it seems to have been removed through a wide cut. The police eventually catch some of the mysterious 'amputees' who confess that they used this meat to make a substitute for 'pirozhki' (dumplings), which they immediately sell on the market".

The geographical area of the famine, to which foreign press correspondents were not allowed to travel until the autumn of 1933, covered the Ukraine, the rich plains of the Don, the Kuban and the North Caucasus, as well as part of Kazakhstan. As already mentioned in the abbreviated review in the previous chapter, in the spring of 1933 the death toll reached twenty-five thousand people a day. The most aberrant thing is that while millions of peasants starved to death during that year, the Soviet Government continued to export abroad eighteen million quintals of wheat for the "needs of industrialisation".

In eastern Ukraine, the plains of the Don and Kuban rivers were inhabited by Cossacks and Ukrainian peasants. The Don Cossacks were Russian, but the Kuban Cossacks were of Ukrainian origin. It has already been seen that during the civil war the Cossacks had mostly fought against the Bolsheviks. Subsequently, there were uprisings in 1922 and 1928. As early as November 1929, several divisions had been deployed in the Don to reinforce the North Caucasus Military District. Unlike the peasant villages, the Cossack "stanitsas" were settlements that could have more than 40,000 inhabitants, so they could not be controlled by a handful of policemen. The Cossacks' struggle against collectivisation was bitter, and the effects of the famine were felt there later than in other areas. After the visit of the Kaganovich and Yagoda commission in November 1932, the Don and the Kuban were declared special military emergency zones.

In Poltavskaya, a stanitsa in the Kuban Delta that had been blacklisted for sabotage, an uprising broke out. The rebels murdered party activists and members of the NKVD (which was part of the OGPU) and temporarily controlled the town, which could only be recaptured after heavy fighting. By January 1933 a special commission was operating with powers to impose forced labour and to evict, deport and even execute those who resisted. It was announced that Poltavskaya had fallen into the hands of the kulaks and that all but a faithful few would be exiled. Once a state of war was declared, an exemplary operation was carried out and publicised so that everyone would know what to expect. Similar actions were undertaken in Umanskaya, Urupskaya, Medveditskaya, Mishativskaya and so on. Some 200,000 inhabitants of sixteen stanitsas were deported to the far north; but the fate of those not deported was even worse, for they had to face starvation. Various testimonies report that there were so many dead in the Kuban that they could no longer be buried. One witness tells of groups of children huddled on street corners, shivering with hunger and cold, and eventually dying in the streets. A description by an engineer who worked on the railways gives an idea of the extent of the slaughter in the area:

> "At the beginning of 1933 two mysterious trains left every morning before dawn from Kavkaz station in the North Caucasus in the direction of Mineralny Vodi and Rostov. The trains were empty and had five to ten carriages each. Two to four hours later the trains would return. They stopped for a while at a staging station and then continued along a dead-end spur to an old excavation site. While the trains stopped at Kavkazka or on a side track, all the wagons were locked, looked loaded and were closely guarded by NKVD agents. At first no one paid any attention to the mysterious trains and neither did I. I was still a student at the Institute. I was still a student at the Moscow Transport Institute and worked there temporarily. But one day, the conductor Kh., who was a communist, quietly called me and led me to the trains, saying: 'I want to show you what is in the carriages'. He opened the door of one of the carriages slightly, I looked inside and almost fainted from the horror I saw. It was full of bodies, piled up in all sorts of ways. Later the engineer told me the story: 'the stationmaster had secret orders from his superiors to comply with the requirements of the NKVD and to have two trains with empty freight cars ready every morning. The crews of the trains were guarded by NKVD agents. The trains departed to collect the bodies of peasants who had died of famine and had been taken to railway stations near the villages. The bodies were buried in remote areas beyond the excavations. The whole area was guarded by the NKVD and no one was allowed to approach."

The cities of the North Caucasus suffered severely from the consequences of the famine. For Stavropol, a city with a population of 140,000, the death toll is given as 50,000. In Krasnodar, with a population of 140,000, the death toll was 40,000. In Starokorsunska, a stanitsa of 14,000 inhabitants, only a thousand remained after the famine. Two other stanitsas, Voronizka and Dinska, had similar figures. A dispatch from the British Embassy dated 27 October 1933 summed up the situation with these words: "the Cossack element has been largely eliminated, either by death or deportation".

In R. Conquest's work, which is one of the main sources for this section on the genocide in Ukraine, a chapter entitled *Children* is devoted to a study of the effects of the famine on children. It recounts cases of mothers dying in the streets with their children on their chests, or of seven, eight and nine year olds witnessing the death of their parents and having to try to survive on their own. However, the opposite was the norm, i.e. the children died first. In 1933 the Lithuanian ambassador in Moscow denounced in a report that in the Ukraine the corpses of children could not be found because "the peasants themselves confessed that they ate the flesh of dead children". M. Maskudov, a dissident Soviet demographer, estimates that no less than three million children born between 1932 and 1934 died during the famine. The first to die were mostly newborns.

Based on the 1970 census, Conquest points to significant figures. In 1970 there were 12.4 million people born between 1929-31; yet there were only 8.4 million born between 1932-34. Data from areas where hardship was most severe show the havoc that famine wreaked on children: in some villages only one child in ten survived. Specific figures from one district of Poltava province show that of the 7,113 people who died, 3,549 were children under the age of eighteen, 2,163 were men, and 1,401 were women. Conquest assumes without any doubt the figure of three million dead children and adds a million more, those who lost their lives because of the inhuman conditions of deskulakisation, so that, according to his estimates, a total of more than four million children died. He notes, moreover, that this figure does not include many children whose lives were ruined and who survived for years as best they could.

Many of these abandoned children ("bezprizornii") formed gangs of petty criminals. Some sources confirm that as early as 1932 confidential orders were given to shoot those who stole from passing trains stopped at stations. This problem of flocks of feral children did not diminish after the famine, so that the possibility of physically eliminating them, sometimes by shooting, continued to be present from 1934 onwards. Finally, on 7 April 1935, by a decree signed by Kalinin and Molotov, the execution of children from the age of twelve was legalised, yet another brutality of the communist criminals in power in Moscow. Sometimes even younger children were allowed to be executed. In the orphanages where the little criminals were interned, some doctors could certify that eleven-year-olds were actually older than their supposedly forged papers testified, for which they could be sentenced to death. In his eagerness to denigrate Stalin, Trotskyite Walter Krivitsky accuses him of purging even children and confirms that the heading of the decree alluded to "measures to combat criminality among minors." Krivitsky denounces that while thousands of children and young people were sentenced to forced labour and often to the death penalty, Stalin decided to take pictures with children in order to present himself "as the godfather of the children of Russia".

Conquest's total figures for the genocide are as follows: 11 million peasants died between 1930-1937, to which he adds 3.5 million people who were arrested during these years and subsequently died in labour camps. The breakdown he gives of the circumstances of the deaths of these 14.5 million people is as follows: Killed as a result of the brutality with which deskulakisation was carried out, 6.5 million. Killed in the processes of deskulakisation and collectivisation of Kazakhstan, as well as in the subsequent famine, 1 million. Famine deaths in 1932-33: 5 million in Ukraine; 1 million in the North Caucasus; 1 million elsewhere. According to this author, this is a conservative estimate, i.e. a low estimate, which certainly does not reflect the truth. These figures come from various works by Soviet scholars and writers, because in 1986, when *The Harvest of Sorrow* was published, Moscow still did not allow the investigation of the criminal acts perpetrated against millions of people.

Aware of their crimes, the Soviets tried to conceal from Western countries the slaughter they were carrying out and, once it had been perpetrated, even denied that it had taken place. However, despite the fact that potential witnesses were barred from the famine areas, word of what was happening in the USSR got out in both Europe and America. Newspapers such as the *New York Herald Tribune, Manchester Guardian, Daily Telegraph, Le Matin, Le Figaro, Neue Züriche Zeitung, Gazette de Laussana, La Stampa* and others of lesser repute published more or less adequate reports. However, there were many accomplices who, consciously or unconsciously, collaborated in concealing the truth. One such case is that of Édouard Herriot, a radical socialist who served three terms as Prime Minister of France. During August and September 1933 Herriot visited the USSR and spent five days in the Ukraine, where he was treated to banquets and other entertainments. He was given a tour of previously "tidied up" areas. His conclusion was that there had been no famine in Ukraine and he attributed the allegations heard in France to anti-Soviet propaganda. On 13 December *Pravda* published his statements, according to which Herriot "categorically denied the lies of the bourgeois press about the famine in the Soviet Union".

The scandalous actions of Walter Duranty, the Moscow correspondent of *The New York Times*, deserves a separate paragraph. In his eagerness to conceal the truth, he intentionally lied over and over again in his reports from Moscow and thus became an accomplice to the genocide. Why he did so is obvious. The role played by *The New York Times*, whose owner, Adolph Simon Ochs, a Zionist Jew in the service of the bankers who imposed the Federal Reserve, had married his daughter to Arthur Hans Sulzberger, another Jew who has since come to control the paper, has already been discussed several times. Since the bankers who had devised the Federal Reserve were the same ones who had financed the Bolshevik Revolution, it is easy to understand that Walter Duranty was in the service of the conspirators, who had just put Franklin Delano Roosevelt in the White House and had among their priorities that the new president should recognise the Soviet Union as soon as possible.

Another journalist who had the courage to report the truth, Malcolm Muggeridge, correspondent for the *Manchester Guardian*, accused Duranty of being "the biggest liar of any journalist I have known in fifty years of journalism". The impact of Walter Duranty's reporting on American public opinion Duranty's reports could not be countered. To ensure Duranty's prestige, he was awarded the Pullitzer Prize in 1932 for his laudatory articles on the Soviet Union. In November 1932, he reported that "there was neither famine nor any sign that there would be one". On 23 August 1933, he wrote: "any information about famine in Russia today is either an exaggeration or malicious propaganda". According to Duranty, it was emigrants who, encouraged by Hitler's rise to power, "told false stories about famines, which were circulated in Berlin, Riga, Vienna and other places where the enemies of the Soviet Union, describing the USSR as a country of ruin and despair, were making last-minute attempts to avoid recognition by the United States".

The curious thing about the Walter case Duranty is that in private he had no qualms about admitting the truth. According to Conquest, Duranty confessed to Jewish journalist Eugene Lyons, a correspondent for UPI (United Press International), that he estimated the number of famine victims to be around seven million. Lyons, a communist who initially worked for the Soviet agency TASS, also initially concealed the terror of the famine, but years later, disillusioned, he was able to rectify the situation and acknowledged the facts. Walter Duranty, then, wrote exactly the opposite of what he knew, which demonstrates the chutzpah and duplicity of the flamboyant Pulitzer Prize winner. Conquest quotes verbatim these words written on 30 September 1933 by the British chargé d'affaires in Moscow: "According to Mr. Duranty, the population of the North Caucasus and the lower Volga has fallen by about three million in the last year, and the population of the Ukraine by four or five million.... Mr. Duranty believes it is possible that during the past year as many as ten million people have died, directly or indirectly from food shortages in the Soviet Union".

Knowing full well that Holodomor had been a planned event and that the criminals who ran the Soviet Union had intentionally exterminated millions of human beings, on November 16, 1933, just after the genocide had been perpetrated, Franklin Delano Roosevelt, the illuminati Freemason who in 1935 approved the introduction of the one dollar note plastered with Freemasonry symbols, established diplomatic relations with the USSR as if nothing had happened.

PART 6
THE MOSCOW TRIALS AND
THE PURGE OF TROTSKYISM

While the Nuremberg trials have gone down in history as a necessary event and enjoy an embarrassing prestige, the Moscow trials are today utterly discredited. The need to lay all the atrocities of communism on Stalin's shoulders has led historians and propagandists of all kinds to proclaim that the trials were a "show", a macabre spectacle staged by Stalin. This is explained by the aim of concealing who Trotsky was and by the need to maintain in the eyes of the new international left the halo of the figures of Lenin and Trotsky himself, who through his dishonest writings was able to impose his version of the Revolution on naive or blind socialists.

In reality, the "show trial" took place in Nuremberg, where the victors, including the now reviled Stalin, gave themselves a moral superiority they did not have to judge the vanquished: Dresden, Hamburg, Hiroshima, Nagasaki are glaring examples of war crimes unparalleled in history for which no one has ever been held accountable. At Nuremberg, evidence was massively falsified and the work of lawyers was obstructed at every turn. The prosecution was largely composed of Jews who had emigrated from Germany, and witnesses who could have favoured the defendants and compromised the prosecutors were prevented from coming forward. Lawyers were unable to examine the prosecutors' evidence and had to hand over their documents to the prosecutors. In 1948 Britain's chief prosecutor, Sir Hartley Shawcross, declared: "The Nuremberg trial has become a farce, I am ashamed to have been an accuser at Nuremberg as a colleague of these men, the Russians. American judge Wennerstrum, who resigned from office, declared that his participation in the Nuremberg infamy was a disgrace to him and to American justice. Torture of the accused, which in the case of the Moscow trials is invoked again and again to discredit them, was routinely practised in the German trial.

Many Jewish writers have devoted themselves to proclaiming the innocence of those convicted in the Moscow trials. On the other hand, Trotskyist historians like Pierre Broué and so many others ignore or prefer to ignore what Trotsky really stood for. Robert Conquest, the Sovietologist whom we shall continue to quote, does not make the slightest allusion to the financiers of Trotsky and the Bolshevik revolution either. In his exposition and analysis of the facts, Conquest does not take into account the fact that the Soviet Union had been a work of international Jewry. This is a serious problem, for only by considering who was behind Trotsky can one get a proper picture of the significance of Stalin's purges and other capital events that eventually triggered the Second World War. We cannot disregard this fundamental circumstance which we have been denouncing throughout our work and, for this reason, we will continue to contemplate it in the following pages. In other words, it cannot be forgotten that Trotsky represented the international conspirators who sought World Government and that Stalin, having opted for national communism, had become an impediment which, initially, had to be removed at any price.

Since the Soviet Union was the work of international Jewry, thousands of Jews occupied, as we know, the leading positions. Many of them, especially in finance, diplomacy, the police and the army, were Trotskyites whom Stalin needed to control, since they were a threat to him: as long as Trotsky was alive, his restoration to power was the main objective. The existence of an opposition coordinated by Trotsky from abroad is admitted by historians and cannot be denied. Murder and terror were the antidotes used by Stalin to combat the Trotskyist opponents, to whom he applied the same medicine that Lenin and Trotsky had previously prescribed for class enemies, considered "enemies of the people". Stalin, as will be seen, proved to be a Machiavellian, cruel politician of unequalled cunning, who exercised the monopoly of violence without any scruple or consideration, in an absolutely ruthless manner.

The fact that Stalinist purges were gradually displacing Jews and putting more Russians in power led to accusations of anti-Semitism, but in fact Stalin had no problem surrounding himself with Jews as long as they helped him fight his political enemies. In 1946, just after the end of the war, the United States presented Stalin with a new plan for World Government that had been sketched out by two Jews, David Lilienthal and the celebrated Bernard Baruch. This proposal saw the light of day in the pages of *The Bulletin of Atomic Scientists* and was based on the monopoly of atomic violence. The Jewish scientists who supported the World Government: Albert Einstein, Robert Oppenheimer, Leo Szilard, Walter Lippman, Niels Bohr, James Franck, Eugene Rabinovitch, Hy Goldsmith, Hans Bethe and Harold Urey came from international socialism and Zionism. Stalin again refused to submit, and for the third time in his thirty years of dictatorship he was again accused of anti-Semitism. Finally, as will be seen in another chapter, he was assassinated in 1953.

To begin the account of the events leading up to the Moscow trials, let us recall first of all that the Trotskyist opposition fragmented for tactical reasons after the failure of the attempts to displace Stalin, and thus various subdivisions took place. It has already been seen that in the autumn of 1927 the Trotsky and Zinoviev bloc, defeated in the internal struggle within the party, tried to mobilise the masses, which was a challenge to Stalin, who was not satisfied until he succeeded in expelling them from the party. Zinoviev was later readmitted, but Trotsky was eventually deported with his most loyal followers. It was not until 1930 that another attempt was made to challenge Stalin. Then Martemyan Ryutin, a man from Bukharin's entourage, was accused of producing a document of some 200 pages, rediscovered and printed in the Gorbachev era. The text consisted of thirteen chapters, four of which attacked Stalin, who, as Trotsky had done years earlier, was accused of being "the gravedigger of the Revolution".

It was believed that a group ("Ryutin Platform") had formed around Ryutin that was plotting against Stalin. On 30 September Ryutin was expelled from the party and shortly afterwards arrested. However, on 17 January 1931 he was acquitted and it was subsequently decided that he would be reinstated. At a Politburo meeting in the spring of 1931 Stalin called for the death penalty to be applied to party members. Until then, all kinds of opponents had been killed at will, but the Bolsheviks did not apply the death penalty among themselves. Apparently, in order to prevent the revolution from devouring its children, as in the case of the French Revolution, Lenin had asked that party members not be executed.

Instead of accepting the defeat of their theses, in June 1932 Ryutin and a group of emboldened officials called for a conference of the Union of Marxist-Leninists. In this new document it was pointed out that Stalin and his clique would not give in voluntarily and should be removed by force as soon as possible. Stalin interpreted these words as a call for his assassination, and on 23 September 1932 Ryutin was arrested again. Stalin would have wished to eliminate this avowed adversary without further contemplation; but the matter was discussed in the Politburo, where Sergei Kirov argued against his death sentence and was supported by Ordzhonikidze, Kúibyshev, Kossior, Kalinin and Rudzutak. Molotov was hesitant, and only Kaganóvich supported Stalin's claims, who had to abide by the majority decision. Nevertheless, at the Control Commission of the Central Committee, which met between 28 September and 2 October, it was decided to expel Ryutin's group from the party. They were accused of being "degenerates who had become enemies of communism and the Soviet regime, traitors to the party and the working class". Ryutin was sentenced to ten years in prison and twenty-nine members of his platform received lesser sentences.

Another resolution adopted by the plenum was the expulsion from the party of those who knew of the existence of the counter-revolutionary group and had not given notice; among these were Zinoviev and Kamenev, who were again expelled and deported to the Urals. Shortly afterwards Ivan Smirnov, who had recently been readmitted to the party, was also arrested and sentenced to ten years' imprisonment. Trotskyist professor Vadim Rogovin, author of several books on Stalin, admitted in a lecture at the University of Melbourne on 28 May 1996 that in 1931 Smirnov had established contacts in Berlin with Trotsky's son Leon Sedov, with whom he had agreed on the need to coordinate efforts. Two others sentenced to five-year terms were Ivar Smilga and Sergei Mrachkovsky. On 12 January 1933 the Plenum of the Central Committee resolved to proceed with a severe purge within the party, suggesting that the ramifications of the Ryutin affair were serious and continued to trouble Stalin. Throughout 1933 more than eight hundred thousand members were expelled and another three hundred and forty thousand were expelled during 1934.

Evidence that the Trotskyite opposition was involved in this plot to unseat Stalin can be found in the book by General Walter Krivitsky, head of the Military Secret Service in Western Europe, who before his assassination in 1941 published *In Stalin's Secret Service (*1939) in New York, a book published in Spain by NOS under the title *Yo, jefe del Servicio Secreto Militar soviético (*1945). Krivitsky, a Jewish Trotskyite whose real name was Samuel Gérshevich Ginsberg, writes in the aforementioned work that the secretary of the Party cell within the Military Secret Service Department (a Trotskyite, of course) summoned him to "a secret meeting at which our chief, General Berzin, was to report on the Ryutin affair". Krivitsky points out that, since this was highly confidential, other members of the cell (evidently non-Trotskyists) did not attend the meeting. Krivitsky admits that Berzin, who was to be purged in 1938, read them extracts from Ryutin's underground programme "in which Stalin was described as a great agent provocateur, a destroyer of the party and a gravedigger of the revolution in Russia". Berzin confirmed to them at that meeting that "Ryutin's group intended to fight for the overthrow of Stalin as head of the Party and the Government"[13].

The Kirov assassination

It is a universally accepted fact that the assassination of Sergei Mironovich Kostrovich, alias Kirov, was the event that served as the trigger for Stalin's purges against the Trotskyists. Once again Robert Conquest is the main investigator of what happened and is thus an unavoidable source of information, although not always convincing. Conquest presented his conclusions in *Stalin and the Kirov Murder* (1989); but also in *The Great Terror. A Reassessment* (1990) devotes a chapter to the analysis of the famous assassination, which, according to him, "deserves to be called the crime of the century", since during the next four years the most conspicuous leaders of the Revolution were shot for their responsibility in the crime and

---

[13] Krivistky himself acknowledges in his book that at the end of 1938, thanks to the help of Léon Blum, President of the French Council of Ministers, and his Minister of the Interior, Max Dormoy, both Jews like himself, he managed to flee France, where he was being harassed by the NKVD. Once in the United States, assisted by another Jew, the journalist Isaac Don Levine, he published the book we have been discussing. In October 1939 he travelled to London under the false name of Walter Thomas and in January 1940 is said to have revealed secrets of great interest to MI5. It is believed that he may have revealed the identities of two notorious Soviet agents, Donald Maclean and Kim Philby. After Trotsky's assassination, Krivitsky returned to New York in November 1940, where he was eventually executed by Stalinist agents on 10 February 1941.

"several million people", Conquest states, "were condemned for their complicity in the vast conspiracy behind the Kirov assassination".

The 17th Congress of the Communist Party of the Soviet Union was held in Moscow from 26 January to 16 February 1934. It seems that many regarded Kirov as the favourite, and some delegates were in favour of placing him as General Secretary, but he resigned on the grounds that this would call into question the party's policies. Apparently, this attitude of Kirov's denotes his loyalty to Stalin. Moreover, between one hundred and fifty and three hundred delegates of the nearly two thousand attending the Congress voted against Stalin's membership of the Central Committee; although this was not reflected in the official tally, according to which there were only three votes against Stalin and four against Kirov. Considered the best orator in the party, Kirov controlled the Leningrad organisation; but in the end it was Stalin who was acclaimed as party leader. The Central Committee, of which Yuri Pyatakov became a member, was made up almost entirely of veteran Stalinists, although Trotskyists such as Sokolnikov, Bukharin, Rykov and Tomsky were among the candidates. Kirov was elected not only to the Politburo, but also to the Secretariat, which included Stalin, Kaganóvich and Zhdánov.

According to Conquest, Kirov believed that the Trotskyist opponents had conceded defeat and accepted the situation definitively, so he argued to Stalin that the best way to disintegrate them was to bring about a reconciliation within the party. In fact at the 17th Congress Bukharin and Rykov, who were considered rightists, had taken the floor. Zinoviev, Kamenev, Pyatakov and Radek, the last two of whom were supposedly ex-Trotskyists, had also addressed the Congress. All had shown a willingness to be unanimous. Even one of the most prominent Trotskyists, Christian Rakovsky, an internationalist Jew who, like Trotsky, considered the theory of socialism in one country to be opportunist and very harmful, announced his submission to the party in a telegram published in *Izvestia* on 23 February 1934. He was thus allowed to return to Moscow, and in March he was received at the station by Kaganóvich. In a letter published in *Pravda* in April 1934, entitled "There Should Be No Mercy", he publicly admitted his mistakes and, surprisingly, portrayed Trotsky and his followers as "Gestapo agents". In 1935 Rakovsky was even appointed ambassador to Japan.

Apparently, then, despite what had happened at the 17th Congress, Stalin had accepted Kirov's proposals, although it is very likely that in reality it was only a ploy, since his secret police had infiltrated the entourage of Trotsky and his son Sedov, and reports compromising the oppositionists were regularly sent to him from Berlin and Paris. In July 1934 the OGPU was incorporated into a new body, the NKVD (People's Commissariat for Internal Affairs), which was headed by Génrij Yagoda, whose real name was Enokh Gershevich Yehuda, who in turn appointed as his deputy director another Jew, Yakov Saulovich Agranov (Yankel Shmayevich), a Chekist of the old school who had led Trotsky's brutal repression of the Kronstadt rebels in 1921.

In September 1934, in Kazakhstan, Kirov was involved in a car accident, which according to some sources was considered an attempt on his life. Two months later, at 16:30 on the afternoon/evening of 1 December, Sergei Kirov was assassinated at the Leningrad party headquarters in the old Smolny Institute. In those latitudes the day in winter has few hours of daylight and when Kirov arrived, at four o'clock in the afternoon, the falling snow contrasted with the darkness of the night. Before going up to his quarters, he lingered with Mikhail Chudov, the second secretary of the Leningrad Provincial Party Committee, and his closest associates, whom he consulted about a report. The assassin, Leonid Nikolayev, after showing his pass to the guards stationed outside, had entered earlier without any trouble and was waiting for him hidden in the toilets on the third floor, from where he had observed his arrival by car. Nikolayev had worked there and knew the building well enough. In theory, Yuri Borisov, the bodyguard who had escorted him to the main entrance, should have gone up to the office with his boss, but he did not. Nor were the guards who were usually posted in the corridors in place. As Kirov made his way alone through the corridors to his work office, Nikolayev found the opportunity to appear behind him and shot him in the neck with a Nagant revolver. Some versions indicate that the criminal tried to commit suicide, as it was discovered that there was a second shot in the ceiling. In any case, Nikolayev fainted and fell to the ground next to his victim, and was soon arrested.

Naturally, Borisov, who was known to be very loyal to Kirov, was immediately summoned for interrogation. On the morning of 2 December, Agranov called the NKVD in Leningrad from Moscow and gave instructions to Volovich to have Borisov driven to Smolny. The journey was made in a truck. Next to the driver sat an NKVD officer and in the back was Borisov with another policeman. According to the version given by Conquest, when the truck was driving along Voinov Street, the man next to the driver swerved and crashed the car into the wall of a warehouse. It was later reported that Borisov died as a result of the accident, but in reality, according to this version, he was hit by iron bars wielded by the two officers who were escorting him, who in turn were later liquidated.

Different versions of the assassination of Kirov have circulated in Europe and to this day none has established with certainty how the events occurred and who was or were behind them. The official version, which was accepted by Western countries at the time, stated that Nikolayev had acted on the orders of Zinoviev and Kamenev. In the first of three trials held in Moscow between August 1936 and 1938, these old Bolsheviks were accused of involvement in the crime. The third trial, held between 2 and 13 March 1938 and known as the Trial of the Twenty-One, established the version that was to last until 1956, according to which Zinoviev and Kamenev, in concert with Trotsky, had planned the assassination. The trial proved that Yagoda, the NKVD chief, instructed Ivan Zaporozhets, the second-in-command of the Leningrad NKVD, to facilitate the crime by removing obstacles.

From 1956 onwards, the campaign to discredit Stalin began in the USSR and throughout the world, which was to lead, among other things, to the rehabilitation of numerous Trotskyists who had been condemned during the purges. Nikita Khrushchev delivered a speech on 25 February 1956, considered "secret" because it was addressed to the 20th Congress of the CPSU in closed session, which marked the beginning of the review of the thirty-year Stalinist period. The full text was not published in the USSR until 1988, but copies were distributed to regional party members and several foreign governments. The appearance since then of new documents on the Kirov case has allowed another version to gain momentum, according to which it was Stalin who instigated Kirov's elimination. Conquest, our main source on the matter, maintains the thesis that Stalin, after the evident support shown by the XVIIth Congress for the figure of Kirov, conceived an absolutely Machiavellian plan of extraordinary shrewdness, which enabled him to eliminate both his main opponent and the Trotskyite opposition at the same time. If this was so, his capacity for intrigue, his skill in handling and controlling the situation and the characters, was unprecedented, and Stalin must therefore be placed in history as a genius of perversion.

A third possibility, which in this writer's modest opinion is the most plausible, would be a synthesis of the two previous ones. That is, Kirov would have been the victim of two conspiracies: on the one hand, the Trotskyist opposition considered him a man loyal to Stalin who could be an obstacle on their way to regaining power in Russia, hence their interest in liquidating him; on the other hand, knowing the intentions of his opponents, Stalin would have decided to let them act, facilitate the crime, allow them to assassinate the leader who could legally challenge him for power, in order to accuse them later and begin a ruthless purge against them. In order to carry out this plan, Stalin undoubtedly needed the collaboration of Yagoda, who necessarily had to follow his secret orders. In his February 1956 speech, Khrushchev noted that the circumstances surrounding Kirov's assassination "still concealed many inexplicable and mysterious things that required careful examination". Five years later, on the occasion of the 22nd Congress in October 1961, Khrushchev returned to the subject and, this time publicly, said: "Great efforts are still needed to find out who is to blame for the death of Kirov. The deeper we study the materials connected with his death, the more questions arise.... A full investigation into the circumstances surrounding this complicated case is underway. It was not until 1988 that Yagoda was officially implicated. Stalin's responsibility was then hinted at. The official report alluded to it in these words: "Stalin's involvement in the assassination is highly probable, but there are no documents to confirm it.

Matthew E. Lenoe, in *The Kirov Murder and Soviet History*, reproduces the text of the confrontations between Nikolayev and four of those arrested: Shatsky, Kotolynov, Yuskin and Sokolov, organised by the NKVD between 18 and 20 December 1934. Below is a fragment of the confrontation between the assassin Nikolayev and Kotolynov after they confirmed that they knew each other personally:

"Question to Kotolynov: Do you confirm that you were a member of a counter-revolutionary Zinovievist-Trotskyist organisation?
Answer: Yes, I confirm that it was. [...]
Question to Nikolayev: Did you belong to a counter-revolutionary Zinovievite-Trotskyite revolutionary organisation and who recruited you?
Answer: I did belong to a counter-revolutionary Zinovievite-Trotskyite counter-revolutionary organisation. I was recruited by Kotolynov; this was in September 1934 in the building of the Polytechnic Institute, where Kotolynov was studying.
Question to Kotolynov: Do you confirm that you recruited Nikolayev for the Zinovievist-Trotskyist organisation?
Answer: No, I deny it.
Question to Nikolayev: Did Kotolynov propose to you on behalf of the Zinovievist-Trotskyist organisation to kill comrade Kirov, did you accept the proposal and under what circumstances did it take place?
Reply: Yes, a proposal to kill Kirov was made to me by Kotolynov in the name of the Zinovievievite-Trotskyite counter-revolutionary organisation. I accepted the proposal in September 1934, the proposal was made at the Polytechnic Institute where I went to meet Kotolynov.
Question to Kotolynov: Do you confirm Nikolayev's statement that he killed Kirov on your orders?
Answer: No, I deny it. [...]"

At the trial Kotolynov accepted his contacts with the counter-revolutionary Zinovievievite-Trotskyite opposition, but maintained his denial of involvement in the murder of Kirov. This confrontation was supervised by two Ukrainian Jews Lev G. Mironov and Genrij Samoylovich Lyushkov, accompanied by a third Chekist of Russian origin named Dmitry Dmitriev. Both Mironov, whose real name was Kagan, and Lyushkov ended up as victims of Stalin. The former, who, according to Conquest, was depressed at having to persecute the old Bolsheviks, was head of the Lubyanka Economic Department and was eventually liquidated by Yezhov in 1938. The second, a bully with a reputation for sadism who had been a chekist since 1920, was appointed in July 1937 head of the NKVD in the Russian Far East, where he commanded some 30,000 elite troops. When the great purge was at its height, Yezhov ordered him to return to Moscow, but he defected in June 1938 with valuable secret documents and went to Japan, where he admitted to Japanese officials that he was a Trotskyite. Lyushkov organised with Japanese support a serious plot to assassinate Stalin, but was discovered. Finally, in 1945 he disappeared without a trace.

As for the Jewish Chekists, we know that from Lenin's time onwards the great majority of Chekists were Bolsheviks of Jewish origin. So were the main chiefs of the NKVD who carried out the Stalinist purges under Yagoda. Many of them were Trotskyists who were forced to play a double game. Here are some of them. The head of the NKVD Special Operations Department was Karl V. Pauker, a Jew whose real name was never determined with certainty. Pauker, who in December 1934 arrested Kamenev on Yagoda's orders, was eventually denounced and shot in 1937. At the head of the OGPU Special Department, which covered the Army, Yagoda placed another Jew, Mark Isayevich (Isaakovich) Gay (Shpoklyand), who was executed by Yezhov after Yagoda's fall from grace. The head of the all-important Foreign Department was Abram Aronovich Slutsky, who was poisoned in February 1938 on Yezhov's orders. Slutsky's two most trusted officers, Boris Davydovich Berman and Mikhail Spiegelglass, were also Jewish. Georgi A. Molchanov, head of the Lubyanka's Department of Secret Policy, was one of the few Russians who held important positions in Yagoda's NKVD. Other noteworthy senior Jewish NKVD officials included Lev N. Belsky (Abram M. Levin), Lev Borisovich Zalin (Zelman Markovich Levin), Grigory (Izrail) Moiseyevich Leplevsky, Zinovi Borisovich Katsnelson and Pyotr Gavrilovich Rud. Almost all of them ended up as Stalin's victims for one reason or another after serving him in the purges.

On 21 December 1934, after several days of confrontation and interrogation, the NKVD already pointed out that, in addition to the murderer Nikolayev, there was a "Leningrad Centre" linked to Zinoviev, who had already been expelled from the party on several occasions and readmitted after pledging allegiance to the official line. At the head of the group was Ivan I. Kotolynov. The next day a list of those arrested was published, the most prominent names being those of Zinoviev and Kamenev, followed by G.E. Evdokimov, who had belonged to the Secretariat, Zalutsky, Fedorov, Kuklin and Safarov. On 29 December Nikolayev, Kotolynov, Shatsky, Yuskin, Sokolov and other accomplices were sentenced to death and executed. It was publicly announced that they had admitted at the trial that the motive for the murder of Kirov was his replacement by Zinoviev and Kamenev. On 15 and 16 January 1935 Zinoviev, Kamenev, Evdokimov, Bakayev, Kuklin and fourteen others were tried in Leningrad on charges of forming the "Moscow Centre", from which Kotolynov's "Leningrad Centre" had been politically supported. The court, presided over by V.V. Ulrich and whose prosecutor was Andrei Vyshinsky, who two years later became internationally renowned for his work on the Moscow trials, sentenced Zinoviev to ten years' imprisonment. Evdokimov received eight years and Kamenev five. The other sentences ranged from five to ten years.

These convictions were only the preamble to a tragedy which has gone down in history as the "Great Terror". Stalin's manoeuvres to prepare for the complete purge of Trotskyists throughout the country began at once. On 1 February 1935 the Central Committee Plenum elected Mikoyan and Chubar to the places left vacant in the Politburo by the deaths of Kirov and Kuibyshev. In the key party posts Stalin placed the men who were to be his top collaborators during the purges: Nikolai Yezhov became a member of the Secretariat, and on 23 February he was also appointed head of the party's Control Commission. A few days later, the young Stalinist Nikita Khrushchev, Kaganhovich's protégé, became the party's first organising secretary in Moscow. In June Andrei Vyshinsky became Prosecutor General. On 8 July 1935 Georgi Malenkov was placed as Yezhov's principal deputy chief and deputy director of the Central Committee's Cadres Department. In the Caucasus was Lavrenti Beria, a criminal of the worst kind who knew how to hide his cards until the end, as will be seen in due course.

While these movements were developing, from July 1935 to August 1936 there was a period of relative calm which seemed to indicate that the waters were calming down, although in reality there was a groundswell. In February 1935 a commission was set up to draft a new constitution, in which Bukharin and Radek participated. The text was ready in June 1936. Freedom of speech and of the press, inviolability of the home and of the secrecy of correspondence, freedom of assembly and demonstration, prevention of unjustified arrests, were some of the guarantees contained in the document, which became a dead letter as soon as the whirlwind of arrests and murders began. This façade of apparent normality allowed Stalin to take control of the Secret Police and other mechanisms of power. In fact, as early as 31 March he gave instructions to Yagoda and Vyshinsky, who offered him some eighty names. Stalin ordered them to prepare a trial against the Trotskyists and to submit the concrete proposal to him. In April the interrogation of Smirnov, Mrachkovsky and Ter-Vaganyan, leaders of the so-called "Trotskyist-Zinovievist Centre", began.

The arrests that preceded the first of the Moscow trials began in early 1936. Valentin Olberg, a Jew of Latvian origin, and several teachers at the Gorky Pedagogical Institute were arrested in January. A group of students from the Communist Youth (Konsomol) in the town of Gorky had admitted in late 1935 that there was a conspiracy to assassinate Stalin. The NKVD accused Olberg of recruiting teachers and students. For three days, between 25 and 28 January, Olberg was interrogated and eventually signed a statement admitting that he had been sent by Trotsky to organise the assassination attempt. In *The Great Terror. A Reassessment* Conquest, he gives Alexander Orlov's version in *Secret History of Stalin's Crimes* (1955), according to which Olberg was an agent provocateur of the NKVD itself.

Orlov recounts that, invoking party discipline, Olberg was asked by the NKVD to confess that he was a link between Trotsky and Gorky's group.

He was told that it was only an assignment and that, whatever the verdict of the court, he would subsequently be released and get an appointment in the Far East. Olberg, according to this thesis, signed everything that was asked of him; however, Valentin Olberg never regained his freedom and on 24 August 1936 he was sentenced to death along with other Trotskyists and executed. In our opinion, it is likely that Olberg was a double agent, and it does not seem logical that a man of his experience would be so naive as to sign a statement that could have brought him the death sentence.

Certainly, Stalin succeeded time and again in infiltrating the entourage of Trotsky and his son. The best proof of this is that he succeeded in assassinating them both. We shall see later that Lev Sedov's most trusted man was the NKVD agent Mark Zborowski, a Jew who called himself Etienne and was even in charge of editing the famous *Opposition Bulletin*. Valentin Olberg also managed to get into the entourage of Trotsky and his son Sedov. However, the claim that he was a Trotskyist agent working for the NKVD always comes from Trotskyist sources[14]. The fact that Conquest gives full validity to Alexander Orlov's thesis does not prevent us from questioning it, since it does not deserve any credibility. It is an exercise in shameless cynicism for a criminal like Orlov, himself a ruthless executor of the murders ordered by Stalin, to write a work on Stalin's crimes.

The Secret History of Stalin's Crimes, the above-mentioned work by Alexander Orlov, was published in the United States in 1953 in order to make money. In Spain it was published in Barcelona two years later, in 1955. The stories Orlov tells are usually known to him second-hand. One of his main sources was the Jew Abram Slutsky, an alleged Trotskyite infiltrated into the Foreign Section of the NKVD. Orlov was also Jewish, born in Belarus, and his real name was Leiba Lazarevich Felbing. He committed numerous crimes in Spain on Stalin's orders. He was in charge of purging the leaders of the POUM. He himself directed the kidnapping and assassination of Andreu Nin. He was also one of the main architects of the theft of gold from the Bank of Spain. These facts will be the subject of the next chapter. In 1939 he warned Trotsky in an unsigned letter that an agent called "Mark", in reality Zborowski, had infiltrated his organisation in Paris. Alexander Orlov, Walter Krivitsky, Max Shachtman, Pierre Broué are examples of writers who

---

[14] In an article published in 1972 in *Studies in Intelligence* Rita T. Kronenbitter, a pseudonym under which perhaps a Trotskyist hides, reports on the activities of Valentin Olberg in Trotsky's entourage. Kronenbitter places Olberg in Germany as early as 1927, where he works for *Inprekor* (International Press Correspondence), a Comintern publication. In letters written in 1929 to Trotsky, who was in Turkey, Olberg tells him that he has left the agency because he opposes Stalinism and has joined Trotsky's movement in Berlin. In May 1930, although some of Trotsky's friends express a certain distrust of Olberg, both Trotsky and his son Sedov already entrust him with the names and addresses of their main supporters in Moscow, in the Baltic countries and elsewhere. Kronenbitter admits that Trotsky's letters, found in the Harvard archives, show that he has full confidence in the Latvian Jew and his wife, who had also joined the movement.

present in their works an ethical gulf between Stalin and Trotsky. The former is always a dictator, an unscrupulous criminal, which is not debatable; the latter, however, is presented as a man of integrity, whom they put forward as the Messiah of the international working class.

In February 1936 Isak Reingold, another Jew who was chairman of the cotton union and a friend of Sokolnikov (Brilliant), was arrested. He was accused of being a Trotskyite and of being connected with Kamenev. According to Orlov, in order to force him to confess, orders were given to arrest his family in his presence. It should be remembered that the arrest of family members was one of Trotsky's favourite devices. In March 1921 he ordered the wives and children of the Kronstadt sailors to be taken hostage and threatened the mutineers with murder. In June there were further arrests: Moissei Lurje, Nathan Lurje, Fritz David and Berman-Yurin were arrested. The last two admitted that they had visited Trotsky and had received orders to kill Stalin. All of them would eventually be shot, but Robert Conquest, again citing Orlov as a primary source and again lending credibility to his claims, accepts that the latter two were NKVD agents. In *Secret History of Stalin's Crimes* Orlov reproduces Mironov's (Kagan) account to a trusted interlocutor (supposedly Abram Slutsky, Orlov's main source) of his conversation with Stalin regarding Kamenev's refusal to confess:

"'Do you think Kamenev will not confess?' Stalin asked, with a slyly annoyed look on his face.
'I don't know,' Mironov replied. 'He does not yield to persuasion'.
'Don't you know?' Stalin asked with affected surprise, staring at Mironov. 'Do you know how much our State weighs, with all the factories, machines, the army, with all the armaments and the navy?'
Mironov and all those present looked at Stalin with surprise.
Think about it and tell me,' Stalin asked. Mironov smiled, thinking that Stalin was preparing to tell a joke. But Stalin had no intention of joking. He looked at Stalin rather seriously. 'I'm asking you, how much does all this weigh?' He insisted.
Mironov was confused. He waited, still confident that Stalin would turn it all into a joke; but Stalin continued to stare at him in expectation of an answer. Mironov shrugged his shoulders and, like a schoolboy taking an examination, said in a hesitant voice, 'No one can know this, Yosif Vissarionovich. It is in the realm of astronomical figures'.
Well, can anyone resist the pressure of an astronomical weight?' Stalin asked sternly.
No,' Mironov replied.
Then don't tell me again that Kamenev, or this or that prisoner, is capable of resisting this pressure. Don't come back to inform me,' said Stalin to Mironov, 'until you have Kamenev's confession in this case.

Eventually both Zinoviev and Kamenev surrendered, testified and accepted the trial. Conquest relates that Yagoda had them locked in cells and that Zinoviev's physical condition was very bad. As for Kamenev, he explains that threats against his son, whose arrest was ordered in his presence, began to weaken him. Again quoting Orlov, Conquest writes: "In July, Zinoviev, after a whole night of interrogation, asked to speak to Kamenev, and when they discussed the matter they agreed to go to trial on condition that Stalin would confirm to them in front of the Politburo his promises that neither they nor their followers would be executed. This was accepted. However, when they were brought before the so-called Politburo meeting, only Stalin, Voroshilov and Yezhov were present. Stalin explained to them that they formed a commission authorised by the Politburo to hear the case". Although disturbed by the absence of other members, it appears that the prisoners accepted Stalin's terms and were guaranteed the lives of themselves and their families. The source for this information is another Jewish Trotskyite, Walter Krivitsky, who claims that a member of Zinoviev's family told him that Zinoviev had capitulated in order to save his family.

The Trial of the Sixteen

Before turning to the first of the trials against the Trotskyist opposition, it may be helpful to the reader to summarise in advance how the opposition was structured. The combined high command of the opposition, the "Right-wing and Trotskyist Bloc", was built on three different layers or levels. This was due to the belief that if one was discovered, the others could continue to operate underground. The first of these layers was the "Trotskyist-Zinovievite Terrorist Centre", headed by Zinoviev, responsible for organising and directing terrorist activities. On the second level was the "Trotskyist Parallel Centre", whose top representative was Pyatakov. The organisation and direction of sabotage actions rested with this parallel centre. The third and perhaps the most important stratum was the "Rightist and Trotskyist Bloc". Its main figures were Bukharin and Krestinsky, and it included most of the high-ranking members of the combined opposition forces.

At 12:10 on 19 August 1936 the first of the trials, the "Trial of the Sixteen", began. A comprehensive report of the sessions before the Military College of the Supreme Court of the USSR was published the same year by the People's Commissariat of Justice and is available to the Internet today. The court was presided over by Vassili Ulrich, an army jurist. The Prosecutor General of the USSR, Andrei Vyshinsky, acted as prosecutor. The defendants were divided into two groups. In the first were eleven leading Bolsheviks who had already in 1926-27, when Trotsky and Zinoviev were expelled from the party, formed the "united opposition bloc". The second group consisted of five members of the Communist Party of Germany who had emigrated to the USSR. In this first trial, ten of the sixteen defendants were Jews, hence Trotsky accused Stalin of anti-Semitism.

The presiding judge asked the defendants if they had any objections to the composition of the court or the prosecutor. After a refusal, he announced that the defendants had declined the services of lawyers for their defence, so that they were personally granted all rights, i.e., the right to ask questions of witnesses and other defendants, to ask the court for clarification of the proceedings, to make speeches in their defence.... They also retained the right of final appeal. The clerk of the court, A. F. Kostyushko, then read out the charges against the defendants, whom he named in this order: G. E. Zinoviev, L. B. Kamenev, G. E. Evdokimov, I. N. Smirnov, I. P. Bakayev, V. A. Ter-Vaganyan, S. V. Mrachkovsky, E. A. Mrachkovsky and E. A. K. K. K. Khamenev. A. Dreitzer. E. S. Holtzman, I. I. I. Reingold, R. V. Pickel, V. P. Olberg, K. B. Berman-Yurin, Fritz David, (I. I. Kruglyanski), M. Lurje and N. Lurje.

After recalling that some had already been sentenced to prison terms in January 1935, Secretary Kostyushko referred to new circumstances established since then and outlined the statements made by the defendants. On Zinoviev, he said that under the weight of evidence presented by the authorities he had admitted that "...The main aim pursued by the Trotskyist-Zinovievite centre was the murder of leaders of the CPSU, and in the first place of Stalin and Kirov. As for Reingold, he said that in July 1936 he had declared that the main aim was "...to change by violence the leadership of the CPSU and the Soviet Union". The confessions of the defendants were presented one after the other in order to maintain that it had been established that the Trotskyist-Zinovievist centre was a terrorist organisation which sought to seize power at any price. This was followed by new testimonies of the defendants on the murder of Kirov, which led to the conclusion that the same Trotskyist-Zinovievievist centre was responsible for the crime. The secretary's exposition ended with the reading out of another block of statements which led to the conclusion that the united Trotskyist-Zinovievievist centre was also working on the murder of other party members, such as Voroshilov, Zhdanov and Kaganovich.

1) That between 1932-36 a united Trotskyist-Zinovievite centre organised in Moscow sought to seize power by assassinating the leaders of the CPSU and the Government. 2) That Zinoviev, Kamenev, Evdokimov and Bakayev had joined with the Trotskyists Smirnov, Ter-Vaganyan and Mrachkovsky, thus forming the united Trotskyist-Zinovievite centre. 3) That during the period 1932-36 the united centre had organised terrorist groups and prepared attacks to assassinate Comrades Stalin, Voroshilov, Zhdanov, Kaganovich, Kirov, etc. 4) That one of these groups, operating on the instructions of Zinoviev and Trotsky and led by Bakayev, had assassinated Comrade Kirov on December 1, 1934.

Already at the end of his exposition, the court clerk added: "L. Trotsky and his son L. L. Sedov, both of whom are abroad, having been exposed by the materials of the present case as having directly prepared and personally guided the work of organising in the USSR terrorist acts against leaders of the CPSU and the Soviet State, in the event of their being found on the territory of the USSR, they will be subject to immediate arrest and will be tried by the Military College of the Supreme Court of the USSR". Finally, Kostyushko gave the names of a number of future defendants: Gertik, Grinberg, Y. Gaven, Karev, Kuzmichev, Konstant, Matorin, Paul Olberg, Radin, Safonova (wife of Ivan Smirnov), Faivilovich, D. Shmidt and Esterman, who, since the investigation in respect of them was continuing, had been set aside in view of a separate trial.

The presiding judge then asked the defendants whether they accepted the charges, which they all did. Only two of them, Smirnov and Holtzman, made some qualifications. The former accepted his membership of the united centre and his contacts with Trotsky. He accepted that he had received instructions to organise attacks and his responsibility for the actions of the united centre, but refused to accept his personal participation in the preparation and execution of terrorist acts. The second defendant accepted the same charges as Smirnov, but also denied personal involvement in terrorist acts. After these two defendants had been heard, the chairman proposed a short recess of fifteen minutes and adjourned the session momentarily until 13:45.

Sergei V. Mrachkovsky, Trotsky's close collaborator since the creation of the Red Army, was the first to testify. He detailed the history of the formation of the Trotskyist-Zinovievievist centre and admitted that after his return from exile in 1929 he had appeared to accept the official party line, although his intentions were to continue the struggle with other members of the opposition. The prosecutor asked whom he was referring to, and Mrachkovsky mentioned the names of Smirnov and Ter-Vaganyan. He also admitted that as early as 1931 the group was openly considering terrorist actions and pointed out that Smirnov, after a trip to Berlin, had brought instructions from Trotsky's son, L. Sedov, who had said: "Until we remove Stalin, there will be no possibility of regaining power". Vyshinsky then asked him to clarify this sentence: "What do you mean by the expression 'until we do not remove Stalin? Mrachkovsky replied: "Until we kill Stalin. At that meeting, in the presence of Smirnov, Ter-Vaganyan and Safonova, I was commissioned to form a terrorist group, that is, to select reliable people. The same assignment was given to Dreitzer. That period, 1931 and 1932, was spent in inducing and preparing people to commit terrorist acts". Mrachkovsky specified that Trotsky sent an emissary named Gaven who conveyed the need to form a united centre for the organisation of terrorist acts. The prosecutor interrupted this interrogation and turned to Smirnov:

"Vyshinsky: A question for Smirnov: Do you corroborate that in 1932 you received a message from Trotsky through Gaven?
Smirnov: I received a message from Trotsky through Gaven.
Vyshinsky: Also, did you receive verbal information from the conversation with Trotsky?
Smirnov: Yes, also verbal conversation.
Vyshinsky: Do you, Smirnov, confirm before the Supreme Court that in 1932 you received Trotsky's order from Gaven to commit acts of terrorism?
Smirnov: Yes.
Vyshinsky: Against whom?
Smirnov: Against the leaders.
Vyshinsky: Against which ones?
Smirnov: Stalin and others".

Mrachkovsky confirmed that by the end of 1932 the bloc of Trotskyists and Zinovievites was already formed and implicated Isak Isayevich Reingold. He stated that he went to Moscow in 1932, where on Smirnov's orders he contacted Reingold, who headed the Moscow terrorist group, with the object of reaching an agreement with him for the union of forces. Continuing his testimony, Mrachkovsky stated that in December 1934, while in Kazakhstan, he received from Dreitzer a letter from Trotsky written in invisible ink, in which it was said that it was urgent to hasten the assassinations of Stalin and Voroshilov and that in case of war a defeatist position should be adopted and advantage should be taken of the confusion. The letter was signed "Starik" (the old man). Mrachkovsky claimed to know Trotsky's handwriting very well, so he had no doubts about its authorship. Since Smirnov denied his personal involvement in the preparation and execution of terrorist acts, the prosecutor then inquired about Smirnov's role in the terrorist centre, and Mrachkovsky reiterated that everything was done with Smirnov's knowledge. Mrachkovsky also confirmed that Zinoviev, Kamenev, Lominadze (who had committed suicide the previous year), Ter-Vaganyan and others were part of the united centre, which led the prosecutor to seek confirmation from Zinoviev:

"Vyshinsky: When was the united centre organised?
Zinoviev: In the summer of 1932.
Vyshinsky: For what period of time did it work?
Zinoviev: In fact until 1936.
Vyshinsky: What were their activities?
Zinoviev: His main activities consisted in the preparation of terrorist acts.
Vyshinsky: Against whom?
Zinoviev: Against the leaders.
Vyshinsky: Against Comrades Stalin, Voroshilov and Kaganovich, was it your centre that organised the assassination of Comrade Kirov, was the

assassination of Sergei Mironovich Kirov organised by your centre or by some other organisation?
Zinoviev: Yes, for our centre.
Vyshinsky: In this centre were you, Kamenev, Smirnov, Mrachkovsky and Ter-Vaganyan?
Zinoviev. Yes.
Vyshinsky: So you all organised the assassination of Kirov?
Zinoviev: Yes.
Vyshinsky: Is that how you all murdered comrade Kirov?
Zinoviev: Yes
Vyshinsky: Sit down".

The next to testify was Grigory E. Evdokimov, who confessed to being a member of the united centre and to having personally approved the murders. Since he had already been sentenced to eight years' imprisonment, the prosecutor reminded him that at his trial on 15-16 January 1935 he had denied that he had anything to do with the murder of Kirov. "Did you lie then?" asked Vyshinsky. "I did mislead the court," Evdokimov replied. This defendant confirmed that the instructions came from Trotsky and that he and Smirnov, Mrachkovsky and Ter-Vaganyan had agreed in the summer of 1932. He added that in the town of Ilyinskaya, where Zinoviev and Kamenev lived that summer, a conference was held in which Bakayev and Karev also took part. At this conference it was decided to form the Moscow and Leningrad centres in order to combine the terrorist groups. Evdokimov stated that, at Zinoviev's suggestion, Bakayev was entrusted with the organisation of terrorist acts.

"Vyshinsky: Defendant Bakayev, do you confirm this?
Bakayev: During that conference Zinoviev said that the Trotskyists, on Trotsky's proposal, had decided to work to organise the assassination of Stalin and that we should take the initiative in our own hands.
Vyshinsky: Zinoviev said this?
Bakayev: Yes.
Vyshinsky: Did Zinoviev say that you should take the initiative?
Bakayev: At that conference I was ordered to organise a terrorist action against Stalin.
Vyshinsky: And you started to prepare it, did you?
Bakayev: Yes.

The name of Grigory Sokolnikov (Girsh Yankelovich Brilliant), the Jewish Trotskyite who in December 1917 was appointed director of the state bank and set in motion the looting of all deposits, was mentioned for the first time. Evdokimov stated that in the summer of 1934 Sokolnikov attended a meeting in Kamenev's Moscow flat, at which, besides himself and Kamenev, Zinoviev, Ter-Vaganyan, Reingold and Bakayev were also present.

Evdokimov admitted that at that conference it was decided to hasten the assassination of Kirov. The morning session on 19 August ended with this interrogation:

"Vyshinsky: Was the murder of Kirov prepared by the centre?
Evdokimov: Yes.
Vyshinsky: Were you directly involved in the preparations?
Evdokimov: Yes.
Vyshinsky: Did Zinoviev and Kamenev take part in the preparations with you?
Evdokimov: Yes.
Vyshinsky: On instructions from the centre Bakayev went to Leningrad to see how the preparations were progressing. Is that right?
Evdokimov: Yes.
Vyshinsky (to Bakayev): Did you meet Nikolayev in Leningrad?
Bakayev: Yes.
Vyshinsky: Did you deliberate on the need for an understanding to assassinate Kirov?
Bakayev: There was no need to come to an understanding with him, since the instructions for the assassination had already been given by Zinoviev and Kamenev.
Vyshinsky: But Nikolayev told you that he had decided to assassinate Kirov, did he?
Bakayev: He said so, and so did other terrorists. Levin, Maldelstamm, Kotolynov, Rumyantsev.
Vyshinsky: Did they discuss the murder of Kirov?
Bakayev: Yes.
Vyshinsky: He confirmed your determination, what was your attitude to it?
Bakayev: I encouraged it.

In the afternoon session four defendants were questioned: Dreitzer, Reingold, Bakayev and Pickel. The first, Ephraim A. Dreitzer, head of Trotsky's bodyguards, had been one of the organisers of the 1927 demonstrations. When Trotsky was exiled to Alma Ata, Dreitzer organised communications with the Trotskyist centre in Moscow. In the autumn of 1931 he took advantage of an official business trip to Berlin to contact Trotsky's son, whom he met twice in a café on Leipziger Street. Dreitzer repeatedly pointed to Smirnov as "the conductor" and declared himself surprised that he denied the evidence. The prosecutor therefore asked Zinoviev to confirm Smirnov's role, which he did at length: "Smirnov, in my opinion, carried out more activities than anyone else and we had him as the undisputed head of the Trotskyist bloc, as the man best informed of Trotsky's views". Zinoviev reiterated that he had personally negotiated with him two or three times. In October 1934 Dreitzer's sister brought him from Warsaw a German film magazine in which, as agreed with Lev Sedov, there was a message from Trotsky written in invisible ink with instructions to prepare terrorist acts against Stalin and Voroshilov.

The most remarkable and novel feature of Isak Isayevich Reingold's interrogation was the mention of Rykov, Bukharin and Tomsky, whom he implicated in the conspiracy. He said that they had been negotiated with as representatives of "the right-wing deviation". As Evdokimov had done in the morning session, Reingold cited Sokolnikov as a member of the Trotskyist-Zinovievite centre. To the disgrace of Bukharin and company, Reingold added that there were two terrorist groups led by two "rightists", Slepkov and Eismont. Another revelation of interest from this defendant was that Zinoviev and Kamenev had a plan to appoint Bakayev as head of the NKVD when they came to power. According to Reingold, after the seizure of power, Trotsky would be brought back from abroad and with his help all Stalinists would be removed from the party and the government. There followed the interrogations of Ivan Petrovich Bakayev and Richard Vitoldovich Pickel, which added nothing significant, for both of them ratified what had been stated during the day.

The morning session on 20 August began with Lev Kamenev (Leiba Rosenfeld), one of the two big shots of this first trial, who accepted that the terrorist conspiracy was organised by himself, Zinoviev and Trotsky. Kamenev, who, according to R. Conquest, "began his statement with some dignity, but sank as the interrogation progressed", not only confirmed the involvement of Sokolnikov (Brilliant), whose name had been mentioned by Reingold, but also implicated Radek and Serebryakov:

> "... Among the leaders of the conspiracy another person must be named, who was one of the leaders, but who, in view of the special plans we made in connection with it, was not engaged in work of a practical kind. I mean Sokolnikov.
> Vyshinsky: Who was a member of the centre, but whose participation was kept strictly secret?
> Kamenev: Yes, knowing that we could be discovered, we appointed a small group to continue our terrorist activities. For this purpose we appointed Sokolnikov. It seemed to us that on the part of the Trotskyists this work could be carried out satisfactorily by Serebryakov and Radek."

As for the relation of the Zinovievites to other revolutionary groups, among them were the so-called "rightists", to whom Reingold had referred at the afternoon session of the previous day and whose top leader was Bukharin. Kamenev said, and I quote:

> "In 1932 I personally conducted negotiations with the so-called 'leftist' group of Lominadze and Shatsky. In this group I found enemies of the party leadership ready to resort against them to the most resolute

measures of struggle. At the same time Zinoviev and I myself maintained contact with the former 'Workers' Opposition' group of Shlyapnikov and Medvedyev. In 1932, 1933 and 1934 I personally maintained relations with Tomsky and Bukharin and sounded out their political feelings. They sympathised with us. When I asked Tomsky about Rykov's state of mind, he replied: 'He thinks the same as I do'. In reply to my question as to what Bukharin thought, he said: 'Bukharin thinks the same as I do, but he follows somewhat different tactics: he does not agree with the party line, but follows the stratagem of persistently rooting himself in the party in order to win the confidence of the leadership."

At the request of the prosecutor, the court proceeded to hear Professor Yakovlev, a witness who corroborated Kamenev's statement and added that in 1934 he had a conversation with him in the course of which he asked him to organise a terrorist group at the Academy of Sciences. Yakovlev admitted that he had accepted the assignment and said that Kamenev had told him at the time that there were other groups with instructions to commit terrorist acts, namely in Moscow against Stalin and in Leningrad against Kirov. Yakovlev said that the Rumyantsev-Kotolynov group had been commissioned to assassinate Kirov.

Next it was the turn of Grigori Zinoviev (Gerson Radomylsky), the other big fish in the conspiracy. Again, Conquest alludes to the state of mind of this defendant: "He appeared cowed. The eloquent speaker was barely able to speak. He looked bloated and grey and breathed like an asthmatic'. Zinoviev stressed that in reality there were never any substantial differences between Trotskyists and Zinovievites. In his statement he implicated Tomsky and Moissei Lurje (alias Alexander Emel), an envoy of Trotsky. He also mentioned Ivar Smilga, a veteran who had been a member of the Central Committee in Lenin's time. Zinoviev, like other defendants, pointed to Smirnov as a key player. A significant passage from his statement follows:

"... We were convinced that the leadership had to be replaced at any price, that it had to be replaced by us and by Trotsky. In this situation I had several meetings with Smirnov, who has accused me here of often telling falsehoods. Yes, I often told falsehoods. I began to do so the moment I started the struggle against the Bolshevik party. While Smirnov took the road of fighting the party, he too tells lies. But it seems that the difference between me and him is that I have firmly and irrevocably decided to tell the truth at this late stage, whereas he seems to have taken a different decision."

The prosecutor asked Zinoviev to confirm that Smirnov had been Trotsky's chief representative in the USSR since 1931, which he confirmed, and he further stated that when he and Kamenev went into exile after the Ryutin case, Bakayev and Smirnov were left in charge of terrorist activities.

Zinoviev, confirming Evdokimov, declared that in 1934 he had sent Bakayev to Leningrad to find out how the preparations for the murder of Kirov were going: "I sent Bakayev to Leningrad as a person of our confidence.... On his return he confirmed that everything was going well". Already at the end of the statement, Ulrich, the presiding judge, asked what role Zinoviev had personally played in the preparation of terrorist acts against Comrade Stalin. He acknowledged that he knew of two attempts on Stalin's life in which Reingold, Dreitzer and Pickel had taken part.

Smirnov's former wife, Aleksandra Safonova, was then questioned as a witness and admitted that she was a member of the Trotskyist centre. She said that Smirnov had passed on Trotsky's instructions on terrorism and supported them. Safonova said that one day Mrachkovsky, after an interview with Stalin, told them both about their conversation and said that the only way out was to assassinate him. Safonova confirmed that Smirnov supported this conclusion. Having heard this testimony, Smirnov denied that he had passed on to Ter-Vaganyan, Mrachkovsky and Safonova instructions to adopt terrorism and, despite the statements of all three to this effect, he also denied that, after his interview with Stalin, Mrachkovsky had spoken of the necessity of assassinating Stalin. To prove that there was no enmity between Safonova and Smirnov and to clearly establish their personal relationship in court, the prosecutor asked these questions:

"Vyshinsky: What were your relations with Safonova like?
Smirnov: Good morning.
Vyshinsky: Anything else?
Smirnov: We were intimately related.
Vyshinsky: Were they husband and wife?
Smirnov: Yes.
Vyshinsky: Were there personal resentments between you?
Smirnov: No."

During the afternoon session, statements were taken from three other defendants: Smirnov, Olberg and Berman-Yurin. The first, although a personal friend of Trotsky and one of the leaders of the organisation since its formation, refused to accept his direct participation in terrorist activities. At the risk of being too long, we reproduce below an interesting and lengthy exchange of questions and answers between the prosecutor and several defendants:

"Vyshinsky: Did you have direct communication with Trotsky?
Smirnov: I had two addresses.
Vyshinsky: I ask you, was there any communication?
Smirnov: I had two addresses.
Vyshinsky: Answer, was there communication?
Smirnov: If having two addresses is called communication?

Vyshinsky: What do you call him?
Smirnov: I said I had two addresses.
Vyshinsky: Did you maintain communication with Trotsky?
Smirnov: I had two addresses.
Vyshinsky: Did you have personal communication?
Smirnov: No personal communication.
Vyshinsky: Was there mail communication with Trotsky?
Smirnov: There was communication by mail with Trotsky's son.
Vyshinsky: Was the letter you received through Gaven sent by Sedov or by Trotsky?
Smirnov: Gaven brought a letter from Trotsky.
Vyshinsky: This is what I am asking you: did you have communication with Trotsky, yes or no?
Smirnov: I say that I wrote a letter to Trotsky and received a reply from him.
Vyshinsky: Is this communication or not?
Smirnov: It is.
Vyshinsky: So there was communication?
Smirnov: There was.
Vyshinsky: Did you give instructions to the group?
Smirnov: No, I did not.
Vyshinsky (to Mrachkovsky): Mrachkovsky, did Smirnov give you instructions?
Mrachkovsky: Yes, instructions were given to me at the beginning of 1931, on his return from abroad.
Vyshinsky: What did he say?
Mrachkovsky: That it was necessary to start selecting reliable people, that we had a very serious job ahead of us, that those selected had to be determined people. He said this in his flat.
Smirnov: Was it in my flat? Where is my flat?
Mrachkovsky: This was in 1931 in Pressnya.
Vyshinsky: Did he visit you in Pressnya?
Smirnov: Not in Pressnya itself, but in that district.
Vyshinsky (to Zinoviev): Defendant Zinoviev, you said that Smirnov talked to you about terrorism on more than one occasion. Did you talk about the need to commit terrorist acts?
Zinoviev: Right.
Vyshinsky: So what Mrachkovsky said about the terrorist group is true?
Zinoviev: Yes.
Vyshinsky: Defendant Smirnov, do you think that Ter-Vaganyan, Mrachkovsky and Evdokimov are lying?
Smirnov: (does not answer.)
Vyshinsky: What do you recognise?
Smirnov: I admit that I belong to the underground Trotskyist organisation, that I met Sedov in Berlin in 1931, listened to his views on terrorism and passed these views on to Moscow. I admit that I received

Trotsky's instructions on terrorism through Gaven and, although I did not agree with them, I communicated them to the Zinovievites through Ter-Vaganyan.

Vyshinsky: And despite your disagreement, you remained a member of the bloc and worked in the bloc?

Smirnov: I did not officially leave the block, but in fact I did not work.

Vyshinsky: So when you passed on instructions you didn't work?

Smirnov (no answer).

Vyshinsky: What do you think, when an organiser transmits instructions, is it work?

Smirnov: Of course.

Vyshinsky: Did you participate in the bloc?

Smirnov: Yes.

Vyshinsky: And you admit that the bloc held terrorist positions?

Smirnov: Yes.

Vyshinsky: Do you also admit that you held this position in connection with instructions received from Trotsky?

Smirnov: Yes.

Vyshinsky: And it was you who received these instructions?

Smirnov: Yes.

Vyshinsky: So it was you who persuaded the bloc to adopt terrorism?

Smirnov: I passed on the instructions on terrorism.

Vyshinsky: If you confirm that, after receiving instructions from Trotsky, the position of the bloc was that of terrorism, should it be said that the bloc adopted the position of terrorism after you received Trotsky's instructions and passed them on to the members of the bloc?

Smirnov: I received these instructions, communicated them to the Trotskyists and Zinovievists, and they formed the centre. Although I did not agree, I did not officially leave the bloc, but in fact I was not a member of the bloc.

Vyshinsky (to Ter-Vaganyan): Ter-Vaganyan, did Smirnov leave the bloc?

Ter-Vaganyan: No.

Vyshinsky (to Mrackovsky): Mrachkovsky, did Smirnov leave the bloc?

Mrachkovsky: No.

Vyshinsky (to Dreitzer): Dreitzer, did you know that Smirnov had left the block?

Dreitzer. If giving instructions to organise terrorist groups is leaving the bloc, then yes.

Vyshinsky (to Evdokimov): Evdokimov, did you hear that Smirnov had left the bloc?

Evdokimov: No, on the contrary; he remained a member of the group and worked actively in it.

Vyshinsky: Did you share terrorist views?

Evdokimov: Yes, he shared them.

Vyshinsky (to Kamenev): Defendant Kamenev, what do you know about Smirnov leaving the block?
Kamenev: I confirm that Smirnov was a member of the bloc all along.
Vyshinsky: Defendant Smirnov, that closes the cycle".

Seeing that they all declared against him, to the effect that he had been the head of the Trotskyists in the conspiracy, Smirnov turned to them sarcastically and said, "You want a leader? Fine, take me!"

Valentin P. Olberg, indicated as an agent provocateur in Trotskyist sources, was the next to give evidence. Vyshinsky asked him to say how long he had been connected with Trotskyism, and Olberg admitted that he had been a member of the organisation since 1927 and that in 1930 he had established contact with Trotsky's son through Anton Grilevich, editor of Trotsky's German-language pamphlets. He stated that from May 1931 to the end of 1932 they met weekly, sometimes even twice a week. The meeting places were a café on Nürnbergerplatz or Sedov's flat. Olberg explained that Sedov's wife Susanna brought from Copenhagen a letter from Trotsky addressed to his son, authorising Olberg's trip to the USSR. The prosecutor asked him what he knew about a certain Friedmann and Olberg replied that he was a Trotskyite who was also dispatched to the USSR.

"Vyshinsky: Do you know that Friedmann was connected to the German police?
Olberg: I heard about this.
Vyshinsky: Was the link with the German police systematic?
Olberg. Yes, it was systematic. Trotsky knew about it and had his consent.
Vyshinsky: How do you know that Trotsky knew and consented?
Olberg: One of the lines of connection was maintained by myself and I established it with Trotsky's approval".

The accused then proceeded to explain the three trips he made to the USSR. The first time, in March 1933, he entered on a false passport in the name of Freudigmann and remained in the country until July. He admitted that the purpose of the trip was to prepare and carry out the assassination of Stalin. Olberg lived secretly in Moscow for six weeks and then went to Stalinabad, where he taught history. Lacking documents to prove his military service, he was forced to return abroad and went to Prague, where his younger brother, Paul Olberg, lived. From the Czech capital, he reported what had happened to Sedov, who promised to get him a better passport. In Prague, according to the official version, Paul Olberg had connections with a certain Tukalevsky, a Gestapo agent who worked as director of the Slavic Bookshop of the Czechoslovak Foreign Ministry. Valentin Olberg stated that for 13,000 Czechoslovak crowns Tukalevsky offered him a passport in the name of Lucas Parades, Consul General of the Republic of Honduras in

Berlin, who had arrived in Prague. The money was forwarded to him by Trotsky's son, and Olberg thus obtained a new passport. Vyshinsky then produced the passport in court and asked Olberg to confirm whether it was the same document, which he did. Olberg thus re-entered the USSR in March 1935, but was unable to stay there for as long as he wished because he had travelled on a tourist visa. He returned to Germany and stayed there for three months until he was able to obtain a time extension for his Honduran passport. In July of the same year, he tried again. After a short stay in Minsk, he went to Gorky, where he made contact with the Trotskyists Yelin and Fedotov and got a job at the Gorky Pedagogical Institute. There he worked on the attempt on Stalin's life, which was to take place on 1 May 1936.

> "Vyshinsky: What prevented you from implementing the plan?
> Olberg: The arrest.
> Vyshinsky: Did you inform Sedov about the preparations for the terrorist action?
> Olberg: Yes, I wrote several times to the Slomovitz management and received a letter announcing that our old friend insisted that the diploma thesis should be submitted on 1 May.
> Vyshinsky: Diploma thesis? What is this?
> Olberg: The Assassination of Stalin.
> Vyshinsky: And who is the old friend?
> Olberg: The old friend is Trotsky".

The last defendant of the day was Konon Borisovich Berman-Yurin (alias Alexander Fomich), who was asked by the presiding judge to recount the instructions he had received abroad before travelling to the USSR. Berman-Yurin stated that in 1932 he had personally visited Trotsky in Copenhagen and had received direct instructions from him to attack Stalin. The first contact with Sedov was also established, as in the case of Olberg, through Anton Grilevich. The statements of this defendant deserve attention, for he explained in detail the circumstances of the meeting and the conversation with Trotsky in Copenhagen. He said that he arrived in Copenhagen at the end of November 1932, where he was met at the station by Grilevich, who led him to Trotsky. At the leader's request, Berman-Yurin justified his Trotskyite militancy at length, after which he went on to discuss the situation in the USSR. Trotsky, according to the accused, said that Stalin must be physically destroyed, that other methods of struggle were no longer effective, that people ready for anything, ready for personal sacrifice, were required to carry out this historic task. Berman-Yurin explained that the first conversation ended because Trotsky left the house and he remained in the flat awaiting his return, which was in the evening. The conversation then continued and Trotsky expressed the necessity that Kaganóvich and Voroshilov should also be killed.

"Vyshinsky: What other issues did you touch on besides terrorism?

Berman-Yurin: Trotsky expressed his views on the situation in the face of possible intervention against the Soviet Union. He clearly adopted a defeatist attitude. He said that the Trotskyists should join the army, but that they would not defend the Soviet Union.

Vyshinsky: Did he convince you?

Berman-Yurin: During the conversation he paced nervously from one side of the room to the other and spoke of Stalin with exceptional hatred.

Vyshinsky: Did you give your consent?

Berman-Yurin: Yes.

Vyshinsky: Is that how your conversation ended?

Berman-Yurin: I also talked to Trotsky about the following. After giving him my consent, he said I should prepare to go to Moscow, and since I would have contact with the Comintern, I should prepare the terrorist action by taking advantage of this contact.

Vyshinsky: Did Trotsky not only give you instructions in general, but formulate your task concretely?

Berman-Yurin: He said that the terrorist action, if possible, should be timed to take place at the Comintern Plenum or Congress.... This would have tremendous international repercussions and would provoke a mass movement all over the world. It would be a historic political event of world importance. Trotsky said that I should not contact any Trotskyists in Moscow and that I should do the work independently. I replied that I did not know anyone in Moscow and that it was difficult for me to imagine how I could act in these circumstances. I said that I had an acquaintance named Fritz David and asked if I should not contact him. Trotsky replied that he would instruct Sedov to clear up this matter and that he would give me instructions in this regard."

Berman-Yurin travelled to Moscow in March 1933. Sedov ordered him to contact Fritz David to prepare the attack. Both believed it possible to commit the attack during the 13th Plenum of the Communist International (Comintern). Fritz David was to provide an entrance for Berman-Yurin and Berman-Yurin was to shoot Stalin. The plan failed because the entrance was not obtained. It was decided to postpone the attack until the Congress of the International, which was scheduled for September 1934: "I," Berman-Yurin declared, "gave Fritz David a Browning pistol and bullets. Before the opening of the Congress he informed me that he had not got a ticket for me, but that he would be at the Congress. We decided that he should be the one to carry out the terrorist action." The plan failed again, for, although Fritz David was seated in a box, he could not get close enough to Stalin to shoot him.

Several sources indicate that in 1936 Stalin had known about Berman-Yurin's interviews with Trotsky for years. Rita T. Kronenbitter (see note 14) published in *Studies in Intelligence* an article entitled "Leon Trotsky, Dupe of the NKVD", *a* secret document declassified years later in the CIA's

"Historical Review Program". This work reveals the extent to which Soviet agents had Trotsky under their control at all times. "All they know about my movements is what they learn from the newspapers", Trotsky had foolishly declared in 1932. The fact is that already in 1931 the OGPU had infiltrated Trotsky's circle through the Sobolevicius brothers, two Lithuanian Jews. The fact that the agents Stalin sent to Trotsky were Jews suggests that he trusted them, which facilitated the rapprochement. The Sobolevicius brothers: Jack Soble and Dr. Robert Soblen, known among the Trotskyists as Adolph Senin and Roman Well respectively, visited Trotsky in Turkey between 1929 and 1932, where they gained his confidence. Trotsky regarded them as loyal supporters and probably never even knew they were brothers. In December 1932 Jack Soble saw Trotsky for the last time in Copenhagen. Senin-Soble, having passed on to the NKVD all the information about Trotsky's movements in the Danish capital, where he had gone to give a series of lectures, left the Trotskyist movement and disappeared.[15]

The morning session on the 21st began with Edouard Solomonovich Holtzman, who had joined the Trotskyist organisation as early as 1926 and had a special relationship with Smirnov, whom he had known since 1918. The prosecutor wanted to establish that the meetings between Smirnov and Holtzman took place regularly in the flat of Smirnov's mother. Holtzman admitted that he had travelled to Berlin, where he telephoned Sedov and arranged to meet him at the "Zoologischer Garten". Since they did not know each other, they agreed that they would carry copies of the *Berliner Tageblatt* and *Vorwärts* in their hands. Trotsky's son took him by car to a flat, where Holtzman handed him a report and the secret code. During the months he was in Berlin the meetings went on and on, until they finally met in Copenhagen, where they travelled separately for security reasons. In the Danish capital he met Trotsky, who asked him to inform him about the feelings and attitude of the party members towards Stalin. Again this defendant confirmed that during the conversation Trotsky had spoken to him about the need to get rid of Stalin. Holtzman tried to argue in court that he did not share Trotsky's views on terrorism; but the prosecutor made him confess that he nevertheless continued to belong to the Trotskyite organisation knowing that terrorist actions had been decided upon.

Then came the turn of the two Lurjes, whose relationship is uncertain, as it seems that they were not brothers. Nathan, the first to testify, a Trotskyite since 1927, admitted that he had come to the USSR from Berlin

---

[15] The Sobolevicius brothers were also known as Sobolev and Sobol. The eldest, Robert Soblen (Roman Well), was editor in 1927 of the *Arbeiter Zeitung* and later of *Bolschevistische Einheit*, extreme left-wing organs in Germany. The names Jack Soble and Robert Soblen, by which these Jewish brothers are known, were the names they adopted in the United States, where they continued to work as Soviet agents during the post-war years. In 1957 Jack Soble and his wife Myra were arrested, accused of being part of an espionage network known as "Mocase". Both were tried and imprisoned.

on a mission to commit terrorist acts. Nathan Lurje declared that hatred of Stalin and the leadership of the CPSU had been central to the training he had received from the organisation in Germany. During the trial it was established that, after arriving in Moscow in 1932, Nathan contacted Konstant and Lipschitz, two Trotskyists he had met in Germany, to whom he passed on the instructions he had received from the organisation through Moisei Lurje. Konstant let him know that they already had a terrorist group involving a German engineer and architect named Franz Weitz, who, according to Konstant, was a member of the NSDAP who in August 1932 informed him that there was a possibility of an attack on the USSR Defence Commissar, Comrade Voroshilov. From September 1932 to March 1933, the car in which Voroshilov was travelling was observed coming and going, but the possibility of assassinating him by shooting was eventually dismissed, as the car was moving fast. A bomb was later considered, but the attack was also unsuccessful. Nathan Lurje testified in court that he was then sent to Chelyabinsk, where he worked as a surgeon, until January 1936, when he went on a scientific mission to Leningrad. While in Moscow he met Moisei Lurje, who gave him instructions to attack Comrade Zhdanov. Moisei Lurje (Michael Larin), a Jewish economist and Comintern confederate, whose daughter Anna Larina married Bukharin in 1934, confirmed in his statement that he had been in contact with Nathan from April 1933 to January 1936 and that both were Trotskyists who had been commissioned to assassinate the Stalinist leadership. The morning session of 21 August ended with Vagarshak Arutyanovich Ter-Vaganyan, who in addition to implicating Smirnov again and accepting that he received instructions from Zinoviev and Kamenev, offered two new names, the Trotskyist historians Zeidel and Friedland.

The last of the accused, Fritz David (Ilya-David Israilevich) alias Kruglyansky, was questioned at the afternoon session on 21 August. He entered the USSR with instructions received from Trotsky to attempt to assassinate Stalin. Fritz David contacted only Berman-Yurin, who was also carrying out instructions directly from Trotsky. The two of them drew up concrete plans to assassinate Stalin. The first scenario chosen was the 13th Plenum of the Executive Committee of the International; the second, the 7th Congress of the International (Comintern). Both failed. In the first case, Stalin did not attend the plenary. In the other, as has been said in examining Berman-Yurin's statement, Fritz David, was able to get into the Congress, but could not approach Stalin. Vyshinsky summarises the defendant's statement thus: "We can therefore summarise. You were a member of the Trotskyist organisation and met Trotsky personally. Trotsky himself instructed you to go to the USSR to commit terrorist acts and warned you to keep strict secrecy. This explains why he did not contact anyone except Berman-Yurin. Together with Berman-Yurin, who had received similar instructions, he made preparations for an attempt on Comrade Stalin's life and chose the Seventh Congress in 1935 as the opportune moment. Thanks to the contacts he had in the Comintern he managed to enter the Congress with the purpose of committing the act, but he was unable to do so because of circumstances beyond your control."

At the end of the interrogations, Prosecutor Vishinsky issued a report announcing that further proceedings were to be instituted:

"In the preceding sessions some of the defendants (Kamenev, Zinoviev and Reingold) have referred in their testimony to Tomsky, Bukharin, Rykov, Uglanov, Radek, Pyatakov, Serebryakov and Sokolnikov as being, to a lesser or greater degree, involved in the criminal counter-revolutionary activities for which those involved in the present case are on trial. I consider it necessary to inform the court that yesterday I gave orders for the launching of an investigation into the information of the defendants concerning Tomsky, Rikov, Bukharin, Uglanov, Radek and Pyatakov, and that, in accordance with the results of this investigation, the General Prosecutor's Office will institute legal proceedings in the matter. In relation to Serebryakov and Sokolnikov, the authorities are already in possession of materials implicating these persons in counter-revolutionary crimes, and, in view of this, criminal proceedings are being instituted against Sokolnikov and Serebryakov."

The next day, 22 August, this statement was printed. The same day, after reading it, Mikhail Tomsky (actually Honigberg) wrote a letter to Stalin denying all the charges and shortly afterwards committed suicide. The Central Committee, to which Tomsky was a candidate, denounced his suicide a day later and attributed it to the fact that he had been framed.

The day of the 22nd also had morning and afternoon sessions. The morning session was entirely for the prosecution. In a lengthy speech, the prosecutor described the Trotskyist-Zinovievite centre as a gang of despicable terrorists and accused Trotsky, Zinoviev and Kamenev of being sworn enemies of the Soviet Union, whose main methods were double-dealing, deception and provocation. Vyshinsky considered that the counter-revolutionary terrorist activities, among which he insisted on emphasising the assassination of Comrade Kirov, had been fully proved. Having dropped the masks of the accused, he concluded, "I request that these mad dogs be shot - every one of them." The afternoon session on the 22nd and the two sessions on the 23rd were devoted entirely to hearing the pleas of the sixteen defendants. When Fritz David, the last to speak, had finished, it was already 19:00 in the evening and the court retired to consider the verdict. On 24 August, at 14:30, the presiding judge, Vassili Ulrich, read the sentence condemning all the defendants to the supreme penalty, which entailed firing squad execution and confiscation of all property.

If, as Orlov and Krivitsky claim, it is true that Stalin promised Zinoviev and Kamenev that they would not be executed, he evidently reneged on his promise, since twenty-four hours after the sentence was made public it was announced that the execution was to take place. In *The Great Terror*, Robert Conquest again refers to Alexander Orlov's account of Zinoviev's last moments. According to the latter, on 20 December 1936 Stalin gave a small banquet for the NKVD chiefs to mark the anniversary of the creation of the Cheka. When everyone was already drunk, the Jew Karl V. Pauker, responsible for the security of the Kremlin, the Politburo and Stalin himself, who was to be arrested in March 1937 and executed on 14 August of the same year, slavishly parodied Zinoviev's pleas before being shot for Stalin's amusement. Using two officers as guards, he played the role of Zinoviev as he was dragged to execution. Hanging from the arms of the guards, moaning and pleading, Pauker/Zinoviev fell to his knees and clutched at the boots of one of the guards shouting, "Please, for God's sake, comrade, telephone Yosif Vissarionovich!". Stalin laughed and Pauker repeated his performance. With Stalin laughing his head off, Pauker/Zinoviev offered a new scene and raising his hands and crying said: "Listen, Israel, our God is the only God!" Stalin was choking with laughter, and signalled to Pauker to finish his performance. It is significant, in any case, that Zinoviev, supposedly an atheist like the rest of his Judeo-Bolshevik colleagues, who had been engaged in destroying Christian churches and murdering the religious of this faith, invoked the God of Israel before he died.

As for the claim that the charges brought against the defendants were trumped up and that the whole thing was a sham, we think it does not hold water. The allegations were carefully examined by various British lawyers, who found them convincing. International journalists present at the trial also gave full credibility to the proceedings. It was only later that anti-Stalinist or Trotskyist writers began to go to great lengths to discredit the Moscow trials. Trotsky himself wrote that "the Trotskyists were playing in the USSR exactly the same role as the Jews and Communists were playing in Germany". Moreover, documents have been found in the Harvard archives which prove beyond doubt that Trotsky and his son Sedov were associated with the anti-Stalinist bloc when it was in formation. The Trotskyist writer Vadim Rogovin in his book *1937: Stalin's Year of Terror* admits that the anti-Stalinist bloc was already formed in June 1932. The contacts of Trotsky and his son with representatives of the leaders of the Trotskyist-Zinovievist centre and the existence of the conspiracy are thus undeniable facts. The infiltration of the entourage of Trotsky and his son Sedov is fully proven and was so deep that even the edition of the famous *Opposition Bulletin* came to be in the hands of Mark Zborowski, Etienne, the NKVD agent who introduced Sylvia Ageloff to Ramon Mercader, who seduced this Trotskyite and was thus able to get into Trotsky's house and assassinate him.

The Pyatakov trial

Preparations for the second trial announced by Vyshinsky began immediately. Sokolnikov was arrested on 26 August. Two weeks after the executions, on 8 September 1936, Bukharin and Rykov were confronted with Sokolnikov in the presence of Kaganovich, Yezhov and Vyshinsky; but on 10 September *Pravda* reported in a small paragraph that the charges against Bukharin and Rykov had been dropped for lack of evidence. Thus Bukharin retained his position as editor of *Izvestia* and both remained candidates for the Central Committee. According to some sources, the refusal to pursue proceedings against them was due to pressure from various members of the Politburo. On 12 September Georgi Pyatakov was arrested, and on 22 September it was Radek's turn. While these arrests were taking place, Yagoda's position was wavering. According to Orlov, Yagoda, convinced that Zinoviev and Kamenev would not be executed, had been deceived by Stalin. Subsequently, he was to be accused of protecting some of the defendants and of having obstructed the interrogations. On 25 September Stalin and Andrei Zhdanov sent a telegram from Sochi to Kaganovich and Molotov in which they considered it urgent and necessary to place Yezhov as head of the Commissariat of Internal Affairs, indicating that Yagoda was distrusted. On 26 September Nikolai Yezhov became the new Commissar for Internal Affairs and a member of the Central Committee.

The fact that Yezhov was Russian did not, however, mean that the predominance of Jewish leaders in the NKVD had been ended. On 30 September, the Jew Matvei Davydovich Berman, considered one of the fathers of the Gulag, as he had been in charge of the Administration of the Labour Camps since 1932, was appointed deputy director of the NKVD. Expelled from the party in 1938, Berman was executed on 7 March 1939. His brother Boris Davydovich also held an important position in the Foreign Department of the Lubyanka. Four other Jews: Mikhail Iosifovich Litvin, Isaak Ilich Shapiro, Vladimir Yefimovich Tsesarsky and Semen Borisovich Zhukovsky were among Yezhov's first appointments. His secretary, Yakob Deych, was also Jewish, as was Yakov Saulovich Agranov, one of Yagoda's men who remained in the NVKD and was head of the team of interrogators who began preparing for the retrial. He himself was eventually shot on 1 August 1938, accused of being a Trotskyite and an enemy of the people.

Of the seventeen people who appeared in court, accused of being part of the so-called Anti-Soviet Trotskyist Centre, Pyatakov, Sokolnikov and Radek were the most prominent figures. The latter had been accused by Trotsky of having betrayed Yakov Blumkin, the Jewish terrorist who on Trotsky's orders had assassinated the German ambassador Wilhelm Mirbach on 16 June 1918. Blumkin, who had been Trotsky's secretary, was in Turkey in 1929 and was selling Hebrew incunabula stolen from synagogues in the Ukraine, southern Russia and state museums. Part of the money was given to his boss to finance a spy network in the Middle East. Trotsky then handed him a secret message for Radek. The GPU got wind of the interview and set a trap for him. Elizabeth Zarubina (actually Lisa Rozensweig), an agent of Jewish origin who in the United States took the name Lisa Gorskaya, had been having an affair for weeks with Blumkin, who was arrested with her in a car and subsequently executed. Yagoda, who together with Menzhinsky headed the operation, most likely warned Radek that the GPU knew about it. Trotsky accused Radek of treason, but it is almost certain that Radek denounced Blumkin as a measure of self-protection. As for Sokolnikov, in the *Secret History of Stalin's Crimes* Orlov reports an interview with Stalin, in which he allegedly promised to save his life in exchange for his collaboration. Robert Conquest does not find this version very credible, since Sokolnikov knew what had happened with Zinoviev and Kamenev. About the third man, Pyatakov, the Trotskyist writer Pierre Broué writes that he had left the opposition in 1928 and was considered a deserter. In *Les Procès de Moscou,* Broué writes: "He had become so odious to the people of the Trotskyist opposition that Sedov, at a meeting in Unter den Linden in Berlin, had publicly rebuked him. Broué therefore considers everything Pyatakov said at the trial to be irrelevant.

In December 1936 the detainees began to collaborate. Conquest writes that Stalin personally visited Radek at the Lubyanka and had a long conversation with him in the presence of Yezhov. Relying again on Orlov, Conquest states that after the interview with Stalin, Radek became the interrogators' most valuable collaborator. At the end of December, Bukharin was given copies of Radek's statements incriminating him in terrorist acts and other crimes. From then on, as a result of the accusations against him, Bukharin had to face continuous confrontations with Radek, Pyatakov, Sokolnikov and other defendants. On 16 January 1937 his name ceased to appear as editor of *Izvestia.* By the beginning of January the prosecution already had hundreds of pages of evidence of the seriousness of the plot, so that on 23 January 1937 the trial against the new batch of Trotskyists, designated as the "Anti-Soviet Trotskyist Centre", could begin and continued until 30 January.

Eight of the seventeen defendants were again Jewish. Knyazev, Pushin and Arnold were assisted by lawyers. The others - Pyatakov, Radek, Sokolnikov, Serebryakov, Livshitz, Muralov, Drobnis, Bogulavsky, Rataichak, Norkin, Shestov, Stroilov, Turok and Hrasche - chose to conduct their own defence. The reading of the indictment took up the first hour of the opening session. In summing up, Prosecutor Vyshinsky recalled that in the previous trial, through the statements of Zinoviev, Kamenev and other defendants, the existence of a "reserve centre" organised around Pyatakov, Radek, Sokolnikov and Serebryakov, which operated under direct instructions from Trotsky, had been established. The prosecutor claimed that the main task of this centre was to overthrow the government of the USSR and that they were assisted in this by foreign states, namely Germany and Japan. According to Vyshinsky, the investigation had established that L. D. Trotsky had entered into negotiations with leaders of the NSDAP with a view to unleashing a war against the Soviet Union. All the defendants pleaded guilty.

The US Ambassador to Moscow, Joseph E. Davies, who was a lawyer, attended all the sessions of the Moscow trials. In his work *Mission To Moscow he* is completely convinced of the guilt of the defendants. On 17 February 1937, in a confidential report to Secretary of State Cordel Hull, he wrote: "To suppose that this trial was devised and staged as a project of dramatic political fiction would be to presuppose the creative genius of a Shakespeare and the staging genius of a Belasco". In the same report, Ambassador Davies reported that he had spoken to almost all members of the diplomatic corps and that, with one exception, they were of the opinion "that the proceedings clearly established the existence of a political plot and conspiracy to overthrow the Government".

The first to testify was Georgi (Yuri) Pyatakov. On the famous quarrel of 1928, considered definitive by P. Broué, Pyatakov mentioned it in the context of an interview with Sedov in 1931 and declared: "Sedov said that Trotsky had never doubted that, despite our quarrel at the beginning of 1928, he had in me a reliable comrade-in-arms". The prosecutor wanted to establish that the 1931 meeting with Trotsky's son had taken place and had the following dialogue with the defendant Shestov:

"Vyshinsky: Did you meet Pyatakov in Berlin in 1931?
Shestov: Yes.
Vyshinsky: Did the defendant Pyatakov inform you about his meeting with Sedov?
Shestov: Yes, he did.
Vyshinsky: Do you confirm what Pyatakov has just said about your interview with Sedov?
Shestov: Yes, I can confirm that.

Pyatakov then informed the court about the receipt at the end of November 1931 of a personal letter from Trotsky written in German and signed with the initials "L. T." The letter, the defendant recalled, began with the following words: "Dear friend, I am very glad that you have followed my instructions..." the missive insisted on the necessity of eliminating Stalin and his collaborators by any means and on the urgency of uniting in the struggle all anti-Stalinist forces. Pyatakov then referred to a second trip to Berlin in mid-1932. Again he met Trotsky's son, who expressed his father's impatience that everything was going too slowly. He specifically recalled Sedov's words: "You know what kind of a man Lev Davydovich is, he is roaring and raving, burning with impatience to see his instructions carried out as soon as possible, and I can offer him nothing concrete from your report. Pyatakov declared that at the end of 1932 he had given Kamenev his consent to join the reserve centre, which began to operate in 1933. Vyshinsky then asked under whose leadership the parallel or reserve centre operated. "From Trotsky", the accused replied.

> "Vyshinsky: What practical measures did the centre carry out during 1933 and 1934?
> Pyatakov: It was in 1933-34 that organisational work developed in the Ukraine and Western Siberia. Later the Moscow group was formed. Work was done in the Urals and all this work began to take shape in the fulfilment of Trotsky's instructions.... In the Ukraine the work was carried out by Loginov and a group of people connected with him and developed mainly in the coal industry. Their work, mainly, consisted in starting up coal furnaces which were not yet fit for operation and in delaying the construction of very important and costly parts of the coal and chemical industry...."

It must be considered that the accused was in 1933-34 the most trusted man of Serge Ordzhonikidze, a Georgian friend of Stalin's who held the post of People's Commissar of Heavy Industry. Pyatakov was therefore in a privileged position to organise sabotage activities in industry and other areas of production. At the request of the prosecutor, the accused then gave an account of sabotage activities throughout the USSR of which he had become aware, which took place in mining, the chemical industry, power stations, construction, etc. As the story progressed, the names of the people directly involved appeared: Drobnis, Shestov, Muralov, Bogulavsky, Rataichak, Norkin. In Kemerovo, the city through which the Trans-Siberian passed on its way to Vladivostok, an important chemical, fertiliser and manufacturing industry had developed. Norkin was sent there on orders from Piatakov.

> "Vyshinsky: Comrade Chairman, let me ask Norkin a question.
> The President: Defendant Norkin.
> Vyshinky: Defendant Norkin, do you remember the conversation with Pyatakov about stopping work in the chemical industry in case of war?
> Norkin: It was quite clearly stated that preparations had to be made, so that defence industry enterprises could be crippled by explosions and fires.
> Vyshinsky: Do you remember when Pyatakov told you this?
> Norkin: In 1936, in Pyatakov's office in the People's Commissariat.
> Vyshinsky: Do you remember the details, was there any reference to the cost of human lives?
> Norkin: I remember that it was said that the loss of human lives was generally unavoidable and that certain actions could not prevent the death of workers. This order was given.
> Vyshinsky: Defendant Pyatakov, do you remember if you said this to Norkin?

Pyatakov: That's right. I don't remember the exact words, but that was the idea. The idea was to paralyse the Kemerovo industrial complex in the event of war; perhaps we talked about concrete ways of doing that, and, of course, the loss of human lives was considered. I told Norkin that there would be a cost in human lives that had to be reckoned with.
Vyshinsky: Did you contemplate this as inevitable?
Pyatakov: Of course.

There follow some significant passages in relation to a very important section of this chapter: that of Hitler's financing. As will be seen from the statements of the defendants in this second trial, Trotsky's contacts with Nazi leaders were in pursuit of a limited war against the USSR which, theoretically, was to end in a draw: it was to serve to overthrow Stalin and put him back in power. In reality this tactic was not new: already in 1905 Trotsky, Parvus and company had worked for the defeat of Russia against Japan as a means of seizing power; and Lenin too had opted for defeatism during the world war. Stalin and National Communism were disrupting the plans for World Government; but this time, with Communism already established in Russia, the USSR was not to be defeated: it was merely a matter of redirecting the situation. The international Jewish bankers, who from the beginning had financed Trotsky and communism, could not accept that overnight Stalin, a stranger, should have upset the plan whose initial outline dated back to the founding of Adam Weishaupt's Illuminati. Wall Street financiers had agreed that Hitler must discover for himself the hidden purposes behind his financial assistance to the NSDAP. When "Sidney Warburg" reported on his interviews, Rockefeller was especially interested in Hitler's statements about the Communists. Warburg himself asked Hitler several times about his intentions in international politics. On one occasion the future Führer told the young Warburg: "Your friends in America have an undoubted interest in our party gaining power in Germany.... I do not care what motives impel them to help me; but they must be well aware that without sufficient financial means I can do nothing." Remembering this, Pyatakov's statement can be better understood:

> "Vyshinsky: Were members of your organisation connected to foreign intelligence services?
> Pyatakov: Yes, they were. I must go back to the line designed by Trotsky to make it clear....
> What did Trotsky demand then?
> Pyatakov: He demanded definite acts of terrorism and sabotage. I must say that among Trotsky's followers there was considerable resistance to the instructions on sabotage activities..... We informed Trotsky of the existence of these views; but he replied in a sharply worded letter that the instructions on terrorism and sabotage were not fortuitous, were not merely one of the intensive methods of struggle he proposed, but an

essential part of his policy and of his present line of action. In the same directive he expressed - this was in mid-1934 - that now that Hitler had come to power it was quite clear that his idea about the impossibility of building socialism in one country had been completely justified, that war was inevitable, and that if we Trotskyists wanted to maintain ourselves as a political force, we should in advance, having adopted a defeatist position, not only passively observe and contemplate, but actively prepare the circumstances for this defeat. But in order to do this, cadres had to be formed, and these could not be created just by talking. Consequently the necessary sabotage activities had to be carried out."

On page 53 of the *Report of the Court Proceedings* in the case of the Anti-Soviet Trotskyist Centre, published in 1937 in Moscow by the Military College of the Supreme Court of the USSR, there is the following passage from the statement:

"Pyatakov: I remember that Trotsky said in his directive that without the necessary help from foreign states, a bloc government could never come to power or seize it. It was therefore necessary to make preliminary agreements with the more aggressive states, such as Germany and Japan, and that he, Trotsky, had already taken the necessary steps himself to establish contacts with the German and Japanese governments."

Later, on page 55 of the *Report of the Tribunal's Proceedings*, Pyatakov's startling revelations confirm an approach that makes sense of the past and the future that was to follow:

"...In a conversation Trotsky had told me that he considered it absolutely necessary to organise terrorist and other acts, but that he would have to consult with his comrades Rykov and Bukharin, which he subsequently did and then gave me an answer on behalf of all three.... At the end of 1935 Radek received a long letter with instructions from Trotsky. In it Trotsky advanced two possible variants for coming to power. The first was the possibility of our achieving it before the war, and the second, during the war. Trotsky visualised the first variant as the result of a concentrated outburst of terrorist actions, as he put it. What he had in mind was a simultaneous chain of terrorist attacks against a number of leaders of the CPSU and the Government, and of course in the first place against Stalin and his closest collaborators. The second variant, which in Trotsky's opinion was the most likely, was a military defeat. Since, as he said, war was inevitable, and moreover in the very near future - a war first of all with Germany, and possibly with Japan - the idea was to come to an agreement with the governments of these countries and thus ensure that they would look favourably on the coming to power of the bloc. This meant making a series of concessions to these countries on terms agreed in advance, in order to win their support for keeping us in power. But since the question of defeatism, of sabotage activities in the rear and in the army during the war, was put to us bluntly, Radek and myself were very uneasy and worried. It seemed to us that the reasons for Trotsky's betting on the inevitability of defeat were his isolation and his ignorance of the real conditions, his ignorance of what was going on here, his ignorance of what the Red Army was like; and therefore he held such illusions. Both Radek and I therefore decided that a meeting with Trotsky must be attempted."

This meeting allegedly took place in Norway in December 1935; but since Trotsky denied it, a plethora of Trotskyist and anti-Stalinist writers, including Robert Conquest, in theory a relatively objective source, have undermined the credibility of Pyatakov's statement about his interview with Trotsky in Oslo, which takes up seven pages of the *Tribunal's Report of Proceedings*. It is fully established that Pyatakov managed to travel to Berlin in December 1935, where he was to conduct Soviet Government business. According to his statement, after contacting an agent of Trotsky's, Bukhartsev, in the Berlin Tiergarten (zoo), he obtained a German passport and flew to Norway. He took off from Tempelhof on the morning of 12 December and landed at Oslo's Kjeller airport at 3 p.m., where a car was waiting: "The journey took probably about thirty minutes and we arrived on the outskirts. We got out of the car and went into a small, well-furnished house, and there I saw Trotsky, whom I had not seen since 1928'. During the meeting, which lasted about two hours, Trotsky revealed to him that he had held talks with Nazi leader Rudolf Hess and that they had reached agreements on cooperation.

Conquest, relying as usual on the opportunist and unreliable Alexander Orlov, accuses Stalin of having personally added this story to the script. Apart from Trotsky's word, which is logically worthless, the evidence adduced to deny Pyatakov's trip are two newspaper reports published in haste, at the behest of God knows who, a year after the events, i.e., while the trial was in progress, namely on 25 and 29 January 1937. The first, which appeared in the newspaper *Aftenposten*, reported that no civilian aircraft had landed at the airport in December 1935. The second, published in *Arbeiderbladet*, the newspaper of the Norwegian Social Democratic Party, stated that no aircraft had used airport between September 1935 and May 1936. For his part, Trotsky personally intervened from Mexico and challenged Stalin to request his extradition to a Norwegian court, "where the truth could be judicially established". Evidently, a parallel trial abroad was the most Trotsky could hope for. To counter the information in *Aftenposten*, at the end of the 27 January session the prosecutor asked the court for permission to say the following:

"Vyshinsky: I have a request to the court. I took an interest in this matter (the flight to Oslo) and asked the Commissariat for Foreign Affairs to make an enquiry, since I wanted to verify Pyatakov's testimony also from this side. I have received an official communication, which I request to be added to the court record.

(Read) 'The Consular Department of the People's Commissariat for Foreign Affairs hereby informs the Public Prosecutor of the USSR that, according to information received by the Embassy of the USSR in Norway, the Kjeller airfield near Oslo receives throughout the year, in accordance with international regulations, aircraft from other countries, and the arrival and departure of aircraft is possible also during the winter months'".

There is not space for a lengthy review of Pyatakov's statement of his conversation with Trotsky in Oslo, during which the need for a coup d'état was emphatically expressed; but we cannot fail to quote verbatim a few passages, among which the famous contact with Rudolf Hess stands out:

"Pyatakov:...He told me that he had come to an absolutely definite agreement with the German Fascist Government and with the Japanese Government and that both would take a favourable attitude in the event of the Trotskyist-Zinovievite bloc coming to power..... He told me that he had had extensive negotiations with the Vice-President of the German National Socialist Party, Hess. It is true that I cannot say whether there is a signed agreement or whether it is only an understanding, but Trotsky presented it to me as if the agreement existed..... What does the agreement amount to if it is to be briefly explained? In the first place the German fascists promise the Trotskyist-Zinovievievite bloc a favourable attitude and their support in the event of its coming to power. In return the fascists are to obtain the following compensations: a generally favourable attitude towards German interests and towards the German government in all questions of international politics; some territorial concessions to be made, in particular, there was veiled talk of territorial concessions which would have to do with non-resistance to the Ukrainian bourgeois-nationalist forces in the case of their self-determination.

Vyshinsky: What does this mean?

Pyatakov: It means in a veiled way what Radek stated here: if the Germans were to install a government - not a government headed by a German governor-general, but a government headed perhaps by a hetman (Ukrainian military chief) - it would in any case be they who would be self-determining and the Trotskyist-Zinovievievite bloc would not oppose it. This would basically mean the beginning of the break-up of the Soviet Union. The next point of the agreement concerned the way in which German capital would be enabled to exploit the raw material resources it needed from the USSR. This was to be the exploitation of gold mines, oil mines, manganese mines, forests and so on. In a word, it had been agreed in principle between Trotsky and Hess that German capital would be admitted and would receive the necessary economic supplement, although the concrete forms of this participation would be the subject of further study."

Vyshinsky: What about cases of diversion in the event of war?

Pyatakov: This was the last point. I remember it well. In the end it was the most painful point, which in a general way clearly shows our true face. It had also been raised in the agreement between Trotsky and Hess.... In the event of a military attack it was necessary to co-ordinate all the destructive forces of the Trotskyist organisations which would act within the country under the leadership of German fascism. The work of diversion and sabotage carried out by the Trotskyist organisation inside the Soviet Union should be carried out according to Trotsky's instructions, which would be in concert with the German General Staff....."

Already in the last part of the interrogation, the prosecutor asked the accused to give an account of his participation in the organisation of terrorist acts. Pyatakov maintained his attitude of calm cooperation and gave details of the places where the actions had been carried out and of the leaders to be assassinated, among whom were Stalin, Molotov, Yezhov and others. The names of the Trotskyists involved in the design, planning and execution of the actions: Radek, Sokolnikov and Serebryakov, Norkin, Livshitz, Rataichak, etc. appeared again and again throughout the statement and confrontations between the accused followed one after another. After Pyatakov's turn, it was Karl Radek's turn.

What the first declarant had said could be contrasted and confirmed during the interrogation of Radek, who proved to be one of the most convincing and cooperative of the accused. He admitted having received three letters from Trotsky: one in April 1934, one in December 1935 and a third in January 1936, the contents of which coincided with Pyatakov's statements. However, Vladimir Romm, a correspondent for TASS and *Izvestia* in the United States who appeared at the trial without being charged, added that in August 1933 he had delivered to Radek in his Moscow flat a letter from Trotsky hidden in the dust jacket of a book, a very popular novel entitled *Tsusima*. During the trial Radek admitted that Romm had been used as a secret liaison. On the content of the 1934 letter, the defendant stated that Trotsky considered that the coming to power of fascism in Germany had changed the whole situation, since it meant war in the future, inevitable war. Trotsky," explained Radek, "had no doubt that this war would result in the defeat of the Soviet Union. This defeat, he wrote, was to create favourable conditions for the rise to power of the bloc." The prosecutor sought redundancy as a way of highlighting the seriousness of Rádek's concepts and responsibility. Here is the quote:

"Vyshinsky: So you were interested in hastening the war and you wanted the USSR to be defeated in this war? How was this stated in Trotsky's letter?

Radek: Defeat is inevitable and will create the conditions for our accession to power, therefore we are interested in unleashing the war. The conclusion is: We are interested in defeat.

Vyshinsky:...The letter you received from Trotsky in April 1934 spoke of war, that war was inevitable, that in this war the USSR, in Trotsky's opinion, would suffer defeat, that as a consequence of this war and this defeat the bloc would come to power. And now I ask you: In these circumstances, were you for the defeat of the USSR or for the Victory of the USSR?

Rádek: All my performances during those years demonstrate the fact that I worked for defeat.

Vyshinsky: Were their actions deliberate?

Rádek: Apart from sleeping, I have never in my life performed any unintentional actions.

Vyshinsky: And wasn't this, unfortunately, a dream?

Rádek: Unfortunately, this was not a dream.

Vyshinsky: Was it a reality?

Rádek: It was a sad reality".

The prosecutor asked whether Pyatakov, Sokolnikov and Serebryakov were informed about Trotsky's letter. Radek replied in the affirmative, and Vyshinsky immediately asked the above-mentioned defendants to confirm this, which they did. As to the 1935 letter, the prosecutor asked him for a summary, and Radek said among other things that the inevitable defeat in the war meant replacing Soviet power with what Trotsky called "a Bonapartist government", which, in the defendant's opinion, meant serving foreign finance capital. Radek stated that in this letter, in addition to recognising the conditions concerning the Ukraine, Trotsky envisaged the cession to Japan of the Amur region and the Maritime Province. The necessity of supplying Japan with oil from Sakhalin was also mentioned. Radek even confessed in court that he had sometimes had the feeling that his organisation was becoming the direct representative of foreign intelligence services. "We are no longer the masters of our actions at all," he said.

The trip to Oslo was also confirmed by Radek, who confirmed Pyatakov's statement that they had agreed on the necessity of visiting Trotsky. Pyatakov justified it," clarified Radek, "by saying that Trotsky had completely lost his sense of reality and was setting us tasks that we could not carry out, so it was necessary to go and see him by any means possible and talk things over with him". Radek told the court that when Pyatakov returned from Oslo he asked him a series of questions concerning foreign policy. Pyatakov replied that Trotsky had assured him that the war was not a matter of five years, but that it was a matter of war in 1937, a conclusion he had reached through his conversations with Hess and with other semi-official persons in Germany with whom he had dealings. According to Radek, Trotsky told Pyatakov that "the military preparations had been completed and that it was now a question of securing diplomatic means for Germany, for which a year would be needed. The object of these diplomatic efforts was, in the first place, to secure Britain's neutrality".

Everything concerning terrorist activities, including the murder of Kirov, was also acknowledged. Prosecutor Vyshsinky, no doubt already thinking of the third and final trial, the Trial of Twenty-One, which finally took place in March 1938, asked him to inform the court about the conversations with Bukharin, who was to be the main protagonist in that trial. "If you mean the talks on terrorism," Radek replied, "I can list them concretely. The first took place in June or July 1934, after Bukharin had returned from work at *Izvestia*. At that time Bukharin and I were conversing as members of two centres which were in contact. I asked him if he had taken the path of terrorism and he replied that he had. I asked him who was directing this activity and he replied that it was himself and Uglanov".

Before leaving this accused, one crucial fact in his statement must be emphasised: the mention of the names of two servicemen. In the course of his testimony, Radek said that Corps Commander Vitovt Putna, the Soviet military attaché in Britain who had been arrested a few months earlier, had come to see him at the request of Marshal Tukhachevsky. Putna had been summoned earlier, but not Tukhachevsky. During the afternoon session Radek, in a long exchange with Vyshinsky, tried to exonerate the Marshal completely and declared that Tukhachevsky had no idea "neither of Putna's criminal activities nor of my criminal activities". Radek referred to Tukhachevsky as a man absolutely devoted to the Party and the Government; however, the damage was already done and was so understood by those present at the trial.

It is not possible to go into the statements of the defendants in this second trial at length, as we have to keep things short. Even so, we do not renounce to select a few more passages that may provide something new. As to the statement of Yakov Livshitz, the next to testify, it should be said that in addition to giving new details about the relations of Pyatakov, Radek and Smirnov with Trotsky, he gave concrete details of terrorist actions in collaboration with Serebryakov, Knyazev and Turok. Oil distribution and railways were the main targets. Livshitz revealed that he knew that Knyazev and Turok were in connection with the Japanese secret services. The latter admitted to prosecutor Vyshinsky that in January 1935 he had received 35,000 roubles from the Japanese intelligence service, of which he kept 20,000 for his organisation and personally handed over the rest to Knyazev in May 1935. "Defendant Knyazev, is this correct?" - The prosecutor asked. "Yes, I received it," he answered. In *The Great Conspiracy Against Russia* Michael Sayers and Albert E. Kahn note that Livshitz himself was an agent of Japanese Military Intelligence and that he regularly passed information about Soviet railways to Japan.

The appearance of Grigory Yakovlevich Sokolnikov (Brilliant) added nothing new, although it did serve to identify new groups involved in terrorist activities. Sokolnikov, Commissar of Finance from 1923-26, had been removed by Stalin and appointed ambassador to London, a post he held from 1929-32. He admitted that in the autumn of 1934 he had learned from Kamenev that there was a plan to assassinate Stalin and Kirov and that Kamenev himself had explained to him Trotsky's defeatist positions. He reported on an interview with Pyatakov in January 1936, in the course of which Pyatakov gave him details of Trotsky's meeting with Hess at which the defeatist position was offered in exchange for German aid. Let us look at two specific questions on issues related to the socio-political and economic system:

> "Vyshinsky: Was I right when I wrote the following in the formulation of the charges: 'The main task of the parallel centre was to force the overthrow of the Soviet Government with the aim of changing the existing social and political system in the USSR...' Is this formulation correct?
> Sokolnikov: Yes, correct.
> Vyshinsky: Further on I say in the imputation: 'L. D. Trotsky, and with his instructions the parallel Trotskyist centre, wanted to gain power with the help of foreign states in order to restore the capitalist system of social relations in the USSR...' Is this formulation correct?
> Sokolnikov: Right..."

Next came Alexei Shestov, a mining engineer who until 1927 had been involved in printing and disseminating Trotskyist propaganda. In 1931 he was appointed director of the Kuznets coal mines, considered among the largest in the world, a position which enabled him to travel that same year to Berlin as part of a trade mission headed by Pyatakov. There he met Trotsky's son, who informed him that propaganda was being introduced into the USSR through H. Dahlmann of the multinational Frölich-Klüpfel-Dahlmann, a company which, in addition to financing Trotsky, was working on mining projects in the Urals and Siberia. Shestov, at Sedov's suggestion, met Dahlmann in Berlin, who proposed that he extend his collaboration with the Trotskyists and suggested that he commit acts of sabotage. Shestov became a member of the German secret service under the code name of Alyosha. However, R. Conquest, in his eagerness to discredit the trials and undermine their credibility, claims that this Trotskyist was an agent of the NKVD.

When asked by Vyshinsky, Shestov explained that in order to carry out sabotage actions he recruited the engineer Stroilov, who agreed to join the organisation and presented him with a plan: the aim was to interrupt the construction of new mines and the reconstruction of old ones; to reduce production and cause losses through accidents, explosions and fires; to intensify the destruction of machinery, and so on. Shestov added that they stole dynamite and kept it in a secret depot in order to have a reserve of their own. Asked what they intended to do, the accused replied: "To cause explosions in the mines". Shestov recalled that in 1934 an explosion took place in this mine and caused the death of several children, children of miners who were playing nearby. Stroilov confirmed everything. Already at the end of the interrogation, the accused also admitted that he gave instructions for the commission of a bank robbery in Anzherka, in which he took part. The loot amounted to 164,000 roubles and he himself managed this money.

The statement of Leonid Serebryakov, deputy director of the Railway Administration, focused in particular on explaining how goods train traffic was disrupted in order to disrupt the daily delivery of goods. In response to a question from the presiding judge, he admitted that they had even discussed with Livshitz the possibility of blocking the main railway junctions during the first days of a hypothetical mobilisation. The president himself asked Livshitz to confirm this statement and to specify when the conversation took place. Livshitz confirmed Serebryakov's statement and gave the date 1935. Both defendants admitted that the orders came from Pyatakov.

The statements of Yakov Drobnis, M.S. Bogulavsky, Mikhail Stroilov and Nikolai Muralov reiterated and elaborated on the statements of other defendants. The chemical complex at Kemerovo was the primary target of the actions of Drobnis, Stroilov and Norkin. Stroilov admitted that several Trotskyists, including himself, collaborated with the German Intelligence Service and admitted in court that he had betrayed his country. Muralov, from his early days a leading member of Trotsky's military faction, considered himself at the trial a faithful soldier of Trotsky. Probably because of this he had been replaced by Klementi Voroshilov at the head of the strategic Moscow Military Garrison,. Muralov admitted that, in collaboration with Shestov, he had tried to assassinate Molotov in 1934 by causing a car accident; but the attempt failed because Valentine Arnold, the Trotskyite who was driving the vehicle and was to give his life for the cause, chickened out and slowed down when he was supposed to crash into a ditch.

As regards the statements of Ivan Knyazev and Yosif Turok, two Trotskyists who, as stated above, collaborated with Livshitz with the Japanese Intelligence Service, the most important was their information about the sabotage of the railway system in the Urals, where Knyazev was the chief. He told the prosecutor that he had enlisted as a Japanese agent in September 1934 and confirmed that in talks with Livshitz they had agreed that it was necessary to combine all forces hostile to the Government and the Party and that they were determined to "stab each other in the back" in order to bring about the defeat of their country in the event of war. Vyshinsky forced him to recall specific accidents they had caused. The accused recounted several and even recalled the train numbers. He referred to a provoked derailment in which twenty-nine Red Army soldiers lost their lives and as many were wounded, fifteen of whom were seriously maimed. The prosecutor referred to two other specific accidents: the first on 7 February 1936 between Yedinover-Berdiaush; and the second on 27 February at the Christaya Chumlyak station. Knyazev was responsible for organising both. Yosif Turok, who also held an important position in the Traffic Department in Perm and on the Ural Railways, testified that he received direct orders from Livshitz to cause derailments, and confirmed what his colleague had stated.

Ivan Hrashe, Gavril Pushin and Stanislav Rataichak, three Trotskyists connected with German espionage, were senior executives in the chemical industry and committed their misdeeds in this field. Hrashe had entered Russia in 1919 disguised as a Russian prisoner of war and worked initially as a spy for Czechoslovakia, but later switched to the German Intelligence Service. Pushin, a German agent since 1935, worked at the Gorlova chemical complex, from where he passed on sensitive information about chemical companies and specifically about nitrogen work. Stanislav Rataichak was the head of the Central Administration of the Chemical Industry. The passage follows in which the prosecutor confronts the three to clarify their espionage activities:

"Vyshinsky: Were you connected with espionage?
Rataichak: Yes, I was.
Vyshinsky: Through whom?
Rataichak: Through Pushin and Hrashe.
Vyshinsky: Defendant Pushin, is it correct that Rataichak was connected through you to an espionage organisation?
Pushin: Through me and also directly.
Vyshinsky: Defendant Hrashe, was Rataichak connected through you with agents of the German Intelligence Service?
Hrashe: Yes, he was connected with agents of the German Intelligence Service.
Vyshinsky: And you were connected with them?
Hrashe: Yes.
Vyshinsky: As an agent?
Hrashe: Yes.
Vyshinsky: What did your activity consist of?
Hrashe: In the transmission of secret information in connection with the chemical industry.
Vyshinsky: Was this known to Rataichak?
Hrashe: Yes, he was my boss.
Vyshinsky (to Rataichak): Did you consistently pass on to the German Intelligence Service materials that you possessed by virtue of your position?

Rataichak: Yes, I was the head of the Central Administration of Chemical Industry.
Vyshinsky: Was there sabotage activity?
Rataichak: Yes.
Vyshinsky: Was there espionage?
Rataichak: Yes.
Vyshinsky: Did you participate in terrorist organisations?
Rataichak: No.
Vyshinsky: Were you aware of the existence of terrorist organisations?
Rataichak: I knew Trotsky's line through Pyatakov".

At four o'clock in the afternoon of 28 January 1937 the inclement speech of the prosecution began. Vyshinsky recalled that the Trotskyists' connections with the Gestapo had already been exposed during last year's trial, but that in the present trial they had been brought out in full measure. He accused the Trotskyists of having reached "the limit, the last frontier of political rot and the abyss of degradation". The prosecutor said that "one could not speak of a political party, but of a gang of criminals, simply the agency of foreign intelligence services." Growing increasingly indignant, Vyshinsky claimed that the Trotskyists were worse than the Whites and had "fallen lower than the worst followers of Denikin and Kolchak." The prosecutor used the syntagma "Trotskyist Judas".

In addition to Bukharin and Rykov, the accused Drobnis had implicated Christian Rakovsky, another important Trotskyist leader of Jewish origin. Referring to the events of 1918, which culminated in the attempted assassination of Lenin, outlined in the previous chapter in connection with the disagreements over the Brest-Litovsk Treaty, the prosecutor said the following:

".... It was Pyatakov and company who in 1918, in a period of extreme danger for the country of the Soviets, conducted negotiations with the revolutionary Socialists to perpetrate a counter-revolutionary coup d'état and arrest Lenin, in order to place Pyatakov as head of the Government and chairman of the Council of People's Commissars. It was through the arrest of Lenin, through a coup d'état, that these political adventurers wanted to pave their way to power."

The prosecutor concluded by asserting that what the defendants had said had been verified by experts. The evidence, moreover, had been proven by preliminary interrogation, confessions and testimonies, so there was no room for doubt. Vyshinsky said that any shortcomings or failures in the trial were due to the fact that the defendants had not told the full extent of their knowledge or all the crimes they had committed: "I am convinced," he said, "that they have not told even half the truth of what constitutes the horrible history of the dreadful crimes against our country. After summarising the most serious offences, he concluded with these words: "You judges, the main charge in the present trial is treason".

There followed the lawyers of those who had requested legal assistance and the final pleas of the remaining defendants. Pyatakov ended his speech with these words:

> "Citizen judges, I only deeply regret that the chief criminal, the recalcitrant and obstinate criminal, Trotsky, is not sitting with us in this dock. I am deeply conscious of my crime and I dare not ask for clemency, I will not even have the effrontery to appeal for mercy. In a few hours you will pass sentence. Here I stand before you in filth, crushed by my own crimes, stripped of everything by my own fault, a man who has lost his party, who has no friends, who has lost his family, who has lost even himself. Do not deprive me of one thing, citizen judges, do not deprive me of the right to feel that in your eyes I have found the strength, though too late, to break with my criminal past."

The verdict was delivered at 3 a.m. on 30 January 1937. Except for Sokolnikov, Radek, Arnold and Stroilov, the rest of the defendants were sentenced to death. On 31 January, *Pravda* reported that, after the sentence was announced, 200,000 people demonstrated against the defendants on Red Square, where, in temperatures of minus 27 degrees Celsius, they were cheered by Khrushchev and Shvernik. According to a recent version, Radek and Sokolnikov were killed in May 1939 by cellmates. Stroilov and Arnold were eventually shot in 1941.

It remains for us to record one last death, that of Serge Ordzhonikidze, the Commissar of Heavy Industry, with whom Pyatakov had been the closest collaborator. According to some sources, Ordzhonikidze had complained to his friend Stalin that the NKVD was arresting his men without being informed. On 17 February 1937 he had a conversation with Stalin that lasted several hours. The next day, at 5.30 p.m. he was dead. Some sources speak of suicide, others of murder. An official medical report signed by G. Kaminsky, Commissar for Health; I. Khodorovsky, head of the Kremlin Medical-Sanitary Administration; L. Levin, adviser to the aforementioned Administration; and S. Mets, doctor at the Kremlin Clinic, attributed the cause of death to paralysis of the heart.

The purge in the NKVD and the Red Army

On 9 January 1937, seriously compromised by the events in the USSR and with the prospect of the impending trial, Trotsky arrived in Mexico accompanied by his closest collaborators. He had received an invitation from one of the founders of the Mexican Communist Party, the painter Diego Rivera, who was a member of the Central Committee. On 9 February the

American Committee for the Defence of Trotsky organised a rally in New York which was attended by some seven thousand people. It had been planned that he would read a speech over the telephone, but the connections between Mexico and New York failed and the text had to be read by the Trotskyite Max Shachtman, a Jewish writer. It was later discovered that the failure of the telephone lines had been caused by a Stalinist operator. In the speech, Trotsky called for an international commission to investigate the charges against him in the Moscow trials.

We have repeatedly denounced in this work where Trotsky's power came from. Naturally, then, an international campaign was immediately set in motion to discredit the trials and rehabilitate his battered figure. A torrent of statements, leaflets, pamphlets and newspaper articles began to flow in Europe and America. The most famous American media, usually in the hands of wealthy Jews, published in their pages reports and contributions by Trotsky's friends and admirers, who mainly spread the thesis that it was all just Stalin's revenge against Trotsky, the true representative of the international working class. In addition to the radio stations, *Foreign Affairs Quarterly, Reader's Digest, The Saturday Evening Post, the American Mercury, The New York Times* and other important publications were at Trotsky's service.

In connection with this international campaign, on 11 March 1937 Ambassador Davies wrote in his diary: "...Another diplomat, Minister --- (he declines to name him), made a clarifying statement to me yesterday. In discussing the trial, he said that the defendants were undoubtedly guilty, that those of us who had attended the trial agreed on this; that the outside world, through reports in the press, however, seemed to believe that the trial was a scam (a facade, in his words), that although we knew it was not, it was probably just as well that the world believed it to be so". In other words, well-known powerful forces were working to hide the truth about the Fifth Column in the Soviet Union.

Although Stalin was ruthlessly decimating the conspirators and all those who could oppose him, the plot had not been completely crushed and remained dormant. Between the end of February and the beginning of March the sessions of the seventy-member Central Committee plenum were held. Yezhov reported on police matters, Zhdanov on party organisation, Molotov on economic matters, and Stalin made the political report. Stalin lamented that there were "deficiencies in the party's methods of work for the liquidation of Trotskyites and other two-faced people". Among the central items on the agenda was the fate of Rykov, Lenin's successor as Soviet Premier, and Bukharin, who had chaired the International (Comintern). Yezhov implicated them in the Zinoviev and Pyatakov conspiracies. Both appeared before the plenum and tried to defend their innocence. On 26 February they denied for the umpteenth time all the charges against them. Bukharin even dared to make a speech in which he accused Stalin and

Yezhov of being the sole conspirators and of plotting to install an NKVD regime that would give unlimited power to Stalin. Both were insulted and booed. A subcommittee composed of Stalin, Molotov, Voroshilov, Kaganóvich, Mikoyan and Yezhov prepared a resolution stating that the NKVD had proved that both knew about the counter-revolutionary activities of the Trotskyist Centre and other rightists in their own circle. Arrested on the spot, they were transferred to the Lubyanka. At another of the sessions, Stalin severely criticised Yagoda, who was subjected to a severe interrogation by the members of the Committee. Among other things he was asked why he had protected Trotskyist traitors. The Plenum of the Central Committee considered that the facts had shown that "the Commissariat of Internal Affairs had failed for at least four years to expose the enemies of the people". On 5 March a final speech by Stalin closed the Plenum.

From this point onwards events were precipitated. On 18 March 1937 Yezhov summoned all the NVKD chiefs to the Lubyanka and delivered a devastating speech against Yagoda. Days earlier almost all the department heads had been dismissed or arrested, sometimes in their own offices, sometimes in their homes at night or at the stations when they left Moscow. Only Abram Aronovich Slutsky, a Trotskyist friend and confidant of Krivitsky and Orlov, remained momentarily in the Foreign Department. Walter Krivitsky recounts one of the scenes of this famous meeting on 18 March, in which Artur Khristyanovich Artuzov and his friend Slutsky engaged in a battle of accusations to save themselves in front of Yezhov. Artuzov accused Slutsky of being Yagoda's man. Krivitsky's source is evidently Slutsky himself. The somewhat lengthy quotation gives an idea of the atmosphere of the meeting:

"Having thrown his comrade to the wild beasts, Artuzov triumphantly descended from the rostrum.
Slutsky, who was head of the Foreign Section, stood up to defend himself. He, too, knew what was at stake. He began quite calmly, realising that everything was against him.
- Artuzov has tried to paint me as Yagoda's closest collaborator. I, comrades, was of course Secretary of Party Organisation within the OGPU; but was Artuzov or I the member of the OGPU Presidium? I ask you: could anyone at that time have been a member of the highest body of the OGPU without enjoying the full confidence and approval of Yagoda? Artuzov claims that for my good services under Yagoda and as organisational secretary I received a special allowance. According to Artuzov, I used this allowance to establish contact between Yagoda's organisation and his leaders abroad. But I claim that this special allowance was granted to me at Artuzov's own insistence. For many years Artuzov has maintained friendly relations with Yagoda.
And then Slutsky unloaded his main blow:

-I ask you, Artuzov, where did you live? Who lived next to you? Bulanov? Wasn't he among the first to be arrested? And who lived just below you? Ostrovsky. And who lived right next to you, Artuzov? Yagoda! And now I ask you, comrades, who in the circumstances of the time could have lived in the same house as Yagoda without enjoying his absolute confidence?"

Conquest provides further examples of the purge that took place in the NKVD under Yezhov. Chertok," he writes, "Kamenev's interrogator, threw himself from his flat on the twelfth floor. Some officers shot themselves or committed suicide by jumping from their office windows. Others left impassively, among them Bulanov, Yagoda's secretary, arrested at the end of March". Conquest states that three thousand of Yagoda's NKVD agents were executed in 1937. Molchanov, Mironov (Kagan) and Shanin, who had been department heads under Yagoda, were denounced as right-wing conspirators. Two other chiefs, Pauker and Gay, both Jews, were subsequently charged with espionage. On 3 April it was announced that Yagoda himself, who after leaving his post at the Commissariat of Internal Affairs had been appointed Commissar of Post and Communications, had been arrested.

The Cheka had been run from its inception by a Jewish mafia. When its founder, the Polish Jew Felix Dzerzhinsky (Rufin), died in 1926, Vyacheslav Menzhinsky, also Polish but of aristocratic origin, took his place. Trotsky wrote in his memoirs that Menzhinsky was "the shadow of a man" and presents him as a weak man, a "nobody" under Stalin. Officially, in May 1934 he died of a heart attack, but in reality he had been assassinated on the orders of his right-wing confidant Yagoda, who had joined the conspiracy in 1929 and was a secret member of the Trotskyist-Rightist bloc.

In *The Great Conspiracy Against Russia* Michael Sayers and Albert E. Kahn explain in detail how the assassination took place. According to these authors, "Yagoda's role in the conspiracy was at first known only to the three leaders of the right-wing bloc: Bukharin, Rykov and Tomsky. In 1932, when the right-wing and Trotskyist bloc was formed, Pyatakov and Krestinsky also knew of Yagoda's role". From his post as vice-president of the OGPU, Yagoda, besides appointing Trotskyist Jews as special agents, protected the conspirators, which he himself confirmed at the 1938 trial. Yagoda declared that the coup d'état had to coincide with the outbreak of war. There are times," he confessed to Bulanov, "when one must act slowly and with extreme caution, and there are times when one must act quickly and suddenly". Poisons were one of his preferred methods. His main collaborator was Leo Levin, a Jewish doctor who in 1953 was among the group of Jewish doctors arrested by Stalin before he was assassinated. Informed by Yagoda of the existence of the conspiracy, Levin, on instructions from his boss, warned Ignati N. Kazakov, the doctor treating Menzhinsky's bronchial asthma, that his patient was a living dead man, that he was wasting his time with him, and that he should not allow him to return to work. Kazakov recounted this conversation at the 1938 trial. Levin's words, quoted by Sayers and Kahn, were as follows: "...By allowing him to return to work, you are making an enemy of Yagoda. Menzhinsky is in Yagoda's way and Yagoda has an interest in getting him out of the way as soon as possible. Yagoda is a man who stops at nothing". In short, Kazakov succumbed and told Levin that he would carry out orders. On 10 May 1934 Menzhynsky died and was replaced at the head of the OGPU by the Jew Génrij Yagoda, who at the trial declared: "I deny that in causing the death of Menzhinsky I was acting from motives of a personal nature.... I aspired to the post of head of the OGPU in the interests of the conspiratorial organisation". This explains why in 1937 there were so many Trotskyist and Jewish agents in the NKVD.

The first arrests in the Red Army had already taken place in 1936. On 5 July Dimitri Shmidt, a Jewish commander commanding a tank unit in the Kiev Military District, was arrested by the NKVD without consulting or notifying his superior, the Trotskyite General Iona Emmanuilovich Yakir, who was also Jewish. Yakir went to Moscow to protest, and Yezhov showed him materials, presumably confessions by Mrachkovsky, Dreitzer and Reingold, implicating Shmidt and B. Kuzmichev, head of an Air Force unit, in an attempt to assassinate the Commissar of Defence, Kliment Voroshilov. Shmidt and Kuzmichev were among those named in the Zinoviev Trial who had been shelved as the investigation continued. During the trial, both Reingold and Mrachkovsky had linked them to a Trotskyist military group. Both moved in the orbit of General Yakir. On 14 August another corps commander, Vitaly Primakov, was arrested, and six days later, on 20 August, Vitovt Putna, who had arrived in Moscow from London, where he was stationed as a military attaché, was arrested. Putna admitted the existence of several Trotskyist groups. During the autumn of 1936 there were even rumours that a trial was to take place against Trotskyist army commanders.

For all that, it is certain that Stalin knew already when he closed the Central Committee Plenum on 5 March 1937 that the conspiracy had the support of a section of the army, within which nested many military men who owed their careers to Trotsky and were loyal to him. The Secret Service of Military Information had managed to safeguard its independence since Trotsky's days as War Commissar and, according to Krivitsky, "was one of the last instruments to fall into the hands of the Secret Police". The Red Army generals had been able to escape the purge the political opposition had been undergoing since Stalin's consolidation of power; however, after Yagoda's arrest on 3 April, everything began to move swiftly. Anatoli Gekker, another Jewish Trotskyite who in 1924 had been political commissar for the communist regions of China and was commander of an army corps, was arrested in April (shot on 1 July). The Chinese Red Army was led by two other Jews, V. Levichev and Yakov (Yan) Gamarnik. At the time of his arrest, Gekker held important positions in espionage and was head of the Red Army's Foreign Liaison. In the same month of April, another corps commander, Ilia Garkavi, commander of the Ural Military District, was also arrested. It so happened that both Gekker and Garkavi were married to two sisters of the wife of the Jewish general Iona E. Yakir. Yakir and fellow Jews Boris Feldman and Yan Gamarnik were among the leading Trotskyist generals in the conspiracy. Yakir went to Voroshilov and inquired about the situation of his brothers-in-law. He was also received by Stalin, who told him that other detainees had made serious accusations against them; but that if they were innocent they would be released.

Between 22 and 25 April Mark Isayevich (Isaakovich) Gay (Shpoklyand) and Georgi Prokofyev were forced to testify about the connections of Marshal Tukhachevsky and other officers with Yagoda, their former chief, who at that stage rejected the accusations. Gay, former head of the NKVD Special Department, had interrogated Dmitri Shmidt. The second, Prokofyev, former deputy head of the NKVD, Yezhov had been replaced by Matvei Berman, another Jewish Chekist. On 27 April A. I. Volovich of the Operational Department also implicated Tukhachevsky in a plot to seize power. Yezhov's interrogators also succeeded in getting Putna and Primakov to testify against Tukhachevsky, Yakir, Feldman and other military men. On 28 April 1937 *Pravda* published a scathing appeal to the Red Army to fight against internal and external enemies. This biased warning was evidently understood by those who knew what it meant: the purge was beginning.

Walter Krivitsky (Samuel Gérshevich Ginsberg), the Jewish Trotskyite who was still head of the Military Secret Service in Western Europe and who, in his own words, was "one of the executing arms of Stalin's intervention in Spain", had been summoned to Moscow by Yezhov. There he lived through the events from the beginning of March until 22 May 1937 in anguish, for he was convinced that he would be arrested and would not return to The Hague, where he lived with his family. Despite cynically denying his membership in the opposition, his work *I, Chief of the Soviet Military Secret Service* is an apology for Trotskyism and Trotskyists, "idealists who are the last hope for a better world". It contains first-hand accounts of the atmosphere at the parade on Red Square on 1 May, the day he saw Marshal Tukhachevsky for the last time. Observed by all," writes Krivitsky, "Tukhachevsky was the first to arrive at the tribune where the military were seated. The second to arrive was Marshal Yegorov, who did not dare to greet him and took his place beside him. Gamarnik, Deputy Commissar of War, arrived later and did not even look at them.... When the military parade was over, the soldiers were to remain in their places to watch the civilian parade, but Tukhachevsky left without a word, with his hands in his pockets".

Tukhachevsky, an officer of the Tsar who had been a Freemason since the age of eighteen, was taken prisoner by the Germans in 1915. Officially, he managed to escape shortly before the revolution began, although there is a possibility that he was released intentionally, as he changed sides immediately. In 1918 he joined the Bolshevik Party and was soon with the adventurous around Trotsky, the war commissar, who made him commander-in-chief of an army at the age of 25. Thanks to his military training, he immediately stood out among the inexperienced commanders of the Red Army. In March 1921, already a renowned civil war hero, he led, with Trotsky, the massacre of the sailors at Kronstadt. In the face of fierce resistance from the mutineers, "every house had to be blown up", Tukhachevsky himself declared. The subsequent repression was ruthlessly executed and mass shootings were carried out. In 1922 Trotsky put Tukhachevsky in charge of the Red Army Military Academy. In the same year he took part in the negotiations with the Weimar Republic that led to the signing of the Treaty of Rapallo. Tukhachevsky had therefore had a number of relations with German military officers. With Trotsky's progressive loss of influence, Marshals Budyenny and Voroshilov were Stalin's new men. The group of generals close to Tukhachevsky, including Yakir, Kork, Feldman Uborevich and Gamarnik, the latter a personal friend of the German generals Seeckt and Hammerstein, felt the change in power. Another man close to the group was Vitovt Putna, military attaché in Berlin, Tokyo and London.

M. Sayers and A. Kahn, relying on the revelations of the Trial of Twenty-One, discussed in the next section, write in *The Great Conspiracy Against Russia* that, from the organisation of the right-wing and Trotskyist bloc, "Trotsky had seen Tukhachevsky as the best card in the whole conspiracy, to be played only at the last strategic moment". According to the statements of defendants and witnesses at the trial, Trotsky maintained his relations with Tukhachevsky mainly through Krestinsky and the military attaché Putna. During the trial a conversation between Bukharin and Tomsky came to light in which the former asked: "How does Tukhachevsky visualise the mechanism of the coup? To which Tomsky replies: "This is a matter for the military organisation". Ideally, the coup d'état should have coincided with the beginning of the longed-for attack by Germany. It seems that even the possibility had been contemplated that Tukhachevsky, using the politicians as scapegoats, might seek popular support and establish a military dictatorship. In this connection Bukharin told Tomsky: "It may be necessary to work out a procedure which will present them as guilty of defeat at the front, which will enable us to win over the masses through patriotic slogans.

By early 1936 Tukhachevsky, before travelling to London as his country's representative at George V's funeral, had received the coveted title of Marshal of the Soviet Union. On his way to Britain, he confidently made stops in Warsaw and Berlin, where he established contacts with Polish and German military officers. Things began to get complicated in August with the trial of the Trotskyist-Zinovievist terrorist bloc and even more so with the subsequent arrests of Pyatakov and Radek. Alarmed, Tukhachevsky contacted Krestinsky. Both then realised that the acceleration of events meant adapting the plan to the new and changing circumstances, and that it might be necessary to execute the coup d'état first. Krestinsky promised that he would urgently send a message to Trotsky. The text was sent in October and said: ".... A large number of Trotskyists have been arrested; but, even so, the main forces of the Bloc have not yet been affected. Action can be taken, but for this it is essential for the Centre that foreign intervention should be hastened.

In November 1936, in the context of the Eighth Extraordinary Congress of Soviets, Tukhachevsky and Krestinsky were able to meet and talk. Both saw that the arrests were continuing and the Marshal was very uneasy: the arrest of Putna, the fall of Yagoda and his replacement by Yezhov showed that Stalin was getting to the roots of the plot. Tukhachevsky was in favour of hastening events without delay before it was too late. Krestinsky met Rosengoltz and both agreed that Tukhachevsky was right. A further message was therefore sent to Trotsky, explaining that Tukhachevsky proposed to act without waiting for the outbreak of war. Trotsky's reply arrived at the end of December, in which he agreed. In fact, after Pyatakov's arrest, Trotsky had come to the same conclusion and had written so in a letter to Rosengoltz which intersected with the letter he had received. Thus, with the acquiescence of the old leader in exile, Tukhachevsky was given carte blanche.

From the statements of the defendants at the March 1938 trial, it became known that during the months of March and April 1937, preparations for the coup were speeded up. Sayers and Kahn, using the trial as their main source of information, state that a meeting between Krestinsky, Tukhachevsky and Rosengoltz took place at the end of March in the latter's Moscow flat. The marshal reportedly announced at the time that the action could take place in mid-May and that the coup plotters were working on a number of possible courses of action. According to Rosengoltz, one of the possibilities envisaged was for a group of soldiers to take over the Kremlin telephone exchange and kill the leaders of the Party and the government. According to this plan, Gamarnik would occupy the headquarters of the Commissariat of Internal Affairs and it would be up to him to liquidate Voroshilov and Molotov.

Just in time the government began to take measures that enabled it to abort the plot. On 8 May 1937 a decree reinstated the old system of dual or shared command, which gave enormous power to the political commissars. This system had been put in place during the civil war to control military officers who were not trusted because they had served in the Tsarist army. On 9 May, these commissars were instructed to increase their vigilance. Meanwhile, in early May Tukhachevsky was summoned by Voroshilov. Those who saw him after the interview with the Defence Commissar describe him as unusually gloomy and depressed. A few days later he was summoned again by Voroshilov, who coolly informed him of his dismissal as deputy to the Defence Commissar and his transfer to the Volga Military District. Between the 10th and 11th, this and other changes of posting were officially announced. Yakir, whose position in the Ukraine was to be paramount, was transferred from Kiev to Leningrad. On 14 May, V. Primakov, who had been detained since August last year, after being beaten and deprived of sleep, finally denounced Yakir and later Tukhachevsky and others. Putna, too, after being tortured, implicated Tukhachevsky on the same day, May 14. On 15 May, Boris Feldman was arrested and initially denied the charges. After severe interrogation, he signed a full confession about the conspiracy, denouncing Tukhachevsky, Yakir, Eideman and others. On 16 May August Ivanovich Kork, a general who had commanded the Moscow Military District and who since 1935 had headed the Frunze Military Academy, was arrested. Although he initially denied the charges, on 18 May he eventually signed a confession in which he acknowledged that Avel Yenukidze had recruited him into the right-wing conspiracy, connected with Putna and Primakov's Trotskyite group.

Finally, on about 24 May Stalin, after consultation with Molotov, Voroshilov and Yezhov, ordered Tukhachevsky's arrest and expulsion from the Central Committee. On 28 May it became known in the army that the case had been handed over to the "investigative organs". Tukhachevsky's interrogation was personally conducted by Yezhov, assisted by Z. M. Ushakov, a Chekist with a reputation for sadism, and by Grigory (Izrail) Moiseyevich Leplevsky, another Jew, one more, who was the new head of the Special Section of the Main Administration of State Security (GUGB) of the NKVD. On the 29th the Marshal accepted charges of espionage, of connections with the Germans and of having been recruited by Yenukidze for the conspiracy. On the same day, General Ieronim P. Uborevich, who was in Minsk, was ordered to travel to Moscow and was also arrested. Confronted by Kork, he denied the charges, but eventually confessed after being tortured. The death of General Yan Gamarnik occurred on the 31st and his fate has been the subject of various accounts. According to some accounts, Gamarnik was tortured and killed; others claim that he shot himself to death. On the same day, 31 May, Iona Yakir, the last of the conspirators, was arrested. Conquest reveals that he wrote from the Lubyanka to the Politburo demanding his immediate release or an interview with Stalin, to whom he wrote promising his innocence. Conquest transcribes an excerpt from his letter: ".... My whole conscious life has been spent in working selflessly and honestly in the sight of the party and its leaders..... Every word I say is innocent and I will die with words of love for you, the party and the country, with unlimited faith in the victory of communism". The Sovietologist adds that Stalin wrote about this letter: "scoundrel and prostitute". Voroshilov added: "an absolutely accurate description". Molotov signed this comment and Kaganóvich added: "for traitor and scum, a punishment: the death penalty". Under nine days of harsh interrogation, Ushakov finally got a detailed confession from Yakir.

At eleven o'clock in the morning of 11 June 1937, the accused were brought before a special military tribunal of the Supreme Court of the USSR. In a session held behind closed doors, all the military men involved in the plot were sentenced to death. The verdict was announced on the 12th and the sentence was carried out on the same day. In the official communiqué, published in *Pravda* on the 11th, it was stated that "they were accused of breaking their military obligations and their pledge of loyalty, of treason against their country, of treason against the peoples of the USSR and of treason against the workers, the peasants and the Red Army." In Voroshilov's report, also published in *Pravda* on June 15, the executed servicemen were associated with Trotsky and were accused of preparing the assassinations of the Party and Government leaders and of espionage.

The repression unleashed during the following months against the conspirators' relatives and against anything that smacked of Trotskyism within the Red Army was on a massive scale. Wives, children, brothers, sisters and relatives of the convicted soldiers were arrested and interned in concentration camps. Robert Conquest claims that the wives of Yakir, Kork, Gamarnik and Tukhachevsky were subsequently eliminated, as were relatives of other executed servicemen. In the days and weeks following the trial, some 20 generals from the Moscow barracks were executed. More than fifty corps and division commanders and about a thousand officers were arrested. The purge at the Kremlin Military School and the Frunze Academy was rigorous. In the Kiev Military District, considered the "Yakir's nest", between six and seven hundred officers were arrested. Conquest's data for the Navy are also impressive: of the nine Fleet admirals, only one (Galler) survived the purge. His family members and numerous subordinate officers also suffered the consequences of the NKVD-organised cleansing operations. According to this historian, the purge continued throughout 1938. A second purge of the army began in January, with a new round of arrests affecting senior commanders and officers, including Marshal Yegorov. A second wave came at the end of July, when more than a dozen army, air force and navy generals were purged.

Given the facts, it remains to contemplate Germany's role in the whole affair. This is a tricky task, as some historians seem more interested in hiding the truth than in seeking it. Unfortunately, Robert Conquest, a schoolmaster, is one of them. Conquest considers the Moscow trials as "show trials" ( ). Despite having an impressive wealth of information, he insists on drinking from contaminated sources, which he gives credibility when they allow him to maintain his thesis that Stalin fabricated everything and that there was no Trotskyist conspiracy. Andrew Roberts in *"The Holy Fox" A Life of Lord Halifax*, a work to which we will return in another chapter, liquidates the purge of Trotskyists in the Red Army in these words: "Stalin's purges of June 1937 had virtually decapitated the entire officer corps of the Army. Five of the seven marshals and a majority of generals and colonels were shot in a paranoid Stalinist bloodthirsty spasm". In other words, despite the evidence that Trotsky had been the creator of the Red Army and had placed his trusted men, mainly Jews, in key positions; despite the knowledge that the internal power struggle had been unleashed after Trotsky's displacement by Stalin, the official historians prefer to ignore it all and, of course, are silent about the Jewish bankers who financed Trotsky, whose figure they preserve unsullied. Thus the subject is reduced to "Stalinist paranoia", "bloodlust" and "show trials". Very academic and professional explanations.

On the conspirators' relations with the Germans, Conquest accepts as the most probable version the one offered by Walter Hagen in a book published in Linz in 1950, the German title of which is *Die geheime Front. Organisation, Personen und Aktionen des deutschen Geheimdienstes (The Secret Front. Organisation, Persons and Actions of the German Secret Service)*. This work was translated into French in 1952 under the *title Le Front Secret* and a year later *The Secret Front* was published in English. The version of Hagen assumed by Conquest is in a nutshell as follows: Reinhard Heydrich in late 1936 proposed to Hitler and Himmler to present a forged dossier of Tukhachevsky's contacts with the German military in order to provoke the purge and damage the potential of the Red Army.

First of all, since it is a matter of crediting the value of the source, it must be said that Walter Hagen is the pseudonym of Wilhelm Höttl, a lying and dishonest character who, after Germany's defeat, did whatever his country's enemies asked of him. Mark Weber, director of the Institute for Historical Review, in the article "Wilhelm Höttl and the Elusive Six Million" provides a wealth of interesting information about this individual. A member of the NSDAP, Höttl was employed from 1939 in the Reich Security Main Office (RSHA). In 1945 the Americans arrested him in Austria and for several years he worked as an intelligence agent for the United States. In April 2001, the CIA published the extensive Höttl file, which contained a detailed report on him. The report, entitled "Analysis of the Name File of Wilhelm Höttl", was compiled by Miriam Kleiman and Robery Skwirot, two government investigators of the IWG (Interagency Working Group). These documents establish that Höttl was a totally unreliable informant who routinely fabricated information to satisfy those who were willing to pay him. In their report, the two government investigators write: "Höttl's file consists of approximately six hundred pages, one of the largest ever brought to light. The size of the file is due to Höttl's career as a post-war intelligence dealer, good and bad, to anyone willing to pay him. Reports link Höttl to twelve different intelligence services: United States, Israel, Soviet Union,

Britain, France, Yugoslavia, Austria, Romania, Vatican, Switzerland, West Germany and Hungary."

As soon as he was captured, Höttl began working for the OSS (Office of Strategic Services), the predecessor of the CIA. In the words of the two researchers, "Höttl served the interests of his captors". It was then that, while in the service of US intelligence, Höttl, at the request of the American prosecutor, made a sworn statement to the Nuremberg tribunal that Adolf Eichmann had told him that the Nazis had killed six million Jews. In 1949, a US intelligence officer warned against the routine use of Höttl for any purpose and referred to him as "a man of low nature and poor political record, whose use in intelligence activities, however profitable they may be, constitutes short-sighted US policy". In 1950 a new CIA message referred to Höttl as an "infamous intelligence fabricator". In April 1952 his reports were considered "worthless and possibly exorbitant or false".

To complete the picture of this unpresentable source, there are numerous intelligence reports linking him to Simon Wiesenthal, the famous Nazi hunter. A January 1950 report by the US Army's Counter Intelligence Corps (CIC) mentions that Wiesenthal "has engaged the services of Wilhelm Höttl". Finally, in July 1952, the US Army stationed in Austria severed relations with Höttl completely and in a letter warned: "Dr. Höttl has long been known to this Headquarters and other Allied military organisations in Austria as a producer of intelligence information. His reports usually consist of a fine web of facts, exaggeratedly made up with lies, deception, conjecture and other false types of information. This organisation will have absolutely nothing to do with Dr. Höttl or any other member of his current entourage. He is persona non grata for American, French and British personnel in Austria."

In all humility, we honestly believe that to accept as true historical facts that come from sources such as this is a discredit to those who do so. Relying on Höttl/Hagen, Conquest writes that the creation of the documents Hitler sent to Stalin was "a time-consuming work of art". According to his version, in March 1937 Heydrich and Behrens directed the forgery of a thirty-two-page dossier of letters exchanged over a year between the German high command and Tukhachevsky. Engraver Franz Putzig, a passport forgery technician, did the work, to which was attached a photo of Trotsky with German officers. The German secret service allegedly obtained a signature of Tukhachevsky from 1926, which, conveniently imitated by graphologists, was used to forge letters. The dossier was allegedly presented in early May to Hitler and Himmler, who approved the operation. According to Conquest, a photocopy of this forged document was sent to Prague, and President Edvard Benes confirmed the existence of the plot to the Soviet ambassador. Moreover, Conquest continues, "a secret agent of Heydrich was put in touch with a Soviet Embassy official, showed him two pages and demanded money for the delivery of the rest. The official flew immediately to Moscow and returned with full powers to share the entire dossier. Half a million marks were paid (although these were later found to be forgeries). By mid-May, the documents were in Stalin's hands". In other words, the whole thing was a hoax by Hitler, a trap into which Stalin and his henchmen naively fell.

Since the matter required it, we were able to obtain a copy of one of the editions of the Hagen/Höttl work in order to examine this source directly. So we have *Le Front Secret*, published in 1952 in Paris, translated from the German by Albert Thuman. Under the heading "Heydrich's greatest coup: He gives Stalin the dossier against Tukhachevsky", Höttl, the producer of intelligence stories, tells the bizarre story of the fake dossier on Tukhachevsky. He begins by revealing that Heydrich was interested in the services of the white general N. Skoblin, despite knowing that he was a double agent who, as a member of the expatriate All-Russian Military Union (ROVS), was also working for the Soviets. Thus Skoblin, who later facilitated the abduction of General Miller, the leader of the Whites, would have become a triple agent. In one passage of the account, Höttl writes: "It is thanks to him (Skoblin) that Heydrich learned from the end of 1936 of an alleged plan of Tukhachevsky to seize power in Russia with the help of the Red Army and to eliminate Stalin by suppressing the entire Soviet system". The idea that the triple agent Skoblin provided the Gestapo and the NKVD with information about Tukhachevsky is not original: Höttl/Hagen takes it from the Trotskyite Krivitsky, who had already in 1939 expounded it in *In Stalin's Secret Service*. In any case, these words about Tukhachevsky implied that the plan existed. Höttl, who realises this, immediately demonstrates his ability and adds: "Was this information well-founded? It is better to leave the question open. And there is little hope that it can ever be answered, since the head of the GPU, Nicolai Yezhov, who provided the elements of the affair to Vyshinsky, was subsequently subjected to a similar accusation and succeeded the Red Napoleon before the execution squad. In other words, to make the whole tangle even more tangled, Höttl/Hagen insinuates that the only one who could have revealed the truth, Yezhov, was shot.

Then, because the facts are stubborn, Höttl/Hagen again acknowledges that there was a rift within the Red Army and writes that, before Heydrich presented his plan to him, "Hitler had already discerned that the internal division which threatened to break up the Soviet regime was an opportunity for Germany. There was the possibility of decisively weakening the Soviet Union and two ways to achieve this: either to support Tukhachevsky against Stalin and thus contribute to the elimination of Bolshevism, or to surrender Tukhachevsky to Stalin's vengeance and thus cripple Soviet military power. It was undoubtedly easier for Germany to contribute to Tukhachevsky's liquidation than to assist him in a coup d'état against the masters of the Kremlin". This approach fits in perfectly with what we have been saying, i.e., the Trotskyists were counting on the army to seize power and aspired to have Hitler help them to do so.

However, a few qualifications are in order. First of all, it must be said that it is not true that the "elimination of Bolshevism" was intended. It was the old Bolsheviks who were encouraging the coup, the old guard of Jewish revolutionaries who had rallied around Trotsky since the latter, after his release by the Canadians thanks to his friend Bernard Baruch, had entered Russia from New York. It was the communism represented by Trotsky that interested the finance international. The big financiers wanted the triumph of the opposition, and proof of this, as we have seen, was the role being played by the press in the United States and in Europe. Recall that Radek testified at the trial that Trotsky had told Pyatakov that the military preparations had been completed and that it was now a question of "assuring Germany of Britain's neutrality by diplomatic efforts". However impatient the Trotskyists may have been, it is only natural that without this assurance Germany would not risk it.

In the plans of the conspiracy was to get rid of both Stalin and Hitler, who had been financed, among other things, to attack Stalin. Trotsky and his supporters conceived of a war that would serve to bring them both down. The French ambassador in Moscow, R. Coulondre, reportedly warned Hitler on 25 August 1939 that in the event of war the real winner would be Trotsky. It is very likely that if Hitler had attacked the USSR in 1937, the United States, Britain and France, under the umbrella of the League of Nations, would have declared war on Germany for having initiated a war of aggression. In fact, that is what happened two years later: as is well known, when Germany and Russia partitioned Poland in 1939, London and Paris declared war on Germany, but not on the USSR. The really scandalous thing is that Stalin not only took his share of Poland, but also annexed Estonia, Latvia and Lithuania, invaded Finland and then occupied Bessarabia and northern Bukovina. All with impunity. It was logical, therefore - and Höttl/Hagen is right in this respect - that Germany opted for the less risky option.

It is quite another matter whether he needed to falsify evidence by means of a spectacular set-up, as those who insist that the military were not part of the Trotskyist conspiracy claim. To conclude our refutation of this source, let us look in summary at the facts as reported by Höttl/Hagen, who writes that the forgery began in April 1937 and that the Gestapo was assisted by NKVD agents. To top it all off, Höttl/Hagen adds that Hermann Behrens, Heydrich's assistant, thought that they were instruments of the Soviet Secret Police. In a cellar in Prinz-Albrecht Straße, Höttl/Hagen says, 'correspondence of all kinds was produced and staggered over the years'. Thus, receipts from Soviet generals, letters and other documents were stamped with the corresponding stamps of the German generals. Interestingly, Wilhelm Canaris, head of the German Intelligence Service

(Abwehr), a British agent, a traitor, as is well known, is kept out of the operation. Höttl/Hagen claims that Heydrich, in his eagerness to implicate Canaris, "fabricated letters in which one could read the Abwehr chief's thanks to Tukhachevsky and several Soviet generals for information received from the Red Army". Conquest, who uses Höttl/Hagen only when convenient, claims that a copy of the dossier was given to the Czechs. Höttl/Hagen, however, says exactly the opposite. He admits that they had initially been considered, but that the option was dismissed. According to his version, "Behrens travelled to Czechoslovakia under a false name and held a preliminary interview in Prague; but in the end this route seemed too uncertain to Heydrich. The Czechs refused, in fact, to say exactly what stages the documents would follow in their transmission; there was no guarantee that the dispatch would not be intercepted by some follower of Tukhachevsky. Heydrich therefore opted for a direct approach through the Soviet Embassy in Berlin.

We cannot dwell any longer on this bizarre story. Bernard Fay, a Harvard-educated French historian who was director of the National Library during the German occupation of France (1940-1944), states categorically that Hitler provided Stalin with documents that enabled him to proceed with the great military purge. Fay's interest as a source lies in the fact that, working for the Vichy government and with the approval of the Gestapo, he seized the secret archives of the Grand Orient in Paris and Masonic lodges throughout France. President Petain himself commissioned him to do this work, which enabled him to publish a monthly publication, *Les Documents Maçonniques*. Fay learned, for example, that Admiral Canaris had warned the British General Staff before Hitler launched the offensive in France in May 1940. Robert Conquest himself notes that in January 1937 the *Pravda* correspondent in Berlin, V. Klimov, reported that in German Army circles there was talk of connections with the Red Army, especially with Tukhachevsky. On 16 March 1937 the Soviet Embassy in Paris sent a telegram to Moscow warning of plans in the German Army "to promote a coup d'état in the Soviet Union by using persons in the Red Army high command". In our opinion, it seems clear that the Gestapo was aware of the generals' plot and had an interest in warning Stalin of a real conspiracy.

Moreover, Stalin learned that Germany would not attack the USSR shortly before the purge of the Red Army began. Much to the chagrin of the Trotskyists and those who encouraged them, especially in the United States and Britain, Stalin and Hitler succeeded in reaching a trade agreement which had been forged in secret. Despite all the attempts of the Trotskyists to prevent the success of the efforts, Stalin had faith in an agreement with Germany and had sent David Kandelaki to the Berlin Embassy as a commercial attaché. In December 1936, at his own risk, Kandelaki contacted Dr. Schacht and explored the possibilities of the agreement. Schacht reportedly made it a condition that Moscow stop supporting the activities of the Communists in Germany, which was infested with Trotskyites who pasted posters in the streets of Berlin at night with the slogans "Down with Hitler and Stalin!" and "Long live Trotsky!" Kandelaki travelled to Moscow and consulted with Stalin. On 29 January 1937 Kandelaki met again with Schacht and verbally formulated to him Stalin and Molotov's proposal to open direct negotiations.

Proof of how badly the agreement went down was once provided by the head of the Military Secret Service in Europe, Krivitsky. His words when he learned of it are worth quoting: "...A bombshell exploded over me. It was the strictly secret news that Slutsky sent me about the signing of an agreement between Stalin and Hitler, brought by Kandelaki". Krivitsky adds that David Kandelaki had arrived in Moscow in April accompanied by "Rudolf", a subordinate of Slutsky who acted as a secret representative of the NKVD alongside Kandelaki. (About this "Rudolf" it must be said that he was a Jew named Viliam Guenrijovich Fisher, alias Abel Rudolf, who remained in the Secret Service until he was captured by the FBI in June 1957.) So much importance was attached to Kandelaki's success that he was received directly by Stalin. Proof of the value the Nazis also attached to the agreement is that Hitler had also personally received Kandelaki. Naturally, the foreign powers and the powers that operated in the shadows to overthrow Stalin opposed this German-Soviet agreement.[16]

Before turning to the Trial of the Twenty-One, we can therefore conclude that after the trial of Pyatakov and Radek, there can be no doubt that the aim was to provoke a war in order to eliminate Stalin and put Trotsky in power in the USSR. The statements made at the trial by Sokolnikov and Radek about "fascism as the best organised form of capitalism" were undoubtedly concessions made to the strategy of Stalin, whose Machiavellianism and political cunning reach the highest heights. It is evident that Stalin knew that the conspiracy had its origin in international high finance, the main beneficiary of the plunder of Russia, of the concessions on resources and of investments in the country. All this had been achieved through his agents, who were the very men who were trying to regain power by provoking war with Hitlerite Germany, which was being

---

[16] On Kandelaki's mission to Berlin, Burnett Bolloten, in his monumental work *The Spanish Civil War: Revolution and Counterrevolution*, explains in a lengthy note that, in addition to the trade agreement, Kandelaki proposed a political agreement that Hitler rejected. The document "Kandelaki Mission", from the German Foreign Ministry, fell into the hands of the Allies. The document dated 11 February 1937, which was finally made public in 1983, contains the words of Yevgeni Gnedin, a member of the Soviet Embassy in Berlin, who in the course of the negotiations expressed "regret that the two countries... could not come to a better understanding". Gnedin claimed that he had gone to Germany "with specific instructions to study the possibilities of an improvement" in their relations. In another significant comment, Gnedin said that "although the Comintern and the Soviet Union had the same ideology, the "Realpolitik" of the USSR had nothing to do with the Comintern".

allowed to rearm for this purpose. Stalin, while progressively eliminating opponents, found it convenient to present them as German and Japanese spies, although in reality they served other interests.

The claim that fascism is the best organised form of capitalism is a fallacy that does not hold water. Today it is an indisputable fact that "democracies" are the façade adopted by international capitalism, which uses neo-liberalism and globalisation to completely annul the sovereignty of countries. The Second World War served to criminalise forever the nationalism of states that claimed to be sovereign and opposed the domination of international Jewish banking. In reality, Germany, Japan, Italy and Spain did not want to sell out to the market, they refused to submit to loans and sought to protect their economies, their industry and their resources from the predation and plunder of the "banksters", who aspired and aspire to own everything. Yesterday and today, the most advanced form of capitalism is based on the manipulation of credit perpetrated by the lending bankers, patrons of the so-called democracies, in which they have established the system of usury and debt as an ideal paradise for their operations.

The Trial of the Twenty-One

Shortly before the Trial of Twenty-One began in Moscow, Stalin's long hand reached out in Paris to Lev Sedov, the son of Trotsky and Natalia Sedova, his second wife. A Ukrainian Jew working for the NKVD, Mark Zborowski, had gained his full confidence and betrayed Sedov in the nick of time. According to John J. Dziak, author of *Chekisty: A History of the KGB* and a renowned expert on defence and intelligence, Zborowski was recruited in 1933 and was part of a group of agents who assassinated important enemies of Stalin, including Ignace Reiss (1937), a Trotskyite Jew and friend of Walter Krivitsky, Andreu Nin (1937) and Krivistky himself (1941). To get into Sedov's circle in Paris, Zborowski, known as "Etienne", befriended Jeanne Martin, Sedov's wife. So much confidence did he inspire that he became secretary to Trotsky's son and even stored part of Trotsky's archive in his own home. From this it is easy to imagine the extent to which the NKVD had accurate information at its disposal.

In his reports, Zborowski used code names: "Old man" (Trotsky), "Sonny" (Sedov), "Polecats" (Trotskyists). In a January 1937 report filed by the NKVD, Etienne wrote: "Sonny, during our conversation in his flat on the subject of the second trial and the role of the defendants, declared: 'Now we should not hesitate. Stalin must be killed. On 8 February 1938 Lev Sedov suffered an attack of appendicitis and Etienne persuaded him to go to a small clinic in Paris run by Russian émigrés. He immediately informed the NKVD where Trotsky's son was, who, despite being successfully operated on the day of his admission, died in great pain on 16 February. After his son's death, Trotsky launched an investigation. Meanwhile, Etienne became the leader of the organisation in Paris and continued to edit the *Opposition Bulletin* with the Jewish Trotskyist Lilia Estrin Dallin (Lilya Ginzberg), codenamed "Neighbour". Some historians consider Mark Zborowski to be the most imposing Soviet spy of all time.

For a complete picture of the Trotskyist conspiracy, it remains to review the famous Trial of Twenty-One, the last of the Moscow trials, officially called the "Trial of the Trotskyist-Rightist Bloc". The new Yezhov team spent almost a year preparing for it. Abram A. Slutsky, the Trotskyite of the Foreign Department, "collaborated" until 17 February 1938, when he was liquidated. His executioner, Mikhail Frinovsky, declared before his execution in 1940 that Yezhov had ordered him "to eliminate him quietly". Frinovsky summoned Slutsky to his office and, while they were talking, an official entered and applied a chloroform mask. He was then injected with poison and afterwards it was announced that he had died of a heart attack. In addition to the aforementioned Frinovsky, the man who acted as Yezhov's right-hand man was the Jew Isaak Illich Shapiro, head of Yezhov's Secretariat and of the new Section for Investigation of Particularly Important Cases. Yezhov's third assistant was Leonid Mikhailovich Zakovsky (Genrij E. Shtubis), a cruel Latvian who used the whip.

The trial began on 2 March 1938 and ended on the 13th. Once again, the tribunal was presided over by V. V. Ulrich presided and the prosecutor was Vyshinsky. The *Report of Court Proceedings in the Case of the Anti Soviet Bloc of Rights and Trotskyites*, which contains an English translation of the full text of the proceedings, published in 1938 by the Commissariat of Justice, is available on "Internet Achive" for readers who would like to read our brief summary. The charges against the "Right-wing Trotskyite Bloc" included: relations with foreign states for the purpose of obtaining armed assistance; espionage activities for the benefit of these states; acts of sabotage in industry, railways, agriculture, finance and other branches of the socialist state; acts of terrorism against Party and Government leaders. The accused were: Nikolai Bukharin, Alexei Rykov, Nikolai Krestinsky, Christian Rakovsky, Génrij Yagoda, Arkady Rosengoltz, Vladimir Ivanov, Mikhail Chernov, Grigori Grinko, Isaac Zelensky, Sergei Bessonov, Akmal Ikramov, Fayzulla Khodzhayev, Vasily Sharangovich, Pavel Bulanov, Prokopy Zubarev, Lev Levin, Dmitry Pletnev, Ignaty Kazakov, Venyamin Maximov and Peotr Kryuchkov. Except for Rykov, the main leaders of the Bloc: Bukharin, Krestinsky, Rakovsky, Yagoda, Rosengoltz were Jews. In addition to leading the Bloc together with Rykov, Bukharin was accused of plotting to seize power in 1918 and of wanting to kill Lenin.

Arrested at the end of May 1937, Nikolai Krestinsky, a Jewish convert, as revealed by V. Molotov himself, came as a surprise, for he did not corroborate the confession made in the preliminary statement and pleaded not guilty. President Ulrich repeated the question, "Do you plead guilty?" to which the accused replied, "Before my arrest I was a member of the Communist Party of the Soviet Union and still am." Ulrich read the charges again, but Krestinsky insisted: "I have never been a Trotskyite. I have never belonged to the bloc of Trotskyists and rightists and I have never committed a single crime." After this intervention by the accused, there was a short break.

This Krestinsky, it should be remembered, was Commissar of Finance between 1918 and 1922, until he was succeeded by Grigori Sokolnikov (Brilliant). While in charge of finance, these two Trotskyists, together with the also Jewish Leonid Krasin (Goldgelb), who died in London in 1926, worked side by side with the top representative of the Jewish finance international, Olof Aschberg, the banker of the revolution, who opened a bank in Moscow to handle wire transfers and later founded the Ruskombank, whose chief operating officer was Max May of J.P. Morgan's Guaranty Trust. Krestinsky was appointed ambassador to Germany, a very important post considering that the victory of communism in Germany depended on the triumph of Trotsky's internationalist theses. As we know, Krestinsky had been director of the "Gokhran" (State Treasury for the storage of valuables), from where he organised the logistics of the biggest plunder in history. All seized loot went to the Gokhran and was sorted there for future export, at which point the ubiquitous Olof Aschberg, who between 1921 and 1924 processed huge quantities of gold, platinum and diamonds from the Gokhran, was again involved.

After a twenty-minute recess, the session resumed with the statement of Bessonov, a revolutionary socialist who in 1918 had, like Trotsky and Bukharin, opposed the Brest-Litovsk peace. From his post as counsellor in the Berlin Embassy he acted as a liaison between Sedov and Trotsky. Bessonov, who had been arrested on 28 February 1937, gave a detailed and precise statement. Among other things he alluded to a meeting between Trotsky and Krestinsky in October 1933. When questioned by Vyshinsky about Krestinsky's refusal to acknowledge that he was a Trotskyite, he smiled: "Why are you smiling," the prosecutor asked him. His reply was: "I am smiling because the reason I am here is that Nikolai Nikolayevich Krestinsky appointed me as a liaison person with Trotsky. Apart from him and Pyatakov, nobody knew about it. If Krestinsky had not told me about this in December 1933, I would not be in the dock." Vyshinsky immediately questioned Krestinsky about these statements, who insisted that he was not a Trotskyite and that he had never discussed Trotsky with Bessonov.

> "Vyshinsky: This means that Bessonov is not telling the truth and that you are telling the truth. Do you always tell the truth?
> Krestinsky: No.
> Vyshinsky: Not always. Defendant Krestinsky, you and I will have to examine serious questions and there is no reason to lose our temper. Consequently, isn't Bessonov telling the truth?
> Krestinsky: No.

Vyshinsky: But you don't always tell the truth either, do you?
Krestinsky: I did not always tell the truth during the investigation.
Vyshinsky: But in other circumstances do you always tell the truth?
Krestinsky: I am telling the truth.
Vyshinsky: Why this disrespect for the investigation? Why did you tell falsehoods during the investigation? Explain.
Krestinsky: (No answer.)
Vyshinsky: I do not hear your answer. I have no more questions.

When the defendant insisted that Bessonov was lying and that he was telling the truth, the prosecutor asked Bessonov for more details. He alluded to another conversation with Krestinsky, namely one held in Moscow in May 1933. "Under what circumstances?" asked Vyshinsky. Bessonov said: "After I returned to Moscow from England with the entire trade delegation, I was appointed Counsellor to the Embassy in Germany. Before taking up this post, I had a long conversation with Pyatakov and Krestinsky". Again the prosecutor asked Krestinsky to confirm this testimony, but again he repeated that he had never been part of the Trotskyist bloc. Extracted from the work *Le Procès de Moscou*, by the Trotskyist Pierre Broué, whose paraphrases invite us to presuppose that everyone is lying and that the only one who tells the truth, as long as he is able to maintain his recalcitrant position, is Krestinsky, we reproduce an unabridged fragment of the interrogation which allows us to appreciate the expertise of the prosecutor Vishinsky:

"Krestinsky: I was not part of the Trotskyist centre because I was not a Trotskyist.
Vyshinsky: Wasn't he a Trotskyite?
Krestinsky: No.
Vyshinsky: Hasn't it ever been?
Krestinsky: Yes, I was a Trotskyite until 1927.
President: At the beginning of the hearing, you replied to one of my questions that you had never been a Trotskyist. You stated that.
Krestinsky: I have declared that I am not a Trotskyist.
Vyshinsky: So you were a Trotskyite until 1927.
Krestinsky: Yes.
Vyshinsky: And in 1927 when did you stop being a Trotskyist?
Krestinsky: Before the 15th party congress.
Vyshinsky: Remind me of the date.
Krestinsky: I made my break with Trotsky and the Trotskyists on 27 November 1927, when, through Serebryakov, who had returned from America and was in Moscow, I sent a virulent letter containing a harsh criticism.
Vyshinsky: We don't have that letter in our register. We have another letter. Your letter to Trotsky.

Krestinsky: The letter I am referring to is in the possession of the examining magistrate, as it was seized during the search of my home and I ask that this letter be attached to the file.

Vyshinsky: There is in the file a letter dated 11 July 1927 which was found in his house at the time of the search.

Krestinsky: But there is another one from 27 November...

Vyshinsky: There is no such letter.

Krestinsky: It can't be.

Vyshinsky: We are here at the court hearing and you did not tell the truth during the investigation. You stated in the preliminary investigation that you were not formally part of the centre, but that you were part of the centre in a general way. Did you acknowledge this during the investigation?

Krestinsky: No, I didn't recognise him.

Vyshinsky: In your statements (ff. 9 and 10) you said: 'formally I was not part of...' So can it be understood that you were part of it in a non-formal way? Is that correct?

Krestinsky: In no way was he part of the Trotskyist centre.

Vyshinsky: Can it be said that you have made false statements?

Krestinsky: I have just stated that the testimony I gave was not accurate.

Vyshinsky: When I questioned him during the preliminary investigation, he didn't tell the truth?

Krestinsky: No.

Vyshinsky: Why didn't you tell me the truth? Did I ask you not to tell the truth?

Krestinsky: No.

Vyshinsky: Did I ask you to tell the truth?

Krestinsky: Yes.

Vyshinsky: Why then, although I asked you to tell the truth, did you persist in telling lies, had them recorded by the examining magistrate and signed them right away? Why?

Krestinsky: I made false statements in advance, before you questioned me, in the preliminary investigation.

Vyshinsky: And have you kept them?

Krestinsky:... then I kept them because I was convinced from my own experience that I could no longer, until the court hearing, if there was a trial, invalidate the statements I had made.

Vyshinsky: And you think you have now succeeded in invalidating them?

Krestinsky: No, this is no longer the important thing. What is important is that I declare that I do not recognise myself as a Trotskyist. I am not a Trotskyist.

Vyshinsky: You stated that you were in a special conspiratorial situation. What do you mean by "special conspiratorial situation"?

Krestynsky: You know very well that...

Vyshinsky: Do not call me as a witness in this matter. I ask you what "special conspiratorial situation" means.

Krestinsky: I said so in my statement.

Vyshinsky: Don't you want to answer my questions?

Krestinsky: This sentence where I say that I am in a special conspiratorial situation is written in my statement of 5 or 9 June, which is false from beginning to end.

Vyshinsky: I am not asking you that, and I beg you not to be hasty in your answers. I am asking you what it means: I am in a special conspiratorial situation.

Krestinsky: That does not correspond to reality.

Vyshinsky: That's what we'll see in a moment. I want to go into the meaning of the statement you made saying that you were in a special conspiratorial situation.

Krestinsky: If it were true, I would say that being a real Trotskyist, I take every precaution to hide my membership of Trotskyism.

Vyshinsky: Perfect, and to hide it, it is necessary to deny its Trotskyism.

Krestinsky: Yes.

Vyshinsky: Now, you claim not to be a Trotskyist, but isn't that to hide the fact that you are a Trotskyist?

Krestinsky (after a silence): No, I declare that I am not a Trotskyist".

The prosecutor then called Arkady Rosengoltz, another Jew who had been an army officer with Trotsky during the civil war. He then went through the Commissariats of Transport and Finance. As ambassador to Britain between 1925 and 1927, he oversaw Soviet espionage. A member of the Central Committee of the Communist Party of the Soviet Union, he was appointed Commissar for Foreign Trade in 1930, a post he held until June 1937. On 7 October he was arrested. Krestinsky, who had not been feeling well, collapsed. Vyshinsky asked him to listen and he replied that after taking a pill he would feel better, but asked not to be questioned for a few minutes.

"Vyshinsky (addressing Rosengoltz): Defendant Rosengoltz, did you know that Bessonov was a Trotskyite?

Rosengoltz: No, I didn't know that.

Vyshinsky: Did Pyatakov recommend it to you?

Rosengoltz: I had no conversation with him on this issue.

Vyshinsky: But did you know that Bessonov was a Trotskyite?

Rosengoltz. I heard about it from Krestinsky.

Vyshinsky: What did Krestinsky tell you about Bessonov?

Rosengoltz: That he was a Trotskyite and that he helped him in his Trotskyite activity.

Vyshinsky: Who told you?

Rosengoltz: It's Krestinsky who told me.

Vyshinsky: Krestinsky personally?

Rosengoltz: Yes, Krestinsky personally.

Vyshinsky: Do you remember what year it was?

Rosengoltz: I can't say exactly.

Vyshinsky: About 1933?

Rosengoltz: Yes, approximately.

Vyshinsky: In what circumstances and on what occasion did he say this to you?

Rosengoltz: He spoke of the collaborators of the People's Commissariat for Foreign Affairs who helped him in this work, and mentioned among others Bessonov.

Vyshinsky (To Krestinsky): Defendant Krestinsky, have you heard this statement?

Krestinsky: I deny it.

Vyshinsky: Deny?

Krestinsky: I deny.

Vyshinsky: Did I hear correctly?

Krestinsky: You heard right.

Vyshinsky: I have no further questions".

Again Rosengoltz and later Grigori F. Grinko provided evidence of Krestinsky's guilt, but he stood firm in his position. Grinko was arrested on 13 August 1937 while he was Commissar of Finance, a post he held from 1930 to 1937. On 5 February 1937 Grinko had affixed his signature to the inconsequential and useless receipt issued by the Soviets for the 7,800 boxes of gold from the reserves of the Banco de España. After the morning session and a two-hour recess, the afternoon session began. A new defendant, Rykov, confirmed the guilt of Krestinsky, who again categorically denied any knowledge of illegal activities. Finally, the session ended on 2 March with the testimony of Mikhail A. Chernov, the former Commissar of the Ministry of Internal Affairs of the Russian Federation. Chernov, former Commissioner for Agriculture, whose contact man within the bloc was Rykov, basically confirmed Chernov's statement.

The next day, 3 March, began with the testimony of Vladimir Ivanov, former Commissar for the Timber Industry, whose testimony is very relevant. At the beginning of his interrogation Ivanov stated that between 1913 and 1916 he had been an agent of the Ojrana, the Tsarist secret police, under the code name "Samarin" and spy number 163, and that in 1915 he had been ordered to infiltrate the Bolsheviks. After the triumph of the revolution, Ivanov took his place with the left communists and connected with Bukharin, who on one occasion told him that he had differences with Lenin on fundamental questions and that he was working on organising cadres who might be prepared to take action against Lenin. The prosecutor's next questions were:

"Vyshinsky: How did Bukharin expect to take action against Lenin? How was he preparing to act?

Ivanov: I was in quite an aggressive mood. He was just waiting for the right moment to come. He wanted to have his own paintings.

Vyshinsky: What for?
Ivanov: To overthrow Lenin
Vyshinsky: How did you intend to overthrow him?
Ivanov: Even by physical methods".

Thus Ivanov admitted to having been involved in the activities of the Left Communists against Lenin, who were working in part, he declared, on the orders of British agents, something which Bukharin denied when confronted by Ivanov. In connection with this statement by Ivanov it is worth recalling that the previous chapter contains the section "Trotsky and the Attempted Assassination of Lenin", in which the alleged involvement of Bruce Lockhart, Lord Milner's man, and Sidney Reilly, the famous British spy, in the attempted coup d'état of 1918 has been discussed. After the cross-examination of Ivanov and Bukharin, the court proceeded to the cross-examination of Prokopy Zubarev, which concluded the morning session of 3 March.

Finally, at six o'clock in the evening, the chairman proposed to take up Krestinsky's testimony; but Vyshinsky intervened to announce that he wanted first to put some questions to Christian Rakovsky, the Bulgarian Jew who had been chairman of the Council of Commissars of the Ukraine until July 1923, and later ambassador to London and Paris. A staunch internationalist, Rakovsky, like Trotsky, rejected the construction of socialism in a single country. After the suicide in November 1927 of Adolph Joffe, the stubborn Jewish Trotskyist who had organised the revolution in Germany, and after the defeat of the Trotskyist opposition in December of the same year, Rakovsky went into exile after being expelled from the Comintern, the Central Committee and the CPSU. The prosecutor immediately asked him to explain the contents of a letter written to him by Krestinsky in 1929. Rakovsky replied that he was asking him to return in order to preserve the Trotskyist cadres within the party and to continue the activities. This was followed by an unexpected development, for Vyshinsky admitted that Krestinsky was right and that he had found among the documents the letter of 27 November 1927 to which the defendant had referred. The prosecutor asked the court for permission to give a copy of it to Krestinsky and another to Rakovsky. "This is the letter," nodded Krestinky. Rakovsky, after examining it, also remembered it. Vyshinsky read out several excerpts, and Rakovsky agreed with the prosecutor that the letter contained criticism of the incorrect leadership, the political line and the tactics employed. All this, the text said, "had to be rectified in order to restore and win back the confidence of the masses and influence over the masses".

"Vyshinsky:...What do we find here? To me it looks like an evaluation of the tactical line of the Trotskyists from the point of view of the interests of the Trotskyist political struggle within the party, and not a break with Trotskyism.

Rakovsky: Yes, that's right; I fully confirm it.

Vyshinsky (To Krestinsky): Have you listened to Rakovsky's detailed explanation of what you call the abandonment of Trotskyism? Do you consider Rakovsky's explanation to be correct?

Krestinsky: What you say is correct.

The President: Do you confirm what Rakovsky said?

Krestinsky: Yes, I confirm.

Vyshinsky: If what Rakovsky says is true, will you continue to mislead the court and deny that the testimony you gave at the preliminary investigation was true?

Krestinsky: I fully confirm the statement I made at the preliminary investigation.

Vyshinsky: No more questions for Rakovsky. I have a question for Krestinsky. What, then, is the meaning of the statement he gave yesterday, which can only be regarded as a display of Trotskyite provocation before the court?

Krestinsky: Yesterday, under the influence of an anxious feeling of false shame, because of the atmosphere and the fact that I am in the dock, and also because of the painful impression made on me by the reading of the indictment, all aggravated by my unhealthy state, I could not tell the truth, I could not say that I was guilty. And instead of saying: yes, I am guilty, I said almost mechanically: no, I am not guilty.

Vyshinsky: Mechanically?

Krestynsky: Before world public opinion, I did not have the courage to admit that all along I have led a Trotskyist struggle. I beg the court to record that I acknowledge myself absolutely and unreservedly guilty of all the serious charges against me, and that I admit my full responsibility for the treason and felony I have committed.

Vyshinsky: No further questions for the defendant Krestinsky for the time being".

From the statement of Alexei Rykov, a former prime minister who was an alcoholic, his information about the Ryutin Platform stands out. He said that Tomsky, Bukharin, Vasily Shmidt and Uglanov had been responsible, that Ryutin had only stood up for them and that Yagoda's protection had saved the main culprits. The prosecutor asked him to elaborate on his relationship with Yagoda and confronted them both during the interrogation. Reviewing this statement, it should be noted that Rykov, Ivanov and Bukharin admitted in court that they had organised and encouraged the uprisings of the kulaks. After an allusion by Rykov to Bukharin, the latter, at the prosecutor's request, declared that he had sent to the North Caucasus a certain Slepkov "for the purpose of raising insurrections. The job then was to sharpen by all means the discontent of the kulaks with Soviet power, to stir up this discontent, to organise cadres and to organise actions, including armed insurrections." Both Rykov and Bukharin added that also in Siberia they had an agitator, Yakovenko, who carried out the same work of agitation and insurrection with the help of partisans in the region. The leading role in the interrogation was taken at many points by Bukharin, the real leader of the Bloc, who time and again during the days of the trial was confronted by the defendants who mentioned him. Vyshinky asked Rykov if he knew the terrorist Semyonov and he admitted: "One day I visited Bukharin and his flat and found a stranger sitting there who left as soon as I arrived". The prosecutor asked if the man was Semyonov and the answer was yes. Bukharin admitted at Vyshinsky's insistence that he was connected with Semyonov and that Semyonov, on his instructions, was preparing in 1932 with other revolutionary socialists attempts on the lives of Stalin and Kaganóvich. To finish with Rykov, it remains to add that, supported by Krestinsky and Rosengoltz, he confirmed at length the participation of Tukhachevsky and other generals in the bloc. From these statements come the details of meetings in Moscow and epistolary contacts with Trotsky on the need to accelerate the coup d'état, which have been recounted above.

The first to testify the next day, 4 March, was Vasily Sharangovich, former first secretary in Belarus. In his statement he gave details of sabotage in rural areas. He referred to an intentionally provoked anaemia in Belarus in order to eliminate thousands of horses, necessary for defence functions. The accused gave a figure of thirty thousand horses killed as a result of these disruptive activities in agriculture. After Sharangovich, it was the turn of the Uzbek leader Fayzulla Khodzhayev. His confession about receiving orders in 1936 to work with the British for the secession of Uzbekistan, which was to become a "British protectorate", is noteworthy for its novelty:

"Khodzhayev:... But in relation to the Central Asian republics, the nearest powerful country was England. We had to reach an agreement with her. We rightists, he (Bukharin) said, will take part in this, but you are closer to the frontier, therefore you must establish relations yourselves.
Vyshinsky: Near which border?
Khodzhayev: Afghanistan. There is a British representation there. Bukharin said that since it is a question of the capitalist nations helping us to achieve power and you gain your independence, we must promise something, give something.
Vyshinsky: Give what? Promise what?
Khodzhayev: Giving means accepting a British protectorate, at the very least. There is no need to mention economic aspects, of course. Uzbekistan, with its five million people, could not become an independent state between two giants, the USSR on the one hand and Britain on the other. We should move closer to one side or the other. If you move away from one shore, you have to move towards another.
Vyshinsky: Is this what Bukharin said?
Khodzhayev: That's how I understood it.
Vyshinsky: And Bukharin pointed to England as the new shore?

Khodzhayev: That's how I understood it".

Following this statement, the chairman adjourned the session until 6 p.m. The prosecutor then questioned Arkady Rosengoltz, former Commissioner for Foreign Trade. The prosecutor then questioned Arkady Rosengoltz, former Commissar for Foreign Trade, whose statement was continuously contrasted with Krestinsky. Rosengoltz revealed that in 1925 he had asked Trotsky to admit that the theory of the "permanent revolution" was wrong, but he had categorically refused to admit it. After reporting meetings with Lev Sedov in 1933 in Felden and in 1934 in Karlsbad, Rosengoltz immediately mentioned Krestinsky as the bearer of instructions. According to this defendant, Trotsky was initially convinced that war would break out in 1935 or 1936. When it became clear that it was not going to happen, the coup d'état was chosen. Rosengoltz alluded to the meeting in his flat with Tukhachevsky and Krestinsky at the end of March 1937, which has already been mentioned above in connection with the purge in the army. Rosengoltz pointed to Krestinsky as the politician who was negotiating with the Marshal. On these relations let us look at an excerpt.

> "Vyshinsky: Defendant Krestinsky, is it true that you systematically urged Tukhachevsky to carry out the coup d'état?
> Krestinsky: As early as November 1936 I had been strongly in favour of precipitating the coup. I did not have to hurry Tukhachevsky, because he was of the same opinion and had himself explained it to the Rightists, to me, to Rosengoltz and to Rudzutak, and had asked our approval to carry out the action without waiting for an armed attack. There was therefore no need to rush him. We were in complete agreement on the question of the coup."

Vyshinsky asked Rosengoltz to expand on his preliminary statement about Gamarnik's role. The accused confirmed that they had had an interview in which the general expressed confidence in his political prestige within the army and expressed his belief that he could take over the Commissariat of Internal Affairs during the coup with the help of some daring commanders, among whom he mentioned Goryachev. Thanks to his position as Commissar for Foreign Trade, Rosengoltz, he explained, used diplomatic mail to finance the Trotskyist movement. He mentioned among the most important operations one carried out by Krayevsky, who gave Trotsky $300,000 stolen from Commissariat funds. On this subject of the financing of the Trotskyist organisation, Krestinsky was asked by the prosecutor for further information.

> "Krestinsky: We Trotskyists had by then become accustomed to receiving regular sums in hard currency.

Vyshinsky: Were they used to receiving money from foreign intelligence services?
Krestinsky: Yes, this money was for the organisation's work in various countries abroad, for the publication of literature and so on.
Vyshinsky: What is the etcetera?
Krestinsky: For travel expenses, for agitators, for the maintenance of certain professionals in different countries...".

In the course of this new intervention, Krestinsky, the ambassador in Berlin, revealed that between 1923 and 1930 they had obtained 250,000 gold marks annually. He admitted that in 1928 he received a letter from Trotsky via Reich, written from Alma Ata, where he was in exile, giving him instructions to receive money from the Germans. Krestinsky specified that his relationship had been with General Seeckt, who at that time resigned, so he had to establish contact with his successor. It was Seeckt himself who put him in touch with Hammerstein, Reichswehr Chief of Staff. Since the link was established with the German Army and not with the Government as a whole, "with Hitler coming to power," he said, "and with Hitler endeavouring to subordinate the Army, and with a certain attitude of distrust on the part of some of the Army chiefs towards Hitler's attempts to penetrate the Reichswehr, the German Government could no longer be identified with the Army, and it became necessary to contemplate that not only the Reichswehr, but the German Government as a whole became the other party to our agreement". Krestinsky went on to clarify that in exchange for money, the Germans received espionage information they might need during an armed attack.

The evening session ended with the statement by Christian Rakovsky, whose intervention would merit space that is no longer available. Rakovsky asked for permission to make a few introductory remarks, which turned into a speech full of relevant information. His first remark was as follows: "Trotsky, so to speak, is the guiding principle in all these conspiracies, in all these felonies and betrayals against the Soviet Union, against the leaders of the Government and the Party". That said, he divided his disloyal activities into two periods, in the middle of which was his exile. Rakovsky confessed his membership of the British Intelligence Service and said that Trotsky had been associated with British Intelligence since 1926. Recalling that he had travelled to Japan in September 1934 as head of a Red Cross delegation, he alluded to important contacts with Ambassador Yurenev, a lifelong Trotskyite, in connection with negotiations relating to the sale of the East China Railway Company, a deal in which the Trotskyists stood to gain. At this point Chairman Ulrich moved to adjourn the meeting until eleven o'clock the next morning.

On 5 March the Chairman asked Rakovsky to conclude his introductory remarks, and he ended by recounting an interview in which a person whose name he did not reveal expressed his discomfort at Trotsky's interference in the Chinese question. This person began his conversation by saying: "We know that you are a supporter and close friend of Trotsky. I must ask you to tell him that a certain government is dissatisfied with your articles on the Chinese question and also with the behaviour of the Chinese Trotskyists. We have a right to expect different behaviour from Mr. Trotsky. Mr. Trotsky should understand what is necessary for such a Government." We understand that the Chinese question was stirring up antagonism between Japan and Britain. Rakovsky pointed out without going into details that a provoked incident could be used as the desired pretext for intervention in China, so he wrote to Trotsky to this effect, since the Trotskyists were in touch with both secret services. The prosecutor pointed out at this point that while Krestinsky was connected with the German Secret Service, Rakovsky spoke of connections with the Japanese and British Intelligence services. At Vyshinsky's request, the accused explained in detail how he had been recruited by the British SIS (Secret Intelligence Service). Vyshinsky asked him also to inform the court of what he knew about Trotsky's own connection with the SIS.

> "Rakovsky: It was just before Trotsky's exile to Alma Ata. At first he was to be sent to Astrakhan, but he managed to get it changed to Alma Ata. When I visited him in his flat in Granovsky Street, I found him very pleased with the change. I was surprised. After all, it was several days' journey from Frunze to Alma Ata (there was no railway there then). He replied: "But it is closer to the Chinese border", and pointed to some maps. He gave me to understand that he intended to escape. I asked him how he could organise the escape across western China, through deserts and mountains, without resources. "The Intelligence Service will help me," Trotsky replied. He then told me in strict confidence that he had established criminal contact with the SIS in 1926.
> Vyshinsky: Through whom?
> Rakovsky: Through one of the representatives of the Lena gold mining concession.
> Vyshinsky: Did he have anything to do with the concessionary firm?
> Rakovsky: At that time he was the chairman of the Main Board of Dealers.
> Vyshinsky: So when he was chairman of the Board of Concessionaires he established contact with the British Intelligence Service through a representative of the Lena gold mines.
> Rakovsky: Absolutely correct....".

Rakoksky stated that he met Trotsky in 1903 and that the friendship grew until he became his close friend, both personally and politically. At one point in the interrogation Rakovsky let understand that Germany and Japan were only instruments. To anyone who could understand, Rakovsky implied rather more than he said. The question that initiated this topic was: "For whose benefit are you Trotskyists waging this struggle against the Soviet state? The answer was: "To seize power". When the prosecutor asked him to admit that they intended to destroy the socialist order, Rakovsky disagreed and pointed out that he could not openly say that they wanted to return to the capitalist system, that this was not the aim they had in mind. "On what premises and on what historical prognosis were they acting?" asked Vyshinsky. "A very indefinite prognosis, this was an adventure, if you could seize power, very well, if not..." The prosecutor did not let him conclude his argument and pretended that he would testify in a way that favoured his thesis, but Rakovsky insisted:

"Rakovsky: There was no ideological premise at all.
Vyshinsky: There was no ideological premise at all?
Rakovsky: No.
Vyshinsky: And the aim was a furious struggle against the socialist state for the purpose of seizing power? And in the long run, in whose interest?
Rakovsky: Citizen prosecutor, if I tell you that we wanted to seize power in order to hand it over to the fascists, we would not only be the criminals we are, we would also be mad. But...
Vyshinsky: But?
Rakovsky: But when we thought it was possible to take power and keep it without handing it over to the fascists it was foolishness, it was utopia.
Vyshinsky: Consequently, if you had succeeded in seizing power, would it inevitably have fallen into the hands of the fascists?
Rakovsky: I fully share this view.
Vyshinsky: So they wanted to seize power with the help of the fascists?
Rakovsky: With the help of the facists.
Vyshinsky: If the facists got power for you, in whose hands would it have been?
Rakovsky: History knows.
Vyshinsky: No, leave history alone".

This fragment is, in our opinion, absolutely significant. Rakovsky could go no further in his insinuations, for he would have had to say that the use of the fascists was a mechanism for regaining power, that to this end they had financed Hitler and were enabling the rearmament of Hitlerite Germany, and that what they intended in the long run was to return to serving the interests of the Jewish finance international, which had backed communism in order to appropriate the resources of Russia through the work of its "revolutionaries". When the prosecutor said he had no further questions, Rakovsky asked for permission to say a few words and recalled that for eight months he had refused to testify and that when he decided to plead guilty it was to make "a full, complete and frank statement". The chairman announced a twenty-minute adjournment.

As for the next accused, Isaac Abramovich Zelensky, who since 1931 had been head of the Central Union of Consumer Societies (Tsentrosoyud), we will say only that he claimed to have been involved in promoting agitation among the kulaks and in sabotage activities intended to produce discontent among the population. To this end, he worked to de-supply the shops and the market with basic necessities: salt, butter, eggs, sugar, corn and other basic consumer goods. At the end of the interrogation, the chairman suspended the session, which resumed at 6 p.m. with the testimony of an Uzbek leader, Akmal Ikramov, who had been the first secretary of the Central Committee of the Party in Uzbekistan since 1929. This defendant was confronted with Bukharin, Zelensky and Khodzhayev on sabotage and terrorist activities, but we will spare his testimony, as it does not add anything new and we need to devote space to Nikolai Bukharin, the most important defendant in the trial.

Apart from Bukharin's (Dolgolevsky's) leadership of the Trotskyist-Rightist Bloc, it is of interest what was revealed in the trial about his involvement in the plot to assassinate Lenin. In this work, it will be recalled, it was argued at the time that Trotsky, disagreeing with Lenin's decision to sign the Treaty of Brest-Litovsk, was behind the events. Let us look, then, at a few moments from Bukharin's very long statement. After the accused had accepted the charges, Vishinsky began the interrogation. The prosecutor initially dwelt on aspects already established in the previous trials, for example, the readiness of the Trotskyists to cede territories of the USSR to Germany and Japan or the participation of the Bloc in insurrectionary activities. When asked to explain his involvement in the murder of Kirov, Bukharin denied it, as did Rykov when confronted with the former.

Vyshinsky asked them to sit down and asked Yagoda. Both Rykov and Bukharin," said the former NKVD chief, "are lying. Rykov and Yenukidze were present at the meeting where the assassination of S.M. Kirov was discussed". The prosecutor then pretended a laconic answer and insisted on asking, "Did the defendants Rykov and Bukharin have any connection with the assassination?" The answer was: "Direct connection". Vyshinsky took the opportunity to ask Yagoda: "Did you as a member of the Trotskyist and right-wing bloc have any connection with the murder?" Yagoda replied: "I had. The prosecutor did not leave the subject of terrorism and went on to inquire about the guidelines emanating from Trotsky in connection with the assassination of leading figures. Asked whether, as a member of the right-wing and Trotskyist bloc, he was in favour of terrorist acts, Bukharin admitted that he was. Suddenly Vyshinsky inquired:

"Vyshinsky: Weren't you in favour of the assassination of our party and government leaders in 1918?
Bukharin: No, I was not.
Vyshinsky: Were you in favour of Lenin's arrest?

Bukharin: His arrest? There were two plans. Of one I informed Lenin myself. On the second, I kept silent for reasons of discretion, of which, if you like, I can give details. It took place.
Vyshinsky: Did it take place?
Bukharin. Yes.
Vyshinsky: What about the assassination of Vladimir Ilyich?
Bukharin: The first time it was proposed to keep him under arrest for twenty-four hours. There was this formula. But in the second case...
Vyshinsky: But what if Vladimir Ilich resisted arrest?
Bukharin: Vladimir Ilyich, as you know, never entered into armed conflicts. He was not a fighter.
Vyshinsky: So you hoped that when he was arrested Vladimir Ilich would not resist?
Bukharin: You see, I can mention another case. When the Left Socialist Revolutionaries arrested Dzerzhinsky, he did not offer armed resistance either.
Vyshinsky: It always depends on the circumstances, so in this case you were counting on the fact that there would be no resistance?
Bukharin: Yes.

The prosecutor wanted to know whether in 1918 there were also plans to arrest Stalin. The accused clarified that there had been talks about arresting Stalin and Sverdlov. Vyshinsky interrupted the questioning at this point and announced that at the end of the session or during the next day's hearing he would ask the court to call a number of witnesses in connection with the plan to arrest and assassinate Lenin. He mentioned Yakovleva, Ossinsky and Mantsev, members of the so-called "Left Communists" group, and Karelin and Kamkov, members of the Central Committee of the Socialist Revolutionaries. After deliberation by the court, the court decided to grant the summons of these witnesses.

Bukharin had asked at the beginning of his interrogation that, as was done with Rakovsky, he should be allowed to consider certain circumstances. The chairman, after warning him that he should not take advantage of the occasion to defend himself, as he would have an opportunity to make the final plea, granted his request. The accused went back to the beginnings of his counter-revolutionary activity, spoke of the evolution of methods of struggle and the formation of groups and cadres. In connection with the hierarchy of the opposition which he headed, he explained his relationship with Tomsky (Honigberg), who had committed suicide in August 1936, and with Rykov when both of them, like himself, were members of the Politburo and the Central Committee. He then went on to explaining his contacts with Zinoviev, Kamenev and Pyatakov and commented on the scope of the so-called Ryutin Platform. Both the prosecutor and the chairman interrupted him, telling him that he was "beating around the bush" and to get to the point. Bukharin then gave news of an illegal conference held in Moscow in 1932, which was attended by agitators and saboteurs like Slepkov or Yakovenko, scattered all over the country, to report on their activities. The session ended without Bukharin having finished his presentation.

At eleven o'clock on the morning of 7 March Bukharin resumed his account. He referred to the formation of conspiratorial groups within the army and mentioned the role of Yenukidze, who told him in 1932 that "in the higher ranks of the Red Army, right-wingers, Zinovievites and Trotskyites had already joined forces". Among those mentioned by Yenukidze, the accused cited Tukhachevsky, Kork, Primakov and Putna. In connection with the coup d'état, he admitted that the rightists as early as 1929-30 had conceived what he called a "palace coup", for the plotters were in the Kremlin. Later in the statement Vyshinsky asked: "Defendant Bukharin, did you engage in negotiations with Radek about the Ukraine? The defendant clarified that not in negotiations, but in talks. Bukharin explained that Radek informed him "about Trotsky's negotiations with the Germans, which envisaged territorial concessions in exchange for aid to the counter-revolutionary organisations". Bukharin was quick to point out that he was against territorial concessions and did not consider himself bound by Trotsky's instructions. The prosecutor did not accept this disassociation and began a series of confrontations with Rykov in order to prove their responsibility for the negotiations. The negotiator had been the Jewish Freemason Lev M. Karakhan (Karakhanyan), one of the leading Bolshevik astrologers, who together with Ttrotsky and Joffe was part of the Soviet delegation at Brest-Litovsk as its secretary. Karakhan was ambassador to Poland in 1921, to China from 1923-26 and to Turkey from 1934 onwards, until he was arrested and executed on 20 September 1937 along with Yenukidze and others, for which reason he could not be present at the trial. Between 1927 and 1934 Karakhan was deputy commissar of Foreign Affairs. The Commissar was also a Jew and a Freemason, Maksim Litvinov (Meyer Hennokh Wallakh), in theory a Trotskyite, who, surprisingly, remained at the head of the Commissariat for nine years. This hasty summary done, there follows a passage from the interrogation in which Bukharin was confronted by Rykov:

> "Vyshinsky: Defendant Rykov, did Karakhan start negotiations on his own initiative?
> Rykov: He undertook them on Tomsky's instructions and initiative, but Bukharin and I supported this initiative when we were informed of the negotiations.
> Vyshinsky: They supported not only the negotiation, but also the initiative, i.e. the whole thing.
> Rykov: None of us are children. If you don't support these things, you have to fight against them. You can't play with neutrality in this kind of thing.

Vyshinsky: Therefore it can be established that Karakhan conducted negotiations with the German fascists with Bukharin's knowledge. Defendant Rykov, do you confirm this?

Rykov: Yes.

Bukharin: What do you mean by Bukharin's knowledge? It is not true that I knew he was going there.

Vyshinsky: I'm not talking about going there. Do you know what initiative means?

Bukharin: I can guess remotely.

Vyshinsky: Remotely? I see that your position forces you to make remote assumptions that are very clear.

Bukharin: It is possible.

Vyshinsky: The defendant Rykov has just testified to the court in front of you that Karakhan started negotiations with the Germans not on his own initiative, but on Tomsky's.

Bukharin; But neither Rykov nor I knew this.

Vyshinsky: But you supported him later when you found out?

Bukharin: Rykov has already declared that in such cases there can be no neutrality. If I did not put an end to the negotiations, then I supported them. But this is a paraphrase of what I said: if I did not disapprove of them, I approved of them.

Vyshinsky: So, defendant Bukharin, do you take responsibility for the Karakhan negotiations with the Germans?

Bukharin: Undoubtedly.

Bukharin later stated that in the summer of 1934 he asked Radek to write to Trotsky and tell him that he was going too far in the negotiations. He commented that he feared that the Germans might end up reneging on any preliminary agreement. He also expressed doubts about Tukhachevsky. He was wary that he might harbour Bonapartist tendencies: "In my conversations I always referred to Tukhachevsky as a potential little Napoleon. And you know how Napoleon behaved towards so-called idealists. Vyshinsky replied: "And you consider yourself an idealist?" Continuing on this subject of negotiations and plans for a coup d'état, the accused reported on three conversations held in 1935 after Karakhan's arrival in Moscow from Turkey: the first with Tomsky, the second with Yenukidze and the third with Karakhan himself. Of the first, he said that he asked Tomsky "how the mechanism of intervention was visualised". The answer was: "This is a matter of the military organisation that is going to open the front to the Germans". This statement generated an exchange of questions with the prosecutor, who demanded to know exactly what "opening the front" meant.

It was in this context that the issue of blaming the military for the defeat came up, opening up the possibility for politicians to launch a patriotic slogan campaign to win over the masses. Vishinsky said indignantly, "playing with patriotic slogans, speculating with them, pretending that someone had committed treason, but that you were patriots...". The prosecutor then asked him whether he had touched on the subject in the interviews with Yenukidze and Karakhan. The accused said that the Germans had asked Karakhan for a military alliance and the annulment of the USSR's mutual assistance pacts with Czechoslovakia and France. Karakhan, according to Bukharin, agreed to the second demand. Vyshinsky insisted on the concept of "opening the front" and asked whether this had been contemplated with Karakhan. The prosecutor accused Bukharin of being the promoter of the idea, and Rykov confirmed: "I first heard the idea of opening the front from Bukharin's mouth.

It was finally the turn of the witnesses requested by the prosecutor. Varvara Nikolaevna Yakovleva was the first to enter. Yakovleva in March 1918 was working in the Moscow Cheka. The first thing she did was to accept participation in the group of "Left Communists", whose organiser and leader was Bukharin. Vyshinsky asked her to recount the main anti-Soviet activities of the group, and she explained that a small Council was formed in Moscow of which she was secretary, until she was replaced by Mantsev when she left for Leningrad. She acknowledged that in the Moscow Council discussions it was decided to fight against the supporters of peace with Germany. She referred to a speech by Stukov, recorded in the minutes book of the Moscow Regional Council, in which Stukov said that they should not shrink back and pointed already to the possibility of going as far as the physical elimination of Lenin, Stalin and Sverdlov. She added that she and Mantsev realised that the group was compromised by the written record of illegal activities and chose to remove from the minutes book the pages recording the intervention of Stukov, who later told them that his intervention had been approved by Bukharin. Yakovleva told the court that Bukharin himself confirmed to her that he supported Stukov. As this witness's statement is not to be missed, we give her the floor:

"Yakovleva:... At the same time Bukharin told me that he (Stukov) was not the only one who thought like this, that Bukharin had had a frank conversation with Trotsky on the subject and that Trotsky also thought that the political struggle on the question of war and peace had just begun, that the Left Communists should contemplate the possibility of the struggle reaching beyond the limits of the party, and that allies who could be trusted should be sought. Trotsky had told Bukharin that the Left Socialist Revolutionaries, whose position on the question was quite clear, could be such allies. Bukharin also said that Trotsky believed that the struggle should take more aggressive forms, involving not only the replacement of the government, but its overthrow and the physical elimination of the leaders of the party and the government. He immediately mentioned Lenin, Sverdlov and Stalin. Bukharin informed me that in the course of the conversation Trotsky had frankly told him that his intermediate position on the question of signing the peace was only a tactical manoeuvre, that he simply did not dare to come out actively in favour of the Left Communists, that is, against the signing of the peace, because he was a new man in the party, and if he publicly adopted the position of the Left Communists it would be said that he had entered the party in order to fight Lenin. During this conversation, when he spoke to me about Trotsky's position and possible allies, Bukharin also referred to Zinoviev and Kamenev. He said that they both maintained a vacillating attitude on the question of war and peace, and that during the discussion on the question they had repeatedly expressed to him in private conversations that they were in favour of the approach of the Left Communists. Bukharin said that Zinoviev and Kamenev did not dare to declare themselves openly against Lenin, since they had compromised their position on the question during the October days.... He said that Zinoviev and Kamenev, like Bukharin and Trotsky, thought that the political struggle on the question of war and peace went beyond the confines of the party....."

Yakovleva went on to give precise details of what happened in 1918, such as an interview with Zinoviev at the Astoria Hotel, where she was taken by Bukharin to hear the Bolshevik leader's opinion for herself. She also alluded to the departure from the government of the Left Socialist Revolutionaries because of their opposition to the signing of the peace treaty. He said that in February 1918 Bukharin and Pyatakov contacted the Left Socialist Revolutionaries to get them to agree to form an alternative government with the Left Communists. In the end, the Left Socialist Revolutionaries staged the July revolt with their own forces, since the Left Communists practically ceased to exist as an organisation. After Yakovleva's presentation, the prosecutor began to contrast with Bukharin some of the witness's assertions:

"Vyshinsky: Defendant Bukharin, were you the organiser and leader of the group called Left Communists in 1918?
Bukharin: I was one of the organisers.
Vyshinsky: Did you speak openly about the arrest of Lenin, Sverdlov and Stalin?
Bukharin: There were talks about arrest, but not about physical extermination. It was not in the period before Brest-Litovsk, but after. Before the Brest-Litovsk Peace the main orientation of the left communists was to achieve the majority within the party by legitimate means.
Vyshinsky: What legal means?
Bukharin: Debates, voting at meetings and all that.
Vyshinsky: And when did this hope disappear?
Bukharin: After the Peace of Brest-Litovsk. I want to clarify this in order to refute Yakovleva's statement. She speaks of a period before Brest-

Litovsk, which makes no sense because then we and the Trotskyists had a majority in the Central Committee and were confident of achieving a majority within the party. To talk of conspiratorial activities at that time makes no sense. At that time I spoke with Pyatakov, when Karelin and Kamkov proposed to form a new government.

Vyshinsky: When was this?

Bukharin: It was before the Peace of Brest-Litovsk. They proposed to form a government by arresting Lenin for twenty-four hours."

This reply enabled the prosecutor to establish that, although Bukharin pretended to deny it, before the Peace of Brest-Litovsk there had been talks to overthrow Lenin's government.

"Vyshinsky: I ask you, before the conclusion of Brest-Litovsk, were there negotiations with the revolutionary socialists to arrest Lenin?

Bukharin : Yes.

Vyshinsky: And were there also negotiations after the Brest-Litovsk Peace?

Bukharin: After the Peace of Brest-Litovsk there were negotiations".

Once the plans to arrest Lenin had been confirmed to Sverdlov and Stalin, Vyshinsky went a step further and entered into questioning on the subject of Lenin's physical elimination, for which he confronted Bukharin with Yakovleva, who stated that Bukharin had told her that physical elimination was not out of the question. Bukharin then asked for permission to put questions to the witness and the chairman granted it, but immediately adjourned the session. When the hearing resumed in the afternoon, Ulrich eventually thwarted Bukharin's questioning of Yakovleva, as his questions were unrelated to the case and the accused violated Article 257 of the Criminal Procedure Code, the text of which was read out by Chairman Ulrich. The defendant argued that since he was conducting his own defence, he needed to ask certain questions. Gradually, the presiding judge and the prosecutor became more permissive, and Bukharin ended up questioning all the witnesses without any problems. Valerian V. Ossinsky was the next to testify and confirmed Yakovleva's statements about the plans of the Left Socialist Revolutionaries to seize power through armed action. Ossinsky confirmed that there were plans to assassinate Lenin, Sverdlov and Stalin.

"Vyshinsky: How did you know that the bloc of conspirators intended to assassinate Lenin, Sverdlov and Stalin in 1918?

Ossinsky: First by Yakovleva and then by Bukharin.

Vyshinsky: Did Bukharin personally corroborate this intention?

Ossinsky: Yes.

Vyshinsky: And what was your attitude to that?

Ossinsky: What was my attitude? Do you want to know my political attitude or my subjective attitude? Whatever, I leave my subjective attitude aside. Since I did not oppose it, consequently I agreed to it.
Vyshinsky: And you didn't inform anyone about it?
Ossinsky: I did not inform anyone.
Vyshinsky: No further questions".

Vasily Nikolayevich Mantsev, the third witness of the group of Left Communists, who was one of their leaders, then entered. Mantsev declared that Bukharin considered that Lenin's Soviet Government was betraying the interests of the proletarian revolution and confirmed the statements of his colleagues. On the destruction of the Moscow Council minutes containing the speech in which Stukov advocated the assassination of Lenin, he said that he and Yavovleva tore them out of the minutes book on Bukharin's instructions: "He proposed that these minutes should be taken out of the book in order to conceal the conspiratorial activities of the Left Communists. Bukharin refused to accept the testimonies of the three witnesses who implicated him in the plot to assassinate Lenin and accused them of lying. An excerpt from this interrogation follows:

"Vyshinsky: Did you have occasion to visit Trotsky and talk to him about this matter?
Mantsev: Yes, I visited Trotsky and told him about this.
Vyshinsky: Did Trotsky speak to you about the need to assassinate Lenin, Stalin and Sverdlov?
Mantsev: Yes, Trotsky talked about that.
Vyshinsky: Consequently, when Bukharin declares that the initiative also came from Trotsky, is he telling the truth?
Mantsev: Yes, in this case he is telling the truth.
Vyshinsky: Does this mean, can it be said, that Trotsky together with Bukharin were planning to kill Lenin, Stalin and Sverdlov?
Mantsev: Yes, that's true.
Vyshinsky: How did you come to know about this plan?
Mantsev: I heard about it personally from Yakovleva, from Trotsky and others.
Vyshinsky: Did Trotsky talk about the need to assassinate Lenin and Stalin?
Mantsev: Yes, he did.
Vyshinsky: Did Bukharin tell you that he himself incited the assassination of Lenin and Stalin?
Mantsev: This was a decision".

Boris Davidovich Kamkov, a Jewish member of the Central Committee of the Revolutionary Socialists in 1918, was the next witness. Perhaps the reader remembers that this Kamkov, one of the revolutionary socialists who presided over the sessions of the Fifth Congress of Soviets in

July 1918, was responsible for publicly rebuking the German ambassador during one of the sessions of the Congress. Two days later Mirbach was assassinated by the Jew Yakov Blumkin. Kamkov began his statement by referring to a meeting with Bukharin at the Smolny Institute, where he told him that the position of the Bolshevik Party, as a result of the attitude towards the Brest-Litovsk Peace, was becoming complicated and had reached very serious levels: "he said that they were discussing the possibility of creating an anti-Brest government consisting of Left Communists and Left Socialist Revolutionaries under the chairmanship of Pyatakov". For the revolutionary socialists, this witness said, peace was unacceptable and they were prepared to make it impossible by any means. He confirmed that they had the support of the Left Communists in the assassination of Ambassador Mirbach, executed directly by Blumkin, Trotsky's most trusted confidant, in order to frustrate the Peace of Brest-Litovsk. Here is an excerpt from the interrogation:

> "Vyshinsky: By the way, did you, as a member of the Left Socialist Revolutionaries, participate directly in the assassination of Mirbach?
> Kamkov: I did.
> Vyshinsky: Were the left communists aware of the preparations for the Mirbach assassination and the July revolt?
> Kamkov: Yes.
> Vyshinsky: Completely?
> Kamkov: Completely, according to the information I received from Karelin, as I stated in the preliminary investigation.
> Vyshinsky: Yes, of course, according to one or the other information.
> Kamkov: That's what I wanted to say.
> Vyshinsky: This is quite clear. I ask you: Was Bukharin in particular - as leader of the Left Communists - aware that the revolutionary socialists were preparing a revolt, which actually broke out in July 1918?
> Kamkov: According to what Karelin told me, I was aware of it.
> Vyshinsky: Were you fully aware?
> Kamkov: Most probably not partially, but completely".

Vladimir Alexandrovich Karelin, who like Kamkov was also a Jew, as Bruce Lockhart states with absolute certainty in *Memoirs of a British Agent,* was the last of the witnesses called by the prosecutor. Also a member of the Central Committee of the Left Socialist Revolutionary Party in 1918, he entered the courtroom at the request of Chairman Ulrich. Karelin admitted that he and Kamkov and Proshyan had negotiated with Bukharin as leader of the Left Communists. According to this witness, in December 1917 there was hope that Bukharin's group might eventually control the Central Committee of the Communist Party. He mentioned Trotsky's famous phrase: "Neither war nor peace", which implied the breakdown of the Brest-Litovsk negotiations. Karelin said that in December/January 1918 the Soviet representation was enlarged and that he personally was a member of the delegation. He mentioned Marc Nathanson (Isaac Sternberg), a Jewish leader of the revolutionary socialists who was part of Lenin's government. Nathanson was also a member of his party's Central Committee and, according to Karelin, it was he who informed them that it had been agreed with Bukharin that negotiations would break down and lead to a revolutionary war. Karelin claimed that he himself, together with Nathanson and Proshyan, conducted the negotiations with the group of Bukharin, Radek and Pyatakov, the result of which was to lead to a coalition government after the fall of Lenin's government. This witness also confirmed that the assassination of the party and government leaders was contemplated. This part of the interrogation is worth quoting.

> "Vyshinsky: Bukharin said that the assassination of the ambassador...
> Karelin: That the terrorist action against German Ambassador Mirbach would be a shocking and effective step towards breaking the Peace of Brest-Litovsk.
> Vyshinsky: Was the attempt on V. I. Lenin's life on 30 August 1918 by the revolutionary socialist Kaplan connected with the plan to assassinate Lenin, Stalin and Sverdlov?
> Karelin: Yes, the July revolt of the Left Socialist Revolutionaries was to entail immediate contacts with the Right Socialist Revolutionaries.... Proshyan, who was in charge of the combat organisation of the Left Socialist Revolutionaries, made a report to the Central Committee in which he said that Bukharin's insistence on a terrorist act had been accentuated. And I must say that, although this has been hidden and concealed for twenty years, the Central Committee of the Left Socialist Revolutionaries was informed about these developments.
> Vyshinsky: Informed of what?
> Karelin: That the right-wing revolutionary socialists, through their combat organisation, were preparing an attack on Vladimir Ilich Lenin.
> Vyshinsky: Does this mean that the Central Committee of the Party of Left Socialist Revolutionaries had information about the preparations for Lenin's assassination?
> Karelin: Yes
> Vyshinsky: And what did Bukharin have to do with it?
> Karelin: According to Proshyan, who was negotiating with Bukharin, Bukharin urged to accelerate the terrorist action...
> Vyshinsky: Do you confirm that the preparations of the right-wing revolutionary socialists for an attempt on Lenin's life were carried out in collaboration with Bukharin?
> Karelin: With the Left Communists. We looked upon Bukharin as the leader of the Left Communists".

Naturally, these very serious accusations forced the prosecutor to ask Bukharin about Karelin's statement. "Answer: "I categorically deny any connection whatsoever". Vyshinsky replied, "Moreover, Yakovleva testifies that in 1918 you agreed to the plan to arrest and assassinate Comrades Lenin, Stalin and Sverdlov. Karelin testifies the same. Ossinsky testifies the same, and Mantsev testifies the same. I ask you: Who gave you instructions to organise this crime; what intelligence service gave you these instructions?" Bukharin insisted: "I completely deny this fact." The prosecutor said he had no more questions and asked Karelin to sit down, but Bukharin asked to question him. In his eagerness to disassociate the group of Left Communists from the July 1918 plot, he asked the following question:

> "Bukharin: Does citizen Karelin know that during the Moscow revolt of the Left Socialist Revolutionaries one of the most important persons who took part in the practical operations, from the point of view of combat technique, against the Left Socialist Revolutionaries was the Left Communist Bela Kun?
> Karelin: I heard about it personally from left communists. As for Bela Kun, I know that at that time he was a left communist, a member of this group who took part in the crushing of the revolt of the left socialist revolutionaries, and in particular, Bela Kun sent a detachment that fought near the telegraph office, which had been taken over by a detachment of the socialist revolutionaries. But this was already when the failure of the revolt was clear. So we interpreted it as an abandonment of the sinking ship".

These allusions to Bela Kun are a discovery. From this statement, then, it is clear that before going to Hungary in the autumn of 1918, where he claimed to be Lenin's man for Central and Western Europe, he had taken part during the summer in the conspiracy led in the shadows by Trotsky, the aim of which was to overthrow Lenin's government. The fact that he changed sides when he realised that the coup had failed shows once again what a criminal he was. Let us remember that Trotsky himself did something similar. In *Memoirs of a British Agent* Bruce Lockhart, with calculated ambiguity, refers that Leiba Bronstein (Trotsky) was waiting in the suburbs of Moscow with two regiments of Latvians and armoured cars.

Knowing the statements of these five witnesses, it is necessary to draw a conclusion about facts which the official historiography intentionally omits. In chapter seven of this work it was noted that Trotsky and his supporters lost a vote in the Central Executive Committee on February 24, 1918, which accepted Germany's conditions for the Brest-Litovsk Peace. Thanks to Yakovleva's statements, it is now perfectly understandable why Trotsky locked himself in his room and even refrained from taking part in the vote: "he did not dare to stand actively for the Left Communists... because he was a new man in the party... and one would say that he had entered it to fight Lenin". In his circumstances it was convenient to use one or more front men. Lenin's criticisms of Trotsky's attitudes, of his lack of principle, of his "continual swerves", were shared by many within the party. In reality Trotsky, the "partyless" one, understood Marxism as a conspiracy for permanent revolution, to achieve, not the dictatorship of the proletariat, but the dictatorship over the proletariat and over all social classes. He served those who had financed him throughout his career as a professional revolutionary. His aim was that of his sponsors: the World Government, announced in the *Protocols of the Elders of Zion*. Trotsky, a Freemason since 1897, a member of the Order of B'nai B'rith and a high-ranking illuminati, proved capable of rallying thousands of Jews around him, as evidenced by the fact that he could count on the Bund and his SR co-religionists when necessary. The main actors in the 1918 coup attempt and the attempt on Lenin's life were almost all Jews working for Trotsky, a fake who for some of his admirers was "the greatest Jew after Christ".

After the sessions of 7 March, an essential day which made it possible to establish the profound significance of historical facts which remain hidden or silenced, the hearing resumed on the 8th with the interrogation of the poison doctors. They were tried for the following crimes: the first, already mentioned above, was that of Menzhinsky, Yagoda's predecessor, perpetrated in May 1934 by Kamkov, who was following Levin's instructions. In the same month Levin and Pletnev murdered Gorky's son Maxim Peshkov. Later, these two doctors also killed Valerian V. Kuibyshev and, finally, the writer Maxim Gorky himself, one of the founders of socialist realism, who had earned Trotsky's personal enmity. Dr. Levin confessed in a lengthy statement that he and Yagoda had been the organisers of these deaths. Yagoda tried to disassociate himself from certain specific events, but his resistance gradually weakened.

The afternoon session began with the statement of Pavel P. Bulanov, Yagoda's private secretary, who had worked with him since 1929. The accused testified that he had known since 1931 that his boss was connected with the rightists and Trotskyists. Everything said in the morning session about Yagoda's involvement in the poisoning crimes was confirmed by his former secretary. The prosecutor asked him to give details about sending money to Trotsky and Bulanov mentioned that in 1934 he had delivered on Yagoda's orders $20,000 to a man sent by Trotsky and that up to 1936 there had been four or five deliveries of money to the same person. The details revealed by Dr. Levin and Bulanov are substantial, but there is not space for a more extensive review.

"What do you wish to say about your crimes?" With this question the presiding judge opened the long exposition of the deposed NKVD chief, who began by acknowledging that his membership of the Bukharin-Rykov bloc dated back to 1928 and that very few people knew about it. His main job was to protect the secrecy of the bloc from rightists and Trotskyists, who asked him to place active members of the organisation in leading positions in the OGPU. Yagoda confirmed that they used the kulaks and promoted their insurrections. On the so-called "palace coup", he acknowledged that, until Hitler came to power, it was considered the best option and that his position as vice-president of the OGPU was key, as he had the technical means to execute the coup, i.e. the Kremlin guard and the military units, which were the centre of attention. Later he said: "In 1933 the centre, the bloc of Trotskyists and Zinovievites, was organised and took shape. Through Rykov I learned that the bloc was connected with the Mensheviks and, through Bukharin, with the revolutionary socialists. Yenukidze kept me informed about the centre's decisions. It was thanks to him that I learned in January 1934 that there were preparations for a coup d'état, which entailed the arrest of the 17th Party Congress, which was in session". Yagoda admitted that he protected a group of his followers who worked for foreign intelligence services and that Karakhan informed him in 1935 about his negotiations with German fascist circles, carried out on the instructions of the right-wing and Trotskyist bloc. In his account before the court, he also accepted his participation in the cover-up of terrorist actions, among which he mentioned the assassination of Kirov. On the appointment of Yezhov as head of the NKVD, he stated the following:

> "...When Yezhov was appointed Commissar for Internal Affairs, it became clear that all the activity of our group and of the bloc of rightists and Trotskyists would be discovered. Yezhov had already begun to tear apart the cadres of the conspirators and, of course, he could reach the centre of the bloc and me personally. Therefore, in order to save our organisation, to save Rykov, Bukharin and others, we decided to assassinate Yezhov. The poisoning was carried out by Bulanov, as he himself has confessed to the court. I deny some of what he has said, but that does not change the facts and the essence of the matter."

The session on the 8th ended with the statement of the accused Peotr Kryuchkov, Gorky's secretary. Kryuchkov fully confirmed his preliminary statement and confessed to having treacherously murdered Maxim Gorky and his son Maxim Peshkov on the orders of Yagoda, who told him that the great heads of the conspiracy Kamenev, Zinoviev, Bukharin and Rykov considered it "necessary to diminish Gorky's activity". The accused told how he had arranged for Gorky and his son to contract serious respiratory diseases, which, properly treated by doctors Levin and Pletnev, led to the deaths of both of them.

On 9 March, the court continued to hear the statements of the rest of the killer doctors. Sixty-six-year-old Dmitry Pletnev, a cardiologist of great reputation who was considered an eminence in his speciality, was the first defendant to speak. Ignaty Kazakov testified after his colleague. Methods and techniques used for the commission of their crimes were explained in detail in court by both doctors. Particularly relevant was the latter's statement regarding the murder of Menzhynsky. Finally it was the turn of the last of the accused, Venyamin Maximov-Dikovsky, who admitted that he had been appointed Kuibyshev's secretary by Yenukidze and that from this position he had helped the doctors. Statements by witnesses and several scientists and medical doctors who were part of a commission of experts requested by the prosecutor's office finally brought to light the actions of the poisoning doctors.

When it appeared that the court was about to retire, prosecutor Vyshinsky asked for permission to put some questions to Rosengoltz, who at the time of his arrest had in his back pocket a piece of paper with prayers hidden inside a piece of bread. The prosecutor asked the court for permission to read out the text in order to ask the defendant for an explanation. The verses were verses from Psalms LXVIII and XCI. The first one read: "Let God appear, let his enemies be scattered: let those who hate him flee before him. Like smoke that vanishes, drive them away: and as wax melts with fire, let the wicked be destroyed before the presence of God". Here is the second psalm: "He who dwells in the secret place of the Most High shall abide under the shadow of the Almighty. I will say to the Lord, you are my refuge and my fortress, in him I will trust. He will protect you from the snares of the hunters and from the foul pestilence. He will defend you under his wings and you will be safe under his feathers. His loyalty and his truth will be your armour and your shield. Thou shalt not be afraid of any terror in the night: nor of the arrow that flieth by day. Nor of the pestilence that moves in the dark: nor of the disease that sweeps at noonday".

"Vyshinsky: How did this get into your pocket?
Rosengoltz: My wife put it in my pocket one day before I went to work. She said it was for luck.
Vyshinsky: And when was this?
Rosengoltz: Several months before my arrest.
Vyshinsky: And you carried this "good luck" in your pocket for several months?
Rosegoltz: I didn't even pay attention.
Vyshinsky: But did you see what your wife was doing?
Rosengoltz: I was in a hurry.
Vyshinsky: Did he tell you this was a family talisman for good luck?
Rosengoltz: Something similar.
Vyshinsky: And you volunteered to be the custodian of a talisman? There are no more questions.

The prosecutor looked at the people attending the public hearing, some of whom burst into derisive laughter. Of course, there is nothing objectionable about having faith and hope in God. What is objectionable is that Rosengoltz and his wife continued to pray to the God of Israel, the one who had chosen them from among all the peoples of the earth, while their Jewish-Bolshevik colleagues were preaching atheism, persecuting Christians and demolishing churches. After this shocking episode, President Ulrich suspended the session for an hour and announced that it would resume behind closed doors. In this session Rakovsky, Krestinsky, Rosengoltz and Grinko gave evidence about their relations with foreign countries and gave the names of official representatives they contacted, which had not been disclosed in open court at the direction of the presiding judge.

The day of 11 March was devoted to final speeches and pleas. Vyshinsky spent the whole morning in a very severe speech, in which he reviewed various proceedings since Lenin's time and examined the facts that had been proved. He showed in no uncertain terms his contempt for the defendants, for whom he spared none of the worst epithets. With the exception of Rakovsky and Bessonov, he demanded the death penalty for the rest of the defendants, who "deserved to be shot like dirty dogs". In the afternoon, the doctors' lawyers tried to shift all the blame for their defendants' crimes onto Yagoda. Then followed the pleas of the other defendants, which lasted until 21:25 on the following day, 12 March. One after the other, after reviewing their revolutionary past, they acknowledged the gravity of their crimes. At 4.30am on 13 March, after seven hours of deliberation on the verdict, the court passed sentence. All the defendants were sentenced to death except Pletnev, who got 25 years; Rakovsky, sentenced to 20 years; and Bessonov, to 15 years. All three were eventually executed in September 1941.

As we have seen, a campaign to protect the figure of Trotsky, a historical figure whose discredit is beyond doubt, was orchestrated during the years in which the Moscow trials were held and has continued to the present day. Numerous articles in the famous Wikipedia, in an effort to falsify history, insist on presenting everything as a fabrication and deny any credibility to the Moscow trials. However, diplomats, journalists and writers attended the sessions, held in the October room of the House of Trade Unions, which held about 300 people, and confirmed in their reports that the existence of the plot could not be doubted. The International League for Human Rights and the International Law Association publicly supported the trials. Ambassadors and members of parliament from several countries confirmed in their writings the plausibility of the trials. Denis Nowell Pritt, for example, an MP in the Commons who was a judge and well versed in procedural law, went to Moscow as a correspondent for *the News Chronicle* in London. In his articles he defended the credibility of the trials and expressed his conviction that the guilt of the defendants had been fully established. It has already been noted that Joseph E. Davies, the US ambassador, wrote again and again in his confidential reports that the authenticity of the conspiracy had been proven. The Czech ambassador Zdanek Firlinger also insisted to his government on rigour and respect for procedural rules. All in all, it must be concluded that the claim that the whole thing was a show is untenable and exposes those who maintain it.

Yezhovschina

The terror unleashed in the Soviet Union as a result of the brutal repression that followed each of the trials is known as the "Yezhovschina", i.e. the Yezhov era. Robert Conquest and his followers estimate that there were some six million arrests and about three million executions. Other historians consider these figures exaggerated and far from reality. It has already been said that one of the reasons for questioning Conquest's figures for this period is the continued use of Trotskyist sources, often Jewish authors, evidently interested in magnifying the repression. Alexander Orlov, for example, writes that a week after the execution of Zinoviev, Kamenev and company, Stalin ordered Yagoda to select and shoot five thousand opponents interned in the camps. In any case, whether this is true or not, terror, already ingrained in the habits of communism from the first days of the revolution, was widely used before and after Yezhov's time.

Considering the duration of the Trotskyite conspiracy, its criminal methods, the means used and the extent of its organisation, it seems a miracle that Stalin was able to survive and remain in power. There is no doubt that the conspirators met their match, for it was only by outsmarting, outwitting and outwitting his enemies that the Georgian managed to defeat those who wanted him dead. Purges, terror and massive repression were the main measures taken to liquidate any opposition. On 30 July 1937, the Politburo approved Operative Order 00447, which established quotas of people to be arrested and shot. According to the authors of *The Black Book of Communism*, during 1937 and 1938 the NKVD arrested 1,575,000 people, 84% of whom were convicted in the course of these years. Of these convicted persons, 51%, or 681,692, were executed. These figures are, as can be seen, considerably lower than those given by Conquest. Bearing in mind that they are generally based on official data, it is likely that the actual figures are somewhere in between.

The purge of party cadres became known thanks to Khrushchev's "secret report". According to it, Yezhov sent in 1937 and 1938 three hundred and eighty-three lists to Stalin containing thousands of names of more or less important party figures whose execution required his approval. An article published on 10 January 1989 in *Moskovskaya Pravda* claimed that on 12 December 1937 alone Stalin and Molotov approved 3,167 death sentences. According to Khrushchev's report, the purge in the party affected 98 of the 139 members of the Central Committee. Another figure referred to the delegates who took part in the 17th Party Congress in 1934: of the 1,966 who attended, 1,108 were purged. The cadres of the Communist Youth (Komsomol) were also subjected to severe repression: of the ninety-three members of their Central Committee, seventy-two were arrested. In general, the regional and local party and Komsomol apparatuses were overhauled. Government representatives accompanied by NKVD agents arrived in the provinces with the mission of, in the words of *Pravda*, "smoking out and destroying the nests of Trotsky-fascist bedbugs". With Khrushchev as the leader of the Ukrainian Communist Party, more than 100,000 people were arrested in 1938 and a large majority were executed. Of the two hundred members of the party's Central Committee in Ukraine only three survived.

On the cultural front, writers, journalists, actors, theatre people and other intellectuals were also purged: some 2,000 members of the Writers' Union were arrested and deported, if not executed. The repression again extended to religious beliefs, and it was also decided to act against "the last clerical remnants". The January 1937 census revealed that 70% of the population, against all odds, remained believers. Of the twenty thousand churches and mosques that were still more or less active in 1936, only a thousand remained open for worship in 1941. Thousands of priests and almost all the bishops were locked up in concentration camps and executed in large numbers.

CHAPTER IX

REPUBLIC, REVOLUTION AND CIVIL WAR IN SPAIN

PART 1
RELIGION AND THE CHURCH IN SPAIN

The religious persecution unleashed in Spain between 1931-39 is only comparable to that practised by the Bolsheviks in Russia. Therefore, before dealing with the specific events that took place during the Second Republic and the Civil War, a brief preamble on the role of religion and the Church in the history of Spain, a nation that has been mistreated for centuries and attacked with all kinds of infamy and slander by its many enemies, precisely because of its role in the defence of Catholicism, is necessary. We know that anti-clericalism in Europe and in the world was an essential part of the great conspiracy planned by Freemasons and illuminati against all religions. It has already been said that intellectuals such as John Robison and Abbé Augustin Barruel were attacked and discredited for denouncing the plot through their works. The new order based on economic and political liberalism, established after the French Revolution of 1789, in addition to mortgaging the power of nations and consolidating the dominance of international bankers, was to be the ideal breeding ground for attacking anything that had to do with traditional values. The effects of this new order were to be devastating for Spain.

Christian civilisation in Europe had its greatest champion in Spain. The clash of civilisations that took place in the Peninsula during the Middle Ages was decisive in preserving Europe from the spread of Islam. The fundamental impulse and force underlying all the kingdoms during the centuries of reconquest was faith in Christ; but so was the idea of Spain, a fact ignored by some undocumented and/or ill-intentioned separatists. The two were closely linked. Hispania, the toponym by which Rome alluded to the whole of its peninsular provinces, was a point of reference for the Goths and continued to be so for later Christian kings, as can be seen in countless medieval texts and documents.

Isidoro of Seville, in his historical work *Varones ilustres de España (Illustrious Men of Spain)*, considers all the inhabitants of the Peninsula to be Hispanic. The romances that deal with the last Gothic king allude to him as king of Spain: "Don Rodrigo rey de España/ por la su corona honrar/ un torneo en Toledo/ ha mandado pregonar" (Don Rodrigo king of Spain/ for the honour of his crown/ a tournament in Toledo/ has ordered a proclamation). In the *Poem of Mío Cid* it is said that the capture of Castellón "will be the talk of all Spain". The Count of Barcelona, prisoner of the Cid, refuses the food offered to him and assures that he will not eat a morsel "because of what he has in all Spain". The Catalan chroniclers pay tribute one after another to the idea of Spain. Pere I of Catalonia-Aragon tells the foreign crusaders who come to defend the Christian faith at the battle of Navas de Tolosa that they are too late because "the kings of Spain" have already defeated the Muslims. In 1283, Pere II asked a Catalan knight to appear with him in Bordeaux in a duel against the French, and invoked "the honour of us and of you and of all Spain". Bernat Desclot, author of the oldest of the four Catalan chronicles, in the face of the invasion of Catalonia by the French in 1285, appeals to the importance of having "totes les osts d'Aspanya hi fossen" (all the troops of Spain) symbolically present to defend Catalonia. Ramon Muntaner, the most patriotic of Catalan chroniclers, wrote: "Si aquests reys d'Espanya (Castile, Aragon, Majorca and Portugal) qui son una carn e una sanch, se tenguessen ensemps, poc duptaren tot l'altre poder del mon" (If these four kings of Spain, who are one flesh and blood, were to unite, they would not have to fear any other power in the world). Jaume I the Conqueror in his *Llibre dels feyts* explains the reasons why he helped his son-in-law, Alfonso X the Wise, to crush the uprising of the Moors of Murcia: "La primera cosa per Deu, la segona per salvar Espanya" (The first thing for God, the second to save Spain). His grandson Jaume II in 1304 referred to the damage that the war between Castile and Aragon would do to "tota Espanya". In his *Estoria de Espanna or First General Chronicle*, Alfonso X the Wise speaks of his "Estoria de las Españas... de todos los reyes dellas" (History *of Spain...* of all the kings of Spain). The famous *Eulogy of Spain* written by the Wise King, which concludes: "O Spain! no ha lengua nin ingenno que pueda contar tu bien" (There is no tongue or wit that can tell of your goodness), is well known among Hispanists. In 1446 Alfons el Magnànin arrived in Naples. Between the two towers of the Castel Nuovo, a magnificent military and residential building built on his orders, there is an arch commemorating his grand entrance into the city, on which he had the inscription "Alfonsus Rex Hispanus" engraved, although for the Neapolitans he was always the King of Aragon.

With the Catholic Monarchs and the discovery of America, Spain enters modern history with a new dimension: the idea of Spain, longed for centuries by the most eminent men, has become a reality; but in addition, the sons of the reconquest, converted into conquerors, with an energy and vital impulse unprecedented in history, colonised the Americas and spread Christianity in them. The foundation of towns and cities gives an idea of the immense work done by the Spaniards. Only Rome has built more than Spain in the course of history. The magnificent buildings of colonial architecture in so many towns in Latin America are an indelible example of the building efforts of the conquistadors. The Indians were considered free citizens and the Spaniards mixed with them, thus giving rise to the essential feature of Spanish colonisation: mestizaje (mixed race).

If we look at what happened with British colonisation, for example, we see that the Australian Aborigines, who had lived in Oceania for thousands of years, were exterminated. The genocide was carried out on the ideological basis of Darwinism: it was concluded that the indigenous Australians were savages and evolutionarily inferior. While in British-colonised America there are practically no Indians left, in Spanish America Indians made up 63% of the population at the end of the 18th century. Today, in Peru, Guatemala and Bolivia, Indians still make up a large majority. However, Spain has suffered for centuries from an endless campaign of attacks and has been dragging along a "Black Legend". Hollywood, on the other hand, has been responsible for presenting the extermination of the North American Indians as a logical fact: the Seventh Cavalry always appears as a regiment of legend whose soldiers naturally liquidated the Indians because they were savages.

The creation of the Tribunal of the Holy Office of the Inquisition is undoubtedly linked to the origin of the black legend. The expulsion of the Jews from Spain and the religious wars against Protestantism in Europe were the decisive events that provoked a well-planned propaganda campaign to discredit the Spanish Inquisition and combat the champion of Catholicism. It was of little use that Charles V and Philip II were once again the main defenders of Europe against the threat of the Turks and Islam: the victory of Lepanto put a stop to Turkish expansionism in the Mediterranean and constituted a victory for the whole of Christendom. In 1567 a pamphlet appeared in French, German, English and Flemish translations that sparked the campaign against Spain in general and the Inquisition in particular. The author, who signed it with the pseudonym Montanus, claimed to have been a victim of the Tribunal of the Holy Office and described a series of tortures and occult practices. It is now known that Montanus was a forger. Each of the cases that the Inquisition had during its three hundred and fifty years of existence has its own register, the details of which have been recorded on tapes and are now available to researchers in the library of the University of Salamanca.

In 1994, four internationally renowned historians publicly debunked the myth of the Spanish Inquisition before the BBC cameras: Henry Kamen, professor at universities in Spain, Great Britain and the United States and member of the Royal Historical Society; Jaime Contreras, professor of Modern History at the University of Alcalá de Henares, a world specialist in the Inquisition and the Counter-Reformation; José Álvarez-Junco, professor at the Complutense University of Madrid who directed the Iberian Studies seminar at Harvard University's Center for European Studies; and Stephen

Haliczer, an American historian of Jewish origin, professor at the University of Illinois specialising in Spain, Italy and the Catholic Church, starred in the documentary *The Myth of the Spanish Inquisition*, available online for anyone interested.

Haliczer states the following; "In reality the Spanish Inquisition used torture infrequently. In Valencia, for example, I have found that out of 7,000 cases only 2% experienced some form of torture and in general not more than fifteen minutes, and less than 1% were subjected to a second torture session, i.e. more than once. I did not find anyone who was tortured more than twice". Henry Kamen confirms that the Spanish Inquisition tortured less than other European courts and denounces that most of the images of their torture methods reproduced hundreds of times are false. The behaviour of the interrogators was well established in their "Instructions" and those who did not observe the procedures were dismissed. In the whole of the 16th century, he claims, the Inquisition executed between 40 and 50 people in the non-peninsular territories of the Spanish empire, including America. During the same period in England, where damaging public gardens could carry the death sentence, more than 400 people were executed. Kamen states that the prisons of the Inquisition in Spain were the most decent, an assertion confirmed by Professor Haliczer: "I have found examples of prisoners in secular prisons blaspheming in order to be transferred to Inquisition prisons and thus escape the ill-treatment they received in secular prisons". Professors Contreras and Kamen agree in pointing out the rigour with which the Spanish Inquisition examined the subject of witchcraft. While between 1450 and 1750 thousands of people accused of witchcraft were burned in Europe, in Spain the Inquisition was looking for evidence: "Remember," Kamen points out, "that the inquisitors were often university lawyers, and lawyers demand evidence. When evidence was not found, witchcraft was considered by the Inquisition to be an imaginary crime, a hoax for which it could not be prosecuted. Kamen states that the number of people executed for heresy in Spain, including false converts, is minimal compared to other non-Catholic countries. Finally, both Contreras and Kamen provide devastating figures for the falsifiers of reality and history: the number of victims of the Tribunal of the Holy Office during the 350 years of its activity varied between 3,000 and 5,000. During the same period, more than 150,000 witches were burned in Europe, a fact that is rarely reported. Since we are about to study the Spanish Civil War, another comparison could be made: during the month of November 1936 alone, the Madrid Defence Junta executed more people without trial than the Spanish Inquisition did in its entire history.

Until the 19th century the Church in Spain played a unifying role, which was to some extent a legacy of the Middle Ages. The conquest and colonisation of the New World was conceived as an evangelising mission and the role of the Church in America and Spain was relevant in all areas. In *The Spanish Labyrinth* Gerald Brenan acknowledges the Church's positive attitude to social issues and even speaks of its socialist tendencies in 17th century Spain. Brenan writes that "all doctors and theologians agreed that the hungry had the right to rob the rich if he had been denied charity" and quotes the great theologian Domingo de Soto, who in 1545 preached that "on pain of mortal sin, the rich are obliged to give in alms whatever they have no absolute need of". Father Mariana, one of the great theologians and historians of the time, declared that the state should oblige the rich to distribute their surplus land or, if this was not possible, to rent it so that it could be properly cultivated. In other words, once merged with the state, the Catholic Church tried to impose its moral ideas.

Many of the missionaries in America were enthusiastic about the fact that the Indians easily assimilated the Christian doctrines. It seems that in Peru the Indians worked the land collectively and this was considered by some evangelisers as a valid model applicable in Spain. In his *Historia natural y moral de las Indias* (Seville 1590), the Jesuit José de Acosta describes the economic system of the Incas and considers it superior to the system of competition and private property that was being imposed in Europe. Gerald Brenan acknowledges that the much reviled and hated Jesuits put into practice with the Guarani Indians the ideas of collectivisation of the land in their thirty missions or "reductions"[17] in Paraguay, Argentina and Brazil, which, according to Brenan, "are the first historical example of the organisation of a communist state by Europeans". Another religious man with socialist ideas praised by Brenan is the Franciscan Francisco Martínez de la Mata, considered a social agitator in the 17th century. His *Discursos* was published in 1659 and was republished by the enlightened Campomanes in 1775 in his *Discurso sobre la educación popular de los artesanos y su fomento (Discourse on the popular education of artisans and its promotion).* Martínez de la Mata proclaimed himself "servant of the afflicted poor and procurator of galley slaves". In his search for solutions to the crisis and decadence of the century, he even proposed the creation of a bank credit institution for agriculture with branches in every town.

The debate over land ownership and productivity had thus begun in the sixteenth century and became more acute during the eighteenth century. On the role of the church during the 16th and 17th centuries, Gerald Brenan writes the following:

---

[17] For a century and a half, about fifty thousand Indians were led by fifty Jesuits in these "reducciones", communities in which there were common and private properties. The Indians had a family life and were allowed to own private property. Orphans and widows were taken into a "casa de resguardo". While in Europe the death penalty was common in all countries, the Jesuits abolished it in their missions and prohibited cannibalism. The order of expulsion of the Jesuits decreed by Charles III in 1768 led to the gradual dissolution of these communities.

"The Spanish Church was a levelling institution. Its close relations with the State inspired it with an interest in social and political questions which no other church in Christendom has ever had, and to its influence was largely due the astonishing success of colonisation in America and the humanity in the methods by which, after the first violence of the conquest, conflicts between the colonisers and the natives were settled. Their missionaries returned to Spain with great practical experience of social problems. On the other hand, the intense idealism of the monastic orders meant that their weight was generally in favour of the humble (in America, the Indians; in Spain, the workers) against the powerful and the rich. It is not surprising, then, to find that the Spanish Church went further than any of the Protestant churches of its time in providing a platform for the free discussion of social theories of a certain communist character".

However, despite the good intentions and ideas formulated by some enlightened minds, agriculture in Spain was unproductive and backward. Most of the land was in the hands of the Church and the nobility. The peasants worked land that was not theirs, which could not be bought and sold freely because of its link to property. The lands of the Church were fully depreciated; those of the nobility were mostly governed by the regime of entailed estates. Thirdly, there were the properties of the municipalities, which were common property that could be leased to neighbours. The rentiers thus based their wealth on the rents they collected from the peasants who worked their land.

From the Middle Ages onwards, civil legislation protected the property of the Church, stipulating that "all things that are or were given to the Church by kings or other Christian faithful should always be kept and kept in the possession of the Church". The ecclesiastics exploited their properties through direct cultivation or through the cession of cultivation to second persons with different types of contracts. In Galicia there was a type of lease called "foro", which was a form of hereditary emphyteusis, as the peasant could not be evicted. This form of possession was also introduced in Castile in the 14th century and was called "censo". In Asturias, the Basque Country and Navarre the prevailing system was that of "sharecropping". In the Basque provinces, contracts were sometimes oral and passed down from father to son. During the 17th and 18th centuries, some settlers who had leased land from the Church sublet it from the Church with a large percentage of profit: sometimes they received up to twenty times more than what they paid. This is how the "subforados" came into being.

In the 18th century, in some provinces of Castile around 75% of the properties were ceded. With a view to improving productivity, many ecclesiastics took an interest in agronomy in order to disseminate knowledge among peasants that would stimulate agricultural development. However, the Enlightenment, aware of the backwardness of Spanish agriculture, focused their attention on the depreciated property that could not be sold, mortgaged or ceded, as it belonged to the Church and the municipalities. The greatest productivity problems were in the large estates of Extremadura, Andalusia and southern Castile. Enlightened figures such as Campomanes, Carrasco, Olavide, Floridablanca and Jovellanos presented various agrarian reports that sought to act on the amortisation of land in the hands of the Church. Jovellanos, in the *Report of the Economic Society*, was convinced that if the King asked the prelates of his churches "to promote by themselves the alienation of their territorial properties in order to return them to the people, either by selling them and converting the proceeds into census levies or public funds, or by giving them in forums or emphyteusis, they would run eagerly to do this service to the fatherland".

The national role that the church had historically played in Spain was once again evident during the War of Independence. When the Spanish people took up arms against the French, they did so in communion with the priests and friars, who led the Partidas de Cruzada, the name given to the groups of clerical guerrillas who began the fight against the invader. The regulations of these partidas were written by the Discalced Carmelite Manuel de Santo Tomás. It was the clergy as a whole who fought the war and supported it with their possessions. The list of priests and religious of the regular and secular clergy who took up arms against Napoleon is very numerous, so much so that, from Galicia to Catalonia and from Andalusia to Navarre, there was no Spanish region without its guerrillas led by canons, priests or friars. While many wealthy nobles and bourgeoisie were Frenchified, the people were led by the Church, whose representatives formed part of the provincial and local juntas. The provincial juntas of Seville, Toledo, Cuenca, Zamora and Santander were presided over by their bishops. In Valencia, Cádiz, Huesca, Murcia and Galicia the bishops were also members of the Boards. Three bishops were members of the Central Junta and two cardinals were presidents of the Regency.

The problems for the Church and the beginning of its disengagement with the people and the poor arose as a result of the disastrous agrarian policies of the liberals and, specifically, the famous Mendizábal disentailment of 1836. This anticlerical and anticarlist law dissolved religious congregations and confiscated the Church's agricultural properties. According to Brenan, "by depriving the clergy and friars of possession of land, it effectively cut them off from the people, forcing them to think of other means of enrichment and driving them into the arms of the wealthy classes". Mendizábal, commissioner of supplies since 1817, was supposed to organise in 1819 the supplies for the fleet that was to leave Cadiz to quell the rebellion for independence in America; but instead he devoted himself to preparing the revolution of 1820 with Rafael de Riego, his Freemason brother. As we know, Mendizabal appears in *Coningsby*, Disraeli's novel whose protagonist is Lionel Rothschild. Juan de Dios Álvarez Mendizábal, described as the son of a marrano from Aragon, was a Rothschild man, a

Jewish Freemason who adopted a Basque surname to hide his origin and who became rich in London by speculating in debt bonds thanks to his friendship with Nathan Rothschild. In 1835, when the Spanish government awarded Lionel Rothschild, Nathan's son, the Order of Isabella the Catholic, Mendizabal was appointed Minister of Finance. The Duke of Wellington said at the time that Mendizabal was nothing more than "an outpost of the Rothschilds".

Liberals judged the collectivist ideas of the 16th and 17th centuries, which favoured state ownership and a degree of communal management, to be outdated. They condemned, of course, solutions based on national land ownership. One of the few who opposed Mendizábal's law was Flórez Estrada, who proposed that the latifundios and communal properties should be nationalised and handed over to those who worked them, which, in his words, "would promote a collectivist solution to the agrarian problem, in accordance with the Spanish tradition". The consequences of the disentailment were disastrous and caused serious damage to farmers, who were stripped of the Church lands they had cultivated for centuries. Many of them, ruined, fell into destitution and destitution. Church property was sold at ridiculous prices, as was communal land in the municipalities, depriving the peasants of pasture, game, firewood and charcoal. The result of the disentailment was an increase in the number and size of large estates, which became the property of the nouveau riche, wealthy bourgeoisie who were only interested in their own financial gain. Obviously, agricultural production declined, as the new owners, who were absentee landlords and lived in the cities, had no interest in making improvements and were generally only concerned with establishing new leases. The peasants were thus left at the mercy of this new class of landowners, the only ones who had been favoured by the application of liberal doctrines which were completely unsuited to the conditions and interests of the country. Thus began the breeding ground for anarchist and Marxist doctrines to take root years later among the Spanish peasantry.

The first to realise that liberalism obeyed the economic interests of international bankers were the Carlists, who were radically opposed to a new doctrine whose main preachers were the Freemasons. For them, the Liberals' agrarian policy was an attack on the nation's traditional and secular values. The peasants of northern Spain understood this and rose up unanimously in favour of Don Carlos. In 1833 the religious question and the land question were linked: while the liberals relied on the Freemasons, the Carlists relied on the Jesuits. Freemasonry, whose role in the French Revolution has already been studied, penetrated Spain through enlightened circles: the Count of Aranda became Grand Master. From then on, its introduction was gradual, and it can be said that during the 19th century it became a revolutionary international of the middle classes, although from 1848 onwards there was already talk of Red Freemasonry.

Many members of the military belonged to these secret societies, which is why most of the plots and pronunciamientos were hatched in the lodges, which spread enormously during the liberal triennium. After the death of Ferdinand VII, the liberals managed to defeat the Carlists through Masonic soldiers and politicians such as Espoz y Mina, Espartero, Álava, Toreno, Alcalá Galiano, Argüelles, Mendizábal, Istúriz, among others. The machinations of the Rothschilds, who had obtained the exploitation of the Almadén mercury mines from Toreno, were decisive in the defeat of the Carlists. The Rothschilds knew that if Don Carlos had reigned in Spain they would not have retained the mining rights[18]. But the Rothschilds did not only gain control of Almadén: the Liberals also took control of the Río Tinto and Peñarroya mines, where copper, lead, zinc and other raw materials necessary for the industrialisation of Europe were extracted.

When the First Republic was proclaimed in 1873, which the Freemasons themselves called the "Masonic Republic", the Carlists had already taken up arms in May 1872. For them, the Republic wore an apron. As confirmed by Grand Master Miguel Morayta in *Masonería Española*, Figueras and Pi i Margall belonged to the Order of the Carbonarii, Salmerón sympathised with Freemasonry, and Castelar belonged to the Order. The main insurrectionist generals in 1868 were also Freemasons: Domingo Dulce, Ramón Nouvillas, Francisco Serrano and Admiral Bautista Topete, under whose command the fleet in Cadiz had risen. Serrano, "the pretty general" who won the battle of Alcolea Bridge, formed the provisional government and was Regent of the Kingdom until the arrival of Amadeo I of Savoy, the Freemason king who had been brought to Spain by General Prim, who was also a Freemason.

The Carlists saw the hand of heretics, Freemasons and Jews behind the liberals. In 1872, as in the War of Independence, with a romantic and quixotic sentimentality, rooted to some extent in the Spanish soul, thousands of young men and peasants from the Basque Country and Navarre returned to the struggle led by priests and friars. The case of the parish priest of Hernialde, the famous priest Santa Cruz, described by Pío Baroja in his novel *Zalacaín the adventurer*, whose cruelty and bravery went hand in hand, is famous. There is a thesis that Freemasonry, faced with the possibility that the reigning anarchy would facilitate the proclamation of Charles VII,

---

[18] Henry Coston denounces in *The Europe of the Bankers* that the Spanish liberal Freemasons handed over Spain's natural resources to the Rothschild family. According to Coston, Almadén and Indria (Austria) were the only deposits in Europe of mercury, a mineral needed to refine silver from impurities. The Rothschilds knew that whoever controlled them would have a monopoly on the mercury market. Nathan Rothschild sent his son Lionel to Madrid to take over the mines. Bidders had submitted sealed bids to the Ministry of Finance. Unknown to us, Lionel learned that the best offer was that of Banca Zulueta, and by offering only five reales more he won the bid. Thus, on 21 February 1835, Lionel Rothschild and the Count of Toreno signed the contract that entailed a loan to fight the Carlists.

decided to support Pavia's coup against the Republic in order to avoid a greater evil. In fact, on 17 March 1875, General Pavía declared the following before the Cortes: "Ah Señores diputados! If I had not carried out that act, the month of January might not have ended without Don Carlos de Borbón entering Madrid".

Apostles of atheism bring the Internationale to Spain

Disagreements with Marx over the organisation of the International had prompted Bakunin to organise in September 1868 a revolutionary secret society, which he called the Alliance of Social Democracy, at the top of which was the International Hundred Brothers, another secret society he had founded earlier in Naples. In October, Bakunin, who like Marx, Trotsky and Lenin was a high degree Freemason, sent to Spain on an evangelising mission an Italian engineer named Giuseppe Fanelli, another Freemason whom he had met in Ischia in 1866 and who belonged to his International Brotherhood. When in December of the same year the Alliance of Social Democracy applied for admission to the International, its application was rejected by the General Council. Bakunin then realised that Marx wanted to get rid of him and that German Jews affiliated to the International were trying to discredit him, so in 1869 he wrote his *Polemic against the Jews*, in which he denounced that Marx was being financed by Jewish bankers.

Fanelli, who had fought against the Pope under Garibaldi and was a close friend of Mazzini, both 33rd degree Freemasons, arrived in Barcelona and from there began his mission in Spain. One of the first Spanish anarchists was Tomás González Morago, whose father was a Carlist. Anselmo Lorenzo, who was also a Freemason, says that González Morago embraced anarchism because it seemed to him to carry out the teachings of the Gospel. In the spring of 1870 the Alliance of Spanish Social Democracy was founded, whose first congress was held in June at the Ateneo Obrero in Barcelona. This congress was attended by ninety delegates representing thirty-six localities. The Spanish Regional Federation of the International was born, which would later adopt the statutes of the Jura Federation of the International, drafted by Bakunin.

Marx's supporters in Spain, who were called "authoritarians", were in the minority and adopted the name "communists", while the Bakuninists called themselves "collectivists". Bakunin's struggle with Marx was thus transferred to Spain, and in December 1871 he sent his son-in-law Paul Lafargue, who spoke perfect Spanish, having been educated in Cuba. Lafargue immediately attacked the Alliance of Social Democracy and accused it of being a secret society. On 12 and 13 September the International had held a conference in London which gave new powers to the General Council, controlled by Marx. This Council dictated the right of admission to the International and had forbidden the existence of secret societies within the International. In order to get the Spanish police to arrest the anarchist leaders, Lafarge published the names of the main Spanish leaders of the International in the newspaper owned by the Marxists in Madrid, *La Emancipation*. The Bakuninists reacted by expelling the "authoritarians". Finally, at the Hague Congress in September 1872, Marx succeeded in having Bakunin expelled from the International and moved the General Council to New York to prevent his enemies from wresting control of the organisation from him. González Morago and Farga Pellicer called a congress which took place on 26 December 1872 in the Moratín Theatre in Córdoba, where the Spanish Bakuninists reaffirmed the aims of the anarchist International.

From these years onwards the "apostles" of anarchism, whose anti-clericalism was one of their hallmarks, began to spread the new doctrine of liberty, equality and justice. The first general strike in Spain took place in 1873 in Alcoy, where eight thousand workers were employed in paper mills. Through this revolutionary action the anarchists aimed to achieve the eight-hour day. The mayor, who tried to mediate, sided with the bosses, so groups of workers gathered in front of the town hall. The police unloaded and a day-long struggle began. The victory went to the workers, who shot the mayor, cut off his head and those of the guards who died in the fighting and paraded them around Alcoy. It can be said that from this moment on, violence and fanatical hatred of the Church became a constant feature of the anarchist movement. In October 1910 the CNT was born in Seville, which was to become the main fighting force of Spanish syndicalism.

As Bakunin had rightly denounced, the fact that the Marxists had the support of the international Jewish bank led to the victory of communism in Russia, which placed the leadership of the international revolutionary movements in the hands of the Judeo-Bolsheviks. In March 1919 the Third International was born in Petrograd. Trotsky's first aim, as we have seen, was to spread the revolution to Germany, Hungary and Austria. However, the social conditions in Spain also put it in his sights. The Spanish Communist Party was founded on 15 April 1920. Between 19 July and 7 August of that year the Second Congress of the Communist International was held in Moscow. It was then that Lenin prophesied that the second proletarian revolution would take place in Spain and that it would be supported by the proletariat in arms. After this announcement the international revolutionaries began to devote attention to events on the Peninsula. The first congress of the PCE met in Madrid on 15 March 1922 and already approved the policy of the united front with the socialists and anarchists, which Isidoro Acevedo, the Spanish representative at the Fourth Congress of the International, attended by sixty-one countries, announced in his speech at the congress sessions in November 1922. Jules Humbert-Droz, the Swiss representative, spoke on 4 December and stressed the need for the PCE to work with the anarcho-syndicalist organisations and the UGT.

The anarchists, impressed by the Bolshevik revolution, were ready to collaborate with the communists in 1921. Andreu Nin and Joaquín Maurín travelled to Russia and without authorisation federated the CNT with the Third International. It is assumed that they must have known nothing then about the massacre of anarchists in April 1918 and about Trotsky's responsibility for the criminal repression of the Kronstadt sailors in March 1921. Soon Ángel Pestaña, who had also gone to Russia, brought back proof of what had happened in Kronstadt and of the war of extermination against the Russian anarchists, so that Nin and Maurín's action was disavowed. In June 1922 a congress chaired by Juan Peiró was held in Zaragoza. The CNT reaffirmed its will to follow the path of libertarian communism, rejected any connection with the Moscow International and attended the congress of the International Syndicalist International (IWA) in Berlin. During the years of Primo de Rivera's dictatorship, Nin and Maurín organised a small communist party in exile. For their part, the anarchists created the Iberian Anarchist Federation (FAI) in 1927, a powerful secret association, whose leaders constituted a mysterious political elite that became part of the leadership of the anarchosyndicalist central.

PART 2
HARASSMENT OF THE MONARCHY
AND OVERTHROWING IT

After the fall of three great European monarchies as a result of the First World War and the Revolution in Russia, all that remained was to finish the job in Spain, a country whose Catholicism had been a stumbling block since the 16th century. Spain had not only expelled the Jews, but also colonised and Christianised America and for centuries had been the defender of the Catholic faith in Europe. For all this, it had done more than enough merit for the World Revolutionary Movement to prepare against it the battle to put an end once and for all to the Monarchy and to religion. As has been outlined, the process of de-Christianisation of the working classes required divorcing them from the Church, their traditional ally. The damage caused by the disentailment of ecclesiastical property was irreparable, for it led to a separation that was accentuated by the stupidity and hypocrisy of the ecclesiastical leadership. The exemplary attitude of many priests and friars who humbly continued to support the poor was of no avail, since the hierarchy, ignoring the teachings of Jesus Christ, decided to link itself to the rich in order to defend its privileges. Scepticism and contempt thus grew among the poor and the middle classes. Before the advent of the Republic, the process of disaffection with everything to do with the Church affected even believers, as evidenced by the fact that the percentage of churchgoers was falling.

An intelligent Jesuit, Father Vicente Andrade, organised the first Catholic workers' unions in 1861, which were affiliated to the International Catholic Labour Movement, but unfortunately neither bishops nor employers were able to support this initiative. The pontificate of Leo XIII (1878-1903), however, allowed Father Andrade's initiatives to receive the recognition they deserved. In 1891 the encyclical *Rerum novarum* denounced the oppression and subjugation of the poor by "a handful of very rich people". In addition to demanding fair wages, the encyclical recognised the right to organise and advocated the creation of Catholic trade unions. The Spanish hierarchy was instructed to organise Catholic centres and aid societies to deal with cases of sickness and forced unemployment. Most of the expenses were to be covered by the employers. In the north of the peninsula, these Catholic unions became operational and were grouped into a National Council of Catholic Workers' Corporations, presided over by the Archbishop of Toledo. These organisations assisted the sick, the unemployed, the elderly and in rural districts gave interest-free loans to peasants. Other Catholic trade unions were associated in the Federación Nacional de Sindicatos Católicos Libres, founded in 1912 by two Dominican fathers. The south and east of Spain, where anti-religious sentiment had taken hold and the Catholic movement was almost non-existent, was another matter.

These Catholic trade unions were, of course, supported during the dictatorship of Primo de Rivera. In addition, the general secured the collaboration of the UGT, whose secretary, Francisco Largo Caballero, won over Indalecio Prieto and accepted the dictator's offer. Largo became a state councillor, a post from which he tried to broaden his base to the detriment of the CNT, which was being persecuted. Caballero was illiterate until the age of 24 and was already a member of the union when he learned to read and write in 1893. It was not until 1934 that, while in prison because of his participation in the Asturias revolution, he began to read Marx, Engels, Trotsky, Lenin and Bukharin at the age of sixty-seven. It seems that it was then that Largo Caballero became enthusiastic about the Russian revolution, despite the fact that it had led to civil war, the ruin of the country and nearly twenty million dead.

With the support of the socialists of the UGT, Primo de Rivera extended the labour legislation that had established the eight-hour day in 1919 and created joint committees to adjust wages, which benefited the working class. In this way he tried to keep the workers away from anarcho-syndicalism. Unemployment was virtually ended through a policy of public works, but the debt increased. If the dictator had dared to expropriate and parcel up the large estates which supported rural anarchism, he might have deactivated the strength of the CNT in the south of the peninsula; but the cost of expropriation had to be borne, and this would have meant more public debt. On the other hand, its dependence on the landowning class and the army did not allow it to deal with this question.

The dictatorship had counted on the support of the Catalan bourgeoisie, terrified by the anarchy that had prevailed in Barcelona. Puig i Cadafalch, president of the Mancomunitat, and other members of Cambó's Lliga Regionalista offered their support to Primo de Rivera in exchange for Catalonia's autonomy. Although the conservative bourgeoisie benefited from the development of Catalan industry and finance, the failure to keep the promise was a mistake that heightened the tension and had serious consequences for the Lliga. The general did not want to see reality and repeatedly claimed that the Catalan problem did not exist. The dictator not only refused to advance the idea of autonomy, but also banned the use of Catalan in schools and in official communications. Nor was it allowed to fly the senyera or dance the sardana in public. All this gave the victory on a plate to the left-wing parties in favour of the Republic.[19]

---

[19] Miguel Primo de Rivera died in Paris on 15 March 1930 in circumstances that have not been clarified, as the Spanish embassy doctor, the Jew Alberto Bandelac de Pariente, a member of the Universal Israelite Alliance, did not allow an autopsy to be performed on his body. Death, unexpected and sudden, as he was not ill and his diabetes was treated

Fourteen months without respite

As soon as the dictatorship fell, an unbridled campaign of attacks on the monarchy and the king began. Moreover, although communism had not yet taken significant root in Spain, insidious propaganda depicting the Russian revolution as a triumph of the working class began to appear in the cinemas. In these circumstances Alfonso XIII offered power to General Dámaso Berenguer, who on 30 January 1930 was sworn in as President of the Council and also took over the War portfolio. His main objective was to organise parliamentary elections as soon as possible. The Junta Central del Censo (Central Census Board) immediately sent a letter to the Government in which it considered it essential to rectify the census. Niceto Alcalá Zamora and Ángel Ossorio y Gallardo supported the Board's demand with their signatures. The need to proceed with this update delayed the convocation for some months, which led anti-monarchists and revolutionaries to denounce the fact that the nation was still under an illegal dictatorship regime.

The trade union agitation instigated by communists, anarchists and socialists became progressively more pronounced. In April 1930 a grandson of Karl Marx, Jean Longuet, a French socialist nicknamed "Johnny" who had founded the newspaper *Le Populaire*, arrived in Madrid. He came with the mission of passing on instructions for action to the Spanish revolutionaries. This character, an expert in conspiracies, was the son of Jenny Marx and Charles Longuet, Marx's most trusted agent in the Paris Commune, who ended up marrying his daughter. Jean Longuet (Johnny), a brazen man who, despite declaring himself a pacifist, had supported the granting of war credits during the First World War, was already a convinced Zionist when he travelled to Spain: four months later, on 6 August, together with the Jew Léon Blum, he supported Zionist positions at the Congress of the Socialist International in Brussels, where the British government was asked to help Jewish immigration and colonisation of Palestine.

Gradually, social and labour unrest grew. On 23 June a general strike broke out in Seville, which was supported a few days later in Malaga. During the same month there were stoppages and strikes in the construction sector in several capitals. In July strikes were also called in Santander, Gerona,

---

and under control, surprised him in his hotel room while he was reading Spanish letters and newspapers. The Spanish ambassador in the French capital, Quiñones de León, a well-known Freemason, was in frequent contact with him. According to José Luis Jerez Riesco, the night before his death Primo de Rivera dined with a Jewish Mason of Sephardic origin whose identity he does not specify. Bandelac de Pariente, a Sephardic Jew born in Tangiers, was the first person in Spain to inject salvarsan, a preparation of organic arsenic used in the treatment of syphilis and relapsing fever, also called 606 (because it was the result of 606 experiments). Its discoverer, a German-born Jew named Paul Ehrlich, called these preparations 'magic bullets'. It seems that in an internal communiqué the lodges considered the death of the ex-dictator "appropriate".

Langreo, Malaga and other cities; but the most important event took place on 17 August in San Sebastián: representatives of all the Republican parties met at the Republican Circle and reached the "San Sebastián Pact", an agreement to overthrow Alfonso XIII and proclaim the Republic. No written record was kept of the issues discussed or the agreements reached, but it was learned from an unofficial note published in the newspaper *El Sol* that there was "unanimity" in the resolutions adopted. The Socialist leader Indalecio Prieto had attended the meeting in a personal capacity, and the note called on the PSOE and the UGT to add "their powerful support to the action which the forces opposed to the present political regime are determined to undertake together". Both organisations confirmed their support in October.

Ángel Rizo Bayona, Grand Master of the Spanish Grand Orient, was the one who conceived the idea of the pact to overthrow the Monarchy. This is according to César Vidal and José A. Ayala Pérez, Rizo's biographer. Alejandro Lerroux himself confirmed that Rizo had been the ideologist of the Pact of San Sebastián. This Freemason, who in 1929 was a lieutenant commander, also conceived the idea of "floating lodges" to gain control of the Navy. Grand Master Diego Martínez Barrio personally authorised him to proselytise among Navy personnel. In 1930, Rizo was promoted to the 32nd rank and was charged with preventing any reaction against the proclamation of the Republic. To prove his effectiveness, suffice it to say that on 14 April more than three thousand members of the Ferrol Squadron who were in Cartagena demonstrated in the streets in favour of the Republic. Alejandro Lerroux, Manuel Azaña, Álvaro Albornoz, Marcelino Domingo, Ángel Galarza, Santiago Casares Quiroga, Eduardo Ortega y Gasset (the philosopher's brother) and Niceto Alcalá Zamora, all of whom were present in San Sebastián, were also Freemasons. They were joined by three Catalan representatives: Jaume Aiguader, who was also a Freemason, Macià Mallol and Manuel Carrasco, who were promised appropriate treatment of the Catalan question.

In *Memorias de mi paso por mi paso por la Dirección General de Seguridad*, published in 1932 and 1933, General Emilio Mola, who was in charge of the General Directorate of Security until the proclamation of the Republic, tells how he experienced from the inside those times of permanent conspiracy, of which the Police had a great deal of information through its agents. During the months of September and October, the storm was brewing. The republican parties that were part of the revolutionary movement were so obsessed that they thought that anarchists and communists would collaborate with them in exchange for mere recognition, and so they recklessly used them as instruments on their way to power. On 3 October Mola sent a long circular letter to all the governors, prophetically warning them of the danger of this attitude:

"The mass of the workers, and in particular the organisations made up of anarchists, anarcho-syndicalists, are the propitious material for revolt and action, not because they are interested in a change of the 'monarchist-bourgeois' regime for a 'republican-bourgeois' one, but because once the dikes which maintain the present social state are broken and the nation is plunged into the chaos of revolution, they know perfectly well how difficult it will be to bring the masses back to discipline. And since, on the other hand, through the crisis only the workers' organisations would have gained in strength and prestige, the time would be ripe to establish a proletarian regime.... It really seems incredible that men of experience and culture should have fallen into the temptation of seeking the support of the CNT in order to make the revolution; but, unfortunately, this is the case."

In *Lo que yo supe, the* first of the three books that make up Mola's *Memoirs,* the director general of Security confirms that he learned in late November 1930 that preparations for a revolutionary coup were already well advanced: weapons had been distributed and there were committed military officers, including generals, in Madrid, Valencia, Logroño, Huesca and Jaca. The UGT and some communists had pledged their participation. The names and portfolios of the members of the future provisional government, which had been agreed within the Revolutionary Committee, were also known. Among other details concerning the plans for action, it was learned that Captain Fermín Galán would act in Jaca with armed peasants and troops, so Mola, who knew him personally, decided on 27 November to write him a letter to desist. "My distinguished captain and friend" were the affectionate terms with which he addressed him. In a significant passage he declared that the plot had been discovered: "The Government knows and I know of your revolutionary activities and your plans to revolt with troops from this garrison: the matter is serious and could cause you irreparable damage". Among other warnings, Mola also reminded him that the Code of Military Justice could be applied to him. What Mola did not know was that months earlier, in mid-September, Fermín Galán, with his right hand "on the Gospel of Light", had taken an oath before his brothers in the Iberian Lodge. Juan - Simeón Vidarte, deputy secretary of the PSOE between 1932 and 1939, a 33rd degree Freemason whose initiatory name was "Erasmo", reproduces Galán's oath in *No queríamos al Rey:* "I solemnly swear before the Great Architect of the universe and before you, my brothers, that the day I receive orders from the Revolutionary Committee I will proclaim the Republic in Jaca and fight for it even if it costs me my life".

Nobody in the General Directorate of Security believed that Galán would go ahead after learning that the conspiracy had been uncovered; but the young captain did not want to see reality and thought he could impose the Republic on Spain. In the early hours of Friday 12 December 1930, in the company of several captains, including Ángel García Hernández and

Salvador Sediles, and countrymen led by local Republican leaders, Galán revolted the garrison of Jaca. The military governor, General Urruela, and the chiefs and officers who did not join in, were imprisoned. Two carabineros who refused to be disarmed were shot. The sergeant commanding the Guardia Civil post was also killed. The rebels then headed for Huesca in two columns: one boarded a military train and the other marched by road with lorries and cars. A small detachment commanded by General Las Heras tried to prevent the advance and there were further casualties, including Captain Mínguez of the Guardia Civil. The general was also wounded in the scuffle. Finally, at Cillas, the clash with the government forces ended with the rebels disbanding.

The police learned that, among other revolutionary elements, two communists, an engineer named Cárdenas and the student Pinillos, were in Jaca. It seems that on Thursday 11th Casares Quiroga was in Zaragoza on his way to Jaca. He was supposed to tell Galán that the Revolutionary Committee had decided to postpone the action until the 15th, but the notice arrived late. The hesitation of the UGT in Saragossa and the differences of opinion within the CNT in Madrid also contributed to the failure of the attempted coup. On Sunday, the 14th, a summary court martial, in application of the Code of Military Justice, condemned captains Fermín Galán Rodríguez and Ángel García Hernández to death, who were shot the same day.

The extent to which Captain Fermín Galán was a hallucinated man is revealed by writings in his own handwriting that were found in Jaca. General Mola published photocopies of them in *Tempestad, calma, intriga y crisis, the* second volume of his *Memorias*. In hastily written pages full of crossings out, the young captain sketched out several decrees and orders. Here is a small sample of some of his follies:

> "Given the present circumstances which require a firm and secure unity of command without subdivisions which could disturb the unity of doctrine which inspires us in the rational development of things, with the clear vision that we have of them, I come to dispose:
> Article 1 All the powers of the revolution are concentrated in my authority".

In other articles written separately, Captain Fermín Galán, in an irrefutable demonstration of his supreme stupidity, stated the following:

> "Article 1: The death penalty without cause shall be imposed:
> a) anyone who in any way hinders, conspires or arms against the emerging regime.
> b) anyone who attempts to change the existing order by himself by threatening the life of persons and the safety of property.

(c) anyone who takes abroad silver, gold or wealth of any kind, including specific or artistic values.

Article 2 The revolutionary juntas shall set up, under their superior instruction, a Revolutionary Tribunal, which shall hear and punish, with the assistance of the National Guard, all the offences referred to in the preceding article.

Article 3° I will punish with all rigour any neglect or leniency that I find in the fulfilment of this decree on the part of the revolutionary authorities".

The rashness of Galán, clearly a young megalomaniac ready to liquidate anyone who did not accept his conditions or his "existing order", led to the failure of the Cuatro Vientos coup, which took place on Monday the 15th. Had the young captain been patient, both uprisings would have coincided, as the Revolutionary Committee had surely intended. A leading protagonist of the aerodrome adventure was Ramón Franco, brother of General Franco, one of the most colourful and reckless characters of the revolutionary movement, who in January 1926 had become a national hero thanks to his flight in the *Plus Ultra* seaplane from Palos de la Frontera to Buenos Aires. Ramón Franco was also a Freemason and had been initiated into the Plus Ultra lodge, hence the name of the plane.

Mola, constantly informed of his wanderings, had arrested him in October after discovering that he was trying to buy arms in Eibar and Saint-Etienne, but Franco managed to escape to take part in the coup. At six in the morning, General Queipo de Llano, Commanders Hidalgo de Cisneros, Pastor and Roa, Captain González Gil, a Mason affiliated with the PSOE, and other officers arrived in two cars at Cuatro Vientos. Ramón Franco arrived shortly afterwards. The guard put up no resistance and the troops were awakened with the announcement that the Republic had been proclaimed. The telegraphist sent the following dispatch to all the airfields: "The Republic has been proclaimed in Madrid, reveille". A lieutenant marched with two trucks and troops to the Retamares powder magazine, where two companies of Engineers joined the rebellion and allowed bombs to be transferred to Cuatro Vientos. Meanwhile, Major Roa had printed the proclamations that were to be dropped on Madrid. Ramón Franco was to bomb the Royal Palace and took off from the base with this intention, but when he flew over Madrid and saw that the Oriente and Armería squares were full of children playing, he gave up and returned to the airfield.

After what had happened in Jaca, when the government learned in the early hours of the morning that the aviators at Cuatro Vientos had risen up, it agreed to declare a state of war in Madrid. When it later became known that general strikes and acts of violence had begun in numerous cities, the declaration was extended to the whole of Spain. A general strike was planned for Madrid, but the call failed because of dissension among the Socialists of the UGT. Troops were immediately ordered to march on the air base. The ringleaders of the attempt then realised that their reckless adventure had failed and fled to Portugal without warning the soldiers, who shot back a cavalry patrol sent by General Orgaz. Since the rebels did not give up their attitude, cannon shots were fired over the airfield. Faced with this measure, the peasants fled and the rebels raised the white flag and surrendered without putting up any more resistance. The Revolutionary Committee had even drawn up a manifesto that ended with the cries of "Long live Spain with honour! Long live the Republic!" and was signed by Niceto Alcalá Zamora, Alejandro Lerroux, Fernando de los Ríos, Manuel Azaña, Santiago Casares Quiroga, Indalecio Prieto, Miguel Maura, Francisco Largo Caballero, Marcelino Domingo, Luis Nicolau d'Olwer, Álvaro de Albornoz and Diego Martínez Barrio, all of whom assumed the functions of the Provisional Government.

Despite the constant harassment to which he was subjected, in January 1931 the Berenguer government confirmed its decision to call a general election and set the date for 1 March. The general, a convinced constitutionalist, believed in good faith that a return to legality would quell the unrest and instability that the enemies of the Monarchy were relentlessly promoting. The government was prepared to lift the state of war, re-establish constitutional guarantees, abolish press censorship and allow electoral propaganda. The fiasco came when the Republican parties announced that they would abstain. This was a further setback for the Government, which addressed public opinion in a press release in which it refused to "penetrate into the background of the motives behind the abstentionist campaign" and stated "once again its impartiality in the electoral contest" while expressing its "fervent desire to guarantee an election with free voting and an accurate result". On 7 February 1931 the government published the decree of convocation, which set the date of 1 March for the elections of deputies and 15 March for those of senators. The date of 25 March was also set for the Cortes to meet in Madrid.

Many Republicans received the news abroad. After the Jaca and Cuatro Vientos uprisings, the revolutionary leaders who had not been arrested went into exile. Since Paris was one of the centres of emigration, there were Spanish spies there to keep an eye on them. Among many others in the French capital were Ramón Franco, who joined the Grand Orient through French Masons, Indalecio Prieto, Queipo de Llano, Marcelino Domingo, Martínez Barrio. The latter arrived in February from Gibraltar. General Mola learned through his agents that through French Freemasonry they had made contact with Russian communism and were in negotiations with the Soviet delegation in Vienna, where they were negotiating a credit of four million pesetas. They were thinking of depositing one and a half million pesetas in a bank as a guarantee fund to insure the military pay: "They are risking their lives, but not their stew", Franco is said to have said. The other two and a half million were to be used to buy weapons. Cárdenas and

Pinillos, the two inseparable communists, also appeared there in February. According to Spanish police reports, they had held talks with representatives of the Central Revolutionary Junta at the Wien Back Hotel in Vienna and were preparing to take action on the day of the elections.

That was how things stood on the afternoon of Friday 13 February when Álvaro de Figueroa y Torres, Count Romanones, and Manuel García Prieto, Marquis of Alhucemas, two monarchist liberals, triggered the crisis that led to the fall of the Government. Both intended to issue a note to the press in which they considered the abstention of the Republican parties to be a disastrous precedent, since it could mean the death of the parliamentary system. They announced that they would take part in the March elections with the intention of going to the Cortes to demand its dissolution and the calling of new constituent assemblies. About the Count of Romanones, Juan -Simeón Vidarte revealed in *No queríamos al rey* that he was a Freemason, who had been secretly initiated by Sagasta, Grand Master of the Grand Orient of Spain and Grand Commander of the Supreme Council of the 33rd degree. In view of the situation, Berenguer called Cambó to find out his attitude. The leader of the Lliga told him that he intended to abstain. When Cambó was warned by the Count of Romanones of the step he and his colleague were going to take, he published this communiqué in the Barcelona press:

"The constant assistance that I and those who share with me the leadership of an important political force have been giving to the government is well known. In the face of the long-announced legislative elections, we confined ourselves to formulating a request for guarantees of electoral sincerity, which were substantially accepted in their basic points. In spite of the granting of these guarantees, and almost coinciding with them, the declarations of abstention from the elections began which, after reaching all the revolutionary groups, extended to notorious monarchical and governmental personalities. Even after such a delicate situation was created, we understood, as we understand today, that we should not abstain from participating in the elections, but in view of the declaration of the leaders of the only two forces of the liberal party that had not declared themselves abstentionists, it seems clear that the Parliament that has been called will only last for the few days that the Count of Romanones and the Marquis of Alhucemas take to put into practice the purpose that they express in their note. And in such a situation it is better, in my opinion, to face the political problem resolutely from now on, avoiding the inconveniences and notorious dangers of the interim regime to which its postponement would give rise".

No one understood why the liberal leaders had waited until the last moment to announce a decision they had surely been mulling over for some time. Their attitude was to give rise in the coming days to an inclement press campaign aimed once again at discrediting the king and the monarchical institution. On 14 March, the crisis was over. The government resigned and, in order not to compromise his successors, General Berenguer proposed to the king that he sign a decree suspending the deadlines set for the elections of deputies and senators and the convening of the Cortes. As an alternative to elections for a constituent Cortes, those who had caused the crisis proposed a government of monarchical concentration presided over by Admiral Juan Bautista Aznar, which would include three Catalan ministers proposed by Cambó. Before leaving for Madrid, Francesc Cambó defined the situation perfectly. According to his analysis, Spain was in a pre-revolutionary situation in which "all the elements of political and social dissolution were acting with unbridled activity". For the leader of the Lliga, General Berenguer's government had increasingly given "the impression that it was not foreseeing and directing events, but was merely the plaything of the men who were provoking and administering them".

On the 15th Cambó met with the king and Berenguer. On the same day, the monarch offered power to Santiago Alba, but the latter refused. For his part, the Count of Romanones announced in conversations with journalists that he was going to try to form a government of "clear and definite leftist significance" that would convene an "arch-constituent" Cortes. The Executive Committees of the UGT and the PSOE reiterated on the 15th the need for a break with the past and called for the Republic. On the 16th the consultations continued and José Sánchez Guerra, a veteran politician, accepted the king's commission. Sánchez Guerra's actions included a visit to the Modelo prison, where the leaders of the revolutionary movement were imprisoned. Officially it was said that he had gone to ask for their support and to offer them posts in the government he planned to form.

A very different version is offered by the then Director General of Security in *Calma, tempestad, intriga y crisis*. Emilio Mola claims that Sánchez Guerra's son, Rafael, was not only a member of the Republican Party, but also a leading member of the conspiracy. Rafael Sánchez Guerra was in the car with his father when he went to the Modelo. It was he who warned him that the directors of the revolutionary movement were preparing a coup for the following morning. In reality, therefore, the purpose of the prison visit was to ask them to postpone the action out of patriotism. Public opinion accepted the first version and was divided between those who protested that they were "handing the king over to his enemies" and those who applauded the initiative, even though the political prisoners were said to have rejected Sánchez Guerra's initiative. In his *Memoirs*, General Mola gives the details known to the secret service of how the revolutionary movement was to be carried out on the night of Monday the 16th to Tuesday the 17th.

The duration of the crisis was logically very dangerous, as General Berenguer and his closest collaborators understood. At around noon on the 17th, Sánchez Guerra arrived at the palace, supposedly with the list of the new government he intended to propose to the king. Half an hour later he announced to journalists that he was declining the commission, even though he had not encountered any difficulties regarding the convening of the constituent Cortes. My advice to His Majesty," he declared, "was to call Mr Melquiades Álvarez, in case he should find the support of the left that I have not found. Hours later, the latter also found himself incapable of putting together a viable government and rejected Alfonso XIII's proposal. In these circumstances of confusion, the Minister of the Interior, Leopoldo Matos, decided on the same day to re-establish prior censorship of the press. In the afternoon, leading royalists held a meeting at the Ministry of the Army at which those responsible for the crisis imposed their criteria. Among the points of discussion, the issue of elections was a decisive one. Contrary to the opinion of General Berenguer, who argued that elections to the Cortes would not only give the government constitutional legitimacy, but would also provide a monarchist majority, the opinion of those who proposed municipal elections first prevailed.

Again thanks to Mola, who experienced the crisis from the front row, we learn that Berenguer proposed the Duke of Alba for President of the Government, but the liberals opposed him: "The Count of Romanones," writes Mola, "supported by the Marquis of Alhucemas, defended the candidacy of the Captain General of the Navy, Mr Aznar. He was a man of no significance in politics and of high representation. What the count did not say, although he probably thought it, was that Aznar, lacking his own criteria and because of his affection for him, would be his plaything". Berenguer tried by all means to disassociate himself from the government, but he was finally persuaded to agree to continue in the concentration government as minister of the army.

Admiral Aznar arrived at the palace at around 10 a.m. on Wednesday the 18th and was given the task of forming a government. It was only a protocol visit, as everything had been decided the previous afternoon. Before midday the ministers arrived to take the oath of office. The Count of Romanones was appointed Minister of State and the Marquis of Alhucemas, Minister of Justice. On the 19th the first Council of Ministers took place, which issued a declaration announcing the total renewal of town councils and provincial councils as a prior step to the calling of general elections. The government offered maximum guarantees of loyalty in the elections and declared itself determined "not to tolerate or leave unpunished the slightest disturbance of public order".

When the instability caused by the crisis was still in the air, the court martial against the rest of those involved in the December uprising, sixty-three in all, began on 13 March in Jaca. The occasion was used by

Freemasonry and revolutionaries of all kinds for a campaign of agitation throughout the country. Of course, the executed captains, Galán and García Hernández, had already become martyrs for freedom. After three days of trial and thirty-two hours of deliberation, the court handed down sixteen sentences, ranging from six months to twenty years in prison, one life sentence and a death sentence for Captain Salvador Sediles, who had fled to France and was tried "in absentia". The executives of the Socialist Party and the UGT published a manifesto calling for amnesty. The Madrid City Council, the National Federation of Students, the Ateneo Científico and other institutions asked the Government to advise the pardon. The medical students marched to the Puerta del Sol giving "vivas" to the Republic and "mueras" to the King. The Government, without even bothering to consult the Minister of the Army, General Berenguer, rushed to propose to the King that he exercise the right of pardon.

Exactly one week later, in the midst of the municipal election campaign, the court martial of the six signatories of the December manifesto who had not fled began: Niceto Alcalá Zamora, Miguel Maura, Fernando de los Ríos, Álvaro de Albornoz, Francisco Largo Caballero and Santiago Casares Quiroga. The Aznar government, displaying unprecedented political stupidity, had set 20 March as the date for the trial. The attempt to hold the hearing in the Supreme Court was another folly, as the trial turned into a demonstration of Republican exaltation. The prosecutor accused the defendants of conspiracy to military rebellion. The spectacle that unfolded during the days of the sessions was delirious: the defendants took advantage of their statements to hold rallies that were greeted by the public with thunderous ovations. On occasion, subversive shouting broke out, and the president of the tribunal, General Burguete, was unable to impose the slightest decorum.

Finally, on the 23rd, sentence was passed and, although fifteen and eight years' imprisonment had been requested, they were all sentenced to six months and one day in military correctional prison for "incitement to rebellion". The law of suspended sentences was applied to them and at five o'clock in the afternoon the following day they were released. Since the morning a crowd had been waiting in the streets for the release of the republican leaders, who were carried out of prison on the shoulders of bullfighters and hailed as heroes. To bring the month of March to a fitting end, the medical students of the Spanish University Federation called a demonstration for the 25th. Among the students were armed workers and serious clashes between demonstrators and the forces of law and order degenerated into a shooting battle: two people died, a student and a civil guard. The student strike soon spread throughout the country.

The bloodless coup d'état

Sunday 12 April 1931 was a sunny and calm day. The municipal elections were held normally. Since newspapers did not work on Sundays, there were no newspapers on the streets on Monday. At two o'clock in the afternoon the Ministry of the Interior announced that the monarchists had won 22,150 councillors and the republicans 5,875. Although the figures were incomplete, all the indications were that in rural areas, in villages and medium-sized towns, the monarchist candidates had won by a wide margin. However, as the day progressed, the figures from the big cities began to come in, where the Republicans had clearly won. When President Aznar arrived mid-afternoon at the Castellana Palace for the Council of Ministers, he was approached by journalists, who asked him if a crisis was imminent. His response was as follows: "Crisis? What more crisis do you want than a country that goes to bed a monarchist and wakes up a republican?" This completely incomprehensible and imprudent statement, inadmissible since it was made by the President of the Government before he had even met with his government, shows that a defeatist attitude was immediately adopted.

On the government meeting, it seems that there were different opinions. Some ministers appealed to the information received and were in favour of dealing with the situation until the general elections were called. Finally, without considering that the nature of the elections was not political, the Council took the decision to hand the king a note presenting the resignation of the government so that the monarch could decide. Don Alfonso, for his part, had already received the Count of Romanones and the Marquis of Alhucemas in the morning. It would undoubtedly be of great interest to know the content of these conversations, since according to Juan -Simeón Vidarte, Romanones was the instigator of the king's surrender. General Mola reveals that Alfonso XIII, without the knowledge of the Government, sent an emissary to the Duke of Maura to make representations to the Revolutionary Committee. What were these representations ? The fact was that rumours soon began to circulate in Madrid that the king was going to abdicate.

Already on Monday night, with the first evening newspapers on the streets, the intelligence services informed General Mola that the Revolutionary Committee had asked its co-religionists in the provinces to get the people out on the streets to frighten the Government and force the King to leave as soon as possible. The same agent added two brief pieces of information in his note: the Minister of Public Instruction, José Gascón y Marín, was in intelligence with the Republicans. The second was that another minister, whose name the informant could not find out, had asked the Committee to abandon its revolutionary attitude. That same night, while the exiles were hurrying back to Spain, the members of the Revolutionary Committee met at Alcalá Zamora's house and drew up a manifesto which began thus. "The representation of the Republican and Socialist forces in coalition for joint action feels the unavoidable need to address Spain to emphasise to it the historic significance of the day of Sunday, April 12. There has never been an act in our past comparable to that of this day...". It then called on the state institutions, the government and the armed forces to "submit to the national will" and scorned "the rural vote of the fiefdoms". The manifesto concluded with the declaration that they were prepared to act with energy and speed to "establish the Republic". Signing the text were Niceto Alcalá Zamora, Fernando de los Ríos, Santiago Casares Quiroga, Miguel Maura, Álvaro de Albornoz, Francisco Largo Caballero and Alejandro Lerroux. As the night wore on, excitement grew in Madrid and a vociferous crowd demanding the Republic completely filled the Puerta del Sol.

On Tuesday 14 April the word "Republic" appeared on the pages of all the newspapers. The pressure increased with the confirmation that the Republicans had won in practically all the major cities. In Eibar, the elected councillors marched to the Town Hall and in front of a crowd of ten thousand people raised the tricolour flag and proclaimed the Republic. There is a more detailed account of the proclamation in Barcelona. The Arxiu Nacional de Catalunya (National Archive of Catalonia) recently discovered unpublished notes by Joan Alavedra, secretary to Francesc Macià and Lluís Companys, which provide new information. On the evening of the 13th, the ERC leadership met on the terrace of the Hotel Colón. In addition to Companys and Macià, there were Joan Lluhí, Pere Comes, Jaume Aiguader, Joan Casanelles, Joan Casanovas, Josep Dencàs and Ventura Gassol. They discussed for hours the strategy to follow. Macià was not in favour of waiting for the legislative elections, like some politicians in Madrid, but of taking action.

The next day, Companys, Nicolau Battestini, Josep Bertran de Quintana, Ricard Opisso and Amadeu Aragay, who had met at the Ariel bookshop, whose owner was Casanellas, decided to go to the Town Hall, where they had arranged to meet Macià. At the door, a ceremonial officer, Puigdomènech, asked them where they were going. "Once inside, Companys ordered Ribé, the ceremonial chief, to summon the city guard. "At your orders, Mr Mayor," the official replied ironically. "I find this very cold," Companys commented. Then Battestini said, "See if we can warm it up", and began to shout, "Long live free Catalonia! Down with the monarchy! Long live the Republic!". They went upstairs and entered the office of the mayor, Antonio Martínez Domingo. Amadeu Aragay i Daví, who like Companys was a prominent member of Freemasonry, then took the stick and gave it to Companys and said: "Here, Lluís, you are now mayor!" They then went to fetch a Republican flag and at about half past one in the afternoon Companys went out onto the balcony to proclaim the Republic in front of a few passers-by.

According to Josep Tarradellas, Companys was hasty because he was afraid that Aragay would beat him to it and proclaim the Republic. In other words, the desire for relevance and prominence guided the steps of this adventurer, whose political actions were almost always dominated by rapture (rauxa) rather than wisdom and sanity (seny). The historian Hilari Raguer recounts that in 1917, when elected councillor for Raval, Companys accused Carrasco i Formiguera, also an elected councillor for Barcelona, of being a separatist and demanded that he shouted "Long live Spain! Azaña, in his eagerness to discredit Lluis Companys, also recalls this fact in his *Memorias políticas y de guerra (Political and War Memoirs)*.

According to Alavedra, Macià was upset when he learned that Companys had taken away the limelight that he too had sought. An hour later, Macià arrived at the Town Hall and said to him, and I quote: "Companys, I will never forgive you for this". Then from the same balcony he looked out over the increasingly crowded Plaça de Sant Jaume and proclaimed the Catalan state with these words: "In the name of the people of Catalonia, I proclaim the Catalan state, which, in all cordiality, we will endeavour to integrate into the Federation of Iberian Republics...". Cheers erupted in the square and the Marseillaise was sung. Macià then crossed the square and entered the Diputació Provincial, now the palace of the Generalitat, and addressed the crowd again from the balcony: "In the name of the people of Catalonia, I proclaim the Catalan State, under the regime of a Catalan Republic, which freely and cordially desires and requests the collaboration of the other brother peoples of Spain in the creation of a Confederation of Iberian Peoples, and offers to free them from the Bourbon Monarchy. Here and now we raise our voice to all the free states of the world, in the name of liberty, justice and peace of nations". All this, of course, was another demonstration of political adventurism, for they had not consulted with anyone and it had nothing to do with what had been agreed in the Pact of San Sebastian, where the federal state had not been even remotely considered. The construction of a federal state was an idea that could take decades to mature: once again the "rauxa" characterised the actions of yet another Catalan politician.

In Madrid the proclamation of the Republic was still not forthcoming, although very important steps had been taken during the morning. The King commissioned the Duke of Maura to draft a manifesto stating that he would leave Spain and await the outcome of the deliberations of a constituent Cortes, indicating that he had not given up all hope of returning. The monarch asked the Count of Romanones to sound out Alcalá Zamora's intentions and request a truce. The reply was that the king had to leave before sunset, since after that time he could not answer to the masses. While these steps were being taken, Admiral Aznar was out of the game, as usual. General Berenguer, Minister of the Army, was trying to find out how things stood in the main garrisons.

At around half past three in the afternoon, General Sanjurjo, Director General of the Guardia Civil, met at the home of Miguel Maura with various members of the Revolutionary Committee, which was an unmistakable sign that he wanted the support of the Guardia Civil, which was guaranteed by Sanjurjo. The Monarchy's fate was sealed. Flocks of Madrilenians were already invading the streets of the capital, cheering for the Republic. Posters abounded with portraits of Galán and García Hernández, the "martyrs of freedom". Large Republican flags were flying from the Communications Palace. At around four o'clock in the afternoon, the ministers met in the Interior building and learned that the king had been given an ultimatum, and one of the main concerns of some of them was the need to guarantee the life of Alfonso XIII and his family. The Count of Romanones said that he was personally responsible for this. And he could answer for it, since he had already agreed with the Committee how the monarch would leave Madrid.

On taking leave of the ministers, the King read them the manifesto commissioned in the morning from the Duke of Maura, in which he made some corrections in his own handwriting. Before five o'clock in the afternoon, the Government ended the meeting, and it was then that the events in Barcelona became known. The words that Alfonso XIII addressed to the Spanish people, which, surprisingly, the provisional government allowed to be published on the 16th, were these:

"The elections held on Sunday clearly show me that I do not have the love of my people. My conscience tells me that this deviation will not be definitive, because I have always tried to serve Spain, my only concern being the public interest even at the most critical junctures. A king can err, and no doubt I did err at times; but I know very well that our country has always shown itself generous in the face of guilt without malice.
I am the king of all Spaniards and also a Spaniard. I would find ample means to maintain my royal prerogatives, in effective struggle with those who fight against them. But I resolutely wish to distance myself from anything that would be to set one countryman against another in fratricidal civil war. I do not renounce any of my rights, because more than mine, they are a deposit accumulated by History, of whose custody it will one day ask me to give a rigorous account.
In order to know the authentic and adequate expression of the collective conscience, I commission a Government to consult it, convening Constituent Courts, and while the nation speaks I deliberately suspend the exercise of the Royal Power and separate myself from Spain, thus recognising it as the sole mistress of its destiny.
I also now believe that I am fulfilling the duty dictated to me by my love for my country. I pray to God that other Spaniards will feel it as deeply as I do and fulfil it".
"Alfonso R. H."

The king could have mentioned in his farewell speech that the elections had been municipal, and he could also have alluded to the broad victory of the monarchist candidates; but he chose not to do so. In reality, he had been abandoned by the monarchists themselves, who had consented to a coup against themselves after having won an electoral victory. Avoiding "fratricidal civil war", the main objective of his departure from Spain, had been achieved for the time being. Before sunset, King Alfonso left Madrid by car for Cartagena, where he arrived before dawn. There he embarked for Marseilles. The Queen and the princes, except for Don Juan, who was studying at the San Fernando Naval Academy, left by train the following day from El Escorial.

At seven in the evening, Eduardo Ortega y Gasset was already celebrating with the masses from the balcony of the Ministry of the Interior and announcing that the proclamation of the Republic was imminent. Around the same time Alcalá Zamora, Azaña, Largo Caballero, Albornoz, Lerroux and company left Miguel Maura's home and headed for the Puerta del Sol to take power. More and more red and republican flags appeared in the streets, waved by groups singing the Marseillaise and giving "vivas" to the Republic and "mueras" to King Alfonso. "Que no se ha idoo, que lo hemos echao" and "un, dos, tres, muera Berenguer" were some of the most frequently chanted phrases. When the members of the Revolutionary Committee entered the Ministry of the Interior, they were greeted as the government, although in reality the takeover took place the following day without negotiations and without any opposition. After several attempts to seize power by force, a bloodless coup d'état had triumphed in Spain.

The Provisional Government was constituted as follows: President of the Government, Niceto Alcalá Zamora; Minister of Foreign Affairs, Alejandro Lerroux; Minister of Justice, Fernando de los Ríos; Minister of the Interior, Miguel Maura; Minister of Finance, Indalecio Prieto; Minister of Public Works, Álvaro de Albornoz; Minister of Education, Marcelino Domingo; Minister of the Army, Manuel Azaña; Minister of the Navy, Santiago Casares Quiroga; Minister of Economy, Luis Nicolau d'Olwer; Minister of Labour, Francisco Largo Caballero. All were Freemasons with the exception of Indalecio Prieto and Miguel Maura. Nicolau d'Olwer, who usually passes for a non-Mason, belonged to the Grand Lodge of England. The fact that Alcalá Zamora was a Catholic has been used to deny his membership of Freemasonry. In reality he was a Mason who obeyed a foreign lodge, perhaps the Grand Lodge of England or B'nai B'rith. Both Léon de Poncins in *Histoire secrète de la Revolution Espagnole* and the Jewish magazine *Kipá*, in a report of 16 May 1931, reveal that three members of the provisional government, Alcalá Zamora, Miguel Maura and Fernando de los Ríos, were Marranos. On 12 June 1931, *L'Universe Israelite* reported on a reception with full honours offered by President Alcalá Zamora to two Jews: Dr. Kibrik and Dr. J. Jaén, the great shabbetay rabbi of Buenos Aires, to whom he promised a law in favour of the Jews, who were to be granted Spanish citizenship. The rabbi even dared to ask him to hand over Santa María in Toledo in order to convert it back into a synagogue.

It remains to add a comment on the departure from Spain of the royal family. After having cut off the heads of the kings of France and having massacred the Romanovs, it is evident that to put an end for ever to the oldest monarchy in Europe, whose history had made it one of the most hated, was for Freemasonry a temptation difficult to resist. When the Count de Romanones was told that if they did not leave Spain before sundown, they could not "answer for the masses", there was a clear hint that there were characters ready to use revolutionary fanatics to assassinate the kings. However, a secret agent working for the General Directorate of Security, Mauricio Carlavilla, had passed information to General Mola in January 1931 which literally stated: "English Freemasonry has imposed on Spanish Freemasonry respect for the life of the king in the event of the triumph of the revolution. This imposition has caused deep displeasure in the lower strata of Spanish Freemasonry and has had to be imposed by the designs of the high degrees".

When on 19 November 1931 the Cortes tried the king "in absentia", with the Count of Romanones in the role of defender, the MP José Antonio Balbontín said in his speech that "it was a widely held opinion that the escape or departure of D. Alfonso de Borbón had been consented to, prepared and facilitated by the provisional government of the Republic". Alcalá Zamora, who was no longer President of the Government, asked to speak from his seat and claimed sole responsibility for having saved the monarch's life: "I could not consent and could not want the Republic to be born dishonoured, taking power in the shadows of the night, in which mobs, of whatever origin or tendency, would come with havoc, with indignity, with tragedy, to stain the first dawn of the Spanish Republic". Alcalá Zamora's flowery speech ended with him taking responsibility for having allowed King Alfonso to flee: "...to these effects, as with everything that is blame, reproach or guilt, the only one responsible is me". When it seemed that things were going to stay that way, Manuel Azaña, by then already President of the Government, asked for the floor to also claim for himself and the other members of the Revolutionary Committee the decision to spare the life of Alfonso XIII:

> "Very gracious, Mr. Alcalá Zamora, very gentlemanly, very self-sacrificing what you have just said, claiming for yourself sole responsibility for what was done on 14 April with regard to the King; but it would be a manifest injustice and lack of loyalty to your Lordship if this Government did not solemnly declare that everything that was done that afternoon and that night was by common agreement, with all sharing in the responsibility.
>
> ... And I would also like to point out that when we were still only a Revolutionary Committee, and the means and acts that could bring about

the Revolution were being discussed, it was the unanimous agreement of the Revolutionary Committee, now the Government, that the royal persons should not be touched, that the entire royal family should be spared, and that we should not stain the purity of our intentions with the repugnant act of shedding blood which, once the Monarchy had been overthrown, was of no use to us".

PART 3
THE SECOND REPUBLIC

The steps taken in Spain to overthrow the Monarchy were very similar to those that had been taken in Russia, where in February 1917 a Provisional Revolutionary Committee became the Provisional Government overnight. Before the Judeo-Bolsheviks staged their first coup d'état, there was the coup of Kerensky's Masonic Provisional Government, which overthrew the Tsar and forced his abdication. As in Spain, almost all members of the Russian Provisional Government were Freemasons, and they also pledged themselves to elections for a Constituent Assembly that would draft a constitution. The promised elections were held in Russia in November, eighteen days after the coup by Lenin, Trotsky and their cronies. When the new Assembly met in January 1918, the Bolsheviks were in the minority, so Lenin declared that the Soviets were more democratic than the Parliament. They then shot the elected parliamentarians and staged another coup d'état, which put an end to the Constituent Assembly. In Spain too, when the election results went against them, socialists, anarchists and communists tried to overthrow democracy by a revolutionary coup d'état in 1934, as will be seen below.

All over the world, Masonic lodges greeted the advent of the Second Spanish Republic with euphoria. *The Official Bulletin of the Spanish Grand Lodge* published an article entitled "Salutation to the Republic", which reads: "...As Spaniards and Freemasons who contemplate as law the liberal structure of a new State born of the immortal principles that shine in the East (allusion to the temple of Solomon), we must feel satisfied.... To the Freemasons who make up the Provisional Government, to the senior staff, the majority of whom are also Brothers, our encouragement goes with them". In another editorial article, entitled "Our greeting to the Republic", which appeared in issue 19 of the *Official Bulletin of the Spanish Grand Orient*, it is literally stated: "...By the thrust of Masonic ideals, the guiding nations of our time have been forged; only with the intense love of those ideas taught in our workshops, can a new Spain be structured, capable of a high historical destiny". In June 1931, *the Official Bulletin of the Supreme Council of Grade 33* for Spain and its Dependencies published an article entitled "The new regime. The Republic is our heritage", in which we read in allusion to the Republic: "...perfect image, modelled by brilliant hands, of all our doctrines and principles. No other phenomenon of political revolution could be more perfectly Masonic than the Spanish one". In Mexico, the magazine *Cronos*, the mouthpiece of the lodges, published an article signed by José L. Oliveros, which stated the following: "Spain is already a Masonic lodge comprising four fifths of the Iberian peninsula. It is a temple to freedom, goodness and virtue, erected on the memorable 14th April 1931, under the presidency of Worshipful Master Alcalá Zamora".

In European countries, too, various publications celebrated the Masonic triumph in Spain. The Viennese journal *Wiener Freimaurer Zeitung*, for example, confirmed: "A long cherished wish of the Brethren of the Spanish Grand Orient has just been realised.... Those of us who know the high leaders of Spanish Freemasonry have no doubt that they will make the best of such exceptional circumstances". The *Bulletin de l'Association Maçonnique Internationale* disclosed unequivocally in its July-September 1931 quarterly issue that the assembly of the Spanish Grand Orient, held on 5 and 6 July, "had elected its high dignitaries among whom the names of three ministers, a civil governor, a state councillor, a mayor, four high officials and ten deputies to the Cortes are noted."

For its part, the Spanish Grand Lodge wanted more power for the Brethren and in number 8 of its *Official Bulletin*, corresponding to the first half of 1931, regretted that the posts in the diplomatic corps had not yet been monopolised: "...It is no secret that Freemasonry dominates almost entirely in the Provisional Government as well as in the high posts. It seemed reasonable that in mobilising the embassy staff, Freemasons should, under the circumstances, have been chosen. This would have considerably smoothed out the administration; and yet it is not so understood.... See, then, the Minister of State, who knows that Freemasonry dominates in Europe and America, whether it would be in the best interest of the Republic to take a resolution in this sense for the good of the country."

The tide of Freemasons is flooding in

A publication by the Consejo Superior de Investigaciones Científicas, *La apostasía de las masas y la persecución religiosa en la provincia de Huelva 1931-1936*, authored by Juan Ordóñez Márquez, provided surprising data in 1968 on the Masonic affiliation of the men of the Republic. Part of the following information comes from this work. To understand the abundance of names and posts, it should be borne in mind that the Second Republic had as many as twenty-six governments. There was only one President of the Government who was not a Mason, Joaquín Chapaprieta, an independent who presided over the Council of Ministers between September and December 1935 and headed two governments.

Eleven were the Masonic presidents of the Council of Ministers who headed twenty-five governments. The first, Niceto Alcalá Zamora, held office from April to October 1931 and was later appointed president of the Republic. He was succeeded by Manuel Azaña, who, according to Mauricio Carlavilla, had belonged to an irregular lodge for political action presided over by Marcelino Domingo, according to the "cuadro lógico" seized by the police from the Círculo Mercantil, where the irregular lodge was based.

Azaña, who was officially initiated into Freemasonry on 5 March 1932 under the symbolic name of "Plutarco", presided over three governments from October 1931 to September 1933, and another two from February to May 1936. When he left the Presidency of the Government, he replaced Alcalá Zamora as President of the Republic. The next was Alejandro Lerroux, whose symbolic name was "Giordano Bruno", succeeded Azaña and presided over six governments: he was president of the Council from September to October 1933, from December 1933 to March 1934, from March to April 1934, from October 1934 to April 1935, from April to May 1935, and from May to September 1935. Ricardo Samper Ibáñez, a member of the Rotary Club, replaced Lerroux from April to October 1934. Diego Martínez Barrio, a 33rd degree Mason and Grand Master of the Spanish Grand Orient, was a constant presence in one capacity or another in all the Republican cabinets and was President of the Government from October to December 1933. When the civil war broke out, he presided over a cabinet on 19 July that lasted little more than an hour. It was the shortest-lasting government in Spanish history. Manuel Portela Valladares, a 33rd degree Mason, his symbolic name was "Voluntad", presided over two governments: the first lasted fifteen days, from 14 to 30 December 1935; the second, from December to February 1936. Augusto Barcia, a 33rd degree Mason whose symbolic name was "Lasalle", presided over the Council from 10 to 13 May 1936. Santiago Casares Quiroga, whose symbolic name was "Sain Just" and in 1929 was already a Mason of the 18th degree, presided over the Government from 13 May to 19 July 1936.

All the presidents of the Government during the Civil War were also Freemasons. The first of these, José Giral, "Nobel", was in office from 19 July to 4 September 1936, when he was replaced by Francisco Largo Caballero, who belonged to the Grand Orient of France: for this reason some sources, not locating him in the Spanish lodges, do not count him as a Freemason. Largo Caballero presided over two governments: the first from 4 September to 4 November 1936; the second from 4 November 1936 to 16 May 1937. Lastly, we have Juan Negrín. In *Juan Negrín*, Gabriel Jackson writes that his name appears in Lorenzo Frau's *Diccionario de la Masonería*, and quotes Aurelio Martín, who in his study *La Segunda República, Grupo Parlamentario Socialista* says that Negrín was initiated in Germany during his student years, which is confirmed by Juan-Simeón Vidarte in *Todos fuimos culpables*. This socialist claims that Negrín himself confessed to him that he had been initiated in Germany and that he regularised his situation when he was elected to the Cortes of the Republic. Dr. Negrín headed during the last two governments of the Republic: from 17 May 1937 to 5 April 1938, and from 5 April 1938 to 6 March 1939.

As for the presidents of the Generalitat de Catalunya: Francesc Macià, Lluis Companys, Josep Irla and Josep Tarradellas, all four were also Freemasons. The first, Francesc Macià, travelled to the USSR at the end of

1925 to ask the Third International for help. Not understanding at all what was happening there after Lenin's death, he met the Trotskyists Bukharin and Zinoviev. In a letter to a Cuban friend, dated 15 January 1926 in Bois-Colombes, Macià writes that they both undertook "to underwrite financially all the expenses of organisation, preparation and propaganda for the revolution in Catalonia and throughout Spain". Macià died on Christmas Day 1933 and in a strange Masonic ritual his heart was removed, which was guarded by Tarradelllas in exile in order to give it to the family.

The Freemason brothers took over all the ministries. During the first two years of the left-wing government, the Ministry of Justice was continuously occupied by Fernando de los Ríos, who had been promoted by Freemasonry to the 33rd degree in June 1931; Álvaro de Albornoz, who had previously been Minister of Public Works; Casares Quiroga and Juan Botella Asensi. After the two years of the right-wing biennium, the Freemasons regained the important Ministry of Justice in May 1936 in the person of Manuel Blasco Garzón, whose symbolic name in the Fe lodge was "Proudhon". Blasco Garzón had been Minister of Communications and the Merchant Navy since the triumph of the Popular Front in February. The Ministry of War was controlled by Freemasons during the Socialist-Azaña biennium. Azaña, who combined the Presidency of the Government with the War portfolio, was succeeded in the post by Juan José Rocha García, a 33rd degree Freemason whose symbolic name was "Pi y Margall". Subsequently, Rocha was also Minister of the Navy, Minister of State and Minister of Public Instruction. The next Masonic Minister of War was Vicente Iranzo Enguita, who also served as Minister of the Navy and Minister of Industry and Commerce. His replacement was the Grand Master of the Spanish Grand Orient, Martínez Barrio. Subsequently, two other Masons, Lerroux and Casares Quiroga, held the post. The Ministry of the Navy was only in the hands of non-Masonic ministers for half a year during the five years of the Republican period. It included Casares Quiroga, Giral, Companys, a member of the Lealtad lodge in Barcelona, Iranzo, the aforementioned Rocha and Gerardo Abad Conde, a Freemason of the 33rd lodge who adopted the symbolic name of "Justicia" (Justice). Abad Conde presided over the Board of Trustees that seized the Jesuits' property. In the Ministry of the Interior, all the ministers were Masons with the exception of Maura. We cite only some of the Ministers of the Interior whose names have not yet appeared in this review: Manuel Rico Avelló, who adopted the symbolic name of "Roma" and was also briefly Minister of Finance between 30 December 1935 and February 1936; Rafael Salazar Alonso, who as well as Minister was also Mayor and President of the Provincial Council of Madrid; Eloy Vaquero Cantillo, alias "Cavour", who would also be Minister of Labour, Health and Welfare; Juan Moles Ormella, Minister of the Interior from 13 May to 18 July 1936. The State portfolio was in the hands of at least five Masonic ministers: Lerroux, Samper, Rocha, Barcia and Fernando de los Ríos.

Since the Masonic ministers surrounded themselves with Masonic brothers, it can be said that the Order succeeded in controlling the State Administration, which was flooded by an unstoppable tide. At the risk of tiring the reader, we will mention in conclusion a few names from an endless list of high-ranking Masons in the Republic: Emilio Pardo Aguado, of the Danton triangle of intellectuals, 33rd degree Mason and member of the Sovereign Council of the Spanish Grand Orient, "Desmoulins" to the brethren, was civil governor of Madrid and undersecretary of Communications, a Ministry of which he became minister for a few months; Pedro Rico López, 33rd degree, symbolic "Madrid", was mayor of the Spanish capital; Jaume Aiguader Miró, of the lodge Rectitud de Barcelona, mayor of Barcelona; Rodolfo Llopis Ferrándiz of the lodge Ibérica de Madrid, was director general of Primary Education, extremely sectarian; Mateo Hernández Barroso, 33rd degree, "Newton", Director General of Telegraphs; Eduardo Ortega y Gasset, symbolic "León", first civil governor of Madrid; José Salmerón García, symbolic "d'Alembert", Director General of Public Works; Pedro Armansa Briales, of the Pitágoras lodge in Málaga, State Councillor; Dionisio Carreras Fernández, "Sócrates", of the Ibérica lodge, Minister of Culture; Antonio Pérez Torreblanca, "Diógenes", Director General of Agriculture; Benito Artigas Arpón, "Juliano", Director General of Trade and Tariff Policy; José Domínguez Barbero, "Henri", Minister of the Court of Auditors; José Jorge Vinaixa, "Vergniaud", State Councillor; Casimiro Giral Bullich, 18th grade, "Platón", Councillor of the Generalitat de Catalunya; Manuel Torres Campañá, "Juvenal", Undersecretary of the Interior and of the Presidency of the Council; José Moreno Galvache, "Lucrecio", successively Undersecretary of Agriculture, Industry and Public Instruction; Nicolás Sánchez Balástegui, "Pestalozzi", Government Delegate for the Guadalquivir Water Services; Ramón Carrera Pons, Commissioner General of Catalonia; Fernando Valera Aparicio, "Plotino", Director General of Agriculture and Undersecretary of Justice; Pedro Vargas Gurendiaín, "Pi", 18th grade, Undersecretary of Communications; Sidonio Pintado Arroyo, "Juvenal", Minister of Culture; Gabriel González Taltavull, "Schopenhauer", 18th grade, member of the Court of Guarantees; Rafael Blasco García, "Sigfredo", grade 13, substitute member of the Tribunal de Garantías; Luis Doporto Machori, "Teruel", civil governor of Valencia and Minister of Culture; Clara Campoamor Rodríguez, Director General of Beneficencia. We have left many names unmentioned, as it would be pointless to continue.

Anti-clericalism

Since the emergence of liberalism in the 19th century, episodes of anticlericalism, associated from the beginning with Freemasonry, had been on the rise in Spain. No one expected, however, that the burning of churches and convents would reappear only a month after the Masonic-Republican coup d'état. On 5 May, statements by the King appeared in the monarchist newspaper *ABC* which became the sensation of the moment. The newspaper's editor, Luca de Tena, had travelled to London to interview the monarch, with whom he had a personal friendship. Alfonso XIII's remarks were in no way provocative or inflammatory, quite the contrary: "I will not put the slightest difficulty in the way of the Republican Government", the king said with commendable moderation. Here is a quote from this interview from *The Spanish Tragedy 1930-1936*, by the Hispanist Edgar Allison Peers:

> "Monarchists who wish to follow my advice will not only refrain from placing obstacles in the way of the Government, but will support it in all its patriotic initiatives.... Above formal ideas about Republic or Monarchy stands Spain.... I may have made mistakes, but I have only thought of the good of Spain.... I rejected the offers made to me to maintain myself and to reign by force.... For Spain I made the greatest sacrifice of my life when I discovered that it no longer wanted me".

Allison Peers believes that it was not the sentiments expressed in the interview that alarmed Republican opinion, but the fact that the editor had travelled to London to obtain it and that Luca de Tena expressed his loyalty to the Parliamentary Monarchy. When only a few days later, on 7 May, the press published a belligerent, and according to some, provocative and anti-government pastoral letter by Cardinal Segura, Archbishop of Toledo, anti-clerical sentiments and feelings were further exacerbated. The Cardinal Primate of Spain, who had acquired a certain social prestige for his humanitarian work in Las Hurdes, did not shrink from praising King Alfonso's role as defender of faith and tradition and warned the faithful that "the enemies of the kingdom of Christ were advancing":

> "If we remain silent and idle, if we allow ourselves to fall into apathy and timidity, if we leave the way open to those who seek to destroy religion or expect benevolence from our enemies to achieve the triumph of our ideals, we will have no right to regret when the bitter reality shows us that we had the victory in our hands, but we did not know how to fight like brave warriors, prepared to perish gloriously."

While the *ABC* newspaper referred to the pastoral as irreproachable, the Minister of Justice, the Socialist Fernando de los Ríos, harshly condemned it, and the government asked the Holy See to remove Cardinal Segura from the archdiocese. The atmosphere continued to heat up days later. On Sunday 10 May the members of the newly founded Círculo Monárquico Independiente held their first meeting in a flat in Calle de Alcalá to elect their Committee. Someone took it upon himself to spread the word that a conspiracy against the Republic was being hatched. According to one version, passers-by were outraged to hear the strains of the royal march;

according to another, royalists were provoking from a balcony of the building. The end result was that a mob began to shout at those in the house and, despite the arrival of the Guardia Civil, proceeded to set fire to the cars of the members of the Círculo. When the monarchists tried to go out into the street, the booing, insults and aggression began, and they were trapped inside. Things got so bad that the Minister of the Interior, Miguel Maura, arrived on the scene and tried to calm the mob. The result was unexpected, and the expletives turned against him: "Let's finish him off! Let's finish off his father's son! Down with the son of the monarchist!

The masses continued to gather in and around Calle de Alcalá. Suddenly someone instructed the people to march to the *ABC* offices in Calle Serrano. Thousands of people converged and joined the demonstration. On the way they set fire to the kiosk of the Catholic newspaper *El Debate*. They then recognised Leopoldo Matos, Minister of the Interior in the Berenguer government, pounced on him, tore his clothes and beat him. The lynching was prevented by the escort service he still had. In front of the newspaper's headquarters, hundreds of people threw stones at the windows and some poured petrol on the walls with the intention of setting fire to the newspaper. The civil guards took cover inside the building and from there fired into the air, which served to disperse the crowds. Incomprehensibly, the Ministry of the Interior, in order to calm the people, who were still very agitated, announced in the evening that the newspaper *ABC* had been suspended, its offices searched and its editor imprisoned. It was a premonition of the government's inability or unwillingness to act.

The next day, 11 May, the attacks on the church began. At half past ten in the morning, a group of men set fire to the Jesuit church in Calle de la Flor, in the centre of the capital. When the firemen arrived, the crowd watching the fire prevented them from putting it out until the church was razed to the ground. A mob with red flags then proceeded to set fire to the church-convent of the Carmelites, in Plaza de España; the Jesuit residence, in Calle Alberto Aguilera; the convent of the Mercedarians, in Bravo Murillo; the Maravillas school, in Cuatro Caminos; the Sacred Heart school, in Chamartín, and other buildings that were more or less destroyed. The attacks on the Church soon spread throughout the country: Valencia, Alicante, Murcia, Granada, Seville, Huelva, Cordoba, Cadiz, Malaga and other cities and towns in Spain saw their churches, convents, schools, seminaries, asylums and reformatories burnt to the ground. In Malaga, the fires went on for two days without interruption. There, the Episcopal Palace, the Jesuit residence and the Augustinian, Carmelite and Marist convents were set on fire. Several churches containing valuable works of art were also destroyed. Shops and public buildings also went up in flames. It is very difficult to accept that all these events could happen simultaneously in such distant places without the existence of a hidden hand. Gerald Brenan states in *The Spanish Labyrinth* that in six major cities alone, Madrid, Seville,

Valencia, Malaga, Granada and Murcia, one hundred and two churches and monasteries were completely destroyed. The total number of church buildings attacked throughout the country exceeded 200.

While all these displays of hatred and intolerance were extremely alarming, even more serious was the reaction of the government, which was not only incapable of taking effective measures to put a stop to the terror unleashed by the manipulated and led mobs, but blamed everything on the royalists: "These reactionaries," said the official report, "have deliberately chosen to provoke riots and defy the people. Despite the fact that the newspapers most loyal and devoted to the Republic contradicted the Government's accusation in their reports, there was no rectification, quite the contrary: the application of martial law served to suspend *ABC* and the Catholic daily *El Debate*, which was an incentive for the anti-clerical masses to persist in their attitudes.

To further embolden anticlericalism, on 18 May the bishop of Oviedo, Dr. Múgica, was invited in a restrained manner to leave Spain "because of the eminently political character that the bishop gave to his visits to the cities of his diocese". And there was still more: ignoring a letter dated 3 June in Rome and addressed to the Prime Minister by the Spanish metropolitans, in which the vexations suffered were recorded, the Cardinal Primate, Pedro Segura, was ordered to be expelled. On 14 June, two weeks before the elections, Cardinal Segura was arrested while on a canonical visit to the convents and parishes of Guadalajara. Taken to the Civil Government police station, the governor himself, León Trejo, banished him "by order of the Provisional Government of the Republic". He was given ten minutes to write a letter of protest to Alcalá Zamora and was placed in solitary confinement in the convent of the Vincentian Fathers at. The following day he was taken to the border at Irún.

The Constitution of the Second Republic

A decree of 3 June 1931 called general elections for deputies to the Constituent Cortes, which were held on the 28th of the same month. The minimum voting age was set at 23. Despite what had happened in May, the enthusiasm for the Republic, in which so many Spaniards had placed their hopes, materialised in results that favoured the Republican parties and were a catastrophe for the monarchists. The UGT and the Socialists had 117 deputies in Parliament, but the left-wing Republicans formed the largest group in the Cortes with 145 seats. The parties included Esquerra Catalana, led by Macià and Companys; Acción Republicana, led by Azaña; the Radical-Socialist Party, which included Marcelino Domingo and Álvaro de Albornoz; and the Republicans of Galicia, whose leader was Casares Quiroga. Among the right-wing Republicans, the most important was Lerroux's Radical Party, with 93 deputies. The parties that had not wanted the Republic won some 50 representatives, of whom only 19 were monarchists. The Freemasons, who were active in different political parties and sometimes apparently disagreed, were united by their anticlericalism and hostility to the Catholic Church. María Dolores Gómez Molleda notes that in the first Cortes one hundred and fifty-one of the four hundred and seventy deputies were Masons.

In the same month of June the CNT was holding a congress in Madrid and no sooner had Parliament been constituted than a telephone workers' strike broke out which lasted for weeks and left the country without service. In addition, the trade unionists assaulted the telephone exchange on Gran Vía with guns. Police on horseback charged the assailants and the attempted takeover of the building failed. Employees affiliated to the CNT switched to the UGT because of the threat of being fired. A week later very serious riots broke out in Seville. On 20 July a general strike was declared and one man died as a result of the clashes. During the funeral there were further shootings: three more people were killed and many were injured. The authorities closed the centres of the trade unionists and communists and proceeded to arrest their leaders, which led to further clashes. A trade union centre where armed men had built up a stronghold was destroyed by artillery fire. Martial law was declared and the city was even guarded by armed aeroplanes. Eventually the situation calmed down, but by the end of the month the death toll had risen to thirty and more than two hundred wounded. These events showed that a bourgeois republic was not the aim of the anarcho-syndicalists and communists, but a stage on the road to the triumph of the revolution.

Prior to the election of the new Parliament, the interim government published an outline or preliminary draft constitution that was to serve as the basis for parliamentary discussion. From July to December the debate on the Magna Carta occupied the elected deputies. When on 9 December 1931 the President of the Cortes, Julián Besteiro, promulgated the Constitution of the Second Republic, the Government must obviously have felt enormous satisfaction; however, it was clear that it could not be the Constitution of all Spaniards. There were too many Freemasons, and the legislators lacked the courage of vision, the will for consensus and harmony, and the intelligence to understand that between the Spain desired by Freemasonry and the Spain desired by the Catholic Church there was a third, in which millions of citizens lived who were waiting for a pact to emerge from negotiation. The first twenty-five articles were approved after reasonable discussions, but when the time came to draft the twenty-sixth, which dealt with the situation of the Church in the new State, the crisis occurred that brought down the Government. The Provisional Government had set up a legal commission which had drafted an article declaring the Church to be separate from the State; but it was considered a special corporation under public law which could have its own schools and, under certain conditions, could teach religion in State schools. Canonical marriage would be legal and public ecclesiastical functions could be exercised on the oath of allegiance to the Republic. Most Catholics would have accepted this. Unfortunately, the Cortes considered these concessions too broad.

José Ortega y Gasset had warned of the need to properly value the traditional importance of the Church and the role it had played in Spanish history: "in dealing with a historical and international body such as the Church, we must be generous in view of the forces of the past that it represents, but we must also act with caution". The philosopher ended by declaring that the 1931 Constitution was "lamentable and without feet or head or the rest of the organic matter that usually lies between the feet and the head". There were more Republican intellectuals who warned of the error. Gregorio Marañón, for example, one of the most committed to the Republic, considered the Constitution "unworkable". The Masonic deputies acted in a unified manner and followed the instructions they received from the lodges, of which there is abundant published documentation. Freemasonry demanded that the religious orders should be dissolved and their assets nationalised. Here, as one example of many that can be provided in this regard, is an extract from the session of 11 October 1931 from *the Bulletin of the Grand Lodge of Spain*:

> "The Grand Master (Francisco Esteva) presented to the Council the need for the Grand Lodge to contribute by its action to ensure that the religious question is forever aired in Spain, to which end he proposed that a telegram be sent to the President of the Council to the effect that the Masonic deputies be urged to fulfil their duty.... The proposal was unanimously approved, and it was agreed that the telegram should be sent for publication to the daily press throughout Spain. It was also agreed to address the lodges, informing them of this agreement and requesting them to support this work, also sending telegrams to this effect and promoting strong anti-clerical action in secular life.

The demand for the dissolution of the religious orders was accompanied by another irrational demand: the closure of all religious schools. If the country's educational needs had really been prioritised over anti-clericalism, it would have been considered that the state could not do away overnight with schools that housed hundreds of thousands of pupils. Closing religious schools was tantamount to depriving the country of half of its secondary schools. Gerald Brenan gives figures on the state of primary education in the capital alone: "In Madrid, for example, 37,000 children were educated in state schools, 44,000 in public schools, most of them run by religious orders, and 45,000 had no education at all. To fill the gap in religious schools, 2,700 new state schools were needed." In *Anarquía y Jeraquía*, Salvador de Madariaga described the catastrophic consequences of the inhibition of religious orders in education. Anyone could foresee that to implement the claims of anti-clerical Freemasonry would require a great deal of money and years of planning. Despite the propaganda of the Republican parties, when the Social-Azharist or Masonic biennium came to an end in 1933, the achievements in the field of education were still very poor and the nation lacked the necessary schools. It seems clear that the Masonic Republic was looking for a fight by so blatantly attacking the Church; but at the same time it was recklessly and unwisely digging its own grave, for it was losing the support of the middle classes, essential if it was to avoid its own collapse.

It was in October 1931 that the debate that made Manuel Azaña the man of the moment took place in the Cortes. The discussion centred on Article 26 of the Constitution, which provided for the dissolution of all religious orders and the nationalisation of their assets. On the 8th, Fernando de los Ríos, Minister of Justice, took the floor and, honouring his status as a marrano, asked for "a tribute of respect and homage to the Jews in this first hour devoted to talking about the religious problem". Gil Robles warned that at the first opportunity he would propose a constitutional reform if the article was approved. In his speech on the 10th, Alcalá Zamora asked that account be taken of the fact that Catholics were the majority in Spain, that legislation should not be passed against them, but that they should be taken into account. He also threatened a revision of the Constitution if the text was approved. The Socialists, through Jiménez de Asúa, presented a dissenting vote on the 13th proposing the permanent prohibition of any religious order in Spanish territory, the dissolution of existing orders and the nationalisation of their assets.

On the 13th, Azaña, a declared enemy of the religious orders, made one of the most spectacular speeches in the history of the Second Republic. In his opinion, it was not a religious problem, but a political one. "Spain has ceased to be Catholic", he said with British phlegm, although he immediately acknowledged that there were millions of practising Catholics in the country. He must have been well aware of the political and emotional charge contained in these words, which, he said, meant protection for the Republic. For Azaña the proscription of religious orders was tantamount to eliminating a fear. With a certain cynicism, he compared the reform of the religious orders to a surgical operation: "Think that we are going to perform a surgical operation on a sick person who is not anaesthetised and who in the onslaught of his own pain can complicate the operation and make it fatal; I don't know for whom, but fatal for someone". He then pointed directly to the Jesuits as the order that should die without delay. At the end of his speech, he expressed himself with crystal clarity on the issue of education: "At no time, under no circumstances will my party or I subscribe to a legislative clause under which the service of education continues to be handed over to the religious orders. Never. I am very sorry; but this is the true defence of the Republic. Don't come and tell me that this is contrary to freedom, because this is a question of public health". The discussion of the article went on all night and, with just over half of the deputies in the Chamber, it was approved on the 14th at seven in the morning by 178 votes in favour and 59 against.

As mentioned above, the affair provoked a governmental crisis: Alcalá Zamora and Miguel Maura left the government and Azaña became the new president of the second government of the Republic, which was to last until the Constitution was approved in December. Barely a week into his presidency, Azaña submitted to the Cortes the Law for the Defence of the Republic, which was passed on 21 October. This law contradicted the fundamental rights that the Constitution was intended to recognise and guarantee, and until it was repealed on 29 August 1933 following the passing of the Law of Public Order, it became the fundamental rule for public liberties. The law allowed the Minister of the Interior to prohibit demonstrations or public acts and to suppress associations. Any activity considered anti-republican could be repressed, fined or punished by exile. Thus, for example, the defence of the Monarchy could be considered an aggression against the Republic. The law could repress not only strikes, riots or violent acts, but also the dissemination of subversive information or rumours, which could lead to the suspension of any media outlet. Naturally, abuses of all kinds could be committed by the government under the protection of this odious and anti-democratic law, which was bitterly attacked from all sides, as it was clear that the measures were similar to those of the Dictatorship.

Before promulgating the Constitution, the Cortes Constituyentes staged a spectacular trial "in absentia" of Alfonso XIII, which became the sensation of the autumn. The travesty of a trial began at dusk on 19 November and lasted until 4 a.m. the following day. A committee charged with examining the monarch's alleged guilt presented its report, according to which the king was guilty of high treason against the Spanish people, a crime for which he deserved the death penalty. Capital punishment being ruled out on principle, the Cortes was recommended to imprison him for life if he returned to Spain, and death if he persisted in "his acts of rebellion". The main charges levelled against King Alfonso were: 1. Abandonment of his duties as a constitutional monarch. 2. Acceptance of the 1923 coup d'état. 3. Lèse majesté towards the people. Complicity in administrative corruption. Perhaps the intention of the prosecution, which was described by the monarchist *ABC* as a "spiteful and unnecessary act of persecution", was to further inflame anti-monarchist sentiments. The paper was suspended for three days and fined a thousand pesetas for expressing this opinion. Nothing could be done against the opinion of *The Times*, which in its 27 November edition expressed itself in these terms:

"From his accession to the throne in 1902 until 1923 the king cannot be accused of the first offence, since all the decrees of this period were signed by the responsible ministers. As for the second offence, the document presented by Count de Romanones shows that, in September 1923, abdication - which would have been desertion, since the king was obliged under oath to serve the country as a soldier - was the only alternative to acceptance of the military dictatorship, which, moreover - and this is so obvious that it cannot be disputed - had at that time the sympathy of the majority of the country. As for the crime of lèse majesté towards the people, no one seems to understand what this means, and this accusation has not even been sustained before the courts. Nor was there any attempt to adduce evidence of complicity in administrative corruption."

The social-Azharist or Masonic biennium

Once the Constitution had been approved on 9 December 1931, the Cortes proceeded to elect the President of the Republic. The names of two great intellectuals, Manuel Bartolomé Cossío and Rafael Altamira, author of *Historia de España y de la civilización española*, a work of international prestige, were put forward. Niceto Alcalá Zamora was finally chosen and took office on 11 December. Two days later, the diplomatic corps was received. The dean was the Pope's Nuncio and, sarcastically, it fell to him to deliver the official speech. The situation could not have been more pathetic: the Government had expelled and deposed the Cardinal Primate and the Vatican had denied the Spanish ambassador to the Holy See permission. The church was being separated from the state and its institutions attacked, the religious orders dissolved, and the expulsion of the Society of Jesus had been announced.

By decree of 23 January 1932, the Society of Jesus was dissolved and its property seized by the State. The long-cherished dream of Freemasonry had come true. A few days earlier *El Debate*, "a newspaper," said Azaña, "that does great harm to the Republic by its intention, its organisation and the catechism that surrounds it", had been closed sine die, which served as a warning to the rest of the press to moderate their criticisms, which they did. In 1935 Salvador de Madariaga, an intellectual not at all suspected of sympathising with the Church, in his essay *Anarchy and Hierarchy* wrote the following about the dissolution of the Jesuits: "The Second Republic has ruined a magnificent opportunity to direct the problem of secondary education towards a satisfactory solution. Obsessed by its anti-clericalism, it has shamelessly closed down the only type of school which, even with its imperfections, bore some resemblance to a secondary school". At the time of its dissolution, the Society had about seventy residences and thirty colleges throughout Spain. The college of Sarriá had near Barcelona a School of Ecclesiastical Studies, an Institute of Chemistry and laboratories of Biology and Experimental Psychology. Also notable were the theological studies at the Colegio de Comillas and the astronomy studies in Granada. The Church of the Sacred Heart in Barcelona maintained five workers' patronages and educated some 1,200 children. In Burgos there was also a patronato with 1,500 members, including accommodation, pension schemes, a welfare system, a savings bank, and day and evening classes. Throughout the country the Jesuits had organised educational and social systems.

On 20 February of that year, the Extraordinary General Assembly of the Spanish Grand Orient met in Madrid. Léon de Poncins, author of several books denouncing the instrumentalisation of Freemasonry by Judaism and Communism, the driving forces behind the World Revolutionary Movement, published *Histoire secrète de la révolution espagnole* in 1938. In it, he reproduced in full the report or minutes of the famous extraordinary convent, held at a time when the stranglehold on the Republican government was at its zenith. Significant excerpts follow, several of which refer to the strict Masonic discipline of brethren in political posts.

> "The Worshipful Master of each lodge shall warn the Masonic Brethren that they must renew a verbal or written promise to be ready at all times to appear before their respective judges to explain and justify the uprightness of their Masonic conscience in all acts of their Masonic or profane life..... Masonic Brethren who refuse to renew such promises or who fail to respond within the time limit which shall be fixed shall be expelled from the Order.... The Worshipful Masters shall watch over the oath taken by their Brethren before the Altar with all solemnity...".
>
> "The Lodges and Triangles shall establish files for all Freemason Brethren, indicating their usual occupation, the jobs they hold or have held in the State or in private companies and the reasons for their departure, and their service record with the merits of their Masonic work. This record shall be especially complete and detailed for those Freemasons who hold political office by popular election or by appointment by the Government.
>
> "Masonic authorities are under the obligation to enforce with the necessary frequency the duty imposed upon Freemasons holding public office, to reiterate the oath, to explain and justify Masonically their public conduct to their superiors. And since, in public office, Masonic duties may be failed, both by action and omission, this means that the Mason holding such office is obliged not only to explain and justify any action which may appear objectionable or doubtful, but also to receive Masonic directives and to take them into account."
>
> "The Masonic Brethren in public office shall be reminded of their duty of fraternal love and tolerance, and they shall be careful to place this Masonic fraternity above all differences which may separate them in political struggles.

It was in this context that the first Holy Week under republican rule arrived. Most of the traditional processions were cancelled. Seville, where the most famous ones were held, experienced those days with sadness, but calmly. The campaign to remove the crucifix from schools, hospitals, charities and all official establishments had already been unleashed and hardly a cross was to be seen. In contrast, kiosks and bookshops prominently displayed an abundance of pornographic literature and Marxist texts. The latter were often sold in front of churches. Another significant feature of social life on the first anniversary of the Republic was the great increase in begging. The *Times* correspondent reported this on 22 March 1932 for English readers: "The streets of Madrid and many other cities are so infested with beggars that it is almost impossible to walk a hundred yards without being accosted not only by the usual blind and maimed, but by groups of two or three men begging for charity with blankets or large handkerchiefs".

It should be remembered that 1929 had seen the famous crash on the New York Stock Exchange and in 1932 the world depression was at its height. In Spain, the prices of agricultural products had fallen as a result of the crisis and a large amount of land was no longer under cultivation. This was one of the reasons for an unprecedented rise in unemployment. Between 1931 and 1932 anarcho-considicalism created a revolutionary situation in the countryside. At last, the much-trumpeted agrarian reform, which had been pending since the Enlightenment had detected the problem, began to be discussed in the Cortes. It was approved in two parts, in July and September 1932. Endowed with annual credits from the State, an Agrarian Reform Institute was set up, which provided for the possibility of expropriating any farm of more than 22 hectares that was not being worked. The nobles lost their estates without right of claim, although they were compensated according to their declaration of income; but since this had been falsified... The *Spanish Labyrinth* attributes the delay in tackling the agrarian question to the different approaches of socialists and republicans. The former advocated that the expropriated land should be worked collectively. The latter wanted to divide the land into individual plots. The difference," Brenan writes, "was more than an abstract principle: it involved the future of Spanish socialism and bourgeois republicanism". Meanwhile, the revolutionary atmosphere in the countryside prevented the implementation of projects in practice.

On 10 August two outbreaks occurred simultaneously. In Madrid a group of aristocrats and retired royalist officers tried to capture the Post Office building in the Plaza de la Cibeles early in the morning. They were unaware that they had been betrayed and were waiting for them. There was a brief scuffle in Alcalá Street, watched by Azaña from a balcony of the War Ministry, and the rebels were arrested. On the same day the Sanjurjada took place in Seville, which had also been known beforehand. It was a botched military insurrection, supported only by a very minority section of the monarchist right wing. General Sanjurjo, the director general of the Civil Guard who a year earlier had refused to support the king, even published a manifesto in which he regretted his loyalty to the Republic and proclaimed himself captain general. Anarchists and communists declared a general strike and began setting fire to numerous aristocrats' houses and various clubs. The offices of the *ABC* newspaper were once again set ablaze. The rebellion failed with a roar, causing ten deaths, almost all of them on the rebel side. Sanjurjo tried to escape to Portugal, but was arrested in Ayamonte.

The fire lit by the attempted coup spread throughout Andalusia. Socialists, communists and trade unionists were quick to declare protest strikes in the big cities. In Granada the riots were particularly serious and in the Albaicín the church of San Nicolás was razed to the ground. Some try to equate the Sanjurjada with what happened in Asturias and Catalonia in October 1934, but the comparison does not hold water. In reality, the left emerged stronger after the coup, which served to repress and dismantle right-wing organisations and close dozens of publications: in Madrid alone, eight newspapers were suspended for an indefinite period, including *ABC, El Debate* and *Informaciones*. When Primo de Rivera banned newspapers, he had been accused by the Republicans of not respecting freedom of the press. General Sanjurjo was later sentenced to death, but was pardoned on the initiative of Alcalá Zamora and sentenced to life imprisonment. The Sanjurjada was mainly a protest against land reform and against the Catalan Statute, which was to be approved by the Cortes.

The Statute of Autonomy of Catalonia, given the importance of the Catalan question in the history of Spain, could be discussed at greater length if we had more space. After the proclamation on 14 April 1931 of the Catalan state, which was to be incorporated into a Federation of Iberian Republics, Macià was warned from Madrid that he had to rectify his position if he wanted the Republic to be viable in Spain. Days later, the ministers Marcelino Domingo, Luis Nicolau d'Olwer and Fernando de los Ríos travelled to Barcelona and convinced him that he had to renounce the Catalan Republic and present a draft Statute for Catalonia to the Cortes. The Governing Council of the Catalan Republic was to adopt the historic name of the Government of the Generalitat. However, the cries of "Visca Macià! Mori Cambó!" had resounded through the streets of Barcelona on the 14th. The windows of Cambó's house were stoned during the night. The leader of the Lliga, who had been bedridden with fever, woke up frightened and decided to take a train and go into exile in Paris, where he was to remain for two and a half years. Allison Peers, a Hispanist in love with the literature, history and culture of Catalonia and translator into English of numerous works by Ramon Llull, including *Blanquerna*, asks the following question in her book *Catalonia Infelix*: "Could they not now forget the personal and political differences between them and form a Macià-Cambó coalition government, which would have united the best brains in Catalonia? Apparently not, but it was a pity". If Professor Allison Peers' advice had been put into practice, the disaster of 1934 could perhaps have been avoided; but the time of the moderates had passed.

The workers' and revolutionary movements in Catalonia were the strongest in the country. Lenin's prediction about Spain was not ignored by anarchists and communists, who were fighting for revolution and not for a bourgeois Republic. None of this, however, worried the Catalan nationalists, who began to work enthusiastically on the drafting of the Statute of Autonomy. On 24 May, elections were held among all the Catalan councillors and the Provisional Deputation of the Generalitat was set up, which produced the eleven deputies who were to form the statute's drafting committee. On 20 June, eight days before the general elections for the Cortes, the preliminary draft of the Statute of Núria was ready. On 2 August it was submitted to a referendum and, with a 75% turnout, it was approved with 99% of the votes. Four hundred thousand women, who did not have the right to vote at the time, supported it with their signatures. On 14 August Maciá personally took it to Madrid; but the Cortes, caught up in debates on the text of the Constitution, put it on hold until 6 May 1932, when it began to be processed.

During the nine months that the Statute was on hold in Madrid, the revolutionary parties and trade unions were warming up their engines. The general elections of June 1931 confirmed the Esquerra of Macià and Companys as the leading political force in Barcelona and Catalonia. The fact that Companys, who left the mayor's office in Barcelona to become civil governor, had been an advocate of thieves, gunmen and other criminals, elements who could not have joined any party or workers' union, but who were accepted in the CNT, had helped him to establish very good relations with the anarchists. From his position as governor he kept the city relatively calm: "Since you," he said cynically to his old friends, "are not prepared to make your revolution, why don't you let us make ours and take advantage of the freedom given you by the new regime to make your propaganda?" He was forgetting that propaganda by deed was the favourite of the anarchists. During the summer, strikes, sabotage and clashes with the police began, who were attacked from windows and street corners in a kind of guerrilla warfare. The civil governor was even asked to disarm the police and arm the people. In September 1931, a two-day general strike was declared, bringing the city to a complete standstill.

Months later, in January 1932, trade unionists, communists and anarchists staged an uprising in Catalonia that was to spread throughout Spain. The movement was organised by the FAI and supported by a Trotskyite party, the Communist Left, which had split from the official Communist Party and had dragged along most of the Catalan communists. Its leaders were Andreu Nin, Joaquín Maurín and Juan Andrade. The FAI proclaimed libertarian communism in the Upper Llobregat and public buildings were occupied in Berga and Manresa. In some places agricultural properties were divided up. The revolt was quelled with much bloodshed. Azaña denounced categorically that the revolutionary movement had been subsidised from abroad. In fact, Soviet propaganda and foreign money had been flowing into Spain through Barcelona for some time. More than a hundred of the revolutionary leaders were arrested, among them Durruti and Ascaso, and deported without trial to Spanish Guinea.

But let us move on to the Statute. In the text submitted to the Cortes, Catalonia was defined as an autonomous state within the Spanish Republic. Catalan would be its official language, although the use of Spanish as the language of communication with Madrid was envisaged. The Statute established legislative and executive powers in the field of education. The Generalitat claimed for itself the power to establish the territorial division of Catalonia and freedom for local councils. It also established that young Catalans would do their military service in Catalonia in peacetime. The main issues at the centre of the debate, which was to last until September 1932, were language and education. The first battle was over the co-official status of Castilian. In the end, the Catalan deputies had to accept the following wording: "The Catalan language, as well as the Castilian language, shall be official languages in Catalonia".

The debate on education occupied the whole month of July and gave rise to heated speeches. The article in question was seriously amended. The final wording gave the Generalitat control over fine arts services, museums, bookshops, monuments and archives, with the exception of the Archives of the Crown of Aragon; but it did not grant it its greatest aspiration: exclusive jurisdiction over the University. University autonomy was accepted, but as the only university in Catalonia, it had to be governed by a board that ensured equal rights for professors and students of both languages and cultures. The Catalans argued that this went against the spirit of the Statute because it destroyed the unity of the education system and because it encouraged racial distinctions that led to enmity. Azaña agreed with them and tried to get the opposing sector to modify its approach, but was unsuccessful. These were the discussions at the time of the Sanjurjada. During the second half of August, the approval of articles progressed rapidly and the provisions relating to municipal and administrative organisation were approved. The recovery of the old Catalan civil code was also accepted to the great satisfaction of the Catalan deputies. The vote was held on 9 September and the Statute of Autonomy of Catalonia was approved by a large majority. On 11 September, a date laden with historical connotations, the Catalans returned. On the 25th President Azaña was acclaimed in Barcelona, where he formally handed over the Statute to the Catalan authorities. On 20 November 1932, the first elections for the new Catalan Parliament were held and were won by Esquerra Republicana. The historic name of Corts was avoided because of its monarchist connotations.

While the nationalists sought to advance in the construction of their newfound autonomy, the revolutionary movement was still determined to prevent social peace. In January 1933 García Oliver, leader of the FAI, led a new armed uprising in Barcelona, Lérida and Valencia. Among other things, it demanded the release of those deported to Africa a year earlier. As then, attempts were made to occupy important public buildings, but again failed and the anarchist leaders, from whom much weaponry was confiscated, were again arrested. Large quantities of bombs were discovered in Barcelona and the government declared the CNT illegal and closed down its premises, although it lacked the strength to maintain the illegalisation.

But the event that was to mark the Government seriously took place in a miserable village, Casas Viejas, near Jerez de la Frontera. The Andalusian anarchists had called a general strike in Andalusia in support of the uprising in Catalonia, which did not materialise. On 11 January, an old anarchist nicknamed Seisdedos, aware of the plans for a general strike, decided to act on his own. After encouraging his friends and family, they all took part in a parade through the streets of the town armed with rifles and clubs. At the anarcho-syndicalist centre they proclaimed libertarian communism and then, after intimidating the mayor, besieged the Guardia Civil barracks and demanded the surrender. The post sergeant contacted Cádiz and Medina Sidonia to request reinforcements. The government, alerted to what was being planned in Andalusia and Catalonia, was ready and ordered troops to be sent. Meanwhile, the rebels of Casas Viejas, who had amassed pistols, ammunition and explosives, began the battle and mortally wounded three guardsmen. Shortly after midday, reinforcements arrived and the town was even flown over by planes. Seeing the scale of the device. Seisdedos and his men withdrew to their homes. A house-to-house search began, but some houses refused to surrender. The nucleus of the resistance was organised in the house of Seisdedos, whose daughter, Libertaria, was reloading her father's rifles while he continued firing. The assaulting troops suffered heavy casualties and darkness fell without the anarchists surrendering. During the night the forces of law and order stockpiled bombs and machine guns with the intention of putting an end to the rebels, but they did not act until they received permission from the Ministry of the Interior, whose minister was Casares Quiroga. The house was mercilessly razed to the ground: after being bombed, it was doused with petrol and set on fire. Seisdedos, Libertaria and six others were killed. The other houses that resisted suffered the same fate and another twenty people lost their lives. By seven o'clock in the morning it was all over.

As details of what happened in Casas Viejas became known, indignation spread throughout the country. The Republic was accused of acting as well as or worse than the Dictatorship. The government's prestige plummeted and never recovered. The Socialists, partners in Azaña's government, were also badly hit. In the spring the CNT returned in Barcelona and declared a massive construction strike that lasted for eighteen weeks. In solidarity with their Catalan comrades, general strikes were declared in Zaragoza, La Coruña, Oviedo and Seville. In the steel foundries of La Felguera (Asturias) two thousand eight hundred CNT workers, practically the entire population, began in the spring of 1933 a heroic strike in solidarity with the dismissal without compensation of elderly comrades. They resisted for nine months and the bosses, faced with the serious losses that their obstinacy caused them, finally gave in.

Azaña had announced that he would call municipal elections in April with the new census, which included women; but in view of his waning popularity he reneged on his promise and on 23 April called only by-elections in some two and a half thousand rural districts which in April 1931 had been monarchist, so that their representation had been cancelled. Azaña, who called these towns the "rotten burghs", feared that the results could be understood as a vote of no confidence in his administration. And so it was, for of the sixteen thousand councillors at stake, only some five thousand went to government candidates. It can be said that from then on the political crisis was in crescendo and calls for the resignation of the government were heard with increasing frequency in the Cortes, where during the month of May the Law on Congregations and Religious Denominations, which implemented the anti-clerical articles of the Constitution, was debated.

On 12 June Azaña ended up reshuffling the government, with Companys joining as Minister of the Navy. It was to be the last government of the Cortes Constituyentes: in September he resigned. The most notable event of these months was the creation of the Tribunal of Constitutional Guarantees. Otherwise, the government's unpopularity only increased. Strikes were continuous, unemployment remained as high as ever, and the prisons were much more crowded than during the Dictatorship: the CNT alone held some 9,000 prisoners. The Republic had failed to solve the problems of the peasants and workers and, moreover, had completely disappointed the middle classes, including the monarchists, who were subjected to all sorts of outrages: even the postmen had been ordered not to deliver to the aristocrats the mail that continued to reach them under the titles of nobility, which had been abolished. The latest demonstration of sectarian intolerance had been a considerable purge within the civil state administration for the crime of "incompatibility with the regime".

The centre-right governs without CEDA

The fall of Azaña in September gave way to a short-lived government headed by Lerroux, which lasted from 12 September to 8 October 1933. It was overthrown by a motion of confidence tabled on 2 September by Indalecio Prieto. The Grand Master of the Spanish Grand Orient, Diego Martínez Barrio, presided over the government that was responsible for overseeing the electoral process after the dissolution of the Cortes, announced by Alcalá Zamora, President of the Republic.

On 19 November 1933, general elections were held for the first ordinary Cortes of the Republic, the first in which women were allowed to vote. Twenty-six political parties obtained parliamentary representation. The most voted party was José Mª Gil Robles' CEDA, with 115 deputies, followed by Lerroux's Radical Republican Party (PRR), with 102. The Republican left was a resounding failure: only half a dozen deputies were elected. Azaña managed to keep his seat by a miracle, thanks to the fact that he stood in Bilbao for the district of Indalecio Prieto, who, against his party's instructions, maintained the coalition with Azaña's Republicans. In Catalonia, Esquerra Republicana dropped from 46 to 17. Many of its votes went to La Lliga Regionalista, which became Lliga Catalana after Cambó's return, and won 24 representatives. It seemed clear that Spanish society was opting for moderation and stability. Other right-wing parties with notable results were the Spanish Agrarian Party (PAE), with 30 seats; the Traditionalist Communion (CT), with 20; the Conservative Republican Party (PRC), with 17; Spanish Renovation (RE), with 14; the Basque Nationalist Party (PNV), with 11. The Communist Party of Spain (PCE) and the Spanish Falange (FE) both won one deputy and entered the Cortes for the first time. The CNT had campaigned for abstention.

Before the publication of the election results, a transport strike had been heating up the atmosphere in Barcelona. On 8 December it turned into a revolt and the police went so far as to place machine guns in some squares. Anarcho-syndicalist uprisings broke out in various parts of the country. General strikes were declared in La Coruña, Zaragoza and Huesca. In many towns in Aragon and in the vineyards of La Rioja, libertarian communism was proclaimed. In Barbastro and other towns in the area, barricades were erected and attempts were made to take over public buildings, leading to clashes with the Guardia Civil. In Calatayud and Granada, convents and churches were set on fire. Suspected revolutionaries caused an accident on the Barcelona-Seville train and 19 people died as a result of the sabotage. The government declared a state of alarm, and within three or four days the situation calmed down. This was the backdrop to the formation of Lerroux's first government.

It would have been logical for the winning party, i.e. the CEDA, to try to form a government. A coalition between Lerroux's Radical Party and that of Gil Robles could have brought stability from the beginning of the legislature; but the President of the Republic entrusted Lerroux with the formation of the government. It should be borne in mind that Gil Robles was a young lawyer of thirty-five with very little political experience, while Lerroux was an old dog seasoned in a thousand battles. Moreover, the fact that Gil Robles was a Catholic leader alerted Freemasonry, which immediately unleashed a campaign against him. From the outset, it was the lodges that branded him a fascist. Already during the election campaign, Freemasonry feared that its anti-clerical victories could be compromised. The Spanish Grand Lodge warned the "dear brethren" to be vigilant: "...The life of our Order is at stake in this struggle. It is our threatened ideals that we must defend. In their name we propose to our sister lodges that they join with local organisations and make alliances to fight wherever necessary against the reaction that threatens us". In a circular dated 22 March 1934, the Spanish Grand Orient considered the victory cedista as the triumph of fascism:

> "By virtue of the basic principles of our institution, we are obliged to repulse against everything that signifies dictatorship, and being at this time the most serious and imminent danger in this Order that of Fascism, all Freemasons, individually and collectively, must take care to prevent the development of this force, which under its modern name covers in Spain our traditional enemies."

However, neither did the CEDA's victory mean dictatorship nor was Gil Robles a fascist, since he had on numerous occasions declared his acceptance of the republican regime. In fact, the young right-wing leader was convinced that within the framework of the Republic it was possible to agree on a consensus Constitution that would be accepted by all Catholics. Gil Robles' followers criticised Alcalá Zamora for not counting on him initially, accusing him of treating him inconsiderately because he had a personal dislike of him; but Gil Robles said he was willing to collaborate with Lerroux's centrists, who on 16 December presided over an almost single-colour government that did not include a single Cedista minister. In any case, there was a price to pay for CEDA support: Lerroux's government, despite the fact that the PRR had been characterised by its anti-clericalism and had voted in favour of the secularisation of education, halted the replacement of religious schools with secular ones. Land expropriation processes were also reviewed, and landowners who had been arbitrarily dispossessed recovered their estates. This caused some ten thousand peasants who had received land to lose their settlements.

In February 1934 Francisco Largo Caballero, president of the UGT, a trade union that had collaborated with Primo de Rivera's dictatorship, began to adopt radical positions that were to make him the man of the masses: "The only hope of the masses," he said in February, "is social revolution. Only it can save Spain from fascism". In four years the UGT had grown from 300,000 to 1,250,000 members and was the only union that could compete with the CNT. From this position of trade union strength, Largo Caballero tried to create an organisation in which all the parties of the working class could converge: the Alianza Obrera (Workers' Alliance).. The CNT refused to join and the communists, who were then behaving like furious revolutionaries, also refused to participate. With these approaches the position of the Socialists vis-à-vis the Lerroux government was one of frontal confrontation.

The beginning of March saw the beginning of the governmental crises that were to follow one after another as a result of the stubbornness of Alcalá Zamora, who continued to ignore the winner of the elections. On 23 January 1934 Grand Master Martínez Barrio, who was a member of the PRR, resigned as Minister of War and became Minister of the Interior; but on 3 March, in accordance with instructions from the lodges, he resigned in protest at the drift of the government, which needed the support of the CEDA deputies. His resignation led to the fall of the government. Once again Lerroux was asked by the President of the Republic to form a new Council of Ministers. Gil Robles then expressed his scepticism: "I doubt that he can survive a month". He was not far wrong, for the government was formed on 3 March and fell on 28 April.

The CNT welcomed him with a general strike in Zaragoza which lasted four weeks, during which the Aragonese capital was paralysed. Another strike was called in Valencia, but there the CNT's strike funds ran out and it could not last. It was not the strikes, however, that brought about the downfall of the new government, but the attempt in April to enact a law reinstating the death penalty. The Minister of Justice, Ramón Álvarez Valdés of the Republican Liberal Democratic Party, defended the bill, arguing that the reintroduction of capital punishment was the only way to put an end to the crimes that were constantly occurring in the country's major cities. Coinciding with the 300th anniversary of the Republic, the minister had the temerity to indulge in an attack on the "martyrs of the Republic", the "heroes of Jaca". A huge scandal then broke out in the Chamber, which spread throughout the country and led to the resignation of Álvarez Valdés. He was replaced by Salvador de Madariaga, an independent who had joined the government as Minister of Public Instruction and who incomprehensibly accepted the post. The final straw for the government came with the draft Amnesty Law, which proposed pardoning those who had committed crimes before December 1933, including General Sanjurjo and his fellow insurrectionists in Seville. The law was passed, but at the end of April rumours spread that the President of the Republic refused to accept it. He finally signed it, but promptly published a letter explaining his disapproval at length. Lerroux felt disavowed and on 28 April he resigned. Only five months had elapsed since the elections and the left rushed to demand new elections. This time too, Alcalá Zamora did not want to go to Gil Robles and entrusted the formation of the government to Ricardo Samper, also of the PRR,. Salvador de Madariaga hastened to leave the Executive.

With the arrival of summer, tensions shifted to Catalonia, where Colonel Maciá had died on Christmas Day 1933 and since 31 December Lluís Companys had been president of the Generalitat and the new Esquerra strongman. As the Statute of Autonomy gave the Generalitat powers over municipal elections, local elections were held there on 14 January, which were won by Esquerra Republicana. In April 1934, the Catalan Parliament passed a new agrarian law, the "Llei de Contractes de Conreu", known in Madrid as the Ley de Cultivos. The landlords protested vehemently and went to seek support from the State Government, which put the matter in the hands of the newly created Tribunal de Garanties Constitucionals (Court of Constitutional Guarantees). This Court, composed of politicians representing all parties, ruled in June that the Catalan Parliament lacked the power to legislate on the issue, and the Cultivation Law was declared inapplicable. A crisis then began that ended in the disaster of 6 October. The Catalan parliament defied the Madrid government and ratified the law. The left-wing Republican parties in the Cortes sided with Esquerra Republicana, but the Lliga Catalana backed the government. President Companys declared that "not a comma" of the law would be altered. President Samper challenged him to apply it. As things stood, the Cortes closed for the summer recess.

In order for the reader to understand the matter, it is necessary to explain that most of the land in Catalonia was in the hands of small landowners who ceded their land to peasants called "rabassaires". In the sharecropping contracts, expenses and profits were shared by the owner and the tenant. Most of the leased land was devoted to vine cultivation, so the duration of the contracts was linked to the life of the vines. When three quarters of the vines had ceased to produce, "rabassa morta", the land returned to the owner, who could or could not renew the contract. Non-renewal meant dispossession of the land. The rabassaires had learned to prolong the life of the vines and in the past they made them last for fifty years. The phylloxera plague in the 19th century killed the old vines and a type of plant was introduced whose life was about twenty-five years and required more care. During the European war the prices were so high that there were no disputes for the renewal of the contracts; but when the bad harvests came and the price of wine began to fall, some rabassaires could not fulfil the contracts and were dispossessed. They organised themselves into a syndicate whose founders included Companys. Protected by Esquerra Republicana, they pledged to vote for it in the elections. Since everything has its price, Macià, before his death at Easter in 1933, had addressed a rally to fifteen thousand farmers and promised them legislation to help resolve the issue. In June, unrest began in the countryside and the landlords were met with armed groups of malcontents attacking their property. A month later, in July 1933, the draft bill that was to be passed in April 1934 entered Parliament. The law, which pleased the farmers more than the landowners, although impartial observers admitted that it was intended to resolve an injustice, provided for arbitration tribunals and facilitated the acquisition by tenants of land they had worked for fifteen years.

The decision of the Court of Constitutional Guarantees highlighted the confrontation between Esquerra Republicana and Cambó's Lliga

Catalana, which in January 1934 had left Parliament in disagreement with the way in which Companys had been elected president of the Generalitat. The Lliga, while accepting that reform of the existing law was necessary, disagreed with the way in which tenants could acquire land. Instead of seeking the Lliga's good offices to mediate with the landowners, Esquerra Republicana accused them of having encouraged President Samper to take the Cultivation Law to the Court of Guarantees and branded their attitude as reactionary and unpatriotic. A political victory thus turned into a loss of prestige in the eyes of public opinion, especially when the president of the Generalitat described the Court's ruling as an attack on Catalonia's autonomy.

Before the end of the summer, the passions unleashed were more than enough to overcome sanity. Companys lost no opportunity to violently attack the Government of the Republic. At a rally held in Gerona on 2 September he expressed himself in these terms: "This government, which is charged with leading the Hispanic peoples, is no longer loyal to the Constitution. It cannot shake off the mantle of imperialism and the education it has received from the Monarchy. These men are not liberals, they cannot understand the federal idea. If in Madrid they cannot create the Hispanic ideal, we will proceed to create the Catalan nationality". Article 13 of the Constitution, which Companys was obliged to comply with, stated with crystal clarity: "In no case shall the Federation of autonomous regions be admitted". It is clear, then, that it was the president of the Generalitat who was not loyal to the Constitution. Worse still, Companys was not alone, as some Socialists were increasingly expressing their threats not to respect the rules of the game. Months earlier, Largo Caballero, in a clear allusion to the dictatorship of the proletariat, had formulated Lenin's famous question: "Freedom for what? Azaña himself increasingly expressed himself as a revolutionary in his speeches. For Azaña, the Esquerra government in Catalonia "was the only republican power" in the whole country and the only "bastion" against the return of tyranny. All of them forgot or scorned the votes deposited at the ballot box. After having been legislating and governing for two and a half years, nine months after the triumph of their political opponents, the "democrats" of the left did not accept the parliamentary game and wanted to seize power by revolution.

As if there were not enough problems, the Basques also raised their own. The Basque nationalists, outraged by the anti-clericalism of the Constitution, had left the Cortes, but with the new legislature they returned. They wanted religious control in their community and aspired to have their own representatives in the Vatican, so many had voted for the CEDA. However, they moved to the left when they realised that the centre-right government was not favourable to their claims to autonomy. The Basques decided to hold elections in their local councils as a sign of protest against an economic imposition that went against their claims for an economic agreement. The Madrid government banned the elections and tried to prevent them by force when they were being held. All Basque town councils resigned and demonstrations demanding autonomy proliferated in the Basque Country. Finally, its deputies in Parliament followed the example of the Esquerra Republicana and left the Cortes. That was the state of affairs in September 1934.

For their part, the Socialist leaders disagreed over the strategy to be followed. The supporters of Largo Caballero were prepared to unleash a revolution against the Government of the Republic, but this was not shared by Indalecio Prieto, who did not see how it could succeed. The control that Largo Caballero exercised over the UGT tipped the balance on his side. The revolutionary approach of the UGT leader was also shared by Companys, the president of the Generalitat, who was prepared to lead the uprising in Catalonia. In connection with these rumours, it was announced that seventy crates of arms had landed in Asturias and the government reported arrests in connection with the discovery of large quantities of ammunition[20]. In view of the situation, a State of Alarm was decreed throughout Spain. Municipal elections due to be held in the autumn were again cancelled.

Gil Robles, who had told his followers on more than one occasion that his accession to power was only a matter of time, considered that the moment to lead the government had arrived. On 11 September the daily *El Sol* published these words of the Catholic leader: "The path is clear before us. Not a moment more! We want nothing for ourselves, but we will no longer tolerate the continuation of this state of affairs". It seemed clear that Gil Robles would withdraw his support for Samper in order to reclaim the government. This was the understanding of the Asturian proletariat, which prepared to go on general strike. On 1 October the leader of the CEDA made a speech in Parliament in which he condemned the successive governments of the last eleven months, which had failed to interpret the will of the people: "We have given them our support," he declared, "but we feel that we cannot continue to do so any longer. We are prepared to do our duty". This sentence, highlighted by *El Sol* in its 2 October edition, could only be understood in

---

[20] On the subject of the arms, it seems that they came from government arsenals. Echevarrieta, a Basque financier and friend of Indalecio Prieto, had placed the order with the Consortium of Military Factories in 1932 with the intention of putting them in the hands of the Portuguese revolutionaries. The delivery was thwarted and they remained hidden in Cadiz until 1934 when, with the permission of the Minister of War, almost certainly the venerable Brother Martínez Barrio, they were loaded on board *La Turquesa*, supposedly bound for Bordeaux. On the way, the ship stopped off the Asturian coast and disembarked them. The police got wind of this and were able to seize at least some of them, mainly cartridges. These weapons were supposed to end up in Madrid, but due to the surveillance it was decided to distribute them in Asturias. Among them were five hundred Mauser rifles, twenty-four machine guns and thousands of hand grenades. Since the cartridges had ended up in the hands of the police, a train of ammunition was forged and sent from the Toledo arsenal to Asturias to make up for the loss.

one way by the government, which resigned. Once again the President of the Republic began consultations and once again refused to entrust the formation of the government to Gil Robles. The criticism voiced by the Cedistas against Alcalá Zamora was resounding, and the indignation was monumental: not only would their leader not be president, but he was not even going to join the government. The person chosen by Alcalá Zamora was once again the seemingly indispensable Alejandro Lerroux, "Don Ale", who gave three CEDA ministers a place in the government. Gerald Brenan finds in *The Spanish Labyrinth* a justification for Alcalá Zamora's decision. According to Brenan, "the left-wing parties warned the President of the Republic that if any member of the CEDA entered the government, they would see this as a declaration of war against them". According to this British Hispanist, the left-wing parties put pressure on Alcalá Zamora to dissolve the Cortes.

The left reacted as if there had been a coup d'état, but in reality the only thing that had happened was that the party that had won the elections had entered the government with three ministers, and that was all. No democratic country in the world would have accepted censorship of the party with the most votes. It was incomprehensible and unacceptable. In *The Spanish Tragedy* Allison Peers refers to this circumstance with words of astonishment: "The left would have been the first to complain if they, as the majority group, had been excluded from power. Why, then, being in principle democrats, and having been rejected by the electors, should they have to breathe fire and carnage, and claim that what they had not been able to win by legal means should be obtained by repugnant means?" In reality, no one accepted the decision of the President of the Republic, whose enemies increased on the left and on the right. Miguel Maura, former Minister of the Interior in April 1931, issued a written denouncing Alcalá Zamora as a "traitor". Other former colleagues angrily criticised his actions and announced that they were breaking off relations with him. Azaña also decided to leave Parliament in protest at the actions of the President of the Republic, but his motives were far from clear.

On 5 October a general strike was declared throughout the country, called by the UGT; in Asturias it reached such intensity that Martial Law was proclaimed and the army was called in to reinforce the Guardia Civil. In all the big cities the strike was felt intensely. In Madrid the military ran some trains, trams and buses, but communications of all kinds were disrupted. Only *El Debate* and *ABC* were able to publish as they were not controlled by the unions. Citizens were warned not to go out on the streets between 8 p.m. and dawn. There were no acts of violence in Madrid for the time being.

Companys' coup d'état in Catalonia

The general strike in Barcelona was developing without violence and with an uneven following. The municipal and regional authorities held a meeting on the evening of the 4th and President Companys announced that he had received assurances from Madrid that martial law would not be declared in Catalonia. The Generalitat had taken responsibility for maintaining public order. The 5th passed without any incidents worthy of mention in Barcelona, and in the afternoon it seemed that the strike was beginning to die down, as the CNT had not supported the socialists' call. On the 6th, however, a suspicious proclamation entitled "The Catalan Republic" began to be distributed in the early hours of the morning. It appealed to the Catalan people to be ready. The pamphlet ended with the words, "To arms for the Catalan Republic!" Another event that did not bode well was the occupation of the Fomento de Trabajo Nacional at the Puerta del Angel, an event led by the Alianza Obrera. The Alianza Obrera was a confluence of socialists, Trotskyists and nationalists. A proclamation was drawn up there and posted in the streets of the city centre. The text began as follows: "The insurrectionary movement of the Spanish proletariat against the coup d'état has acquired an extraordinary extent and intensity...". Once again, blatantly, the entry of three Catholic ministers into the government was described as a coup d'état. The proclamation announced: "the proclamation of the Catalan Republic will undoubtedly have an enormous influence, will provoke the enthusiasm of the working masses all over the country and will boost their combative spirit". The text ended with the exclamations "Long live the revolutionary general strike! Long live the Catalan Republic!"

At 9 a.m. on the morning of the 6th, the President of the Generalitat had already decided to betray the Republic, as he showed Josep Dencàs, Minister of the Interior, two optional texts to address the Catalan people: one, drafted by Joan Lluhí, a Freemason who was Minister of Justice; the other he had written himself. Dencàs opted for the second and asked Companys if he should give the order to mobilise and distribute arms. After receiving the president's permission, he ordered Miquel Badia to distribute arms to the "escamots". Dencàs, another Freemason who belonged to the Immortality lodge in Barcelona, had participated in the founding of Esquerra Republicana de Catalunya in 1931. He and Badia were the leaders of Estat Català, the youth movement of Esquerra Republicana founded by Macià. Estat Català had a military organisation of some 3,500 men, the escamots, who wore green uniforms and represented fanatical nationalism. Badia, who was also a Freemason and had participated in an assassination attempt on Alfonso XIII in 1925, was the head of the Generalitat's General Commissariat of Public Order, in other words, the chief of police. His acolytes called him "capitá collons" (captain bollocks). These two men were Companys' closest collaborators.

According to a report by General Domingo Batet, "short and long arms were publicly distributed and armed groups began to circulate". The Minister of the Interior ordered the concentration of some four hundred squad officers at the Generalitat. Miquel Badia was put in charge of the escamots and Commissioner General Coll i Llach had three thousand two hundred assault guards at his orders in case they were needed. Emissaries were sent all over Catalonia with mobilisation orders, aimed especially at the rabassaires. At five o'clock in the afternoon, a meeting was held in the palace of the Generalitat, and at half past six the ministers were in their offices. At the same time, groups of escamots and nationalist militants appeared in the Plaça de Catalunya. A demonstration was soon organised and headed for the Plaça de Sant Jaume, where a crowd of people gathered and spread out into the adjacent streets. Amid shouts and exalted cheers, President Companys appeared on the balcony and pronounced these words:

"Catalans!

The monarchist and fascist forces that for some time now have been trying to betray the Republic have achieved their goal and have seized power. The parties and men who have made public demonstrations against the scarce liberties of our land, the political nuclei who constantly preach hatred and war against Catalonia, are today the support of the present institutions. The events that have taken place have given all citizens the clear impression that the Republic, in its fundamental democratic principles, is in the gravest danger. All the genuinely republican forces in Spain and the advanced socialist sectors, without distinction or exception, have taken up arms against this bold step by the fascists.

Liberal, democratic and republican Catalonia cannot be absent from the protest that is triumphing throughout the country, nor can it silence its voice of solidarity with those who, like itself, are fighting in the Hispanic lands, sometimes to the death, for freedom and rights. Catalonia raises its flag high and calls on everyone to do their duty and to pay absolute obedience to the Government of the Generalitat, which from this moment on breaks off all relations with the adulterated institutions. At this solemn hour, in the name of the people and of Parliament, the Government over which I preside assumes all the powers of power in Catalonia, proclaims the Catalan State of the Spanish Federal Republic, and by re-establishing and strengthening relations with those who lead this general protest against fascism, invites them to establish in Catalonia the Provisional Government of the Republic, which will find in our Catalan people the most generous impulse of fraternity in the common yearning to build a free and magnificent Federal Republic.

We feel strong and invincible. We will keep anyone at bay, but everyone must restrain himself by submitting to the discipline and instructions of the leaders. The Government, from now on, will act with unrelenting energy to ensure that no one tries to disrupt or compromise its patriotic aims.

Catalans! the moment is serious and glorious. The spirit of President Macià, restorer of the Generalitat, accompanies us. Each in his place and Catalonia and the Republic in the hearts of all.

Long live the Republic! Long live freedom!"

After the speech, the Minister of Culture Ventura Gassol, another Esquerra Republicana mason leader, encouraged everyone to announce the proclamation throughout Catalonia on behalf of the Government of the Generalitat. The Catalan flag was then raised to applause. A group from Estat Català protested and demanded their flag, the four-coloured flag with the star. From the balcony they were asked for discipline and urged to follow the president's orders. In his anger, Companys telephoned General Batet and announced that he had just proclaimed the Catalan state. Batet replied: "As a Catalan, as a Spaniard and as a man of humanity, I am very sorry for what has happened, because it is a blow to my head. I can't resolve such a serious matter in a moment...". Having said this, he asked for time to reflect and demanded that the agreement be communicated to him in writing, so Companys sent him this communiqué through the Director of Labour Joan Tauler: "Your Excellency, as President of the Government of Catalonia, I request you to place yourself at my command to serve the Federal Republic that I have just proclaimed. Palace of the Generalitat, 6 October 1934". Tauler asked him if there was an answer and Batet replied: "Not at the moment. In any case, later."

Whichever way you look at it, Companys, as in 1931, showed that good sense, sanity and prudence (seny) were not qualities that adorned his person. It was definitely foolishness and rapture (rauxa) that presided over his opportunistic and adventurous actions[21]. In 1931 he was only an elected

---

[21] It is generally accepted that "seny" is the best of the Catalans' qualities. Paradoxically, however, at decisive moments in their history they have suffered from leaders who have let themselves be carried away by the "rauxa". See the case of Canon Pau Clarís, conseller en cap of the Generalitat, who threw himself into the arms of Cardinal Richelieu and allowed France everything that Spain did not want to be allowed. On 16 January 1641, this calamitous character proclaimed the Catalan Republic under the protection of France; but only a week later, the same Pau Clarís appointed Louis XIII Count of Barcelona and sovereign of Catalonia. Louis XIII occupied the country militarily and the French took political and administrative control. The Catalans also paid the invading army's expenses. The traitor Pau Clarís died a month later, in February 1641, but his lack of seny caused Catalonia irreparable damage.

The history of what happened with the much-maligned Philip V also deserves a brief commentary. Certainly, when the first Bourbon entered Spain via Irún, he hastened to appoint a viceroy for Catalonia. He was immediately warned that what he had done was illegal, since he had first to swear the Catalan laws. The king then hastened to make amends for his mistake by convening the Parliament of Catalonia, and in less than a year he appeared in Barcelona to swear in the Catalan Constitutions, an act that took place in the Saló del Tinell on 14 October 1701. The sessions of the Cortes lasted until 14 January 1702 and, in accordance with law and custom, the Catalans accepted their sovereign. Philip V not only swore them in, but also granted new privileges, including a Court of Contracts, where royal decisions would be judged before being applied in Catalonia, and limited permission for them to trade with America. The minister Melchor de Macanaz

councillor; but in 1934 Lluís Companys was not only the leader of Esquerra Republicana, but the president of the entire Catalan people, who undoubtedly deserved to be better represented. Companys had not only betrayed the Republic, of which he was the greatest exponent in Catalonia, but, with his stupid act of rebellion, he betrayed all those Catalans who were in favour of respect for the legality of the republic and the statutes. An analysis of the content of the text shows that it was full of lies: there was no other betrayal of the Republic than his own. As for the announcement that "advanced socialist sectors, without distinction or exception, had taken up arms", it indicated that Companys was aware of the coup d'état planned by the socialists and was participating in it with his rebellion. Very significant is the invitation "to those who lead this general protest against fascism to establish in Catalonia the Provisional Government of the Republic", since Manuel Azaña was in Barcelona and many thought at the time that he was the person designated by the conspirators to preside over the Federal Republic. In fact, he was one of the people arrested after the failure of the coup throughout Spain.

At around 10 p.m. General Batet announced to the president of the Generalitat that he was in favour of legality and issued a proclamation declaring a state of war. Faced with Companys' refusal to accept the demand for surrender, the movements began. The large square of Catalonia was occupied by Batet's troops, who soon reached the Plaça de Sant Jaume. Two artillery pieces, an infantry company and a machine gun company converged there. Pérez Farràs, commander of the Mozos de Escuadra, ordered to fire. A commander and a soldier were killed and another six soldiers and a captain were also wounded after this first skirmish. Entrenched in the palace of the Generalitat, which had been fortified with machine guns, the Catalan leaders tried to hold out while waiting for reinforcements. Josep Dencàs made a general appeal and appealed to the rabassaires in particular via Radio Barcelona; but the help he demanded never arrived. At four in the morning, the Generalitat airfield was occupied by forces loyal to the Republic. The greatest resistance was at the Centro Autonomista de Dependientes de Comercio and the Comandancia General de Somatenes, where artillery was used to reduce the rebels. Shortly after 6 a.m. on 7 October, Companys and the ministers who accompanied him, with the exception of Dencàs, who fled with money through the sewers and managed to get abroad, decided to

wrote: "The Catalans achieved all they wanted, for there was nothing left for them to ask for, nor anything special to give the king, and so they became more independent of the king than the Parliament of England". In 1704, an attempt to land Anglo-Dutch troops in Barcelona failed because no Catalans joined the invaders. When in 1705 Archduke Charles' landing was successful and Barcelona surrendered on 9 October, the Catalan elites, under the bayonets of the occupying troops, changed sides, betraying the oath they had sworn, and declared themselves Austracists. The consequences of this reckless act of disloyalty were disastrous for the future of Catalonia and for the whole of Spain.

surrender in the face of the evidence that the people did not support them. The president of the Generalitat addressed the Catalans and announced their capitulation. Forty-six people were killed and 117 wounded in the clashes in Barcelona.

As a result, autonomy was suspended. The pleas of Francesc Cambó, who argued that it was not the entire Catalan people who had violated the Statute, but Esquerra Republicana, were to no avail. Cambó repeated that the Lliga could be trusted to administer Catalonia's powers loyally and recalled the enmity between the two parties with these words: "For three years they have humiliated and insulted us. When Mr. Dencàs' papers were examined by the police, a list was found, in which there were twenty-eight people who were to be shot if the rebellion triumphed. I was one of them. Undoubtedly, these revelations by Cambó highlight the totalitarian nature of the coup plotters.

Bloody coup d'état and civil war in Asturias

Far more catastrophic was the revolution that broke out simultaneously in Asturias, where a coup d'état organised by socialists, communists and anarchists turned into a civil war that lasted two weeks. The general strike of the UGT continued throughout Spain on the 6th. While in Madrid there was fighting in the streets, in Asturias the miners were preparing to take Oviedo. The headquarters of the October revolution was in Madrid, where Largo Caballero directed operations. The exits and entrances to the capital were tightly controlled and the expected weapons could not arrive. Many of them had been discovered and seized weeks earlier. There were plans to blow up the Ministry of the Interior and there were also plans to take over the Presidency of the Government and other centres of power, but the insurrection in Madrid failed. Nor were the objectives achieved in the provinces, although in some there was heavy fighting. In Cantabria, for example, the insurrectionary strike lasted until the 16th. There were serious clashes with a death toll of eleven in the region. In the north of Castilla-León, fighting in the mining areas was fierce and artillery was used. After Asturias and Catalonia, it was in the Basque Country that the October uprising was most virulent. There the insurrection lasted a week and claimed 40 victims, most of them among the insurgents. On the 5th, the industrialist Dagoberto Rezusta and the traditionalist MP Marcelino Oreja Elósegui were murdered in Eibar, crimes that caused great indignation. On the same day Carlos Larrañaga, a well-known Carlist, was also murdered in Mondragón.

In Asturias, the actions were on such a scale that one has to speak of a civil war. Gerald Brenan considers the Asturian revolution to be the first battle of the civil war. "The October revolution, I have said and written many times, ended the Republic". These words written in *My historical-political testament* by Claudio Sánchez Albornoz, one of the great Spanish historians and President of the Government of the Republic in exile between 1962 and 1971, allow us to properly assess the historical significance of the revolutionary uprising. Since 1912, the miners in Oviedo, Gijón and surrounding towns had been affiliated to the UGT and the CNT. They were well organised: they had their own newspapers and cooperatives, as well as other recreational societies. In Gijón and La Felguera, with its important iron foundry, the CNT was predominant, while in Oviedo and Sama the UGT socialists were in the majority. The Communists managed to capture one of the CNT unions and also established themselves in Asturias. When Largo Caballero founded the Alianza Obrera, the Asturian CNT, unlike in Catalonia and other regions, joined it. Moreover, the Comintern encouraged the Communist Party of Spain to form alliances with other parties in order to achieve a united front. All this helped the Alianza Obrera in Asturias to become the Frente Único, the prototype of the Popular Front.

According to Brenan's figures, in the whole of Asturias some 70,000 workers participated in one way or another in the revolution, of whom 40,000 belonged to the UGT, 20,000 to the CNT and 9,000 were communists. Experiments in libertarian communism were put into practice in La Felguera (municipality of Langreo) and in the poorest neighbourhoods of Gijón,. The uprising began on the 5th in Mieres, in whose Town Hall the Socialist Republic was proclaimed, and in Sama de Langreo, where socialist militiamen under the orders of Belarmino Tomás assaulted the Civil Guard barracks on the 5th and some seventy guardsmen who were defending it were killed. From these towns the leaders of the rebellion coordinated the actions. A power cut in Oviedo in the early hours of the morning of the 5th was the agreed signal for the socialist Ramón González Peña, who chaired the first Revolutionary Committee, to enter the city at the head of the rebels. Something went wrong and the blackout did not take place, so the capture of Oviedo was delayed. On the 6th the armed uprising began with simultaneous attacks on thirty-one Civil Guard barracks. Telephone and telegraph communications were cut off and thousands of men, ready for anything, headed towards Oviedo. On their march they spread out to occupy all the towns and cities they passed through. In Trubia, twelve kilometres from the capital, the revolutionaries occupied an arms factory and seized thirty thousand rifles, numerous machine guns and some cannons.

For three days Oviedo was the scene of continuous fighting. As soon as the loyalist troops were dislodged from the buildings they were protecting, they were set on fire. The Banco Asturiano, the Campoamor Theatre, the Instituto de Enseñanaza Secundaria and the University were set on fire and suffered considerable damage. The destruction at the University was almost complete: the library, which contained valuable bibliographic collections, and the Natural History Museum were burnt. Numerous paintings and works of art were lost. The walls and sober Renaissance façades remained standing. Curiously, the statue of the Asturian Fernando de Valdés Salas, the famous inquisitor general of Philip II and founder of the University, was respected despite the fact that the cloister it presides over was razed to the ground. The cathedral was also badly damaged: the famous holy chamber, a magnificent Romanesque work begun in the 9th century, was dynamited and important relics disappeared. On the 9th, the city was taken over by the attackers. Only in the governor's palace, where about a thousand soldiers and policemen had taken refuge, was there any resistance. They could not be helped because from the windows of private houses, snipers fired on anyone who approached to try to alleviate the situation of the besieged, which shows that, unlike in Barcelona, there was popular support.

General Eduardo López Ochoa, who commanded the loyalist troops in Asturias, fought a fierce battle with 400 men near Avilés. Once the uprising was under control there, he tried to go to Oviedo to help his men, but the destruction of the bridges and the blocking of the roads with trees made it impossible for him to help. The reinforcements sent by the government: Regulars and troops of the Foreign Legion commanded by Colonel Yagüe, landed near Gijón, a city which fell into the hands of the government forces on the 10th. López Ochoa also received other reinforcements that arrived en masse in Asturias from all points of the compass. On the 12th, General López Ochoa's troops, marching into Oviedo from the west, met up with Yagüe's troops on the outskirts of the city. The battle for control of the Asturian capital was fierce and the fighting in the streets lasted for three days.

Three Revolutionary Committees were formed, which actually coordinated the numerous committees that had been set up in the various localities. The first was chaired by the socialist Ramón González Peña and was made up of four socialists, two anarchists and two communists. González Peña blew up the safes of the Bank of Spain on 9 October and when things began to get ugly he and other members of the Committee fled, taking with them fourteen million pesetas requisitioned from the branch. A second Revolutionary Committee was then formed, chaired by Teodomiro Menéndez, also a socialist, although most of its members were from the PCE. These communists denounced the defeatist attitude of the socialists and issued a report denouncing that they had abandoned them and that they had fled "making millions". On this subject, the aforementioned work by Juan Ordóñez Márquez contains the words of Ángel Valverde, a radical deputy who was appointed governor general of Asturias after the revolution. In the course of a banquet offered to him by his party on 13 February 1936, Valverde related the following in relation to González Peña: "... it is certain that of the fourteen million he seized, he only handed over five million to the Revolutionary Committees and tried to flee with the rest, until he was arrested by the same rioters, who seized the money he was carrying. The fact is completed with the detail that almost all the money recovered by the public forces was taken from the families of the leaders - Graciano Antuña, Amador

Fernández, etc. -. Even dirtier was the action of another leader, Largo Caballero, whose cowardice led him to deny any participation in the movement". The Communist-majority Committee was only in charge on 12 October, since the Socialists immediately formed the third Revolutionary Committee, chaired by Belarmino Tomás. Back in their barracks in the mining areas of Mieres and Sama, these leaders realised that the uprising had been defeated, and on the 18th Belarmino Tomás met with López Ochoa to agree on the surrender, which took place on the 19th. The general himself recounts details of the agreements in *Memorias de un soldado (Memoirs of a Soldier)*. Belarmino Tomás requested that "in no way should the indigenous Moorish troops be allowed to enter the towns, as they were truly afraid of them because of their customs and because of what was said about them".

This general was called "the executioner of Asturias" by the propaganda. The fact that he was a Freemason gave rise to all kinds of comments. Ordóñez Márquez states in *La apostasía de las masas y la persecución religiosa en la provincia de Huelva 1931-1936* that he had to account for his actions at the head of the anti-revolutionary forces before the Council of Seven of the International Masonic Association in Brussels, where he was probably irradiated. Prosecuted and imprisoned in March after the victory of the Popular Front,, he was transferred to the Military Hospital of Carabanchel because of an ailment. There he was insulted and threatened by leftist patients and doctors. On 3 April 1936, Teresa León, Rafael's companion Alberti, wrote in *Ayuda*, the newspaper of the Socorrro Rojo Internacional: "López Ochoa, unscrupulous adventurer, his cruelty was well known... responsible for hunting fugitives, raping women, crushing children.... Repulsive figure... Sick in Carabanchel? Perhaps out of fear of being executed by the masses? On 16 August 1936 they went to look for him, took him out in his pyjamas and riddled him with bullets on the hill of Almodovar. Then they cut off his head with a large knife and stuck it on the bayonet of a militia woman's rifle. The criminals then went through the streets of Madrid, in the style of the French Revolution, holding aloft the skewered head of the general, who, to their derision, was subjected to insults and spitting. His assassination is considered a Masonic revenge. The official version of the Republican authorities, unable to arrest the executioners, was that he had died in the Military Hospital of Carabanchel "as a result of an old ailment".

The defeat of the Socialist-led coup d'état, instead of bringing about the collapse of the Left, served to strengthen it thanks to the campaign which Socialists and Communists, supported by Freemasonry, organised inside and outside Spain. The government was accused of infinite cruelty in its repression and, as usual, the usual accusations of inquisitorial and intolerant Spain were made. Once again, Juan -Simeón Vidarte acknowledges the facts: "Freemasonry, the Second International, the League of the Rights of Man (a

Masonic creation) informed the world of the crimes committed by Spanish fascism. The socialist and communist parties of the whole world sent the Spanish government their strongest protests. The French socialist deputy Vincent Auriol organised, together with the president of the Belgian Socialist Party, Émile Vandervelde, an international campaign." Both the Frenchman Auriol and the Belgian Vandervelde were Freemasons.

It cannot be denied that after the crimes committed by the revolutionaries there were brutal episodes of repression. The historical antagonism of the miners against the Guardia Civil gave rise to episodes of hatred on both sides. The fact that the Civil Guards who resisted in their barracks were killed when they surrendered gave rise to a thirst for revenge among the members of the Benemérita. There were numerous summary executions. Hugh Thomas denounces in particular the methods of Lisardo Doval Bravo, a Guardia Civil officer who was appointed delegate of the Ministry of War for public order in the provinces of Asturias and León. His mission was the "persecution of the elements responsible for the crimes perpetrated in the revolt". The government allowed his actions to remain outside judicial control, as he was given a document granting him the necessary autonomy and special jurisdiction so that he could carry out his duties without hindrance. At the beginning of December he was dismissed, not for having exceeded his powers, but for having shown copies of the orders he had received to monarchist leaders to restrain himself from repression.

In *The Spanish Holocaust*, Paul Preston reports a conversation between General López Ochoa and the socialist Juan -Simeón Vidarte, two Masonic brothers, in which the former explains that he ordered the shooting of legionnaires who beheaded and hanged prisoners with whom they were furious, which led to an altercation with Colonel Yagüe. In the same conversation reproduced by Paul Preston, López Ochoa explains that he ordered the shooting of six Moors who had been looted, raped and murdered, which caused him problems with the Minister of War, who asked him for explanations: "How dare you shoot anyone without the formation of a War Council?" To which he replied, "I have subjected them to the same court martial to which they subjected their victims." Perhaps the difference between one brutality and another is that, normally, the authorities sought out or persecuted those who had previously committed crimes.

Then there was the absolutely gratuitous anticlerical violence, which appeared again and again in the actions of the revolutionaries until it ended in the unspeakable orgy of bloodshed and hatred that took place during the civil war. From the first days of the uprising in Asturias, all kinds of religious were killed for no reason: the priests of Rebollada and Valdecuna were killed on the 5th, the former by gunshots. On the same day, in Mieres, the revolutionaries killed two students and two Passionist novices. A parish priest was also killed in Mieres on the 5th. Another parish priest in Mieres, the parish priest of San Esteban, was arrested and shot on the 6th. On the same day, also in Mieres, the convent of the Passionist Fathers was attacked and set on fire, two of whom died at the hands of the militiamen. The crimes in Mieres were not yet over, as on the 7th the monastery of Santo Domingo, which had been occupied the previous day, was set on fire. Six seminarists who had fled the fire and were in hiding were discovered and shot. On the 8th, six friars who had been kidnapped were killed in Turón. On the same day, the militiamen killed the vicar general, Juan Puertas, and the bishopric's chamber secretary, Aurelio Gago. In Santullano, a Jesuit and another friar were also killed on the 8th. The list on the 9th begins with the so-called martyrs of Turón, the main communist stronghold in Asturias where the Workers' and Peasants' Republic, based on the dictatorship of the proletariat, was proclaimed. There, nine priests of La Salle were shot next to the cemetery, and another Passionist also died with them. Other victims on the 9th included the parish priest of Santa María la Real and three more religious in Santullano, one of them a Jesuit. On the 10th the parish priest of Olloniego was killed. On the 12th the superior of the Carmelite convent in Oviedo was shot. In all, thirty-four priests and religious died in Asturias; but to these must be added those who were killed elsewhere during the October uprising. In the province of Palencia, to give just one more piece of information on this matter, on 6 October a Marist Brother was stabbed to death in Barruelo; in Muñecas the parish priest was killed. All these religious have been identified, but their names have been withheld so as not to tire the reader.

Victims throughout the country as a result of the coup d'état and the war that ensued were very high. Months later, the government made public the official figures for Asturias, which have been revised and slightly modified by various historians. The toll is as follows: 1,335 people lost their lives, of whom 1,051 were civilians; 100 were officers and members of the Guardia Civil; 98 were soldiers; and 86 were policemen. The wounded numbered 2,961, two thirds of whom were civilians. 730 public and private buildings were destroyed or badly damaged, to which must be added 58 churches and 58 bridges. As for the weapons captured, the figures are as follows: 89,354 rifles, 33,211 revolvers, 41 cannons, 10,824 kg. of dynamite, 31,345 bombs, 97,322 cartridges, 50,585 dynamite cartridges, 255,375 revolver cartridges. The figure of thirty thousand detainees gives a good idea of the massive support for the uprising. The prisons were filled to overflowing and, as it was impossible to house so many prisoners, internment camps were built.

To conclude this nefarious episode in the history of the Second Republic, we give the floor to the republican Salvador de Madariaga, whose words, written in his work *España. Ensayo de historia contemporánea*, we endorse them in their entirety:

"The uprising of 1934 is unforgivable. The presidential decision to call the CEDA to power was unassailable, inevitable, and even long overdue. The argument that José Mª Gil Robles was trying to destroy the Constitution in order to establish fascism was both hypocritical and false. Hypocritical because everyone knew that the socialists of Largo Caballero were dragging the others into a rebellion against the 1931 Constitution without any regard for what Gil Robles was or was not trying to do; and on the other hand, it is obvious that President Companys and the entire Generalitat also violated the Constitution. With what faith are we to accept as heroic defenders of the Republic of 1931, against its more or less illusory enemies on the right, those who in order to defend it destroyed it? (...) With the rebellion of 1934 the Spanish left lost even the shadow of moral authority to condemn the rebellion of 1936".

From crisis to crisis towards the Popular Front

That the PSOE and ERC had tried to seize power by means of a coup d'état and by using the masses is undeniable. It could be argued that not all socialists shared Largo Caballero's strategy, which is true. Indalecio Prieto, whose position was rather murky, acknowledged in Mexico in 1942 his share of responsibility: "I plead guilty before my conscience, before the socialist party and before the whole of Spain, for my participation in the revolutionary movement of October". There was also a sensible and legalistic sector in the PSOE, personified in the figure of Julián Besteiro, who accused his comrades of "poisoning the workers with false and hate-filled propaganda". But facts speak louder than words, and they prove that a coup d'état had been attempted against the Republic, even though those involved ignominiously denied their responsibility and attributed the uprising to the masses, who had "spontaneously" broken out.

Largo Caballero, Companys, Azaña and the other leaders involved in the coup were arrested. For two months Spain remained under martial law. Catalonia temporarily lost the powers granted to it by the Statute. The winter passed with unusual calm: strikes decreased significantly and a kind of exhaustion settled in the atmosphere. The first of those arrested to be put on the street was Azaña, as his involvement in organising the rebellion could not be proved. He was arrested again shortly afterwards, but was again released. Largo Caballero, who had taken the precaution of remaining quietly at home while the streets of Madrid were being fought in the streets, was also subsequently acquitted. When the courts martial against Ramón González Peña and Teodomiro Menéndez were held in February 1935, the international campaign had already begun, and French Freemason socialists visited their Freemason brother Alejandro Lerroux, President of the Government, to present him with thousands of signatures collected throughout Europe calling for a pardon for the defendants. On 16 February the military tribunals sentenced Peña and Menéndez to death, and in successive days seventeen other members of the Revolutionary Committees received the same sentence.

The day before the sentence, on 15 February, the Conservative Republican Party deputy Dionisio Cano López had presented a bill in the Cortes, backed by twenty parliamentarians, including Calvo Sotelo, Fuentes Pila, Sainz Rodríguez, Ramiro de Maeztu and others, calling on the Government to adopt measures to prevent members of the armed forces from belonging to Freemasonry. It was a stormy session that Viscount Léon de Poncins transcribed in full in his book *Histoire secrète de la révolution espagnole.* Cano Lopez argued that if the military were forbidden to belong to a legally constituted political party, much less should they be allowed to join a secret society whose directives are incompatible with the interests of the homeland to which they have sworn allegiance. This deputy courageously attacked Freemasonry and accused it of being a political party and a secret international organisation that bound its members by an oath of obedience. The proposal was voted in favour, but in practice it became a dead letter due to the victory of the Popular Front. Despite the unquestionable relevance of the proposal, given that many members of the military belonged to Freemasonry, which had attracted them like a magnet since the beginning of the 19th century, Leandro Álvarez Rey, Professor of Contemporary History at the University of Seville and author, among other works, of *Los diputados por Andalucía de la Segunda República 1931-1939,* disqualified those who paid attention to Cano López's speech and branded them as extreme right-wing fanatics or "revisionist pseudo-historians".

Lerroux's PRR ministers declared themselves in favour of the commutation of the sentences. The CEDA, the Agrarian Party and Melquiades Álvarez's Republican Liberal Democratic Party (PRLD) were opposed and announced that they would no longer support the government. Even so, Lerroux recommended the cancellation to the President of the Republic and provoked the crisis. Alcalá Zamora commuted the sentences of twenty-one condemned men and only two were executed: Diego Vázquez, who had blown up a lorry with thirty-two civil guards, and Jesús Argüelles, alias "Pichalatu", who had shot eight civilians. It was of no use for "Pichalatu" to confess at the trial that he was taking orders from the Revolutionary Committee. The real perpetrators of the October revolution would soon be released from prison, as amnesty for all those arrested was the main promise of the Popular Front during the election campaign of February 1936.

Once again, Ordóñez Márquez provides relevant information on the situation of the socialist González Peña in Burgos prison. According to this author, the director of the Burgos prison was the Freemason Julián Peñalver, who was commissioned by the lodges to form a "triangle" of protection around this prisoner, who was also a Freemason. As soon as his death sentence was pardoned, González Peña was comfortably transferred by car from Chinchilla prison to Burgos because the climate of Chinchilla did not suit him. Then, the policeman Mauricio Carlavilla was close enough to him to hear from his mouth the following comment: "By January I will be free; I will be released by a government-bridge presided over by Portela". Under the pseudonym Mauricio Karl, Carlavilla quotes these words in his book *Technique of the Komintern in Spain*.

President Alcalá Zamora affably proposed the formation of a "Government of concentration and concord"; but he found no one capable of achieving this feat. After a week of uncertainty, an original solution was found: "Don Ale" took it upon himself to form a government of thirteen ministers, members of his own party, none of whom was a member of parliament. The fact of having been a minister entitled him to a lifetime pension of 10,000 pesetas. The chances of survival of the new Executive were nil, as it was in a minority and no one was prepared to support it. All parties then began to talk of new general elections. When the government fell on 6 May 1935, barely a month after taking office, Alcalá Zamora was faced for the umpteenth time with the evidence that the only reasonable solution was Gil Robles. Since the failure of the October coup, the CEDA had increased its prestige and popular support, and its membership was growing steadily. The dilemma began to circulate: "Gil Robles or elections"; although some, premonitory, warned: "Gil Robles or chaos". Unperturbed, Alcalá Zamora avoided entrusting Gil Robles with the formation of the government. His usual joker, "Don Ale", managed to preside over another centre-right cabinet in which the CEDA obtained five portfolios, including that of War, which went to Gil Robles. Among the priorities of this government were the drafting of a budget, since there had been none since 1932, and a reform of the Constitution. The Finance Minister, the independent Joaquín Chapaprieta, announced that he would present a balanced budget in October. At the end of July the Cortes took a two-month holiday.

In the same month of July the 7th Congress of the Communist International took place in Moscow, where the strategy of the united front comprising the bourgeois left was fully confirmed and encouraged. Wilhelm Pieck, General Secretary of the KPD (Communist Party of Germany) delivered the opening speech in the great hall of the Palágyi, the Trade Union Hall, on 25 July. Pieck, in the context of his report on the events of October in Spain, mentioned the name of Largo Caballero, which was greeted with thunderous and interminable applause. This German communist claimed the glory of the Asturian operation and "the fighting of October 1934". An article appeared in the daily *Pravda* saluting Largo Caballero, who was hailed as the Spanish Lenin. Communists all over the world knew that a new leader of international communism had been born in Spain. The Seventh Congress of the International (Comintern) did not limit itself to calling for the formation of a Popular Front in Spain, but even outlined the programme to be applied after the conquest of power.

Inexorably, as the summer drew to a close, steps continued to be taken in Spain towards this Popular Front announced at the meeting of the International. In September a new crisis arose: Alejandro Lerroux became Minister of State and handed over the presidency of the Government to Chapaprieta, who, despite lacking parliamentary backing, accepted the post without relinquishing the Treasury portfolio. This government of only eight members, in which Gil Robles retained the Ministry of War, was formed on 25 September and lasted until 29 October. By this time, Gil Robles had ceased to be interested in the Presidency of the Government, and his supporters in the street came to the conclusion that as long as Alcalá Zamora was President of the Republic, there was no chance for their leader. Chapaprieta's second government (the only president of the Council of Ministers who was not a Freemason) lasted until mid-December. His resignation heightened the feeling that the country was heading for new elections. There was no longer any talk of a budget. The President of the Republic then began to manoeuvre to impose a government without the support of the majority party. On 11 December he summoned Gil Robles and told him that he was not going to entrust him with the formation of the government; but he also tried to intimidate him with the threat that he would use the Guardia Civil to repress any adverse reaction from his followers.

As the country's demoralisation grew, Alcalá Zamora absurdly sought a centrist cabinet that had no parliamentary support. Although failure was certain, Manuel Portela Valladares, a Freemason in the Fénix and Liberation lodges of Barcelona and Grand Master of the 33rd degree, brazenly accepted the challenge and presented his government on 14 December. This Worshipful Brother had been chosen to prepare for the general elections. The Government lasted exactly two weeks. It seems that the farce was discovered and a brawl with insults and disqualifications broke out between the president and his ministers, resulting in the dissolution of the first Portela government. The second government was formed on 30 December and was, in effect, in charge of organising the elections. To that end, Portela Valladares also took charge of the Ministry of the Interior. The President of the Republic dissolved the Cortes and called a general election for 16 February 1936.

Alcalá Zamora and Portela Valladares brought about the defeat of the right and the triumph of the Popular Front by means of a suicidal strategy that it is impossible to believe was unintentional. Portela, President of the Government and Minister of the Interior, created the Democratic Centre Party, also known as the National Republican Centre Party, out of nothing. Financing a second candidate of the same party to split the vote and facilitate the victory of the opposing candidate was, as we have seen, the preferred stratagem of the Jewish lobby in the United States.. In the 1936 elections,

Portela's party, bourgeois, moderate and official, could only subtract votes from the right, since the few votes it obtained would always be subtracted from the right-wing parties. Portela's manoeuvre blatantly favoured the Popular Front because the electoral system gave a premium of 80% to the majority candidacy. In other words, the list that obtained one more vote got eight deputies, while the list that obtained one less vote only won two. It was therefore the best method for taking votes away from the right. It was in this way that the votes obtained by Portela's party decided the majority in favour of the Popular Front candidates in several provinces and facilitated their absolute triumph. It is unreasonable to think that Portela Valladares and Alcalá Zamora were so stupid as to ignore the disastrous consequences of their manoeuvre. That is why some historians accuse Grand Master Portela Valladares of obeying superior orders and of having organised the defeat of the right-wing parties.

PART 4
POPULAR FRONT, REVOLUTION AND CIVIL WAR

The election result was very close. In February 265 seats were awarded to the Popular Front, which won 47.03% of the vote, and 185 seats to the right, with 46.48% of the vote. Subsequently, in May, after revisions and repetitions, the final result was given, according to which the Popular Front increased its seats to 285, while the right wing was left with 166. The National Republican Centre Party of Portela Valladares finally won 17 seats. There were 13,553,710 voters, of whom 9,864,783 (72.9%) took part in the elections. The parties with the most seats in the Popular Front were the Socialists, who won 99 seats; Azaña's Republican Left, with 87; and Martínez Barrio's Republican Union, with 37. The Communist Party, thanks to being part of the coalition, went from 1 deputy in 1933 to 17 in 1936. The parties with most right-wing representation were the CEDA, which won 88 deputies; Calvo Sotelo's Renovación Española, with 12 seats; and Manuel Fal Conde's Comunión Tradicionalista, with 9. As can be seen, with practically the same number of votes, the Frente Popular won an overwhelming victory and almost doubled the number of seats of its opponents. The final blow to the defeat of the right was dealt by the Vote Records Commission, presided over by Indalecio Prieto, whose rigging prevented thirty elected right-wing candidates from obtaining their seats. In his *Memoirs* Alcalá Zamora wrote: "In the parliamentary history of Spain there is no memory of anything comparable to the 1936 Minutes Commission".

Although neither the FAI nor the CNT were represented in the Popular Front, the majority of anarcho-syndicalists voted for it, which was decisive. The reason why the anarchists did not abstain as in the 1933 elections was the promise of amnesty, which had been the main propaganda of the Popular Front. The elections were held normally; but once the elections were over, the pressure on the streets began and from the very beginning a revolutionary situation arose. Groups appeared in front of the Modelo prison, raising their fists to proclaim the victory of the Popular Front. In the early hours of the morning of the 17th the Minister of the Interior learned that the agitators in the provinces were leading the rioting masses who dominated the streets and were trying to storm the prisons in order to free the prisoners. In many places the prisons were opened without the local authorities doing anything to prevent it, and thousands of prisoners took to the streets all over Spain. In Valencia, for example, a CNT mob stormed the prison to get the 1934 convicts out. In the early hours of the same morning, reports came in of churches and convents burning in towns in Murcia, Malaga, Seville, Cordoba, Cadiz and Caceres. In Elche, the three churches in the city and the convent of the Poor Clare nuns were destroyed on successive days. In

Alicante, the mayor, a madman, had proposed: "On the 16th, don't let the nuns or the beatas vote; when you see someone holding a right-wing candidacy in his hand, cut off his hand and break it in his face and make him eat it". There, on the afternoon of the 20th, the mob set fire to the churches of Santa María and Nuestra Señora de la Misericordia, the convent of the Sisters of the Blood, the asylum of Nuestra Señora del Remedio and the headquarters of the congregation of San Luis. Three newspapers: *Mas*, of the agrarian right, *El Día* and *Diario de Alicante* were completely destroyed. In the same area of the Levante, in Yecla, churches were set on fire and their ornaments desecrated.

The haste of Portela Valladares, Minister of the Interior and President of the Government, in abandoning his posts when he was receiving reports of serious disturbances, including assaults on some audiencias and deputations and the theft of electoral records, is incomprehensible. General Franco, who had been appointed Chief of Staff by Gil Robles, was in contact in the early hours of 17 February with the Inspector General of the Civil Guard, the Freemason General Sebastián Pozas Perea, whom he asked to consider declaring a State of War to prevent the disturbances from escalating. Faced with Pozas's indifference, Franco went so far as to wake up the Minister of War, General Nicolás Molero Lobo, who was also a Freemason, and asked him to propose to the President of the Council the declaration of a State of War. At ten o'clock in the morning, the Council of Ministers met and General Molero presented the proposal. Portela Valladares initially agreed, but Alcalá Zamora finally asked him to cancel the measure. Some historians believe that through these requests Franco and Gil Robles were in fact attempting to stage a coup d'état. When Spain was already plunged into the tragedy of the civil war, Alcalá Zamora publicly acknowledged what he had refused to accept on 17 February 1936. In the article entitled "Les débuts du Front Populaire", published on 17 January 1937 in the *Journal de Géneve*, he wrote the following:

"From 17th February, and even from the night of the 16th, the Popular Front, without waiting for the end of the counting of the votes and the proclamation of the results, which should have taken place before the Provincial Census Boards on Thursday the 20th, unleashed the offensive of disorder in the streets: it claimed power by means of violence. Some civil governors resigned. At the instigation of irresponsible leaders, the mob seized the electoral documents; in many localities the results could have been falsified".

It is difficult to understand how a civilian governor could resign and leave his post at the moment of greatest responsibility. However, if one considers that the Minister of the Interior himself set an example and abandoned ship in the middle of a storm, things can be understood a little better at. Josep Pla, the Catalan writer and journalist posted to Madrid by *La*

Veu de Catalunya, the organ of Cambó's Lliga, was from 1931 to 1936 the best chronicler of the life of the Republic. In *Historia de la Segunda República española*, a work of almost two thousand pages in four volumes, he gives the following assessment of what happened the day after the elections: "It has been said that 17 February was 14 April. This is not exactly the case. February 17 was an April 14 aggravated by a repeat of May 11". As we know, on 11 May more than two hundred religious buildings were burned throughout Spain.

On the 18th violent disturbances broke out, and assaults, looting and arson continued in many provinces. In view of the seriousness of the events, General Franco visited the President of the Government at the Palace Hotel, where he was residing, and demanded that he take urgent measures to deal with the situation; but he replied that he lacked the energy and was thinking of resigning immediately. Before the end of the day, Calvo Sotelo, accompanied by Joaquín Bau, went to the hotel and asked the President of the Government not to relinquish power, but to use the appropriate legal measures of exception. On the 19th Portela Valladares called General Franco to confirm that he was no longer President of the Government.

The handover ceremony took place on 19 February, before the Provincial Boards had confirmed the election results. The Director General of the Police, the Freemason General Miguel Núñez de Prado, attended the ceremony. According to his comments, "it looked like a Masonic ceremony". Núñez del Prado knew the protagonists well: Portela Valladares, the Grand Master of the Grand Lodge, was handing over the office to his successor, the Freemason Azaña, before the Grand Master of the Spanish Grand Orient and future President of the Cortes, Martínez Barrio. As eyewitnesses, two Masonic generals, Núñez de Prado himself and the Inspector General of the Civil Guard, Pozas Perea. In the first Popular Front government, hastily formed by Azaña without the participation of the Socialists, there were seven other Masonic ministers. "The government seemed to have been born under our auspices", writes Juan -Simeón Vidarte in *Todos fuimos culpables*.

Azaña's first measure was to sign the amnesty decree. President Companys and six of his ministers returned to Barcelona in the odour of crowds. The first thing the Catalan Parliament did was to reaffirm the Cultivation Law. Despite the goodwill of the government, strikes began all over the country on the same day of the 19th. Demands were made for the reinstatement to work of those convicted or dismissed, the payment of wages to all workers arrested during the previous two years, and wage increases. In addition to these corporate strikes, other general, regional or local strikes of a political or solidarity nature were declared. The situation immediately worsened. The employers reacted in many cases by closing down the enterprises. In the countryside, too, the situation became revolutionary, since from the end of February the peasants began to occupy farms in Extremadura, Andalusia and Castile, for it was not in vain that the Popular

Front had promised them land. At the end of March a decree was published authorising the Agrarian Institute to proceed more quickly with the distribution of land. On the other hand, the first targets of popular violence continued as usual to be religious centres. In Madrid, the churches of San Ignacio and San Luis were set on fire, as were the offices of *La Nación*. In Logroño, two churches and four convents were burned. The anticlerical violence was soon joined by a wave of assassinations of politicians and businessmen.

The policy of the Popular Front had been officially adopted in the resolutions of the Seventh World Congress of the Communist International, so the PCE had methodically designed its strategy, which was to enable them to grow from thirty thousand members on the eve of the civil war to two hundred thousand at the beginning of 1937. The Pasionaria, Dolores Ibárruri, as early as the end of 1933, as recorded in the 13th Report of the Plenum of the Executive Committee of the Communist International, had declared: "Our task is to attract the majority of the proletariat and prepare it for the seizure of power. This means that we must concentrate our efforts on the organisation of workers' and peasants' committees and on creating soviets..... The development of the revolutionary movement is extremely favourable. We are advancing along the road which has been indicated to us by the Communist International and which leads to the establishment of a soviet government in Spain, a workers' and peasants' government." The work of infiltration of its cells into the workers' organisations and trade unions was essential.

A key man was to be Julio Álvarez del Vayo, who had returned from Russia in April 1936. While remaining a member of the Socialist Party, Álvarez del Vayo was prepared to follow the Communists' lead. It was he who persuaded Largo Caballero to agree to the merger of the Socialist Youth with the Communist Youth, which took place as soon as the civil war began. The United Socialist Youth (JSU), whose secretary was Santiago Carrillo, joined the Communist Party en bloc. Thus, leaders like Largo Caballero, La Pasionaria and Álvarez del Vayo, although they must have known what was happening in Russia, insisted on proposing the Soviet model as the universal panacea for all ills. On the other hand, propaganda flooded the bookshops, where Lenin translations and books or pamphlets extolling the excellences of life in the communist paradise proliferated. Unfortunately, the Spanish workers were unaware that terror, pillage, hunger, and injustice were the result of the dictatorship imposed on the Russian people by foreign agents.

On 7 April a disconcerting event took place after the opening of the Cortes: the deposition of Alcalá Zamora as president of the Republic, despite the fact that his term of office was due to expire in 1937. Don Niceto, "el Botas", only obtained the backing of five deputies out of the 473 who made up the Chamber. In short, the following happened: the Constitution stipulated that the president had to resign if he twice dissolved the Cortes. Alcalá

Zamora was confident that the dissolution of the Constituent Assembly did not count, as they had been elected before he began his term of office. In fact, Martínez Barrio, Largo Caballero and Azaña himself had implied as much in statements and writings. Alcalá Zamora was convinced that his days as president of the Republic were numbered if the right wing won; however, he was confident that the Republicans and Socialists would judge the second dissolution to have been necessary and right, especially as they had regained power thanks to it, and would therefore allow him to finish his term of office. He was wrong: he was found guilty of having dissolved the Cortes unnecessarily and was constitutionally dismissed. This is how the left thanked him for his political manoeuvring. Naturally, the right, who detested him, abstained from voting. The search for a successor began immediately and, to general surprise, Manuel Azaña allowed his name to be put forward. At a time when the Republican parties lacked men of prestige capable of dealing with the situation that had been created, Azaña was prepared to abandon his responsibilities as leader of the Popular Front and President of the Government.

Before the outbreak of the civil war, the so-called "tragic spring" showed that hatred between Spaniards had reached unbearable extremes: murders in the streets were the order of the day and the atmosphere in the Congress of Deputies was unbearable. The session of 15 April 1936, in which Azaña asked for a vote of confidence in the second Popular Front government, which was to last until 10 May, the date on which Azaña became President of the Republic, has gone down in parliamentary history. Azaña said in his speech that he was calm, that he personified calm. José Calvo Sotelo replied that to speak of calm when there was no security for people's lives was proof of carelessness. "If a State does not know how to guarantee order, peace, the rights of all citizens," said Calvo Sotelo, "let the representatives of this State resign!" Here is a significant paragraph from his speech reproduced *from the Diario de Sesiones de Cortes*:

> "We look at Russia and Hungary, we read and review the pages of their recent history, and, as we know that this was a tragedy, short for Hungary, permanent still for Russia, we want this tragedy to be avoided in Spain, and we say to the Government that this mission is its responsibility, and that to accomplish it it will certainly not lack either the votes or the opinion of those of us who are here. Ah, but if the Government shows weakness, if it hesitates.... we must stand up here and cry out that we are ready to oppose it by all means, saying that the example of extermination, the tragic destruction which the conservative and bourgeois classes of Russia experienced, will not be repeated in Spain".

Amidst insults and threats tolerated by Martínez Barrio, President of Congress, Calvo Sotelo continued his vibrant speech in which he gave figures of what had happened in Spain in the month and a half up to 2 April.

When he gave the figure of 345 wounded and 74 dead, he was interrupted by Dolores Ibárruri, La Pasionaria, who asked him, "How much money have you had to pay the assassins?" Then Margarita Nelken, a German-born Jewess, famous for her appeals to violence, added: "We are going to bring here all those who have been rendered useless in Asturias." Calvo Sotelo replied that as long as the Presidency protected his right, he would say what he had to say. There were further protests and, among other things, Calvo Sotelo was accused of being a cynic, since the violent actions he denounced came from his own ranks.

Finally, on 10 May, Manuel Azaña ceased to be president of the government and became the second president of the Republic. He was elected by an overwhelming majority, although the right wing voted blank. Azaña thus became a kind of hieratic, beatific Buddha with an icy smile who, from the presidency of the Republic, gazed impassively at the ruin of Spain. On the 10th a sort of interim government was formed under Augusto Barcia which lasted three days, until the formation on 13 May of the fourth single-colour government of the Popular Front, whose president was Santiago Casares Quiroga. The Socialists continued to be uncooperative. If for the uninitiated what had happened had been unexpected, it was not unexpected for Largo Caballero, judging by some astonishing statements made while he was in prison for his part in the October uprising. Edward Knoblaugh, the American correspondent in Spain for the *Associated Press*, one of the world's leading news agencies, visited him in his cell to interview him. An excerpt of the interview appears in the book *Correspondent in Spain* (1937). Knoblaugh, whose work was translated into Spanish thirty years later, confesses that he almost laughed when Largo Caballero told him this:

> "We will win at least two hundred and sixty-five seats. The whole existing order will be transformed. Azaña will be to me what Kerensky was to Lenin. In five years' time the Republic will be so organised that it will be easy for my party to use it as a springboard to achieve our aim. Our aim is a Union of Soviet Iberian Republics. The Iberian peninsula will again be one country. Portugal will join, we trust peacefully, but we shall use force if necessary. Behind these bars you have the future master of Spain! Lenin declared that Spain would be the second Soviet Republic of Europe, and his prophecy will come true. I will be the second Lenin who will make it come true".

Knoblaugh adds that, faced with such a sensational statement, he wanted to make sure that Largo Caballero would not deny it. Before sending it to New York, he showed him the text in the presence of Máximo Fernández, one of his lieutenants who was fluent in English, and "Largo willingly approved it". The headline of the interview appeared on the front page of *La Prensa*, a Spanish-language New York newspaper.

A few days before Azaña's accession to the Presidency of the Republic, the May Day celebrations had been held, at which Largo Caballero appeared as the man of the revolution. He led the demonstration in Madrid, where workers shouted "Long live the Red Army!" and images of the right-wing leaders, Calvo Sotelo, Gil Robles, Antonio Goicoechea and others were dragged or displayed hanging from gallows. "The revolution we want can only be made with violence", proclaimed Largo Caballero openly, who from 6 April had had his newspaper, *Claridad*, a well-edited evening paper in which the inevitable triumph of socialism was frequently announced. In his articles and statements Largo tirelessly repeated his slogans. In April the resolution of the Madrid socialist group had appeared in *Claridad*: "The proletariat must not limit itself to defending bourgeois democracy, but must ensure by all means the conquest of political power, in order to carry out, from there, its own social revolution. In the period of transition from capitalist society to socialist society, the form of government will be the dictatorship of the proletariat." While the Spanish Lenin was preparing to remove the Republican bourgeois from power, the other Socialist leader, Indalecio Prieto, accused him of practising "infantile revolutionism" and was in favour of collaborating with the Republicans. Prieto gave a speech in Cuenca that was very well received by the Republican newspaper *El Sol*, which considered him to be the true statesman that the Republic needed; however, the speech was rejected on the spot by the socialist youth, who threatened him, González Peña and Belarmino Tomás, who accompanied him. In Ecija they were met with gunfire and were nearly killed. This was the atmosphere in Spain.

The accusation that José Antonio Primo de Rivera's Falange practised "counter-revolutionary terrorism" is often made by Marxist historians. Certainly, the Falange, which failed to win parliamentary representation in 1936, swelled its ranks with young people from right-wing parties who, tired of the moderation of their parties, were ready to respond in the streets to their Marxist and anarchist enemies: it was the dangerous "dialectic of fists and guns". Now, it is indisputable that since April 1931 the street had been taken over again and again by arsonists, thugs and other revolutionary radicals. Stanley G. Payne clarifies who and how the violence and murders of political opponents began.

In *Falange. A History of Spanish Fascism*, Payne notes that when the first issue of *F.E.*, the Falange weekly, appeared in December 1933, the socialists threatened the vendors and the publication disappeared from the streets, so that SEU students had to sell it protected by squads of activists. Before this harassment, the first murder had been committed on 2 November 1933: a state official who was a supporter of the JONS was stabbed to death in Daimiel. A month later, the car in which Ruiz de Alda, pioneer of Spanish aviation and co-founder of the Falange, was travelling was stopped and set on fire as it passed through Tudela: Ruiz de Alda managed to save his life.

On 11 January 1934, the young Falangist Francisco de Paula Sampol was shot dead during the sale of the fifth issue of the weekly. Four other Falangists were killed before the end of the month. On 9 February 1934, Matías Montero, a twenty-year-old student who had been one of the three founders of the Sindicato Español Universitario, was shot five times as he was returning home after helping to sell *F.E.*. Francisco Tello, a worker affiliated to the PSOE and the Socialist Youth, was arrested while still carrying the murder weapon and sentenced to twenty-three years; but in February 1936 he was released amnestied by the Popular Front. None of these assassinations against the incipient fascist movement met with any response, so that some gave the Falange the nickname "Funeraria Española" and its leader the nickname "Juan Simón el Enterrador" (Juan Simon the Undertaker). The newspaper *ABC* wrote that the new party bore more resemblance to Franciscanism than to fascism. José Antonio's only response to the assassination of his friend was a press release stating: "Falange Española is nothing like an organisation of criminals, nor does it intend to copy the methods of such organisations, however much unofficial encouragement it receives". The assassinations continued and in March 1936 two more Falangists were killed in Madrid. José Antonio himself was the target of an attack in the same month: a bomb was thrown through the windscreen of his car in the centre of Madrid, but the occupants were unharmed. The need to respond to the attacks became a clamour. An SEU student wrote a letter to José Antonio telling him that if *F.E.* continued with its intellectual and literary tone it was not worth risking his life to sell it. It was at this point that reprisals were organised and the Falangist gunmen entered the scene.

Impunity had been common for violent leftists, usually invested with a moral hyper-legitimacy. However, José Antonio Primo de Rivera was "arrested as a fascist", according to the record of his arrest, and was imprisoned on 14 March 1936 in the Modelo prison in Madrid. Six weeks after his imprisonment, a search of his home was carried out and two loaded pistols were found. During the trial on 28 May, José Antonio indignantly declared that the whole thing was a farce and that the guns had been deliberately placed there by the police. Despite the fact that everything smelled of a frame-up, José Antonio was convicted of illegal possession of weapons. On 5 June he was transferred to Alicante, where he was to be executed on 20 November. Along with José Antonio, numerous leaders of the Falange, the only party viciously persecuted by the Republican authorities, were arrested. As a result of these arrests, violent actions by Falangists against Republican and Socialist leaders proliferated in March. The first attack was on the PSOE deputy Luis Jiménez de Asúa, who was shot outside his home: he was unharmed, but one of his bodyguards, Jesús Gisbert, was killed. On 15 March, the day after the Falangist leader went to prison, Largo's house Caballero's house was shot at by unknown assailants.

On 7 April, a basket containing a bomb was delivered to Eduardo Ortega y Gasset's house, the explosion of which did not cause any casualties but did cause damage to the house. On 13 April, Manuel Pedregal, the Supreme Court judge who had been investigating the case of the attack on Jiménez de Asúa, was assassinated outside his home. On 7 May, Captain Carlos Faraudo, instructor of the Socialist Youth militias, was assassinated in Madrid. Six people, allegedly Falangists, were arrested in connection with the crime.

Alongside this violence, Marxist historians omit to mention the murders of young Falangists which took place all over the country from March to July 1936. Since the figures for the dead and wounded presented by Calvo Sotelo in Congress went up to 2 April, we give some data only up to this date. On 6 March, four bricklayers who were members of the Falange were killed in Madrid for not joining the strike and working on the demolition of the old bullring. In retaliation, the Falangists killed several communists gathered in a tavern. On the same day, on the 6th, in Puebla de Almoradiel (Toledo), the right-winger Miguel Sepúlveda was murdered and shot with a gunshot to death. The mayor forbade his Catholic burial the following day and the Falangists went to his house to demand permission, but were shot at. Two of them, Ramón Perea and Tomás Villanueva, were killed and seven others were wounded. On the same day, a member of the SEU who had been shot by the police a few days earlier was killed. On 9 March Jesús Álvarez died in Palencia: he defended himself with a gun when he refused to be searched by militiamen and was killed by an assault guard. On 11 March Marxist gunmen murdered two law students in Madrid. The following day, 12 March, the action was repeated: militiamen of the Socialist Youths frisked passers-by with guns and murdered two students, José Olano and Enrique Valdovel, who identified themselves and were considered fascists. What happened in Jumilla on the 16th deserves a few lines: A socialist worker who had had altercations with right-wing people was found dead. All the people identified as Falangists and right-wingers were arrested. The prison was stormed by a crowd demanding the surrender of the detainees. Two of them were stabbed to death and one guard was shot dead. Two other Falangists, Pedro Cutillas and Jesús Martínez, were attacked with machetes that had been taken from the Guardia Civil, then beaten and dragged away. On the 18th there were three events in three different places: in Mendavía (Navarra) militiamen led by the mayor shot two Falangists and killed Martín Martínez de Espronceda; in Boñar (León) Manuel Montiel was beaten because he was considered a Falangist; in Mula (Murcia) the mayor of Acción Popular, José Martínez, was found murdered. On the 19th in Avila twenty people beat up the young Falangist Ramón Ferrer, who was seriously injured. On the same day in Cordoba three other Falangists were beaten up by a socialist group. Other types of murders and violent actions could be cited in this list, which would complete the picture of a real civil war.

Then there were the murders among the revolutionaries themselves. Among the most notable in April were those of the Badia brothers. Miquel, the "capità collons", and his brother Josep were murdered in Carrer Muntaner in Barcelona by members of the FAI. It seems that the anarchists hated them for their methods at the head of the Generalitat police. Another paradigmatic example occurred shortly before the outbreak of the war. Seventy thousand construction workers in Madrid began an indefinite strike, decided in assembly by the CNT and the UGT. Armed strikers forced shopkeepers to serve them, occupied restaurants and ate without paying. The socialist Clara Campoamor, in *La revolución española vista por una republicana (The Spanish Revolution as Seen by a Republican)*, describes these events in this way:

> "From mid-May until the outbreak of civil war, Madrid lived in chaos. Workers ate in hotels, restaurants and cafés, refused to pay their bills and threatened the owners.... The workers' wives placed their orders in the grocery shops without paying for them, because they were accompanied by a brave man with a revolver. In broad daylight on the outskirts of the city and even in the centre, small shops were looted and goods were taken under the threat of guns."

Trouble arose among the strikers when the UGT accepted arbitration by the Minister of Labour, while the CNT decided to continue. The anarchists accused the communists and socialists of being "strikebreakers". Revolts broke out between the two sides. On 9 July five people were killed at the gates of the workplaces, three from the CNT and two from the UGT. In this atmosphere, the CNT machine-gunned a café that served as the Falange's headquarters and three Falangists were killed. The conflict between the UGT and the CNT was repeated at the same time in Malaga, where on 10 July the anarchists assassinated the communist Andrés Rodríguez, head of the UGT. The response was an attack on Ortiz Acevedo, a Cenetista leader, but the dead was one of his sons. On the 11th, before the funeral of the communist Rodríguez, the socialist Ramón Reina was assassinated. The violence continued until the 15th and the governor ordered the closure of the premises of the two workers' centres.

The assassination of Calvo Sotelo

The elimination on 13 July 1936 of José Calvo Sotelo, leader of the parliamentary opposition, was a scandalous and extremely serious act, as it was a provocation behind which the Socialist Party was behind. Some versions attempt to falsify history and justify the event as revenge for the assassination on the 12th, in reality only five hours earlier, of Lieutenant José del Castillo, a Freemason who trained the illegal militias of the Socialist

Youth. This is an inadmissible interpretation. María Moliner's *Diccionario de uso del español* offers this definition of vengar: "To cause harm to a person in response to another (daño) or to a grievance received from them". Those who killed Calvo Sotelo had not received any harm from him. The assassination of Lieutenant Castillo, on the other hand, could be described as revenge, since his men had killed Andrés Sáenz de Heredia, a cousin of the founder of the Falange. Lieutenant Castillo himself had personally seriously wounded José Llaguno Acha, a young Carlist militant. From then on Castillo was in the crosshairs of both Carlists and Falangists. Hence the discrepancies over who his assassins were. According to Paul Preston, he was killed by the Falangists, but Ian Gibson points to members of the Madrid Tercio de Requetés as the perpetrators. It is not valid, therefore, to argue that the lieutenant's comrades took revenge on an innocent person who had nothing to do with the aforementioned events. In reality, taking advantage of the situation, the assassins were used. Lieutenant Castillo, Andrés Saénz de Heredia and José Llaguno were pawns who sacrificed themselves among themselves; but José Calvo Sotelo was one of the rooks that the right wing had in the game being played in Spain, which could only be knocked down with the support of other important pieces.

It is not only for his tragic death that José Calvo Sotelo deserves to be remembered. While still very young, he proved his worth and his status as a statesman. In 1924, for example, he drew up a Municipal Statute which, in the opinion of Professor Alfonso Bullón, author of the work *José Calvo Sotelo*, "is the freest rule of government that the municipalities have had in Spain, the one that has given them the most powers, in which women's suffrage was contemplated for the first time". Minister of Finance in 1925 at the age of only 32, he was the author of an attempt at tax reform that contemplated progressive taxation. His policy was aimed at combating tax fraud and trying to ensure that the privileged were taxed according to their assets, which earned him the enmity of the most immobilist sectors, who called him "the Bolshevik minister". A reaction against him forced him to desist and to denounce "the obstinate quietism of the conservative classes". Calvo Sotelo promoted specialised public banking and under his mandate the Banco de Crédito Local was created. He also created the Banco Exterior de España and promoted a major reform of the Banco Hipotecario and the Banco de Crédito Industrial. A measure of great interest that made him powerful enemies abroad was the creation of the oil monopoly CAMPSA (Compañía Arrendataria del Monopolio de Petróleos S. A.), which provoked a confrontation between the regime and the big oil companies. These international trusts were trying to take over the oil monopoly in Europe and could in no way accept an oil monopoly in Spain. In the fall of Primo de Rivera, the Anglo-Dutch company Royal Dutch-Shell played an important role. Henri Deterding, director of the trust, met with the dictator and with Calvo Sotelo himself, to whom he warned: "There you are, the monopoly may be born, it will live for one or two years, because there will be no lack of supplies; but afterwards there will be no one to supply you". In *Política económica de la Dictadura, a* work from which some of the above information is taken, Professor Juan Velarde considers that Calvo Sotelo was a magnificent Finance Minister.

On 15 April 1931, José Calvo Sotelo went into exile in Portugal; but he was elected for Orense in the June elections. He hoped that with his deputy's seat he would be able to return to Spain without the danger of being imprisoned, as had been the case with the PRI ministers who had not left the country. When he learned that he would not be able to take his seat, but would instead go to prison, he decided to remain in exile. In September 1933 Calvo Sotelo was elected a member of the Tribunal of Constitutional Guarantees by the Bar Associations, but again he was not allowed to return. He was unable to participate personally in the November 1933 elections, but he sent a recording which was broadcast at the event at the Royalty cinema in Madrid and could be heard on the radio throughout Spain: "Spaniards, Madrileños! - said Calvo Sotelo, "listen to the distant voice of an exiled compatriot, whom the same people who deny Spain its honour, its history and its faith are trying to deny all political rights. Far from you geographically, but close to you spiritually, I am a poor exile, despite the suffrage twice favourable, twice withheld. To build a people you need centuries and heroes, to undo it you only need two years and any monster at the helm". Calvo Sotelo was again elected to parliament, but before returning he had to wait a few more months before he could take advantage of an amnesty.

The first thing he did on arriving in Madrid on 4 May 1934 was to visit his father. After the February 1936 elections, Calvo Sotelo again had to fight bitterly for the deputy's seat he had won to be handed over to him, as the notorious Minutes Commission tried to steal it. In protest at the arbitrariness of the Commission, the right-wing deputies decided to abandon it in order not to legitimise it with their presence; but he appeared in the Cortes to defend his seat, and did so with such brilliance that the Republicans did not dare to annul it, despite the protests of the Socialists and Communists. Finally, in the early hours of 3 April, Calvo Sotelo won his seat "and with it - in the words of Professor Bullón - his passport to death". In fact, several Popular Front deputies had threatened him on several occasions before he was assassinated.

Chaos was the word repeatedly used by European journalists reporting on the Spanish situation; but, because of the press censorship imposed by the government, Spaniards were not informed of what was going on. It was only through the denunciations of Calvo Sotelo and Gil Robles that the figures of the disastrous reality were known, because censorship could not be exercised over the speeches of the deputies. It was in the session of 16 June 1936 that both Gil Robles and Calvo Sotelo denounced the misrule that prevailed and provided new data. According to the former, between 16 February and 15 June there had been 113 general strikes and 228 partial strikes in Spain; 160 churches had been destroyed and 251 fires had been put out in religious buildings. Gil Robles gave a figure of 269 dead and 1,287 wounded; but the historian Juan Blázquez today offers verified figures with names and surnames that put the number of people killed and wounded during the five months of the Popular Front at 454 and 1,638, respectively.

Calvo Sotelo stressed the government's obligation to ensure public order and denounced its bias in enforcing the law. He accused certain parties of encouraging violence with "senseless propaganda" and specifically quoted Largo Caballero, who two days earlier had declared in a speech that the policy of the Popular Front was only admissible for them as long as it served the programme of the October revolution. This was followed by Dolores Ibárruri, who called for the imprisonment of those who opposed the revolutionary policies and "those who with unparalleled cynicism, full of blood from the October repression, come to demand responsibility". It was in the context of the replies that Pasionaria, without having a turn to speak, shouted: "This is your last speech", words that are not recorded in the session diary, but which have been ratified by numerous attendees.

Worse were the words uttered against Calvo Sotelo in the parliamentary session of 1 July. Ángel Galarza, a Freemason socialist who frequented the Luis Simarro lodge in Madrid, raised the tone of Pasionaria's threat and said exactly the following: "Thinking of his lordship, I find everything justified, including the attack that will deprive him of his life". It should be borne in mind that the person justifying the assassination of a member of parliament was no insignificant character, but a specialist in criminal law who had been state prosecutor general. Later, as minister of Gobernación, Galarza was to become one of the main perpetrators of the Paracuellos massacres. Unsurprisingly, this unspeakable threat unleashed a scandal, during which Dolores Ibárruri was heard to say: "They have to be dragged in". Martínez Barrio intervened to say that the deputy's words would not appear in the journal of sessions; but Ángel Galarza replied: "These words, which will not appear in the journal of sessions, will be known to the country and will tell us all whether or not violence is legitimate".

After this blatant display of lack of principle and infamous legitimisation of assassination and violence in general, it seems clear that those who sought to take Calvo Sotelo's life were not just any pawns. An author as unsuspicious of right-wing sympathies as Gerald Brenan writes: "There was only one possibility of Largo Caballero taking power, and that was that the military would rise up, that the Government would give arms to the people to put down the uprising, and that the people would win the struggle. Consciously or unconsciously he and his party were calculating their game on the possibility of a military insurrection". In other words, with the assassination of Calvo Sotelo the PSOE capitols intended to provoke the military uprising and take advantage of it to seize power. If Brenan's assessment is correct, it would be once again the strategy of civil war, repeatedly proclaimed by Trotsky and Lenin as the ideal means of getting rid of class enemies.

A series of facts show that the material assassins of Calvo Sotelo were merely the executors of a plan that had been considered from higher up. At the end of June, the Director General of Security, José Alonso Mallol, master of ceremonies of the Constante Alona lodge that had outlawed the Falange and ordered the arrest of José Antonio Primo de Rivera, ordered the two policemen who were Calvo Sotelo's bodyguards to be changed. On 29 June Rodolfo Serrano de la Parte, a friend of Casares Quiroga, and a Freemason named José Garriga Pato were appointed new bodyguards. Days later, they received instructions from the head of personnel of the General Directorate of Security, Lorenzo Aguirre Sánchez, who ordered them to simulate protection in the event of an attack on Calvo Sotelo if it took place in a central location, but to finish it off if it took place in an unfrequented place, in the event that the attack failed. From all this it can be inferred that the idea of killing Cavo Sotelo existed before the assassination of Lieutenant Castillo. This was confirmed by the Freemason Urbano Orad de la Torre, the military officer who directed the bombing of the Cuartel de la Montaña after 18 July, who in September 1978 confessed to *El País* that Freemasonry had taken the decision to assassinate Calvo Sotelo on 9 May 1936.

The policeman Rodolfo Serrano was repulsed by the order received and made contact in the corridors of Parliament with the Carlist deputy Joaquín Bau Nolla, a close friend of Calvo Sotelo. Serrano had access to Congress as a bodyguard. The deputy summoned the policeman to a café in Calle Alcalá, where Serrano specified his information. After telling Calvo Sotelo what he knew, Bau visited the Minister of the Interior, Juan Moles Ormellla, who was also a Freemason, and told him what he had found out without mentioning the source of the information. On the morning of 8 July, Calvo Sotelo and Bau visited Minister Moles together, who did not pay much attention to them, so Calvo Sotelo, who managed to get a new escort assigned to him, made him responsible for whatever might happen to him.

Lieutenant Castillo was assassinated at half past nine on the night of the 12th. In *La Masonería en la España del siglo* XX, a work coordinated by J. A. Ferrer Benimeli, it is confirmed that the game was played by Freemasons, since, in addition to Lieutenant Castillo, there were: Juan Moles Ormella, Minister of the Interior, and José Alonso Mallol, Director General of Security. Lorenzo Aguirre Sánchez, chief of staff of the Directorate General of Security, had applied to join the Freemasons and after the outbreak of the war joined the Communist Party. The aforementioned work reports on the meeting of a dozen officers of the Assault Forces, where there was talk of taking revenge without stating what it was to consist of. Mallol was present for about a quarter of an hour, listening without saying a word.

Everything suggests that Mallol contacted the Minister of the Interior, Moles Ormella, who authorised arrests at the homes of prominent right-wingers.

At around two o'clock in the morning on the 13th, several vans with assault guards and PSOE militants with lists of Falange activists left the Pontejos barracks. The last van, number 17, was not commanded by an Assault officer, but by a captain of the Guardia Civil, Fernando Condés Romero, another Freemason who was the head of La Motorizada, the name of an armed group of Socialists who acted as an escort for Indalecio Prieto. This van was the one that drove to Calvo Sotelo's home in Calle Velázquez. It was later revealed that another van had gone to Gil Robles' house, but they did not find him because he was in France. After identifying themselves to the guards in charge of the night watch, Condés and several men went up to the house.

It was half past two in the morning. The family was startled awake by the ringing of the doorbell and voices demanding that the police open the door. After entering the house, Captain Condés, who was in civilian clothes, said that he had to search the house and immediately announced to Calvo Sotelo that the Directorate General of Security had ordered his arrest. Calvo Sotelo tried to make a phone call to find out who had given the order, but Condés would not allow it. It was of no use for the head of the National Bloc to argue that he had parliamentary immunity. He was promised that he would be able to plead his case at the Directorate General, so he finally agreed to leave his home. His wife repeatedly asked him not to leave. Before leaving, Calvo Sotelo, who suspected the worst, told her: "in five minutes I will call you from the Directorate General of Security if these gentlemen don't take me away and shoot me four times". About twenty people took part in the arrest, half of whom did not belong to the Assault Guard. Among the socialists who accompanied Condés were Santiago Garcés and Francisco Ordóñez, who held positions of great responsibility during the war, and José del Rey Hernández, who had been reinstated in the corps after his expulsion for having taken part in the uprising of October 1934. Del Rey was one of the bodyguards of the socialist Margarita Nelken.

The account of what happened in van number 17 comes from an eyewitness, the assault guard Aniceto Castro Piñeiro, who was on duty at the Pontejos barracks when at midnight he saw Captain Fernando Condés arrive in civilian clothes along with several of Indalecio Prieto's regular bodyguards. This guard went in the vehicle, but did not go up to the house. According to his version, Captain Condés and José del Rey sat in the front next to the driver, Orencio Bayo. Calvo Sotelo was on the third bench between Aniceto Castro and another guard. The assassin, Victoriano Cuenca, another socialist who was Indalecio Prieto's bodyguard, sat behind him and when they reached the junction of Ayala and Velázquez streets, he took a pistol and shot him twice in the back of the head. Calvo Sotelo fell face first between the seats. Nobody said anything and those in front didn't bother to look back. The van continued on to the East Cemetery, where the employees were ordered to open the gates. Once inside the cemetery, they left the body on the ground, in a place near the morgue. On the way back, the driver, worried about what the employees on duty at the cemetery had seen, said: "I suppose they won't give us away", to which Condés replied: "Don't worry, nothing will happen". José del Rey added: "Whoever says anything commits suicide, we'll kill him like that dog".

Hours before the murder was made public, the socialist media were well aware of what had happened. At eight o'clock in the morning, the gunman Victoriano Cuenca spoke to Julián Zugazagoitia, "Zuga", a PSOE deputy and editor of *El Socialista*, whom he informed of what had happened. Captain Condés, for his part, contacted the socialist deputy Juan -Simeón Vidarte and informed him of the crime that had been committed. Instead of doing their duty and denouncing the facts to the authorities, the socialists remained silent and complicit. Vidarte advised Condés to find a place to hide and he did so at the home of the socialist deputy Margarita Nelken.

The Government refused permission to install Calvo Sotelo's funeral chapel in the Academy of Jurisprudence, of which he was president, so the burial was held directly in the cemetery where the body had been laid to rest. At five o'clock in the afternoon, the coffin, accompanied by a crowd of people and right-wing personalities, was buried. Before the crowd, Antonio Goicoechea, one of the leaders of Renovación Española, spoke a few words for history: "Before this flag placed like a cross on your chest, before God who hears and sees us, we take a solemn oath to consecrate our lives to this triple task: to imitate your example, avenge your death and save Spain, which are all one and the same, because saving Spain will be avenging your death and imitating your example will be the surest way to save Spain". No member of the government had the decency to attend the funeral ceremony. After the funeral, some of those present tried to demonstrate, but were broken up by gunfire from the Assault Guards, who killed five people and wounded some thirty.

Martínez Barrio suspended the scheduled session of the Cortes on the 14th. On the 15th a meeting of the Standing Committee was held and the right wing expressed its desire to leave Parliament. Indalecio Prieto, who knew the truth from the first moment, limited himself to describing the events as "an outrage by the security forces". However, the assassination of the leader of the opposition by members of the PSOE, the most important of the parties that made up the Popular Front, was unthinkable in any democratic regime. The use of public force to protect criminals made what had happened even more unacceptable. Instead of taking measures against the socialist organisations, the government proceeded to close the headquarters of Renovación Española, that is, the headquarters of the party in which the victim was a member. The discredit of the Republic, which had generated so many illusions and expectations among Spaniards, had reached its peak. The enquiries into the assassination of Calvo Sotelo inevitably led to the arrest of Captain Condés, identified by his widow in a photograph; but on 25 July members of the Socialist youth movement turned up at the Supreme Court and took the case papers.

Failed coup

It is well known that the assassination of Calvo Sotelo was the trigger, the spark that ignited the fire that burnt Spain for almost three years. It is true that the plans for the uprising had existed beforehand, but that crime precipitated everything. Perhaps it was this precipitation that led to the initial failure and, consequently, to civil war. The military insurrection that Largo Caballero wanted in order to seize power had taken place and, moreover, as the Spanish Lenin had foreseen, it was going to unleash the workers' revolution. It was therefore a question of taking advantage of it to defeat the rebels and impose the dictatorship of the proletariat so often announced. After the initial failure of the military uprising, everything was in favour of the republican leaders to put down the rebellion in a short time, which would facilitate a thorough purge of the army and civil society. However, disorganisation, the inability to coordinate the heterogeneous forces that made up the Popular Front and, in short, infighting, once again led to chaos, which took the form of a dual power in Republican Spain. During the first few weeks, the Republican government, which had been waiting for the coup, had a quick victory within its grasp. If it had been able to act swiftly and in a coordinated manner, the military uprising would have been short-lived: most of the generals, the air force and the Guardia de Asalto had remained loyal. The fleet remained in the hands of the government after the rebels' initial failure. The industrial resources were theirs, and the Banco de España's gold reserves, the fourth largest in the world, were available as a guarantee for managing the economic costs of the war.

Casares Quiroga's first measure was to resign as president of the government. Immediately, in the early hours of 18-19 July, Azaña asked Martínez Barrio to try to form a government that would ensure the loyalty of the military leadership and avoid civil war. This was the so-called "lightning government", composed only of Republican ministers, which, in the face of the hostility of the Socialists and Communists, who demanded arms to fight the military, collapsed within a few hours and did not even take office. On 19 July, José Giral Pereira, the third Masonic president in less than twenty-four hours, managed to form the government without the participation of the Socialists; but under pressure from the trade unions and left-wing parties, he decided to distribute arms to the workers' militias and decreed the dissolution of the army and the police in order to proceed on 4 August with the creation of the "volunteer battalions". Thus, according to the Marxist historians P. Broué and E. Témime in *La revolución y la guerra de España*, "legality vanished in the face of the clash of social forces". This government was to last until 4 September 1936, when Largo Caballero finally became President.

Nationalist historiographers confirm that by the evening of 20 July General Mola, "the director", saw the rebels' cause as lost, and that if it continued it was because of the drive of the requetés and the Falangists, whose determination to fight was unstoppable. The pessimism was justified if one considers the situation. The army from Africa, which was due to land en masse in the hours after the coup, could not cross the strait, as the seamen and NCOs had shot the rebel commanders and officers, and the ships that were to transport Franco's men to the mainland had been placed under government control. In Andalusia, where the strength of the trade unions and the left-wing parties was overwhelming, Queipo de Llano had momentarily gained control of Seville with 180 men, which was almost a miracle; but his chances of holding on were very slim without help. In the most important regions, the most industrial, where commerce and most of the population and resources were concentrated, the uprising had been crushed: Madrid, Asturias, Cantabria, the Basque Country, Catalonia, Valencia and the entire eastern coast had been lost. The insurgent forces had been cut in two and their chances of contact were nil, as the fleet anchored in Tangiers dominated the Strait and prevented the arrival of reinforcements from the Moroccan army. To top off the disastrous situation for the rebels, General Sanjurjo, who according to plans was to be the head of state if the coup succeeded, died on 20 July in Portugal when the plane that was to take him to Burgos crashed on take-off. The government therefore had the best pieces in its hands to win the game.

The coup leaders' chances of survival were decided between 18 and 25 July. This was acknowledged by the Nationalist leaders to Harold Cardozo, the correspondent of the *Daily Mail,* a British newspaper that supported the Nationalists. Cardozo published *The March of a Nation* in 1937, in which he recounts his experiences as a journalist during the first year of the civil war. Three facts were considered vital to keep the uprising alive: the control of the Ferrol naval base, railway communications in the rebel territory, the possession of Seville and the ports of Cadiz and Algeciras. The fact that General Mola was able to retain the Ferrol base was vital for the rebels. Vice-Admiral Indalecio Núñez Quijano supported the uprising after initial doubts, so he was dismissed and replaced by Rear-Admiral Antonio Azarola, second in command at the base, who had been Minister of the Navy under Portela Valladares. After the triumph, the mutineers court-martialled him and shot him for opening the arsenal to the "Marxist masses".

The fighting at the base and in the city was extremely hard, to the point that the city changed hands half a dozen times. Multiple battles broke out in the surrounding area and in the centre of Ferrol between loyalists and Falangist and Carlist volunteers. Inside the base the confusion was even greater. On both the cruiser *Almirante Cervera*, which was in dry dock, and the battleship *España*, the crews engaged in fighting inside the ships. On the third major ship, the destroyer *Velasco*, its crew did not mutiny: some 30 were shot after the rebels won victory. The Nationalists finally seized the base. Franco thus had a nucleus of the Navy that helped lift the blockade of the Strait of Gibraltar and participated from the sea in the bombardment of Irún, whose capture at the end of August was essential to cut off the connection with France for the northern provinces.

The operation of the railway lines in the provinces where the conspiracy had triumphed was crucial for Mola. The general strike called by the trade unions was being massively followed by the workers and the trains were at a standstill. Key to keeping the rebel forces operational was securing the transport of fuel from Vigo and Ferrol to Burgos, Pamplona and other rebel capitals, the easternmost of which were Huesca, Zaragoza and Teruel. General Mola signed a decree threatening those who did not immediately return to work with the death penalty under martial law. His second measure was to set up a technical committee of railway engineers, to which he gave military power and rank. Simultaneously, throughout the territory under Nationalist control, the Guardia Civil was given the task of getting the workers out of their homes and ordering them to return to work without delay. The measure was effective and within twenty-four hours long trains with petrol tanks were running throughout the area controlled by General Mola.

As for how Queipo de Llano took Seville, "la Roja", and the ports of Algeciras and Cadiz, Harold Cardozo gave the version of the protagonists, whom he interviewed days later to send his chronicle to *the Daily Mail*. According to this correspondent, Queipo, who had 180 soldiers under his command, captured the Maestranza de Artillería to control the weapons, ordered the strategic points to be occupied and succeeded in intimidating the Sevillian population. In response to the call for a general strike, numerous armed communist and anarchist workers had erected barricades and set fire to churches and noble houses. Queipo's bluff could only be maintained for a short time, so the arrival of the army from Africa was vital. Soon messages were received from Cadiz and elsewhere about concentrations of armed syndicalists. From the suburbs of Seville and from Cadiz, the Guardia Civil telephoned for help, as they were being harassed.

When Queipo learned that the uprising in the fleet had failed and that the ships that were to bring Franco's troops were patrolling the Strait of Gibraltar, he continuously moved his garrison to make it appear that he had more troops than he really did and placed machine guns at key points. Cardozo recounts that it was dawn when Franco was able to send a plane to Seville with eleven legionnaires under the command of Captain Luis Meléndez. As soon as he got off the plane, the captain mounted the machine gun he had brought with him in the cab of a large six-wheeled truck, ordered his men to get in and headed for the Captaincy. There he was told the districts where the Reds were. He asked for a map and drove at high speed towards the concentration points. The vehicle became a whirlwind of fire going from one place to another, firing on the concentrations of trade unionists. Several times the colour of the truck was changed, giving the impression that there were many attackers. Word began to spread that the Legion had arrived and the armed men disappeared from the streets. The Guardia Civil and the Assault Police, taking advantage of the panic created, seized large quantities of arms and ammunition from the trade union headquarters, which were distributed among the Requesetes and Falangist volunteers. Three of the legionnaires were killed and two were badly wounded. Meléndez was also wounded in the left hand. A few more planes landed before nightfall. In successive days, about 100 soldiers arrived daily and the position of the rebels in western Andalusia was strengthened, although the triumph of the uprising was consolidated in successive days at Granada as well. As is well known, ruthless repression began there immediately, which will be discussed at the end of this chapter.

The revolution

As Spain was divided by the outcome of the coup, state power in the provinces where the uprising had been defeated shifted to the street. Burnett Bolloten details in *The Great Deception. The Left and its Struggle for Power in the Republican Zone* to what extent the revolutionary forces wrested all the levers of authority from the state. The control of ports and frontiers, usually in the hands of carabinieri, guards and customs officers, was taken over by workers' committees. In the navy, seventy per cent of the officers were executed by their own men and authority was left in the hands of seamen's committees. In various areas of the state administration, committees led by anarcho-syndicalists and socialists were also imposed. The courts of justice were replaced by revolutionary courts, and in many places the court archives were burned. Prisons and penitentiaries were raided and prisoners were set free. Because of all this, it can be said that the Government, presided over by Giral, possessed only nominal power, since real and effective power was divided into multiple fragments and scattered in cities and towns where the revolutionary committees exercised control. Essential services such as post and telegraphs, radio stations, telephone exchanges came under the control of workers' committees. UGT and CNT workers began to expropriate and collectivise. Notarial archives were destroyed in many places. Means of transport: railways, trams, buses, ships; water, electricity and gas services; factories, industries and mines; cinemas and theatres; newspapers and printing presses; hotels, bars and restaurants, etc. were seized or controlled by workers' committees.

The petty bourgeoisie was not spared the cataclysm caused by the revolution: shopkeepers, artisans and small manufacturers were also expropriated by the anarcho-syndicalists of the CNT and often the UGT. In Madrid the trade unions took over the premises and tools of carpenters and shoemakers, collectivised hairdressers and beauty salons and established equal pay for owners and employees. In Barcelona the reorganisation of barbershops and hairdressers was even more drastic. In *The Spanish Civil War: Revolution and Counterrevolution, an* impressive twelve hundred page work covering a three-year period, Burnett Bolloten writes that "nine hundred and five hairdressers and barbershops were closed and their staff and equipment concentrated in two hundred and twelve larger establishments, where the expropriated owners worked with the same rights and duties as their former employees." The anarcho-syndicalists collectivised the wholesale fish and egg trade. In the slaughterhouse they imposed a control committee which cut out the middlemen. The dairy industry was collectivised and also the central fruit and vegetable market. It can be said that the trade unions interfered in almost all the usually bourgeois areas. Some members of the middle class, fearing that they would lose control of their businesses for good, accepted the new situation in one way or another in the hope that they would be able to regain their property once the revolutionary earthquake had passed. Bolloten defines the frustration of the middle classes in these words: "The middle class had not made projects and saved for years, had not struggled to survive the competition of big business, to see their hopes of independence ruined in a single day. If they had expected anything from the revolution, it would have been freedom from competition and a larger share in the wealth of the country, but not expropriation and a worker's wage". In the countryside, too, the tenant farmers and humble landlords felt the same discouragement as the small manufacturers and shopkeepers.

Catalonia, spearhead of the revolution

It was in these circumstances that the Communist Party, despite its small representation in the Cortes and its small membership, succeeded in arousing the sympathies and hopes of the middle classes in only a few months. In both town and country, thousands of petty bourgeois came under its protection without ever joining the party. The communist penetration of Spain had been the object of special attention of the International (Comintern) at a session on 27 February 1936. One of the main measures adopted for this purpose was the dispatch to Spain of two Jewish communists, Bela Kun and Solomon Abramovitch Losovsky. We have already written a great deal about the former. The latter was a leader of the Red International Trade Union and a member of the Jewish Anti-Fascist Committee. Salomon Losovsky was one of the Zionists who lobbied

Roosevelt to enter the war. Eventually, as will be seen, he was executed by Stalin in 1952. In March these two men arrived in Barcelona in the company of Heinz Neumann, another Jew who, accused of Trotskyism, was also liquidated by Stalin in 1937. Their mission was to prepare the creation of a revolutionary military committee and the formation of cells that were to serve as the basis of the future Red Army. The fruit of his work was to be reaped half a year later, when with the arrival of Moses Rosenberg, the Soviet ambassador of Jewish origin sent by Stalin, the PCE became decisive. Before this was possible, the libertarian revolution had to make way.

When, on 19 July, a combination of civil guards, storm troopers and workers of all persuasions defeated the military coup plotters, the revolution began in Barcelona. Generals Goded, Fernández Burriel and other high-ranking military officers were shot on 12 August in front of some five hundred people who shouted "Long live the Republic!"; but by then power and justice were already revolutionary and in Catalonia there was no authority other than that of the various committees that had sprung up all over the country, whose highest expression would be the Central Committee of the Anti-Fascist Militias of Catalonia, set up a few days later. On the afternoon of 20 July, Juan García Oliver, Buenaventura Durruti and other anarchist leaders went to the palace of the Generalitat with weapons in hand and without having slept for two days. The president of Catalonia, as Juan García Oliver wrote in *Dans la tourmente. Un an de guerre en Espagne*, told them: "You have won and everything is in your power. If you have no need of me, if you do not want me as president, say so now and I will become one more soldier in the anti-fascist struggle". According to Miquel Serra Pàmies, Companys was given to theatrical scenes: "They gave him fits, he pulled his hair, threw things, took off his jacket, tore his tie, opened his shirt". However, during those days he was very prudent and his government accepted all the decisions of the Anti-Fascist Militia Committee. Later, Companys addressed the Catalans on the radio and announced that the government would "impose discipline with the collaboration and help of the workers' organisations and the anti-fascist political parties with which it had reached an agreement." From then on, he limited himself to doing nothing that could alter the disturbing revolutionary order.

In *Why We Lost the War*, FAI leader Diego Abad de Santillán acknowledges that they opted to keep a puppet president: "We could have stayed alone, imposed our absolute will, declared the Generalitat defunct and put the real power of the people in its place". In reality, their intention was to gradually liquidate the Republicans in Catalonia and Aragon. If they kept Companys, it was out of prudence, because they were momentarily interested in the presence of the petty bourgeoisie in the new revolutionary organs of power until the fall of Saragossa. In this way, Esquerra Republicana placed three delegates on the Central Committee, the rabassaires, one, and Acció Catalana, another. The POUM (Andreu Nin's Trotskyite party) and the

PSUC (the Catalan Stalinist Communists) had one representative each. Santillán and Aurelio Fernández were both members of the FAI. For the CNT, García Oliver, Durruti and Asens were members of the Central Committee. The UGT also had three representatives. Thus, although the Generalitat continued to exist, the real government of Catalonia was this Central Committee, the only effective power. In his radio address Companys had promised that he would "impose discipline". Since his party was part of the Committee, he should therefore be held responsible for the "revolutionary discipline" that was imposed on the population.

In application of the revolutionary order, most of the churches in Catalonia were burnt down during the first few days. In Barcelona, on the afternoon of the 19th, the magnificent church of Santa Maria del Mar was burnt, followed by the Gothic church of Santa Anna, Santa Maria del Pi, La Merced and the Baroque church of Belen. It can be said that, except for the cathedral, which was saved thanks to the intervention of the Generalitat, all the churches in the city were burnt down. The Christ that crowned the Tibidabo mountain was also demolished. There was also the more or less complete destruction of convents, monasteries, seminaries, publishing houses, bookshops and the headquarters of conservative parties. The same thing happened all over Catalonia, with the exception of Tarragona Cathedral. In Vic, one of the most traditional Catalan cities, at least forty churches and religious buildings were burned, including the cathedral. In Sitges, in Sabadell, in Puigcerdà all the churches were destroyed. The methods of destruction were similar everywhere: cars or lorries driven by revolutionaries went from place to place, killed the parish priest or the priest if they found him, poured petrol all over the building and set fire to it. If anyone dared to object or protest, they were usually shot on the spot. On 22 July 1936 *La Vanguardia* published a decree issued by President Companys stressing the importance of "completing the annihilation of the fascist nuclei throughout Catalonia". Already in 1931 Azaña had expressed how little these acts of vandalism mattered: "All the convents in Madrid are not worth the life of a Republican".

The destruction was accompanied by all sorts of barbarities. The arsonists and the spectators who encouraged them often staged shameful displays of jubilation. They amused themselves by dressing up statues of Christ and the Virgin Mary in militia costumes or adorned themselves in sacred garb. Desecration of tombs and niches in the floors of many churches was a constant. The mummified bodies of nuns and friars were removed. Among other macabre obscenities, skulls were played football with. A dozen skeletons of nuns and friars were placed on the steps of the Carmelite church and left exposed in front of the church doors, some standing, some reclining. Professor Allison Peers, who, as has already been said, deeply admired Catalonia and the Catalans, recounts with restrained rage in *Catalonia Infelix* the murder of friends, scholars like himself of a culture to which they had devoted part of their lives. Among them he remembers the bishops of Lérida and Barcelona. He especially deplores the murder of the director of the Montserrat choir, a man of eighty-two, an eminent musician, a specialist in patristics, who was unable to escape to Italy with other members of the community.

The violence in Catalonia during the first two months following the uprising shocked locals and strangers alike. Although official spokesmen declared that everything was normal and that the authorities were in complete control, for two long months the reign of terror was everywhere. Workers roamed the streets all day with rifles and pistols. Thanks to the seizure of the barracks, weapons were issued to all those who wanted them. Tens of thousands of rifles were distributed in Barcelona, Madrid, Malaga and the cities where the coup had failed. Political and common prisoners found themselves on the streets and with guns in their hands as soon as they were released. Broué and Témime speak of "a spontaneous movement, a real 'mass terrorism' in terms of both the number of executioners and the number of victims". These authors, in accordance with the Marxist argument that only the proletariat is the people, consider that power "had passed to the people" and on this basis ideologically justify the violence, i.e. "the immediate liquidation without trial of the class enemies branded as 'fascists' in those circumstances". In this way all kinds of "fascists" were killed on the spot if there was no militant with authority to prevent it. Here is an excerpt from the work of these Trotskyist authors:

> "The ride almost always unfolded according to the same sinister plot. The victim, designated by a 'vigilance' or 'defence' committee of a party or a trade union, was arrested in his house at night by armed men, taken by car outside the town and dumped in an isolated corner. In this way perished, victims of real arrangements of political accounts, priests, bosses, small and big, political men, bourgeois or reactionaries, all those who, at one time or another, disputed with a workers' organisation: judges, policemen, prison guards, informers, tormentors, gunmen, or, more simply, all those whom a political reputation or a social situation marked out in advance as victims. The 'class frontier', moreover, was not always sufficient protection: thus, in Barcelona, workers' militants were also assassinated: the secretary of the UGT dock workers, the communist Desiderio Trillas, denounced by the CNT as a 'cacique of the docks', the head of the UGT section of the Hispano-Suiza factory".

This text confirms that mafia thuggery existed: personal vendettas, looting and unmitigated murder were legitimised in the name of the revolutionary order imposed on the entire population. G. Brenan points out that Juan Peiró, secretary general of the CNT in two periods and Spanish Minister of Industry from November 1936 to May 1937, denounced the excesses in *Llibertat*, the newspaper he edited, from which he called for the need to organise repression. "In the name of honour revolutionary", Peiró demanded an end to the "macabre dance of every night" and described those who "kill for the sake of killing" as "modern vampires", "fascists in a latent state".

On 1 August the *Times* correspondent wrote: "Behind the surface there lurks in Barcelona the terrible story of the searches of houses by purification squads, the abduction of individuals and whole families and their subsequent murders in lonely places, the murder of nuns and priests". An insightful and intelligent witness to the revolution was Franz Borkenau, an Austrian of Jewish origin who had been a member of the German Communist Party and an agent of the Comintern, who entered Catalonia via Port Bou on 5 August[22]. In *El reñidero español* Borkenau published his "Diario revolucionario" (Revolutionary Diary), in which he recorded the impression he got when he arrived in Barcelona at night, with the streets taken over by armed men, many of whom were walking with a girl on their left arm: "Few people on the Passeig de Colón. And then, as we turned the corner of Las Ramblas, a tremendous surprise arose: before our eyes, like a flash of lightning, the revolution unfolded. It was overwhelming. As if we had entered a different continent...". Once the first shock had worn off, Borkenau realised that on the street the militiamen could arrest anyone and demand that he prove he was not a fascist if he did not want to be arrested or even executed. Carrying right-wing books, conservative newspapers or proof of having been to Italy or Germany could have dire consequences. Impartial observers put the number of dead found in the streets every dawn at around a hundred. The socialist Clara Campoamor wrote in *La revolución española vista por una republicana* that the bodies were taken to the Hospital Clínico, which served as the city morgue. Campoamor put the number of corpses collected in fifty-two days at six thousand. According to the *Times* correspondent, in the last week of July, a dozen or more bodies were found every day on the La Rabassada road alone.

As things stood in the rearguard, the response needed against the rebels was slow in coming. Perhaps, if action had been taken immediately, Zaragoza, whose possession was vital for maintaining communications between Madrid and Barcelona, could have been taken; but this was not achieved throughout the war. While in the Nationalist zone the trains ran almost immediately and order and discipline were imposed immediately, in

---

[22] Franz Borkenau, disillusioned with both communism and Marxism, turned to sociology. He made two trips to Spain. On the second he had problems with members of the PCE. In January 1937 he was suspected and denounced as a Trotskyite. Arrested and tortured, he was finally released. The work we are discussing was published in 1937, after his second trip, under the title *The Spanish Cockpit*. Gerald Brenan, author of the preface to the American edition, considers Borkenau's work to be "a model of what a study of a revolution should be and one of the best books ever published about Spain". Borkenau died in 1957.

the Red zone the strike lasted more than a week. Since there was no professional army, it became necessary to organise a militia. Almost from the very beginning, the divergent views between the communists of the PSUC, in favour of the "army system", and the anarchists, in favour of the "militia system", became apparent. The idea was to organise columns made up of CNT members and sympathisers, controlled by the anarchist organisations and led by elected political commissars. Within the columns, centurias of 100 men were formed. In order to march towards Saragossa, the Durruti Column of about three thousand militiamen was hastily organised and left Barcelona amid general enthusiasm on the morning of 24 July 1936. The only military officer by profession was the Freemason Enrique Pérez Farràs, commander of the Spanish Army who in 1931 had been appointed head of the Mozos de Escuadra by Macià, who showed his pessimism from the outset. In the following days the Central Committee formed other columns, but it was not an easy task, as partisan quarrels and rivalries over the possession of arms soon arose.

Borkenau writes very interesting pages about Durruti's march on his way to the Aragon front. On 10 August he obtained documents that allowed him to leave Barcelona in a car belonging to the Central Militia Committee, accompanied by a driver and an armed escort, in pursuit of the anarchist column. As he passed through the villages, he found that the churches had been burnt down without exception and that political committees were operating in them, imposing terror. This was a fact not only peculiar to Catalonia: in all the cities and towns of Spain, as has been said, committees of all kinds proliferated, operating under different names: popular war committees, public health committees, defence committees, executive committees, revolutionary or anti-fascist committees, workers' committees... Borkenau noted that the POUM was the strongest party in Lérida, which was due to the fact that Maurín, one of its leaders, was originally from this province. Once in Fraga, where Farràs's intervention helped them obtain a room and bed, Borkenau found out that Durruti had ordered the arrest of all those suspected of reactionary activities, who were taken to prison and shot. The villagers, mostly anarchists, told him in the tavern what had happened: "Making the significant gesture of crossing his throat with his fingers, one man tells us that thirty-eight fascists have been executed in the village; it is evident that they have enjoyed it immensely. They have killed neither women nor children, only the priest, his most active adherents, the lawyer and his son, the judge and a number of rich peasants". Borkenau adds that as a result of the massacre, the rich and the Catholics in the neighbouring village revolted, so a column of militiamen went there and executed another twenty-four people.

Durruti set up his War Committee in Bujaraloz, where he waited for the arrival of the *Red and Black* and *Karl Marx* columns before attacking Zaragoza. His delay only allowed the enemy to reinforce their positions.

Each passing day made it more difficult to take the city. In the end, neither the Durruti Column nor any other ever reached Zaragoza, so their most notable achievements were the collectivisations. On 11 August Durruti issued a proclamation in Bujaraloz that completely abolished property. All property without exception was to be distributed by two Committees, the War Committee and the People's Committee. In Sariñena, north of Bujaraloz, the regulars, including the notary, were executed as usual. In his house and in offices next to the square, the documents of rural property and other financial matters were kept. They were all burnt in a bonfire in the middle of the square so that no trace of the property rights remained. This symbolic act, which was repeated in other localities, signified the abolition of property and the liquidation of the previous social and economic order.

The collectivisation of land encouraged by Durruti and his column began with the slaughter of the big landowners. In many areas of Aragon libertarian communism was established and money was abolished. The collectivisations involved up to half a million people. There has been much debate about whether the rural collectivisation was voluntary or forced. Anarchists have been arguing that it was a voluntary collectivisation movement; however communists and republicans claim that in most cases it was imposed by force. Among neutral observers there are opinions to suit all tastes. Franz Borkenau considers that, except in La Mancha, collectivisation was imposed on the peasants by terror, despite the fact that the peasant trade union organisations of the UGT and the CNT had spoken out in favour of the voluntary nature of agrarian collectivisation. In any case, in Catalonia the rabassaires, many of whom had land thanks to the Law of Cultivation, opposed collectivisation head-on.

It was in those August days that a shocking massacre took place in Barbastro, near Sariñena, instigated by Durruti, who had gone to the town at the beginning of the month because of the mistaken shooting of three anarchists from Barcelona. Durruti, enraged by the death of the Catalans, reproached the local Committee, demanded that they put an end to the cassock and pointed the finger at the bishop. Recently, the facts have been made public thanks to the film *Un Dios prohibido (A forbidden God)*. It all began on 20 July, when the house of the Claretian Community of Barbastro was attacked by CNT militiamen. Sixty people lived there: nine priests, twelve brothers and thirty-nine students. The three superior fathers were taken away and shot on 2 August. The rest were transferred to the Pious Schools, where they were imprisoned along with nine Piarists and nineteen Benedictines. The jailers brought them prostitutes in order to provoke the apostasy of the young seminarians, who had been forbidden to pray. Meanwhile, the bishop, Monsignor Florentino Asensio, was arrested. Locked up on 8 August at in a cell in the Town Hall, he was cruelly tortured. He was savagely tortured: multiple wounds and amputations were inflicted to slowly bleed him dry. Amid mockery and laughter, they cut off his genitals. On 9 August, when he was executed with a group in the cemetery, he blessed those who shot him. On 12 August the six Claretian professors were shot. The seminarian Faustino Pérez left these words written on a chocolate wrapper: "Six of our companions are already martyrs. Soon we hope to be martyrs too. But first we want to state for the record that we die forgiving those who take our lives and offering them for the Christian ordination of the working world...". The rest were executed on 13, 15 and 18 August.

Along with the three superiors, a gypsy, Ceferino Giménez Malla, known as "El Pelé", died on 2 August, arrested for reprimanding some militiamen who were beating a priest with their butts. Since they found a rosary on him, he was taken to prison and condemned. He was offered to be spared if he gave up the rosary, but he refused. He died a consistent death with the rosary in his hand, shouting "Long live Christ the King". One can speak without exaggeration of the extermination of the clergy of Barbastro during the civil war, since eighty-eight percent of the priests were martyred. Lay believers did not escape the anticlerical hatred: about eight hundred died throughout the diocese for the simple fact of being Catholic. In all, twelve bishops and one apostolic administrator, 4,184 secular priests and seminarians, 2,365 religious and 296 nuns were killed during the Spanish civil war.

Companys had called for "the complete annihilation of the fascist nuclei throughout Catalonia". It is not known whether he considered Catholics to be among them, although for the anarchists it made no difference. On the other hand, there was only the justice imposed by the dynamics of the revolution, from which those who were not considered part of the "people" could expect little. The courts of justice were closed and the magistrates had been killed or had fled. In Barcelona, militiamen led by the Freemason lawyer Angel Samblancat ransacked the Palace of Justice and threw files and crucifixes out of the windows. A Justice Committee was set up, composed of left-wing lawyers, which dismissed all the officials and set itself up as a Revolutionary Tribunal. Judges, prosecutors and the president of the Tribunal were appointed by the parties and trade unions. At the very least, it was a step forward in the aim to abolish the practice of promenading.

The situation in Madrid

On 18 July Sebastián Pozas Perea, the Freemason general of the Civil Guard, ordered the immediate arrest of any soldier who left his post. Pozas, who spent the night in the Gobernación controlling the garrisons, was key to the failure of the coup. In the afternoon, Dolores Ibárruri, the Communist deputy for Asturias, addressed the people of Madrid and the whole of Spain on behalf of the PCE from a makeshift radio studio in the Ministry of the Interior, urging them to defend the Republic. Shortly afterwards the Casares

Quiroga government resigned. On the 19th the formation of Martínez Barrio's government became known and the word "treason" spread from mouth to mouth. Thousands of people in the streets demanded arms from the government.

At about half past twelve in the morning, General Joaquín Fanjul, accompanied by his son and Commander Mateo Castillo, arrived in civilian clothes at the Cuartel de la Montaña to take charge of the uprising in the capital. Instead of going out to take the key points, he made himself strong there while waiting for reinforcements to arrive from Burgos and Valladolid, as the rebellion failed in the garrisons of Campamento, Getafe and Cuatro Vientos. At dawn on the 20th the barracks began to be bombarded by aircraft and artillery. At around 11 a.m. the surrender took place. According to sources, the number of dead ranged from 500 to 900, many of whom were executed on the spot. General Fanjul, his son and Colonel Fernández de la Quintana were taken prisoner. On 18 August the general and the commander were shot. Fanjul's son, José Ignacio, was killed four days later in the Modelo prison by militiamen.

The first military campaign of the civil war took place in the Sierra de Guadarrama during the last week of July and early August. The coup generals initially thought that the capture of the capital would give them victory. General Mola tried to break through the mountain passes in order to fall on Madrid from the north, but failed due to the rapid reaction of the Popular Front troops: a combination of the disbanded military units, anarchist and communist militiamen, and civil guards and storm troopers. The rebels were unable to make any progress and the northern front in Madrid was stabilised until the end of the war. Both sides shot their prisoners. The fighting was fierce in the Altos del León and Somosierra, where thousands of combatants lost their lives, among them Fernando Condés and Victoriano Cuenca, two of Calvo Sotelo's assassins. The Falangist leader Onésimo Redondo also died on 24 July in the Segovian village of Labajos, where he was riddled with bullets by a group of anarchists after arriving by car, thinking that it was a nationalist zone.

The Giral government, formed after the short-lived "lightning government", showed its weakness from the outset. As in Catalonia, the division of powers made it inoperative, so Giral's role was similar to that of Companys. In Madrid, too, barracks and armouries were looted. Women and men with rifles on their shoulders took over the streets, although not as completely as in Barcelona. As everywhere else, prison doors were opened, allowing political and common prisoners to go free. The mobs began their rampage on 19 July. In the Torrijos neighbourhood, in front of the Dominican church, the faithful were shot at as they were leaving the church and several people were killed and wounded. Soon the dense smoke from the fires was rising into the sky in different parts of the capital: the churches of San Nicolás, San Cayetano, San Lorenzo, San Andrés and the Escuelas Pía de San Fernando were the first to burn. On the 20th the bonfires were rekindled and the cathedral of San Isidro ended up converted into a large brazier in which canvases and valuable works of art were consumed.

The worst, however, were again the cold-blooded killings in the streets. Every morning the bodies of people who had been taken from their homes were collected. The Aravaca cemetery, some ten kilometres from Madrid, became one of the executioners' favourite places. In just a few days, more than three hundred Madrilenians were killed there alone. In the distribution of power in Madrid, each party or trade union claimed a share. They all had their checas, their prisons, their own independent "armies". In the districts, libertarian athenaeums functioned, where criminal actions of all kinds were organised. The militiamen took possession of large, powerful cars in which they went to look for their victims and went for rides. Two weeks after the murders had been carried out with impunity, the Director General of Security, Manuel Muñoz Martínez, a 33rd degree Freemason who had replaced his brother Freemason José Alonso Mallol, called a meeting in early August at the Círculo de Bellas Artes, attended by all the parties and trade unions that made up the Popular Front. A Provincial Committee of Public Investigation was set up to direct repressive policy, and it was agreed that this Committee could "execute" without limitations or formalities whenever it saw fit. Subsequently, this Provincial Committee was organised into sections or tribunals and functioned until November 1936 in the cellars of Bellas Artes.

Among the crimes authorised by Manuel Muñoz, the venerable brother who was in charge of the General Directorate of Security, is the first mass shooting of the Civil War, studied by historian Santiago Mata, who in *El tren de la muerte: investigación de la primera masacre de la guerra civil* (2011) narrates the events and analyses the international impact they provoked. The crime took place on 12 August 1936, the day on which nearly two hundred people were machine-gunned. They came from Jaén, where the prisons were overcrowded and some 800 prisoners were locked up in the cathedral. To ease the situation, on the night of 11 August, a train with 250 prisoners left for Alcalá de Henares, guarded by civil guards. At the passing stations, the mobs stoned the train and insulted the passengers. Arriving on 12 August at Santa Catalina station, the train was stopped by militiamen who demanded that the prisoners be handed over. It was around midday when, after a long communication with the Ministry of the Interior, the head of the force guarding the train withdrew the guard and the occupants were left in the hands of the mob.

The convoy was taken to a branch of the ring road near a place called El Pozo del Tío Raimundo (Uncle Raimundo's Well), the prisoners were taken down in groups and, placed next to an embankment in front of three machine guns, they were killed. Among the victims were the bishop of Jaén, Manuel Basulto Jiménez, the vicar general of the diocese, Félix Pérez

Portela, and the bishop's sister, Teresa Basulto, the only woman on the expedition. "This is an infamy! -I am a poor woman", she exclaimed. Then she was told: "Don't hurry, you will be killed by a woman". A militia woman called Josefa Coso, "La Pecosa", stepped forward and executed her on the spot. Two hundred men had already been machine-gunned when a young man of nineteen, Leocadio Moreno, miraculously managed to stop the execution. He and about forty others were spared. Santiago Mata located Leocadio when he was already ninety-four years old. According to Mata, diplomatic documentation has revealed that the massacre seriously discredited the Republic, as many diplomats stopped considering it a state governed by the rule of law and began to protect Spanish citizens in their embassies.

The defeat of the rebels in Extremadura left Franco and Mola disconnected. After the failure at Guadarrama, the capture of Badajoz was a priority objective, as they were still thinking of winning Madrid. From the beginning of August, rebel planes bombed the city, where the hunt for right-wingers had been the norm. Knowing that the Nationalists were approaching, the militiamen wanted to storm the prison and kill the prisoners, but the guards prevented them from doing so. On 6 August, civil and assault guardsmen rose up. Colonel Puigdengolas' troops and the militiamen put down the rebellion and imprisoned the rebels. On the same day, eleven people were shot: priests, Falangists and several retired soldiers.

On the 7th, Zafra, Almendralejo and Villafranca de los Barros fell into the hands of the Army of Africa, and on the 11th troops entered Mérida. Severe repression was practised in these places and hundreds of people were executed. The fall of Mérida unleashed a wave of reprisals throughout the province: between 7 and 13 August hundreds of right-wingers were in turn shot in the Republican zone. On 13 August, Yagüe's troops reached the walls of Badajoz and the population began to flee en masse. Puigdengolas went to Portugal and abandoned the fight. On the 14th, the assault on the walls was fierce. To shouts of "Long live death!" the legionnaires advanced with bayonets drawn. Once in the city, the fighting was merciless. The last point of resistance was the cathedral, where a machine gun fired from the tower until the ammunition ran out. When they reached the top, the legionnaires ignored the surrender of the militiaman and threw him into the void. The Moors did not want to enter the cathedral, but they staged Dantesque scenes of extreme cruelty outside: they shot those who had taken refuge in the temple on the steps of the cathedral and finished them off with a shotgun blast or slit their throats with their knives. Alerted by the shots, Captain González Pérez-Caballero and another captain went to the scene and ordered the slaughter to stop. Drunk with blood, the Moroccans ignored the orders, so both captains even drew their pistols. The Moors then dispersed and began looting shops and businesses.

Before nightfall, the city had been taken. There were no prisoners: those who had surrendered were unceremoniously shot. About fifteen hundred people managed to flee through the Palmas gate and entered Portugal. The military could not halt their advance and repression soon passed into the hands of the Falangists, whose leader was Arcadio Carrasco, and the Civil Guards. Republican propaganda about the extent of the repression originated with René Brut, who on 16 August was still in Seville and arrived in Badajoz on the 17th, where he captured images of numerous bodies of the executed in the cemetery, many of which had already been cremated and burnt. Recent research puts the number of bodies that were taken to the cemetery between 13 and 18 August at around 500, including 44 Nationalist soldiers and 220 Republicans, 70 carabineros and 180 militiamen. During the month of August, however, the shootings continued, so that a further 300 dead victims of the repression must be added. Figures have now been provided on the number of people repressed in Badajoz between 1936 and 1945: it is estimated that around a thousand people were shot in these nine years as a result of summary trial convictions.

The Badajoz massacre had worldwide repercussions thanks to Jay Allen, an American journalist and friend of Negrín and Álvarez del Vayo. He was the one who invented the lie about the massacre in the Badajoz bullring without ever having been to the city. This correspondent gave a figure of four thousand dead, which has been accepted by many historians. The truth is that Allen wrote his articles from Tetuan and arrived in Madrid in October, when the city could fall into the hands of the Nationalists. Then the government of Largo Caballero again used the capture of Badajoz for propaganda purposes and invented a bullfight with prisoners instead of bulls, which would have been attended by ecclesiastical dignitaries, nuns in white robes and friars. The international propaganda campaign served the Republic well to cover up what was happening in Barcelona, Madrid and other cities such as Malaga and Valencia. Borkenau, who arrived in Madrid on 24 August from Valencia, wrote that the news had spread in the city that the insurgents in Badajoz had machine-gunned 1,500 prisoners in the bullring.

As a result of the atmosphere created, a crowd gathered in front of the prison had demanded the immediate execution of all the detainees in the Modelo prison. The Minister of the Interior, Pozas Perea, allowed agents of the General Directorate of Security and militiamen commanded by Elviro Ferrer Obrador to enter the Modelo to search important prisoners. On 21 August, a new search was ordered in the Fomento prison. Felipe Emilio Sandoval, alias "Dr. Muñiz", entered at the head of some forty CNT militiamen. The search was interrupted, so it was resumed on the 22nd, the day on which related officials entered on duty. What happened is very unclear, but it seems that a fire in the cellars of the prison caused chaos and led to the arrival of new groups of militiamen. At around 7 p.m., a people's tribunal was organised which succeeded in executing right-wing personalities, among them the following: Republican leader Melquíades Álvarez; José Mª Albiñana, head of the Spanish Nationalist Party; Manuel Rico Avelló and José Martínez de Velasco, both former ministers of the Republic; Julio Ruiz de Alda, Falangist and pilot on the Madrid-Buenos Aires flight of the "Plus Ultra"; Generals Osvaldo Capaz and Rafael Villegas; a brother of José Antonio Primo de Rivera... A total of thirty prisoners were "executed" by this tribunal.

There is a pattern that is inexorably repeated throughout contemporary history. When the prisoners in prisons are revolutionaries condemned during the rule of conservative governments, they take to the streets as soon as a "democratic" or left-wing government comes to power. The storming of the Bastille set the first precedent, which was later repeated in the revolutions of 1848 and in Russia during the Bolshevik Revolution. In Spain, as we have seen, in 1931 the Republic granted amnesty to those arrested for the Jaca uprising, and in 1936 the Popular Front won the victory with the promise to free those arrested for the Asturias uprising. On the other hand, it was different when the prisoners were not revolutionaries but rightists or conservatives. In this case, revolutionary justice demanded that they be exterminated. In September 1792, during the famous prison massacre, about six hundred people were killed in Paris. At the time, the criminals made Masonic signs on their victims to save the lives of the sect's brethren. In Spain, what happened in the Modelo prison was only the preamble to what was to happen shortly afterwards, when the biggest massacre of the whole war was organised in Paracuellos.

The union of the forces in Africa with those in the north was followed by the final offensive on Irún, which ended on 4 September. The occupation of Fuenterrabía and Irún, which was set on fire by the defenders and turned into a heap of smouldering ruins, severed the connection with France and led to the collapse of the Guipuzcoan front. These events made people in Madrid realise that the war effort had to put an end to the dual power. Those in favour of restoring the republican state demanded a solid government, supported by a strong army. On 26 August, *Pravda* correspondent Mikhail Koltsov, a Jew whose real name was Mikhail Efimovich Fridlyand, interviewed Indalecio Prieto, one of the first to realise the gravity of the moment. At the end of August, Prieto, who was in favour of the Socialists entering the government, was determined even to support his opponent, Largo Caballero, because he believed that he was the only man respected by the working masses who could form a government. In *Diario de la Guerra de España* Koltsov reproduces an excerpt from the interview: "The opinion I have of him (Largo) is known to all. He's an imbecile who wants to pretend to be clever. He is a disorganiser and a muddler who wants to pose as a methodical bureaucrat. He is a man capable of bringing everything and everyone to ruin. And yet, today, he is the only man, or at least the only useful man to put at the head of a new government." Prieto was willing to collaborate and work with Largo Caballero, for he believed that he was the last card: "There is no other way out for the country. Nor is there any other way out for me if I want to be useful to the country".

The PCE and the PSUC shared Prieto's approach, since it was also that of Stalin, who was then in the midst of a purge of Trotskyists after the first of the Moscow trials. In order to be the wild card, Largo Caballero had to renounce for the moment his announced "dictatorship of the proletariat". From *Claridad*, he had criticised Giral's mobilisation decrees and had defended the Leninist thesis of the "people in arms". He did not share the views of those who wanted to put aside the revolution in order to win the war, although the harsh reality of the defeats would give him pause for thought. However, on 27 August Largo Caballero presented his views to Koltsov and, besides sharply criticising Giral, expressed his conviction that the popular forces united around the anarchist and socialist trade unions would eventually seize power. Koltsov interpreted that, unlike Prieto, the Spanish Lenin was still thinking of a "workers' government".

On 27 August, four days after the executions of Zinoviev and Kamenev, Moses Rosenberg, the Soviet ambassador known as Marcel Rosenberg, arrived in Spain. According to Nahum Goldmann, president of the World Jewish Congress, Rosenberg, who was to be liquidated by Stalin in 1937, was a Zionist Jew who criticised non-Zionist communist Jews. Between 1920 and 1930 he was a counsellor at the Soviet Embassy in Paris and then secretary of the League of Nations in Geneva, where, with a salary of over $25,000, he owned a luxurious mansion, two limousines, a collection of secretaries and a young bride. During the time Stalin trusted him, Rosenberg wielded so much power that, although he was only an ambassador, he attended meetings of the Council of Ministers, a rarity in the history of international relations. Rosenberg's influence was felt from the very beginning.

Pierre Broué confirms in *La revolución y la guerra en España* that Largo Caballero was determined to seize power. According to this author, an assembly of UGT and CNT leaders "culminated in the creation of a Provisional Committee charged with carrying out the coup d'état and the installation of a Junta presided over by Largo Caballero", from which the Republicans would be excluded. Clara Campoamor confirms this and adds that Álvarez del Vayo, spokesman for the Committee, warned Azaña, who threatened to resign. Broué claims that Rosenberg's intervention averted the crisis and stopped the Provisional Committee, which was determined to do without Azaña. The Soviet ambassador, Broué writes, warned of the international consequences of an action that "took away the argument of 'legality' from the friends of Republican Spain and seemed to give the lie to rebel propaganda by presenting to the eyes of the world a government of 'reds' that would no longer be covered by any republican and parliamentary fiction". It was therefore Rosenberg who, in place of the "workers' government", proposed at that early stage of the war a Popular Front government with Republican ministers, presided over by Largo Caballero.

On 4 September the first government of Largo Caballero was born, which was to last for exactly two months, until 4 November 1936. The Secretary General of the UGT, in addition to the Presidency, took over the War portfolio. Five other socialists joined the government, which also included two communists, five republicans and a member of the PNV. The anarchists did not want to participate, because, according to *Solidaridad Obrera*, "the masses would be frustrated if we continued to cohabit in institutions whose structure is of a bourgeois type". Thus Largo Caballero presided over the government that Indalecio Prieto had been calling for, and he was put in charge of the Ministry of the Navy and Air Force.

Largo Caballero and Negrín present gold to Stalin

Almost everything has been said about foreign intervention in the Spanish Civil War. The Nationalists received massive aid from Fascist Italy, both in arms and men. It should be noted, however, that when the first Italians of the CTV arrived, the international brigadists had already been in Spain for two months. National Socialist Germany's assistance focused on armaments, although advisors and the airmen of the famous Condor Legion also arrived. Portugal sent a group of volunteers, the Viriatos, but its main contribution was logistical: the use of its territory at the beginning of the war was essential for the Nationalists. Salazar knew that a Popular Front victory could lead to a federation of Iberian republics under the red banner of international communism. For its part, the Republic received massive aid from the USSR and, to a lesser extent, from France, which helped the Popular Front from the outset: by early September 1936 France had already sent some forty aircraft and other armaments. Mexico also sent arms to the Republic. Little known is the attempt by the Republican government to buy arms from Germany. Between 1 and 4 August 1936 Augusto Barcia, "Lasalle", a 33rd degree Freemason, was at Berlin; but if the Republican anti-fascist Freemasons had no scruples about negotiating with the Nazis, Hitler did and refused to sell them anything.

As for the economic aspects of foreign aid, the first thing to note is that national Spain lacked financial resources. On 25 July two Germans living in Spanish Morocco, A. P. Langenheim and E. F. Bernhardt, arrived in Bayreuth with a request for aid. F. Bernhardt, arrived in Bayreuth with a request for help. When they told Hitler that Franco had only the gold deposited in the Bank of Tetouan at his disposal, he replied that it was better to keep it. From this very first moment, the German Führer trusted him and agreed to grant an initial credit to the Nationalists. Mussolini also granted credits to the rebels with the sole guarantee of a final victory which at the time was very uncertain. Other aid came from Juan March and other Spanish bankers, although American and British companies also granted loans with the backing of Catholics in their countries. In September the national side set up its own Banco de España in Burgos. As for the resources of the Popular Front, it has already been said that they were very important, as they were in possession of all the foreign exchange reserves, gold and silver of the Bank of Spain. Their management was lamentable, disastrous, for they paid for all their purchases in advance, in gold and in cash, until they had exhausted all their funds. While the Republican governments surrendered themselves completely into Stalin's arms, Franco's government was always able to maintain its independence.

Perhaps the only issue of foreign intervention in Spain that remains unclear is that of the elimination of the Trotskyists, which took place simultaneously with the trials and purges in Russia. It is an obscure episode, generally poorly studied and little understood. The prolongation in Spain of the internal struggle among the Soviet communists had a perverse influence on the politics of the Republican side and on the war. It was a crucial issue that conditioned the USSR's involvement in favour of the Republic. When national communism was defeating internationalism and in Russia Stalin was winning the game against his enemies, Spain became a piece that everyone wanted to collect and no one wanted to lose. In September 1936 the Trotskyists saw in Spain a possibility of underhandedly opposing their enemy, the last chance, perhaps, of gaining a base of international resistance. The options were slim, but whether through the International Brigades, or by taking control of the government of the Republic, or by provoking a world war, Trotskyist agents, and there were plenty of them, could try. The idea of creating a Trotskyist communist state in Spain existed and was welcomed by the secret forces supporting Trotsky.

Stalin, who knew the ramifications of the conspiracy he was fighting through the purges, never lost sight of the men operating in Spain. Almost all of them were Jews, as usual, proving once again that the world revolution was from the beginning an enterprise controlled and led by international Jewish agents.. Just as official historiography has concealed the historical significance of the Moscow trials and the self-righteousness of the Trotskyists, so it is silent on the true nature of the Spanish episode. Stalin was ambitious for Spain from an "imperialist" point of view. The Peninsula constituted geopolitically a strategic position of the first order. That was precisely why Britain could not accept Stalin's control of it. Gibraltar, "Gib" as the British say, the symbol of British power, together with Suez one of the two keys to the Mediterranean, was too important. Before he was assassinated on Stalin's orders in 1941, Krivitsky (Samuel Ginsberg), the Trotskyite Jew who in 1936 was head of the Soviet Military Secret Service, wrote: "The story of the Soviet intervention remains the most momentous mystery of the Spanish Civil War".

With the formation of the Largo Caballero government, Stalin's intervention in Spain accelerated sharply. Krivitsky devotes a chapter of his book to commenting on and explaining how this came about. Since he is a source of great interest, as he was for years in intimate contact with USSR policy in Europe, we shall take important information from his pages, always bearing in mind that he deeply hated Stalin. Krivitsky never reveals who were the Trotskyist agents in Spain and presents his colleagues as idealists aiming at the liberation of the international proletariat. He states emphatically that Stalin wanted to make Spain a soviet republic federated with the USSR and regrets that so many naive people thought that his policy was connected with the world revolution. Among these naive people were thousands of foreign communists who, expelled from their countries, lived as refugees in the Soviet Union. Stalin took the opportunity to get rid of these old revolutionaries and send them to Spain, where they arrived convinced that the Spanish civil war could unleash the world revolution.

Thanks to Krivitsky, it is known that at the end of August three Spanish officials travelled to Russia to buy arms, but were not immediately taken to Moscow, but were held in their hotel in Odessa. In the meantime, the Politburo met, where Stalin finally presented his plan for intervention, which was to be done covertly to avoid becoming involved in a war. A special courier was flown to Holland, where Walter Krivitsky, camouflaged as an antiquarian, was residing. He received these instructions: "Immediately extend your operations to cover the Spanish civil war. Mobilise all agents and all available facilities for the rapid organisation of a system for purchasing arms and transporting them to Spain. A special agent is dispatched to Paris to assist you in this work. There he will be introduced to you and will work under your supervision."

On 14 September 1936, Yagoda, whose links with the Trotskyists had not yet been discovered, convened on Stalin's orders a conference at the Lubyanka. It was then decided to coordinate the activities of the PCE with the Soviet intelligence services. The meeting was attended by Mikhail Frinovsky, then in command of the military forces of the OGPU, which was part of the NKVD; Abraham Aronovich Slutsky, head of the foreign division of the OGPU; and Semene Petrovich Uritsky, general of the Red Army General Staff and nephew of Moisei Salomonovich Uritsky, who had been murdered in 1918 in the context of the infighting between Lenin and Trotsky. All four were Jews and all of them were eventually purged as Trotskyists and executed by Stalin. It was at this conference at the Lubyanka that the man who was to organise the OGPU in Spain was appointed, a veteran of Slutsky's department whom Krivitsky refers to as "Nikolsky, alias Schwed, alias Lyova, alias Orlov", another Jew who was known in Spain as Alexander Mikhailovich Orlov, though his real name was Leiba Lazarevich Felbing. The historian Burnet Bolloten points out that Stanley G. Payne provided him with a copy of a note signed by Orlov himself in 1968, according to which his appointment by the Political Bureau had taken place on 26 August 1936, so that the date of 14 September given by Krivitsky is not correct as far as this appointment is concerned. In fact, Orlov had already left for Paris with his wife, Maria Roznetski, also an NKVD agent, and his daughter, whom he left behind in the French capital. On 15 September he was already in Spain. Burnett Bolloten notes that Orlov may well have been one of the Soviet officers who accompanied Ambassador Rosenberg on his visits to Largo Caballero.

Two days before Orlov's arrival, an astonishing event had taken place: the Minister of Finance, Juan Negrín, had ordered by decree the transfer of most of the Banco de España's gold reserves to the USSR. According to Krivistsky, the Jew Arthur Stashevsky, who passed for a simple commercial attaché in Spain, was working "to place control of the Republic's finances in Soviet hands". Stashevsky, writes Krivitsky, "discovered in Juan Negrín a sincere collaborator in his financial plans". It was he, therefore, who persuaded Negrín to hand over the gold to him. Juan Negrín was married to a Jewish woman of Ukrainian origin, Maria Fidelman Brodsky Mijailova, the daughter of a wealthy businessman who had been living in Germany since the end of the 19th century. In order to conceal his Jewish origin, Negrín and his wife decided to register their children under the maternal surname of Mikhailov instead of Brodsky. After his flight from Spain, Negrín went into exile in Bovingdon, near London, where he was frequently visited by the Soviet ambassador, Ivan Maisky, a Polish-born Jew who frequented him regularly. Negrín invited Maisky and his wife to spend weekends at his home.[23]

Since Krivitsky's credibility was denounced by the Stalinists, Burnett Bolloten, an English historian of Jewish origin, wanted to check the reliability of Krivitsky's assertions. In *The Spanish Civil War: Revolution and Counter-Revolution,* Bolloten demonstrates from four different sources that Negrín was indeed a close friend of Stashevsky's and was married to the Jewess Maria Fidelman Brodsky, by whom he had five children. Louis Fischer reports that Stashevsky was a friend of Negrín's who advised him on economic matters. Álvarez del Vayo confirms that Negrín and Stashevsky had a "true friendship". Santiago Garcés Arroyo, whom Negrín put in charge of the SIM (Military Information Service) in April 1938, acknowledges that Negrín got on very well with the Russians, especially with Stashevsky, "with whom he had breakfast and lunch every day". Mariano Ansó, a minister with Negrín, notes that Stashevsky appreciated his "irresistible talent and charm". Arthur Karlovich Stashevsky, born in Mitau, was actually a Latvian Jew

---

[23] In his memoirs Maysky writes: "From then on Bovingdon became our regular place of rest at weekends". In February 1953 Maisky was arrested. Accused of espionage, treason and involvement in the Zionist conspiracy, he escaped execution thanks to Stalin's assassination. Beria, who was trying to seize power, had thought of him as a future foreign commissar. In 1955 Maisky was released and exonerated of his charges.

called Girshfeld or Hirshfeld, who under the pseudonym "Verkhovsky" laid the foundations for the founding of the international Bolshevik brigades. In 1920, during the Civil War, he was head of the secret service on the Western Front, and in peacetime he organised the intelligence network in Western Europe on the orders of the Czech Presidium, for which he was awarded the title of "Honorary Chekist". With this CV, there can be little doubt about his Trotskyite affiliation. Stalin executed him in 1937.

Largo's executive Caballero did not inform the President of the Republic of the transfer of the gold. Largo himself justified his decision on the pretext that Manuel Azaña "was in a truly lamentable spiritual state". Although Article 2 of the Decree stated that the Cortes would be informed, they were never notified. The Decree, dated 13 September 1936, stated that the abnormality produced by the military uprising made it advisable to adopt measures to "safeguard the metal reserves of the Banco de España, the basis of public credit". Article 1 of the Decree read as follows: "The Ministry of Finance is authorised, at such time as it deems appropriate, to order the transport, with the greatest guarantees, to the place it deems most secure, of the stocks of gold, silver and banknotes held at that time in the central establishment of the Banco de España". In other words, when the Nationalist troops had not even approached Madrid - the siege of the Alcázar of Toledo ended on 27 September - it was considered that the safest place to deposit the gold was Moscow. On the 14th carabinieri forces showed up at the Banco de España, with the collaboration of the director general of the Treasury, Francisco Méndez Aspe, a man Negrín trusted at. The directors Martínez Fresneda and Álvarez Guerra denounced what was being done as illegal and resigned. According to various sources, the chief cashier of the Banco de España committed suicide in his office.

Spain's reserves of 707 tonnes of gold were then the fourth largest in the world. Of this, 510 tons were handed over to the Soviet Union and the rest was deposited in French banks in order to guarantee payment for armament purchases. Before the gold left Spain, Stalin sent Orlov a coded radiogram in Moscow: "Together with Ambassador Rosenberg, I arranged with the head of the Spanish Government, Largo Caballero, to send Spain's gold reserves to the Soviet Union on a Russian steamer. Everything must be done with the utmost secrecy. If the Spaniards demand a receipt for the shipment, refuse, I repeat, refuse to sign it, and say that an official receipt will be given to you in Moscow by the State Bank. I hold you personally responsible for the operation. Almost two months elapsed before the gold arrived in Moscow. The proceedings began at 11.30 p.m. on 15 September with the transport of 7,800 crates to the Cartagena naval base. Each box contained some 65 kilos of pure gold. The cargo was deposited in the powder magazine at La Algameca and remained there for a month, until 22 October. Considering that Cartagena was under the control of the Government of the

Republic until the end of the war, it is obvious that the reserves would have been perfectly stored there.

Stalin had thought that "one Russian steamer" would be sufficient for transport, but Orlov found that more ships would be needed, so he moved to Cartagena and ordered the Soviet naval attaché to confiscate incoming ships. He ordered them to be unloaded quickly and to stand by. During the nights of 22, 23 and 24 October 1936, Soviet tankers from the Archena base, commanded by a Jewish commander named Semion Moiseyevich Krivoshéin, loaded the gold onto the ships *Kim*, *Khrushchev*, *Neva* and *Volgoles*. The Minister of the Navy, Indalecio Prieto, who was in charge of the naval base, must necessarily have been aware of what was happening there. By 10 a.m. on 25 October, the operation was over. Méndez Aspe asked for a receipt, but Orlov replied that it would be issued in Moscow once the gold had been weighed. To reassure the director general of the Treasury, Orlov told him that he could send a Treasury representative on each of the ships.

Months later, in 1937, Krivitsky spoke to the four Spanish officials, who were still in Moscow, staying at the Metropol Hotel with their passports withheld. If they leave here when the war is over," Slutsky told him, "they can count themselves lucky. For now they have to remain in our hands." The ships sailed from Cartagena for Odessa, where they arrived on 2 November with the Spanish treasure in their holds. The dock where they docked was cordoned off by special troops. OGPU officials transported the crates to the tracks for days and filled the wagons of several armed convoys that took the cargo to Moscow. In March 1937 Slutsky and Krivitsky were walking in Red Square and Krivitsky told him about the arrival of the gold. To give him an idea of the quantity, he told him: "If all the boxes piled up on the Odessa docks had been placed side by side here in Red Square, they would have covered it completely from end to end. Stalin gave a banquet in the Kremlin to celebrate the success of the operation. He then declared: "The Spaniards will no more see the gold than anyone can see their own ears". The USSR, therefore, did not grant any credit to the Republicans and more than collected in advance all the aid it sent to Spain.

In *Weapons for Spain. The Untold Story of the Spanish Civil War*, Gerald Howson sheds definitive light on how Stalin swindled the Republic out of hundreds of millions of dollars through arms sales. Howson demonstrates how the Soviets falsified the accounting books and arms prices, since the dollar was then exchanged at 5.3 roubles and they set the exchange rate for the Spanish at 2.5 roubles to the dollar. Thus the Republican government paid twice as much for the arms as they were worth. In Howson's words, "of all the swindling, cheating, stealing and treachery that the Republicans had to endure, the unscrupulous conduct of Stalin and the high officials of the Soviet nomenklatura is surely the most sordid, the most treacherous and the most indefensible".

Government flight and mass killing of prisoners

Soviet intervention gave the communists a strength and power they had previously lacked. The PCE's connection with Stalin's intelligence services gave it additional advantages over the other parties. Moreover, it can be said that they had three more ministers, since Rosenberg acted in the Councils of Ministers as a sort of vice-president, and the Socialists Negrín and Álvarez del Vayo acted in harmony with them. As soon as the military advisers began to arrive, his dominance increased even more. On Rosenberg, Luis Araquistáin confirms that he acted like a viceroy who gave daily instructions to Largo Caballero on what to do and whom to appoint or dismiss. Burnett Bolloten quotes a very significant text from Ginés Ganga, a left-wing socialist deputy: "This gentleman (Rosenberg) used to carry in his pocket a collection of slips of paper conceived in these or similar terms: X, head of such and such a division, should be dismissed and Z appointed as a substitute; so-and-so, an employee of Ministry A, is not performing properly, he should be replaced by B; M should be imprisoned and prosecuted for disaffection; and so on all the time". In all the technical military personnel in Spain numbered about two thousand men, of whom only the pilots and tank officers went into combat. The Russians were staff members, instructors, engineers, chemical warfare experts, aircraft mechanics, radio operators or artillery experts. All of them were closely watched by the NKVD.

The International Brigade, the real army of the Comintern, was recruited by the local Communist parties, integrated into the Communist International, where many internationalist followers of Trotsky were still trying to influence, despite the fact that since 1930 Stalin had been carrying out various purges. Moreover, the Military Secret Service, still infiltrated in 1936 by numerous Trotskyists, had secret checkpoints in Europe where foreign communists who had enlisted were reinvestigated. It should be emphasised that the purge of the Red Army in Moscow took place in the late spring of 1937 and that in September the conspiracy against Stalin was at its height. The Trotskyists were engaged in a life-and-death battle to oust Stalin from power, and naturally they intended to impose themselves on events in Spain, which was to become another arena for their confrontation.

The control of brigade volunteers, many of whom came to fight for the Republic and the world revolution, continued in Spain, where they were spied on by political commissars. According to Krivitsky, their passports were taken away and rarely returned, as foreign passports, especially American passports, were highly prized by the NKVD. A Comintern Executive Committee document dated autumn 1937, when the purge of Trotskyists in Spain had already taken place, indicated the need to "watch over the selection of volunteers to prevent the introduction into the Brigades of agents of the fascist and Trotskyist information services and spies". In Spain there were two prisons reserved for brigadists, one in the Horta district of Barcelona, where in 1937 there were six hundred and twenty-five prisoners, and another in Castellón de la Plana. The training base was established in Albacete, where the Frenchman André Marty, nicknamed "the butcher of Albacete", was in charge of ensuring the orthodoxy of the communist volunteers. He himself admits in a report to the Central Committee of the French Communist Party that he did not hesitate and ordered the necessary executions: about five hundred.

After the liberation of the Alcázar of Toledo, the Nationalist troops began to approach Madrid. Meanwhile, international communist volunteers were landing in the Mediterranean ports and from France were entering Catalonia, where the revolution had reached its zenith and was beginning to weaken. There, after the formation of the first government of Largo Caballero, the Generalitat was also trying to put an end to the dual power, which required the dissolution of the Central Committee of the Militias. The anarchists finally agreed on 26 September and, although they had remained outside the Madrid government, they accepted to enter the Government of the Generalitat, whose "conseller en cap" was Josep Tarradellas. In this "Consell de Govern" formed on 28 September, all the parties and trade unions were represented, including the POUM, Andreu Nin's Trotskyist party, which won the Justice portfolio. The POUM had dared to criticise the August 1936 trial in Moscow, the first of the three trials, and had come out publicly in defence of the victims. The anarchists, for their part, managed to gain control of the economy, supplies and health. The formation of the new Government of the Generalitat meant in theory the end of the organisms of revolutionary power. On 1 October the Central Committee of the Militias was dissolved and, in a manifesto, adhered to the policy of the Generalitat. On 9 October a decree approved by Nin and the CNT "consellers" put an end to the local committees throughout Catalonia.

After the step taken in Catalonia, it would have been inconsistent for the anarchists to refuse to join the Madrid government. The UGT, the PSOE and the PCE demanded it, so in October, coinciding with the arrival of the first Russian officers and planes, negotiations began. The CNT newspapers called for the formation of a National Defence Council. The military defeats and the threat to the capital finally decided the leaders of the CNT and the FAI, who agreed to join the government, despite the commotion their decision caused in the libertarian movement. At first they demanded six ministerial portfolios. Largo Caballero finally offered them four: Justice (García Oliver), Health (Federica Montseny), Trade (Juan López) and Industry (Juan Peiró). The restoration of the state was thus completed with the approval of the anarchists.

The second government of Largo Caballero and twenty-fourth of the Second Republic was formed on 4 November 1936, when the rebel troops were already in the vicinity of Madrid. Negrín held the Treasury portfolio and Prieto the Navy and Air Force portfolios. Largo Caballero, in addition to the Presidency, also retained the War portfolio. Manuel de Irujo and Jaume Aiguader represented the Basque and Catalan nationalists. All the parties were in the government except the POUM, whose participation was vetoed by the PCE, which followed instructions from Moscow. A month later, pressure from the Catalan Stalinists of the PSUC and Soviet advisers led to the dismissal of Andreu Nin as Minister of Justice of the Generalitat. For some historians, this measure initiated the counter-revolutionary process.

On the evening of 6 November, in the first hours of the attack on Madrid, Largo Caballero and his ministers fled shamefully without announcing it to the population. On their way to Valencia, the official caravan was stopped in Tarancón by a hundred anarchist militiamen, who insulted and threatened the ministers and Ambassador Rosenberg, who was fleeing with them. The anarchist ministers' explanations were to no avail: forced the retinue to retreat. Finally, they were able to make a detour to the south of Madrid and managed to continue their flight. When they reached the capital of the Turia, the CNT-FAI in Valencia branded them "cowards and fugitives". Two days later, the newspapers were allowed to give the news of the transfer of the Government of the Republic to Valencia "to organise the definitive victory ". The government communiqué announced that, before leaving, the Madrid Defence Junta, chaired by General Miaja, had been formed.

With the arrival of the first Soviets, a decree of 6 October had created the General Commissariat of War, which established the figure of the commissar, the government's representative in the army, who was defined as the right arm of the command, "the sentry, the watchful eye", the political educator of the soldiers and officers, "the comrade and the model". The commissars were to be, according to the PCE, "the nerve and soul of the people's army", although their opponents referred to them as the "red chaplains". The Communists took over half of the posts in the Defence Junta, which was formed on 7 November, and thus became the masters of Madrid.

On the evening of 9 November, the city seemed lost. In addition, hunger was becoming another enemy to be overcome: to get hold of a loaf of bread, one could queue from midnight to noon at times. Panic was widespread and the roads were full of fugitives. From the west and south, Franco's forces arrived without encountering resistance. In the opinion of Edward Knoblaugh, Associated Press correspondent in Madrid. Franco could have taken the city that afternoon, but he did not, the entry did not take place, perhaps because it was felt that more troops were needed. In the opinion of foreign military observers, about 150,000 men were needed to take a city like Madrid, and Franco did not want to take the newly mobilised fifth troops to the front, as they had not completed their training period. By the time he decided to go in three days later, it was too late, as thousands of brigadiers who had received training in Albacete were arriving in the capital.

With control of the city in the hands of the Communist Party and the Soviets, and fearing that the prisoners might be released, the prisons were emptied and the largest organised genocide in Spanish history was committed in Paracuellos del Jarama, Torrejón and Aravaca. Although some estimates put the number of victims executed during the massacres as high as 12,000, most scholars put the figure at around 8,000. It was the German diplomat Felix Schlayer, who was acting as Norwegian consul and chargé d'affaires in Spain in Madrid, who discovered the events and denounced them. Schlayer, a sixty-three-year-old tough guy who had lived through the horrors of the First World War as a German officer, sported an elaborate nineteenth-century moustache that gave him the appearance of a Prussian "Junker". His courageous determination and impressive bearing often intimidated his interlocutors. Although has sought to discredit Schlayer for his sympathies towards the Nationalists, his work *Diplomat im roten Madrid*, published in 1938 in Germany after his expulsion from Spain, was an indisputable testimony that revealed in Europe the massacre perpetrated by the government of the Republic. Santiago Carrillo, one of the main perpetrators of the crimes against humanity at Paracuellos, referred to him as "that Nazi".

In Madrid alone, there were some two hundred checas operating. Some were official, but most were controlled by political parties, trade unions and committees. It can be said that any organised militia group, whether anarchist, socialist or communist, considered itself authorised to detain, interrogate and, if necessary, execute those suspected of anti-republicanism. As a result, diplomatic headquarters soon became a refuge for thousands of people seeking protection. By October, Schlayer had nine hundred people housed in the Norwegian "asylum". Aurelio Núñez Morgado, the Chilean ambassador and dean of the diplomatic corps, had more space in his embassy buildings and exceeded the previous figure by several hundred. The head of the Argentine mission, Edgardo Pérez Quesada, also played a leading role. When he knew for certain what was going on, Pérez Quesada sent a strong report to Buenos Aires, of which he gave a copy to the British chargé d'affaires, who forwarded it to the Foreign Office.

In this atmosphere, Schlayer began to take an interest in the prisoners at the end of September and decided to make regular visits to the prisons where the detainees were crowded. The fact that his legation's lawyer, Ricardo de la Cierva, was imprisoned was one of the reasons for his concern. His example was followed by the representatives of Chile, Argentina, Great Britain, Austria and Hungary, which was a respite and a relief for the detainees. While the government was still in Madrid, the removal of prisoners from the prisons began at the end of October. The Director General of Security, Manuel Muñoz, the 33rd degree Freemason whose hands were already stained with the blood of the victims of the "death train", signed an order to execute thirty-two prisoners from the Ventas prison on 28 October in the Aravaca cemetery, Among them were the Falangist Ramiro Ledesma and the Generation of '98 intellectual Ramiro de Maeztu, author among other works of *Defensa de la Hispanidad* and *Don Quixote, Don Juan y la Celestina,* an excellent literary essay on the three universal figures of Spanish literature. Arrested in July, Maeztu wrote during his captivity *Defensa del Espíritu (Defence of the Spirit),* a posthumous work of which fragments were lost. On the same day, another 29 prisoners from the Modelo were also shot in Aravaca. On the 29th, fifty more were taken out of the famous checa de Fomento and executed on the Boadilla road.

On 1 November, the Jew Koltsov (Efimovich Fridlyand), alias Miguel Martinez, supposedly a correspondent of *Pravda,* but in reality adviser to the Red authorities and the Defence Board, discussed with the political commissars the fate of the prisoners. Koltsov proposed shooting them. Again on the orders of Manuel Muñoz, seventy-nine prisoners were taken from the Ventas prison and shot in Aravaca. Days later, on 3 November, another sixty-six prisoners were executed in Carabanchel Alto. In the early hours of the morning of the 5th, two lorries loaded with prisoners left San Antón prison, another from Porlier prison, and a large expedition from Modelo prison. Ian Gibson, author of *The Assassination of García Lorca,* in his work *Paracuellos: How it happened,* argues that Koltsov was the instigator and responsible for the Paracuellos massacres. Koltsov was considered to be a man of Stalin's utmost confidence, but despite this, he was denounced at the end of 1937 by André Marty, the highest authority of the International Brigades, who accused Koltsov of contacts with the Trotskyists of the POUM and his wife, Maria Osten, of being an agent of the German intelligence service. Forced to return to the USSR, Koltsov was eliminated on 2 February 1940.

The executions in Aravaca had to be suspended due to the proximity of the nationalist troops. Torrejón and Paracuellos were then chosen as the places to continue with the executions. When the government fled, the Defence Junta appointed the communist Santiago Carrillo, leader of the JSU and son of the socialist Wenceslao Carrillo, as adviser for Public Order. Segundo Serrano Poncela was placed as his deputy. On the afternoon of 6 November, shortly before Carrillo's inauguration, large-scale sackings were carried out from the Modelo and Porlier prisons. The prisoners were executed at the foot of the Cerro de San Miguel, at the top of which is the village of Paracuellos, near the Jarama River. In the early hours of the morning of the 7th, the largest round-ups took place: 1,600 people left the Modelo prison, of whom 300 were taken to Alcalá de Henares and the rest were slaughtered en masse in Paracuellos. On the same day, the 7th, there were two more massacres: a very large one from the San Antón prison and a smaller one from the Porlier prison. The victims of the latter were shot in the walls of the Almudena cemetery. After the war these bodies were exhumed and taken to the cemetery of Paracuellos. The massacres continued during the night of 7-8 November: expeditions from the Modelo and Porlier prisons were led back to Paracuellos. The magnitude of the previous massacres exceeded forecasts, so that there were not enough graves prepared and those shot the day before remained unburied. The villagers were forced to dig new trenches, into which the bodies were dragged by hooks and ropes pulled by horses and mules. Because of the pile-up of corpses in Paracuellos, the next shipments were sent to Soto de Aldovea, in the municipality of Torrejón de Ardoz, where an old irrigation channel one hundred and fifty metres long was used to bury the dead. Once the war was over, four hundred and fourteen corpses were exhumed and transferred in individual coffins to the cemetery at Paracuellos. Of these, only a few could be identified.

Félix Schlayer writes in *Diplomat in Red Madrid* that he went to the Modelo on the morning of the 7th, accompanied by delegates from the International Committee of the Red Cross. He found the prison surrounded by cobblestone barricades and guards and militiamen with bayonets drawn at the entrances. Inside he saw a large number of buses. He wanted to speak to the director, but he was at the Ministry. The deputy director told him that the buses were there to pick up officers and take them to Valencia. He immediately went to the Directorate General of Security, but the venerable Brother Manuel Muñoz had fled with the government. He asked who the new person in charge was and was told that Margarita Nelken, the Socialist deputy of Jewish origin, had been installed in the director general's office since the morning. He asked for an interview with her, but was told she was not in. Schlayer understood that she did not want to see him.

Faced with the impossibility of seeing Nelken, the diplomats, who had not been informed by the government of their departure from Madrid, organised a meeting at the Chilean embassy and decided to go to the Ministry of War to meet José Miaja, general-in-chief of the Defence Junta. He received them at 17:30 and promised that he "would not let the prisoners be touched in the slightest". Schlayer asked about his lawyer, Ricardo de la Cierva, who had been killed two hours earlier, and Miaja assured him that he would do all he could for him. The diplomat returned to the Modelo at six in the evening and learned from the director, with whom he had a good relationship, that Ricardo de la Cierva had been handed over to a communist called Ángel Rivera, who had orders for the transfer of hundreds of prisoners to Valencia. Before the long day was over, Schlayer picked up the Red Cross delegates again, as they had managed to get an interview with the new head of Public Order, Santiago Carrillo, with whom they had a long conversation. Carrillo told them that he knew nothing about the release of prisoners from the Modelo prison and showed his willingness to protect the detainees. Schlayer says that he was certain that Carrillo was lying to them, so that during the night the most dire omens came to his mind. The next day he went to the Modelo again and the director tried to justify himself personally by showing him a letter from the General Directorate of Security, ordering him to hand over 970 prisoners, selected by his guards, for transfer to Valencia. Schlayer writes, "The possibility of a horrible crime in which I had hitherto been unable to believe was beginning to take shape in me".

With great difficulty, the Norwegian chargé d'affaires managed to make telephone contact with the directors of the San Miguel prison de los Reyes (Valencia) and the Chinchilla prison (Albacete). He then learned that in the last fourteen days they had not received any prisoners from Madrid. In the following days Schlayer tried to locate the crime scene and his investigations led him initially to Torrejón, specifically to Soto de Aldovea, where there is an 18th century fortress, the castle of Aldovea. He travelled there in the company of the Argentinian Edgardo Pérez Quesada, with whom he had shared his enquiries and with whom he agreed to accompany him. Arriving at the castle, Schlayer asked the militiaman who was on duty where those who had been shot had been buried. The man, who must have been a blessed man, began to point the way, but the diplomats asked him to accompany them. He took his rifle and led them to the old ditch, where there was a strong smell of decay. In some places, limbs could be seen sticking out or boots were showing. Schlayer and Pérez Quesada estimated that there were between five and six hundred corpses there.

A few days later, the German diplomat travelled with his driver to Paracuellos. When, after several enquiries, he managed to get close to the place of the executions, he met a young man who had just come from ploughing with two mules. He then used the same tactic as in Soto de Aldovea and, as if it were a known fact, asked: "Where did they bury all the people who were executed on Sunday? The young man replied: "There, under the Four Pines, but it wasn't on Sunday, it was on Saturday". Schlayer insisted: "How many of them were there? The peasant replied that there had been many. "Was it about six hundred?" he asked again. "More," replied the young man, "they were coming buses all day long, and all day long the machine guns were heard." The diplomat wanted to approach the Four Pines, but three men with rifles guarded the place. Schlayer writes: "I clearly saw two newly erected parallel hills of earth, running from the road to the river bank, each about two hundred metres long."

In short, Schlayer not only provoked diplomatic intervention, but also sought the support of Dr. Henry, a delegate of the International Red Cross. Together they took photographs, sought testimonies, interviewed people who had been forced to dig graves, visited prisons and talked to members of the Defence Board. Fearing an international scandal, the executions and executions were temporarily halted. The thousands of prisoners still remaining in the Modelo were transferred to the prisons of Porlier, San Antón and Ventas. Another event that led to the temporary cessation of the killings was the appearance on the scene of the Sevillian anarchist Melchor Rodríguez, who was appointed Prison Delegate on 10 November. Schlayer, who met him on several occasions, has very kind words for Melchor Rodriguez in his book and devotes a small section to him entitled "Anarchist or apostle? This anarchist, one of many idealists who came up against an atrocious reality, on taking office renounced his monthly salary of fifteen hundred pesetas, "even though he had no other source of income", writes the consul, "and lived on the charity of his friends". The new delegate radically cut off the sacas; but it took him only four days to learn that the communists had again executed prisoners taken from the prisons without his authorisation. He demanded exemplary punishment, but the Minister of Justice, also anarchist García Oliver, did not back him up, so Melchor Rodríguez resigned from his post.

From 17 November, the round-ups for Paracuellos resumed. The Red Committee of the Civil Guard had imprisoned disaffected members of the Institute in a cell called "Spartacus", located in a convent in Santa Engracia street. On the afternoon of 19 November, supposedly to be transferred to Guadalajara, some two hundred guardsmen of all ranks left for the Almudena and Vicálvaro cemeteries, where they were executed. On the 22nd, a smaller number of prisoners were removed from the San Antón prison. On the 24th, hundreds of prisoners of all ages and professions left Porlier for Paracuellos. On the 25th, 26th, 28th and 29th, hundreds of new victims were taken from this same prison, including a whole family, that of the well-known notary Alejandro Arizcún Moreno. Of his four children who were shot, the youngest was a student and only seventeen years old. Again from the San Antón prison there were large round-ups on the 27th and 28th.

The playwright Pedro Muñoz Seca was released handcuffed at eight o'clock in the morning of the 28th together with Fr. Guillermo Llop, prior of the Brothers of San Juan de Dios in Ciempozuelos. Although the Republic was supposedly a regime of freedoms, Muñoz Seca, for being a monarchist, for being a friend of the king and for writing against the Republic, had been arrested on 29 July in Barcelona, where on the 17th *La tonta del rizo* had premiered at the Poliorama theatre. Admitted to San Antón prison on 6 August, he had remained there for almost four months. On 26 November a people's tribunal was formed in the prison itself, which condemned him to death for being a monarchist, anti-republican and Catholic; three very serious crimes indeed. At 1 a.m. on the 28th he went to confession to the priest Ruiz del Rey, who died with him, and at 4 a.m. he wrote a letter to his wife, in the final paragraph of which he left these words: "I am sorry to give you the displeasure of this separation; but if we all have to suffer for the salvation of Spain, and this is the part that has fallen to me, blessed are these sufferings". In the postscriptum he alluded to his recent confession: "As you will understand, I am very well prepared and clean of guilt".

More than two hundred and fifty people, including about a hundred religious and about twenty university professors, were shot on the second day. Also on the same day, on the 30th, a very large number of people were taken out of the Ventas prison. These were the last massacres of the month of November, but the macabre ritual of executions continued during the first four days of December. Prisoners were taken from San Antón on all four days. Sixty-four people left the Ventas prison on their way to death on the 2nd and another sixty on the 3rd. New expeditions with destination Paracuellos left Porlier on the 1st, 2nd, 3rd and 4th of December. Fortunately, the so-called "red angel" was again requested by the Minister of Justice. Melchor Rodríguez accepted for the second time the post of government delegate for Prisons on the condition that no prisoner would be allowed to leave the prison without his written consent. From then on, the murders ceased.

In the search for responsibility, several names are mentioned by historians. If we accept Ian Gibson's thesis, the proposal to exterminate the prison population came from the Jew Koltsov, and he would have been the direct instigator, although the orders came from those who were in charge. Another possible ideologue of the massacres was the Argentine Victorio Codovilla, a Stalinist who was the highest representative of the International in Madrid. The initial order authorising the first sackings before the government left Madrid came from the Minister of the Interior, Ángel Galarza, the Freemason socialist who had publicly justified the assassination of Calvo Sotelo in the Cortes. Once the Defence Junta was set up, the orders came from the new Minister of Public Order, Santiago Carrillo, who was politically responsible, even though the idea had not been his.

According to the *Minutes of the meetings of the Madrid Defence Junta*, at the session of 15 November Carrillo said that he had total and absolute responsibility for everything relating to the prisoners. The orders, however, were usually signed by Segundo Serrano Poncela, his collaborator and right-hand man, who personally visited the Modelo prison on 7 November and ordered, in the purest Leninist style, that "military men, career men and aristocrats" should be selected. In the background were those who, although they had responsibility, did not have the decency or courage to confront the communists, who, in tune with the Soviet henchmen, were directing the whole operation. Among these was the Minister of Justice, Juan García Oliver. Finally, it cannot be ignored that the President of the Government was Francisco Largo Caballero, who, whether he knew about it or not, bore ultimate responsibility for the actions of his ministers.

On 8 December, Georges Henry, the Swiss delegate of the International Red Cross, took off from Madrid on a French embassy plane that made the weekly flight from Toulouse to Madrid. His final destination, however, was Geneva, where he intended to present a document containing evidence provided by Edgardo Pérez Quesada and Félix Schlayer on the massacres of prisoners. Travelling with him were journalists Louis Delaprée of the newspaper *Paris-Soir* and André Chateau. Two girls under the age of twelve were also passengers. The plane, a Potez 54, took off in the early afternoon. In addition to the French flag on the tail rudder, the fuselage was clearly marked "Ambassade de France". At Guadalajara a warplane suddenly appeared and approached to reconnoitre it. It seemed to be moving away, but soon returned and strafed Potez 54, which was badly damaged on one wing and the fuselage. Nevertheless, the pilot managed to land the aircraft in a grain field in Pastrana, where it was left upside down with its wheels in the air and some 30 hits. The two girls fared the best. Dr. Henry was wounded in the leg, Chateau was saved by the amputation of a leg, Delaprée died on 31 December after a slow and painful agony. The pilot was unhurt and, of course, was interrogated by the Norwegian diplomat, who gave this version of events in his book:

"... At the height of Guadalajara he crossed head-on with another plane which at first passed him at a considerable distance. It bore the insignia of the Red Government. The Frenchman saluted it as usual by waving his wings, i.e., moving them up and down twice to be recognised, despite the fact that he had large French insignia. The red plane flew past, turned away, circled, came back and came under the Frenchman. He then fired at it from below with his machine gun. Then he made a quick getaway. The frightened French pilot gave me personally this account."

Mikhail Koltsov visited the wounded in the hospitals on 9 December. In his *Diary of the Spanish War* he wrote the version given to him by Delaprée himself before he died:

"We had not been in the air for more than ten minutes. Suddenly a fighter appeared over the side of us. It circled around, apparently watching us at its leisure. It's impossible that it didn't see the distinctive signs. It disappeared for a few minutes and then all at once, from below, through the floor of the cockpit, the bullets began to penetrate. We were hit by the first shots. The pilot was unhurt. He made an abrupt landing. The plane hit the ground very hard, went upright on the bow. Badly wounded, bleeding to death, we fell on top of each other. It seemed to me that a fire started, I could no longer understand anything. A few minutes later, some peasants appeared, broke the hatch and pulled us out carefully.

As early as 1938, William Foss and Cecil Gerahty denounced the perpetrators of the attack in *The Spanish Arena*. In their contemporary books, E. Knoblaugh and F. Schlayer also suggested that it had been an operation by the Soviet Union's secret services. In France, the event shocked public opinion, but the truth was not known because the Republican press claimed that it was "a new savagery by Franco's air force" and launched a propaganda campaign accusing the Nationalists of an attack against the International Red Cross and against France. It is now known that the pilots who carried out the attack were G. Zakharov and N. Shimelkov. A friend of Delaprée's, journalist Sefton Delmer, claimed in the 1960s that Alexander Orlov, the head of the NKVD, had ordered the downing of the plane to prevent reports of the mass murders at Paracuellos del Jarama from reaching the International Red Cross Committee, as the Republic could be accused of crimes against humanity. The Socialist Foreign Minister Julio Álvarez del Vayo must have been particularly interested in concealing the massacres. On 11 December at the United Nations in Geneva, he gave a famous speech in which he accused Germany and Italy of indiscriminate bombing that caused the deaths of thousands of children and women in Spain. At a time when he was trying to win over international opinion, it would have been a serious setback for Álvarez del Vayo, who, like Negrín, was married to a Jewess of Russian origin, if Dr. Henry had handed over the documents in the Swiss city that would have discredited his government in the eyes of world opinion.

Before the end of the year, another incident caused an international scandal that embarrassed the government of Largo Caballero. On 20 December, Baron de Borchgrave, a diplomat acting as Belgium's chargé d'affaires in Spain, left the embassy in his official car and disappeared. His wife, an American national, worriedly called all the journalists she knew and they all began to search for him. Finally, on the 28th, in a mass grave in Fuencarral, his body was found along with those of fifteen other victims. The diplomat had been killed with three shots at close range, two in the back and one in the head. The gruesomely mutilated corpse could be identified by the name of the Belgian tailor on his suit. At first the government said he had been killed in a bombing. In a second version, it blamed international brigades, who had executed him for being a Franco spy. The Belgian government, outraged, protested strongly and threatened to break off diplomatic relations, demanded an official apology, military honours at the funeral, heavy compensation for the family and punishment for the culprits. The Republican Government rejected any responsibility and Largo Caballero submitted the matter to the Hague Tribunal. In Belgium the assassination was compared to that of Calvo Sotelo and led to the resignation of the Socialist Émile Vandervelde, Minister of Health and Vice-President of the Government. Finally, in January 1938 Negrín agreed to pay compensation of one million Belgian francs.

On the subject of propaganda and Álvarez del Vayo's lack of scruples, it must be said that in the early years of the war a well-known figure, Otto Katz, the Jewish communist and Zionist who in 1933 had mounted the entire campaign to frame the Nazis for the Reichstag fire, was in charge of propaganda for the Republic. Katz arrived in Madrid at the end of June 1936 and three days before the military rebellion he went to Barcelona, where he lived through the beginning of the civil war, during which he entered and left Spain on numerous occasions. Paris and London were the cities from which he controlled the Agencia España, which he directed in close collaboration with Julio Álvarez del Vayo, the Foreign Minister of the Republic, who considered him a genius of propaganda.

Initially, Agency Spain was linked to Willi Münzenberg, "the red millionaire", but in 1937 Stalin lost confidence in Münzenberg because of his relations with Trotskyism and Katz became the shadow director. The Spanish Agency, with offices and contacts throughout Europe, maintained an information and disinformation network and carried out other secret tasks. Katz was based in the Paris office, but had the solid support of the Spanish News Agency in London, hence his frequent travels. Not everyone was as accepting as Álvarez del Vayo of Katz's way of running the Spanish News Agency. Jonathan Miles reports in *The Nine Lives of Otto Katz* that Andrés de Irujo, secretary of the Ministry of Justice when his brother Manuel was minister, denounced the lack of scruples of a person "with whom no dealings should be made." Irujo, not knowing who Katz was and who he was serving, believed that any transaction with a character who, from his point of view, did not credibly represent "any political party or organisation and who ignored the problem of Spain and the Spanish people" should be avoided. Irujo would later denounce Agencia España as a propaganda factory without any informative rigour.

Towards Stalinist rule of the Republic

On 21 December 1936 Stalin wrote a letter to Largo Caballero, published on 4 June 1939 in *The New York Times* and quoted by Gerald Brenan and Burnett Bolloten. In it he recommended that he should win over the peasants by solving the agrarian questions and reducing taxes. As for the petty bourgeoisie, he advised him to win them over by preventing confiscations, supporting their interests and introducing republican leaders into the government in order to reassure foreign capital. Stalin was thus pursuing a moderate policy, seeking the backing of the middle classes and the support of France and Britain, a policy which had nothing to do with the revolution advocated by the Trotskyists and anarchists, so often announced by Largo Caballero himself. The PCE, which went from thirty thousand members at the beginning of the war to two hundred and fifty thousand in March 1937, was to be the great beneficiary of this line of action. The battle of Madrid was the circumstance which enabled the Communists to become gradually stronger, more indispensable. The role of the anarchists in the defence of the capital and the power they held both in Madrid and in Barcelona and other cities should not be forgotten, however. They were to become the main stumbling block which sooner or later would have to be removed, since, moreover, they constituted for the Trotskyists the only possible point of support. Only with them could the revolutionary party demanded by Trotsky in his writings on the situation in Spain be formed.

It must be borne in mind, and this is the great mystery that remains unravelled, that behind the scenes there was the internal struggle among the communists who came from all over Europe, whom Stalin controlled through his agents. The inextricable web of betrayals, spies, agents provocateurs, professional criminals, disappearances and assassinations is very difficult to unravel. Historians generally criticise Stalin, the great traitor of the international proletariat; but the dogmatic intellectuals of the Left say not a word about who Trotsky was, whose relationship with the Baruchs, Morgans, Schiffs, Givotovskys and Warburgs is always overlooked and never revealed. Trotsky represents for them revolutionary purity. His betrayal, even greater than that of Stalin, is ignored and the enigma of the shadowy manoeuvres of his agents in Spain has never been revealed.

On the ground, the Communist Party, besides demonstrating its organisational capacity and its mastery of the technique of propaganda, had the power to distribute the arms arriving from Moscow, which enabled it to create out of nothing a magnificent army, the famous Fifth Regiment, which was vital during the almost three months of the siege of Madrid. By the end of 1936 the Fifth Regiment had sixty thousand men in its ranks. Among its founders were the Italian Stalinist Vittorio Vidali, known as Carlos Contreras, the famous Major Carlos, the Regiment's political commissar, and Enrique Castro, its first military commander.

The frontal battle took place during the month of November and the first half of December. The offensives and counteroffensives were fought to the point of paroxysm in fierce hand-to-hand combat. Before he died in December after his plane was shot down, the journalist Louis Delaprée recounted the harshness of the fighting, which was fought from house to house and from floor to floor: "They shot each other at point-blank range, they slit each other's throats from landing to landing...". In the end, the Nationalists were stopped thanks to the arrival of the international brigades, T-26 tanks, artillery and Russian aircraft, which gave the defenders of the capital the extra strength they needed. "No pasarán", the famous slogan coined by Pasionaria, was the slogan that became reality. By January 1937 the failure of the attack on Madrid was irreversible and the front was stabilised until the end of the war.

The Spanish military men put in charge of the defence of Madrid by the government were José Miaja and Vicente Rojo, and alongside them was the top representative of the GRU (Soviet Military Secret Service), a brigadier general who arrived as a military attaché and called himself Vladimir Efimovich Gorev, alias "Sancho", whose real name was Woldemar Roze. According to Pierre Broué, he was the real director of the General Staff and organiser of the defence of Madrid. Gorev must have been in Trotsky's orbit from the beginning: in addition to serving in the Red Army during the Russian civil war, he had worked in Germany as a military organiser, but was also in charge of terrorist acts. When he was arrested in 1923 for being one of the organisers of the "German October", he said his name was Alexander Skoblewsky. In Germany he had a different name in each city. In Berlin he went by the name of General Wolf. According to the German police Gorev-Roze-Skoblewsky was half-Jewish.

Before he was tried in Lepzig, GPU leader Felix Dzerjinsky tried to negotiate his release through Heinz Neumann. Finally, Skoblewsky, who had been sentenced to twelve years, was released in 1925 through a prisoner exchange. His next destination was China, which was another of Trotsky's priorities. There he was to organise the soviets and speed up the revolution. Until the end of 1929 he was in China, where he was called Vysokogorets, but he also had two other aliases, "Nikitin" and "Gordon". In *Das Rotbuch über Spanien (The Red Book about Spain)* he is accused of mass terror and blamed for the deaths of more than half a million people in the Sinkiang region in the northwest of the country. Between 1930 and 1933, under the pseudonym "Herbert", he worked as a military spy in New York. Stalin, in the process of purging the Red Army, ordered his arrest in January 1938 and in the same year he was sentenced to death[24]. Two other Jewish military men who gained fame in the Battle of Madrid were Semion Moiseyevich Krivoshein, alias "Mele", who commanded the tank forces of the Republican army, and Yakov Vladimirovich Smushkevich, who commanded the Soviet air force and was known as "General Douglas". The latter, too, was arrested in June 1941 and executed in October of the same year.

---

[24] Vladimir Efimovich Gorev (Woldemar Roze) was surrounded by Jewish agents. One of them, Sergei Ginzburg, appears under the pseudonym "Sierra Charriba" in the chronicles of the Battle of Madrid. Research in the RGASPI (Archives of Socio-Political History of the Russian State) has uncovered a notebook by Sergei Ginzburg entitled *Mission to Madrid.* It reports a meeting in the vicinity of the Soviet embassy at which General Gorev, accompanied by his interpreter and mistress Emma Wolf, summoned a dozen international and Spanish personalities to announce that he had integrated them all into a special unit: the Mobile Assault Battalion. Wolf translated Gorev's words into English and Spanish, assuring them that the Battalion's entry into action would mean "a new way of waging war, unknown until now". Only the members of the new unit, including Ginzburg, would know of its existence. They were soldiers selected for their skill in combat and for their great physical and intellectual endurance. Ginzburg explains that the Mobile Assault Battalion, based in Madrid, would report directly to Gorev, i.e. Military Intelligence, and would operate anywhere in Spain, as it would be transported by land or air. Gorev announced that the Battalion's missions would be mainly behind enemy lines, which is why it had to be lethal and effective. It would be equipped with the most advanced means and the most modern weapons. The names of some of the international members of the Battalion mentioned by Ginzburg indicate their Jewish origin. Prominent among them are Livshits, Ratner ("John "), Lvovich (the latter two were colonels who were shot with Gorev) and two other guys sitting to the right of the general, old acquaintances of Ginzburg: Rosencrantz and Guildenstern, whom Gorev presented as "two revolutionaries who would be engaged in various tasks connected with their proven experience as international agents". Ginzburg ends by saying that, in any case, he "would not trust them".

One of the world's most famous communists during the defence of Madrid was the legendary General Emilio Kléber. He passed for a naturalised Canadian Austrian, but was a German-born Jew named Manfred Zalmonovich Stern, although he was also known as Lazar Stern, Manfred Stern and Moishe Stern. Stern/Kléber had been in 1929, under the pseudonym Mark Zilbert, head of Soviet espionage in New York, where he coincided with Gorev. An international press campaign portrayed him as the great hero of the international brigades. Krivitsky claims that he belonged to the Red Army General Staff. Kleber commanded the 11th International Brigade, which fought in the battles at the Casa de Campo and the Battle of the University City. Propaganda catapulted him to fame by describing him as the "saviour of Madrid". However, Vicente Rojo, in a letter to Miaja dated 26 November 1936, denounced the "exaggerated" publicity Kléber received, his "contrived" popularity and his "false" leadership skills. Burnett Bolloten quotes excerpts from Rojo's letter in his monumental work on the Civil War: "It is true that your men fight well," he said, "but nothing more, and this is done by many who are not commanded by Kleber". Rojo accused Kleber of falsifying the military situation in his reports, of insubordination, of political ambitions, and warned Miaja of a "low manoeuvre which may displace you from the function which all your subordinates see you perform with enthusiasm."

On New Year's Eve 1936, a dinner was held at Kléber's command post, to which he invited, among others: Máté Zalka, known as General Luckacs, a Jew of Hungarian origin who was commander-in-chief of the 12th Brigade and was actually called Béla Frankl; the poet Rafael Alberti; his companion María Teresa León and her sister, who eventually married Kléber[25]; Colonel Gustavo Durán, a member of the Generation of '27; and a special guest, Major Juan Perea Capulino, a Spanish military officer who became a general. In his work *Los culpables: recuerdos de la guerra 1936-1939*, Perea recounts that Kleber told him that the PCE needed to control the direction of the war and create its own caudillo, a man with a revolutionary political history who had the confidence of the people, who could become generalissimo of the armies of the Republic. You can be that man," offered Kléber. I know, and I tell you within with the greatest reserve, that in these days you will be promoted to divisional general and that you will be entrusted with the command of a large unit on a very important sector of the Madrid front. You dare. The Communist Party will be very glad to see you join its ranks. Think it over. Don't answer me now." Maria Teresa Leon, seated on the right of the Spanish soldier, pinned the party insignia on his breast; however, Perea later refused the offer to the general surprise.

---

[25] This sister of María Teresa León was the enigmatic Spaniard who years later turned up in Moscow with two children and claimed to be the wife of Manfred Stern/Emilio Kléber.

Gerald Brenan writes in *The Spanish Labyrinth* that in January 1937 "Communist pressure on the Government was great and for a moment it was thought that a coup d'état was imminent and that the International Brigades would march on Valencia". If this was indeed the case, a couple of questions might be asked: were Generals Kleber and Luckacs loyal to Stalin and the PCE or were they seeking to stage a coup d'état? Was Kleber trying to win Perea's support and were there ulterior motives in his proposal? On 4 February 1937 Kleber was suddenly removed from command of the 11th Brigade and in the autumn of the same year he was recalled to Moscow and disappeared. Krivitsky, who had worked with him for years and knew his entire family, links his downfall with the purge in the Red Army. It later emerged that Kleber was arrested and sentenced to 15 years' imprisonment on charges of treason committed in Spain. He died on 18 February 1954 in the Sosnovka labour camp.

On 21 February 1937 there was another event that has not been adequately clarified: the withdrawal of Ambassador Moses Rosenberg, who had been recalled to Moscow and eliminated the same year in the context of the anti-Trotskyist purges. His replacement was another Jew, Leon Yakovlevich Khaikis, who had been acting as secretary of the Embassy. He had been one of the officials of the Petrograd Czech in the early days of the revolution. In the early 1920s he became head of propaganda for the Comintern in Central Europe. Under Karl Rádek, he worked alongside Bela Kun. Later he was attached to the Soviet embassy in Mexico and from then on directed the activities of the GPU in Central and South America. Khaikis presented his credentials to Azaña on 16 March, but his tenure was short-lived: in May 1937 he was recalled to Moscow and was also executed in 1938. It is not clear who took his place.

According to socialist Luis Araquistáin there were no more ambassadors. The Trotskyite Pierre Broué and other historians try to explain Rosenberg's dismissal on the basis of an alleged complaint by Largo Caballero about the ambassador's interference in Spanish affairs; but this explanation does not hold water if one considers that in Moscow's eyes the Spanish Lenin had become an obstacle to the Stalinist Communists who did not want social revolution. Stalin would hardly have heeded Largo Caballero's reproach if Rosenberg had acted on his instructions. All the documents show that the Soviet advisers, the Communist ministers and the Socialists Alvarez del Vayo and Negrin were trying to gain control of the government. Had Rosenberg's efforts gone in the same direction, they should not have led to his dismissal and subsequent execution.

Stalin had reportedly received negative reports from his agents about the conduct of Ambassador Rosenberg, so in the letter of 21 December mentioned above he asked Largo Caballero for an appraisal of the Soviet advisers and in particular his opinion of Rosenberg. In the letter of reply, dated 12 January 1937, published in *Guerra y Revolución* by Dolores Ibárruri et al, Largo Caballero wrote:

> "The comrades who have come to help us at our request are doing us a great service. Their considerable experience is very useful to us and contributes efficiently to the defence of Spain..... I can assure you that they are carrying out their duties with real enthusiasm and extraordinary courage. As for Comrade Rosenberg, I can sincerely inform you that we are satisfied with his behaviour and his activities among us. We all appreciate him here. He works very hard, in fact excessively hard, for he exposes his delicate health..."

This reply would show that it was not the complaints or alleged arguments between Rosenberg and Largo Caballero that advised the replacement of the ambassador. Stalin's interest in the attitude of the diplomatic mission would rather indicate that its conduct was not in line with the non-revolutionary direction designed by Moscow. Proof of this is that on 2 February 1937 the Spanish ambassador to the USSR, Marcelino Pascua, had a meeting in the Kremlin with Stalin, Voroshilov and Molotov. In the middle of the interview, Stalin surprised the ambassador by criticising his main representatives in Spain. Marcelino Pascua's notes on the meeting exist in the National Historical Archive (AHN). According to these papers, Stalin told the ambassador that they would send someone less "enfant terrible", someone more "official". As for Antonov-Ovseyenko, he was given to understand that he would be replaced by "someone less revolutionary".

Krivitsky acknowledges that Moscow's main concern at the end of 1936 was to gain control of the International Brigade. As for the second government of Largo Caballero, he defines it as "a precarious coalition of antagonistic political parties". Krivitsky travelled to Barcelona in November and learned from his colleague Stashevsky that Stalin had already thought of Negrín to replace the Spanish Lenin. At the beginning of November the PCE and the OGPU supported Largo Caballero; although they did not control him at will, so they had already thought of a replacement from the beginning. The priority of winning the battle of Madrid put aside the many differences within the coalition government; but in December the Defence Junta withdrew by decree all the powers that the committees had been allowed to retain in the decisive month of November. The Communist Party began to work in the districts to get them to abandon their revolutionary initiatives and submit to the single administration of the Junta. Pierre Broué refers to "violent clashes between the CNT troops and the men of the Communist Party".

On 12 December the Junta decided to militarise all militia units under the authority of Miaja and the communists of the Junta. On this date the trams ceased to be free and rents were re-established. On the 24th the carrying of arms was banned in the capital and security was handed over to government agencies. On 26 December, the Junta's councillor for supplies, Pablo Yagüe, was seriously wounded by CNT militiamen who tried to verify the identity of the occupants of his vehicle. This attack," writes Broué, "provoked the indignation of the communist, socialist and republican press. The CNT newspaper, which wanted to respond to them, was censored; but the culprits, arrested, were acquitted by the people's court. The CNT press accused the CP men of having murdered three of their own, in reprisal, in a neighbourhood of Madrid". As for the POUM, an offensive was unleashed against it which involved the closure of its premises, its radio and its press.

In January 1937 the Stalinist communists were already preparing the struggle for power in the government of Largo Caballero, which was to lead to the events of May 1937 in Barcelona. The revolution had been stopped and the counter-revolution was being prepared, to which Largo Caballero was an obstacle. The Spanish Lenin had proposed in March 1936 the fusion of the socialist and communist parties, which had been enthusiastically welcomed by José Díaz, leader of the communists. A step in this direction had been the union in April 1936 of the Socialist Youth and the Communist Youth, whose initiator was Álvarez del Vayo. This merger was done hastily, without a previous congress, and the big winners were the Communists. Largo Caballero must have thought that the three thousand young Communists would be diluted among the fifty thousand Socialists, but exactly the opposite happened, for after the outbreak of the war, Santiago Carrillo, the general secretary of the JSU, whom Largo called Santiaguito, switched to the Communist Party together with other leaders of the Federation of the Socialist Youth. In this way the JSU became one of the driving forces behind the domination of the PCE.

Instead of the National Unification Congress, Carrillo called a National Conference in January 1937, dominated by his delegates, which succeeded in setting up a National Committee crammed with communists. Only then did Largo Caballero realise his mistake. Jesús Hernández (Public Instruction and Fine Arts) and Vicente Uribe (Agriculture), the communist ministers in the government, held portfolios of little political weight to be able to dominate the Executive. For this reason, the collaboration of two socialists was decisive: Álvarez del Vayo (Foreign Affairs) and Negrín (Finance). The former, who happened to be the prime minister's right-hand man, proved to be a convinced communist, a supporter of the USSR and its international policy. The actions of the latter have already been discussed.

The four anarchist ministers, theoretical representatives of the revolutionary vanguard, were another matter. While in Russia the anarchists were a tiny group which could be eliminated without difficulty by Trotsky and Lenin, in Spain they constituted the most militant elements of the proletariat and were indispensable for the consolidation of the revolution. Trotsky had understood that in principle it was necessary to count on the anarchist masses to take power. In a 1931 article entitled *The Spanish Revolution and Communist Tactics* he had written in relation to the CNT:

"To strengthen this confederation and transform it into a real mass organisation is a duty for every advanced worker and, above all, for the communists". Trotsky then foresaw a two-front struggle within the workers' movement: against the "parliamentary cretinism" of the socialists, and against the "anti-parliamentary cretinism" of the anarchists. Because of his contempt for anarchosyndicalism as a doctrine and as a revolutionary method, he saw no other solution than to wrest the masses from the influence of the anarchists and the socialists: "The anarchosyndicalists," said Trotsky, "can be at the head of the revolution only if they renounce their anarchist prejudices. It is our duty to help them in this respect. It must be assumed that some of the syndicalist leaders will go over to the socialists or will remain on the fringes of the revolution. The real revolutionaries will be with us; the masses will go with the communists, as will the majority of the socialist workers." Five years after the publication of the article, Trotsky could only count in Spain on Andreu Nin's party, the POUM, and the anarchists remained the only possible card to play in opposing Stalin's communism.

The situation of Largo Caballero as prime minister was in a sense similar, since only by relying on the anarchists could he survive the offensive of those who did not want a social revolution. His situation became untenable when Indalecio Prieto's sector also moved closer to the Communists. Whereas in 1936 Largo had advocated union with the Communists and Indalecio Prieto had rejected it, by early 1937 the roles had been reversed: now it was Prieto who called for immediate fusion and Largo Caballero who opposed it. Socialists and Communists agreed on putting an end to the revolution, ending the collectivisations, restoring the state and forming a regular army that could win the war. In January 1937 Santiago Carrillo proposed in Valencia to fight against three enemies: Franco, the Trotskyists and the uncontrolled extremists. The fall of Malaga on 8 February, where lack of discipline, factional fighting and chaos prevailed, favoured the start of the public campaign against the president of the government and the resumption of hostilities between the PCE and the CNT, who accused each other of having brought about the defeat. The communists exploited the disaster in Malaga to the full.

The struggles between communists and anarchists were a fact. Largo Caballero noticed during March that men he trusted, including Álvarez del Vayo, the foreign minister, were betraying him. He informed Azaña of this. The president of the Republic authorised the minister's dismissal; however, the prime minister, aware of his weakness and that the dismissal of Álvarez del Vayo would lead to a government crisis, opted to keep him on. Nevertheless, on 14 April Largo went on the offensive and signed an executive order limiting the powers of the Commissariat of War, a vital body whose appointments he would personally decide.

On the other hand, in the Madrid checas, in a vicious circle of action and reaction, they had begun to murder each other. Melchor Rodríguez, the "red angel", accused the communist José Cazorla, the Junta's adviser for Public Order, of allowing communists to interrogate, torture and kill CNT militants in private prisons. The anarchists accused Cazorla of being "a provocateur in the service of fascism" and demanded his dismissal. The scandal grew and Largo Caballero took advantage of the situation to proceed on 23 April to dissolve the Madrid Junta, which was to be replaced by a Municipal Council. This was his definitive declaration of war on the PCE, as numerous commissars ceased their functions.

Largo Caballero thus tried to take the initiative to regain control of the situation. Since he was still the Minister of War, he proposed an attack in the direction of Extremadura in order to divide Franco's zone again: the plan was to cut off the rebels' communications with the south and thus relieve the situation on the northern front. Both Miaja and the Russian advisers objected on the grounds that Madrid could not be cut off. When Miaja was ordered to send part of the troops from Madrid to the Extremadura sector, the communists asked him to refuse. Faced with this indiscipline, the Minister of War adopted a forceful attitude and forced Miaja to carry out the orders.

At the same time, in Catalonia, the POUM, which in December 1936 had been expelled from the Government of the Generalitat under pressure from the Stalinists of the PSUC, was clearly orienting itself in favour of a revolutionary policy. Through his newspaper *La Batalla* he denounced the retreat of the revolution and the "counter-revolutionary machinations of the CP and the PSUC". On 21 March Andreu Nin gave a speech in Barcelona which was reproduced the next day in *La Batalla*. According to him, the counter-revolutionary process was due to the "political role played by reformism within the revolution, supported by that international organisation which has the cynicism to call itself communist". Nin appealed to the leaders of the CNT and ended by saying that for victory it was necessary to have "only one flag, the red flag of the proletarian revolution. A single government, the workers' and peasants' government, the government of the working class".

The youth of the POUM, JCI (Iberian Communist Youth), were in favour of the dissolution of parliament and in favour of a constituent assembly elected on the basis of factory committees and assemblies of peasants and fighters. The CNT also had a revolutionary opposition current which did not accept the militarisation of the militias. They called themselves "the friends of Durruti" and published the newspaper *El amigo del pueblo*. Their position coincided with that of the POUM and the JCI. Andreu Nin and the party leaders tried to approach the leadership and militants of the CNT in order to organise the defence of the workers' movement and the gains of the revolution. His proposal, outlined in another speech on 25 April, was the formation of a revolutionary united front. To this end, he called for "the revolutionary instinct of the CNT to be transformed into revolutionary consciousness and the heroism of its masses into coherent policy".

These were in fact the aspirations of Trotsky, who from Mexico, not suspecting that Stalin's agents had him in their sights, pontificated in the same vein with a vapid verbiage, as far removed from reality as were the proposals of his Spanish friend. Trotsky had criticised the entry of the anarchists into the Popular Front Government and that of Nin as Minister of Justice in the Government of the Generalitat. Once again, "the old man" was preaching civil war within the civil war. In an article under the pseudonym Crux, written in April 1937 and published belatedly in *La Lutte Ouvriére*, his prescription was as follows:

> "It is necessary to mobilise the masses openly and boldly against the government of the Popular Front. The treachery of these gentlemen who pretend to be anarchists when in reality they are nothing more than liberals must be exposed to the trade unionist and anarchist workers. Stalin must be denounced as the worst agent of the bourgeoisie. We must feel ourselves to be the leaders of the revolutionary masses and not the advisers of the bourgeois government."

Trotsky's brazenness and cynicism, being himself the chief agent of international Jewish capitalism, allowed him to write in the same article:

> "... The victory of the republican army of capital over the fascist army will necessarily mean the explosion of civil war within the republican camp. In this new civil war, the proletariat will not be able to win unless at its head there is a revolutionary party which has succeeded in winning the confidence of the majority of the workers and the semi-proletarian peasants."

While the smug guru of the international proletariat dogmatised from a distance, comfortably ensconced in his Mexican residence, the Spaniards continued to fight fiercely against each other. His proposals and Nin's criticisms of the PCE and Stalin, however, did not go unnoticed.

Civil war on the Republican side and the overthrow of Largo Caballero

Catalonia, where the revolution had reached its peak, was still the bastion where revolutionary structures remained and the armed workers were reluctant to give up their share of power. On 3 April Companys formed a provisional Consell de Govern (Provisional Government Council) presided over by Josep Tarradellas, who was also the Conseller en Cap (Minister of Finance and Education). Artemi Aiguader (ERC), Joan Comorera (PSUC), Josep Calvet (Unió de Rabassaires), Francisco Isgleas (CNT) and Joan J. Domènech (CNT) completed the government. On 7 April PSUC and UGT presented a "Victory Plan " for Catalonia that collided with the revolutionary aims of the CNT and concentrated all arms, security and power in the hands of the Government. On 16 April Companys increased the number of members of the Consell de Govern to ten without altering the balance of political forces.

On 17 April, carabinieri sent by Negrín appeared in Puigcerdà and Figueras with the intention of taking control of the customs offices, which had been in the hands of CNT militiamen since July 1936. Faced with their refusal to withdraw, the situation became tense and a stalemate was reached, so the CNT Regional Committee tried to negotiate. On 24 April, the Commissioner for Public Order, Eusebio Rodríguez Salas, alias "el manco", a former anarchist and poumista militant who had switched to the PSUC, suffered an attack from which he escaped unharmed. On the 25th, Roldán Cortada, a leader of the UGT and member of the PSUC, was assassinated in Molins de Rey. The PSUC organised a mass funeral which turned into a protest against the POUM and the CNT: for three hours the Catalan Stalinist communists paraded with guns on their shoulders. The leaders of the POUM accused the Catalan communists of having organised a "counter-revolutionary demonstration".

The next day the Generalitat sent its police to Molins de Rey. The local anarchist leaders, accused of having participated in the assassination, were arrested. In this atmosphere the spark finally broke out in Bellver de Cerdanya (Lérida), where the carabineros clashed with anarchist militants. Antonio Martín, alias "el cojo de Málaga", fell in the battle along with seven other militiamen. Martín, president of the Puigcerdà Revolutionary Committee and the main promoter of collectivisation in the region, was a former smuggler who had become the head of the customs officers in July 1936. Faced with the rumour that the Ministry of the Interior would order the disarmament of all the workers' groups, on 29 April CNT-FAI groups armed with rifles and hand grenades appeared in the streets of Barcelona. Fearing the outbreak of conflict, the Generalitat cancelled the May Day celebrations. Both *La Batalla* and *Solidaridad Obrera*, the CNT newspaper, called on the workers not to let themselves be disarmed and to stand vigil "with arms in hand".

In Valencia a joint meeting of the CNT and the UGT was held on 1 May. Largo Caballero finally realised that he was being left alone, so his staunchest supporters still tried to appeal to the unity of the two unions. Carlos Baráibar, one of the founders of *Claridad* together with Luis Araquistáin, veiled criticism of the PCE and the USSR and exalted the joint action of a utopian "trade union government". Largo Caballero, who because of his collaboration with Primo de Rivera was never well regarded by the libertarian masses, knew that the anarcho-syndicalists could not accept a regular army without violating their anti-authoritarian principles, so, in order to win them over and seek reconciliation, he had not carried out a complete militarisation of his militias, even though it was one of the constant demands of the communists.

The situation was explosive and the explosion took place on 3 May. At around three o'clock in the afternoon, three trucks with Assault Guards from the Public Order Police under the command of Eusebio Rodríguez Salas, a member of the PSUC who held the post of Public Order Commissioner of the Generalitat, arrived at the Telefónica building with a seizure order signed by Artemi Aiguader, a member of the ERC and adviser on Internal Security. Telefónica belonged to the American trust "American Telegraph and Telephon". The exchange, which according to a decree of the Catalan government on collectivisations had been in the hands of the CNT-FAI since the beginning of the war, perfectly exemplified the duality of powers. All communications were listened to by the anarchists, who found out everything that interested them. Azaña and Companys could not speak freely, as their conversations were sometimes interrupted by the CNT Control Committee. Arthur Koestler, correspondent of the *London News Chronicle*[26], reveals that Luis Araquistáin, ambassador in Paris, and Álvarez del Vayo communicated through their wives, two Jewish sisters of German origin who spoke Yiddish, so that no one could understand them.

Once inside, the guards disarmed the militiamen on the ground floor; but the workers on the upper floors blocked their way with machine-gun fire. Since the CNT was part of the Government of the Generalitat, Rodríguez Salas asked for help and two anarchist leaders of the Control Patrols of the Generalitat's General Commissariat for Public Order, Dionisio Eroles and José Asens, immediately showed up. Eroles had directed the actions of the Control Patrols of the Central Committee of Anti-Fascist Militias after the coup d'état and was responsible for the murder of thousands of people. On 22 October 1936 he had been one of the signatories of the pact of unity of action between the CNT, UGT, FAI and PSUC, so from then on he was the head of service of the General Commissariat of the Generalitat. According to the 4 May edition of *Solidaridad Obrera*, Eroles and Asens "intervened in a timely manner so that our comrades, who had opposed the action of the guards inside the building, would renounce their just attitude." Other sources say that they persuaded the Assault Guards to leave the besieged building.

On learning of the assault, the CNT councillors Isgleas, Capdevila and Fernández demanded the dismissal of Rodríguez Salas and Aiguader, but

---

[26] Arthur Koestler, whose *The Thirteenth Tribe* has occupied an important place in this work, worked in Paris in the Comintern offices of Willi Münzenberg, the great propagandist of the Communist Party of Germany, and was sent to Spain as a spy. His work as a journalist provided him with cover. In Paris Koestler was the assistant to Otto Katz, alias André Simone, the Jewish Communist of Czech origin who had been appointed by Alvarez del Vayo as director of the Agencia Española, the Republic's foreign propaganda office. Both Katz and Koestler received instructions from Münzenberg.

their demand was not met, as the other parties and President Companys opposed it. This led to a general strike and a break in hostilities. Thousands of people had been gathering in the Plaça de Catalunya, and the events of the Telefónica were immediately known throughout the city. The POUM, the Friends of Durruti, the Libertarian Youth and other organisations took up arms and began to build hundreds of barricades. George Orwell, who witnessed the events, describes in *Homage to Catalonia* how the barricades were erected:

> "The construction of those barricades was a strange and wonderful spectacle. With that passionate energy that Spaniards display when they have decided to undertake a task for good, long lines of men, women and small children were pulling up cobblestones, moving them in a wheelbarrow they had found somewhere, and staggering from one place to another under heavy sandbags".

By nightfall, factories, workshops, warehouses and other establishments had stopped their activity. Barcelona was in arms and war had broken out. The anarcho-syndicalists dominated the situation in the working-class neighbourhoods surrounding the city: in the suburbs of Sarrià, Hostafrancs, Sans and Barceloneta many of the guards surrendered or locked themselves helplessly in their barracks. In the commercial area and the Gothic Quarter, the forces were more evenly balanced. President Azaña, who lived near the Catalan Parliament, at 8 p.m., frightened by the intermittent gunfire heard in the surrounding area, ordered his secretary Cándido Bolívar to ask Largo Caballero for reinforcements for his personal guard. Shortly afterwards, it was Aiguader himself who asked the Minister of the Interior, Galarza, to urgently send 1,500 men to put down the rebellion. On Companys' orders, Tarradellas visited Azaña at 11 p.m. to apologise. It took him an hour and a half to make a journey that could have been made in just a few minutes. Azaña himself recounts this in his memoirs:

> "They forced him to get out of the car at all the barricades... and to parley at length, humiliating him. When he wanted to start on the subject of excuses, stressing that he was ashamed as a Catalan, I stopped him by repeating the remarks already made to Bolívar for the president of the Council: 'There is no room for excuses, but to control the mutiny; and as far as I am concerned, to guarantee my safety and freedom of movement'".

The regional committees of the CNT, the FAI, the Libertarian Youth and the Executive Committee of the POUM met during the night and the Poumists tried to convince the anarchists that the time had come to form an alliance against the communists and the government. Various sources give texts of what was said on that historic night. Bolloten reproduces the words of the poumist Julián Gorkín: "Neither you nor we have thrown the masses of Barcelona into this movement. It was a spontaneous response to a Stalinist provocation. This is the decisive moment for the revolution. Either we take the lead in the movement to destroy the enemy within or the movement will fail and that will be our destruction. The choice must be made: revolution or counter-revolution." The leaders of the CNT and the FAI refused and proposed to work to calm things down. It seems that their main demand was the dismissal of the commissar who had caused the provocation.

The next day, Tuesday 4 May, Aiguader again asked Galarza to send 1,500 assault guards, but Largo Caballero, who was fighting a political battle against the communists, did not want to antagonise the CNT and the FAI and give more power to his adversaries in Catalonia. The Minister of the Interior replied to Aiguader that the President of the Government would wait until the afternoon in the hope that the Generalitat could control the situation with its own forces. Meanwhile, supported by the POUM, the Libertarian Youth and the Friends of Durruti, the workers, armed with machine guns and rifles, took control of the city. They attacked the barracks of the Guardia de Asalto and government buildings. A leaflet written by the German Jew Hans David Freund was distributed at the barricades. At the beginning of the war, Freund had entered Spain to participate in the building of the Trotskyist movement. To this end he arrived in Madrid in August, where he contributed to the POUM's German-language radio broadcasts. From the end of 1936 he had been working in Barcelona with the Friends of Durruti under the pseudonym "Moulin". He played a prominent role in the uprising and was arrested at the beginning of August and, like Andreu Nin and other Trotskyists, disappeared.

The counter-attack by the communists and the government forces soon followed and Barcelona was plunged into a civil war within the civil war. Companys addressed the population by radio and called for calm, but to no avail. Meanwhile, Largo Caballero had summoned the CNT ministers of his government to Valencia, where he told them that he feared that the communists would exploit the struggle to overthrow him. He confessed to them that he could not send the forces requested by Aiguader. This could not be done by the government," he said, "because it would mean handing over forces to operate in the service of the one who had perhaps provoked the conflict. Before agreeing to this, it would proceed to seize the public order services, as the Constitution empowered it to do". Largo Caballero proposed that representatives of the CNT National Committee and the UGT Executive Committee should go to Barcelona to try to stop the hostilities. At eleven o'clock in the morning a meeting of the Council of Ministers took place in Valencia. Backed by Indalecio Prieto and the left-wing Republican ministers, the Communists pressured the President of the Government to send reinforcements and to take control of public order and military affairs in the region. Faced with the threat of a government crisis, Largo Caballero promised to take these measures if the situation had not improved by the afternoon.

García Oliver and Federica Montseny, the anarchist ministers who had supported the president's position during the government meeting, arrived by plane in Barcelona at 5 p.m. in the company of the ugetista Hernández Zancajo, a personal friend of Largo Caballero. They all read out on the radio an appeal to their followers to lay down their arms and return to work, but these instructions outraged many libertarians, who felt betrayed by their leaders. At about the same time as the arrival of the cenetista leaders, the POUM publicly declared itself in favour of resistance. Meanwhile, units of the 26th Anarchist Division, the former Durruti Column, assembled in Barbastro under the command of Gregorio Jover with the intention of marching on Barcelona.

At half past nine that night Prieto communicated with Azaña and let him know that the destroyers *Lepanto* and *Sánchez Barcaiztegui*, which were to evacuate the president of the Republic, had left Cartagena at two in the afternoon and that five companies of the air force would arrive in Valencia at three in the morning on their way to Barcelona. Free access to the port from Parliament was Azaña's main concern. Burnett Bolloten provides the testimony of Constancia de la Mora, wife of the head of the Air Force, Hidalgo de Cisneros. According to her, from the beginning of the conflict Azaña had asked the government with "hysterical insistence" to take measures for his personal protection, but only Prieto listened to his pleas. Azaña later complained in his writings that President Largo Caballero did not even try to talk to him.

While Prieto tried to reassure Azaña, emissaries from Valencia met with the Catalan government under the chairmanship of the president of the Generalitat. In order to displace Aiguader and Rodríguez Salas, it was agreed to form a provisional Consell de Govern with four representatives: Esquerra, CNT, UGT and Unió de Rabassaires; but when the CNT proposed that the new government should be formed immediately, the communists argued that "the fire in the streets had to cease completely first". Esquerra and the Rabassaires supported the communists, so at 2 a.m. on Wednesday, the 5th, it was decided to speak again by radio. It was in vain, because all through the early hours of the morning the fighting in the streets continued fierce.

Early on the morning of 5 May, CNT leaders redoubled their efforts to control their supporters. The anarchist leader Diego Abad de Santillán later recalled that he had heard libertarian comrades crying on the phone when they were ordered not to shoot while being machine-gunned. So, despite these attempts, the battles raged everywhere. The proletarian districts were all in favour of the revolt and under the control of the workers, who continued to occupy the barricades. In the old town, where the government forces were concentrated, the clashes were particularly intense: the narrow, winding streets were conducive to barricade fighting. Machine-gun fire and rifle shots could be heard throughout the city and those who risked leaving their shelters were shot down in the streets. In the Plaça de Catalunya, in the adjacent streets and around the Generalitat there were numerous dead and wounded. *Solidaridad Obrera* denounced the following day the existence of "agents provocateurs, the so-called 'pacos' snipers, who from the rooftops of the houses were engaged in firing the weapons they had to carry the alarm in the neighbourhoods where it was quiet." The CNT leaders, aware that Largo Caballero would not resist the pressure of his adversaries for long, returned to the Generalitat and insisted that the new government be formed without loss of time. The radio broadcast the agreements between the CNT and the Generalitat, while demanding the simultaneous withdrawal of the police and armed civilians, but the truth was that the communists continued to delay the constitution of the new Consell de Govern. While they were meeting, the news arrived that the Government of Valencia had decided to seize the public order and defence services.

While negotiations continued in the palace of the Generalitat, Azaña expressed his mistrust of his rescue to Indalecio Prieto in a telegraphic communication, as he did not see how the commander of the *Lepanto* could present himself to him when communications with the port were cut off. In *The Spanish Civil War: Revolution and Counterrevolution*, Bolloten reproduces the lengthy conversation. Here is an excerpt from Azaña's words:

"That I should move to Valencia is a very good thought, but absolutely unrealistic, and this is one of the most serious features of the situation, because it is impossible to get through the gates of the park of my residence, around which machine-gun, rifle and bombs are being fired. In this connection, I must tell you that there are two sides to the problem. One is the anarchist insurrection, with all the serious consequences and deplorable effects which I need not point out to you. The other is the lack of freedom in which the Head of State finds himself, not only to move freely, but also to exercise his function. The first would already be serious and would require urgent and energetic decisions. The second is even more serious and could have incalculable consequences. Since Monday afternoon I have waited as long as I could reasonably expect, until the Government had gathered enough repressive elements to control the situation and free the President of the Republic from his kidnapping.... All these considerations induce me to let you know that I can no longer bear the delay of the Government's decisive intervention in either of the two aspects of the problem, and since the President of the Republic cannot quell the insurrection with the sixty poorly armed soldiers of his guard, he will have to attend personally to resolving the other aspect of the question. You have enough perspicacity and political sensitivity to understand that neither my personal decorum nor the dignity of my function, nor the scandal that is taking place throughout the world, allow the head of state to remain in the situation in which he finds himself...".

He then threatened to inform the president of the Cortes, Martínez Barrio, who was to succeed him in office if he resigned. The insinuation did not go unnoticed by Prieto, who, after deploring the situation, asked for a few more hours of calm. Prieto was informed by Largo Caballero that there was no room for any more delays because they would entail a very grave responsibility, and he therefore proposed that an extraordinary issue of the *Gaceta* should publish the decrees that would allow the Ministers of War and the Interior to take measures to re-establish order. Prieto hastened to contact Azaña again, who reminded him that the circumstances could force him to make irreparable decisions: "only a very rapid and overwhelming action by the Government can avoid them". Bolloten, citing information provided by Hidalgo de Cisneros in Mexico in 1940, writes that Prieto had witnessed President Azaña's pusillanimity on several occasions. Here are Burnett Bolloten's own words: "In 1936, when the President was urging the Government to leave Madrid in view of the growing danger in which the capital was placed, he asked Prieto: 'Does the Government want the Fascists to catch me here?' Irritated by Azaña's haste and his concern for personal safety, Prieto remarked to the head of Aviation, Hidalgo de Cisneros: 'That cowardly faggot is acting like a hysterical whore. To justify the use of such harsh terms the British historian adds, "Known as one of the most eloquent orators of the Republic, Prieto also had a reputation for using foul language in his private conversations." The truth was that Azaña feared assassination in Barcelona, as he knew that the anarcho-syndicalists had not forgotten the massacre at Casas Viejas in January 1933.

The clashes spread to other Catalan cities. The Assault Guard proceeded to clear the Telefónica headquarters in Tarragona, Tortosa and Vich. More than thirty anarchists died in Tarragona and another thirty were killed in Tortosa. Elements of the former Durruti Column, joined by militiamen from the 29th Division of the POUM, stopped at Binéfar, forty kilometres from Lérida, where delegates from the CNT Regional Committee tried to persuade Gregorio Jover not to continue the march, which they succeeded in doing despite news from Barcelona of an attack by elements of the PSUC on Federica Montseny's car, which had been shot at from a barricade.

Finally, the new provisional Consell Provisional was formed in Barcelona. The PSUC-UGT councillor, Antonio Sesé, secretary of the Catalan UGT, whose entry into the Government of the Generalitat had just been announced on the radio, was shot and killed in Caspe Street, opposite the CNT's Public Entertainment Union, as he was on his way in an official car to take up his post. The communists accused "Trotskyist provocateurs in the service of fascism" of the assassination. An hour later, Domingo Ascaso, brother of Francisco, one of the leaders of Spanish anarchism along with Durruti and García Oliver, was killed in combat. The clashes intensified and communist forces violently attacked the France station, which was defended by CNT railway workers. The Friends of Durruti refused to obey the CNT-FAI leaders and chose to continue the fight. In the evening the anarchist philosopher Camillo Berneri and his comrade Francesco Barbieri were found murdered on the Ramblas. Fifteen men with UGT armbands, led by a squaddie in civilian clothes, had taken them from their home at around 6 p.m. They had been taken away by the UGT. At the end of the day Companys and Largo Caballero spoke by telephone and the former agreed to cede Public Order to the Madrid Government, so forces from the Jarama front were sent to Barcelona. The war units sent by Prieto, the Minister of the Navy, were already positioned in front of Barcelona harbour, where French and British warships were also ready to take up positions.

On Thursday, 6 May, the CNT was ready for an agreement: both sides were to abandon the barricades and release the hostages. Companys proclaimed that there were "neither winners nor losers". The population began to take to the streets to try to stock up on supplies or with the intention of resuming their daily tasks; but the shooting did not stop and there was no way for the belligerents to leave their trenches at the same time. In the morning, during a lull in the fighting, the commander of the *Lepanto* appeared in Parliament accompanied by a group of sailors; but Azaña felt that it would be foolhardy to try to leave the building. Azaña himself later wrote: "Prieto kept urging me to go out to the port, taking advantage of ten minutes of calm". Zugazagoitia, who was at Prieto's side when he was trying to convince President Azaña, recounted years later, "On Prieto's face there was a faint sceptical smile." Finally, the President of the Republic decided to leave, but when they were about to leave the Parliament building the fighting, Azaña explains, "flared up more violently than ever". This forced him to postpone his departure for Valencia until the following day.

In the afternoon the fighting resumed and a 75 mm. artillery piece manned by the libertarian youths left several dead when it opened fire on a cinema occupied by Republican guards. Finally, in the CNT-FAI House, the news was received in mid-afternoon that fifteen hundred Assault Guards had arrived in Tortosa, which prompted the anarchist leaders to work through the night to organise the truce. The comrades were ordered to be ready to withdraw at six o'clock on Friday morning, 7 May. Exhausted and feeling that it was useless to continue fighting against the will of their leaders, the men left the barricades in the early hours of the morning and disappeared into the darkness. At dawn the local committees of the CNT and the UGT launched the following appeal. "Let's get to work, comrades!

Meanwhile, Sebastián Pozas, the Guardia Civil general who had joined the PCE, took possession of the Captaincy General and was given command of the troops in Catalonia. At the same time, a caravan of 120 trucks carried 5,000 men sent from Madrid, who entered Barcelona on 7 May. In command of the expedition was Lieutenant Colonel Emilio Torres

Iglesias, former leader of the anarchist column *Tierra y Libertad,* who had arrived by plane. It seems that the CNT itself requested that the force be commanded by this old friend, to make things easier and avoid reprisals. However, the expeditionaries' passage through the towns of Catalonia led to an uprising of police, military and civilians on the government side against the revolutionaries. In Tortosa, the CNT-FAI militants, who had imposed themselves on the communists, received orders not to oppose them. UGT members immediately occupied the city's nerve centres and imprisoned the anarchists. The peasant collectives around Tortosa were invaded and the repression spread to the villages of the region. The bodies of some of the prisoners who were supposedly being taken to Tarragona were later found with bullets in their heads. In Tarragona, where the clashes were as fierce as in the capital, many detainees were killed and their bodies dumped outside the town. In the northern regions of Catalonia, which had a Carlist and conservative tradition, there were also revenge actions.

After a few days the fate of some important people who had disappeared began to become known. Through *Solidaridad Obrera* it became known, for example, that twelve young libertarians taken from their homes in the San Andrés neighbourhood had been murdered. Their bodies had been thrown from an ambulance into the Cerdanyola-Ripollet cemetery, where they were found completely disfigured. Among them was Alfredo Martínez, secretary of the Revolutionary Youth Front. Once the revolution had been put down, the Generalitat gave the official toll of victims of the war unleashed in Catalonia during the days of May. According to its figures, some 500 people were killed and nearly a thousand wounded.

One of the conditions of the armistice was the release of all political prisoners. The fact that the OGPU, the Soviet secret service, had its own clandestine prisons posed an insoluble problem. CNT-FAI and POUM elements detained in official centres were prosecuted for the crime of military rebellion. Others who were not released continued to be imprisoned as government prisoners. The same did not happen with the anarchists and Trotskyists who had ended up in prisons controlled by Stalin's henchmen. Most of them were tortured and killed. This issue deserves more attention and will be dealt with in the next section.

The communists, taking advantage of what had happened, were quick to call for the suppression of the anti-Stalinist Partido Obrero de Unificación Marxista (Marxist Unification Workers' Party), which they held responsible for the bloodshed. The secretary general of the PCE, José Díaz, reproduces in *Three Years of Struggle* the speech he gave at a public meeting on 9 May 1937. From Burnett Bolloten's work, we extract some very interesting excerpts:

"...All workers must know the process which is going on in the USSR against the Trotskyites. It is Trotsky himself who has led this gang of outlaws who derail the trains in the USSR, practise sabotage in the big factories, and do their utmost to discover military secrets in order to hand them over to Hitler and the imperialists of Japan. And when this has been discovered in the process and the Trotskyists have declared that they were doing this in combination with Hitler, with the Japanese imperialists, under the leadership of Trotsky, I ask: is it not quite clear that this is not a political or social organisation with a certain tendency, like the anarchists, the socialists or the republicans, but a gang of spies and provocateurs in the service of international fascism? The Trotskyist provocateurs must be swept away!

That is why I said in my speech to the recently held Plenum of the Central Committee that not only in Spain should this organisation be dissolved, its press suspended and liquidated as such, but that Trotskyism should be swept out of all civilised countries, if those vermin who, embedded in the workers' movement, do so much harm to the workers they claim to defend, are really to be liquidated. This situation must be brought to an end.

In Spain, who if not the Trotskyists have been the inspirers of the criminal putch in Catalonia? *The Battle of* May Day is full of blatant incitements to the putchist coup... This newspaper is still being thrown out in Catalonia... Why? Because the government has not decided to get its hands on it, as all the antifascists are demanding.

If, ten months into the war, there is no firm policy to bring the rearguard up to the level at which some fronts are being placed, I, and I am sure that all anti-fascists will be thinking along with me, begin to think: either this Government puts the rearguard in order, or if it does not do so, another Popular Front government will have to do it".

José Díaz could not understand in 1937 that Trotsky was not "in the service of international fascism", but wanted to use him to regain power in the USSR. This was Trotsky's new mission, which is still not understood in the 21st century thanks to the work of falsifying reality and concealing the historical truth. It has been seen in this work that Hitler himself was financially supported by the same Jewish bankers who had financed the Jewish-Bolshevik revolution. Through a war with Germany, these conspirators aspired to put their agents back in charge of the USSR in order to continue to appropriate its enormous resources, as they had done for the first seven years with Lenin and Trotsky. When in 1932-33 they helped Hitler seize power, they intended to launch him against Stalin, a National Communist who was proceeding with the physical elimination of many Jewish agents of international Communism. Gaining control of Spain would have greatly strengthened the international position of Trotskyism, which, it should not be forgotten, that same May tried to seize power in the USSR by a military coup. Leon Trotsky's hallucinated analysis of the events of May show that he had lost his sense of reality with regard to Spain if he ever had one. The following text is from his writings on the Spanish revolution:

"If the proletariat of Catalonia had seized power in May 1937, it would have found support throughout Spain. The bourgeois-Stalinist reaction would not have been able to muster two regiments to crush the Catalan workers. In the territory occupied by Franco, not only the workers but also the peasants would have sided with the Catalan proletariat: they would have isolated the Fascist army and triggered in it a process of irreversible disintegration. In these circumstances, it is doubtful whether any foreign government would have risked sending its regiments into the inflamed Spanish territory. Intervention would have been materially impossible or, at least, extremely dangerous".

At a meeting of the Cabinet of Largo Caballero on 13 May, the two communist ministers, Jesús Hernández and Vicente Uribe, demanded the dissolution of the POUM. The President of the Council vehemently denied that this party was a fascist organisation as the communists claimed and refused to take action against it. He added that he would not dissolve any party or trade union, since he did not preside over the Council of Ministers to serve the interests of any of its member parties. Naturally, Largo Caballero was right: the POUM was not a fascist organisation. In the Moscow trials, where the existence of a plan to overthrow Stalin by means of a Red Army-backed coup had been proved, the accusation could be justified, since, moreover, Trotskyist contacts with the Nazis had existed. In Spain, however, it did not apply to the POUM, whose leaders were incapable of unravelling the abominable game of Trotsky, an incorrigible fatuous man who, without accepting his defeat and his limitations, was preparing to create the Fourth International.

The two Communist ministers got up and left the Council of Ministers. Prieto, who sat to the right of Largo Caballero, explained after the war that the President of the Government intended to continue the meeting, but he told him: "Look, Caballero, something serious has just happened here, and that is that the ministerial coalition has broken up, since one of the parties that made up the government has left. Consequently, I think it is your duty, without continuing the work of the Council, to report to the President of the Republic and resolve the situation with him". Largo Caballero notified Azaña of what had happened, to whom he gave him to understand that he had no intention of resigning, but that he intended to replace the two Communist ministers. About this interview, Azaña wrote in *Memorias políticas y de guerra*, volume four of his *Obras completas (Collected Works)*: "Largo told me how inopportune the crisis was, because there were reasons of national interest which made the continuation of his government advisable, in order to carry out very important plans whose suspension would be a catastrophe". The most decisive of these plans was the large-scale offensive in Extremadura.

For the past two months, the president of the government and minister of war had been planning a military offensive in Extremadura, which was to begin in mid-May. The crisis had therefore arisen just as the operation was about to begin. Azaña accepted the Prime Minister's arguments and suggested postponing any cabinet changes. It was not only Largo's supporters who were convinced that the operation could have been decisive, but also the military historian nationalist Ramón Salas Larrazábal. Burnett Bolloten reports the views of Salas Larrazábal, who confirms that some 100,000 men were to be involved in the operation, which was the largest deployment of troops ever made. According to Salas Larrazábal, the Republicans' overwhelming initial superiority would have enabled them to reach Badajoz and the Portuguese border.

On hearing of the President of the Government's meeting with Azaña, Negrín and Álvarez del Vayo, the two Socialist ministers married to Jewish women, visited Largo Caballero and, claiming that under the circumstances the Communists could not be dispensed with, informed him that they and Prieto were also resigning. This step not only eliminated Largo Caballero, but also prevented the Extremadura operation. On 15 May Azaña put Largo Caballero in charge of forming a new government, but failure was a foregone conclusion. On 17 May he presented his list of ministers to the President of the Republic. In addition to the Presidency of the Government and the Ministry of War, he took the portfolios of Navy and Air Force. Largo," wrote Azaña, "did not want to leave the government in any way". Only the anarchists could accept that Largo Caballero should retain the Presidency and War. The opposition of the Communists, supported by the Socialists and the Republican Left, forced Largo Caballero to abandon his efforts to hold on to power. The President of the Republic then entrusted Juan Negrín, the man who had been chosen by Moscow months earlier, with the task of forming a new government.

On 17 May the ministers of the fifth government of the Civil War and the twenty-fifth of the Republic were sworn in. In contrast to the previous executive, with 18 members, Negrín presented what was to be the "Government of Victory ", a compressed cabinet with only nine ministers, in which he retained the Treasury. Communists, socialists, Basque and Catalan nationalists and Azaña's republicans shared the portfolios. The anarchists left power. The Ministry of War was renamed the Ministry of National Defence and was taken over by Indalecio Prieto. In Catalonia, too, the CNT ended up leaving the new Government of the Generalitat, formed in June and made up of four councillors from the ERC, three from the PSUC, one from the Unió de Rabassaires and one from Acció Catalana. Negrín's first government lasted until 18 August, when Jaume Aiguader, the Esquerra Republicana minister in Madrid, who held the Ministry of Labour and Social Welfare, provoked a crisis in protest at the withdrawal of the Generalitat's responsibility for industry. In solidarity with him, Manuel de Irujo of the

PNV resigned. A PSUC militant thus entered the government, so that from then on the communists had three ministries.

Trotskyist Jews and Stalinist Jews

Before dealing with the repression that the Communists carried out against the POUM and the anarchists, it is necessary to insist on the underground struggle that was being waged in Spain and in the world between Jewish agents of Stalin and Trotsky. It must always be borne in mind that if the Spanish civil war had not coincided simultaneously with the struggle for power in the USSR between Trotskyists and Stalinists and with the Moscow trials, held between 1936 and 1938, Stalin's intervention in Spain would surely have been different. The exposition of some background and a number of complementary facts will help to understand the events as a whole.

On 3 October 1936, Vladimir Antov-Ovseyenko, the Jewish revolutionary who had led the storming of the Winter Palace in 1917 and was Trotsky's right-hand man in the Red Army, presented his credentials to Companys as consul general of the USSR in Barcelona. The Politburo had appointed him to the post on 21 September. Before that, Ilya Ehrenburg, a Jew of Ukrainian origin who passed for an *Izvestia* correspondent, had been in charge of observing the revolutionary process in Catalonia and reporting to Ambassador Rosenberg. The best calling card of Ehrenburg, about whom there will be occasion to write more in the next chapter, is the savage and criminal harangue he addressed in 1945 to the Red Army soldiers invading Germany. Printed in the pamphlet entitled "Kill", it is a prime example of anti-German racial hatred: "Kill, kill! -Ehrenburg demanded, "There are no innocents among Germans, neither among the living, nor among the unborn. Carry out Comrade Stalin's instructions and crush the fascist beast in its den for ever. Tear with briskness the racial pride of the Germanic women. Take them as legitimate booty. Kill, brave and battle-hardened soldiers of the Red Army!"

This repugnant character, who arrived in Barcelona in mid-August, even reported on Companys' speeches. Of particular importance were the reports of 17 and 18 September, in which he warned of two simultaneous crises: that of the Madrid government with the Generalitat, and that of the Catalan government with the FAI. In his reports, reproduced in *Spain Betrayed: The Soviet Union in the Spanish Civil War (Annals of Communism)* (2001), a work edited by several authors based on documents extracted from the RGASPI (Archives of Socio-Political History of the Russian State), he denounced the intransigence of the anarchists which, in his opinion, threatened the war effort and delayed the production of Catalan industries. It was Ehrenburg who, on behalf of Companys, requested the establishment of a Soviet Consulate in Barcelona. Antonov-Ovseyenko, who arrived accompanied by Soviet advisers, soon established excellent relations with President Companys and sought a compromise between the Communists and the anarcho-syndicalists of the CNT. From the papers of ambassador Marcelino Pascua, we know that four months after his arrival in Barcelona, Antonov-Ovseyenko had already lost the confidence of Stalin, who considered him a Trotskyite. After the events of May, he was ordered to return to Moscow in August 1937. On 10 February 1939, accused of espionage and Trotskyism, he died in Butyrka prison.

On 14 October 1936, Antonov-Ovseyenko wrote a letter to Krestisnky, who had not yet been accused of being a Trotskyite, in which, in line with Trotsky's directives, he expressed his plans to "tame" the anarchists. The text (document 22) appears in the work cited above. It is a long letter, four points of which are reproduced below. The Consul General in Barcelona had infiltrated among the anarchists an agent, whom he refers to as "X", with whom he agreed on the following strategy:

"1. We shall jointly strengthen, by all means, the permanent conciliation commission with the anarcho-syndicalists."

2. We will support the authority of the Companys-Tarradellas government, gradually, by systematically adopting a series of measures that will put an end to the stubbornness of the anarchists.

3. Until steps are taken to disarm the informal elements, we will launch a political campaign on the threat posed by Franco to the revolution, and all that."

4. We will undertake as soon as possible the organisation of a unified division, carefully selecting its commanders and equipping it with arms and uniforms. Weapons arriving from abroad will go as a priority to this division."

The letter ended by noting that relations between the UGT and the CNT were improving, but regretted that the liaison committee was working with difficulties "because of the intransigence of Comorera" (secretary general of the PSUC). The Communists of this party, as we know, were the main point of support for Stalin's policy in Catalonia.

It is obvious that Stalin could not share these plans and neither could he share the criticism of the PSUC. The official policy of the USSR was announced on 17 December in *Pravda* in these words: "In Catalonia, the elimination of the Trotskyists and anarcho-syndicalists has already begun. It will be carried out with the same energy as in the USSR". This alluded to the beginning of the actions of the Soviet secret police, which had its own dungeons and acted outside the Government of the Republic. Two Trotskyists operating in Spain, General Walter Krivitsky (Ginsberg) and Arthur Stashevsky (Girshfeld), Negrin's friend, were called to the Soviet Union in March 1937 to report on the situation. Both met in Moscow, where they learned of the May revolution in Catalonia. The former was convinced that they suspected him and that he would not return to the Netherlands; however, on 22 May he was unexpectedly ordered to return to his post. The latter, according to Krivitsky's account, had a personal meeting with Stalin in April and came away confident, so much so that he dared to meet Marshal Tukhachevsky, who was already in the eye of the storm. Finally, Stashevsky was also allowed to return to Barcelona; but in June he was ordered to return to Russia, which he did in the company of General Ian Berzin, the top Soviet military adviser in Spain, whose nom de guerre was "Grishin". In early August Stashevsky wrote a brief note from prison to his wife, who lived in Paris, asking her to travel to the USSR. Stashevsky was executed in 1937. As for Berzin, a Latvian whose real name was Peteris Kuzis, he was arrested on 13 May 1938 and shot in the cellars of the Lubyanka on 29 July 1938.[27]

While Stashevsky and Krivitsky were in Moscow, Soviet secret service agents carried out a kidnapping in Spain that was to be the forerunner of the disappearances and murders of poumists and anarchists that followed in the wake of the May events. On 9 April 1937 the young Jew Marc Rafailovich Rein disappeared from the Hotel Continental in Barcelona, where he had a room, and was never heard from again. Marc Rein worked as a correspondent for several anti-Stalinist publications, including the Jewish New York daily *Forward*. He was the son of Menshevik leader Rafael Abramovich, one of the heads of the Jewish Bund before the October Revolution. Abramovich, a leader of the Second International in exile in Paris, was a trusted confidant of Leon Blum, the Jewish president of the French government, and thus an influential person. As a result, both Largo Caballero and Companys were forced to give explanations and to start an investigation. It seems that the kidnapping was connected with the third of the Moscow trials, whose main defendants were Bukharin and Rykov. The Spanish government's investigations pointed to the so-called "Information Group", and specifically to the service of Alfredo Hertz, who, according to Julián Gorkín, was "one of the great masters of interrogations and executions". Hertz executed with a shot to the back of the head when he received permission, but his speciality was night-time torture.

Little has been written about Hertz. What we have learned about him deserves the following section. The only source of information that provides interesting data on this character is Jan Valtin, pseudonym of Richard Krebs.

---

[27] The Latvian was already involved in the 1905 revolution, whose leading figures were Parvus and Trotsky. According to historian Victor Suvorov, Berzin was the main organiser of terror during the Russian civil war. Suvorov attributes to him the paternity of the system of taking and shooting hostages in order to put down peasant rebellions and recover deserters. Under Trotsky's orders, he was in charge of eliminating the sailors involved in the Kronstadt rebellion in March 1921. Before being posted to Spain, he had been head of the Military Secret Service. When he was recalled to Moscow in 1937, he was again appointed Chief of Military Intelligence, a post he held until his arrest in May 1938.

In *Out of the Night, an* extensive autobiographical work published in 1941 and translated into English under the title *La noche quedó atrás.* Valtin reveals that Hertz was a Jew named George Mink, who in 1926 had joined the Communist Party in Philadelphia, where he worked as a taxi driver while looting on the docks. His cronies called him "Mink, the harbour pirate". What Jan Valtin did not know was that his real name was Godi Minkovsky, as revealed in *The Venona Secrets,* and that he had come to the United States in 1911 at the age of twelve. In 1927 he settled in New York, from where, on his own initiative, he began sending reports to Solomon Abramovitch Losovsky and offered him his services.

As will be recalled, Losovsky, a leader of the Red Trade Union International and a Zionist, travelled to Barcelona in February 1936 in the company of Bela Kun and Heinz Neumann. In 1928 Losovsky called Mink to Moscow and provided him with a false passport, money and special powers of attorney. From 1930 onwards Mink became part of the GPU's counter-espionage apparatus and moved between Berlin and Hamburg. According to Jan Valtin, who knew Mink personally, in Hamburg, where he was regarded as an unscrupulous gangster, he murdered the defector Hans Wissinger. When Valtin remarked to him that perhaps they had made a mistake, his reply was: "We never make mistakes! We never eliminate innocent men!" Valtin describes Mink in 1931 as follows: "An unusual fellow, young, elegant, with slight Jewish features, cynically arrogant, short in stature, but robust. His mouth was small and cruel, his teeth jagged, and his eyes, greenish-brown, had a vague glint of a wild animal".

At the end of May 1935, staff at the Nordland Hotel in Copenhagen burst into Mink's room when they heard a chambermaid screaming for help: Mink was raping her. Danish police searched her room and found secret codes, forged passports, coded addresses and thousands of dollars. On 30 July 1935, charged with espionage, he was sentenced to eighteen months. Once released, he travelled to Moscow, where only the powerful influence of Losovsky saved him from ostracism for his reckless behaviour. The OGPU then provided him with a passport under the name Alfred Hertz and posted him to Barcelona, where he took up residence in the Hotel Continental, the same hotel where Marc Rein was staying. Hertz/Mink/Minkovsky acted for a time as political commissar of the Thaelmann battalion, the Kléber/Stern battalion, supposedly in charge of surveillance of possible Trotskyists among the German brigadiers. He must have done something wrong, possibly he too was a Trotskyite, since the Stalinist Vittorio Vidali, alias Carlos Contreras, Major Carlos, in his book *Diary of the Twentieth Congress of the Communist Party of the Soviet Union* reports that he was eventually eliminated by Stalin.

Stéphane Courtois and Jean-Louis Panné in *El libro negro del comunismo (The Black Book of Communism)* state that the struggle over the Rein case between the Spanish government and the NKVD reached such an extreme that on 9 July 1937 the Secretary of State, who reported to the Ministry of the Interior under the socialist Zugazagoitia, provoked a confrontation in front of witnesses between his agent (SSI 29) and comrades Hertz and Mariano Gómez Emperador. The latter was a man of the Catalan secret services, which functioned as a camouflaged delegation of the NKVD. Hertz/Mink/Minkovsky's brazenness reached such an extent that the next day he proceeded to arrest the government agent SSI 29, whom he had to release on the orders of his superior, Alexander Orlov (Leiba Lazarevich Felbing), the head of the NKVD.

Two other Jews worked with Alfredo Hertz: Georg Scheyer, alias Sanja Kindermann, who was sent to Valencia to run the Santa Úrsula Czech quarter, and Moritz Bressler, alias Hubert von Ranke, married to Seppl Hermann, widow of Rafael Campalans, a prominent Catalan socialist who had drowned on the beach at Torredembarra in 1933. Seppl Hermann became Seppl Kapalanz, an obvious Germanisation of the surname Campalans. There are testimonies about the horrors of the Santa Ursula prison, from prisoners of the DAS group, German anarcho-considicalists. Helmut Kirschey, one of them, explains that the convent guard staff was composed of Spaniards; however, he adds, "The NKVD-GPU men who interrogated us were all Russian Jews. They spoke Yiddish among themselves, and as this language has many German words in it, we could understand them without any great problems." According to Kirschey the interrogations took place at night: "They woke us up between twelve and two o'clock, when one is most tired and least alert"[28]. Moritz Bressler had been hired in 1930 by Ernö Gerö, alias "Peter ", under whose orders they all worked.

Ernö Gerö, also known as Ernst Singer, was another Jew actually named Ernst Moritsovich Gere, head of the NKVD in Catalonia, who was in turn subordinate to Orlov. Gerö was evacuated to the USSR in 1939 and after the end of the World War became one of the communist leaders in Hungary. Gerö and Hertz, who created a file of all foreigners residing in Catalonia, were the main architects of the kidnapping of Erwin Wolf, Trotsky's secretary, who recklessly entered Spain. According to the authors of the *Black Book of Communism*, Alfredo Hertz had joined the Generalitat's Investigation and Surveillance Corps and controlled the passport department, thus examining entries and exits in Catalonia. Erwin Wolf, whose political

---

[28] Ángel Galarza, the man responsible for the first sackings at Paracuellos, set up the DEDIDE (Special State Information Department) in Valencia. Two of his men, commissioner Juan Cobo and commander Justiniano García, the head of his bodyguard, tortured in the Baylia and Santa Úrsula checkpoints. The Anselmo Lorenzo Foundation has reports on their methods. One reads: "Justin García was involved in these bestial outrages. His speciality consisted of squeezing the neck with both hands, cutting off the breathing. It was a slow strangulation. The veins in the throat would swell and the face would change colour from red to cadaverous white. Numerous detainees who underwent this torture eventually fainted from heart attacks.

pseudonym was "Kiff", born into a wealthy German family of Jewish origin, joined Trotsky before he travelled to Norway. His personal abilities and linguistic skills enabled him to replace Jan Frankel as Trotsky's secretary in November 1935. Frankel, who was, of course, also Jewish, was one of Trotsky's secretaries between 1930 and 1933, and from February to October 1937 he lived with him in Coyoacán.

The Central Committee of the Belgian Socialist Revolutionary Party discussed Erwin Wolf's relationship with the POUM in November 1936. At the end of April 1937, Wolf offered to travel to Spain to assist in the reorganisation and reorientation of Andreu Nin's party. His arrival in Barcelona took place just after the May Days. It has been seen in the previous chapter that Stalin used Jewish agents to infiltrate Trotsky's entourage, who tended to rely on people of his own ethnicity. Most famously, Mark Zborowski, "Etienne", who became Leon Sedov's secretary, necessarily knew of Wolf's plans. Several authors agree that it was he who passed the information about his entry into Spain to the OGPU. In July 1937 Hertz/Mink/Minkovsky arrested Erwin Wolf on the orders of Ernö Gerö. Trotsky's secretary was last seen on 13 September 1937 in the central prison in Barcelona, which was at 24 Puerta del Angel. Then he disappeared. Perhaps he was secretly taken to Moscow for interrogation. In any case, in Moscow or in Barcelona, he was executed. Zborowski would also be instrumental in finally bringing about Trotsky's assassination in Mexico. It all simmered in Spain and specifically in Catalonia, where the "work" of Stalin's Jewish agents against the Trotskyist Jews was brutal and relentless.

It was not only in Spain and the Soviet Union that the confrontation between Trotskyist and Stalinist Jewish agents took place. Stalin's hand reached as far as the Americas, as evidenced by the fact that Trotsky was assassinated in Mexico and Krivitsky in the United States. The head of the Military Secret Service in Western Europe, Krivitsky, was put to the test as soon as he took up his post in The Hague. His colleague and friend Ignace Reiss, nicknamed "Ludwig", a Jew like himself whose real name was Nathan Markovic Poretsky, travelled from Paris to the Dutch capital on 29 May 1937 to announce to him that he intended to leave the service. Krivitsky writes down the advice he gave him: "The Soviet Union is still the only hope of the workers of the whole world. Stalin may be wrong. Stalins come and go. But the Soviet Union will endure. Our duty is not to break away from our posts." In other words, if they regained power, all would be well again.

Krivitisky relates that on 17 July Isaac Spiegelglass, another Jew who had arrived from Moscow with full powers to purge the foreign services, showed him two letters that seriously compromised Comrade Reiss. "You know that you are responsible for Reiss," Spiegelglass told him, "you introduced him to the Communist party and you endorsed his entry into our organisation." The invitation to participate in the assassination of Reiss put Krivitsky between a rock and a hard place. He replied that he wanted "nothing to do with such an enterprise", thus digging his own grave. He also alerted his friend, who managed to escape temporarily. On 10 August Krivitsky was ordered to return to Moscow, and two weeks later, on the night of 4 September 1937, Reiss's body was found in a ditch outside Lausanne with five machine-gun bullets in his head and seven in his body. A forged passport in the name of Hans Eberhardt was found in his pockets. Candorously, Krivistky pretends to convince the reader of the moral superiority of his Trotskyist friends, who "had dedicated their lives to making the world a better place". Although he had always denied being a Trotskyist, Krivitsky confesses that in November 1937 he contacted Trotsky's son through Reiss's lawyer. He also admits that the French Interior Minister in Léon Blum's government, the Jew Marx Dormoy, gave him identity papers and police protection until he managed to flee to the United States.

Repression against poumists and anarchists. The assassination of Andreu Nin

Knowing all these things, we are in a better position to deal with what happened in Spain after the tragic week of May. A wave of terror swept over Catalonia, where arrests and kidnappings of POUMists and anarchists led to torture and murder, the most notorious of which was that of Andreu Nin. When Negrín's government was formed, repression against the POUM began with the suppression of *La Batalla* on 28 May. Attempts were made to arrest Julián Gorkín, who had been the author of the 1 May editorial, which proposed to the CNT the formation of a revolutionary united front and urged the workers not to abandon arms; but the police found neither him nor Juan Andrade, another of the newspaper's promoters. On 11 June, the same day that the Trotskyist generals of the Red Army appeared before the Supreme Court of the USSR, a formal accusation was made against the POUM, according to which "the general line of the propaganda of this party was the suppression of the Republic and its democratic government by violence and the establishment of a dictatorship of the proletariat". Further on the indictment referred to the POUM having "slandered a friendly country whose moral and material support had enabled the Spanish people to defend their independence." Reference was also made to the attack on Soviet justice in connection with criticism of the Moscow trials and contacts with the Trotskyists.

On the night of 16 June all the POUM leaders were arrested in their homes, but Nin was arrested in his office. Since Gorkín and Andrade were still untraceable, their wives were arrested. On 23 June a decree was published announcing the creation of Espionage and High Treason Tribunals, composed of three civilian and two military magistrates. These tribunals were appointed by the government and could hold hearings behind closed doors. On 29 June, a note from the Minister of Justice, Manuel de Irujo, announced that Julián Gorkín, Juan Andrade, Pere Bonet, Jordi Arquer and six other Poumist leaders had been accused of high treason. Ultimately, they would save their lives thanks to the intervention of several international delegations that arrived in Spain to take an interest in them and ensure due process. Tried between 11 and 22 October 1938, they were sentenced to fifteen years' imprisonment. But Andreu Nin, who had been handed over to communist policemen, was not among them.

"What have you done with Nin?" was the question posed by Federica Montseny, the first person to publicly demand news of him. The government confined itself to saying that he had been arrested and was in custody. The Minister of the Interior, Zugazagoitia, admitted that he was in Madrid in a private communist prison. According to P. Broué, "at a Council of Ministers meeting, Negrín questioned the ministers. He declared himself ready to cover up what had to be covered up, but demanded to be brought up to date". Since Nin, a former secretary of the CNT and the Red Trade Union International, was known worldwide in the workers' and trade union movement, the affair had international repercussions. The Minister of Justice, Manuel de Irujo, after failing to locate Nin in any of the government prisons, appointed a special examining magistrate to investigate the disappearance. He ordered the arrest of suspected policemen, some of whom had taken refuge in the Soviet embassy. Days later, a special police brigade tried to arrest the judge himself, prompting an outraged Minister Irujo to threaten to resign in a stormy council of ministers in which the communists, who defended the presence of Soviet technicians and advisors as an expression of "disinterested help", were exposed. As a result, they had no choice but to compromise on the dismissal of the director general of Security, the Communist lieutenant colonel Antonio Ortega, who had been offered as a scapegoat. On 8 August 1937, the correspondent of *The New York Times* wrote "Although everything has been done to cover up the affair, everyone now knows that he has been found dead outside Madrid, murdered".

Some things about what happened are known from the writings of different protagonists. Thus, for example, in *Yo fui ministro de Stalin* Jesús Hernández dissociates himself from Nin's arrest and points out that the decision was taken at a meeting between Orlov, Pasionaria and the secretary of organisation of the PCE, Pedro Checa, who worked for the NKVD services, which is why several historians point to him as one of those responsible for the Paracuellos massacres. The kidnapping and subsequent assassination of Andreu Nin has gone down in history as "Operation Nikolai". Nin was arrested by Catalan police officers from the Special Brigade. After a few hours in the Barcelona police station, he was transferred to Madrid on Orlov's orders. He was immediately taken to Alcalá de Henares, where between 18 and 21 June he was interrogated: he was supposed to sign a false document implicating the POUM in acts of treason and espionage. From this point on, the investigators offered multiple versions of what had happened.

It is generally agreed that on 22 June Andreu Nin was confined to a chalet where he was left in the hands of Orlov and two other Soviet agents, who tried to subdue him for a month. Since we already know Orlov, let us introduce his accomplices. One of them was Iósif Romuáldovich Griguliévich, a Jew born in Vilna into a Crimean Karaite family. The Costa Rican journalist Marjorie Ross in *El secreto encanto de la KGB: Las cinco vidas de Iosif Grigulievich (The Secret Charm of the KGB: The Five Lives of Iosif Grigulievich)* provides surprising facts about this personage who, under the name of Teodoro B. Castro, became Costa Rica's ambassador to Italy and Yugoslavia, where he was to assassinate Josip Broz Tito. Curiously, it was Tito who, as a Serbian delegate to the International, gave him the false passport that allowed him to enter Spain in 1936, where he became known as "Júzik" and "Miguel ". Throughout his career he had other nicknames: "José Ocampo", "Father", "Artur", "Maks", "Daks" and "Felipe". Griguliévich has been identified as the probable perpetrator of Nin's murder.

As to the identity of the second agent, some point to Ernö Gerö, although most historians, including Ángel Viñas, favour Leonid Eitingon, Orlov's lieutenant, another Jew whose real name was Nahum Isaakovich Eitingon, nicknamed "Kotov", "Leonido" and "Pierre". Robert Conquest, Hugh Thomas and Julian Gorkin claim that Eitingon was the lover of Charity Mercader, the mother of Trotsky's assassin, although another acknowledged lover of Charity, Pavel Sudoplatov, denies this. Whether she was or not, Nahum Isaakovich Eitingon recruited her and her friends Africa de las Heras and Carmen Brufau, the three famous Spanish NKVD agents, and organised the assassination attempt on Trotsky's life on 20 August 1940. These three men were thus the ones who allegedly tortured Nin, who stood firm and refused to collaborate with the Stalinist agents. It is not clear whether he died during the sessions or was killed because his condition made it impossible to release him. All indications are that Orlov decided to eliminate him[29]. There

---

[29] In 2013 appeared in Spain *El caso Orlov. Los servicios secretos soviéticos en la guerra civil española* (2013), a work by Boris Volodarsky that we have learned about too late. It seems that this author confirms that the order to kill Andreu Nin came from Orlov and that Grigulievich shot him, although he doubts that he was tortured. We do not know whether this work clarifies Orlov's defection, an indecipherable mystery, since everything indicates that he was serving Stalin well. However, both Eitingon and Gerö were able to inform Stalin about unknown aspects of Orlov's activities in Spain. In June 1938, Orlov was ordered to meet in Antwerp with an NKVD chief, probably Isaac Spiegelglass. He then stole $60,000 from the NKVD operations box and fled with his wife and daughter to Canada. In 1939 he sent an unsigned letter to Trotsky informing him that an agent named "Mark", probably Zborowski, had infiltrated his organisation in Paris. Trotsky thought this was a ploy by Stalin and gave no credence to the warning. In September 1938, at the conference to create the Fourth International in Paris, "Etienne" (Zborowski) introduced Ramon Mercader, the future assassin of Trotsky, to the

is evidence of a telegram sent by "Júzik", probably from Paris, headed by the letter "N", a clear allusion to Nin, which speaks of Nin's assassination halfway along the road from Alcalá de Henares to Perales de Tajuña. Ángel Viñas considers the most likely date of the assassination to be 21 July 1937.

In September 1937, Emma Goldmann, the famous Lithuanian anarchist of Jewish origin, visited Spain in order to find out for herself about the repression against anarchists. She went straight to Valencia. "I discovered," Goldmann later declared, "that fifteen hundred members of the CNT, comrades of the FAI and the Libertarian Youth, hundreds of the POUM and even members of the International Brigades filled the prisons of Valencia." In November *Solidaridad Obrera* gave the figure of fifteen thousand prisoners in prisons in Catalonia, Valencia and other regions of the Republican zone.

On 17 October 1937 Largo Caballero made his last speech in Spain at the Teatro Pardiñas in Madrid. In that famous speech, Largo took the opportunity to denounce the damage that the Nin case had done to the cause of the Republic abroad: "You all know that there have been truly unfortunate cases, which have not yet been cleared up, of people made to disappear by elements that are not the Government, and which have constituted a State within another State". This was the first public denunciation by a Republican leader of the utmost importance of the fact that the Spanish Republic had fallen into the hands of people who were not in the service of the Spanish State. Largo Caballero organised a series of rallies, but was not allowed to speak in public again. The first was to be held in Alicante, but on his way to the city in the company of Luis Araquistán, Rodolfo Llopis, Wenceslao Carrillo and other collaborators, he was arrested at gunpoint. In *Todos fuimos culpables* Vidarte recalls that he asked the Minister of the Interior, Julián Zugazagoitia, "Zuga", whether it was true that Caballero was under police surveillance, to which Zuga, normally restrained in his expressions, replied: "That's nothing, because I'm going to put Largo Caballero and his friends in jail.... My orders are not up for discussion."

On 2 November 1937 Trotsky referred to the lost battle in Spain in a letter to all workers' organisations. It began with these words:

"The world socialist movement is being destroyed by a terrible disease. The source of the contagion is the Comintern, or to put it more correctly, the GPU, for which the Comintern apparatus serves only as a legal cover. The events of the last few months in Spain have shown what crimes the

---

Trotskyite Sylvia Ageloff, an unattractive woman who was seduced by Mercader. Falling passionately in love with him, she followed him to Mexico and introduced him to Trotsky's house in Coyoacán. Orlov, as far as we know, after having been Stalin's executioner, had the nerve to publish in 1953 *The Secret History of Stalin's Crimes*. Both Orlov and Krivistsky make use in their works of information supplied to them at the time by their colleague Abram Slutsky.

unbridled and completely degenerate Moscow bureaucracy is capable of, together with its henchmen of the international scum. This is not about secondary assassinations or unimportant set-ups. It is a conspiracy against the international working-class movement."

This text shows the extent to which Trotsky recognised that he had completely lost his once powerful influence within the Communist International, whose Executive Committee had been in the hands of the Trotskyists Zinoviev and Bukharin. When Stalin placed the Bulgarian Georgi Dimitrov at the head of the International in 1934, the ideological subjection of the Communist parties to Moscow, whose political line advocated popular fronts, was already unquestionably imposed. In contrast, as we have seen, the Trotskyist movements continued to serve the world revolution, initially planned by the Illuminati and outlined by Adam Weishaupt. In July 1938 Rudolf Klement, one of whose pseudonyms was "Frederic", another secretary of Trotsky who was preparing in Paris for the founding conference of the Fourth International, was kidnapped and beheaded. Nevertheless, against all odds, the Fourth International was founded in September 1938.

The situation in Franco's Spain

While the government of the Republic was trailing behind Moscow and the struggles between communists and anarchists had caused chaos and internecine warfare in Catalonia, the Nationalists were preparing to win the north, which would create the necessary conditions for the final victory. It has been said that the Spanish Civil War was the last war fought for the defence of ideals, which must be true, since Spaniards on both sides felt that way and died for them. However, we have seen in this work that the World Revolution was from the beginning the project of conspirators who, after the publication of the *Communist Manifesto*, expanded the theory of the dictatorship of the proletariat and planned to use the masses to achieve their aims. From a distance, any objective observer will admit that the ideals and values for which half of Spain fought were a chimera. Anarchists and internationalists scorned the concepts of God, country, family and property, they advocated a brave new world in which there would be no nations and no social classes. At the same time, republican Spain had adopted the cry of long live Russia and raised the red Rothschild flag with the hammer and sickle, the symbol of the Maccabean revolts. Images of the gods of atheism were displayed in the Puerta de Alcalá. By contrast, the Spaniards on the other side shouted viva España and clung to traditional values, among which religion, homeland and family predominated. One may or may not share these ideals, but in practice they proved to be much more consistent and served to achieve a seamless union.

The correlation of forces in national Spain showed some ideological differences, which were neutralised by the Unification Decree of 19 April 1937. By means of this decree Franco succeeded in dissolving the old right-wing parties, whose influence had waned. Gil Robles' Accjón Popular, which had played no role since the beginning of the uprising, disappeared when Gil Robles himself announced that he was giving up political action. The other monarchist party, Renovación Española, showed no signs of life either, and Goicoechea, its leader, also agreed to dissolve. However, the differences between the Spanish Falange and the Traditionalist Communion were great enough to constitute a stumbling block in the creation of the single party. The Falangists did not initially have any problems with Franco, but their differences with the conservative forces, the Church and the monarchists meant that they were doctrinally distanced from the Carlists, whose battalions of requetés had been decisive in the victory of the uprising. Let us look at it briefly.

It has been said that the requetés were soldiers from another century. They fought "for God, the fatherland and the king", in that order, as proclaimed in *Oriamendi*, the hymn of Carlism, an ideology that had persisted to an astonishing extent and in 1936 was the oldest political force in Europe. These values were the same ones they had defended throughout the 19th century, when time and again they had stood up against liberalism and international Freemasonry. The Carlist pretender, Don Jaime, had issued a manifesto on 23 April expressing the willingness of the Carlists to collaborate with the Republic; however, the serious anticlerical riots of May 1931 were an unmistakable sign that behind the advent of the new regime lurked international atheism and communism, forces considered inhuman and of foreign origin. As soon as they saw the drift of the Masonic Republic, tens of thousands of Carlist volunteers, regardless of what the military did, were ready to take up arms, as their ancestors had done. After the death of Don Jaime on 2 October 1931, Don Alfonso Carlos, his uncle, became the new pretender. Carlism had its organs of expression, which were very combative in almost all the provinces. These included *El Siglo Futuro* in Madrid, *El Correo Catalán* and *El Pensamiento Navarro*, which were censored or suspended time and again despite the freedom of the press guaranteed by the Constitution.

On 31 March 1934, a commission of Carlist and Alphonsian monarchists met Benito Mussolini in Rome, to whom they confessed that they wanted to overthrow the Republic and replace it with a corporate monarchy. The Duce ordered Marshal Balbo to give them 10,000 rifles, 200 machine guns and 1.5 million pesetas. It was also decided that young Carlists would receive training in Italy. On 3 May 1934, Manuel Fal Conde, who had managed to organise Carlism in Andalusia and create an enthusiastic group of hundreds of requetés there, was appointed Secretary General of the Traditionalist Communion. In Navarre and the rest of Spain, the requetés began to receive military instruction. Carlism also had a women's branch, the "Margaritas", which even before the war numbered around thirty thousand. A Carlist Military Junta was set up in San Juan de Luz, and General Sanjurjo was thought to be the head of the movement.

In May 1936 Fal Conde, Sanjurjo and Javier de Borbón, who was acting as regent, met in Lisbon. They supported an army uprising, but decided that if this did not take place they would rise on their own and Sanjurjo would take the lead. Since Mola had begun to organise the military conspiracy, the Carlists met with him in early June and offered him 8,400 requetés in Navarre alone. The problem was that Mola wanted to establish a republic with universal suffrage and the Carlists wanted a Catholic and corporative monarchy. Such differences prevented agreement, and Mola wrote to Fal Conde in these terms: "The price you put on your collaboration cannot be accepted by us. We turn to you because in the barracks we have only men in uniform, who cannot be called soldiers. If we had had them, we would have been on our own. Traditionalism will contribute by its intransigence to the Spanish disaster as effectively as the Popular Front". Fal Conde sought the mediation of Sanjurjo, who asked Mola in a letter to let the Carlists fight under the two-colour flag, as they were not prepared to rise up under the Republican flag. On 12 July they broke off relations with Mola; but the assassination of Calvo Sotelo forced the general to accept the guidelines in Sanjurjo's letter and those he might subsequently give as president of the Government. Having bridged the differences in extremis, the requetés gave the order to mobilise on 15 July. With Sanjurjo's death five days later, any political pact was postponed.

A report dated 28 February 1936 put the number of requetés willing to join the rebellion throughout Spain at more than 25,000. Some sources estimate that on 18 July the number of Red Berets was close to thirty-five thousand, half of whom were in areas where the uprising did not succeed and were therefore neutralised, as was the case in Catalonia, Valencia, Vizcaya and Guipúzcoa. It is estimated that between fifty thousand and sixty thousand volunteers joined the legitimist ranks during the war. In February 1939, 23,000 were still fighting. On the morning of 19 July 1936, thousands of requetés gathered in the Plaza del Castillo in Pamplona. Most of them were simple people from the countryside. Their contribution was key to holding Navarre and reinforcing La Rioja and Zaragoza. They later marched towards Guadarrama and in September 1936 took part in the capture of San Sebastián and the liberation of Guipúzcoa. The tercios de requetés were the best of the volunteers: they were disciplined, enthusiastic, self-sacrificing and brave. They constituted a resolute military shock force that was constantly used, so that six thousand were killed and some thirty thousand wounded during the war. When they took part in the northern campaign, on 19 June 1937 the Carlists fulfilled a century-old dream: to take Bilbao, the city before which

Zumalacárregui, the best of their generals, had fallen in 1835. The entry into Bilbao had a great psychological connotation in Carlist circles.

The Traditionalist Communion had won nine deputies in the February 1936 elections; in contrast, the Spanish Falange had obtained only 6,800 votes and had no parliamentary representation. During the months preceding the military uprising, however, its membership increased significantly and during the war the Spanish Falange became a powerful political organisation. Some sources estimate that it grew to over a million members, while others put the figure as high as two million. Many saw the Falange, which opposed monarchical restoration, as a force for progress against the immobility of the traditionalists. Many Falangists had Republican and/or trade unionist origins, and thus possessed a social sensitivity that brought them closer to the Italian and German allies. In addition, they also created military forces that were organised into militias and grew in size in Castile, Extremadura and Andalusia. If José Antonio Primo de Rivera, arrested and executed in Alicante on 20 November 1936, had been present, things might have turned out differently. Ramón Serrano Suñer went so far as to say that if he had turned up alive in Salamanca the only "Caudillo" would have been him. But in April 1937 the Falangists lacked a leader capable of uniting everyone around him. There were also divisions among the traditionalists, since on 29 September 1936 the last of the kings of the Carlist dynasty, Don Alfonso Carlos, who had died in Vienna, had not designated a successor and had merely appointed a regent.

In these circumstances, General Franco, who had become generalissimo and head of state on 1 October 1936, decided to take the necessary step to create the single party, as had happened in Italy and Germany, in order to avoid internal quarrels and maintain a strong power that would allow him to focus on the war. The aim was to reconcile the ideas of the Falangists, who wanted a thorough overhaul of the state, and the conservative tendencies of the traditionalists. Franco, who had been considered a monarchist, was in fact a pragmatist and realist, so he postponed any decision for or against the monarchy that might divide his supporters. Thus, when in February 1937 Fal Conde tried to precipitate an immediate restoration of the Monarchy, Franco considered it a betrayal and the traditionalist leader had to flee to Portugal. Resistance also arose on the Falangist side, where there were ups and downs that should not be dwelled on now. Manuel Hedilla, who became secretary general of the Falange, tried to oppose unification, but he did not control the different groups and his manoeuvres led to his arrest and that of numerous Falangists. All were tried and four were sentenced to death, including Hedilla, although they were eventually commuted to life imprisonment. Hedilla was later granted further pardons.

The Unification Decree was promulgated on 20 April 1937. The night before, the Generalissimo delivered a speech from the balcony of the General

Headquarters in Salamanca in which he justified the single-party decision. The Decree consisted of a preamble and three articles. The first began as follows: "Falange Española and Requetés, with their present services and elements, are integrated, under my leadership, into a single political entity of a national character which, for the time being, will be called Falange Española Tradicionalista y de las JONS. This organisation, intermediate between society and the State, has the principal mission of communicating to the State the breath of the people and of bringing to the latter the thought of the former through the political-moral virtues of service, hierarchy and brotherhood". The second article stated that "the Head of State, a Secretariat or Political Board and the National Council" would be the directing bodies of the party. The Generalissimo personally appointed all the members of the first National Council, which consisted of fifty members: half were Falangists, a quarter Carlists, five monarchists and eight military personnel. This composition shows that the Falange had become the most favoured organisation. Article 3 stated: "The Spanish Falange and the Requetés are merged into a single National Militia, retaining their emblems and external signs. The National Militia is auxiliary to the Army. The Head of State is the Supreme Chief of the Militia. A general of the Army shall be the direct chief...". A symbolic example of the union was the imposition on the Falangists of the red beret of the requetés as a complement to their blue shirt. The situations that had arisen on the Republican side, where parties, trade unions and committees had their own armed militias, were thus ruled out. Once the unity of the Movement had been organised and guaranteed by the creation of the single party, which heralded a dictatorial structure for the possible new state, all efforts were concentrated on the conquest of the north.

On the myth of Guernica and the Northern Campaign

Biscay was the first objective of the northern campaign, which was carried out in parts. The first ended at the end of April with the occupation of Durango, Eibar and Guernica. The bombing of the latter city by the Condor legion led to the creation of a myth that has been maintained to this day. The events took place on 26 April and the propaganda campaign was responsible for unleashing an international reaction. The greatest exponent of the propaganda operation was Picasso's famous *Guernica*, a painting which, unfortunately, has become a pictorial pamphlet because of the political abuse to which it has been subjected. Among multiple lies, it was said that the bombing lasted three hours and there was talk of thousands of victims. The falsity of these assertions has now been proven: the planes passed over three times and the bombs fell for a few minutes. The argument put forward by Franco's supporters about the burning of the city by "the red hordes" before evacuating it has been considered irrelevant; however, this is what the militiamen habitually did: they did it in Irún and continued to do it in other towns in Cantabria and Asturias. *The New York Times* correspondent wrote: "The retreating Asturians seem determined to leave behind them nothing but smoking ruins and desolation, and when they are finally forced to abandon a town or village..., the rebels find them dynamited and burned to the ground".

As the matter was debated in the House of Commons, where Anthony Eden, the Foreign Office Secretary, was questioned, the nationalists invited an international commission. The delegation, led by an English architect specialising in destruction, visited the city and found that it had not only been bombed, but also burned and dynamited. Much of the damage to the streets was caused by underground explosions at nine different points. In each case, these explosions had occurred near the covers connecting to the main sewage system. The British press continued to take an interest in the Guernica bombing affair. A year later, on 19 April 1938, two British newspapers, *The Daily Telegraph* and *The Morning Post*, published a letter from A. W. H. James, an air force commander and Member of Parliament. A fragment of the text published in these newspapers was reproduced in *La Renaissance de l'Espagne* (1938), a work by the Count of Saint-Aulaire, French ambassador in Madrid and London, who revealed, incidentally, that after the capture of Bilbao, his Freemason insignia were found in the drawers of the lehendakari Aguirre. Commander James visited the city twice and examined it closely. According to him, the versions stating that the city was destroyed by air "come from inexperienced young men, none of whom have been witnesses.... They have not tried to verify, through critical examination on the ground, the stories they have spread. I have verified that Guernica was bombed, but that most of the destruction, about 95 per cent, could only have been due to fire. Nothing is easier to distinguish than the sporadic effects of a bombing and the systematic, house-to-house destruction of the arsonists".

Two historians from the *Gernikazarra* association, Vicente del Palacio and José Ángel Etxaniz, have recently carried out an exhaustive study, in which they establish that 126 people died in Guernica as a result of the bombing. In Dresden, a city bombed by nearly three thousand heavy bombers for three days, more than 200,000 people were massacred as a result of the saturation bombing. However, the Marxist historian E. Témime does not even mention this German town in *The Revolution and the War in Spain*, where he compares the bombing of Guernica with others carried out in World War II on English and Dutch cities. For more than twenty years I have worked as a teacher with thousands of students. Almost all of them knew that Guernica had been bombed and were familiar with Picasso's painting; however, I never found one who knew about what happened in Dresden.

In the midst of the campaign to take Bilbao, General Mola died unexpectedly on 3 June 1937 when his plane crashed on his way back to Vitoria. He was replaced by General Dávila, and on 12 June the famous "Iron Belt" defending the city was broken and the definitive attack on Bilbao began, which fell on the 19th. A large part of the army defending the city retreated westwards and entered Cantabria. In order to try to stop the Nationalist advance in the north, the Republican commanders planned an offensive on Brunete, in the Madrid sector. Nearly 50,000 men were placed at the disposal of the Republican General Staff. On the night of 5-6 July a massive attack was launched and Líster occupied Brunete; but the Nationalists soon recovered and within a few days were in a position to counterattack, so that by the 12th the offensive had been halted and the Republicans were defending the positions.

At the end of the month, part of Franco's troops were able to return north to prepare for the campaign against Santander. The entry of the Navarrese and Italian soldiers into the city took place on 26 August and was enthusiastically celebrated by the mainly conservative population. The Nationalist troops captured some 17,000 prisoners, many of whom were shot,. On 31 August, in their retreat towards Asturias, the Republican militiamen, true to their habits, dynamited and set fire to Potes. On 17 September, with the capture of Tresviso, the last town in Cantabria, the operations in this province came to an end. Finally, the Navarrese brigades entered Gijón on 21 October 1937. It can be said that the fall of this city meant the disappearance of the northern front, although resistance did not completely cease and the clearing operations lasted for some time, which prevented Franco from immediately moving all the troops that had been operating in Asturias.

As resources passed into their hands, the rebels' economic situation became better and better, and neutral observers began to believe that their triumph was only a matter of time. The mines and industry of the north complemented the agricultural and livestock resources. Franco had the sheep and pig herds of Extremadura, the vegetables of Galicia, the cereals of Castile and the produce of the large Andalusian farms. In the national zone, the shops were well stocked and not only was the supply of the army and the population assured, but it was also possible to export part of the production. On the other hand, the Republican government had serious problems in ensuring food for the millions of people who lived in the large cities they controlled. When the war ended, however, the difficulties for Franco's government began, as it had to supply the undernourished masses of Madrid, Barcelona and Valencia, who had suffered for months from a lack of food.

Two decisive battles to win the war

In view of the length of this work, it is necessary to summarise the events that led to the Nationalists' victory. In November 1937 Negrín had moved the seat of government to Barcelona. In this way, the Generalitat reluctantly relinquished its prerogatives and, at the same time, the anarcho-syndicalists could be closely controlled by the SIM (Military Investigation

Service), a terrifying police force feared by all and under Orlov's influence until his defection in July 1938. Negrín and his friends had consolidated themselves to such an extent that they even managed to take over the leadership of the UGT. It was then that the High War Council decided to take the initiative and chose Teruel as its target. By the end of 1937, the Republican army had 575,000 men in one hundred and fifty-two brigades. Had this offensive not taken place, it is almost certain that Franco would again have opted for an attack on Madrid. On 15 December operations began and 40,000 men advanced towards the Aragonese city, which was surrounded while the bulk of the forces continued their advance. The entry into Teruel took place on 22 December, but inside the city they fought house to house until Christmas Day.

Franco decided to accept the challenge and sent a large number of troops there, who managed to stop the Republicans. The battle was fierce and both sides needed to send reinforcements and materials to hold their positions. Nearly 180,000 men were concentrated in a very small area, fighting under appalling conditions as the winter began to bite. Anyone who has been to Teruel knows that it is one of the coldest parts of Spain. The entrenched soldiers had to be relieved every quarter of an hour. Snow, wind and icy roads brought operations almost to a standstill. On 15 January 1938 the weather conditions eased and the Nationalists prepared a counteroffensive, but were unable to start it because the Republicans again went on the attack. Finally, on 5 February, General Yagüe's troops broke through the front and overran the enemy positions. Finally, on 22 February, the Republicans evacuated Teruel, retreated to their initial positions and gave up the battle for lost. Vicente Rojo offered the post to Negrín, who did not agree to replace him. The bravery and bravery with which both sides fought led General Rojo to say that in Teruel "the moral greatness of the Spanish fighter" had been revealed.

As a result of the build-up of troops in southern Aragon, the very dynamics of the operations prompted Franco's army to continue its advance towards the Mediterranean. On 9 March it resumed the attack and the Republican troops, who had barely had time to reorganise, had to withdraw to the other side of the Ebro. Prieto, the Defence Minister, warned the Council of Ministers in alarm: "If the rebels reach the Mediterranean, four-fifths of the army will be in the southern zone". It was then decided to move part of the forces to Catalonia, which was short of troops to be able to mount an offensive. In order to make it possible for troops to march towards Tortosa along the coastal road, the Republican resistance was organised along the Caspe-Alcañiz line. Lérida fell on 3 April. Once again, Azaña's words serve to illustrate how compromised the situation was: "No one has yet explained why they did not reach Barcelona when they took Lérida in March 1938. There was no force between the two capitals".

The debacle intensified the campaign against the Defence Minister, who even before the national offensive of 9 March had been sacked. In *Yo fui un ministro de Stalin* Jesús Hernández, then one of the two communists in the government, provides substantial information for understanding how Prieto's dismissal came about. According to him, Ernö Gerö (Ernst Morisovich), alias Pedro, one of those involved in the assassination of Nin as head of the NKVD in Catalonia, declared at a meeting of the political bureau that it was necessary to "use the loss of Teruel to liquidate Prieto". On the conspiracy against Prieto, Hernandez gives news of a trip to Moscow by Boris Stefanov, alias "Moreno", an anti-Trotskyite delegate to the International who enjoyed Stalin's confidence:

> "Stefanov, who had just made a very quick trip to Moscow, brought with him precise instructions and supported Pedro with these words: 'The comrades of the Casa advise feeding the army with new reserves that will make possible a prolonged resistance in order to maintain the struggle with a view to a possible world conflagration, which would change the whole outlook of the war in Spain. Resist, resist and resist, such is the directive of the (Moscow) House.... Do you believe that with Prieto at the head of the Ministry of Defence this is possible?'"

Prieto, like Azaña, was increasingly in favour of seeking a negotiated solution to the conflict. On 27 February, five days after the evacuation of Teruel, Dolores Ibárruri, La Pasionaria, had already unleashed an offensive against the Minister of Defence, whom, without naming him, she accused of being defeatist, incapable and cowardly. On 16 March 1938, given the general feeling that the war was lost, the French ambassador Eilrick Labonne offered Negrín France's mediation. The President of the Government summoned the Council of Ministers, which met at the Pedralbes Palace in Barcelona under the direction of the President of the Republic to study the proposal. Azaña suggested that it would be advisable to accept the mediation and begin peace negotiations. Knowing that Prieto was as pessimistic as he was, he asked him to inform the Council of the military situation. The Defence Minister admitted the demoralisation of the army, which "was fleeing in all directions, abandoning arms and ammunition".

Rumours of capitulation were spreading in Barcelona, so the PCE, with the support of the secretary of the CNT National Committee, Mariano Vázquez, organised a demonstration which paraded through the streets of Barcelona and headed for the Pedralbes Palace. "The Communist Party," wrote La Pasionaria in her memoirs, "mobilised the people of Barcelona to demand that the Government continue the resistance." The demonstrators entered the palace gardens with uproar. "Down with the capitulating ministers!" and "Out with the Minister of Defence!" were the cries heard during the Council meeting. Zugazagoitia and Vidarte, who had been appointed by the Socialist Executive to represent the party at the demonstration, confirm in their writings that Negrín had known about it beforehand, and it is even possible that he himself had advised the communists to organise the march in order to coerce the president of the Republic.

On 23 March 1938, both the communist newspaper *Frente Rojo* and *La Vanguardia* published an article by Jesús Hernández, Minister of Public Instruction, entitled "Impenitent pessimist". The article, which contained harsh attacks on the Minister of Defence, was signed under the pseudonym Juan Ventura, but the identity of the author escaped no one, least of all Prieto, who on 29 March described before the Council of Ministers as "inadmissible the conduct of the Minister of Public Instruction in attacking me in the way he has done". The Defence Minister announced that he would not resign out of responsibility, although inwardly he must have known with certainty that his days as minister were numbered. Thanks once again to Bolloten's exhaustive work, we can transcribe the words Negrín wrote to him in a letter announcing that he was going to dismiss him:

> "My decision to replace him as Minister of Defence was an exclusively and genuinely personal one. It came to me on the night of 29-30 March after a painful and violent inner struggle. It followed the meeting of ministers on the night of Tuesday the 29th, when you, with your suggestive eloquence, your usual pathos and the authority of your office and your person, completely demoralised our government colleagues by stylising the events with tints of grim despair and presenting them as fatal".

Palmiro Togliatti, the head of the International in Spain whose main mission was to ensure that the PCE faithfully carried out Stalin's instructions, informed Moscow that Negrín had called a meeting of the Socialist leadership, where he declared that Prieto would not continue as Minister of Defence because he was "a defeatist, worthy of being shot".

Thus, faced with the communists and without the support of his party, Indalecio Prieto was dismissed. On 5 April 1938 Negrín's new government was formed, which was to be the penultimate of the Republic, because in August, in the midst of the Battle of the Ebro, a crisis with the Catalan and Basque nationalists, who left the government, forced Negrín to reshuffle his cabinet. In addition to the presidency, Negrín took over the Defence portfolio. On 30 April he formulated his political programme in a thirteen-point document setting out the objectives for which the war would continue and on which an agreement in principle could be reached with the rebels. The programme was widely disseminated in Spain and abroad. Both Negrín and his Foreign Minister, Álvarez del Vayo, who returned to the Ministry to replace Giral, were convinced that a conflict would break out in Europe and that, if they managed to hold out, there was still hope of salvation. The Munich agreements were a setback for all those who, like them, longed for a general war in Europe. Since the Sudeten crisis and the consequences of the agreement are of paramount importance for understanding the events that followed, the reader is referred to the following chapter, where they will be discussed.

On 15 April 1938, Franco's army reached the sea at Vinaroz, dividing the territory of the Republic in two. The collapse of the Aragon front caused despondency among the population and deep demoralisation among the soldiers of the Popular Army, many of whom began to turn to the other side. On 2 June 1938, the Ministry of Defence decided to impose the punishment of desertion on the relatives of the fugitives, in the purest Soviet style. In order to gain time and to try to prevent the National Army from marching on Valencia, General Rojo again planned an offensive. The aim was also to show Europe and the world that the Spanish Republic was not yet defeated. As early as June, plans began to plan the crossing of the Ebro, a high-risk operation that required lengthy preparations, since boats had to be assembled and bridges built to allow the troops to cross.

On the night of 24-25 July, the operation began. The first commandos crossed the river in boats and set up bridgeheads that allowed the engineers to work in relative safety on putting up bridges and footbridges. The advance was fairly rapid: Mora del Ebro and Corbera were occupied at once and the bridgehead reached a depth of twenty kilometres and a length of thirty, covering the whole of the great meander that the river traces between Fayón and Gandesa. Despite the fact that spies had reported the troop concentrations, the crossing of the Ebro surprised the Nationalist commanders. The immediate dispatch of the air force was not enough to prevent some fifty thousand men from crossing the Ebro. The Nationalists retreated on Villalba and Gandesa and managed to hold out. By the time the T-24 tanks were able to cross the river and enter the battlefield, Franco's relief supplies were already at the front. A battle of attrition began that lasted until 15 November. Only three days after the offensive began, Azaña, in secret from Negrín, held a secret meeting in Vic with the British representative in Barcelona, John Leche, whom he asked to propose a peace plan to his government that included the withdrawal of foreign fighters from both sides and the formation of a consensus government without the communists.

It was during the Battle of the Ebro that the Munich Pact was reached on 29 September, which put an end to Republican hopes of war in Europe and foreign intervention in Spain. Franco also followed the meeting in the Bavarian capital with great concern, aware that everything could be at stake there. During the months of August and September the Nationalists launched one attack after another; but the ferocity of the resistance was at its peak and any point in dispute could be captured and recaptured several times. The losses in men and material were enormous: between sixty and seventy thousand fighters were killed or wounded. At the end of October, while the

Nationalist side was preparing to send reinforcements, the Republican soldiers reached the limit of their forces. On 1 November, an attack began that allowed the Republican positions on the heights of the Sierra de Cavalls to be taken, which meant that the entire southeastern part of the area gained after the crossing of the Ebro changed hands once again. Although the front was stabilised again on 15 November, by 15 December 1938 the Republic had lost the battle and the war.

The offensive on Catalonia was not delayed and began on 23 December 1938. The Republic no longer had any reserves and only had about ninety thousand men to defend Catalan territory. The collapse came in the first days of January. The desperation was such that the Barcelona government decided to mobilise all men of fighting age, but it did not have time to do so. When Barcelona was being bombed, it even went so far as to mobilise the fire brigade, whose work was essential in the city. By the end of January 1939, disorder and chaos reigned in the city. In the south, the loss of Tarragona caused thousands of refugees to flee northwards, converging on Barcelona and crowding into the metro stations, which served as a refuge and dormitory. Survival in the city, where Franco's supporters longed for an end to the nightmare, was almost impossible, as there was no food in the shops, no coal, no electricity. Many Republicans, already tired and without hope, also preferred it all to end once and for all.

On 23 January President Negrín and his government left Barcelona. As it was impossible to take all the documents with them, part of the archives were destroyed. By 6 February more than 100,000 people had entered France and hundreds of thousands, including soldiers fleeing with the civilian population, were crowded together near the Perthus and Boulou customs posts. Many of these armed men used their force and seized vehicles at gunpoint, which they later abandoned near the border. The French authorities, overwhelmed, had banned the entry of able-bodied men from 30 January, allowing only women and children to enter. This decision caused panic and many fugitives opted to return. Between 5 and 9 February, the border was officially reopened to the soldiers, whose war material was confiscated. Among the fleeing Republican leaders was the President of the Republic, Azaña, who crossed into France on 5 February. Three days later, so did Negrín and the last government ministers. The members of the General Staff, led by General Rojo, left Spain on 9 February, a few hours before Franco's troops reached the border at Perthus.

According to information that appeared in June 2009 in the *Revista de Catalunya*, Miquel Serra Pàmies, one of the founders of the PSUC on 23 July 1936 and Minister of the Generalitat during the war, managed to prevent the destruction of Barcelona before the retreat. In an extensive twenty-page report, the publication reveals that the USSR and the Communist International had a plan to destroy Barcelona with thousands of tons of trilite and large quantities of artillery ammunition, with which they intended to dynamite factories and infrastructures in the Catalan city.

Casado's coup d'état and new civil war on the Republican side

With Negrín's government in France, the situation in the Republican zone worsened dangerously, since no one had sufficient authority to direct policy and the war. At the Spanish consulate in Toulouse, where the government took refuge, Azaña and Negrín could not reach an agreement. Negrín wanted the President of the Republic to return with him to Spain in order to regain power. There was no way of convincing him. General Rojo had also told the Prime Minister that he did not see what could be done to resist and why the resistance should continue. Negrín, Álvarez del Vayo, Segundo Blanco, a CNT trade unionist who was Minister of Public Instruction and Health, and the communists imposed their views and decided to return to Spain immediately, with or without Azaña. Their idea was to resist to the end rather than accept the unconditional capitulation demanded by Franco. They believed that the armed forces still in the Centre-South zone were sufficient to prolong the struggle for several months, pending what might happen in Europe.

On 10 February 1939 Negrín landed in Alicante accompanied by Julio Álvarez del Vayo, the Foreign Minister, and Santiago Garcés Arroyo, the head of the SIM (Military Investigation Service). Negrín immediately went to Valencia. There he met with José Miaja, head of the army, who was in favour of putting an end to the hostilities. Two days later he took up residence in Madrid in the Presidency building, where he summoned Colonel Segismundo Casado, head of the Central Army, who told him clearly that his forces had no chance of resisting Franco's foreseeable offensive on the capital. Negrín found that, apart from the PCE officers, few chiefs supported the policy of resistance. Fearing that Azaña, who had taken up residence in the Spanish embassy in Paris, would resign and that Britain and France would immediately recognise General Franco, on 12 February Negrín sent Álvarez del Vayo to the French capital to tell the President of the Republic that the government considered his presence in Spain "essential". Azaña refused to prolong a "pointless struggle".

On the 16th Negrín called a meeting of the military chiefs at the Los Llanos air base (Albacete). All except Miaja told him that they shared the opinion of Colonel Casado, who related what was said at this meeting in *Así cayó Madrid*. The truth was that Casado was already in contact with Francoist agents and knew that Franco would not negotiate as long as the Communists were in power. For this reason he told Negrín that Azaña's return and the formation of a new government of Republicans and Socialists in which there were no Communists were necessary. Among the anarchists,

Casado had the support of Cipriano Mera, who commanded an army corps, and of José García Pradas, leader of the Castilian CNT. As for the Socialists, Julián Besteiro and Wenceslao Carrillo were aware of the colonel's plans and approved them. Wenceslao Carrillo and other Socialists even tried to wrest control of the party and the UGT from Negrín's supporters. Casado maintained contacts with the Foreign Office through Denys Cowan, who operated out of the British consulate in Madrid.

On 27 February France and the United Kingdom recognised the Burgos government "de iure" as the legitimate government of Spain, despite the fact that on 13 February 1939 the BOE had published the Law of Political Responsibilities, which was to serve "to settle the faults incurred by those who contributed with serious acts or omissions to forge the red subversion". This law specified that representatives of the army, the judiciary and the Falange would form the tribunals responsible for imposing sanctions. According to its first article, the responsibilities went back to 1 October 1934. With the abandonment of the Second Republic thus consummated, President Azaña announced his resignation in France on the 28th. Despite the fact that events were proving the futility of resistance day by day, on 2 March Negrín made a series of changes and promotions that placed the resources of power in the hands of his communist friends. Colonel Casado was promoted to general, but at the same time Negrín replaced him in command of the Central Army with the communist Modesto, who was also promoted to general. The "mobile shock units" were created and the communists Líster, Galán and Márquez were appointed colonels. In command of the port of Cartagena, home of the fleet, he appointed Francisco Galán. Two other communists, Etelvino Vega and Manuel Tagüeña, were appointed civil governors of Alicante and Murcia. On 3 March 1939, the Permanent Deputation of the Cortes met in Paris and appointed as interim president Grand Master Diego Martínez Barrio, who was also in France.

The military, trade unionists and the cadres of other parties regarded these manoeuvres by Negrín as a communist coup d'état. Indignation was widespread, and on the night of 4 March an uprising took place at the Cartagena base, led by naval captain Fernando Oliva, which was supported by the city's garrison, under the command of artillery colonel Gerardo Armentía, who ended up committing suicide after being arrested. It was the beginning of a new civil war on the Republican side, which was to claim thousands of dead and wounded in a week. In the midst of the chaos and confusion, Admiral Miguel Buiza ordered the departure of the fleet from Cartagena on 5 March. Three cruisers, eight destroyers and other smaller units set course for Bizerte, where they surrendered to the French military authorities. Although forces commanded by the communist Alonso Rodríguez later regained control of the base, the loss of the fleet meant the disappearance of the best means of evacuation available to Negrín's government.

While the PCE politburo gathered in Elda, in the so-called "Dakar position", Colonel Casado took up residence at 7 p.m. on 5 March in the Ministry of Finance. An hour later, the rest of the conspirators arrived and the National Defence Council was set up, which Casado agreed to chair provisionally until the arrival in Valencia of General Miaja, who after some hesitation and hesitation had joined the rebellion. The most important and prestigious figure was the Socialist Julián Besteiro, who was assigned to Foreign Affairs. The Socialist Wenceslao Carrillo took over the Interior. The Council included two men from the CNT, Eduardo Val and José González Marín, a representative of the UGT, Antonio Pérez, as well as two other republicans and a trade unionist. At 11.30 p.m. the 70th Brigade, commanded by the anarcho-syndicalist Bernabé López, occupied the strategic posts in Madrid: the Ministries of Defence, the Interior and Communications, Telefónica, the Bank of Spain and the General Directorate of Security. Thus began the coup d'état.

Once the capital was under control, in the early hours of the morning of 6 March, a communiqué from the Council was broadcast over the radio. Julián Besteiro then spoke, stating that with Azaña's resignation the Republic had been decapitated and Negrín's government lacked legitimacy. The Army of the Republic," he said, "exists with indisputable authority; it takes into its own hands the solution to a very serious, essentially military problem". Besteiro called on Negrín to withdraw and accused him of gaining time "in the morbid belief that the growing complication of international events would lead to a catastrophe of universal proportions". Negrín, who had heard the speech, called Casado over and, giving him the general's treatment, asked him what was going on. Casado replied that he was not a general, but a colonel, as he did not accept the appointment of a government that had no legitimacy. On the morning of 6 March all the Popular Front forces made public statements of support for the coup. Only the PCE remained loyal to Negrín, who had been in Elda since 27 February, protected in the so-called "Yuste position" by an elite guard.

While the communists in Madrid were preparing to do battle with the putschists, in the early hours of 6 March Negrín, Álvarez del Vayo and the PCE leadership began to prepare their departure from Spain. Negrín visited the PCE headquarters in the "Dakar position", where he found that Palmiro Togliatti, the delegate of the International in Spain, was organising the departure of the communist leaders. Five hours before the President of the Government fled, planes began to take off from the base at Monóvar, near Elda. The first to leave the country for Oran were Dolores Ibárruri, Jesús Monzón, Stefanov, alias "Moreno", and the French communist deputy Jean Cattelas. Togliatti later organised the departure of more communists, including Uribe, Líster, Modesto, Hidalgo de Cisneros and other political and military leaders of the PCE. Later, at 2.30 p.m., Negrín's government left Spain for Toulouse.

The Communists in Madrid, because of the breakdown in communications, were unaware of the decisions taken in Elda by the Political Bureau, as well as of the flight of Negrín's government. However, Togliatti, whose reliability is very poor, later wrote that they had been ordered to overthrow the Junta by force of arms. With or without orders, the communist counter-coup was led by Guillermo Ascanio, who commanded a division deployed in the El Pardo area, which began the attack on the Casadist troops. The centre of Madrid became a battlefield where Popular Front soldiers fought each other, as had happened in Catalonia in the days of May. Tanks and artillery fired on the Castellana, Recoletos and other streets in the heart of the capital, which became the scene of a delirious spectacle. For the first two days it looked as if the counter-attack was going to triumph. It was necessary for the brigades of the IV Army Corps, commanded by the anarchist Cipriano Mera, to leave the Guadalajara front on the 9th and enter Madrid. The fighting in the capital lasted until 13 March. In Valencia and other provinces the communists had no plan of action and basically fought to defend themselves. Historians do not agree on the number of dead in this second civil war within the civil war. Julián Casanova claims that there were two thousand between the two sides; but Ángel Bahamonde and Javier Cervera Gil raise the total number of victims of the fighting to scandalous figures and claim that the number of dead was close to twenty thousand, which seems incredible.

Once the internecine war was over, Colonel Casado tried to negotiate an honourable peace, but the basis he presented for negotiations was unrealistic, and on 15 March Franco, who had never really thought of making major concessions, demanded unconditional surrender. Finally, on 26 March the negotiations broke down, so late on 27 March Casado and his Defence Junta moved to Valencia, from where they left Spain on the afternoon of the 29th aboard a British cruiser. Only Julián Besteiro remained in Madrid as the highest Republican authority, waiting in the basement of the Ministry of Finance, where the National Defence Council had been located, for the arrival of the victors.

On repression in national Spain

As is well known, hatred breeds hatred and violence breeds violence. These seeds had been sown abundantly in Spain for years. It is not for nothing that Marxism, as we have seen, preaches hatred and the struggle between classes to impose the dictatorship of the proletariat. The civil war was the ultimate expression of the underlying hatred within Spanish society. Both sides tried to justify their own crimes as a response to much worse crimes committed by their adversaries. Since we have been describing the abominable acts and barbarity unleashed in Republican Spain from the outset, it is necessary before concluding this chapter to consider the repression in Franco's Spain. A repression that took the form of executions and murders, many of which could have been avoided. In fact, when on 2 September 1936 Manuel Hedilla took office as head of the Provisional Command Junta of the Falange Española de las JONS, he wrote several clear indications: "It is necessary to avoid," he advised, "that outrages be committed because of personal feelings, often unconfessable". Hedilla said that it was necessary to ensure that control was carried out in such a way that there were no "innocent victims in the rear of our lines.... No one will be punished without a background check and without an order from the competent authority". Months later, on Christmas Eve 1936, Hedilla made a speech in which he insisted on the need to act with rectitude:

> "And I address myself to the Falangists who are in charge of political and judicial investigations in the cities and above all in the villages. Your mission must be the work of purging the leaders, ringleaders and murderers. But prevent with all your might anyone from indulging personal hatreds, and anyone who, out of hunger or despair, has voted for the Left, from being punished or humiliated. We all know that in many villages there were - and perhaps are - right-wingers who were worse than the Reds. I want arrests of this kind to cease and, where they have occurred, you must become a guarantee for the unjustly persecuted. And wherever you are, be resolutely ready to oppose proceedings against the humble. The Phalanx must stand everywhere with its face held high, in order to be able to defend itself against its many enemies. We want the salvation and not the death of those who in their vast majority were hungry for bread and justice".

Still in the spring of 1937 Hedilla expressed his desire for reconciliation among Spaniards in statements to the newspaper *Il Regime Fascista*. Although they were mutilated by military censorship, in *El Adelanto* of 17 April 1937 one could read this essential idea "...For our deceived workers, our most cordial and Christian forgiveness; forgiveness that means obligation and friendship...". For those of us who look at the facts from a Christian point of view, these words and those quoted above are a model of behaviour which should have been followed by those who made the cross the symbol of their struggle against atheistic communism. Instead of being driven by hatred and intolerance, they were obliged to put temperance, understanding and, of course, charity and forgiveness first; but most of the time they failed to do so.

On the other hand, it must be considered that Franco's repression was exercised over a much longer period of time, since the victory was followed by very hard years for the defeated who remained in Spain. Moreover, the fact that until the end of the war Barcelona, Madrid and Valencia, the major cities, were in the hands of the Republic necessarily meant that the persecution of political opponents was carried out after the victory. Since it was in these cities that the popular-frontists committed the greatest number of murders against civilians, denunciations and denunciations by those who yearned for revenge were inevitable.

Another circumstance to be taken into account is that important urban centres such as Bilbao, Malaga, Santander, Gijón, San Sebastián... were also taken over after having been subject to earlier repression by the Republican forces. were taken over after having been subject to previous repression by the Republican forces. Revanchism also led to persecution and reprisals in these cities after the entry of the Nationalists. In San Sebastián, for example, many detainees were shot without warning. José Herrera, a requeté colonel from Seville, recalls in his appearance in the documentary *Violence in the rearguard* that when they arrived in the Malaga village of Almargen, groups of women flocked to the square through the streets shouting: "Kill them, kill them! They justified their thirst for blood by the fact that they had killed a loved one: their son, husband or brother. This anecdote is significant, as it shows that blood calls for blood and that the feelings of hatred and revenge were uncontainable. In the province of Malaga, where the Republicans had killed more than 2,500 political opponents, the repression was ruthless and thousands of people were shot.

However, Émile Témime, a Marxist historian, acknowledges the following: "Once the first moments of turmoil and picturesqueness had passed, observers agree that Nationalist Spain had an aspect of calm and even, in some regions, of peace, unimaginable in the Republican zone at the same time". Certainly, the macabre spectacle of murders and the dead lying by the dozen in the streets of the cities did not occur on the Nationalist side, or, if you like, it was less sinister because of the direction of the executions exercised by the authorities. The repressive control was achieved earlier and more completely in the Nationalist zone than in the other zone. However, during the first few months there was also a lack of control on the rebel side, and it was then that personal vendettas were carried out and innocent people were arbitrarily eliminated. From executions by firing squad ordered by anyone who thought he was authorised to kill, there was a mockery of justice through "summary instruction" and, from the beginning of 1937 onwards, through courts martial. On both sides, the greatest number of rearguard victims occurred during the months of 1936. On 13 February 1939, as mentioned above, the Law of Political Responsibilities came into force, which, as soon as the war ended, made it possible to prosecute those who had organised subversion since October 1934. The penalties imposed ranged from imprisonment or confiscation of property to the death penalty. The law was amended in 1942 and repealed in 1945. On 1 March 1940, the Law for the Suppression of Freemasonry and Communism came into force and remained in force until 1964.

In any case, mass massacres such as those organised in Paracuellos del Jarama and other places of infamous memory near Madrid did not occur in Spain. There was not even a case similar to that of the Jaén train, when two hundred people who were being transported to Alcalá de Henares were indiscriminately machine-gunned on the spot. Perhaps a comparable case occurred in Cáceres, where in December 1937 the presence of the communist commander Máximo Calvo was discovered. It was concluded that a plot was being hatched to put the city in the hands of the enemy. Some 200 people were implicated in the affair, and after summary courts, they were all shot. There was, however, no collective execution of the 200 people sentenced. The executions began on 25 December 1937, when 35 people were executed. The death sentences continued to be carried out on successive dates until they ended on 20 January 1938.

As Hispanists, we are compelled to end this chapter with a review of the cowardly murder of Federico García Lorca. A despicable crime, like all crimes, which discredited national Spain from the outset and deprived Spanish literature of an incomparable figure, whose work, had he not been murdered, promised to be among the most prolific in our literature, for at the age of only thirty-eight his literary output was already immense. García Lorca's death had repercussions all over the world, since the quality of works such as *El romancero gitano* and *Bodas de sangre* had consecrated him in Europe and America. The Hispanist Ian Gibson wrote his doctoral thesis, *Granada, 1936. The Murder of García Lorca*, on what happened in the city of the Alhambra. This work provides precise data on the repression in Granada, in whose cemetery 2,012 people were shot from July 1936 to March 1939. Half of these deaths took place in two months: in August 1936 alone, 562 people were executed in the cemetery, and another 499 were shot in September. In just one day of this second month, the 22nd, seventy people were killed. These figures confirm, as mentioned above, that it was in the months immediately after the outbreak of the fratricidal war that most people were killed.

Federico García Lorca arrived in Granada on 14 July to spend a few days with his parents and sister at the Huerta de San Vicente, a family property. Everyone knew about it because *El Defensor de Granada*, whose director was a good friend of the poet, gave the news on the front page on the 15th. Days later the civil war began. The rebels took control of the city centre on 20 July, but resistance was organised in the working-class neighbourhood of the Albaicín and the shootings began. On the 22nd Radio Granada issued an ultimatum. Women and children walked down the narrow streets in the direction of the indicated rallying points; but the men refused to surrender and the fighting resumed. Artillery pieces were used to cannonade the Albaicín, so the workers began to raise white flags. By the 24th the resistance was crushed; but Granada was at first an island in an area where the rebellion had failed. On 29 July the Republican air force carried out the first of a series of bombing raids on the city, which not only caused civilian casualties but also caused damage to the Alhambra. On the 30th, numerous militiamen launched an attack to try to regain control of the city. They were repulsed by the rebels and a month-long siege began.

After being threatened in the Huerta de San Vicente, Federico's parents advised him to look for a safer place. They called Luis Rosales, another poet from Granada, a friend of the family. Some of the Rosales brothers were "old shirts" of the Falange. Luis Rosales offered three alternatives to his colleague: move him to the red zone, take him to the house of the eminent composer Manuel de Falla, or put him up in his own house in Calle de Angulo. When Lorca's enemies returned to the Huerta, he was no longer to be found; but the family, intimidated, had no choice but to reveal that he was living at the Rosales' house[30]. García Lorca was distraught to learn that in the early hours of 16 August his brother-in-law, Manuel Fernández-Montesinos Lustau, had been shot. His anguish was justified, as in the afternoon of the same day he was arrested.

At the head of a disproportionate security detail, Ramón Ruiz Alonso, a former CEDA deputy who made the complaint, turned up at the Rosales' house with an arrest warrant stamped with the seal of the Civil Government. None of the brothers were at home. Ian Gibson writes: "Mrs Rosales, dismayed and fearing that Federico would be killed on the spot, in the street, insisted that she would not let García Lorca leave her house without her husband or one of her sons being present". She immediately called Miguel, her eldest son who was on duty at the Falange barracks, and also spoke to her husband. Miguel turned up at the house and decided to go with the poet to the Civil Government, but Valdés Guzmán, the civil governor, was inspecting the trenches on the Jaén front and nothing could be done until he arrived, so Lorca was locked up in the building's outbuildings. When the other Rosales brothers heard what had happened, they immediately marched to the Civil Government accompanied by other Falangists with the intention of confronting the governor.

On 17 August, Angelina Cordobilla, the Fernández-Montesinos' nanny, was sent by Federico's mother to the Civil Government with food for her son, but Valdés Guzmán told her he was no longer there. He lied, as it is almost certain that he remained there from the afternoon of the 16th until the evening of the 18th. Gibson believes that Valdés hesitated about what to do with the writer, given that he was not unaware of his prestige. He therefore contacted General Queipo de Llano, the supreme leader of the rebels in Andalusia, whose verbal excesses repeatedly betrayed his deplorable behaviour and bravado. In the course of his research, Ian Gibson learned that one of Valdés Guzmán's companions in the peña of Bar Jandilla, Germán

---

[30] The head of the family, Miguel Rosales Vallecillos, risked his life and fortune by taking Lorca and others persecuted by José Valdés Guzmán, a Falange commander who had taken command of the Civil Government, into his home.

Fernández Ramos, quoted Queipo de Llano's exact words in response to the civil governor's query: "Give him coffee, lots of coffee", which was tantamount to saying that he should be killed.

With these instructions, Lorca was taken from the Civil Government on the night of 18 August and taken to Víznar, a village nine kilometres from Granada. Nearby, there was a building called "La Colonia", which served as a summer residence for groups of schoolchildren until it was converted into a prison. It was there that García Lorca spent his last moments. It seems, according to Gibson, that in addition to assault guards who, perhaps as punishment, had been forced to take part in the shootings, the criminals were volunteers who "killed for the pleasure of killing". The poet was murdered in the early hours of 19 August in Fuente Grande, a place located between the villages of Alfacar and Víznar, near the infamous Víznar ravine, where there were multiple executions. Three other people died alongside him: Dióscoro Galindo González, a teacher from Pulianas, and the banderilleros Joaquín Arcollas Cabezas and Francisco Galadí Mercal.

The first newspaper to reveal Lorca's death was the *Diario de Albacete,* which in its 30 August edition reported on the front page of the "possible execution of the great poet Federico García Lorca". In the following days the news spread like wildfire around the world. *The Times* of London reported on the case for several days in September. In 1940, Dámaso Alonso, poet and teacher of Hispanists, dedicated the elegiac poem *La Fuente Grande o de las Lágrimas (The Great Fountain or Fountain of Tears)* to his murdered friend. Rafael Alberti, Miguel Hernández, Emilio Prados, poets of his generation, composed poems in memory of Lorca. Antonio Machado also wrote the poem *El crimen fue en Granada: A Federico García Lorca.* With the fragment entitled *El crimen* we would like to end this chapter on the tragedy of Spain:

> "He was seen, walking among rifles,
> down a long street,
> going out into the cold countryside,
> even with early morning stars.
> Federico was killed
> when the light was coming.
> The executioner's squad
> did not dare to look him in the face.
> Everyone closed their eyes;
> they prayed: not even God saves you!
> Dead fell Frederick
> -blood on the forehead and lead in the guts-.
> ... What was the crime in Granada
> Know -poor Granada-, in your Granada".

OTHER BOOKS

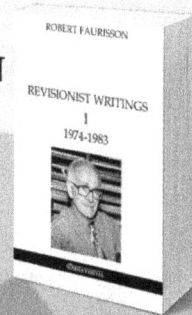

It does not deny, but aims to affirm more accurately. Revisionists are not 'deniers' or 'negationists'; they strive to seek and find where, it seems, there was nothing left to seek or find".

OMNIA VERITAS LTD PRESENTS:

ROBERT FAURISSON

REVISIONIST WRITINGS I

1974-1983

Revisionism is a matter of method, not ideology

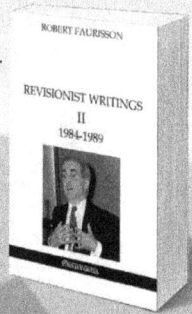

Jewish and Zionist organisations throughout the world are experiencing a tragedy. A myth, from which they have sought to profit, is being exposed: the myth of the so-called 'Holocaust of the Jews during the Second World War'.

OMNIA VERITAS LTD PRESENTS:

ROBERT FAURISSON

REVISIONIST WRITINGS II

1984-1989

Revisionists have never denied the existence of the camps

"By its very nature, revisionism can only disturb public order; where tranquil certainties reign, the spirit of free examination is an intruder and causes a scandal."

OMNIA VERITAS LTD PRESENTS:

ROBERT FAURISSON

REVISIONIST WRITINGS III

1990-1992

Every Frenchman has the right to say that gas chambers did not exist

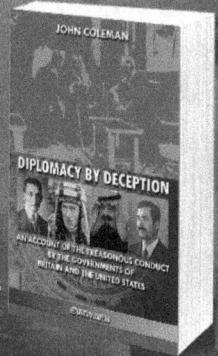

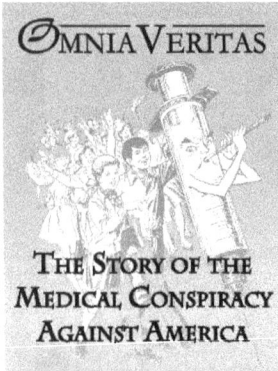

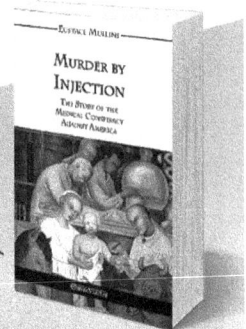

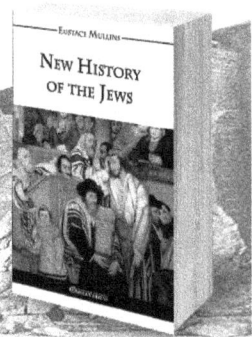

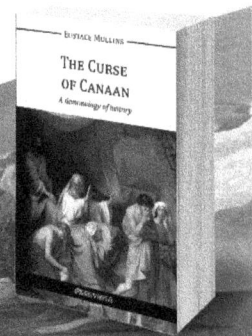

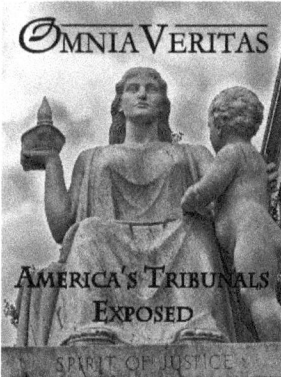

THE RAPE OF JUSTICE
AMERICA'S TRIBUNALS EXPOSED
by EUSTACE MULLINS

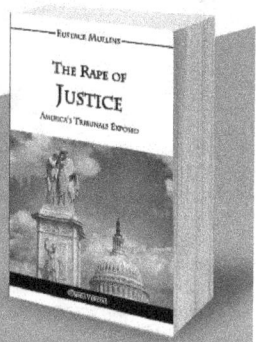

American should know just what is going on in our courts

THE SECRETS OF THE FEDERAL RESERVE
HERE ARE THE SIMPLE FACTS OF THE GREAT BETRAYAL
by EUSTACE MULLINS

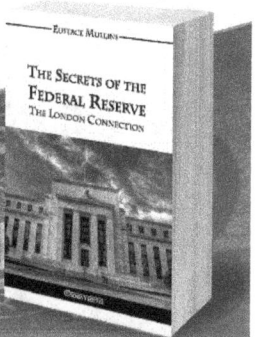

Will we continue to be enslaved by the Babylonian debt money system?

THE WORLD ORDER
OUR SECRET RULERS
A Study in the Hegemony of Parasitism
The peoples of the world not only will never love Big Brother, but they will soon dispose of him forever.
by EUSTACE MULLINS

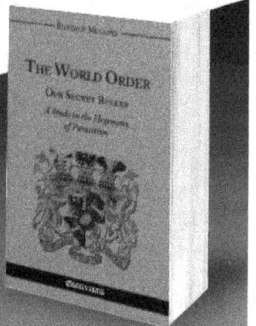

The program of the World Order remains the same; Divide and Conquer

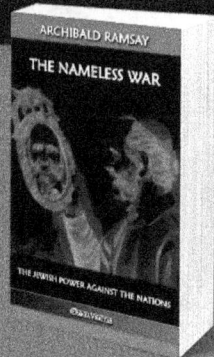

OMNIA VERITAS LTD PRESENTS:

SOLZHENITSYN

The Jews Before the Revolution

"The purpose that guides me throughout this work on the life common the Russians and the Jews consists of looking for all the points necessary for a mutual understanding, all the possible voices which, once we get rid of the bitterness of the past, can lead us towards the future."

The Jewish people is at the same time an active and passive element of History

Omnia Veritas Ltd presents:

An exclusive and unpublished work of EUSTACE MULLINS

BLOOD AND GOLD
History of the Council on Foreign Relations

The CFR, founded by internationalists and banking interests, has played a significant role in shaping US foreign policy

Revolutions are not made by the middle class, but by the oligarchy at the top

OMNIA VERITAS LTD PRESENTS:

THE TRACK OF THE JEW THROUGH THE AGES

One of the most characteristic and significant signs of the hostility of the Jews towards the Europeans is their hatred of Christianity

Indeed it is not surprising that the Church increasingly proscribed Jewish works

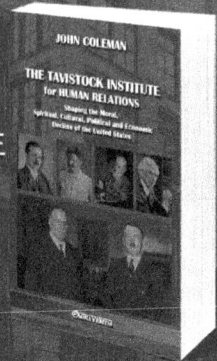

ramcontent.com/pod-product-compliance
Source LLC
urg PA
54270326
00012B/2052